THE STORY
OF
AMERICAN RAILROADS

The Story of
American Railroads

By STEWART H. HOLBROOK

AMERICAN LEGACY PRESS
NEW YORK

This edition is published by American Legacy Press,
distributed by Crown Publishers, Inc.
h g f e d c b a
AMERICAN LEGACY PRESS 1981 EDITION
AMERICAN LEGACY PRESS is a trademark of Crown Publishers, Inc.

Manufactured in the United States of America

Library of Congress Cataloging in Publication Data

Holbrook, Stewart Hall, 1893–1964.
　The story of American railroads.

　Originally published: New York : Bonanza Books, 1947.
　Bibliography: p. 453.
　Includes index.
　1. Railroads—United States—History.　I. Title.
HE2751.H44　1981　　　385′.0973　　　81-8005
ISBN 0-517-001004　　　　　　　　　AACR2

For

MY AUNT JEANETTE

CONTENTS

CONTENTS

ACKNOWLEDGMENT

WHEN I had finished writing this book and reflected on the great number of persons who had given me aid in one form or another, the humbling thought occurred again, as it had before, that a book, no matter who is so bold as to sign it, is more often than not a sort of community, perhaps a national, enterprise. I regret that scores, probably hundreds, of men who aided me in this particular work are not known to me by name. They were the conductors, the brakemen, engineers, firemen, roundhouse men, the baggage masters and news butchers, the station agents and telegraphers with whom I have had occasion to speak, even if briefly, these past forty-odd years. Each of them has contributed something to my layman's casual knowledge of railroads.

Then, there are the railroad men I happen to know, either at first hand or by mail. They are a courteous and freehanded brotherhood, ready to aid, aye, even to cheer on, us outsiders who would write about railroads, although they are quick to damn us, and roundly, should we confuse a mogul and a mikado, or hang the wrong lights on the bobbing end of a train. They are, on the whole, probably more intensely interested in their daily occupation than are the men of any other occupation I could name, offhand or after considerable reflection.

Of these genial persons who have made the way simpler for me I must cite John W. Barriger, Anton Anderson, and Henry B. Willis, all of the Monon Route; O. L. Grisamore, C. E. Kane, and William F. Blye, of the Illinois Central; Donald Ashton and F. T. Darrow(retired), of the Burlington; C. W. Y. Currie, of the New York Central; M. R. Cring, of the Katy Lines; F. H. Johnson, of The Milwaukee Road; R. A. Pearce, of the Alton; I. L. Gordon, of the Reading; George C. Frank and H. L. Skeen, of the Erie; T. J. O'Shaughnessy, of the Rock Island; Lee Lyles, of the Santa Fe; Wingate Cram, of the Bangor & Aroostook; Thomas E. Owen, of the Louisville & Nashville; Leith Abbott, late of the Southern Pacific; and Forrest O. Hayes, Purdy, Mo., a retired veteran of the Pennsylvania and other lines.

In the allied fields I must also mention the help given by B. D. Westfall, Railway Mail Service; W. A. Scheeder, Parmelee Transfer Company; W. A. Eichhorn, American News Company; Richard H. Johnston, Association of American Railroads; Gardner Stratton(retired), F. W. Colson, and the late Harry Gilbert, employes of Pullman; Harley Hallgren, Consolidated Ticket Office, Portland, Ore.; and Henry B. Comstock, editor of *Railroad Magazine*, the Old Reliable in its field.

Then there were a number of people, in no wise connected with railroading, who by their special knowledge were able to supply me with information I would otherwise have been hard put to come by, among them Herbert Cox, Eugene, Ore.; Freeman Cleaves, *New York World-Telegram;* Ernest Haycox, Portland, Ore.; A. H. Holbrook, Colebrook, N. H.; Mrs. Thelma Jones, Wayzata, Minn.; George Jean Nathan, New York City; and George T. Springer, Minneapolis. I might, and do, add that the careful typing of Miss Esther Watson, Vancouver, Wash., rendered the manuscript legible and thus helped to preserve the tempers of editors and typesetters, who often are irritable men.

As always, I am perhaps most in debt to the ladies and gentlemen of the libraries and historical societies, without whom no book of mine would ever have appeared. In respect to the present volume I must thank Charles E. Fisher, Railway & Locomotive Historical Society, Boston; Miss Ruth Porritt, Baker Memorial Library, Cambridge; John G. Weld, The Bostonian Society; Sylvester Vigilante, New York Public Library; Miss Anna Heilmeir, James J. Hill Library, St. Paul; Mrs. Anne McDonnell, Montana State Historical Society, Helena; Miss Eleanor Stephens, State Librarian, Salem, Ore.; Miss Nell Unger, Miss Katherine Anderson, Miss Louise Prichard, and Miss Nellie Fisher, all of the Portland (Ore.) Public library; Miss Barbara Gantz, Reed College Library, Portland; Chapin Foster, Washington State Historical Society, Tacoma; and the Pacific Northwest Bibliographic Center at the University of Washington, one of the unsung glories of the region where I make my home.

I owe much for extending every facility of his group to Robert S. Henry of the Association of American Railroads, who also went far beyond the limits of mere courtesy to make my way easier.

Thanks are due to Milton L. Bernstein, Chairman of the Museum Committee of The Railroadians of America, from whose unique collection the majority of the old prints among the illustrations were taken.

Finally, to Freeman H. Hubbard, good friend, long-time editor of *Railroad Magazine,* and now free-lancing with the fine *Railroad Avenue* already to his credit, I must tender special thanks. Mr. Hubbard gave most freely of his time and of his wide knowledge to advise me, and then not only made available his superb collection of railroadiana but also supervised the collecting and arranging of the illustrations.

Listed in the Bibliography are the works that the author found of particular help.

THE STORY
OF
AMERICAN RAILROADS

CHAPTER I

Panorama

FOR a time in my boyhood I lived on a farm within sound of the Grand Trunk Railway, and went to school in the town of North Stratford, a junction with the Maine Central. The Grand Trunk was not the first railroad I can remember, but it was the one that appealed most powerfully to me, that stirred my imagination beyond compare. Not before and surely never since have I heard the like of the whistle of a Grand Trunk mogul as it moaned up from deep in the forest we called the 'Hegan Woods and came wafting on frosty waves through the brittle air of a December in northern Vermont.

To me those moguls were gigantic locomotives. I firmly believed them to be the largest locomotives on earth, and so did all other boys of the town. They hauled the long freights between Portland and Montreal, and commonly stopped at North Stratford for water. There, on a grade crossing in the very center of the village, one of them stood at dusk every winter night, holding up what town traffic there was while we boys stood to watch the great black monster with its trimmings of ice that told of bitter weather, and listen fascinated to its breathing.

We knew, of course, that this breathing of the locomotive was really some sort of pump that had to do with the airbrakes, but we never thought of it that way, for an engine to a boy of my time was not a machine at all but a living animal, perhaps some species of mastodon, in any case an animal that had lungs and breathed. To us that nervous panting—that *pam-pah, pam-pah*—now slow and even, now hurried, was coming direct from the body and soul of the locomotive, as sentient as any human and twice as wonderful. The engine, you understand, was panting, resting, as a dog rests and pants, gathering strength for the heavy pull ahead, which it knew very well would begin as soon as it had crossed the Connecticut River and started the rugged haul up the valley of the Nulhegan to Island Pond.

Up the 'Hegan valley I've sat in a sleigh and watched, completely spellbound, while one of those vast trains of freight cars came thundering by on

1

its way to Canada. The locomotives must have had exceptionally good headlamps for the era, for I recall that a shaft of light lit up the tracks at Hobson's Mills for what seemed to me a mile or more in advance of the engine. Along with the first glimmer of brilliance came the first rumblings of the heavy train; and soon the very woods, all dark and mysterious and rather sinister outside of that shaft of yellow light—soon the very woods began to tremble and were filled with the rolling thunder of the railroad in action. Then, for a moment that was never quite long enough, the mogul pounded up and past in clouds of steam and smoke, a glow of hellish fire lighting the interior of the cab, where the shadow of the fireman moved against the glow, a silhouetted imp of the Pit, with the endless cars coming along behind bringing the hypnotic rhythm of their clatter.

There was a grade crossing ahead, at the Mills, and the warning that welled up from the dome of the mogul was a warning to all human beings in the 'Hegan Woods, alive or dead, to all animals wild and domestic, to the fishes in the frozen muttering streams, to the birds in the balsams and the owls awing, and to the frightened souls of all Indians who had used this route for a highway before ties and rails had been laid upon it.

The Grand Trunk engines possessed whistles built by a master who was a combination of Thor himself and some brilliant esthete, for he perfected an art form fitted wonderfully to that northern clime and splintery air where an obbligato was supplied by the crackling of Aurora Borealis. The steam shot quickly up from the big round dome on the mogul's heaving back, then a blast of mighty noise shattered the woods and the night, a trump to shame all horn players since Gabriel, to tell the loggers all over Brighton township that the Fast Freight was going through. Yes, sir, that was her. . . . It was a blast to roll on and on over the timbered hills, over the blueberry swamps, over the stark white fields, to inform farmers in Bloomfield and Brunswick, even in Lemington and Canaan, before the echo had worn itself out, that the Grand Trunk was making the 'Hegan Woods with a full head of steam and would soon be over the hump, to drift easily downgrade along St. Lawrence waters. . . .

It was said of these locomotives and trains, and even the timetables cited the fact, that they went either to Montreal on the north, or south to Portland. But we boys knew better than that. They went, we were certain, to a magic and wholly wondrous land for which we had no name, and once there they never stopped rolling. True, they might pause now and again, in the manner of locomotives, for fuel and water, when they would rest briefly and pant. But they never would come to the end of the track. There was no end. The rails, we knew, led on into Canada, reputed to be a big enough country, then on through Canada and to God knew where, the engines whistling at intervals, ringing the bell at intervals, smoking, steaming, pounding, rolling, rolling on to the end of time and the edge of the world. . . .

As I say, we boys did not have a name for that magic country to which all passing trains went. But some of my boyhood friends resolved to see that land and learn its name. So, a bit later they went to work for the railroad, some on the Grand Trunk, some on other lines. Forty years later, which was just the other day, I talked to one who had set out in youth to find the land to which all passing trains went—or, rather, used to go. Gold stripes and stars marched up his blue serge from cuff to elbow. "Yes," he said, "I found out where the place is, though I never got there."

"You know," continued this veteran of forty years on the rails, "you know, when you and I were kids, boys did not go to work on the railroad simply because their fathers did. What fetched them were the sights and sounds of moving trains, and above all the whistle of a locomotive. I've heard of the call of the wild, the call of the law, the call of the church. There is also the call of the railroad—or there used to be in our day. It was the echo of a mogul whistle in these same old 'Hegan Woods that made me a railroadman for life."

We talked some more, this veteran and I, and although he never quite put it into so many words, I understood him well enough; he was telling me that the country where passing trains go is just beyond Oz, where the Round River flows through a notch in the Big Rock Candy Mountains.

If railroads created a dreamworld for boys of my generation, and they most certainly did, it was merely incidental. The main achievement of the railroads was to help enormously to build the United States into a world power and do it well within the span of one man's lifetime. Historians know it, too, though because of the stiff if genteel conventions of their craft most of them have continued for a hundred years to write about our armies and navies and sonorous statesmen, with here and there guarded references to mysterious Economic Factors and forces which, stemming as they do straight from either Heaven or Hell, are amenable to no control by man, be he Democrat, Socialist, or Republican.

I realize as well as any man, and glory in it too, that the smoke that clouded the pretty green at Lexington was important. So were the clouds of burning powder that hung above Gettysburg. Both were freighted with destiny. But neither is more a true symbol of the United States than the plume of white smoke that streamed out behind the first double-header to plow up and over the Rockies carrying the first rail-borne goods and passengers from the Atlantic seaboard to the Pacific shore. The whole great empire of the American West was riding that train of cars.

By turns the railroad was to bedevil and bewilder America. In one of his essays Herbert Spencer, an Englishman who meant more to the United States than to his native land and who thoroughly believed in Steam, said that a volume would be required simply to trace through all of its ramifications the effects contingent upon the act of lighting a fire. These effects, he vowed, were infinite though imperceptible. The effects upon the United States of steam, which comes from water heated over a fire, are also infinite, but most of them are easily perceptible.

For one thing, steam locomotion in the United States harmed one region to build up another. The forces of nature meant little to it. It overcame wind and tide. It abolished the Mississippi River, until then a gigantic fact. It abolished those fearful reaches of the interior that cartographers labeled Great American Desert. All that even the Rockies meant to steam locomotion was merely a little more fire under the boiler.

Steam turned out to be capricious. It proved to be as much a master of what Americans called their Destiny as it was its slave. It carried the individual wherever he would go; and it carried away whole communities who did not want to go anywhere at all. Either that, or it buried them where they were. The railroad made bright green grass to grow in the once busy streets of Nantucket, Salem, and Charleston. It stole, openly and arrogantly, from New Orleans that monopoly of wealth which the Mississippi once promised to pour into her lap. Up in the hills of Vermont and New Hampshire, pine and spruce started to creep across the fields and pastures of deserted farms, to surround even the barns and houses and to strangle them—all because of steam locomotion. By 1880, at the latest, the home of one of my forebears, cleared and built by enormous effort before 1800, was marked by a lonely chimney, slowly crumbling into bright red ruins amid green forest, beside a melancholy hole in the ground, while an apple tree and a bush of lavender struggled for life in what had been the yard. It was only one of hundreds like it.

Steam locomotion was filled with wayward fancies. For some mysterious reason that only professors of economics pretend to understand, it carried wealth and importance past one place to lay them down at another. It passed Oswego, Dunkirk, Sandusky, and Fort Wayne to build a gigantic city at the foot of Lake Michigan. It picked the most impossible building site in California and conjured up San Francisco on the spot. It whistled past old and important places like Fort Vancouver, Tumwater, and Nisqually and made secondary hamlets like Portland and Seattle into cities.

There was no telling what steam would do, and many a fortune was made or lost because of its perversity. Before men realized what was going on, steam had moved the center of population from near the Atlantic seaboard to a point that existed in the school books of the same generation only as deep wilderness. More than one pioneer related, in no more than his middle years, how the last Indian whoop and the last sad cadence of the owl had died in the echo of the first locomotive. Wilderness one year, metropolis the next. It constantly astonished those who had been through it, to their last day, as well it might.

Wherever and whenever the railroad came, the change was often swift to dizziness. As a young fur trader, Gurdon Saltonstall Hubbard climbed an oak tree in a dismal swamp to get his first look at Fort Dearborn, a miserable collection of hovels. A little more than two decades later, he liked to be shaved in the elegant barber shop of the great and gaudy Palmer House, on almost the same spot.

Minneapolis, Portland, and Seattle grew up so rapidly they left the map makers a full ten years, perhaps twenty years, in the rear; while all along the two thousand miles separating those places there grew up one, then two, then three lines of continuous civilization, bolstered on each side by rectangular townships devoted to growing wheat, mining copper, cutting timber—now that wheat, copper, and lumber could be taken to market. "All that land," said a congressman referring to the entire American West, "wasn't worth ten cents until the railroads came."

It was the same everywhere in the country. Following the Civil War the United States started to build so rapidly, so madly, and continued to the end of the century in such a frenzy of exploitation, that it might have wrecked itself had it not been for the railroad. The country did crack several times, but it never quite blew up, or collapsed, and the reason it not only survived but prospered in wealth, in population, and in power was the railroad. Charles Francis Adams, our great philosopher of railroads, said it. "The simple truth was," he wrote, "that through its energetic railroad development, the country was then producing real wealth as no country ever produced it before. Behind all the artificial inflation which . . . so clearly foreshadowed a catastrophe, there was also going on a production that exceeded all experience."

The new element of the railroad, Adams believed, did away with the best of reasoned conclusions. Acting upon undeveloped and almost inexhaustible natural resources, it dragged the country through its difficulties in spite of itself—as if all the fraud, the ignorance, and speculation that greedy men could think up and practice were quite unable, because of the railroad, to precipitate disaster. Every mile of steel laid was quietly adding many times its cost to the aggregate wealth of the country.

What maddened Adams was the "complacency with which a certain class of philosophers mistook the operation of a great, quiet natural force for the results of their own meddling." One school of these professors, he said, attributed the freedom from commercial disaster to their jugglings with paper money. Another clique saw in the great prosperity of the day nothing but a vindication of their own meddling with the tariff. "While socialists talked, however," cried Adams, "the locomotive was at work, and all the obstructions which they placed in its way could at most only check but never overcome the impetus it had given to material progress. . . .*

Although Mr. Adams did not say so, the building of the American railroad system was one of the greatest dramas of modern times. Unlike the

---

* *Chapters in Erie and Other Essays.*

Republic itself, whose founding can be dated well enough for all practical and symbolic purposes as of July 4, 1776, the American railroad system cannot be said to have a birthday. For many years it existed only in the minds of a few visionaries who, try as they did, could make little impression on the great mass of Americans, just then charmed by the wonders of canals. The greatest of these visionaries, or prophets, was an odd genius named Oliver Evans who soon after the Revolution petitioned at least two legislatures for exclusive rights to use what he termed his "improvements in steam carriages" in their states.

A few other prophets were stirring, among them John Stevens of Hoboken, who built a miniature locomotive, which he ran around on a track in the yard of his home. The states of New Jersey and Pennsylvania good-naturedly granted Stevens the charters he wanted, which proposed to build a railroad across those states. Stevens was a veteran of the Revolution, hence they humored him, knowing nothing would come of his aberrations. And nothing did, though the noise he made did prompt a group of Pennsylvanians to send William Strickland to England to learn what he could about the new steam railways there.

England had taken to the steam engine, especially in its locomotive form, with a readiness that seems to have been lacking in America. News of the first English railroads came across the sea, and Strickland and other Americans had seen with their own eyes what was going on. Like an imported virus, the idea at last began to function in American port towns. In 1827 a group of citizens incorporated the Baltimore & Ohio Rail Road Company, and a bit later prevailed on old Charles Carroll, sole surviving Signer of the Declaration, to lean on a spade and turn a sod, while a band played and cannon boomed. In quick succession other railroad companies were organized in New York, Philadelphia, and Charleston.

Boston already had a railroad of a sort, three miles of wooden rails laid on stone ties to move granite from Quincy to the banks of the Neponset River, where the stones would be transported by water to Charlestown, there to form the Bunker Hill Monument. Horses were its motive power. Nor was the Baltimore & Ohio quite ready to take the big step to steam. They fooled around with sail cars and with horsepower in its direct and in its treadmill form. In Charleston, South Carolina, however, a group of railroad builders engaged Horatio Allen, who wanted steam, to run their line. Allen had the first American-built locomotive made in New York and hoisted it aboard his rails where, in December 1830, it pulled the first train of cars ever moved by steam in the United States. This six miles of railroad may properly be said to have fathered all lines since in this country. It was more the true source than the much-heralded, much-pictured race between Peter Cooper's *Tom Thumb* engine and a gray horse, the horse winning hands down.

The success of the South Carolina railroad brought a rash of incorporations in all of the settled regions except New England where, so solid Yankees said, commerce was tied to the sea and always would be. By 1840 there were almost 5,000 miles of steam railroad in the United States, of which Pennsylvania had almost one-fifth, with New York second on the list, followed by Virginia, North Carolina, Alabama, Tennessee, and Louisiana.

In the meantime, competing philosophers had emerged from their lairs to argue what a railroad was. Some said it was merely an improved turnpike, a semipublic way over which, by the payment of a fee, any man might operate his steam engine and carriages. If this contention seems odd today, it did not seem odd to a people who were familiar with turnpikes but had never seen a steam railroad. Other philosophers contended that a railroad was not and could not, with impunity, be considered a turnpike. Chief of this school was the remarkable Jonathan Knight, civil engineer who surveyed for the Chesapeake & Ohio Canal Company, laid out the federal government's National Road, then became engineer for the Baltimore & Ohio. A railroad, he said, could not operate successfully if more than one company ran steam carriages upon it. Since that day Knight's basic philosophy of single ownership has remained unchanged, although on thousands of miles of track more than one railroad operates trains on a rent or lease arrangement.

In the wake of the prophets came the incorporators of railroads. Incorporators were not necessarily builders. Many of these men were simply gull-catchers who had previously discovered easy money in selling stock in companies ostensibly formed for the purpose of digging canals, or building plank roads. The canals were never dug, the planks never laid, and now their railroads were never built. How numerous were these crooks is to be judged by the expression that became current if not popular: "As worthless as railroad stock."

But there were also honest and capable men among the organizers of railroad companies, men who at last had caught the vision of the steam locomotive, and they worked to some purpose to lay the first lines of iron rails. Conservatives were seldom among them. Conservatives at first paid the railroad no heed at all, but presently they roused and in the manner of their kind time out of mind, they fought the innovation. Enlisting both the law and the clergy, to say nothing of hired free-lance orators and makers of "Railroad Disaster" lithographs, the conservatives, or merely the owners of canal stock and stagecoach lines acting like conservatives, fought the railroad with every means ingenious men could devise.

They had lost, of course, before they started to fight. On went the rails, connecting two towns here, another two towns there, and over the rails went dinkey little engines hauling either stagecoaches with flanged wheels, or long boxes. Steam-railroad travel was a novelty, but it was hardly pleasure. No one ever knew, when a brigade of cars left a depot, when or if it would arrive at the other terminal. Farmers piled logs across the tracks. Bulls at pasture, offended by the sight of the puffing engines, charged them head on and butted them from the rails—until Isaac Dripps, boss mechanic of the Camden & Amboy, invented the deadly parent of all cowcatchers, which *speared* the rambunctious bulls and tamed them somewhat.

Passengers discovered they not only had to pay to ride on the cars; they had often to help lift them back onto the rails and to push entire trains over slight grades. Smoke sooted them, cinders burned their broadcloth and bombazine, yet there was no keeping them from riding behind what was soon heralded as the Iron Horse, the animal that was going to change and make America.

Men of outstanding imagination and ability were presently showing interest in the railroad. John Edgar Thomson took hold of the newly formed Pennsylvania Railroad, added a dilapidated line here and there, purchased a state-owned streak of rust, and set his own crews to laying track from Harrisburg to Pittsburgh. When he died in 1874, his road was one of the great systems in the country. Erastus Corning, nail maker of Albany, New York, and associates, got a pot of cash together, purchased ten small railroads, then forged them into the New York Central, one of the wonders of the time. Up in now waking New England, John Poor, on foot and in sleigh, set out to find a route from Portland to Montreal, and then with efforts to be described only as epic, built what became the Grand Trunk. In Georgia, in Tennessee, in Ohio, even in far Minnesota, men of push and determination were connecting their towns with other towns, or with rivers or lakes, laying rails, buying rolling stock, naming their roads ". . . & Pacific" with a superb indifference to the 2,000 or more miles that stretched out beyond the farthest western railhead.

The challenge of the plains and mountains, however, was to be met. Brisk men in New York and California asked the government to help them bridge the continent, and the government donated land and a lot of money and sent soldiers to protect the construction crews from the dismayed Indians who knew well enough what the Iron Horse would do to their buffalo. The Union and the Central Pacific outfits went to work at both ends, making fortunes for a few, impoverishing many more, seducing senators and other noble statesmen into what one voluble critic said were "cunning, craft, chicane, guile, and knavery"; yet, in the end, providing the United States with a steel highway of incalculable value. When impassioned orators spoke of this first transcontinental as a Path of Empire, they were not speaking bombast; it was sober truth. It was also no less than a monument to Grenville Dodge, an able soldier and the greatest railroad builder of his time.

In a little more than two decades, three transcontinental railroads were built with government help. All three wound up in bankruptcy courts.

And thus, when James Jerome Hill said he was going to build a line from the Great Lakes to Puget Sound, without government cash or land grant, even his close friends thought him mad. But his Great Northern arrived at Puget Sound without a penny of federal help, nor did it fail. It was an achievement to shame the much-touted construction of the Erie canal.

Along with the era of feverish construction went the era of buccaneering. Perhaps Uncle Dan'l Drew started it. Perhaps he merely gave it impetus. In any case this drover of cattle who salted his steers, then let them drink their fill before weighing—thus giving us Watered Stock—turned his great talents to railroad speculation, trying his hand first on the New York & Erie. "I got to be a millionaire afore I knowed it, hardly," he liked to say. And so he did. With Jay Gould and Jim Fisk, Jr., Drew wrecked the Erie again and again, and tried to wreck the New York & Harlem, running plumb into old Commodore Vanderbilt, who was too much for him. After looting here and there for more than a decade, Uncle Dan'l softened to the extent of setting aside suitable sums, in the style of so many rascals, for the founding of seminaries of God.

The old Commodore used methods akin to Drew's, yet on an even grander scale, and was so eminently successful that the vast New York Central system, which he and his son William H. built out of lines they clubbed into compliance, was often known simply as Mr. V's Road. Both father and son were of outstanding ability in the business of amalgamating and operating railroads, even though the younger man has been continuously discredited because of a statement which, honest though it was and quite reasonable from his point of view, proved most offensive to the public; for sixty years it has been used against Capital in all its forms. "The public be damned!" said the younger Mr. Vanderbilt, doing his own class more harm than all of the vaporings of Johann Most and the Haymarket anarchists combined.

Raids similar to those of Drew, Gould, and Vanderbilt were being staged in the West. Out where the deer and the antelope are said to play, Ben Holladay, Henry Villard, and a number of other go-getting men were fighting for control of rails and boats in the Pacific Northwest; and the war proved so wide and bitter that reverberations were felt in England, Germany, and Austria, where Lords and Junkers began to wonder why the laying of simple American iron rails could cost so much good European money.

In California a quartet of singularly grasping men named Crocker, Huntington, Stanford, and Hopkins, commonly known as the Big Four, were using the courts, the legislatures, and hundreds of gunmen to build a monopoly out of the Southern Pacific, the Central Pacific, and sundry lines bought under pressure.

Fighting the Big Four in the Southwest were the men of the Santa Fe, virtually a Yankee railroad, owned and run from Boston, operating in the most remote region possible, and using tactics that combined the worst in Dan'l Drew and certain characteristics of the late and unfortunate William Kidd, a sea captain of New York City who was hanged on the 23rd of May, 1701, in England, but not before he had addressed the judge. "My lord," said he, "it is a very hard sentence. . . ." Kidd was a softie compared to the American railroad buccaneers of the late nineteenth century; few of *them*, so far as I can learn, ever asked for quarter—or gave any.

Industrial America of the time was a savage state within the Republic, a state of anarchy operated (nobody ruled) by ruthless men who were thoroughly convinced, if not by Herbert Spencer then by mere observation, that the world would be a better place if there were no weaklings among men. The most efficient way to remove weaklings was to set a pace so swift that only the most rugged characters could keep abreast. Horatio Alger, Jr., a writer of stories for boys, said it again and again, said it one hundred and thirty-five times in as many books, in milder words than Mr. Spencer used but even more effectively than the Master: You did not work Upward & Onward, from Train Boy to Railroad President, by hanging around pool halls and kicking tambourines out of the hands of street evangels. You got to be Railroad President by *getting ahead of the other fellow* and possibly running him down on the way.

Industrial America was a jungle, made for jungle law. Industrial America fanned out to follow the steel rails wherever they went, and the jungle laws went along too. This fact has been much deplored these past sixty years and more by well-meaning if naïve writers who seem to think that Bad Men were running the country, grinding Good Men down into the muck of poverty. Nothing could be farther from the truth, which was that *all* men were competing at a time and in a place when and where the prizes possible were immense and all rules in abeyance. Ethics, conduct, morals, all were pragmatic. The so-called ruthless industrialists, including the railroad operators, were no worse and no better than their fellow Americans who happened to be politicians or preachers, or simply nonentities. The governments, state and federal, were not better and possibly no worse than the men they pretended to govern. Let one not forget that if railroads offered and gave bribes, there were always ready takers.

Let one not forget, either, that it was these ruthless railroad builders and operators, whose morals and principles were average but whose abilities were very great—that it was these men, perhaps more than any other class, who were making the United States into the first industrial nation on earth, ready to take her place in world councils on any subject, whether of commerce or war. If these industrialists are to be damned, and I say they *are* to be damned, it is not because of what they did, but what they didn't do. The world they were building had little place in it for the artist of painting, of letters, of music, nor for the thinker who was other than pragmatic.

Let them be damned and doubledamned for these shortcomings, but not
because they rode roughshod over their fellows.

With America building so frantically, it was natural that the cost came
high. You do not get speed except at an extra cost. America paid for it in
many ways, and is still paying. It began to pay for speed, and greed, in the
1850 period, when disasters on the shoddy and hurrying railroads became
a disgrace. With heavy irony *Harper's Weekly* of June 31, 1858, said it:
"Nobody's murders. The railroads are insatiable. Boilers are bursting
all over the country—railroad bridges are breaking and rails snapping—
human life is sadly and foolishly squandered—but nobody is to blame.
Boilers burst themselves. Rails break themselves. And it may be ques-
tioned whether the consequent slaughter of men, women and children is
not really suicide. . . ."

Those were harsh words, from Mr. Harper's periodical, yet no harsher
than conditions warranted, as the State of New York discovered when it
made an investigation into the operating practices of its railroads. It
learned that a difference of at least five minutes was to be expected of the
watches of engineer and conductor. It found that a train might expect to
encounter an unguarded and wide-open drawbridge either by day or by
night, and that an engineer might well run his train on the supposition
he would find another train out of its scheduled running order at any
old place along the line. So careless had locomotive engineers become
and so erratic their rolling stock, that No. 238 of the two hundred and
fifty regulations that an alarmed New York saw fit to set up, required
that "The engineman must invariably start with care and see that he has
his whole train before he gets beyond the limits of the station."

First Connecticut, then New York, then other states, desperate at
the horrors committed almost daily by the railroads, attempted to stay the
slaughter. Regulations tumbled out of the legislative committees like a
snow storm—and had little more effect. True, equipment did improve
simply from necessity; rails were made better and heavier for the same
reason. Humanitarianism did not enter into it. But inventors were busy.
Janney and his automatic coupler and other devices, Westinghouse with
his air brake, they and a thousand other gadgeteers were offering the roads
marvelous or indifferent or hopeless ideas. Janney and Westinghouse made
an impression, but their fine devices were used sparingly until the fanatic
Alonzo Coffin arose to cry aloud at the murder, and to club the railroads
and the government until the Interstate Commerce Commission came into
being and forced the automatic coupler and air brake on the recalcitrant
railroads.

Another great improver of railroad travel, George Mortimer Pullman,
was made of the same stout stuff as the railroad operators. So was Webster
Wagner. Pullman and Wagner, and half a dozen other men, started sepa-
rately to build sleeping cars, then parlor cars and dining cars, gauding

them with all the art forms beloved of Victorians, including plush and damask and paneled wood, mirrors on every hand and silver-plated cuspidors, thus achieving a true rolling horror on wheels that caught the fancy of the mass of new *eleganti* who were just emerging from the log-cabin era and were likely to confuse elaborateness with beauty, whether in a house design by M. Mansard or a railroad coach by G. Pullman.

Busy as they were with their manufacturing, Pullman and Wagner found time to fight each other, using the same tactics employed by the railroad men—gouging, cheating, suborning perjury, bribing. They also found some time to devote to their employes, especially Mr. Pullman, whose barony near Chicago became the scene of one of the bitterest industrial wars the country has known.

Yet, because of Wagner and Pullman and their competitors, travel on the steam cars grew much better and immeasurably more comfortable.

By 1870 the railroad was safer than it had ever been, and more comfortable. Almost everybody agreed with that. There were also many Americans who thought it was altogether too costly—not the Pullman cars, not even the day coaches, but simply the cost to the public of having any railroads at all. These men were the farmers, mostly farmers of the Midwest, and they had known, and were to know again, some tragically bad times, times when drought killed their cattle, when myriads of grasshoppers appeared without warning to leap at their crops and devour them; times when corn at ten cents a bushel was too expensive to ship, so they burned it for fuel. And, above all, times when speculators and the railroads seemed in combine to rob the farmer of everything he had.

Flitting through the Midwest like a wind running through the wheat, and with no thought of railroads on his mind, Oliver Hudson Kelley, a fanatic with an idea for a social and educational society for farmers, nevertheless founded the Patrons of Husbandry, the Grange, which burgeoned swiftly into a mighty army of rustics in the West and South, then attacked the railroads in force and from all sides. Until the Grangers, no group in the United States had ever been a real challenge to the railroads, grown as arrogant as they were powerful. The Grangers actually tamed the carriers, taught them a few manners, then subsided into the kind of group Founder Kelley had envisioned from the first. It was a happy occasion for all America when the farmers rose against the railroads. When it was over, the lines were better and more useful citizens.

Although railroads were hardly agencies of reform, nevertheless it was they who gave the United States its one and only reform in the important matter of time. Until an October day in 1883, railroads and all else in the United States operated on clocks set by the sun or on some whim held by local commerce or industry. How many different "standard" times there were in the country is not to be known. This situation, which had been no hardship in canal and stagecoach days, became serious with the railroads.

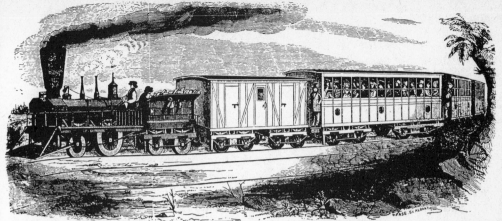

One of the earliest railroad photographs ever taken was the daguerreotype from which this wood-cut of the Albany-Springfield express on the Western Railroad of Massachusetts was copied. It was made in 1842 under the direction of Charles Van Benthuysen.

Peter Cooper's locomotive on a trial run pulls a car-load of B & O directors.

The first locomotive to use a cowcatcher was the John Bull, as it was commonly but not officially called, operated by the Camden & Amboy.

Trestle Bridge and military train, photographed by Matthew Brady during the Civil War.

After more than ten years of agitation, started implausibly enough by the principal of a school for young ladies, Prof. C. F. Dowd, noon of the 18th of October, 1883, was set by the railroads as the moment when four time belts would come into existence—that is, so far as the railroads were concerned.

If you think that the proposal was accepted with joy by the United States, then you do not understand your countrymen. There was plenty of opposition to the time belts, ranging all the way from the federal government, which officially ignored time belts for the next thirty-five years, to the Rev. Mr. Watson, Tennessee preacher, who pounded his dollar watch into pulp with a claw hammer, right in the pulpit, to indicate that the four time belts would make all timepieces worthless because, so it appeared to Mr. Watson, they interfered with God's own ideas about time. Incidentally, and all prophecies to the contrary, the adoption of the time standards was accomplished without an accident to a railroad train.

The time belts were of tremendous advantage to the country, railroads and all else. Another advance was the forming of the Interstate Commerce Commission, stemming from the Granger movement, which helped the carriers to improve their morals and also to protect their employees from needless injury. As for the employees, they were helping themselves, organizing first one Brotherhood, then another, staging or taking part in strikes only when they felt nothing else would do; but when they did strike, they struck with desperate determination. The years 1877 and 1894 were wreathed in the smoke of burning cars and gunpowder, while would-be travelers stayed at home and little freight moved. Out of the violence the railroad unions emerged both strong and stable, to be of immeasurable help in making railroad employees dependable, self-reliant, well-paid, and efficient. For a long period hard liquor was the greatest enemy to good railroad operation. Education and pressure, both by the unions and the carriers, plus the celebrated Rule G, brought such sobriety that for a long time past few Americans have seen a drunken railroad man on duty.

Railroads permeated every last corner of American geography and mind. The trunk lines stretched out to reach Chicago, to reach the Gulf, to reach the West Coast. Branch lines came to the main lines in patterns like the ribs to a fish's backbone. And before the great period of construction had reached its climax, stub lines forked off from branch lines until one would have been hard put to trace all the relationships. Into the second decade of the twentieth century new rails were being laid, although by then, too, many a branch line was finding the going difficult indeed; and soon they were fading, one after the other, as the internal combustion engine took hold of America and started to change its habits once more, just as the rails had changed things seventy-five years before.

A huge book, set in fine type, would not find room even to list the countless occupations brought into being by the railroads. All railroad jobs were, of course, new occupations, and so were many jobs merely associated with railroads. Express service was virtually unknown until a few men like William Harnden, Daniel Niles, and Alvin Adams took to riding the steam cars, carrying inside their tall beaver hats the important and valuable parcels of businessmen who did not like the slowness of the mails, nor consider the postoffice wholly reliable. The individual express men filled a real need. In a little while their business was such as to require them to carry carpetbags, then trunks, until finally they were renting whole cars and the express business became of great importance to the railroads.

The federal government did not favor express companies, and for a considerable period harassed them as lawbreakers; yet, because express did fill a need, it grew famously in spite of all objections and probably had an influence in forcing Uncle Sam to give better service with his mails. The Fast Mail came into being. All America was greatly excited and immensely pleased to see mailbags snatched from stanchions at little depots by the iron arm of the mail car while the train thundered by in full flight. Mail cars were painted prettily. They were marked with the symbol of the Union, flying with her own wings. The Fast Mail train itself was a grand symbol of Progress in an age that was certain Progress led, if not to Utopia, then to a fine condition of things anyway.

In these handsome cars rode young men who sorted letters and papers while the train rolled through the night, while it spanned rivers and crossed mountains, speeding the correspondence of the nation, bringing the far outposts on the Pacific shore twenty-four hours closer to the old settled regions. It was wonderful, and any man who doubted the future was no man to live in America.

From Mr. Pullman's sleeping cars came a new occupation that proved to be a boon to colored men who were chattels no longer but were still not free from their heredity. The Pullman porter grew into a type, a character, as standard and recognizable as that of the policeman, the cowboy, or the commercial drummer.

Other jobs, too, stemmed from the rails, among them jobs to be filled by hundreds of boys and young men who were known as train boys or news butchers, half salesmen, half carnival folk, who walked the rolling trains and hawked their wares, supplying the latest news to literates, and the Facts of Life to adolescents in the form of *Only a Boy* and the snappy *Paris Package*, not to be opened in the cars, and tons of salted peanuts and chewing gum to ruminants.

Telegraphy did not come into its own until its conjunction with the railroad, a fact Ezra Cornell made clear at some effort to himself and to his own great fortune. Telegraphers soon were a race apart, a fraternity comparable to that of the tramp printers in some respects, yet leading to better things. More than one railroad president got his start pounding a key at some obscure junction or way station.

Inspired by the new railroads, the Reno brothers of Indiana invented the profession of train robber, highly thought of and much romanticized for a hundred years, due in part to the spectacular professional technique developed by members of the James and Younger families, together with the hard-riding Daltons and the persistent and determined firm of Evans & Sontag, in some respects the greatest of them all.

Hero though the train robber was to much of America, an even greater hero was the Brave Engineer, the man in the right-hand side of the loco-motive cab, who drove his train safely through night and storm; or tragically into some other train, or washout, or defective bridge or rail. The Brave Engineer largely supplanted the Soldier and the Sailor as what Young America wanted to be when he grew up. Keen-eyed, tanned to leather by the elements that constantly played upon him, the lines in his face marked with soot, the engineer always looked ahead, scanning the bright rails for danger, his mind weighted with responsibility for his charges in the cars, his left arm resting on the throttle. It was his duty to put her through, or to die at his post, and die he too often did, to go into balladry along with the boy upon the burning deck and the kind if inefficient skipper of the doomed *Hesperus*.

He was a great, a magnificent figure to Young America. More than one banker and college president and eminent divine envied him, too, for his was the post they all had wanted and once meant to have, the calling for which superb whistles blew and noble bells rang, to the accompaniment of pounding drivers on the rails. He was the man who put her through, come what might of the weather or other deviltry.

Time was his very god, this man. No matter what the timecard showed, no matter how able the officials, the division superintendents, the dispatchers, switchmen, and fireman, it was at last and finally the engineer who put her through on time. With the coming of the railroad, Time for the first time in history really became an important measure in the lives of most Americans. To be "on time" was "railroad fashion." Even so ordinarily detached a man as Henry David Thoreau, in his cabin in the woods on Walden pond, came to reflect a good deal on Time and The Railroad. "They come and go," said he of the trains that passed his pond, "with such regularity and precision, and their whistle can be heard so far, that the farmers set their clocks by them, and thus one well-regulated institution regulates a whole country. Have not men improved somewhat in punctuality since the railroad was invented? Do they not talk and think faster in the depot than they did in the stage-office?"

Yes, Mr. Thoreau, they did, and do. A thesis that the most punctual peoples on earth are those best served by railroads could doubtless be supported by incontrovertible evidence. In addition, when the railroad is applied to a new country, such as most of America was in 1840, the railroad *demands* that a people be up and coming in all ways, if they would survive. Languor, indolence, beget themselves in no greater degree than does speed, hurry, being on time, or ahead of it. The railroad begat not only speed, but also precision and promptitude. The United States rapidly built itself into a great country by reason of many acquired habits, chief among them stemming, I am convinced, from the very force and urgency of the railroad.

"The stabler of the iron horse was up early this winter morning by the light of the stars amid the mountains," said Thoreau, "to fodder and harness his steed. Fire, too, was awakened thus early to put the vital heat in him and get him off." That was it. The Brave Engineer and his Iron Horse had begun, even in Thoreau's day, to set the pace that was to hurry America to its material triumph. Pious men sought to stop its progress, on the first day of the week; but not even the tablets of Moses, at least in translation, could stop the Brave Engineer from making his run. Plain greed of speculators came nearer to stopping it than did the Fourth Commandment.

Plain greed, in the form and style of watered stock, was the first dangerous disease to attack the railroads, and watered stock was a great and almost continuous scandal for half a century. It laid many a fine carrier low, and put them into bankruptcy courts, where they had no more real need of being than could be imagined. Plain greed also did much good. It tended to consolidate many small or weak carriers into one or another of the big systems which could and did, and do to this day, serve vast regions so well that newer forms of transportation will have a time of it to dislodge them.

Into every last part of the American credo the railroad has permeated. Our ballads and stage plays and movies, our literary fiction, our studies in economics and geography—aye, and politics—all have felt in some degree the effects of the steam carriers. Makers of luggage had to conform to the limitations of seats and shelves in day coaches and Pullman cars. They had also to build well in order to defeat the muscular temperament of baggage men, often called smashers. Inventive minds compounded mixtures to alleviate or prevent the ills suffered from car smoke and gas and the motion of moving cars. Printers sat up nights to devise methods of numbering the endless tickets and bills and forms needed for travel and transportation. Folk living near imposing mountains or beside gorgeous lakes suddenly discovered the Summer Visitor trade and have lived on it ever since. Other folk found their regions salubrious and warm in winter. The railroad was happy to bear these tidings and prompt to carry people thither, while forward-looking man erected huge hotels to accommodate the visitors.

There was no end to the ramifications of the steam cars. Hordes of calculators and orderly thinkers had to pool their resources to formulate the interminable records and the gigantic bookkeeping machine that apportions the proper amounts of passenger income from through tickets to this or that road. Other moles had to burrow into the deep morass of routes and public needs to produce schedules by which a man on the peak end of Florida could travel without delays to Port Angeles on the Olympic peninsula of Washington, or ship a box of fruit from San Diego, California, to Fort Fairfield, Maine, and have it arrive in good condition.

It was the Brave Engineer that the public knew and admired. The public never saw or thought of the railroad bookkeeper, a whole army of him, who had to devise, then to operate the system by which thousands of freight cars, owned by a thousand different roads, could be run over all those roads and their every moment, their every penny of expense and income charged and credited to the proper lines. It gives one a monumental headache just to consider such a task. Next time you watch a passing freight, note the owners of the cars—Wabash, Pere Marquette, Soo, Kansas Pacific, Fruit Growers Express, Central of Jersey, Rock Island, Canadian Pacific. There they roll, all in one string, touring the country, forty-eight states, and nine provinces, all carrying something to somebody from somebody. There is magic in the names on their sides, but they move and are accounted for not by any magic but because of the plodding and accurate work of thousands of men and women who keep the records. Nobody ever found Charley Ross, the Lost Boy, but the railroad people know where their hundreds of thousands of cars are, any week, any day, almost at any hour.

There go your long timbers at forty miles an hour, like battering rams sent against the city from the woods. Back to the woods goes a chair to sit in, or a mackinaw to wear, or a case of fruit to keep scurvy away. The movement is shuttle-like. Always there is something needed at a distant point, and the railroad that does not or cannot carry goods both ways is headed for the courts or the boneyard. Shrewd men in insulated offices look at maps, scan industrial and agricultural statistics, keep one eye on the calendar, another on the weather, in order that the Milwaukee or the Rutland or the Texas & Pacific shall not be caught without cars when time and weather conspire to force movement of whatever is seasonable. They never get into the ballads or the plays, these men, and seldom into the newspapers, but it is because of them that the Brave Engineer puts her through on time.

Coordination of effort has been a notable achievement of American industry and business generally. Nowhere is this factor to be found in better working order than in the American railway system. So smooth, so precise, so punctual is this system that the average person seldom has reason to reflect on it. He is served, whether as passenger or shipper, so well that he takes for granted the complicated and vast network of rail carriers.

This network is a giant, a giant so familiar, so close to our daily lives, that we seldom if ever appreciate its real size. Consider that the United States has 227,335 miles of railroad, almost one-third of the world total.

Included in this American system are 398,730 miles of track. Over these tracks, every day, run 24,000 freight trains and 17,500 passenger trains.

It requires more than one million persons to operate the Class 1 American railroads alone, and of these employees (in 1944) 115,000 were women.* Wages paid in 1944 total $3,853,345,000.

The railroad dollar earned comes from four major sources: 74.2 cents from freight, 19.0 cents from passengers, 1.5 cents from express, and 1.4 cents from the mails; all other sources contribute the remaining 3.9 cents.

Incidentally, American railroads are publishers to the extent of 80 million copies of timetables yearly.

What railroads mean to the financial structure of the country is indicated by their evaluation, set in 1944 at $27½ billions.†

The railroads have usually been run by ingenious men, quick to sense a challenge of any sort, and quick to meet it. Of challenges and other dangers they have had their share, and now, in mid-twentieth century, the challenge of the internal combustion engine is the greatest they have had to face. It seems to be the history of ideas and methods that the steam carriers either will become obsolescent, then disappear, or will survive in some modified form, although still tied to rails. It is certain, I think, that they will survive, even in modified form, for many years. I hope they will survive, nor change too much, either, for to me the steam railroad is the essence of America, the America I have known and believe to be the finest place on earth. Railroads had a great deal to do with making it that way.

To me, the distance between two points is still in railroad mileage, and not by air line or bus line. Perhaps this is as good a sign as any that one does not belong to the younger generation, either in years or in spirit. It is one of the penalties for being born in a time when the Brave Engineer was one of the noblest Americans of them all, when a train of steam cars was magic that took one to all known places, and beyond, even in Oz. I find I bear this particular penalty of age very lightly. I even find room for pity of the generations too young to have known the steam railroad in its heyday, that lasted for some eighty years and cast a sorcery from which I, for one, have never attempted to escape. Let me sing of the magic steam cars of my day, and of two generations before.

---

* Class 1 railroads are those with operating expenses of more than one million dollars annually.

† "Current statistics are not available with respect to institutional holdings of railroad bonds. According to the Interstate Commerce Commission, and based upon testimony submitted to it in 1937 on behalf of the Railroad Security Owners Association, in hearings in Ex Parte No. 123, nearly 56 per cent of the total net railroad funded debt at the end of 1936 (excluding intercompany railroad holdings) was held by insurance companies, banks, endowed educational institutions, and foundations."—*Railroad Finance;* A Report by the Subcommittee on Finance. Railroad Committee for the Study of Transportation. Association of American Railroads. 1947.

CHAPTER II

The Prophets

I do verily believe that carriages propelled by steam will come into general use, and travel at the rate of 300 miles a day.
— OLIVER EVANS, 1813

NEARLY all great innovations seemingly must be preceded by prophets, men for the most part ignored or ridiculed, who have the vision to comprehend the implications inherent in a new discovery or a new invention. Stating something novel, something that differs radically from what is currently believed, is dangerous business. It used to be common practice to feed such prophets a stout dose of hemlock brew, or simply burn them at the stake. In any period the role of prophet is no life of joy.

It is probably true that a majority of prophets become monomaniacs and bores, tramping streets and turnpikes, stopping all who will listen or who can't escape, haunting legislatures, writing tracts and pieces for the papers, ringing doorbells, and standing hat in hand to plead futilely with some wealthy and completely unimaginative nobody for a little cash to aid in transforming the shadowy nimbus into the hard fact of substance.

These prophets, or advance men for the new day, are pretty certain to have a hard time of it, and 'tis little wonder that many of them fell finally into habits of vice, such as the taking of drams. Because they see clearly what their fellows cannot see at all and do not even believe possible, they are set down as fanatics—at best dreamers, lookers at the moon when it is full, sitters on clouds, men who permit their poor wives to drudge, their children to starve, all for the sake of some nebulous idea in a distorted mind. At worst, the prophets of things to come are reviled as agents straight from the pit that has no bottom and are treated as enemies of the established order, as indeed often they are.

One, and perhaps the greatest, disregarded prophet of the steam railroad in the United States was a persistent and cantankerous genius born Oliver Evans in 1755, in Delaware. When he was seventeen he read about the steam engine that James Watt had recently perfected in England, and from that point to the end of his life Evans' great ambition was the utilization of the steam engine, chiefly as a locomotive force. His first work, however, took the form of valuable and rather startling improvements in the machinery of a gristmill operated by his brothers at Wilmington. He also experimented with steam engines of his own construction.

Right after the close of the Revolution, Evans had progressed so far with his steam experiments that he petitioned the legislatures of Pennsylvania and Maryland for the exclusive rights to use his "improvements in flour mills and steam carriages" in those states. Pennsylvania granted the flour-mill part of the petition, and Maryland granted the whole request, showing its complete disbelief in its stated reason that whatever Evans did with steam carriages "could harm no one."

Evans devoted the next thirteen years to developing a steam-propelled carriage. During this period he remained as poor as a dormouse, using what cash came his way for his experiments. He also tried, futilely, to find someone who would put up sufficient money for a practical demonstration. At last he gave up his steam carriage idea for the time, and built a steam dredge, which he prodigiously named Orukter Amphibole and which he drove overland, under its own steam power and to the horror or amazement of all who saw it, from his shop in Philadelphia to the Schuylkill River. A contemporary drawing of the contrivance indicates it to have been startlingly similar to the amphibious automotive machines used in World War II.

Although Orukter Amphibole was a ten days' wonder, it got Evans nowhere. Meanwhile, his steam-milling inventions, which performed every necessary movement of the grain and meal from one part of the mill to another without the aid of manual labor, but which he had failed to introduce successfully were at last being grossly infringed by millers, and Evans spent much of the remainder of his life fighting the pirates of his inventions.

But it was as a prophet of steam railroads that Evans stood almost alone. As early as 1786 he was talking about steam carriages. As early as October of 1813 he was writing to the *Aurora,* a Philadelphia periodical, proposing nothing less than establishment of a railway between Philadelphia and New York City. This was to be "for the transportation of heavy produce, merchandise, and passengers on carriages drawn by steam engines." Nothing like this had been proposed before in America. He went on to suggest that paths be made for the carriage wheels to run on, "with a rail between them, set on posts, to guide the tongues of the carriages so that they might travel by night as well as by day."

It was a tremendous conception that Evans held up before his fellow Americans, and it was too much for them. While they snickered or yawned, he elaborated it. To aid the carriages, he continued, why not lay parallel lines of logs on the ground, flattened on their top sides and with a three-inch plank pinned to them, this to bear the carriages and the engine and to guide the wheels? A friend of his, he remarked, Captain Samuel Morey of New Hampshire, thought there was good sense in the proposal even if no one else did; and Captain Morey had made a suggestion of his own, namely, that the whole length of the railway from Philadelphia to New York be covered with a shed, which would protect the carriages, the ways, the goods, and the passengers from the inclemencies of the weather.

Poor old Evans, and poor Captain Morey, blowers of bubbles, riders of rainbows. Their fellow Americans believed that paresis was already hard upon these two visionaries. Bedlam yawned for them. . . .

Captain Morey returned to his old home in Orford, New Hampshire, there to prove that he really was crazy by puttering with a steamboat; and Evans talked on and on. A wooden railway, he said, and few listened, would be less costly than a turnpike to keep in repair. The speed of the railway would be much greater. People, said he, would travel like birds, 15 miles an hour, 300 miles in a day, and in safety. Everything was in the railroad's favor, and he could not understand, said Evans, how any reasonable man could oppose it. Yet, otherwise reasonable men did oppose it, while other men ignored it.

The good old stagecoach, Mr. Evans, will never be supplanted.

If the Lord had intended us to ride in steam carriages, sir, he would have invented them.

Although for lack of funds Evans was never permitted to build and operate a steam carriage, he continued to his last day to prophesy the steam railroad as America's great method of transportation. The wonder of Evans as prophet is that he saw the railroad in all of its fullness a century later, for his imagination did not halt at the railroad as it was first put into use, as a short line between two neighboring towns, but as a vast network, possibly connecting the Mississippi Valley with the Atlantic Coast. More, he said in print, over these railroads would operate not only freight and common passenger carriages, but carriages that would be set aside for sleeping and for dining. Here was a prophet of the first mark.

In 1819 Evans died, still unshaken in his belief in steam engines hauling carriages on rails. "I do verily believe," he said in his later years, "that carriages propelled by steam will come into general use, and travel at the rate of 300 miles a day. But," he added wistfully, as he thought of the doggedness with which his fellows held to old ways, "one step in a generation is all we can hope for. If the present generation shall adopt canals, the next may try the railway with horses, and the third generation use the steam carriage."

The steam carriage would not have to wait so long, not nearly so long. A few other fanatics had seen something of the same vision that had beckoned to Evans. One of these, John Stevens of Hoboken, was a fanatic of great energy and ability. A veteran of the Revolution, Stevens had been preaching railroads even in Evans' time, and in 1821 he got from New Jersey a charter to build a railroad across that state, and two years later another charter from Pennsylvania to build from Philadelphia to the Susquehanna River.

This looked like progress. But not even the forceful Stevens could pry capital out of the complacent or cautious men of Jersey and Pennsylvania. The noise he made, however, prompted founding of the Pennsylvania Society for the Promotion of Internal Improvements, which presently sent William Strickland to England to learn what he could about the use of the primeval railroads in operation there. In 1826 Strickland made his report which has been hailed as one of the great landmark documents in the philosophy and practice of the railroad in America.* Strickland was of the opinion that the railroad was much to be preferred to the canals, which just then were much the craze in the United States.

While Strickland was in England, the indomitable Stevens, then seventy-six years of age, designed and built with his own hands a steam locomotive, then laid a circular track in the yard of his home, and invited all who would to come and see that steam carriages could be made to run on rails. Toy though it was, this was the first locomotive to run on a track in North America.†

Close on the heels of Strickland's report, and the demonstration in Stevens' yard, the dam of ignorance and apathy that appears in retrospect to have been holding back the application of the idea of steam and rails seemed to burst. Perhaps it was Strickland's report. Maybe it was the snorting toy on the circular track in Hoboken. In any case, it was barely a year until the Baltimore & Ohio Railroad was chartered, and within twelve months more, actual construction of the line was under way, being touched off in a happy occasion, since immortalized in murals, during which old Charles Carroll, sole surviving Signer of the Declaration, grunted slightly as he laid a stone to mark the spot where the first dirt was turned.

But the B&O was not yet a steam railroad. Horses were its first motive power but it soon staged a prize contest "for the best steam locomotive," which was won by Phineas Davis, late of Grafton County, New Hampshire, but more recently of Pennsylvania, who built an engine he called the *York*, loaded it onto a wagon, and took it overland to Baltimore, where it was found a better machine than the four other entries. For his *York* Davis received $4,000 and an offer to go to work for the Baltimore & Ohio Railroad, which he promptly did, becoming manager of the B&O shops and serving until 1835, when he was crushed to death in the derailment of a new locomotive he had designed.

---

* By Robert Selph Henry, in his authoritative *This Fascinating Railroad Business*, Indianapolis, 1942.

† Stevens was no monomaniac, for he was a man of many ideas. He proposed as early as 1815 that the United States Navy go in for armored ships. He drew up a design for a bridge across the Hudson from Hoboken to New York. And before he died, aged 89, he proposed a vehicular tunnel under the Hudson, and an elevated railroad for New York, which he held to be already congested.

Almost simultaneously with the chartering of the B&O there came a sudden burst of railroad excitement. Work was begun on the Charleston & Hamburg from the South Carolina city to the head of navigation on the Savannah River. The State of Pennsylvania, roused at last by the Strickland report, revived John Stevens' charter of 1823 and prepared to go into the railroad business. The Delaware & Hudson, already a going concern as a canal company, branched out into railroads and built a line from Carbondale to Honesdale, sending a man to England to buy four locomotives. A group calling themselves the Mohawk & Hudson started laying track out of Albany with the idea of connecting with the Erie Canal at Schenectady. The New York & Harlaem(sic) was laying eight miles of rail from City Hall northward to the Harlem River. The Boston & Lowell got a charter from the State of Massachusetts. The Chesterfield Railroad got a charter from Virginia and went ahead to lay 13 miles of rail from the coal mines on Falling Creek to the head of tidewater at Richmond. Only a little later (1832) the Portsmouth & Roanoke was incorporated to operate between Portsmouth and Suffolk, Virginia. (Today this latter line is the oldest part of the Seaboard Air Line.)

It would all have done Oliver Evans good, could he have seen the many manifestations of his prophecy.

While the Baltimore & Ohio was fooling around with sail cars and with horse-treadmill locomotives, the Charleston & Hamburg, on the advice of its chief engineer, Horatio Allen, had the first American-built steam locomotive built in New York, at the West Point Foundry, quaintly named it *Best Friend of Charleston,* and in December of 1830 it pulled the first train of cars ever moved by steam on track in the United States. The Charleston & Hamburg, six miles long, may be said to have been the first American railroad as the term is generally understood.

The first trips made on the Charleston road were informal jaunts, to try out the engine and the rails, but in January of 1831 formal operation of the line was begun with a festive occasion. In one of a brigade of carriages attached to the *Best Friend* was placed a small field gun of the United States army, the use of which "had been politely granted by Major Belton," and this was fired at proper intervals as the train sped along, at a rate of 21 miles an hour, over the six miles of flat rails. No less than two hundred persons were hauled on this first formal railroad excursion in the United States, most of whom were stockholders of the railroad and their families.

It was the Charleston road, too, that had the honor of the first locomotive explosion. On the memorable 17th of June, 1831, as the *Best Friend* was being turned around on what was described as the "revolving platform," the Negro fireman, annoyed at the sound made by the escape of steam from the safety valve, tried an experiment. He sat down right hard on the valve lever. For a few moments he was happy at the ensuing quiet;

then the boiler blew up with a roar and was tossed some distance from the rest of the engine, while the Negro, the engineer, a Mr. Darrell, and two other men were injured.

Superintendent Horatio Allen of the line had been forehanded. He had another locomotive on hand, the *West Point,* and this was put into service at once; and Mr. Allen saw to it that its safety valve was so arranged that it was "out of reach of any person but the engineer." The deplorable accident to the *Best Friend,* however, had caused, says a contemporary account, "a feeling of unease in the people of Charleston about the behavior of locomotive engines." This unease on the part of the public, naturally enough, called for prompt action; and the railroad must have had a bright public relations counsel on its staff, for almost immediately it had introduced what it was pleased to call a Barrier Car. Perhaps the Barrier Car was the idea of Superintendent Allen, for he was a most ingenious man: he later became a leading engineer on the Croton Water Works project in New York, did important work on the Brooklyn Bridge and the Panama Railroad, patented a rotary steam valve, and was one of the founders of the Union League Club in Manhattan. In any case, the Charleston & Hamburg's Barrier Car was worthy of such a genius.

This was a flatcar on which was built up a high pyramid of cotton bales, well secured in place with ropes. It was attached just behind the locomotive tender. Should the *West Point* blow up, as the *Best Friend* had done, the hurtling boiler would batter harmlessly—except, of course, for the poor engineer and fireman—against the wall of cotton—or such was the idea. It undoubtedly relieved the unease of the traveling public of Charleston.

The immediate success of the Charleston & Hamburg must have been a big factor in breaking down the wall of sloth that had kept steam transportation on land confined, while steamboats were making wonderful progress. Five years after the *Best Friend* made its epic first trip, there were 1,098 miles of steam railroad in operation in the United States, and by 1839 the figure had risen to nearly 5,000 miles. The South was particularly quick to charter and also to build rail lines. Although in 1839 Pennsylvania led all states with 947 miles of track, and New York was second with 573 miles, there were 363 miles in Virginia, 246 miles in North Carolina, 308 miles in Alabama, 164 miles in Tennessee, and 96 miles in Louisiana.*

The engines and rolling stock of the period were naturally crude and neither very safe nor efficient. Most of the newly emerged lines built their passenger cars in the familiar form of the stagecoach, just as seventy years later the first automobile makers adopted the form of the buggy; but the coachlike carriages were found to be top-heavy on rails and were quickly

---

* Turner, H. S., *A Description of Canals and Rail Roads in the United States,* New York, 1840.

discarded for cars built more like farm wagons. These were gradually lengthened, gradually enclosed, and windows added.

The locomotives of the 1830's came in highly varied designs, some with upright, others with horizontal boilers, and all of them left their crew standing on their feet and open to the weather and the sparks and smoke. The tender was a mere stubby flatcar, on which were a hogshead of water and a pile of wood.

The coming of the railroad, and the rapidity with which it expanded during the 1830's, found a public wholly unprepared, and pretty much confused. What, thoughtful men now asked one another, was a railroad? There had been little thinking on the subject, hence there was no philosophy of railroads. The canal builders and operators, of course, simply damned the new method of transportation on every count they could think of. It was dangerous. It wouldn't work. It was merely a clever method by which smart scoundrels could steal your money more or less legally by selling you worthless stock. The canal men had something there, for a terrible amount of stock did prove worthless. The railroad was also against nature. And, finally, it was against God; and many a preacher found friends among canal and stagecoach men when he opened up full blast on this new curse that a tireless Satan had promulgated to try all Christian men.

Thoughtful souls, however, considered the railroad and wondered what it should be. Was it to be simply a new and improved kind of turnpike, a highway, to be used by any number of transportation and shipping companies? Could any man who had a steam carriage use the rails simply on payment of a fee, as a man could use his wagon on a turnpike for a fee? In 1834 many men thought so, for such was the idea of both the turnpike and the canal. The subject was debated in taverns and in legislatures, and in Pennsylvania the subject became so troublesome that a committee was appointed by the state to study the matter and make a public report.

The committee labored well, and its report was forthright and clear, terming it a fallacy to consider a railroad a turnpike. It would be impossible, the committee thought, by that method to secure "a cheap, constant, and expeditious transportation." The vast outlay of money required to keep up "a constant line of engines and cars on the road" would soon throw the business into very few hands, over whom there would be "no check or control." All the evils of a monopoly would exist, said the committee, without any of its advantages. It visualized also "an occasional understanding between companies" that would produce great fluctuations in freight rates. These might come on suddenly, too, and would "catch distant merchants unawares." Then, there would also be accidents, similar to those caused by racing stagecoaches on the turnpikes, long a scandal to all right-thinking men, but on the railroad these accidents would be more frequent and dangerous because of the increased speed. "The strictest police," said the committee with finality, "could not guard against them."

No, said the committee, a railroad was not to be a turnpike. It must be managed by one company. And to bolster its opinion the committee called for support Jonathan Knight, Esq., first chief engineer of the Baltimore & Ohio Railroad and one of the giants of the early days of the rails. Knight was a man of positive opinions and direct speech, and what he said about the place of the railroad in American life must have settled the matter. With his usual vigor he vowed that ". . . locomotive engines and their trains, managed and ordered by different companies, cannot be successfully run upon the same rail-way; and whoever shall attempt it will assume a fearful responsibility, as jeopardizing, in an imminent degree, and without necessity or the prospect of corresponding benefit, the lives and effects of passengers and others. The great speed and irresistible momentum of these machines and their trains render any other than a unity of management in the highest degree dangerous, if not absolutely impracticable. . . ." *

The man who set down those positive opinions was one of the most notable in the primeval days of railroading. His location work for the Baltimore & Ohio had been particularly remarkable in that he laid out an excellent route at a time when there were no rules to go by, when it was not even known how steep a grade or how sharp a curve a locomotive engine and its trains could handle. Knight, like Allen, the operating head of the Charleston road, had to work pretty much on the trial-and-error system,. and both men appear to have made few errors. Hence, when J. Knight said that a railroad was to be operated by one concern, he was listened to. There seems to have been little if any more public discussion as to what form a railroad should take.

Even with "unity of management" a railroad of the time was none too safe. What must have been one of the earliest fatal accidents to passengers occurred in October of 1836 on the Columbia Railroad in Ohio. A Mrs. Gibson and her child were killed when a car axle broke and let the coach down upon the track while in motion. It was in this period, too, that every train was equipped with a sledge hammer to be used when a rail—then merely a strap of iron on top of wood stringers—suddenly let go and crashed up through the bottom of a car. The conductor or brakeman took the hammer and pounded the loose rail back through the floor. These rail ends were called "snake-heads."

On some of the roads there seems to have been little if any special accommodation for passengers. On June 21, 1837, one of the cars of a train on the Boston & Providence broke down and threw overboard its load of lumber and shingles "on top of which were a number of passengers, two of whom, Dennis Conder and William Kervin, Irishmen, were killed."

---

* *Evidence Showing the Manner Locomotive Engines are Used on Rail-Roads*, Boston, 1838.

The entire period of the 1830's was marked by explosions and other grievous accidents to trains. Typical was one that took place on the Fourth of July, 1839, on the New York & Harlem:

About 10 o'clock in the morning the steam engine which comes into the city with the cars ran off the track opposite Union Park. The steam was already generated to excess, but, unfortunately, the engineer neglected to blow it off. It is also supposed that the water had not been taken in properly at the stopping place. When the engine had thus run off the track, a number of passengers, mostly mechanics, lent their services to get it on again. While thus surrounded, the boiler burst. The chief engineer was blown to pieces— his legs went into Union Park, his arms on a pile of lumber on the other side of the avenue. . . .

Then there were grade crossings, even in that day. One cannot be sure of the first man to arrive at a crossing at the exact moment the train was due, and on time, but it must have occurred before 1840, for in that year the up-and-coming Western Railroad in Massachusetts put up warnings where their tracks crossed highways and turnpikes: "Look Out for the Engine while the Bell Rings." * There appears to have been a shocking indifference, on the part of railroad men, to the disasters occasionally wrought by their trains. An English traveler of the period, T. C. Grattan, related that the train he took out of Philadelphia soon struck a horse and buggy containing two women and failed even to slow down. Later, he said, the conductor casually informed him that one of the women had been killed and the other seriously injured.

In 1836 Harriet Martineau, a woman who spoke her mind, reported that the few railroads in the South were pretty bad. The roadbeds were poor, she said, the engine boilers leaked, and trains were more likely than not to arrive hours late. Possibly she was somewhat prejudiced against railroads by what happened to her on one short trip; sparks from the locomotive burned thirteen great holes in her gown.

Occasionally passengers were obliged to aid the railroad in other ways than by paying fare. George Combe, the English phrenologist, making a trip on the Schenectady & Troy, said that the cars broke down and all hands got off and pushed the train a good third of a mile to the next station There one horse was obtained, and the cars moved on again. Perhaps this was merely an unfortunate day for the S&T, for Captain Frederick Marryat, the popular writer, rode the S&T in that same year of 1837, and he considered it the speediest railroad in all the United States.

If the early roads were crude, learning by trial and error how to control "the great speed" and the "irresistible momentum" of the locomotive engines, so too were the methods used to raise capital to finance the roads.

---

* So said S. A. Howland in his ghastly *Steamboat Disasters and Rail-Road Accidents in the United States,* Worcester, 1840, a hair raiser from first page to last.

In most, but not all, cases, private capital started the venture, and to this was often added varying sums from the public funds. It was believed by many that railroads should somehow be owned both by the government, either state or federal, and the private stockholders. The State of Maryland and the City of Baltimore invested in the Baltimore & Ohio and so continued in the railroad business until 1896, when the city sold its stock, and 1906, when the state did likewise. The State of Pennsylvania owned much of one road for a time, and Georgia, South Carolina, and Tennessee aided roads within their boundaries by taking stock.

But what in time became the classic method of financing railroads was the land grant. Probably the first land grant made by Congress for "internal improvements" was an act of 1796 authorizing one Ebenezer Zane to locate certain lands in the "territory west of the River Ohio in such situations as should best promote utility of a road to be opened by him on the most eligible route between Wheeling and Limestone." Twelve years later Abraham Alfonse Albert Gallatin, Secretary of the Treasury—an able prophet—strongly advocated governmental aid to roads and other internal improvements as being economically sound. Land grants to a number of canal companies were made by Congress in the next few years. Then, in 1835, Congress made the first grant of land to a railroad, the Tallahassee Railroad Company, which set the style for later grants. This one gave the company a right of way of 30 feet on each side of the line, and also the privilege of using timber from public lands, on either or both sides, for 100 feet, and "ten acres for a terminal where the St. Mark's and Wacolla Rivers join." *

By 1840, to select an arbitrary date, the American railroad had come down out of the clouds of prophecy and, in spite of bitter and continual opposition by canal and stagecoach interests, was well on its way to becoming a success. The work of the early prophets and fanatics and monomaniacs was done, but that of the primeval railroad technicians was just beginning.

---

* Haney, Lewis Henry, *A Congressional History of Railways in the United States to 1850*, Madison, Wis., 1908.

From A Pioneer Indiana Railroad

The pride of the New Albany & Salem Railroad (now the Monon) in 1868 was The Admiral, shown here in all her glory. She was built in the little company's shops at New Albany, Indiana.

N. Y. Illustrated News, April 18, 1863

Chicago and Northwestern depot, 1863.

CHAPTER III

Primeval Railroading

*The locomotive engine built by our townsman, M. W. Baldwin, has
proved highly successful . . . working with great ease and uniformity.*
—*Philadelphia Chronicle*, Nov. 24, 1832.

IT WAS probably natural that the attention of the operating men of the
early railroads should have been concentrated on the locomotive. Here
was the machine that put transportation into a new era, that set it apart
from travel over turnpike. A train of wooden coaches pulled along wooden
rails by horses, which was the method employed by a number of 1830
railroads, was not shockingly different from stage coaches pulled along
turnpikes by horses. Only the rails were different. But the steam locomotive, throwing up black smoke, giving off glowing sparks, seeming to
breathe, to snort, to cough and sizzle, and making its own power out of
wood and water, why, this was a startling thing, a new sort of animal, an
object to give pause to any person. The first sight of a steam locomotive in
movement struck the fancy of all who saw it. Applying the first analogy
that came to mind, people called it the Iron Horse, and the iron horse
quickly went into American life and remained there as the most important
machine of the nineteenth century.*

Because England was earlier in experimenting with steam locomotives
and railroads, it was to England that most of the early American railroad
men turned for their machines. In 1831 the first British importations were
put into American service: the *John Bull No. 1* on the Camden & Amboy
and another *John Bull* on the Mohawk & Hudson, which was also using
the American-built *DeWitt Clinton*. Other English machines had by then
or were soon to come for the Boston & Worcester, the Baltimore & Susquehanna, and other lines.

Along with the English locomotives, in many cases, came British engineers to operate them. These men appear to have been the most secretive
persons imaginable, acting as though they considered themselves the
keepers of mysteries so important that only the gods could know them.

---

* The sight of his first locomotive, however, brought to the mind of the writer's paternal
grandfather a different animal. Writing to his home in northern Vermont from Springfield,
Mass., in 1847, he related that the steam cars made his "eyes to bung out" and that they
"come faster than deer ever run."

No doubt they had been so instructed by their employers in England, and those astute men had not forgotten how the secrets of wool- and cotton-spinning machinery had been smuggled to the American colonies and had resulted in stiff competition. In any case, sixty years afterward, Charles H. Chandler, son of a Boston & Lowell Railroad mechanic, recalled his father's experiences with English locomotive men, which began when an English engine arrived in parts and was taken in wagons to Lowell, Massachusetts. The elder Chandler and another skilled mechanic were told to put the parts together and make them run.

Having never seen a locomotive of any kind, and having no diagrams to go by, the two men journeyed to Boston to inspect a new British engine just put into use by the Boston & Worcester Railroad. They were not even allowed to approach it. Thinking that the English mechanic would, of course, make free with information, once he knew that it was for two budding locomotive mechanics—brothers of the rails, so to speak—Chandler explained the reason for their visit. The Englishman froze. No, sir, he would answer no questions at all. No, they could not come near the engine. Chandler recalled that such treatment was universal at the time and Americans learned the mysteries only by sharp observation and even spying methods.

Yet Americans were not to rely very long on English locomotives or Englishmen to run them. John B. Jervis of the Mohawk & Hudson line soon came to the conclusion that the English locomotives, which weighed six or more tons, were too heavy for the American rails then in use; they were tearing up M&H tracks by deflection and wear. Jervis rebuilt one of the imported engines, removing the rigid front axle, with its single pair of wheels, and substituted a front truck with two axles and four wheels. This resulted in better distribution of the engine's weight and also shortened its wheelbase, permitting the machine to take the curves in the track with less wear on wheels and rails.

Jervis had made an important discovery. He had also made the first contribution toward development of what even today is known the world over as the American-type locomotive. (Within the next decade Americans were building locomotives for the British, and the Czar of all the Russias was ordering American-type engines from a Philadelphia concern.) Adding to the Jervis improvement, Henry R. Campbell designed and James Brooks built an American locomotive which, in addition to the four-wheel leading truck, had four driving wheels connected with outside rods, in contrast to the two-driver engines. This locomotive was named the *Blackhawk* and it may rightly be called the ancestor of almost all of the types of American locomotives in use today.*

---

* This might be the place to remark that in the twentieth century locomotives are classified by a method originated by F. M. Whyte, using the wheel arrangement on which to base the classification. Thus the *Blackhawk* would have been known as a "4-4-0"—an engine with four-wheel leading truck, with four driving wheels coupled, and no wheels behind the drivers."

Something of a genius among early American locomotive makers was an ex-jewelry manufacturer named Matthias William Baldwin. And Baldwin became interested in locomotives through the son of another genius, Benjamin Franklin Peale, one of seventeen children of Charles Willson Peale, philosopher, naturalist, and artist, he who had painted eight portraits from life of General George Washington and pictures of other officers of the Revolution, and also and not least, a portrait of Thomas Paine. But in 1831 the elder Peale was four years in the grave, and Peale's Museum, which he had founded, was now operated by his son, best known as Franklin Peale.

Young Peale knew that Matthias Baldwin had built a stationary steam engine, and asked if he could make a small locomotive, one large enough, say, to pull a couple of small cars around a circular track to be set up in the Museum. Baldwin thought he could. He set to work and on April 25, 1831, the little engine snorted and hissed and pulled two cars, each seating four passengers, around the track in Peale's Museum, instantly becoming the greatest attraction in the museum's long and distinguished history.

All Philadelphia felt an urge to ride behind the tiny iron horse that made its own power as it moved; and among the many riders were men interested in the newly incorporated Philadelphia, Germantown & Norristown Railroad, six miles of flat rails on which horses were the motive power. These men asked Baldwin if he could build them a man's size job, an engine to haul freight and passengers on the new railroad. Baldwin allowed that it was possible. He visited the shop of the Camden & Amboy line, where a British locomotive was in process of being assembled, then went home and so to work. Six months later he produced *Old Ironsides*, a 5½-ton job that rolled on wooden wheels banded with thick tires of iron.

Old Ironsides was accepted by the railroad, but its first unofficial run must have been disappointing to everybody. A Mr. Haskell who rode the locomotive with Baldwin himself recalled in later years that the two men alternately rode and pushed all the six miles to Germantown, which proved to be exactly six hours from Philadelphia, according to the speed displayed by *Old Ironsides*. When they attempted a slight rise in the track on the homeward journey, the engine stopped for want of steam. The two men applied themselves to a handy rail fence and presently had raised sufficient power to make the grade and continue on to Philadelphia without further incident.

The railroad operators were frankly dismayed at the performance, and were happy they still had their horses. Baldwin told them not to worry. He worked on the engine to such purpose that on November 24, 1832, the *Philadelphia Chronicle* could report, undoubtedly with truth, that "the locomotive engine built by our townsman, M. W. Baldwin, has proved highly successful." The paper went on to say that the placing of the fire in the "furnace" and raising steam occupied but twenty minutes, then she moved with her tender from the station "in beautiful style, working with great ease and uniformity." She puffed on to some point "beyond Union Tavern," then returned to the city, a total distance of six miles, without a halt. The paper added with pride that *Old Ironsides* had developed a speed of 28 miles an hour.

The PG&N road was immensely proud of its refurbished engine and immediately took space in the local papers to advertise that *Old Ironsides* would haul the cars every day when the weather was good, the horses being reserved for rainy days and for snow. But this first Baldwin locomotive was even better than they knew. Her maker continued to putter with her and a year later she accomplished an astonishing performance: she ran a mile in 58 seconds, and did $2\frac{1}{4}$ miles in 3:22, either of which was a marvel to contemplate.

Matthias Baldwin didn't know it yet, but he was in the locomotive manufacturing business. Other lines were quick to hear of *Old Ironsides*, and sent their men to ask Baldwin for an engine. In the next ten years he built at least one a year and each was better than the one before. Baldwin put good stuff into them, too. Many a Baldwin job of the 1830's was in use for the next three decades and more. A sample of his work at this time was the *Post Boy*, a locomotive built in 1836 for the new Long Island Rail Road. The Long Island used the *Post Boy* until 1852, when it was sold to a Boston foundry. Reconditioned there, it was shipped to Georgia and, still known as *Post Boy*, was put into operation by the Georgia Central and continued to haul trains in Dixie until well after the end of the Civil War.

Baldwin perfected a steamtight metal joint that would carry 120 pounds of steam and not leak, compared to the English joints made of canvas and lead that would not carry 60 pounds pressure. He also began experiments with coal for fuel, perhaps the first in relation to locomotives. He quickly did away with his banded wooden wheels and turned to chilled steel.

Incidentally, and because most American industrialists have been known as efficient men in their lines and almost wholly without other interests, I think it is worth knowing that Matthias Baldwin was not merely a builder of good iron horses. He aided in founding the Franklin Institute for the "improvement of working and living conditions among laboring families." He was an Abolitionist of the rankest sort and in 1835 founded a school for colored children. He even bought paintings and became a member of the Pennsylvania Academy of the Fine Arts and was elected to membership in the austere American Philosophical Society. In 1854 he admitted to partnership Matthew Baird, a man who understood how to take the inventions of others and apply them to practical use, often improving them in the process. It was Baird who first perfected the spark arrester, much needed in the days of wood-burning locomotives; and he also improved the use of fire brick in the construction of boilers. He was a fit man to team with Baldwin.

Because of Baldwin's Abolitionist activities, the locomotives of Baldwin and Baird were under boycott by Southern roads just before 1861, but neither Baldwin nor Baird cared, and before the former's death in 1866, the concern had made and sold more than 1,500 engines, and was well on the way to the top-layer position that the firm enjoys in the mid-twentieth century.

A fair sample of Baldwin's early work is still to be seen in the *Pioneer*, his thirty-seventh locomotive, now in a Chicago museum. It was built in 1836 for the Utica & Schenectady, used several years by that line, then sold in 1848 to the Galena & Chicago Union, where it was named the *Alert* and still later the *Pioneer* again. But the Baldwin job I should have liked to see with the naked eye was the *Tiger*, one of a series of four engines built in 1856–57 for the Pennsylvania Railroad. A handsome lithograph in full color of this splendid locomotive appears in E. P. Alexander's magnificent *Iron Horses* (New York, 1941), and it is something to see. Although the stack, firebox, and part of the steam dome are painted black, the rest of the engine exhausts the rainbow. Wheels and pilot are not only red but vermilion red. The boiler is eggshell blue. The tender is a delicate rose, with the railroad's title done on a flowing ribbon and surrounded by curlicues in gold. The outside of the cab is gorgeous, with scrollwork in gold and underneath the window a painting in natural colors showing a Bengal tiger obviously stalking some unseen prey in a jungle as green as emerald. The name plate, set well forward on the boiler, is in great Barnum-type letters, *TIGER;* another jungle painting appears on the side of the headlight, and to top everything off an American flag flies from a special bronze socket atop the pilot. No doubt the poor engine crew, and the roundhouse wipers, had a time of it keeping this engine in anything approaching its original beauty, but the effort must have been well worth while.

Decoration of locomotives swept the industry in the 1850's and did not die for a quarter of a century. The Taunton Locomotive Works in Massachusetts became especially noted in the field of art. Starting in 1847 with a job called the *Rough & Ready*, Taunton went on to build them gaudier and gaudier until about 1870. Charles E. Fisher, an authority on early locomotives, says that the Taunton people liked the running gear to be painted a variety of colors. Their boilers were covered with Russian iron, the cabs made from walnut or mahogany and well upholstered inside. A deft touch of Taunton was a piece of plate glass fitted over the number or name of the engine.* Taunton became a great locomotive-building center. William Mason of that city went into the business, and while his engines were not so decorative as those of the Taunton works, they were

---

* See, for instance, Mr. Fisher's "Locomotive Building at Taunton, Massachusetts," in Bulletin No. 15. The Railway and Locomotive Historical Society, Boston, 1927.

handsome in form and most efficient. Mason built what is now known as a
Mallet type of engine thirty years before the idea was patented. He also
constructed a number of engines famous in their day, jobs like the
Prometheus for the New Haven, and for various Western lines the *Prairie
King*, the *Mazeppa*, the *Zephyr*, and the *Amazon*.

The man who left his permanent and obvious mark on the American
locomotive, however, was Isaac Dripps, boss mechanic of the Camden &
Amboy, who thought up the cowcatcher or pilot. It appears that the C&A
was having no little trouble with derailments caused by wandering horses
and cattle, who were forever getting onto the Camden's tracks. The line's
superintendent asked Dripps if he couldn't do something to relieve the
situation. Dripps built a low truck and attached it to the front end of the
engine. Sticking out ahead of the two truck wheels were several long and
pointed bars of wrought iron. "That rig," Isaac Dripps declared of the
formidable weapon, "ought to impale any animal that may be struck and
prevent it from falling under the engine wheels."

It did, too. A few days after this first cow-catcher had been installed,
the Camden & Amboy locomotive hit a big and mean bull so hard that the
animal was held by the iron prongs and could be detached only by the use
of block and tackle. Such a cowcatcher was only too efficient, so Dripps
took away the pointed prongs and substituted a heavy bar at right angles
to the rails; this shortly was modified again and became the pilot or cowcatcher much as we know it today. Thus did Dripps contribute a feature
that still sets American locomotives apart from those of almost all other
countries.

All sorts of things were happening to prompt improvements to American
locomotives and rolling stock. In 1836 Pennsylvania was visited by a tremendous plague of grasshoppers. They arrived by the billion and overran
country and city alike. They came in great clouds that darkened the sun.
They came down into the fields and cleaned them of everything that grew.
The several short railroads soon discovered that their trains could not
run over the slippery squashed bodies of the insects. Crews of men armed
with brooms were set to work to precede the trains and sweep the hoppers
from the rails. But more often than not the hoppers were back on the rails
by the time the next train came along. Brooms were attached to the head
ends of locomotives. They soon wore out. Then, some forgotten man hit
upon the idea of sand. He filled a box with dry sand, put it on top of the
locomotive and ran pipes from it down to a point just in front of the
drivers. It worked wonderfully well and since then no American locomotive has been without a sandbox.

The iron horse was beginning to take on its classic form, but it still
lacked a whistle. On the early roads the engineer often hung out a flag on
a pole when it was time to apply the brakes to the cars, and a lookout
sat on the roof of a coach to spy the flag and call the crew to man the

brakes. An improvement was quickly discovered when some curious engineer tried a new type of signaling; he lifted the steam valve on the dome, either with his hand or an iron rod, causing steam to rush out with a loud hissing and thus attract the attention of the train crew. It was doubtless the Englishman, George Stephenson, who first suggested the steam whistle, and whistles were soon an integral part of all locomotives.

But the engine cab was invented by some American, probably a Yankee, for it appears to have first been tried on Massachusetts lines extending north into New Hampshire and was for the obvious purpose of keeping the engine crews from freezing at their posts. The first cabs of all were made of canvas, then wood was adopted.

The early American lines were, of course, so short that night operation was uncalled for.* But the passenger business increased so rapidly that something had to be done about freight, and the answer seemed to be to run passenger trains during the day, freight trains at night. The lustier railroads were also extending their tracks, and presently a trip from one end of the line to the other could not be accomplished in daylight hours. So, a few bold spirits started to run trains after night had fallen. This was considered so hazardous, as indeed it may well have been, that a pilot locomotive was sent ahead of the train, to test the rails. The pioneering Charleston & Hamburg in Carolina was the first to improve on this method. Its chief engineer, mentioned earlier, Horatio Allen, had a small flatcar made. He covered the platform with sand, and on top of the sand built a fire of pineknots. This fire-car was pushed ahead of the night-running engine and gave a sort of weird and jumpy illumination of the track. About 1840 the conventional headlight, burning kerosene and having tin reflectors, came into use.

All or nearly all of the early roads were single-track affairs. As traffic increased, something had to be done about trains passing each other between stations. This was accomplished by the building of turnouts, mere sidetracks of a few yards in length connected at each end with the main line by switches. Because there was no method of communication between stations, a point was selected half way between two turnouts, and a large pole erected, called the center post. Whenever a train moving west was met by a train moving east before the west train had reached a center post, the west train was required to back up to the nearest turnout and take the sidetrack. More than one head-on collision took place between two trains racing for the same center post or turnout. At other times there were bat-

---

*Nor were the lines overly anxious to start night operation. On Oct. 4, 1846, the *New York Tribune* had this to say: "The Housatonic Railroad is requested by a correspondent either to run their trains through in the course of a day or stop them where passengers can find beds. We think this is perfectly reasonable. He says he was among a number who could obtain no accommodation at New Milford, where the train stopped for the night, several ladies having to lie on the floor without beds."

tles between engine crews, and even passengers, of opposing trains, each side insisting it was farthest from the turnout.

The troubles with turnouts and center posts brought attempts to schedule trains at certain hours and a form of timetable came into use. These were called "arrangements of trains" and really did not have much significance. The most optimistic of the timetables were so far from actual performance of trains, then and later, that "to lie like a timetable" became a figure of speech. In the early days, when a train left its home terminal, little or nothing was known of its progress and trials until it returned; and so far as schedules were concerned, it was mostly a case of a train being due at a station when it arrived there.

Probably the first effort to increase knowledge of a train's movements was that of some forgotten station agent who erected a wooden tower at his depot and when he *thought* the cars were about due, he climbed to the tower top and sat there on a perch, spyglass in hand; and there he remained until he could glimpse the distant smoke plume. He then climbed down to announce, either by shouting or ringing a bell, or in some cases by blowing a horn, that Number Four would be along pretty soon. Out of these crude watch towers grew the system of semaphore signaling, with its high ball for a clear track.

The wooden rails topped with strap iron were most unsatisfactory. They were made obsolete by Robert L. Stevens of the Camden & Amboy who whittled out of wood a model for the iron "T"-shaped rail much as we know it today. The "T" rail proved to give the best support for the amount of iron (and later steel) used, and it could also be spiked directly to the ties. It was a great improvement, and Stevens has gone into railroad hagiography for his contribution.

The American railroad builders, it soon became apparent, were individualists, and each road arbitrarily selected a gauge of track and forthwith built its engines and cars to fit, although in a few cases, mostly in the Midwest, the track gauge was built to fit the engines that arrived from eastern manufacturers. The Baltimore & Ohio built to a gauge of 4 feet 8 inches, and so did many of the roads in Pennsylvania and around Boston. But the pioneering Charleston & Hamburg laid its rails 5 feet apart, the Mohawk & Hudson 4 feet 9 inches, the Camden & Amboy 4 feet 10 inches, and the New York & Erie called for a full 6 feet. All of this individualism made for something like chaos in later years and resulted in the celebrated Erie War, of which more in its place.

Several of the budding lines laid their tracks on ties of split granite and quickly discovered the stone to be entirely too rigid for good results. It had no give. The Boston & Providence had begun with wood ties, which were so eminently successful that the Boston & Lowell, the Boston & Worcester and other roads farther west tore up their expensive roadbeds and put in ties of hickory or oak. The use of preservatives began astonishingly early, for in 1833 the engineer of the Cayuga & Susquehanna advised the soaking of crossties in salt solution before they were laid. He had observed, he said, the long life of piling used in the salt beds at Syracuse, New York, and he thought the salt must have something to do with it.

It may have been the progressive Philadelphia, Germantown & Norristown that first broke away from the stagecoach idea of passenger cars. In 1837 this road put into use two cars of startlingly different design. One was named the *Victoria,* the other the *President,* and each rolled on eight, instead of four, wheels, had end instead of middle doors, and for seats benches extending along the sides, with a narrow center aisle. Nor was this all. At each end of this new type of car was a small room some five feet square. One was designed for "such feminine passengers as might wish to make changes of their apparel under conditions of privacy," the other was an out-and-out barroom where thirsty males, who were greatly in a majority in that day of comparative masculinity, could wet their whistles as the cars rolled along. I have no doubt but that many a male took a dram with the explanation it prevented car sickness.

The *Victoria* and the *President* must have found quick acclaim from a public that had been herded like sheep into boxcars or coach-shaped cars and often had to sit on the roof. From this point onward the passenger cars of all American roads quickly changed and took on much of the form we know today. An exception appears to have been the Erie & Kalamazoo Railroad, which operated between Toledo, Ohio, and Adrian, Michigan. This backwoods line had at least one passenger coach shaped much like a Swiss cuckoo clock, with two windows below, one above, and a large and very fancy center door.

Other lines, however, built closely to the form and style of the superb *Victoria* and the *President.* They varied somewhat, in this 1838–40 period, and in length ran from 35 to 40 feet. They were about 8 feet wide. The double seats were so narrow that two adults could only with great politeness sit side by side. From floor to ceiling was not more than 6½ feet. Doors were very small and so were the windows, which of course were nailed tight. Not for several years did all of the cars have the small ventilating holes that some builders thought necessary but others believed would "suck in" sparks and set fire to the inside of the coaches—which actually happened more than once.

In hot weather these "improved" coaches were unbearably humid and smelly and crowded. In cold weather a small stove was installed in one end of the car and these became the cause of cremation of many passengers when the era of railroad derailments and collisions started to push the ghastly steamboat accidents off the front pages of newspapers.

Night travel was worse. The male traveler hung his coat on one of the wall hooks, put his feet up on the seat in front, if there was room, then lay back and went to sleep—if he could. The womenfolk could not be so comfortable, for it was not seemly for them to lift what were known as their extremities off the floor. They merely sat and dozed. At night the cars were lighted by one candle at each end, stuck in candlesticks near the doors.

Two sorts of private cars made their appearance at an early date. One was simply a flatcar on which a buggy or stagecoach was securely fastened for the exclusive use of a family or party outing. The other sort of private car was merely a passenger coach chartered for the occasion. The cost of either sort ran from five to twenty-five dollars, being graduated by the length of the trip; this cost was in addition to the fares of all members of the party.

There was a deal of mighty jerking on the first trains. The cars were coupled to each other with some three feet of chain. Three feet of chain contain immense possibilities; and the engineer, who in early days was a god and ruled the conductor, was no man to worry about the comfort of passengers. When he started his engine, he opened up fast and took up the slack in the coupling chains with gusto and a bang. More than one traveler reported that the starting of a train jerked off every stovepipe hat aboard. Chains gave way to drawbars, then to the link-and-pin coupling.

American railroaders appear to have made steady progress in improving trains. As early as 1840 a distinguished German engineer, von Gerstner, had heard of the progress made by American lines and came over to see it. He was both delighted and impressed. In England, he said, everything had to conform to the ideas laid down by George Stephenson. It was almost impossible to change anything. In the United States, however, "everyone is trying to surpass his neighbor" and out of the rivalry came constant improvements. In England, said the German, all was imitation; in America, all was invention.*

In England they continued to book passengers; that is, the traveler paid his fare at the station where he was to board the train and his name was written in a book kept for that purpose and given to the conductor for checking his passengers. Often the booking agent added certain descriptive phrases, such as "boy" or "old man." And although this system was adopted and used for a time by at least one American railroad, the Philadelphia & Reading, other lines adopted the use of tickets. Some tickets were pieces of stout paper 10 inches by 5 inches. Some lines made use of metallic discs in sizes varying from that of a ten-cent piece to a dollar. Still more roads used cardboard, often glazed and highly colored. There were, of course, many travelers who boarded a train without a ticket, thus presenting the temptation, or the opportunity, to the captain to "knock down" a part or all of the fare collected. In time to come, knocking down

---

* von Gerstner is quoted at some length in John H. B. LaTrobe's *The Baltimore & Ohio Railroad; Personal Recollections*, Baltimore, 1868.

INLAND ROUTE

FOR NORTHERN AND SOUTHERN TRAVELLING.

The Richmond, Fredericksburg and Potomac Rail Road Company, in connection with the other Rail Road and Steamboat Companies on the route, have adopted the following Schedule, by which the daily Mail is now carried.

(NORTHWARD DIRECTION.)

Leave				Arrive at			
Blakely, N. C.	at	5 o'clock,	P. M.	Petersburg,	at	10 o'clock,	P. M.
Petersburg,	"	12 "	A. M.	Richmond,	"	4 "	A. M.
Richmond,	"	4½ "	A. M.	Washington,	"	6 "	P. M.
Washington,	"	7½ "	P. M.	Baltimore,	"	10 "	P. M.
Baltimore,	"	6 "	A. M.	New York,	"	11 "	P. M.

(SOUTHWARD DIRECTION.)

Leave				Arrive at			
New York,	at	4 o'clock,	P. M.	Baltimore,	at	3 o'clock,	P. M.
Baltimore,	"	5 "	P. M.	Washington,	"	8 "	P. M.
Washington,	"	10 "	P. M.	Richmond,	"	2 "	P. M.
Richmond,	"	3 "	P. M.	Petersburg,	"	7 "	P. M.
Petersburg,	"	1½ "	A. M.	Blakely,	"	7 "	A. M.

The whole time required between *Blakely* and *New York*, being Northwards, 54 hours ; Southwards, 57 hours. Between *New Orleans* and *New York*, Northwards, 12 days and 13 hours; Southwards, 13 days and 8 hours. Of the whole distance between Blakely and Baltimore, 126 miles is travelled upon Rail Roads, and 50 miles by Steamboat.

The Stage Travelling, which is conducted by Messrs. J. Woolfolk & Co. and Messrs. J. H. Avery & Co. in the handsomest manner, being now only 6½ miles, is becoming rapidly reduced by the extension of this Rail Road.

☞ Passengers are never in danger of delay, preference being given to such as enter and continue on the line.

By arrangements which this Company is making, Passengers, with their baggage, will be conveyed to and from the Depot, without charge. On the Rail Road, a coach will be especially appropriated to Northern and Southern Travellers; and in general, the Company's Agents will adopt all measures calculated to expedite and facilitate their journey.

Carriages and Horses are safely and expeditiously transported ; enabling those travelling in them, with the additional use of the Potomac Steamboat, and the Petersburg Rail Road, to accomplish, without fatigue to their horses, the journey between Washington and Blakely, N. C. in two days.

☞ The Mail Train leaves Richmond at 4½ o'clock, A. M.; returning, leaves the North Anna at 12 o'clock, M. The alternate Trains for Passengers and Freight, leave the North Anna at 7 o'clock, A. M. and 4, P. M.; and Richmond at 9 o'clock, A. M. and 1, P. M.

All possible care will be taken of baggage, but it will be carried only at its owner's risk.

Rail Road Office, Richmond, May 30, 1836.

Dated at Richmond, Va., in 1836, this must have been one of the earliest timetables in the United States and was issued by the Richmond, Fredericksburg & Potomac Railroad Company. New York to New Orleans called for stage, steamboat and steam cars and the trip required 13 days, 8 hours.

E. & S. RAIL ROAD.

Elizabeth-Port and Bound Brook.

☞ The passenger to assist the Conductor on the line of road whenever called upon. *J. W. Storms* Man'gr

Harper's Weekly, April 5, 1884

Ticket of the Elizabethtown & Somerville Railroad (now part of the Jersey Central) in the 1840's.

MOTHERS LOOK OUT FOR YOUR CHILDREN!
ARTISANS, MECHANICS, CITIZENS!

When you leave your family in health. must you be hurried home to mourn a

DREADFUL CASUALITY!

PHILADELPHIANS, your RIGHTS are being invaded! regardless of your interests, or the LIVES OF YOUR LITTLE ONES. THE CAMDEN AND AMBOY, with the assistance of other companies without a Charter, and in VIOLATION OF LAW, as decreed by your Courts, are laying a

LOCOMOTIVE RAIL ROAD!

Through your most Beautiful Streets, to the RUIN of your TRADE, annihilation of your RIGHTS, and regardless of your PROSPERITY and COMFORT Will you permit this? or do you consent to be a

SUBURB OF NEW YORK !!

Rails are now being laid on BROAD STREET to CONNECT the TRENTON RAIL ROAD with the WILMINGTON and BALTIMORE ROAD, under the pretence of constructing a City Passenger Railway from the Navy Yard to Fairmount!!! This is done under the auspices of the CAMDEN AND AMBOY MONOPOLY!

RALLY PEOPLE in the Majesty of your Strength and forbid THIS

OUTRAGE!

Poster attacking the Camden & Amboy in the 1830's.

became a graft and an art that called for all the ingenuity of the railroads to master—if mastered it ever was.

It was passenger and not freight traffic that kept the primeval railroads running. During 1835 the totàl freight receipts of railroads operating in Maryland increased by $8,400, while the income from passengers jumped up by $139,000. Five years later, in Massachusetts, the railroads gained freight to the extent of $51,000, while cash paid by passengers increased by $148,000. A striking proof that railroads actually created travel is to be seen in the experience of the Charleston & Hamburg in South Carolina. Before that little road was built, passenger traffic between the two towns had been adequately cared for by one two-seated stagecoach, which made only three trips a week. During six months of operation in 1835 the C&H railroad carried 15,959 passengers, who paid more than $53,000 for the privilege. The comparison, in numbers, was 50 travelers as against 2,500 travelers monthly.

A most fortunate thing about the primeval railroads was that, crude as their tracks and rolling stock were, there were few great disasters due to accidents. The average speed was probably not more than 18 miles an hour. Traffic was small. There was little travel at night. And the idea of time schedules and the consequent desire of engineers to "make time," to bring her in "on the advertised," was not present. It seems probable that travel by rail would not have increased so rapidly as it did had their been many wrecks disastrous to human life—the kind of wrecks that, beginning in the 1850's, were a national scandal.

So, the rails multiplied and expanded. It seemed for a time as if every state, every city, every one-horse village in the United States, East and West, North and South, was bound it should be on a railroad, even if it had to build one at home and with home capital.

CHAPTER IV

Railroad Fever

*The railroad will leave the land despoiled, ruined, a desert where only
sable buzzards shall wing their loathesome way to feed upon the carrion accomplished by the iron monster of the locomotive engine. No,
sir, let us hear no more of the railroad.*
    —From a typical oration against railroads, *circa* 1847.

FROM about 1832 to the end of the century epidemics of a disease that
came to be known as Railroad Fever broke out sporadically in the
United States. A really violent outbreak in any particular region was almost sure to be followed by a relapse; and the relapse, in turn, was followed by a condition approaching sanity in which railroads were looked
at realistically.

The inception and progress of the fever came in time to have a pattern.
First, some up-and-coming individual, or simply a fanatical dreamer, said
forcibly that what his home town of Brownsville needed, if it were to share
in America's great destiny, was a steam railroad. He talked the idea to
anyone in Brownsville who would listen or could not get away, and the
more he talked, because of the very nature of one-idea men, the better the
idea seemed to him. It grew and blossomed and burgeoned and even soared,
meanwhile taking on all of the beautiful hues of the sky in the Land of
Opportunity. It also dripped with gold, gold for all of Brownsville, soon
to be a mighty metropolis, teeming with commerce, with industry, with the
stir and bustle of countless travelers.

As the virus of the fever began to circulate, it got under the skins of
several of Brownsville's leading citizens, almost any one of whom was
alert for some new way to turn an honest or at least a respectable dollar.
Yes, sir, no matter how you looked at it, the idea did have possibilities. A
meeting was held, followed by many more, and if temperature rose to the
proper pitch, an application was made to the state for a charter for the
Brownsville Rail-Road Corporation.

The legislature debated. And because Americans of the period had invested a total of $250,000,000 in canals and would-be canals, there were
stout speeches made against granting the railroad charter by the officers
and hired creatures of the canal companies:

Canals, sir, are God's own highway, operating on the soft bosom of the
fluid that comes straight from Heaven. The railroad stems direct from Hell.
It is the Devil's own invention, compounded of fire, smoke, soot, and dirt,
spreading its infernal poison throughout the fair countryside. It will set fire
to houses along its slimy tracks. It will throw burning brands into the ripe
fields of the honest husbandman and destroy his crops. It will leave the
land despoiled, ruined, a desert where only sable buzzards shall wing their
loathesome way to feed upon the carrion accomplished by the iron monster
of the locomotive engine. No, sir, let us hear no more of the railroad.

But a charter was granted to the would-be railroad men of Brownsville,
and to men in hundreds of other places both large and small. So, they sent
out surveyors, or at least lookers-at-the-land, who followed up the creeks
and rivers, noting the grades, putting a stake here, another there, and
finally making a report to the budding corporation: "A line of steam
rail-way cars between Brownsville and Columbia City is entirely feasi-
ble. . . ." The railroad builders then looked at the maps, saw that Columbia City was 20 miles, or at least 18 miles, west of Brownsville, and then
added ". . . & Western" to the corporate title.

Now began the raising of money, the selling of stock or bonds or both in
the projected railroad. Possibly some local practitioner of letters was engaged to write a splendid pamphlet outlining the opportunity offered in
the stock of the Brownsville & Western Rail-Road. He could lay it on
heavylike, too, for each of the corporation's officers could submit some
excellent reason why the road would repay investors manyfold, nor were
they men to halter the lively imagination of a gifted composer of beautiful
prose.

Usually, too, an orator was called into consultation, for this was a period
when sonorous sounds from stump or platform were highly thought of and
most effective. In certain towns, so the record shows, the initial sum
deemed necessary to start construction was raised within a few days after
application of the pamphlet and the oratory to the public pulse. There was
simply no resistance; the virus was so active that no real sales efforts were
necessary. In other places, however, and these were often communities
where money had been raised by selling stock in canals that were never
dug, the going was harder, much harder. In which case, reconditioned
lightning-rod and patent-medicine salesmen were rushed into the breach.
Needy pastors were hurriedly converted to steam, and they presently
could see God's hand on the throttle. A newspaper might be purchased, or
even started, for the express purpose of boosting the Brownsville & Western. Eminent charlatans and eminent honest men, both were quoted as saying that one share of stock in the new venture, costing a mere $1000,
would be worth ten times that amount "in a year's time, mark my words."

Widows and old men and guardians of fools and minors were told how
a thousand dollars would not only help to make Brownsville a leading

city of the nation, but would also return a multitude of rich dividends, now and forever. Rallies were held, if needed, and resistance broken down by the combined assaults of oratory plus food and drink. And when the laying of the first rail—usually a log with an iron strap along its upper side— was done with great ceremony, and the Hon. Member of Congress let out the *vox humana* stop and poured the wondrous magic of his voice over the assembled citizenry, it was a hardheaded and moody man indeed who could not glimpse the setting sun and the Western ocean at the other end of the Brownsville rails. . . .

Gold had not yet been discovered in California when railroad fever first set in, yet the West was beginning to loom large in Eastern eyes. It was a happy, homely place, this new West, and guide books for emigrants to that lovely country were dropping from the presses throughout the 1830's. Listen while J. M. Peck tells the story:

> The backwoodsman of the West has many substantial enjoyments. After the fatigue of the journey west, and a short season of privation and danger, he finds himself surrounded with plenty. His cattle, his hogs and poultry, supply his table with meat; the forest abounds in game; the fertile soil yields abundant crops; he has, of course, milk and butter; the rivers furnish fish and the woods honey. For these various articles there is, at first, no market, and the farmer acquires the generous habit of spreading them profusely on his table, and giving them freely to a hungry traveler or indigent neighbor. . . .*

The railroad, Mr. Peck went on to say—and possibly he meant the Brownsville & Western—would soon bring a market right to the lucky Western farmer's door, and he was echoed by a score of other guiders of emigrants, all of whom reported this or that railroad "almost ready to commence," or "projected," or "planned," or "chartered." The woods and the fields were filled with them, these dreams of naïve men, these projected and planned and chartered and almost railroads. They literally covered the Union, both states and territories.

In Pensacola, Florida, in 1835, stock was being sold in the ambitious Alabama, Florida & Georgia Railroad Company. In Albany, New York, it was the Albany & West Stockbridge; in Delaware, the Andover & Wilmington. In the same period were the Auburn & Syracuse, the Baltimore & Port Deposit, the Bangor & Oldtown, the Bath & Crooked Lake, the Beaver Meadow, the Berkshire & New York, the Boston & Albany, the Boston & Maine, the Boston & Taunton, the Canajoharie & Catskill, the Catskill & Ithaca, the Chillicothe & Cincinnati, the Clinton & Vicksburg, the Connecticut & Passumpsic, the Corning & Blossburg, the West-

---

* Mr. Peck held forth for many pages in his delightful *A New Guide for Emigrants to the West*, published in Boston, 1837.

ern & Atlantic, and the Great Railway Route that was to run from New York City to the farthest spot in Michigan.

It was a great and wonderful dream, this first manifestation of the railroad. Some of the builders, however, must have been a bit skeptical of the business of general railroading, for they planned an auxiliary business— a railroad and something else. The old charters tell the story.* There was the Offerman Rail Way & Mining Company, the Towanda Rail Road & Coal Company, the Georgia Rail Road & Banking Company, the Atchafalaya Rail Road & Banking Company, the formidable Tuscarora and Cold Run Tunnel & Railroad Company.

By the beginning of 1837 at least two hundred railroads were being operated, built, projected, planned, or merely talked about. Most of them managed to get charters. Millions of dollars changed hands for the paper of stocks and bonds, which were often, and with no regard for their actual worth, things of beauty. A right handsome job were the stock certificates of the New Albany & Salem Rail Road Company of Indiana, crisp rag paper bright with green and gold and carrying also a work of art in a depiction of a New Albany & Salem locomotive and four-car train, smoking around a curve in the Hoosier wildwood. Incidentally, a share of the NA&S (later the Monon) cost $50; and its bonds, not nearly so gaudy, could be had for $10 each.

Pictures of locomotives began to appear as decorative patterns on china and glassware. A much-copied sampler pattern showed a primeval engine and tender hauling one car, and the motto God Speed Thee. Small brass medals were struck in honor of this or that railroad, either actual or projected. The construction of the first mile of the Baltimore & Ohio, incidentally a concern that has always known how to achieve good publicity, was greeted by a stirring piece of music, The Carrollton March, written by A. Clifton and performed with notable zest by a band in attendance at the "ceremony commencing the Baltimore & Ohio Railroad, on the Fourth of July, 1828." It was dedicated to the Hon. Charles Carroll, aged ninety, who as the reader will recall, was a signer of the Declaration and a stockholder in the B&O.

In January of 1832 the first issue of the first railroad periodical in the United States appeared, the American Railroad Journal of New York. It remarked editorially that as soon as railroads became common in its vicinity, it might expect to receive a supply of paper stock on time, rather than, as at present, having it delayed many weeks by ice in the canals.

Glassblowers broke out with a line of fancy flasks on which appeared a crude representation of a car or an engine on rails, together with the naïve legend: "Success to the Rail-road." As early as 1831 George Crabb, who

* See Thomas R. Thomson's monumental Check List of Publications on American Railroads before 1841, published by the New York Public Library, 1942.

published *A Family Encyclopedia, or, an Explanation of Words and Things,* felt the time had come to define "Railway," and did so, adding that "many have been commenced and several are already completed." Crabb went on to offer his opinion that the rails were eminently superior to canals.

Newspapers carried success stories about the established lines such as the Camden & Amboy, the Boston & Worcester, and the Chesapeake & Ohio. The latter, determined to outshine the B&O in its "commencing ceremony," prevailed on John Quincy Adams, President of the United States, by efforts that must have been herculean, to step on a shovel to break the first sod. Mr. Adams, an old hand with a shovel, had bad luck with his first dig, being brought up short on a tough root, but the President was just as tough as the root. He took a new stance and this time drove the spade fair home and brought up a clod that might have staggered a ditch digger.

In spite of all of the enthusiasm, there was also a small yet stiff opposition, and a whole heap of lethargy, about railroads. There were, for instance, many rich men who simply could not bring themselves to the belief that the old order really was changing, that the day of the coach and the canal was done, or swiftly passing. These men had come to manhood and to success without the aid of such things as a steam railroad. Every circumstance of their lives was harnessed to the old ways. Now they were being harassed by a lot of strange new fanatics who waved plans, surveys, and charters, and demanded cash for immediate construction of fantastic roads of rails, on which were to run smoking, stinking, dangerous locomotive monsters.

In Boston, as an instance, Editor Buckingham of the *Courier,* who held himself a progressive man, laid into the idea of a railroad from Boston to Albany with scorn and gusto. Wrote he in his paper: "Alcibiades or some other great man of antiquity, it is said, cut off his dog's tail, that quidnuncs might not become extinct from want of excitement. Some such notion, we doubt not, moved one or two of our experimental philosophers to get up a project of a railroad from Boston to Albany—a project which every one knows, who knows the simplest rule in arithmetic, to be impracticable, but at an expense little less than the market value of the whole territory of Massachusetts; and which, if practicable, every person of common sense knows, would be as useless as a railroad from Boston to the moon."

There was another thing to be considered, too. Were railroads moral? Many honest men believed that the railroads would, in some inexplicable manner, have an influence to lower public and private morals. When this question was raised, as it often was in New England, the railroad promoters and builders worked in a purposeful manner on preachers. The Western Railroad of Massachusetts, which became the Boston & Albany and was nowhere near so useless as a railroad from Boston to the moon, ran

into the moral issue and to meet it sent a general letter to parsons in the
Bay State in which it alleged that "the moral effect of Rail-Roads" was
bound to be good and asked, in so many words, that ". . . you take an
early opportunity to deliver a Discourse on the Moral effect of Rail-Roads
in our wide extended country."

In many regions the struggling railroads actually did need the help of
the parsons, and of all other men they could enlist on their side, for the
canal, the steamboat, and the stagecoach lines were combining in a savage
campaign to stop the progress of the rails. One sample of this combination
of interests appeared by the thousand in Philadelphia in the form of a
poster designed by a master of the fear-and-outrage school. It depicts a
steam train labeled "Mon-Op-O-Ly" battering the daylights out of a horse
and buggy on a grade crossing, with death to the occupants of the carriage
both imminent and horrible. A terrified bystander is rushing to a cop
standing at a street corner, undoubtedly to ask him to arrest the Iron
Horse. The text is in keeping. It advises "MOTHERS LOOK OUT FOR
YOUR CHILDREN" and goes on to demand "When you leave your family in health, must you be hurried home to mourn a DREADFUL CASU-
ALTY!" In somewhat smaller type the poster goes on to say that "Rails
are now being laid on Broad Street to Connect the Trenton Rail Road with
the Wilmington & Baltimore Road, under the pretense of constructing a
City Passenger Railway from the Navy Yard to Fairmount!!! This is
done under the auspices of the Camden & Amboy Monopoly!" And then,
in a delirium of type-styles, all of studhorse size, the poster demands
"RALLY PEOPLE In the Majesty of your Strength and forbid this OUT-
RAGE!"

Yet in spite of organized opposition there was no stopping the advent
of the railroad. The fever spread westward rapidly. In 1835 Ohio's first
rail:oad, the Mad River & Lake Erie, was building. In the wilds of Kentucky, Frankfort and Lexington were laying strapiron rails on limestone
slabs to connect those towns. The legislature of Indiana granted charters
to six projected lines in 1832 alone and nineteen more in the next four
years. In Virginia, the Richmond, Fredericksburg & Potomac Railroad
Company found the Old Dominion ready to buy some of its stock. Since
1784 it had been the policy of Virginia to encourage transportation by sub-
scribing to the stock of canal, turnpike, and toll-bridge concerns, and now
it could see no reason why it should not do the same for the railroads. In
1941 the state of Virginia still retained the 2,752 shares of stock in this
pioneer railroad that it had acquired in 1834.

But it was Illinois that decided to go the whole hog, as a state, into the
business of both canals and railroads. Early in 1837 the Illinois legislature committed the state, in what must have been a singularly untram-
meled meeting, to the creation of more than 1,300 miles of railroad, together with the improvement of many rivers, the digging of several canals,

and the construction of many turnpikes. This measure, an omnibus affair cooked up to please everybody in the state and known as the Internal Improvements Bill, provided for the expenditure of $10,250,000 on fifteen projects, in addition to several million dollars already appropriated for construction of the Illinois and Michigan Canal.*

In the entire state of Illinois at the time there lived only a few thousand people. There were no cities, and the spaces between villages and farms were immense. Yet the Internal Improvements Bill was passed after noble lobbying by Stephen A. Douglas and other politicians who owned land in the region. One may wonder how the state would have managed to go about carrying out the measure, but the panic of 1837 arrived promptly and put an end to the biggest single railroad dream of the era. Illinois, however, had incurred a huge debt through the fraud and collusion perpetrated by its swindling officials who had, of course, made jobs for themselves as "surveyors," "land buyers," and "estimators." Only a few miles of rail were laid before the panic struck. The state was left crippled with debt, and the consequent high taxes acted to discourage immigration to Illinois for many years. New settlers passed it by for Wisconsin and Iowa.

The panic of 1837 was sudden, devastating, thorough. Food riots broke out during February in New York and other cities. Stores and flour mills and warehouses were raided and looted. Banks refused to honor their own notes. Hard money went into hiding. In attempts to stem the debacle, public men gave utterances to fatuous noises of optimism, and Daniel Webster was sent through the country to announce, in the great voice that held even his enemies spellbound, that the country was fundamentally sound.† The ensuing depression lasted a full seven years. It mowed down the current inflation to size by immediately tumbling the fantastic prices of land. And it laid many a budding railroad, or railroad corporation—which were not the same thing—into a grave so deep that their very names are to be found only in old records. One can appreciate the feelings of the treasurer of the Syracuse & Auburn, just before it lost its shirt and its locomotive and its rails, when he wrote: "I am almost in despair. Is there no sale for our stock?" There wasn't, and the company was reduced to issuing IOU notes for bills as low as five dollars.

Yet, bad as times were, the dismal year of 1838 saw the beginnings of a now historic line at Petersburg, Virginia, when the City Point Railroad hauled its first load of passengers at 75 cents a head over its nine miles of track. This was the genesis of the present Norfolk & Western, one of the great freight carriers of the nation, which operates in the coal regions of

---

* Paul Wallace Gates tells the incredible story in detail in his *The Illinois Central Railroad and Its Colonization Work*, Cambridge, 1934.

† Not all public men gave out with bilge. In *Niles Register* of Baltimore, on Feb. 25, 1837, Editor Hezekiah Niles found the outlook hideous indeed, and said that he reported it merely "to enable the future historian to trace the downward course of his republic."

six states and in normal times moves 40 million tons of bituminous coal annually.

One of the results of the panic was to put the State of Michigan *into* the railroad business—for a time. It had chartered and given considerable aid to two roads, the Erie & Kalamazoo and the Detroit & St. Joseph. Both roads emerged insolvent from the panic. The state took over and by successive appropriations completed construction of some 150 miles of road. In 1846 the state was happy to sell its railroad to a group of Massachusetts and New York men who had made their fortunes in the China trade and knew a bargain when they saw one, even if the bargain were on land rather than on water. For $1,750,000 they got what had cost Michigan almost $3½ million, and then proceeded to make it the Michigan Central.

As Michigan got into the railroad business, Illinois got out. The latter was glad to pull out from under the dreadful burden. After a dozen more years of political skullduggery, including bribery seldom equalled, it granted a charter to the Illinois Central, and with the charter went a federal land grant, of which more in its place.

The panic of '37 plus the death of a great orator, also made hash of the ambitious Louisville, Cincinnati & Charleston Railroad, begun in 1835 to connect the Ohio River with the Atlantic Ocean. Robert Y. Hayne, he who was rated the only master of words fit to debate with Dan'l Webster, was the moving spirit of this enterprise. Stock was sold in four states, and South Carolina agreed to endorse $2,000,000 worth of its bonds. Tennessee went into it for $500,000. Banking charters were secured in South Carolina, North Carolina, and Tennessee, but Kentucky refused. The panic hit the road hard, but it was being carried on when Hayne died, in 1839. Thus, declared a Southern writer, died the company's dreams.

Though the early part of the 1840's was required to recover from the '37 panic, by the middle of the period the better-managed and financed railroads were making fair progress with expansion and also in improvement of rolling stock and operation in general. One striking advance was that made by Thomas Rogers of Paterson, New Jersey, who invented what he called counterbalancing. He put weights between the spokes of the driving wheels of his locomotives, on the opposite side of the rim from the point where the driving and connecting rods were fastened to the crank pins. This simple procedure was found to make the engine ride wonderfully well and it also reduced the blow on the track occasioned by the revolutions of unbalanced wheels.

Septimus Norris began to enlarge the American type of 4-4-0 locomotive by the addition of a third pair of drivers, making the first engine of the 4-6-0 class. Ross Winans, a young prodigy of mechanics, devised for the Baltimore & Ohio a friction wheel with outside bearings for its railroad cars, and took charge of the company's shops. For the next quarter of a century he devoted his energies to the improvement of B&O engines and rolling stock, inventing the camelback locomotive for use on steep grades, and turning out what were probably the most comfortable passenger coaches of the era.

The federal government was beginning to take some notice of the new railroads. As early as 1834 it was sending mail in closed pouches by train, and in 1838 Congress passed an act declaring all railroads to be post routes, and the carrying of mail became a regular thing, though the railway postal car was still twenty years in the future. As early as 1840 Amos Kendall, Postmaster General, felt obliged to report on the many delays in mail between New York and Boston. Although this route was composed of steamboat, railroad, and stagecoach carriers, and winds, bad roads, and weather had occasioned several delays, it was snow that had held up the mail on the all-rail Boston-Worcester route—nine serious delays in one season.

For any extended journey the traveler was still obliged to use railroad *and* steamboat, and possibly stagecoach and canal boat as well. Competition between the various modes of transportation, and between the various lines, was savage. As usual in such cases, then as now, a fringe of parasites attached itself to legitimate business. One of the forms parasites took in that era was that of the forwarding house. These employed runners to go after trade and held a contract with a railroad line, or a steamboat, or stagecoach, or perhaps all three, by which the forwarding house bought tickets very cheaply and sold them as dearly as the traffic would bear.

The forwarding houses compounded extortion with fraud. Their runners hung around depots and the taverns that were used as stations, and fastened themselves like leeches on any person who appeared to be going on a journey. To secure a passenger, they talked and shouted and even fought each other, with fists, clubs, even guns. When they had hooked him, and hooked is the word, they sold him what purported to be a ticket, a through ticket, that would carry him, say, from New York to Buffalo without further cost. More often than not the fast-talking runner alleged that the ticket also included all meals along the way, and even lodging at stopovers. The tickets were usually elaborate printing jobs embellished with pictures of railroad trains, canal boats, and stagecoaches, all moving with the speed of the wind toward their destination.

But many a victim of the runners discovered on his arrival at Albany that the runner's ticket actually took him only as far as that point. From there on to Buffalo he paid and paid again, and he also paid for any meals and any lodging he had along the way. This slickering quickly made forwarding houses a public scandal. State laws soon made it difficult for them to operate brazenly, so they merely changed their spots and their tactics somewhat and prepared for the gigantic business of handling, in one way or another, a large part of the great immigration from Europe, principally from Ireland and Germany, that was getting into full flood by the end of the 1840's. But by then the more forward-looking of the railroads were establishing their own agencies for the encouragement of emigration from Europe to America and specifically to the gorgeous country along the lines of the railroads immediately interested in settlers.

The panic of 1837 was doubtless a good thing for a more orderly advance of railroads. It had taken a terrible toll. Poor's *Railroad Manual* noted that many roads, especially in the West and South, were abandoned, while others which had never from the day work began paid even the cost of construction were thrown into bankruptcy. It is probable that this was the proper end for these roads. Yet, railroad fever, after its almost deadly setback during the panic, returned to circulation with greater strength, and with better balance, than ever before. Many a budding road, though hard hit, had survived, some of them, true enough, to be gobbled up by other and better-financed lines, and a few to carry on under their original charter title, even if with new officials and directors.

Among the few hardy survivors of 1837, and also of more hell and high water than was common to most American roads, was the New York & Erie Rail Road Company, one that was known and with good reason enough as The Work of The Age.

CHAPTER V

"The Work of the Age"

. . . *Resolved: that we hail the Completion of this gigantic and stupendous work as emphatically THE WORK OF THE AGE.* . . .
—The Board of New York City Aldermen, to the directors of the New York & Erie Rail Road Company, June 13, 1851.

IT WOULD be difficult to discover a citation of merit more deserved than the eye-shattering scroll done in three colors and superlative prose that the City of New York drew up, approved, and on June 13, 1851, presented to the officers of the New York & Erie Rail Road Company. The citation hailed completion of the longest railroad in all the United States and termed it, in the same sentence, not only Gigantic and Stupendous, but vowed in capital letters that it was THE WORK OF THE AGE.

Purple as they are, those are not empty words. The men of the Erie deserved them, and deserved, too, better of fate than the stockjobbers and vultures who laid obscene hands on the road in later years and wrecked it so savagely that generations were to pass before the Erie could recover. The wrecking of the Erie is a well known and much worn story, but its construction, a hundred and more years ago, is something of an epic that has been pretty much buried for half a century.* Into the building of those 450 miles of road across New York state went enough genius and stupidity, enough parsimony and prodigality, and enough heartbreak to have built a railroad not only to the Great Lakes but to the Pacific shore.

What became the Erie Railroad had its inception in the remarkable mind of William C. Redfield, a Yankee harness maker who became a distinguished meteorologist and the first president of the American Association for the Advancement of Science. In 1829 Redfield wrote and published a pamphlet, *Sketch of the Geographical Rout(sic) of a Great Railway,* in which he proposed and outlined a route to connect the canals and navigable waters of New York with the Great Lakes and the Mississippi River. At the time Redfield wrote, there were scarcely twenty miles of steam railroad in the United States, yet he saw even then what steam and

---

* Or since Edward Harold Mott wrote *The Story of the Erie,* published in New York in 1899, a poorly written and organized work, yet complete and authoritative. My own and all other accounts of the Erie must rest heavily on Mr. Mott's gigantic (8 lbs.) book.

50

rails were about to do to and for the country; and he set forth, with uncanny foresight, "nineteen points of superiority of railroads" over the then popular canals.

With his pamphlet Redfield published a map on which he traced the proposed railroad to points on Lakes Erie and Michigan, and by routes which within another two decades became in general the outline of the New York & Erie Rail Road's tracks and terminals. It is improbable that the nineteenth century witnessed any greater example in the realm of material prophecy than Redfield's. His route was to have its eastern end at a point on the Hudson River "accessible at all seasons to steam ferryboats," and proceed to the valley of the Delaware near the northeast corner of Sullivan County, up the valley a way, then over the height of land to the Susquehanna valley, "which it enters at or near the great bend of that river"—and so on to the Tioga, the headwaters of the Genesee, and Lake Erie. The general line of the proposed railroad was to traverse what was known as the Southern Tier of New York counties.

One who found the Redfield pamphlet of particular interest was the Hon. Henry L. Pierson of Ramapo, New York, a well-to-do businessman who had recently seen the opening of the few miles of track in South Carolina that were called the Charleston & Hamburg Railroad. Mr. Pierson's brother-in-law was Eleazar Lord, another successful man of affairs. The two men shared the belief that some sort of communication across the Southern Tier of New York counties would be a fine thing. The northern counties already had the Erie Canal and were prospering famously thereby.

Redfield's pamphlet also set up a running fire of interest in all of the Southern Tier counties; and in 1831 a number of small conventions were held there and attended by such citizens as had caught the railroad fever. At a meeting in Owego an application for a charter was drawn up, and from it stemmed the New York & Erie Rail Road Company. Two years later, or in August of 1833, the actual organization of the company was accomplished and Eleazar Lord elected its first president. The state put up $3,000,000 as a loan. And although the company was incorporated at $1,000,000, only 5 per cent of the subscriptions had been paid and a shortage of cash was to be almost a permanent condition of the Erie during its construction years.

The first ground was broken on the east side of the Delaware River, near Deposit, when all of the amenities proper for such an undertaking were observed—the turning of the First Sod, the moving of a wheelbarrow filled with dirt, the speeches weighted with Destiny, "What now appears a beautiful meadow will in a few years present a far different aspect, that of a track of rails, with cars passing and repassing, loaded with merchandise." But Destiny was preparing a dreadful blow. Within five weeks of the enthusiastic ceremony, there broke out in New York City the most

disastrous fire that town had known. Many of the Erie's heaviest subscribers were ruined by the fire, and their stocks in the budding railroad
remained unpaid for. Almost on top of the fire came the panic, which
began in 1836 and lasted throughout 1837. It drove into bankruptcy many
more of the Erie subscribers and thus, says Historian Mott, was "the Company robbed of whatever cheer and brightness they may have had."

Aye, the cheer and the brightness had gone. In the spring of 1837 all
work on the road was ordered discontinued. The company's debts
amounted to only $13,000, yet there was much less than that in the com-
pany's treasury. A year later, through the influence of Lord and of Walter
Smith, a large land owner at Dunkirk on Lake Erie, a state loan of
$100,000 was secured. A provision of the loan was that work must be
started at once on ten miles of road from Tappan Slote (Piermont) on the
Hudson, building west, and on ten miles of road from Dunkirk, building
east.

Work was resumed and the company began a campaign of asking for
donations of land from private citizens, chiefly on which to build depots
and water stations.* Pressure was also put on stockholders to pay their
subscriptions in full; and greater efforts were made to get new subscribers.
Indicative of the desperation of the company at this period is an incident
related by Jeremiah Rogers of the Erie staff, who was trying to raise
$20,000 by stock sales in Binghamton. One of the wealthiest citizens of
that town was Hazzard Lewis, who had become rich simply by not spend-
ing any money. Rogers found him adamant about buying stock until he
offered Lewis, secretly, a subscription of $1000 for $500. Lewis took it,
and because of that gentleman's great reputation for shrewd dealing,
Rogers was able to place the rest of the stock with Binghamton citizens
without much effort. It was typical of the subterfuges the Erie had to use
to keep money in its coffers.

Surveys and resurveys went ahead, and so did some actual clearing of
right-of-way, and a little laying of track. Hezekiah Seymour, a friend of
President Lord's, was first superintendent of the line and also its chief
engineer. His ideas appear to have dominated the company so far as its
early construction work was concerned. He was known familiarly as the
Oneida Chief and seems to have been a man of energy and decided opinions, not all of which were wholly sound.

The Erie was going to do the thing right from the first. It did not trouble
its head about strap-iron rails, which a number of the primeval railroads
were using. It bought solid iron stuff from the British Iron Company of
England; and at least one batch of castiron rails from the Huron Iron

---

* Sample donations of land from citizens to the company: John Hollenback, East Owego,
6½ acres; John R. Drake, Owego, 9 6/10 acres; Charles F. Johnson, Owego, 15 acres;
Harmon Pumpelly, Owego, 4¼ acres; John Lorimer, Elmira, 9¾ acres; the Corning Company, Corning, 34½ acres; F. E. Erwin, Painted Post, 10 acres; W. B. Jones, Addison, 5 acres.

Company, an American concern in which, possibly incidentally, Walter Smith, a heavy Erie stockholder, was also interested. Contracts for ties were let. These were to be of oak, chestnut, or butternut; 7½ to 9 inches in diameter at the small end, and *9 feet long*, for Lord had set upon 6 feet as the proper gauge.

There have been many stories about the Erie's six-foot gauge. It appears to have been promoted by Lord himself, who had the strong backing of Hezekiah Seymour. The reasons given for adopting this odd measure, rather than the 4 feet 8 inches which was in use by the majority of the American roads, were several.* The six-foot gauge was favored in England which, so the Erie men seemed to think, was the home of master railroad builders. Then, too, the grades of the Erie were bound to be steep and to call for heavy engines to surmount them. There was also in the Erie's charter the strange provision that the line should not connect with any railroad leading into New Jersey, Pennsylvania, or Ohio. Thus did the State of New York seek to protect itself from railroads that might lead trade away from New York City. Both Lord and Seymour believed devoutly in the right and goodness of this provision and thought that by adopting an odd gauge the company could preclude any other railroad from making physical connections with it. This idiotic idea of a gauge different from any other in the United States cost the Erie much in the next 40 years, and finally, in 1878, when something simply had to be done about it, the change was made at tremendous cost.

Still another fetish Lord held, much to the detriment of the company, was that most if not all of the road should be built on piling. He held that a railroad on piles would have no snow drifts, it could not be washed out by floods, frost could not harm it, and besides, a railroad on piles could be laid faster than by grading a roadbed. So, eight of what were described as Crane's Patent Pile Driving Machines, each operated by thirteen men, went ahead with the fantasy on the Susequehanna Division between Binghamton and Hornellsville. The farmers round about were in clover; they supplied white oak piling by the thousands of feet, and Crane's patent battering rams snorted and thumped from morning to night.

It was a heartening sight to the natives. They gathered in big crowds to see Progress and Destiny at work in the pile drivers, and no one was immune, from "the gray-headed veteran of the Revolution to the stripling schoolboy of six or seven." They cheered each and every crew, and at Owego, which went quite mad about the business, a flag was raised that had, in the place ordinarily devoted to the stars, the figure of a locomotive on a railroad of piling. One hundred miles of piling were driven at a cost of $750,000; and perhaps this is the place to remark that no train, no locomotive, not even a track ever laid its weight on these piles which

---

* Present standard gauge is 4 feet 8½ inches.

could be seen, for half a century after, as melancholy monuments to what the historian of Erie delicately termed a "misdirected effort in furthering a worthy cause."

While Mr. Crane's patent rams were pounding down the piles, a little actual progress was being made at the eastern end of the line. Rails on stringers and crossties had been laid from Piermont to Ramapo, and in June of 1841 a "first train" was run over the section behind a locomotive named for that prince of piling and king of wide-gauge, Eleazar Lord.* This portion of the road was pushing hard to get to Goshen, and a rumor got around somehow that the first cars would enter Goshen in July of 1841. They didn't. No cars, not even a sign of a rail had reached Goshen, but on September 23rd they did, and they carried no pay-load but a group of *eminenti* that included, happily, old W. C. Redfield, he who had the first vision of a railroad from the Hudson to the Lakes. It carried also Mr. Washington Irving, the writer, who had previously objected loudly to the building of a pier in the Hudson by the Erie company because he thought it would deflect the river currents to the East shore, where he lived, and damage his property.

The next objective of the eastern division was the line from Goshen to Middletown, nine miles. But the money barrel was empty again. Contractors were warned that they continued clearing and grading at their own risk, and most of the work ceased at once, although a few concerns kept on in the hope that the legislature would come forward with another loan. On the first of April, 1842, the company defaulted on its interest payments to the State and placed itself in the hands of assignees. This time it seemed certain the Erie was done for, that Redfield's vision of a railroad was after all only a vision.

The blow was a particularly terrible one to Middletown, which, in anticipation of becoming a railroad city, had already donated land for a depot. But its stouthearted citizens, led by Samuel Denton, Thomas King, and William Robinson, formed the Middletown Association, raised money and *paid* the Erie then and there for building the nine miles of grade and track to make their town the end of the line. This was done within the year and service of a kind opened in June of 1843. For the next three years and more Middletown was to be the end of the line on the Erie.

For the next three years, too, the New York & Erie Rail Road lay silent with the stillness of death. Rust crept along the fine imported rails. The hundred miles of piling began to warp and to rot. Elsewhere grass and weeds grew high between the ties on the right of way, perhaps the most significantly desolate sight a railroadman's eyes can look upon. Farmers all along the line were holding the bag for ties, for piling, for timbers, for

---

* Mr. Lord, a hardy character, was in and out of the presidency of the Erie so often it might be well to list his terms of office, which were 1833–35, 1839–41, 1844–45.

grading work, for stone. There was no cash to pay them, so they moved almost in a body upon the thousands of dollars worth of material that had been piled beside the grade and removed it. When work was at last resumed in 1845, nothing remained of this stuff. But there was no mystery about its disappearance. Says the Erie's historian: ". . . to this day [1899] evidences of this material may be seen in the dwellings of people of more or less consequence in that part of the State."

The property of the Erie that remained was sold under foreclosure on April 1, 1845. Lord was in as president again, and he announced that $6,000,000 would be required to complete the job. The State of New York, by what monumental lobbying no man now can say, was prevailed upon to cancel the $3,000,000 debt already owed it by the Erie; and the company was permitted to issue new stock to the amount of $3,000,000. A new president was elected, Benjamin Loder.

In the meantime the Erie had piled a gigantic error of omission on top of its fantastic errors of commission. It had been offered for the modest sum of $90,000 the New York & Harlem Railroad, a property that would have given the Erie access to New York City by virtue of the Harlem's rights and properties on Manhattan Island. The Erie did not make the purchase and the little Harlem went on to become, in time, an extremely important part of the New York Central. The chief reason the Erie did not buy the Harlem, it appears, was that the Erie officials believed its boat trip from Piermont on the Hudson down the river to its dock in New York would be of great benefit because travelers might "rest and relax" on the boats either before or after their trip on the railroad. This could well have been the reason for not buying, for the Erie's directorate did have many strange ideas; but still, a road that could not pay for crossties might consider $90,000 too much for any property.

Loder, the new president of Erie, was a native of Westchester, New York, who had made a fortune in the drygoods business. He was a man who made up for his lack of knowledge of railroads by his unquestioned force. And with debts now all cleared and new money rolling in, the work of construction went ahead. The hundred miles of Lord's piling was ignored, and the new line went over different though often adjacent terrain. At last the Erie discovered that a good grade and crossties was the way to make a railroad.

President Loder was determined that the Erie, which for twelve heartbreaking years had raiséd, then wrecked, many a hope and, as yet, in 1845, amounted to little more than a jerkwater affair of 40 miles from the Hudson into the highlands—Loder determined it must and should fulfill the implications in its corporate title and reach the shores of Lake Erie. Quite possibly he was no genius as a railroad builder, but he did hold fast to his determination; and he and his construction and

operating crews were to go through hell, high water, deep snow, and many
a bloody riot before five years more and approximately 500 miles of rail
had been laid.

The one epic of American railroad building that has been well if not
overly reported and romanticized is, of course, that of the Union and the
Central Pacific lines. Theirs is a great story and no decent man should
want to detract so much as one Indian fight from it. It is, in fact, such
a good story and so exciting that it has put almost all other railroad construction feats into shadow.

This is unfortunate. The building of many a road in the first half of the
last century was a great story. They were built at a time when men proceeded by trial and error; there were no rules, no sort of science. Neither
the grading of a roadbed nor the laying down of iron rails had any precedent. Nor had the operation of trains. The stress laid on rolling stock and
rails due to curvature was still somewhere in the future, in an unworked
algebraic equation. So, to a large extent, were the laws of traction that
govern the starting of a load on wheels and its continued motion. As to
grades, nobody knew how much of a hill a ten-ton Rogers locomotive
pulling twenty little freight cars could surmount; nor what would happen
when such a train started down a hill, what with the crude brakes then
in use.

All of these things and many more had to be learned the hard way by
the stubborn men of the New York & Erie Rail Road when, after more
than three years of hiatus, they began, at last, in 1845, to fight their way
westward mile by mile until they came fair to the lake shore at Dunkirk
more than five years later. In all, eighteen years passed before the Erie
achieved what it had set out to do so bravely. Presidents of the Erie and
Presidents of the United States came and went. The old men of the
Revolution died off. The Mexican war was fought. California and the
Oregon Country and Texas joined the Union. Canals were dug, then
abandoned. Mr. Morse perfected his magnetic telegraph. Joseph Smith
was lynched by gentiles, and Brigham Young led the Saints into the land
of Deseret. Slavery came down out of the abstract and became an Issue.
And still the roadbed of the Erie made its way, sometimes on the ground,
again on piling, while Erie waterboys became foremen, then superintendents, and married, had children, and put their own sons to work for Erie.
The Erie was, as the handsome scroll was to say, The Work of the Age,
and it took an age to build it.

From the time of Benjamin Loder onward, however, progress never
stopped. The Erie contractors were aggressive men, slave drivers, too, and
for slaves they managed to secure several thousand Irish who had just
escaped their unhappy land after the great potato famine of '45. A mighty
crew of these lads was put to work on the section through the mountainous

region around Port Jervis on the Delaware. Here not far from Parker's Glen, where the rock cliffs rose almost perpendicularly from the river, the pick of the Irish drilling crews were lowered in great wicker baskets from the high ledges and there suspended in mid-air while the tarriers drilled like devils, then tamped their powder into the holes, lighted the fuzes, and yelled for the boys above to haul them up before the blasts let go. Lives depended both on the ropes and on quick response, and sometimes the ropes broke, again the windlass was slow. And then there was sure to be another wake. . . .

The blasts often hurled gigantic rocks across the river to fall like a blizzard of stones into the Delaware & Hudson Canal, much to the demoralization of canalboat captains. So much damage was done to canal traffic that in 1847 many boatmen refused to run this stretch of the canal at all; and damage suits were brought against the railroad, an accursed thing anyway, according to canalers.

Fights and small riots grew out of the animosity between the railroad construction gangs and the canalers, and at least one murder was done near Lackawaxen when a canaler named Kays was killed by Pat Callaghan, one of the Erie bhoys.

The Irish crews were hard to handle, anyway, especially so when they were not actually at work. On Sundays they swarmed through the countryside to appropriate anything they could move, or destroy it if they could not. They cleaned the orchards of apples, and no potato was safe anywhere. They robbed cornfields, took wood fuel from piles, stripped clothes lines, broke into stores in search of whiskey, and stole chickens and hogs. Protests from the embattled farmers to the railroad were in turn passed along to the contractors, who did little or nothing about it. The looting continued.

Then, there was a small war that was fought in a foothill region called Shin Hollow, just west of Port Jervis. Here the contracting firm of Carmichael & Stranahan was working a big crew of Irish, cutting through a wall of solid rock. The contractors also operated a boarding house, and so did one of the foremen, O'Brien. These places were barn-like structures having a dining room downstairs, with an upstairs loft, reached by outside ladders, for sleeping quarters. In the crew were two factions of Irish, the Far-downers, and the Corkonians, who were mutually poisonous to one another; and also a small number of Germans.

What started the war has puzzled historians of the region. It would seem to be simple enough, if one remembers that two factions of Irish were employed on the same job; and that further, there were present, on the mountain above Shin Hollow, a large number of small shanties in which females known as "widows" sold whiskey and supplied entertainment of a kind often sought by healthy young men. Such a situation, it seems to me, is clue enough to the troubles that began in 1847, when the mixture had fermented sufficiently.

A gang of Far-downers formed on the mountain, marched or staggered in a body upon the Corkonian camp, and attacked them with stones and clubs. The Corks fled, taking their wounded with them. Two days later the Far-downers again attacked, this time armed with several rifles, and drove the Cork lads across Shin Hollow to the contractors' office, where they forced the agent to pay off and discharge the unspeakable men of Cork. One man was killed in the process.

Now the Far-downers, their heads full of dizzying success, turned on the small German camp. Here they met with smaller numbers but excellent organization. The Germans handled the affair coolly and with great vigor, sending the Irish packing.

Following this second raid, work on the Shin Hollow contract was suspended except for the German crew, which posted an armed guard and continued to labor without the loss of an hour. The poor Corks, whom the other Irish had forced to be discharged, still hung around the neighborhood. They were planning to return to their jobs, or at least such was the rumor that reached the Far-downers in their camp. This would not do. On the night of February 3rd, when Shin Hollow was wrapped in sleep, the Far-downers again formed on the mountain, drank right heartily, and staggered once more to the Corkonian camp. They arrived in full strength but so quietly that before the poor Corks knew what was afoot, the other Irish were chopping down the posts that supported the sleeping lofts. Down came the rickety structures, and with them the Corks, while the bloodthirsty Far-downers fell upon them like savages, beating them unmercifully.

This was easy, and wonderful. The Far-downers next turned their attention on what they called the Damned Dutch. The Germans were ready. Captained by an able man named Wisler, they had armed themselves with shotguns several days before; and now Wisler formed them in battle line in the darkness and awaited the attack. When the Irish came up whooping, Wisler had his men hold their fire until the enemy was but a few yards distant. Then they let them have it. The night blazed, and the startled Irish fell back, then fled in rout, many of them to pick shot out of their bodies for weeks to come. The Germans remained alert in their camp, ready for more action if needed.

When morning came, the firm of Carmichael & Stranahan had come to think that the situation was out of hand. Sheriff Welling of Goshen was sent for. He arrived with deputies, found conditions wholly beyond his control, and called for the militia. Captain Peter Swartout and a company of artillery of Deerpark responded. Attired in full dress uniforms, which were all the uniforms they possessed, the battery moved into Shin Hollow in fine formation, wheeled smartly, and set up one small cannon. Captain Swartout called on all rioters to cease and desist in the name of the law. The very presence of the soldiers had an immediate quieting effect, and a number of suspected leaders of the mobs were arrested and held under guard. Some of these men were later fined. The situation was considered so critical that the militia remained on duty a month.

There were other Irish riots too, the most serious of which was at Alfred, west of Hornellsville, on the Western Division of the Erie, where contractor Henry A. Fonda was working a mixed crew of Corks and Tipperaries. While passing through Alfred, one John Pardon and family, Fardowners, were set upon by a gang of the Erie Irish. The Pardons were given refuge by a citizen whose name is given in the record as Paris Green. The mob attacked the home of Paris Green, the militia turned out, the rioters were arrested and brought to trial, and just then all of the remaining Irish in Contractor Fonda's crew massed for an attack on the courthouse. Again the militia saved the day, and without shooting. Yet a night or two later, when Fonda and one of his foremen went into an Irish shanty to quiet a row, the lights went out, two Irishmen died from the gunfire, and the foreman, Kent, died of wounds.

These and other small riots may have slowed the westward course of the Erie's rails, but they did not stop it. Worse than riots were a few ornery native farmers who believed that a railroad was primarily a source of easy money, to be tapped as may. They wanted the railroad, to be sure, to haul their produce to market, and often they also wanted an ungodly lot of money for a tiny strip of their land. The Erie's land agents, often making up with big talk what they lacked in ready cash, were prone to agree to any price asked, and to take the land and let the farmer get his money if he could. Adrian Holbert, a successful farmer of near Goshen, knew how to handle such fellows. The Erie agents had agreed to pay him his price for a right-of-way across his fair meadows. They also asked him to supply ties and piling. Holbert completed his contract, on time and without a sign of cash, and then attempted to get his money. Instead, he got some more Erie promises.

On a June day in 1843 an Erie inspection train came along the rails newly laid on the Holbert place, and the locomotive engineer noted an obstruction on the track. It was a stout rail fence, four rails high, three lengths long, and, lying on a crosstie, his arms around a piece of the fence, was Farmer Holbert, a man, remarks the Erie historian, in whom stubbornness predominated. The engine stopped, and stubborn Farmer Holbert addressed Conductor W. H. Stewart. "This railroad," he shouted, "can't run no cars through my farm until the company settles with me." Nor would he move from his prone position across the tracks of Destiny and Progress. The train crew tried moral suasion, but at last were forced to pick the man up, load him onto the train, and take him to Middletown, running down the rail fence to do so. Next day an Erie agent called at the Holbert farm and settled.*

Some of those farmers must have sat up nights figuring how to trim the Erie. One of them, who had a worthless place on a hill near Middletown, heard that the road was looking for good sources of water for their engines. The road ran through this farmer's place, and at one spot went through a cut where the ground was higher than the locomotive. On a level spot above this site the farmer dug a sizable reservoir, lined it with clay, and by means of small ditches and a little patience, filled the depression with good rain from heaven. Then he called on President Loder of the Erie, who happened to be in Middletown. He told Loder that he, the farmer, was a most fortunate man indeed, in that God had put on his fine farm a wonderful pond of never failing water, fed by deep springs; that the pond was handy to the Erie tracks and that for a consideration of $2,500, modest in view of the circumstances, he would sell to the Erie all rights to the pond.

Loder and Major Brown, the Erie's chief engineer, went to look, and sure enough there was a pond of water sufficient to fill the tanks of all the locomotives possessed by Erie. They paid the man his $2,500, and set a crew to work laying iron pipe from the pond to a tank built beside the tracks. When the valve was opened, the tank filled up wonderfully fast, but in doing so the pond went stark dry, and dry it remained.

Even the Indians got out their knives for the railroad. When the Erie came to the Seneca Reservation in Cattaraugus County, its agents hoped to get a right-of-way for little or nothing, but the chief of the tribe said it would be a matter of $10,000. The Erie agents protested, saying that the land wanted was of no value, no good for corn or potatoes, and that there was no decent timber on it. The old chief reflected a few moments, then remarked, "It pretty good for railroad." The Erie paid.

Much of the country contained what would be called hillbillies today, and in the wild Pike Pond region near Callicoon, some of the natives did not even know a railroad was in the neighborhood until they heard the whistle of the *Pioneer,* first locomotive to run over the line. As the echo rambled on through mountain valleys, the natives took down their rifles and went out to hunt what they thought was some new kind of varmint. John Quick, a famous trapper of Pike County, Pennsylvania, where the Erie touched, heard his first locomotive whistle and went promptly out with a string of traps, big ones, hoping to catch the beast with the uncanny cry. If these things seem preposterous today, time is to blame. The inci-

---

* Nor was the Erie yet through settling with Farmer Holbert. One day in 1884, four decades after the rail-fence episode, an Erie train arrived at a grade crossing on the Pine Island branch just as Farmer Holbert and buggy were bumping across it. He died of his injuries, and a damage suit was on.

dents are vouched for by the best of authority, Historian Mott of the Erie.

Two of the great engineering feats of the era were performed by Erie men. One was the Cascade Bridge across a chasm in the Randolph Hills west of Deposit, and the other the Starucca Viaduct, a 1200-foot stone affair a few miles beyond the Cascade Bridge. Eight hundred men were employed on the latter, and the cost was $320,000, probably the most expensive span in America up to that time. But the Starucca was well worth the cost. In 1947, a century after it was built, the structure still carries the Erie's main line and looks good for another century or two.

Worse than the hillbillies, worse than the difficult terrain, worse than anything else in the early operating days of the Erie were the tremendous snows that blanketed New York State. They piled down onto the tracks four, five, six feet deep on the levels, with drifts of thirty feet and more in the cuts. For a long period one winter ten locomotives and 500 men were required to keep the tracks clear.

President Loder kept the rails moving westward and the wheels turning on them until the main job was finished in 1851. His letters and diaries show him to have been a decent and honest man, and completing the Erie came to be the biggest thing in his life. It also broke him in health.

Loder knew good men when he saw them, and in 1850 he hired one of the real operating geniuses of the day. This was Charles Minot, a Yankee of Haverhill, Massachusetts, son of a judge on the Bay State's Supreme Court. Young Minot had been trained for the law, but the construction of the Boston & Maine Railroad had appealed to him and he had gone to work, carrying a chain and learning the engineering arts. He also picked up telegraphy, learned to operate a locomotive, and by 1850 had become an important man on the B&M. Loder hired him and made him general superintendent of the Erie.

Minot was a large and portly man, genial and direct, with no fuss or feathers, and of an extremely low boiling point. For days his temper would undergo the severest strains without a ripple, then he would blow up like a volcano and his wrath was something to hear. Yet he was liked and respected by both the Erie brass hats and the operating men. He refused a special car such as previous Erie superintendents had enjoyed, and traveled much of the time in an old coach, which he liked to couple just ahead of the engine. Said he could see things needing to be done in that way, and his eyes missed little. There were slides across Erie tracks, and often Erie rails were loose, and more than once Minot and his old coach were shoved off the track, and at least once sent rolling down a bank. Minot did not seem to mind.

The main stem was all but completed when Minot arrived to take charge. One of his first jobs was caring for the elaborate ceremonies that were considered only proper for completion of The Work of the Age. The history of railroading in the last century is filled with accounts of

Opening Ceremonies and they all read pretty much alike; but I think the Erie doings deserve some attention. Not even the Baltimore & Ohio staged such a resounding event. And why shouldn't it be impressive? Here was the longest railroad in the country, more than 450 miles of main line, stretching from the Hudson to the Lakes.

So, on May 14, 1851, the company steamer *Erie* loaded up with eminent Americans in New York City and with whistle blowing and a band playing set off up the river for Piermont, where the party was to take the cars to run across New York to Lake Erie. In the party were no less than one President of the United States, six candidates for that office, and a dozen aspirants for the vice-presidency. And there was also the greatest figure of all, that of Dan'l Webster, nigh seventy now and none too rugged, but still able to operate under his own power, aided by copious drafts of gin and rum and whiskey, which he alleged were good for his stomach.

Millard Fillmore, by grace of God and the death of Zach Taylor President of the United States, was nominal head of the party, and with him were his Secretary of State, Mr. Webster, and 298 assorted statesmen and political catchpoles of varying degrees of importance. Two trains had steam up and were waiting at Piermont, eastern terminus of the Erie, when the boat party arrived. At his own request Mr. Webster was seated in a rocking chair—a depraved custom of Yankees—that was securely fastened to the platform of an open flatcar. In his rumbling, sepulchral voice he said that he did not intend to miss any of the scenery.

The first train took off, but before it got to Goshen the engine had developed trouble. At Middletown Superintendent Minot met the emergency by using the new telegraph line to wire instructions ahead to the Erie roundhouse at Port Jervis to have a locomotive ready. This was done. On went the two trains. Along the Delaware, President Loder pointed out to the visitors the fine rails that were said to be the first rolled in the United States, made at Scranton. Along this portion of the road the first train made 34 miles in 35 minutes, and one can picture old Dan'l, out there in the gorgeous aloneness of his flatcar and rocker, holding his stovepipe hat and batting the hot sparks that fell on his buggy robe like the rain of hell.

The party got an excellent view of the Starucca Viaduct, then certainly the most famous engineering feat since the Erie canal; and a stop was made to permit "a good inspection of this mammoth work of man." Then, on to Susquehanna, where sixteen locomotives were lined up on a siding to let go a salute with bells and whistles, and a procession of Erie employees filed by, "led by a pioneer engineman, Luther Coleman, playing a copper key bugle."

At Binghamton a large crowd greeted the trains. President Fillmore spoke briefly, and old Dan'l stood up on his flatcar to rumble that he was indeed happy to see the "western end of this great work of art," by which he unquestionably meant the New York & Erie Rail Road. A stop overnight was made at Elmira, and here festivities rose to new heights, and "Mr. Webster responded to calls for a speech by a short but eloquent address." One of the crowd noted that the old statesman's voice was hoarse, as why shouldn't it have been? He had made "short but eloquent speeches" all the way from Hudson.

Groggy but determined, the excursion party got on their feet next morning and prepared for the last lap of the journey. So great had been the hilarity, however, that two of the Erie train crew had to be left in Elmira, with substitutes taking their places on the run to Dunkirk and the Lake. Along the route the usual crowds were waiting at the stations, and they unfurled banners, "Welcome to the Iron Horse," and "Strangers Yesterday, Neighbors Today"; and at Dunkirk, the end of the line, the welcome was truly magnificent.

The two trains were coupled together and rolled into town behind a double-header, while church bells rang wildly and the USS *Michigan*, lying in the harbor, let go with 21 guns.

An arch had been built near the railroad depot, and on a pedestal was an old-fashioned plow on which was the legend "Finis." This was the plow that had been used for breaking the first ground on the Dunkirk division of the railroad. Eighteen years had passed since the Erie had set out to reach the Lake; and now that it was here, Dunkirk must mark the event. It did so handsomely.

A table 300 feet long had been set up along Railroad Avenue, and it creaked and groaned with barbecued oxen, pork and beans in 50-gallon containers, bread baked in loaves ten feet long and two feet thick. There was a monstrous clam chowder, too, but Mr. Webster merely sniffed it and remarked to Attorney General John J. Crittenden that chowder was unfit to eat, sir, unless it contained port wine. Mr. Webster was unquestionably in failing health, but his nose still told him whether or not port wine was an ingredient of anything prepared to eat or drink.

There followed a parade, then dinners and speeches. For once in his life Mr. Webster had to be excused, and the reason given was that he was ill, as well he may have been. An eye-witness observed him to be "haggard and disheveled." But the clamor for him was so great that he made his halting way to show himself at a window of the Loder House, took a bow, and uttered a few words so faint that none could tell what he had said. Still, they had seen him, seen this man who had so often stirred the imagination of the whole nation, and one who was present remarked on Webster's "great black eyes, gleaming out of cavernous depths, under heavy brows dark almost to a frown, but with a droop of the eyelids that gave him a look of inconceivable gloom, and smote upon the senses of the spectators with a weird and wondrous fascination." * The aging stateman had only a year to live.

Well, the Erie was built, and now Charles Minot was going to run it. He ran it well, too, first for a period of four years, then after an interim, for another six years. It was Minot who devised the telegraphic method of train operation, unquestionably the greatest single step taken by railroads in their formative era. In his first year with the Erie, Minot had noted a lean and shabby man, an eccentric named Ezra Cornell, who was stringing telegraph poles along the wagon roads in the region around Goshen. Minot, as related, had learned something about telegraphy in Boston. He conceived of it as a fine method by which to regulate train movements.

Minot induced the Erie to set up a line of poles along the railroad's Eastern Division without reference to Morse's patent rights and without knowing how he was to get the machines to operate the wires. He also talked Cornell into supplying the Erie with insulators. Then he attempted to purchase the Morse patent for the Erie line. It was refused, but the Morse concern asked the Erie to become stockholders in the newly formed Telegraph Company and thus acquire the rights. Minot stalled. He also got Cornell to string his wires on the Erie poles, and presently the New York & Erie Telegraph Company was organized to connect New York City with Dunkirk. Rights to use the Morse machines were acquired, the company changed its name to the New York & Western Union Telegraph, and was on the way to being the great monopoly it became. Ezra Cornell, who in his Erie days was glad to get a few free hot cakes at the Occidental hotel in Goshen, became wealthy and founded the university that bears his name.

It has been told how Minot wired ahead to have a locomotive ready for the special that carried the Erie opening celebrants. A bit later in the same year, on September 22, 1851, Minot again used the telegraph. He was on a train bound west, which was supposed to meet and pass an eastbound train at Turner's Station, now Harriman, New York. In that day nobody knew when a train would arrive until it did. After a considerable wait Minot, at best an impatient man, went into Mr. Cornell's telegraph office and asked the operator to inquire of his colleague at Goshen, 14 miles distant, if the eastbound train had passed that point. It hadn't, and Minot dispatched the first telegraphic train order ever sent in America:

---

* It would appear from the record that Webster turned up at a great many railroad opening ceremonies of the period. Among many lesser events, he was present when the Old Colony started operation on Nov. 10, 1845, and rode the first train of the Northern, later a part of the Boston & Maine, in June of 1848.

To Agent & Operator Goshen:
     HOLD EASTBOUND TRAIN TILL FURTHER ORDERS
                                        Charles Minot, Supt Erie

Then he wrote out another order, which he signed and handed to the conductor of his train, W. H. Stewart. It read:

To Conductor & Engineer, Day Express:
     RUN TO GOSHEN REGARDLESS OF OPPOSING TRAIN
                                        Charles Minot, Supt Erie

Conductor Stewart took it to his engineer, who was Isaac Lewis, a man of orderly mind and of little imagination. Lewis read it and then remarked that he'd be damned if he would "run by that thing." Conductor Stewart so reported back to Minot. Without a word Minot put Lewis out of his cab, sat himself down at the throttle, and took the day express to Goshen, while Lewis rode the cushions. The eastbound still had not arrived. Minot telegraphed ahead again, this time to Middletown and, learning that the opposing train had not showed, he mounted to the cab and put her through to Middletown. Once more he repeated the process of wiring ahead, and then drove his engine to Port Jervis, arriving just as the other train pulled in. An hour or more of the westbound's time had been saved by the magnetic telegraph.

Erie officials were quick to see the advantage made so clear by Superintendent Minot. The road presently had special blanks printed for running orders and every Erie depot had a telegraph office. From that time on, except in New England where for one reason or another the telegraph made slow progress, American railroads were increasingly operated by the clicking key in the depot office.

With him from the Boston & Maine, Minot brought a number of good men to the Erie, among them the celebrated locomotive engineers William Hall, Charles H. Sherman, David Carey, and Samuel Veazey. Minot also was quick to find and engage likely men for the Erie telegraph line, one of whom was C. W. Douglas, said to have been the first to take messages by ear rather than by the tape.

It seems probable that the ticket punch was a contribution of the Erie railroad. In the line's early days there were no ticket agents. Each Erie conductor was given a tin box when he started a trip. In it were a supply of tickets and ten dollars in small change. But as travel increased and ticket agents came into being, passengers discovered that they could buy a ticket, say, in Goshen, calling for a through trip to New York; and then, at some station near the end of the line, perhaps at Clarkstown, they would get off and buy another ticket to their destination, this one for only a few miles and at small cost. This and not the first ticket would be surrendered to the Erie boat purser on the way down the Hudson. The Goshen

ticket would be kept and used over and over again, merely repeating the
performance—and with a sizable overall loss to Erie coffers.

Erie conductors caught the idea, and although some of them no doubt
used the situation to their own personal advantage, some one of them devised the ticket punch that made a telltale hole, and the days of cheap
riding were over.

Billy Skelly was the first news butcher on the Erie, and perhaps he was
the first anywhere. He did so well on the Erie trains that he set up a
monopoly to supply all news butchers on that road, then on a few other
roads, and in time Skelly's outfit became a part of the Union News Company. News butchers in those days were as young as ten and twelve years
of age. Skelly's boys were well chosen, and when Horatio Alger, Jr., got
around to the subject, his hero, rightly enough, was *The Erie Train Boy*,
fifty thousand words of immortal prose. The Erie had train waterboys,
too, youngsters who went through the cars with a long-spouted can and
a couple of glasses for the use of customers. The service was a great thing
for traveling germs, but it was free.*

In the matter of switching the Erie lagged a little, using horses for this
work for several years; but the line was first in the van with many other
innovations than those already mentioned. The Erie's agent at Chester,
Thomas Selleck, invented the milk train, which revolutionized the milk
business in New York City. Up to that time (1841) the main supply of the
big city's milk came from swill-fed and brewery-fed cows right in town.
The farmers of Orange County, where Selleck was stationed, sent their
dairy products to New York in the form of heavily salted butter. Selleck
gave a good deal of thought to the subject of milk. He talked leading
farmers like Philo Gregory and Jonas King and John M. Bull into trying
a few shipments of raw milk to New York. Selleck fitted up quarters at
193 Reade street in Manhattan, then went there to handle the shipment.
He found New York families ready, and he sold the 240 quarts in the first
shipment at a premium, and quickly.

Each succeeding consignment of milk over the Erie was larger than
the one before, and all of the Orange County farmers wanted to get in on
the new business. With the coming of hot weather came troubles with
consignments that soured on the way. Farmer Jacob Vail of Goshen rigged
up a hogshead with a coil of one-inch pipe inside, packed the pipe with
cracked ice, then filled the barrel with milk and sent it to Manhattan. The
weather was extremely hot, yet Vail's milk arrived in fine condition. From
that point on milk and not butter became the product of Orange County
dairies.

---

* Although all historical references I have found indicate that train waterboys on the Erie
and elsewhere went out of fashion even before the Civil War, I have drunk water served by
waterboys who passed through the cars of the Boston & Maine Railroad as late as 1904.

Many other Erie agents were avid for business for their company. In 1844 one such in Rockland County, talked the farmers roundabout into shipping a carload of berries by the railroad. Two years later the Erie was running a Berry Special that carried some half a million baskets of strawberries into Manhattan; and the business continued to increase until Long Island and New Jersey farmers entered the market, and the Erie's trade languished.

And finally, it was the Erie on which the foundation of a classic story was built: On a spring day in 1854 Mrs. Silas Horton, who lived along the railroad near Owego, noted that an immense tree had been blown down across the Erie tracks, on a sharp curve of the line. A train was due, was even whistling for the curve. Grabbing the first thing that came to hand, good Mrs. Horton dashed out of the house, and so on down the tracks toward the oncoming train, flagging it down and becoming without doubt the first such heroine in railroad history. Her flag was a pair of her own red woolen undergarments, vulgarly called drawers.

And it is most pleasant, indeed, to report that the Erie Railroad did the proper thing. On June 20, 1854, from his office in New York, President Homer Ramsdell of the company wrote Mrs. Horton to thank her for "the noble and humane conduct evinced by you, on an occasion when the lives and safety of the persons traveling on our mail train were jeopardized by an obstruction on the road." Then, to show that the Erie did things hand-somely, good President Ramsdell enclosed a life pass each for Mr. and Mrs. Horton; and although he made no mention of the specific sort of garment so nobly and humanely used, he added delicately that he was also "sending a dress for Mrs. Horton and respectfully request your accepting the same."

Out of Mrs. Horton's brave deed must have come the countless stories, the poems, the songs, the "true" anecdotes about the flagging down of the Fast Mail or the Lightning Express by waving a pair of red flannel drawers, women's, that have long since become a part of our folklore, and which have been coupled, for the sake of regional glory, with the Maine Central, the Boston & Albany, the Pennsylvania, the Rock Island, and nobody knows what other lines. The Erie event, however, is dated, placed, named, thoroughly documented. All others are unquestionably forgeries.

In the identical year in which brave Mrs. Horton saved the Erie train from disaster, another and much greater tragedy to the road was in the making. This appeared in the form of Daniel Drew, a former drover who is said to have devised the method of salting his cattle well, then per-mitting them to drink copiously just before they were to be weighed in at market. From the practice came the term "watered stock."

As ignorant as he was pious, Uncle Dan'l Drew was also the greatest rascal of his era, which was no mean achievement. Buying into steamboat lines, he soon turned to railroads, and before the beaver-hatted gentlemen of the Erie knew what was afoot, he had acquired Erie stock and slipped onto its board. Three years later he was its treasurer. And presently he brought into the now doomed concern two unusual characters. One was James Fisk, Jr., a Vermont peddler of tinware who later became a partner in the drygoods house of Jordan, Marsh & Company, Boston, and still later went into Wall Street, where he met Drew. Fisk was to become a sort of Barnum of business. The other Drew protege was quiet Jay Gould, who had worked wonders rehabilitating the Rutland & Washington railroad.

The Erie being commonly short of cash, in 1866 Drew advanced it $3,-500,000, taking 28,000 shares of unissued stock and three millions of convertible bonds. Simultaneously he went short on Erie on a rising market, and suddenly unloaded 58,000 shares. When the stock sank from 95 to 50 he took enormous profits.

Old Mr. Vanderbilt went after Erie control, but Drew, Gould, and Fisk set printing presses to working overtime to produce Erie stock certificates —all unauthorized—and the Vanderbilt crowd's millions could not hold out against the deluge of pretty paper. Vanderbilt took a dreadful licking in this deal.

Now the courts were called in. The arrest of Fisk, Gould, and Drew was ordered. Taking along some $6,000,000, the trio emigrated to Jersey City, where they turned Taylor's Hotel into a fort manned by several hundred assorted and armed thugs wielding everything from shotguns to brass knuckles. The war was now transferred from the courts and the hotel to the legislature at Albany which, by the use of bribes, Gould had little difficulty in persuading to pass a bill legalizing an issue of some 50,000 shares of unauthorized Erie stock.

The three buccaneers took their unholy gains and proceeded to start an assault on stock prices, bank credit, and foreign exchange which brought thousands to ruin. Gould and Fisk next turned on old Uncle Dan'l himself, their former mentor, cornered him, and sent him on the way to bankruptcy.

The Erie headquarters were in the gaudy Pike's Opera House at Twenty-third street and Eighth avenue, New York, and were fitted up to suit the so-called taste of Fisk, which was a combination of Byzantine and P. T. Barnum. From here Gould and Fisk continued to juggle Erie matters to their own advantage until the Erie board, desperate at last, managed to oust Gould. Gould's arrest followed on charges of embezzlement. Lawsuits and other legal troubles continued to harass the wrecked railroad. In spite of this, Erie paid a dividend on its common stock in 1873. It was to be the last in sixty-nine years.

Gould turned to other railroads, leaving the Erie to go its halting way. As for Jim Fisk, a notable lecher and show-off, he died with his boots on, in 1872, shot down on the stairs of the present Broadway Central Hotel by Edward Stokes, who had also taken from The Prince of Erie his favorite mistress, one Josie Mansfield, an untalented person whom Fisk had tried vainly to make into an actress. Fisk's death must have been an incomparable relief to the general run of Erie directors and officials, who were conservative in business and of orthodox morality in their private affairs.

CHAPTER VI

Forgotten Genius

John Poor's proposal hit the city like an alarm bell in the night, struck by the hand of a stranger.
—A comment in Portland, Me., *circa* 1843.

MANY an able Yankee left his homeland in the eighteen-forties and after to go West and build or operate the great railroads of the nation. Look into the early history of almost any Western line and you will discover New Englanders among the officials and among the chief construction and operating men. There was one Yankee, however, who remained in his native Pine Tree State to conceive and to push through against rugged opposition the original line that became the Grand Trunk and is now part of the Canadian National, one of the truly great roads (24,000 miles) of North America. The Yankee was John Alfred Poor, a wholly indomitable and tireless man of great and varied talents who ought not to be but is largely forgotten. It was Poor who built the line through the Big Woods.

It was Poor, too, who waked his beloved Maine to the new era brought in by the steam railroad. Born in 1808 at Andover, he taught school at Bethel, then went to Bangor to study law and soon to practice. He possessed considerably more intellectual curiosity than usually is granted to men who build railroads, and presently he was lecturing at the Bangor Lyceum, which he helped to found, and contributing historical articles to newspapers. He spoke and wrote eloquently and well, and these talents were to be of great aid to him in rousing the sluggards of Maine to the importance of the Iron Horse. That he was also a "man of splendid beauty," being six feet two and weighing two hundred and fifty pounds, "of noble and commanding presence, with clean-cut Grecian features," unquestionably prepared him to meet and conquer the opposition and to fit him for the great physical tasks he undertook.

Massachusetts became mildly interested in railroads about 1832; and two years later, when the budding Boston & Worcester was about to run its first train of steam cars, Poor, reading of it in the papers, made the long journey from Bangor to Boston and was present, on April 16, 1834, when the great event occurred. It made a lasting impression, and it there and then gave him also a tremendous and lifelong ambition.

Harper's Weekly, Feb. 27, 1864

Civil War hospital car: cots were suspended by thick rubber bands.

From The Story of the Pullman Car

J. L. Barnes, who had charge of the first Pullman on its first trip, over the Chicago & Alton between Bloomington and Chicago, on the night of Sept. 1 1859.

Webster Wagner, the New York Central's sleeping-car genius, prospered with Vanderbilt support, but was burned to death in one of his own cars in a rear-end collision at Spuyten Duyvil, N. Y. in 1882.

I like to muse on the scene. Here was John Poor, aged twenty-six, a boy of the backwoods, yet of lively mind and no little learning, come from farthest Maine, indeed from that city which Henry Thoreau likened to a star on the edge of night, hewing away at the forest of which it was built—come down from Bangor to see New England's first steam locomotive railway begin its career. Standing in the enormous crowd of sightseers, Poor noted that the engine driver, who like the locomotive had come from England, stepped upon the platform with almost the air of a juggler or a professor of chemistry. Then this important man put his hand upon the lever, moved it slightly, and the monster started moving amid the shouts and cheers of the multitude.

One wonders what this or that one in the crowd thought they were seeing, but one knows what John Poor thought. "It gave me such a shock," he said, "that my hair seemed to start from its roots rather than to stand on end." From that moment to the end of his life Poor often spoke of the impact of that scene upon his mind. The engine, he said, continued to grow into a greatness in his mind that left "all other created things far behind it as marvels and wonders."

I am not certain, but it seems to me that in this scene there is subject matter for a wonderful mural, perhaps to grace the walls of the Grand Trunk station in Portland, Maine, or even of the Canadian National's great station in Montreal. The legend could tell all men that this was "John Alfred Poor, Railroad Genius, 1808–1871, Looking for the First Time on a Locomotive Engine." No one is more worthy of such a mural, for it was he who first envisioned a railroad system embracing all of New England, Quebec, and the Maritime Provinces of Canada, and then went ahead to found such a system. John Poor was a true fanatic, and it was going to take a fanatic to build the railroad he had in mind.

During the remainder of the 1830's the state of Maine talked a good deal about railroads, chiefly in its legislature, which favored a road of iron from Belfast, on the Maine coast, to the city of Quebec. A half-hearted survey was made. Nothing whatever came of it, nor of a later survey from Portland to Lake Champlain. Meanwhile Poor was quietly looking over the land, not merely as a surveyor, but as what today would be called a geopolitician.

John Poor had a broad and remarkable mind. Before he was ready to spread his views of railroads before his fellows, he studied every possible subject that might have a bearing on what he conceived of as not merely a railroad between two points, but as an all-embracing railway system, one that would be of mutual advantage to Canada and to Maine and incidentally, if for no other reason, to other portions of the United States.

Poor first made himself thoroughly familiar with the physical geography of the regions he had in mind; and also with their commercial, agricultural, and manufacturing possibilities. He even studied the habits of the peoples concerned, both Canadians and Americans, and their political and economic notions. After he had digested a monumental amount of printed matter, and looked at countless maps he set out by stage or buggy, and often on foot, to see what the land looked like at first hand and to learn how the people felt about a railroad.

He was concerned not only with the people of Portland and Montreal, the two cities he had picked for terminals of his first line, but with the rustics and backwoodsmen all along the three hundred miles between those cities. He saw and talked with them too. Swamp and meadow, valley and mountain, Poor saw them all at first hand, and their peoples. Chewed by black flies and mosquitoes or frost-bitten, Poor made trip after trip into those three hundred miles of seemingly interminable woods, the Big Woods, the forests of pine and spruce that enclosed the Androscoggin from the sea to its headwaters, that followed the height of land over to the Connecticut's upper reaches, then followed another height of land over to the waters of the St. Lawrence. He stopped at hamlets, logging camps, vilages, stayed overnight at farmhouses, always talking, asking questions, learning what this man and that man wanted, what they thought a railroad could do for them. Likely no region was ever better canvassed, certainly not by one lone man, than was the Big Woods country through which Poor's Atlantic & St. Lawrence Railroad was to pass, in good time.

It may have been and probably was John Poor who first conceived—so far as New England was concerned—of a railroad not as a mere convenience to an old settled community, which was the theory held in Massachusetts and Connecticut, but as a highway that should serve to develop uninhabited or sparsely settled regions, such as this howling wilderness between Portland and Montreal, and make them prosperous through agriculture, industry and commerce. In 1843 he was ready. In that year he wrote petitions for his proposed railroads to the Maine legislature, and a year later dropped everything else to write and speak for his proposals. What he proposed was an international railway to run between Portland and Montreal in the Northwest, and Portland and Halifax in the Northeast. These were simply the beginnings of the system he had in mind. From Montreal the line would be extended to reach Chicago.

The reasons for this road, said Poor, were many. It would first stimulate the growing of agricultural products in the great west and bring them to the finest port on the Atlantic, namely Portland, whose bay had never been known to freeze. It would tap the rich empires of timber and minerals, both in Canada and the United States. It would make for mutuality of interests and hence work for friendship between British Canada and her old enemy, the United States of America. In this regard, it is well to bear in mind that in 1843, when Poor was publicizing his ideas, there was little "mutuality of interests" between the two countries. The International Boundary was the chief item of discord, and even though the controversy had been officially settled by the Webster-Ashburton Treaty, there still was high feeling and resentment on both sides of the line.

Poor's proposal created something of a sensation. In that day, Portland was literally a deserted village, said a contemporary, rich in retired capital, but poor in enterprise and public spirit. The great days of the sailing ships were in the past. Many citizens believed they could see grass starting to grow up through the cobbles of India and Pearl and Exchange Streets. Lights still glowed at night on the headlands, yet comparatively few skippers took their bearings to enter Casco Bay.

With such a setting of incipient decay, it was probably little wonder that Poor's startling proposal for a vast railway system centering in Portland hit the city "like an alarm bell in the night, struck by the hand of a stranger." Within a few weeks Portland and much of Maine and the province of Quebec were excited as never before since the Revolution. Poor went on to hold meetings in Portland and then, true to his idea that people along the route should have opportunity to speak, in villages along the line of his first road, the Portland-Montreal. He appeared in person at Andover, Maine, at Colebrook, New Hampshire, at Canaan, Vermont, and at Sherbrooke, Quebec. In all of them he aroused the natives—then as now hardly a crowd to excite easily—to a pitch bordering on delirium. And in Montreal Poor's message and idea found a ready reception. Montreal was growing fast and felt it might grow even faster if it had a port that were not frozen solid for six months of the year. Portland, the ice-free port of which John Poor spoke so eloquently, might well be the answer.

Poor now engaged James Hall, a professional engineer, to make a survey for the Portland-Montreal line. Hall recommended that the White Mountains be passed by way of the Androscoggin River valley and Dixville Notch; and estimated the cost of building the road from Portland to the Canadian border at $2,250,000, no little of which would go for clearing the right-of-way of one of the thickest stands of timber in Eastern North America. In the meantime Montreal men were stirred to action, and a group headed by A. T. Galt prepared to build the line from that city to meet the Portland line at the border.

Villains, too, were rousing, in Boston. This crowd, having had plenty of time to get wind of Poor's proposal, moved quietly upon Montreal, and before Poor was aware of it, his plan was in danger of being transferred to the Hub of the Universe. It was a most potent group, these Boston men, and they included the Hon. Harrison Grey Otis, the Hon. Abbot Lawrence, and "three hundred and fifty-seven others, certified by the Mayor of Boston to be amongst the most wealthy capitalists and business men of the city." The group also included such hardy Vermonters as Erastus Fairbanks, who was interested in the fact that the route from Boston to Montreal would pass through his home town of St. Johnsbury, where he made weighing scales.

What was more, the Boston group had interests already in one or more of the three existing railroads of the general region—the Vermont Central, the Northern Railroad of New Hampshire, and the Fitchburg; and now, in the very teeth of John Poor's proposal, the Boston group chartered a new line called, with plain notice of intent, the Boston, Concord & Montreal. This was to be the route, so the Boston men informed the Montreal men, that would best serve Canadian interest. Indeed, should the Provincial Parliament be so inept as to give a "preference to a different route, it would be calculated to defer, if not ultimately defeat, the object so much desired by business men in Canada and the United States."

Anyway, that was the way in which the Boston men placed the matter before the Montrealers.

The implied threats of the Boston crowd, to which was no doubt added some fancy lobbying, began to change the ideas of the Canadians. Where at first they had accepted Poor's proposal as the logical one for them, they now began to see that Boston had something to offer. In February 1845, emissaries of the Boston, Concord & Montreal railroad were gathered in the latter city, confident and ready to close an agreement by which the Canadian group should build to meet the line working north from Boston. John Poor, 300 miles away in Portland, first heard of this encroachment on February 4th. At half-past midnight on the fifth he started out from Portland in the teeth of one of the worst storms on record. It was to be a journey the man never forgot, a journey so terrible that Poor was six full months recovering. It was also one of the great epic trips having to do with American railroads. I can think of no other quite so approaching the epic.

As soon as he heard that the unspeakable Boston men were in Montreal, wooing the Canucks toward Boston harbor, Poor sent out a man to ride ahead and arrange for relays of horses; he himself would get to Montreal, and fast. The day of Wednesday the fifth was threatening. A dark and portentous sky hung over Maine, and at about ten that night came a wind that quickly increased to gale proportions and brought with it the first specks of dancing snow.

Before midnight, while Poor was frantically trying to get some necessary papers together, the snow became a blizzard. "The fierce howl of the blast," Poor recalled, "and the clatter of the snow against the window panes and awning posts, made everyone anxious to remain indoors." Family and friends did their best to keep him from starting. Poor said "No," that the turning point in the history of Maine's railroad to Montreal was at stake, and that he must go on, no matter what the weather.

Poor could find but one man in all Portland, a Mr. Cheney, who must indeed have been a redoubtable man, to accompany him. Bundled in furs and with a spirited horse and a good stout sleigh, the two took off into the face of the northeast storm. Part of the time they held to the road, but the road soon disappeared entirely and Poor and his companion were presently rolling over unseen stonewalls, rail fences, and woodpiles, while the horse did its best to dodge the larger drifts.

The snow cut horse and men alike, and they bled. Poor found the only way to protect his eyes was to allow icicles to form and hang down from his eyebrows and then with the end of a finger to melt a small hole through which to see. What tells more of the nature of the storm was the time required to make Teak's tavern in Falmouth Town, seven miles from Portland. It was six hours.

Changing horses at Teak's, eating a hurried breakfast, Poor and Cheney were away with the first streak of dawn. Eighteen inches of new snow rested on the road, but by dark the travelers had reached Mr. Waterhouse's hospitable inn at Paris. Poor discovered he had a frozen nose, and one ear badly frost-bitten. Again the travelers rested, the horses were changed, and Poor tried to prevail on Waterhouse to go ahead to break road. Although Waterhouse was an old Nestor of the region and enjoyed the reputation of being an able man in breaking roads, he was not crazy. He told Poor he would not for anything consider striking out until morning. So, Poor and Cheney stayed over-night.

At dawn they left in the wake of Waterhouse, who drove a powerful tandem team and battered through the immense drifts on the way to Rumford. They found the snow at Rumford deeper than ever, but managed to get half a dozen young men to ride ahead and break a horse track as far as Andover.

All had gone well, so far. But beyond Andover, as Poor well knew, there was to be no road or track of any kind. He had now reached the real wilderness, the country out back of beyond, the Big Woods. For forty miles over the route he must follow to Colebrook in New Hampshire he must make his way as he went, and he must also pass the extreme northern part of the White Mountains through Dixville Notch, a terror of a place, which one traveler reported was like "a titantic gateway to some region of vast and mysterious desolation." *

On they went. They found Andover Surplus and the Umbagog Lake region to be fairly free from drifts, yet even with two strong horses and with a Captain Wallace Abbott breaking road, they could scarcely cover two miles an hour. And so at last they came to the great test of the whole trip, Dixville Notch. At Errol, New Hampshire, before getting to the Notch, Poor found "Captain William Bragg and three others" willing to help him over the height of land. They were going to be needed.

Although the temperature was 18 below zero, hard snow was still riding the wind; and as they approached the Notch gusts came through the deep narrow chasm with terrific force. All Poor could see were "perpen-

---

* See Thomas Starr King's classic and truly wonderful *The White Hills,* 1860.

dicular mountains of snow" through which there was no apparent pass. But Bragg, who was called the Notch-Tender, knew what he was about, and after two hours of hard work by his crew, a path was opened in the gigantic drifts. Slowly, very slowly, with an outrider ahead, the sleigh was got into the Notch and here it met a wind of such force and cold it was not to be described.

The Notch, said Poor, and anyone who has ever been there in winter will believe him, the Notch roared and thundered like a bellows of the gods, as perhaps it was. The air was dark with thickening snow, and all creative forces seemed to have retreated from the spot and abandoned it to the sport of destructive elements. Here, as Thoreau was to find on Mount Katahdin, was Chaos and Old Night. A brave man always, Poor neverthe- less shook with fear as he listened to the wind and caught brief glances of menacing cliffs on all sides. The horses at last were unhitched and led ahead in single file, while Poor and the other men heaved at the sleigh and inched it along up the rise. And thus they passed over the height of land, 2000 feet above the sea, from the waters of the Androscoggin to those of the Connecticut.

It was better going west of the Notch. Poor and Cheney stopped over- night, whether in Colebrook, New Hampshire, or Canaan, Vermont, isn't clear, then crossed into Canada. They reached Sherbrooke on Saturday the 8th, and drove all night and Sunday to reach Montreal early on Mon- day. They were still on the wrong side of the St. Lawrence, which was filled with floating ice. Some time was occupied in finding and convincing a Frenchman that he should ferry the weary travelers across to the main part of the city. It was done, though, and Poor had a chance to sleep an hour or so before he had to act.

It turned out to be a situation of some drama. At ten o'clock that morn- ing the Montreal Board of Trade was to meet for final decision on the Boston proposal. These Canadians had no particular preference for Boston over Portland, or vice versa. But the Boston group had been long on the scene, while Poor had been absent since his first proposal; and it is certain that the Boston group must have represented, to the Canadians, a more substantial interest. But young John Poor was still to be reckoned with.

His great frame and ready mind refreshed by brief sleep after his ter- rible five days in the wilderness, Poor walked unannounced into the Board of Trade meeting. With what must have been great eloquence as well as good judgment, he prevented the Board from adopting the resolution before it, the resolution to adopt the Boston plan, and to agree to recon- sider his own proposal.

Poor told the assembled capitalists of the vast superiority of Portland harbor over any other, including that of Boston. He dwelt upon the fact that Portland was 100 miles nearer to Montreal than was Boston. He stressed the physical features of the route he proposed, saying they were much easier to conquer by rails than the Boston route—which was really a debatable point. And along with his arguments he threw the weight of his likable personality. Then, while the Board still debated, another dramatic incident occurred: Judge William Pitt Preble of Portland, a moving spirit in the Poor enterprise, arrived at the Board's chambers after a five-day trip over the route for which Poor had broken the trail. With him he brought a handsome charter, glittering with red seal and elegant script, for the Atlantic & St. Lawrence Railroad, granted on February 10th by the legislature of Maine.

It seems likely that Poor already had turned the tide in favor of Portland; and now the appearance of Judge Preble and the charter were evidence of such good faith and good business that the Montrealers were wholly won over. They voted for Portland, then went ahead to charter their own end of the railroad as the St. Lawrence & Atlantic.

Poor and Preble returned to Portland in triumph, and the new company went ahead to raise money. On a trip to Boston, Poor was taken suddenly ill, probably from the effects of exposure on his journey to Montreal. For many weeks he lay in bed, delirious; and on recovery could walk only with crutches for several months.

In the meantime, Judge Preble and other staunch men of Portland were keeping up the public interest. They soon had immeasurable aid from the pen of John Neal, the odd and gifted man of letters who had given first and often the sole encouragement to many young writers, including the Quaker John Whittier, and the pagan Edgar Poe. Contributor to most of the leading periodicals of the day, Neal was noted for his support of phrenology and utilitarianism and his unqualified damnation of prohibition. Now he took up the steam railroad and wrote enthusiastically of it, specifically of the Atlantic & St. Lawrence. In a series of powerful articles in the *Portland Advertiser* he discussed the subject from all angles and fortified his arguments for the road by statistics that were "so convincing to his readers that none attempted to question their accuracy."

All of this yeasty eloquence was topped by a mass meeting held in Portland City Hall. Neal acted as secretary. Speakers outdid each other. Enthusiasm rose to a new pitch and the meeting broke up with mighty cheering and the assurance of capital with which to build the Atlantic & St. Lawrence.

John Poor was soon back in harness; and on the Fourth of July, 1846, a huge crowd witnessed a long parade and then six thousand of them congregated under a monstrous piece of canvas to hear Judge Preble and Canadian dignitaries sound off, and ground was broken at Fish Point to start construction of the Atlantic & St. Lawrence. At almost the same time work was begun on the Montreal end of the line. At last Poor's dream was being laid with iron rails and wooden ties!

Progress seemed dreadfully slow at first, at both ends, for money was hard to come by even when it had been promised, once the initial enthusiasm had cooled. At the end of two years only fifty miles of track had been laid in Maine, only thirty miles in Canada. Poor and Preble never faltered, but kept up their drumming. During the second year, and partly because England had reduced her tariff on grain and thus opened a new market for Canadian and American farmers, money became easier. Some of it went into stocks of the two railroad companies.

Early in July, 1851, the road entered New Hampshire from the south and east, not through Dixville Notch as originally planned, but by way of Gilead and Shelburne. It reached and crossed the Connecticut River at North Stratford late in 1852, and in the following February arrived at the international border, just north of Island Pond, Vermont. The Montreal division was completed soon after, and the entire line of 292 miles was theoretically ready for operation in July, 1853. It was also ready for lease to a new concern, the Grand Trunk Railway of Canada, which took over the line on a 999-year contract by which it agreed to pay all bills outstanding and 6 per cent dividends on stock.*

That the new line left something to be desired as a finished railroad is to be seen in an old account of conditions between North Stratford, New Hampshire, and Island Pond, Vermont, as they were in January, 1853, when one of the first trains attempted a run through what are still known as the Nulhegan Woods:

> The road was not ballasted for some distance from North Stratford, and the ties were laid on the snow. Snow started to fall just as the train left town. It labored up the heavy grade for a way, then cut off a portion of the train and the crew proceeded with engine and tender as far as Wenlock. Here they were obliged to leave the tender, and went on as far as Hobson's Mills, where the water gave out.†

When the water played out at Hobson's Mills, Engineer C. W. Mayer remained with the naked locomotive while Conductor Tuttle went forward on foot to Island Pond Village, four miles away. Tuttle had a time of it, for he had to plow through immense drifts and found difficulty even in keeping to the track in the blinding storm. At Island Pond he reported the situation to Superintendent Courser. Courser routed out a gang of men and all hands plodded to the stalled engine. Here they formed a bucket brigade and filled the tank from a brook. It required, said a contemporary, more than one thousand pails of water to do it.

---

* "Over a century has passed," writes Alvin Harlow in his *Steelways of New England,* published in 1946, "but the Atlantic & St. Lawrence still has a corporate existence, most of its stock being held in Europe, though a small quantity of it still pays its comfortable 6 per cent to citizens of Maine."

† Jeannette R. Thompson, *History of the Town of Stratford, New Hampshire, 1773–1925,* Published by Vote of the Town, 1925.

This Stratford-Island Pond portion of the Grand Trunk was very uneven, apparently not unusual in Grand Trunk track at the period. The locomotive engineers commonly had to apply power to run up short but steep elevations of the rails, then to apply the brakes quickly as the rails dipped downward. Bridges were given to washing out without any notice at all. The cut at a place called Blackberry Hill was so poorly done that engine drivers soon learned to slow down to five miles an hour in passing it; if they didn't, off the rails they went. But these defects were soon straightened out. John Poor's dream of fifteen and more years' duration was now the Grand Trunk Railway, set for a long and honorable career.

Poor had been right, too: industry and commerce did follow his rails into and through the Big Woods, the wilderness. Villages founded on industries sprang up almost before the rails had been laid—Mechanic Falls, South Paris, Locke's Mills blossomed beside the tracks. Berlin Mills quickly grew into one of the great pulp towns of the entire United States. Sawmills went up on the river at Bloomfield, Vermont, and the 'Hegan Woods filled to overflowing with roaring men armed with axes and peaveys. Sherbrooke, Canada, grew into a city, Queen of the Eastern Townships, and started to stage an annual fair that brought Canucks and Yankees together by the thousands. Portland and Montreal both prospered; the former town's Old Orchard Beach grew into a resort that was the mecca of Grand Trunk excursions, which gave hundreds of thousands of inlanders their first and sometimes only view of salt water. For more than a score of years Portland was a great port of entry for immigrants from Europe, immigrants both for the Western United States and for Canada; and wheat and other grains from the prairie provinces of the Dominion went to Europe from Portland's ice-free port.

John Poor had done a great service for the northeastern United States and Canada. Yet the Portland-Montreal line, it will be remembered, was only a part of Poor's dream. When the Grand Trunk was in operation, Poor went to work on his plan for the European & North American Railway. This was to carry one from Portland up through Maine, on through New Brunswick, to the farthest point in Nova Scotia. From there great steamers, operating in conjunction with the trains, would carry the traveler to Galway, Ireland, in five days. From Galway special trains were to speed across Ireland to Dublin, then a quick crossing to Holyhead, England, and a rail jump to London.

It was an immense conception. Poor wrote about it, talked it, and finally called a convention to consider the plan. No little enthusiasm was displayed, so Poor founded a weekly newspaper to publicize the idea. It never quite came off. A railroad at last did run up through Maine and so on into the Maritime Provinces, but Poor's vision did not take shape, then or ever. What part of it did take shape was leased to and became the Maine Central Railroad.

Yet Poor had not dreamed in vain. The Grand Trunk, as I have tried to indicate, gave the deserted village of Portland a new and long lease on life, and its influence is felt a century afterward.

Even while he continued to work for his grandiose European & North American, Poor was also busy elsewhere, building or reorganizing a number of railroads, among them the York & Cumberland, the Portland & Rochester, the Belfast & Moosehead Lake, and the Bangor & Piscataquis. In 1870 he got a charter for a road, called, in fearful length, the Portland, Rutland, Oswego & Chicago Railway Company, and was working hard at it as late as the night before he died.

John Poor was a purposeful fanatic, one of the finest examples of that species of man, a man of action as well as of thought. He bought the *American Railroad Journal* of New York and turned it over to his brother, Henry V. Poor to edit, and out of this in time came the celebrated Poor's *Railroad Manual*. He was as fanatical about his native Maine as he was about railroads. Maine was a place, he said, where a man could do twice as much work as any other place on earth. He was the kind of man who believed things like that, too. It was the climate, he said, the very air of the place.

Poor called attention, and perhaps was the first to do so, to what he said were the fertile lands of Aroostook County, a remote and wholly undeveloped part of Maine, and proposed a railroad that in time became the unique Bangor & Aroostook, the great Pulp & Potato line. He wrote an excellent monograph on English Colonization in America (1862) and many papers urging the State of Maine to make geological and waterpower surveys and also to keep general statistical studies of everything pertaining to Maine's agriculture and industry. On the day before he died in 1871 he finished an article on "Railroad Improvements." Thus he died true to the faith he had first known back in 1834, when he saw steam move the wheels of the Boston & Worcester's locomotive engine and the hair on his head "had seemed to start from its roots."

The technical cause of Poor's death, says his chief biographer, was "the breaking down of the walls of the heart"; but he really died, says the same source, of a broken heart, disappointed that his idea of the European & North American did not take shape. One is quite prepared to believe the broken-heart story. Fanatics are likely to be open to such fractures, and John Poor belonged to that company of men, though he was hardly of the wild-eyed variety. He was also a pretty good prophet.

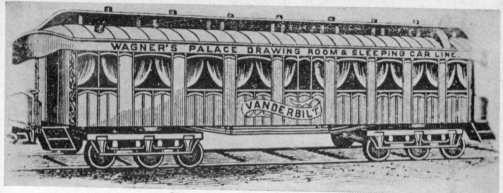

Old print of a Wagner Palace car.

Frank Leslie's Illustrated Newspaper, Aug. 25, 1877

Mr. George Mortimer Pullman explaining car construction to two of the Boston gentlemen of the famous Board of Trade Transcontinental Trip, 1870.

Morning scene in a Pullman-car washroom in 1877, as depicted by an artist for Frank Leslie's Illustrated Newspaper.

CHAPTER VII

The Pennsy and the Central

I was at home, gentlemen, playing a rubber of whist, and I never allow anything to interfere with me when I am playing that game. It requires, as you know, undivided attention.
—COMMODORE VANDERBILT, to a Legislative Committee of Investigation, 1867.

A T ABOUT the same time John A. Poor was rousing the citizens of Portland and Montreal to the need for a line between those cities, the business men of Philadelphia were watching with increasing unease the progress of the New York & Erie Rail Road Company. That progress, as I have tried to show, was slow and often at a standstill; yet the astute men of the Quaker City saw in it a menace. They saw a menace, too, in the faster progress westward of the Baltimore & Ohio rails. Some of them remarked that the new Erie Railroad, together with the long established Erie Canal, threatened to carry the traffic of the northern Midwest to New York City, while the B&O seemed to be heading for Pittsburgh in order to divert western trade from eastern Pennsylvania, and of course to Baltimore.

These were horrible things for Philadelphians to contemplate. Much of the Quaker City still believed it was the biggest and most important city in the United States, a position it had held at the time of the Revolution. But now it looked as if the crude, brash town on Manhattan Island was taking itself seriously. So, on April 13, 1846, after no little discussion, a group of Philadelphia men laid aside their plug hats and gold-headed canes to incorporate the Pennsylvania Railroad. The idea was to build a road to Pittsburgh, and the Pennsylvania legislature put a burr under the new railway magnates by authorizing the hated Baltimore & Ohio to extend its line to Pittsburgh if the new concern failed to reach that rising steel city in good time.

The history of the Pennsylvania Railroad was to be as unlike that of the unfortunate Erie as could be imagined. For one thing, the Pennsylvania had money from the start, perhaps not quite so much as its officials would have liked, but sufficient always to keep things moving. It also had John Edgar Thomson, one of the greatest all-around railroad men America has known. Thomson came to the Pennsylvania soon after it was chartered. Born in 1808 in Delaware County, Pennsylvania, descended from Quaker forebears and son of a civil engineer, he had worked on surveys for railroads in his native state, in New Jersey, and in Georgia. The Camden & Amboy had put him in charge of one of its engineering divisions in 1830. A year later, in order to learn what the Old Country knew of steam railroading, he went to England and Europe, and returned in 1832 to become chief engineer of the Georgia Railroad, with which he remained, doing much brilliant work, until he joined the new Pennsylvania company.

No budding rail line was ever more fortunate in its chief engineer than the Pennsylvania. Thomson was at times a difficult man, taciturn, abrupt to rudeness, and given to doing startling things without consulting his directors; but he also devoted his every thought and energy to building the finest railroad possible. The result was a main line and branches that were laid with a foresight which appears uncanny today, a century afterward.

The first thing, of course, was to get some sort of rail line into Pittsburgh. This must be done quickly, or the B&O might arrive on the scene first. To avoid the heavy cost of building a line between Philadelphia and Harrisburg, the state capital, Thomson made arrangements with the dilapidated Philadelphia & Columbia, the state-owned road, to carry the Pennsylvania's freight and passengers. From Columbia to Harrisburg everything had to go by canal boat. At Harrisburg, Thomson put crews to work building the main line to Pittsburgh; and while this was going forward, the Pennsylvania purchased the state-owned road and extended the rails to Harrisburg. On July 18, 1858, a passenger train passed over the entire route from Philadelphia to Pittsburgh, among its cars being, incidentally, the first smoker ever hauled on an American railroad.

The building of this first section of the Pennsylvania was a feat both of finance and engineering, yet Thomson's greatest days were still ahead. While he was building for Pittsburgh as the goal, Thomson also was thinking of places far beyond that city. Early in the fifties he had by advice and cash encouraged the consolidation of a number of small roads west of Pittsburgh. This was accomplished in 1856 and took form as the Pittsburgh, Fort Wayne & Chicago, which was later leased and eventually bought by the Pennsylvania.

Thomson now had a line from Philadelphia to Lake Michigan. His next move was to acquire the United Railroad & Canal Company of New Jersey, which gave the Pennsylvania terminal facilities on the west bank of the Hudson, with ferries operated to New York City. To protect properties leased or controlled by the Pennsylvania from raids by outsiders, Thomson and associates formed what may have been the first holding company in the country. This was known as the Pennsylvania Company.

Soon into its care went the Cleveland & Pittsburgh, many small lines in Ohio, and then the sizable system known as the Panhandle Route—the Pittsburgh, Cincinnati, Chicago & St. Louis. These additions gave the Pennsylvania a second line to Chicago, a direct line to St. Louis, a second line to Cincinnati, and also tapped much new territory.

Thomson, who died in 1874, and those who followed him, kept the Pennsy expanding and clear of financial buccaneering. While Daniel Drew was looting the Erie for his personal gain, and old Commodore Vanderbilt building up his enormous fortune through manipulation, the Pennsy continued to be operated as a *railroad*, a carrier of goods and people. It never missed a dividend prior to 1946, in which year, according to its annual report, it lost money for the first time in its history. Its public relations, except in the 1877 strike, were better than good. It was the first American railroad to lay steel rails, probably the first to use air brakes and a block-signal system. It also gave some thought to esthetics. Even before the Civil War its conductors were ordered to dress in fine cutaway coats of blue broadcloth, with shiny brass buttons, buff vests, and black trousers. These gorgeous yet dignified characters were noted for their courtesy and ability in a day when many railroad conductors were both surly and arrogant.

When Thomson died in 1874, he left a railroad property sound in every limb, including its leased lines, and so situated geographically that it was then and still is today the greatest carrier in the United States. Even in death Thomson differed from Commodore Vanderbilt. In his will he left his estate in trust, the income to be used to educate daughters of railroad men killed in accidents. It still functions, in Philadelphia, as the John Edgar Thomson Foundation.*

The men in Thomson's wake continued to work for the glory of the Pennsylvania Railroad. Under Thomas A. Scott, George B. Roberts and Alexander Johnston Cassatt, the system grew steadily larger and better. It acquired the Northern Central, running south from Sodus Bay on Lake Ontario to Baltimore, thus moving into the home territory of the B&O, which had invaded Pittsburgh. It took over the Buffalo & Allegheny Valley, extending from Oil City northward, and also the Western New York & Pennsylvania, reaching from Oil City to Buffalo and Rochester, hard in the New York Central's bailiwick. Under Alexander J. Cassatt, though he did not live to see its completion, the Pennsy, for thirty years termi-

---

* Thomson's name is honored in the town of Braddock, Pa. During the panic of 1873 Mr. Thomson had kindly aided Andrew Carnegie by buying $100,000 worth of bonds in a huge steel plant the Scot was building there. When the plant was done, Mr. Thomson was hardly pleased to find that Mr. Carnegie had erected it within as easy distance of the Baltimore & Ohio as it was to the Pennsylvania. Little Andy then performed a neat piece of flattery which is said to have softened the great railroader. On the founding-stone corner of this "Leviathan of Steel," he placed a bronze marker of quiet dignity: "The J. Edgar Thomson Works."

nating on the west shore of the Hudson opposite Manhattan, drove its tunnels under the river and into the heart of New York City. Not only that, the Pennsy now went right on through the city and so eastward. It accomplished this by buying control of the Long Island Rail Road Company, whose lines extended 125 miles east of the big city.

To reach into New England, the Pennsy bridged the East River at Hell Gate and in conjunction with the New York, New Haven & Hartford established through service to the Hub of the Universe on Massachusetts Bay. In 1910 it completed the Pennsylvania Station in New York, a structure covering 28 acres in which more people have become lost than in all of the woods of Maine. You can see a statue of Cassatt in the New York terminal, for it was his idea and much of it was his planning. Underneath the statue are carved credits for the man's "foresight, courage, and ability."

The Pennsy's great rival, the New York Central Railroad, was not the result of engineering and construction crews. It was rather the creature of lawyers and investors, many of whom might be said to be speculators, and was put together on paper under the master mind of Erastus Corning, nail maker and politician of Albany. All of this happened on the first day of August, 1853, when what up to then had been ten small and independently owned railroads lost their identity in the New York Central, certainly one of the best publicized rail lines in the eastern United States, just as the Erie has been the worst publicized; while in the Far West only the Union Pacific, with its hell-and-whooping career of scandal and Indian fighting has made great legend.

The capitalization of the New York Central, at the time of its birth in 1853, was $23,000,000, so vast a sum as to cause a national sensation. The consolidation was a natural one, and had long been in the minds of Corning and his associates, including John V. L. Pruyn; and it may have been hurried somewhat by the fact that the Erie Railroad, through the southern portion of the state, had at last got within sight of Lake Erie. If the northern counties were to prosper, then they too must have a through line between the Hudson and the Great Lakes.

Into the New York Central went the line between Rochester and Batavia, opened in 1837; the Utica-Syracuse line, opened in 1839; the Auburn-Buffalo, opened in 1842; and a couple of gaps that were closed in 1853. In all, as related, ten separate concerns, together with such branches and feeders as they possessed, made up a consolidation having 542 miles of track, which was more than the Erie had. Into it, too, went 187 first-class passenger coaches, 55 second-class, 65 baggage, mail, and express cars, and 1,702 freight cars. At this period it was possible to buy a through ticket from Albany to Buffalo, though the ride called for a number of changes of cars. But nobody, at any price, could get reliable

information regarding the time and movement of trains. These were kept
as secret as matters of state.

All of the allegedly fast express trains between Albany and Buffalo
covered the distance, in theory, in 14 hours, but only in theory. A traveler
who made the journey in May of 1850 left a record of the trip, which was
doubtless just average for the period. He got out of Albany on Saturday
evening, arriving at Utica at 11:30 P.M., where the train drowsed on a
sidetrack until 2 A.M. Sunday, the passengers meanwhile sitting in the
stuffy little coaches in a gloom made only the deeper by one candle at
each end of the car. Nobody, neither conductor, brakeman, nor station
master, would or could tell the travelers when they might be taken further.
Then, two hours after midnight, there was a bustle in the yards, a locomotive was coupled on and away they went, to arrive three hours later in
Syracuse.

In Syracuse the passengers were in for a real wait. Throughout the
morning, then the afternoon, together making up as long a day as any
of the travelers had ever known, they attempted every little while to learn
if and when they should proceed. Nobody knew, and nobody, among the
railroad men, seemed to care, or give it a second's thought. So, for better
than twelve hours the now worn travelers sat around in the cars, not dar-
ing to leave them lest some whim of the railroad masters set the train in
motion. At half-past five in the afternoon the journey was resumed. The
train arrived in Rochester in time to hear the clock strike midnight, and
in Rochester it remained for six hours. This delay seemed to be for lack
of a suitable locomotive. At last an engine was discovered that could
haul the train to Buffalo. Distance: 290 miles. Time: 38½ hours.*

The new consolidated line made immediate improvements in the service.
New cars, new locomotives were purchased. Track was bettered. Passenger
and freight traffic increased rapidly. In fact, business was very good, and
even the panic of 1857, which wrecked more than one railroad, failed to
make dividends disappear. The Central paid on time and paid well. The
road's headquarters were in Albany; and besides Corning, who was president, the officials and directors included Pruyn, he who had drawn up the
consolidation papers and which were considered to form a remarkable
instrument, as no doubt they did; Nathaniel Thayer, scion of a long line
of Congregational ministers of Massachusetts; Chauncy Vibbard, said to
have drawn up the first railroad timetable in America, which he put into
effect on the Utica & Schenectady, of which he was manager; and Isaac
Townsend. Central stock was owned largely by residents of Albany.

As time passed the Central's officers saw that they ought to have a line
from Albany down the Hudson to New York City, but nothing was done

---

* This unhappy traveler's story, though not his name, is related in Chas. F. Carter's *When
Railroads Were New*, New York, 1926. His resentment is to be felt in every line of his account.

about it, and meanwhile there were goings-on in the latter city directed
with ruthless genius by Cornelius Vanderbilt, called the Commodore, an
ex-ferryboat operator who had made a fortune out of Manhattan real
estate and several sales of dubious ships to the government during the
Civil War. In 1862 Vanderbilt was sixty-eight years old, an age when most
businessmen of the day preferred the genteel quiet of board rooms. Vanderbilt preferred the docks and rails and the berserker battles that raged
in such places. His years really counted for, rather than against him;
his shrewdness seemed to increase with age, and his energy never
flagged.

It occurred to the old Commodore, sometime in 1862 or before, that
the New York Central would one day want entrance to New York City.
So he looked into the New York & Harlem Railroad, which had been
kicked around by politicians and speculators ever since it was built in
1832. He also investigated the New York & Hudson, chartered in 1846.
The Harlem had very slowly lengthened its line until it got as far as
Chatham to connect with the Albany & Stockbridge and thus make a
through road from Manhattan to Albany. The New York & Hudson had
worked its laborious way up the river as far as Poughkeepsie and, through
a short leased line, to Troy.

The two small roads looked pretty fair to the Commodore. He went to
work first on the Harlem. Through varied and subtle machinations that are
not even yet fully understood, he pounded Harlem stock down to $9 a
share, then bought a controlling interest. He next turned to the New York
& Hudson and bought control. He was ready now to take on the New
York Central.

Many writers of railroad history relate that Vanderbilt had shown
such genius in acquiring the Hudson and the Harlem and in sending the
stocks of those two roads soaring, that the directors of the New York
Central were "happy to lay that road at the Commodore's feet," to do with
as he pleased, in order to make it a successful property such as the Harlem
and the Hudson. But that is not the way it happened, according to two
writers of such different outlook as Edward Hungerford, official historian
of the New York Central,* and the late Gustavus Myers, author of *History
of the Great American Fortunes,* which is a biased but careful and accurate book. Hungerford relates that the Central had made it a practice
to give freight and passengers to the Hudson road only when the river
was frozen, and the boat lines, with which the Central had working agreements, were unable to run. This was, of course, all right and proper, but
the Commodore didn't like it. The Central had also refused to pay a
"bonus" that the Commodore thought was due him. What was perhaps

---

* *Men and Iron, The History of the New York Central,* New York, 1938, an uncritical yet
accurate and readable work.

worst of all, the Central's officials had treated the Commodore in a brusque manner.

Now, no man living could treat old Vanderbilt in a brusque manner or refuse him his "rightful bonus" and not live to regret it. These things were sufficient, even though Myers says Vanderbilt set out to wreck the Central simply because he wanted to control it. The motive hardly matters, anyway, but the method by which the job was accomplished was in the best tradition of that piratical day, and worked about as follows:

During the cold months of the year, as related, and only then, it had been the custom of the Central to pass on its freight and passengers to the Hudson River road at Albany, for transfer to New York. During the cooler months of late 1866 the Commodore kept quite warm with his rage at the unspeakable Central. Then, on January 14, 1867 he gave an order to his Hudson River Railroad stopping all trains at East Albany, almost two miles from the Albany depot. This made the transfer of freight and passengers a very complicated, not to say almost impossible, business. There, just beyond the bridge across the river, the Hudson's trains stopped, the fires in the locomotives were banked, the freight and baggage dumped out on the ground, and the passengers ordered out of the coaches.

An immediate howl went up from the public and the New York Central. The Legislature appointed a committee to look into the matter. The committee waited on Vanderbilt and demanded to know why he refused to run his trains across the river, as in the past. And then the old man gave them the works. He showed them, to their great astonishment, an old law which had never been invoked or repealed and by then long forgotten, which specifically prohibited the New York & Hudson Railroad from running trains across the river. Nor had Vanderbilt had anything to do with the passage of this law. It had been put onto the books by the influence and at the instigation of the New York Central in the early days, to prevent any competing line west of Albany.

The legislative committee was temporarily speechless. The Commodore was having a wonderful time. After a few minutes one of the committee was able to give voice, if but meekly. "But why, Mr. Vanderbilt," he enquired, "why do you not run the trains across the river as you used to do?"

"I was not there, gentlemen," replied the Commodore, indicating that whatever had been done was the work of his operating men.

"But what did you do when you heard of it?"

"I did not do anything."

"Why not? Where were you?"

"I was at home, gentlemen, playing a rubber of whist, and I never allow anything to interfere with me when I am playing that game. It requires, as you know, undivided attention."

It must have been superb drama. The gorgeous old corsair was never in better form. What the committeemen thought of it is not of record, but they assuredly went away knowing they had met a man who neither sought nor gave any quarter.

Well, the stock of the New York Central Railroad began to slide downward, and when it had reached a point that the Commodore deemed right and proper, he stepped in and bought it in copious quantities. On December 11, 1867, when he was seventy-three, he became president of the consolidated railroads, known for many years to come as the New York Central & Hudson River. He retained his little New York & Harlem in the Vanderbilt family, leasing it to the larger line for what was said to be a good round sum.

Though he was already well past the biblical ceiling of age, a decade of life yet remained for the Commodore, and this was long enough for him to compose a mighty system of rails. He visioned Buffalo, not as almost all other railroaders of New York had visioned it—as a western terminus—but merely as a stop on the way to Chicago, yes, and beyond. He bought into the Lake Shore & Michigan Southern, which had an almost gradeless line from Buffalo to Chicago, and when the Black Friday panic of 1869 came along and Lake Shore shares were thrown into the market, he was there to buy them. Soon he became president of that line also, a perfect extension for the New York Central.

There remained another road, the Michigan Central, which looked to the Commodore like a useful line for his purposes, and he set out to get it. Because the Michigan Central had an odd, and for a time as exciting and dangerous a career as any road one could name, it ought to be cited if only as a horrible example of political inheritance. It is also a story as fantastic as it is forgotten.

The Michigan Central had begun as a state-owned road. Like most such affairs, it got nowhere other than into disastrous bankruptcy. It was then taken over at bargain rates by a group of Boston men, as related elsewhere. The Boston men did not realize it, but along with the tracks and rolling stock they acquired the milch cows of farmers who lived by the way.

During the years when it had been a creature of politics, the Michigan catchpoles who acted as its managers had, of course, been most considerate of the sensibilities of the voters. When a hog or a cow was killed by a locomotive on the state-owned line, settlement was made promptly and generously, usually for about three or four times the value of the liquidated animal. The simple, honest agrarians along the road were quickwitted enough to know Opportunity when it loomed on the steel rails in the form of the Iron Horse. They began to feed their oldest and poorest stock handy to the tracks and often, it is said, plumb between the rails. Never before nor since have Michigan farmers received so much for their livestock.

When the road became the Michigan Central, privately owned and operated, its officials took some pains to prevent their locomotives from running into farm animals. And the locomotive engineers, even if they had no great disinclination to running down Durhams and Berkshires, did have a respect for what a good solid cow or even a good hog could do to the light engines then in use. They used all the care possible.

But the animals of farmers along the Michigan Central continued to be hit and killed—as why not, when they had become so used to feeding between the very rails? The company at first tried to pay a fair valuation for the killed stock. Then, when these prices did not please the farmers, the company fenced its tracks and announced that henceforth only one-half the market value would be paid for any animal killed on the tracks. This, said the farmers, was gross and cruel imposition by a monster of Capital.* No farmers since 1775, they told each other, had been so put upon. Right soon stations and other property of the Michigan Central were damaged in one way or another. Journal boxes were filled with sand. Switches were tampered with. The rails were often slick with grease. Obstructions were found on the tracks, sometimes too late to prevent derailments. The road countered by sending out handcars ahead of its trains, to clear the ties, logs, and boulders from the tracks. Next, the farmers took to stoning trains as they passed through cuts, or at night. It became common knowledge that the bucolics of Southern Michigan had sworn to kill a few passengers, as a warning not to travel by Michigan Central.

Both passenger and freight traffic fell away. Employes quit after a few engineers and brakemen had been fired on. By late 1850 the harassed officials of the road could see disaster just ahead, unless something drastic were done. They decided on one more attempt. This time *they* would attack. Putting a crew of amateur detectives to work, the dicks learned that one Fitch, a leading citizen of Michigan Center, and a saloonkeeper of that place named Filley were the leading agitators. Fitch, it seemed, had been turned into an enraged farmer with a grudge against the company because he had failed to get a construction contract from it.

The homemade dicks made further progress. Several of them joined the conspirators, and one was even selected to set fire to the Michigan Central depot at Niles. On April 10, 1851, the undercover men were ready to spring their trap. That night a special train arrived at Michigan Center, and some seventy-odd railroad detectives and county deputy sheriffs piled off and made a quick roundup of thirty-six persons, a majority of whom made damaging confessions. Their trial was the sensation of the Midwest

---

* In Wisconsin, at a later date, farmers not only had their cake but ate it too. Around Wittenberg, on the then Wisconsin, Lake Shore & Western, I am told by Archibald Whisnant, many cows were killed by trains in the 1880's. The section foreman of that portion of the line, George Gates, had instructions to bury the dead creatures as soon as possible. But news of a cow struck traveled fast, and usually before Gates could complete burial, two or more farmers and their families would be sitting patiently on the tracks, waiting for Gates to be done and gone, when they would disinter the carcass for beef.

in 1851, lasting from May into October and calling for such eminent counsel as William H. Seward, for the defense. An even dozen of the simple, honest farmers were convicted.

Twenty years later, when Commodore Vanderbilt got around to the Michigan Central it was a prosperous and well-run line into Chicago and had a number of excellent feeder lines. The Commodore bought a heavy interest in it, also bought the new Canada Southern, which operated from Buffalo to Detroit north of Lake Erie, and leased the Canada to the Michigan Central.

The old Commodore continued, almost to his last day to buy into this or that railroad which he thought he could use. He also had time for other things, one of which was to run the finances of his New York Central exactly as he wished. Any fair observer must admit that he probably conducted these affairs much better than any other Central director could, better perhaps than anyone else in the United States.

The old man looked over the rolling stock of his big railroad and came to the conclusion that the locomotives were too gaudy—that is, all except the one named Commodore Vanderbilt, which, in spite of considerable decoration, he appeared to think was all right. The engines were gaudy in that day, running to much brass and bright paint, plenty of scroll work; and occasionally portraits of eminent Americans, or landscape scenes, appeared on the tender or on the sides of the headlight. The Commodore ordered all such trumpery removed. Plain black and metal finish were best, he said. But he felt that the terminal facilities of his roads in New York City were very mean, not in keeping with the fine system he was making better by the month. In 1870, when he was seventy-six years old, he ordered that a new and grand depot be erected in Manhattan, as well as a gargantuan freight house.

For the freight house, down came the trees in St. John's Park, up went a great fortress of brick, in front of it an imposing pediment in bronze, cluttered with bas-reliefs of steamboats, Conestoga wagons, railroad trains, and a gigantic figure of the Commodore himself. It was all stupendous, even elegant, and Mr. Hungerford, historian of the Central, remarks humorously that it was the only such gaud attached to a freight house anywhere on earth.

For the Grand Central Depot, for that is what it was to be called—the first of several on the same site—construction was begun in 1870 and finished in 1871; the completed structure contained the almightiest train shed in the world—600 feet long, 200 feet wide, 100 feet high. Twelve tracks ran into the shed. The great room was lighted by huge chandeliers of gas jets, which could be automatically ignited by an electric spark. To keep this imposing room free of train smoke and gas, the Central adopted the flying-switch method of bringing its cars into the station: a short way from the depot, the engine speeded up, uncoupled itself from the train, dashed onto a side track well ahead of the cars, while a switchman stood ready to throw the switch and thus send the train into the station on the main line. With brakemen at each post, the engineless train then rolled on momentum and down a slight grade into the shed and was brought to a halt at the proper place by the combined and excellently coordinated efforts of the brakemen.

The flying-switch system was used at the Grand Central for many years, and appears to have worked well and without accidents. The same could not be said of the grade crossings on the streets coming into town. Accidents happened there in great plenty. They shortly became a public scandal and continued until the tracks were fenced off for a number of blocks north of the terminal.

With two fine terminals in New York, Vanderbilt set out to improve the road elsewhere. He had a clear vision of the immense traffic the line was to handle in future years, and he sought to make ready for it by four-tracking the Central all the way from Albany to Buffalo. Two tracks for passenger service, two for freight, that was the idea, and no better idea was ever held by a railroad man. New bridges went in here and there. So did new stations, enginehouses, shops. The Commodore did not merely plan these things on paper; he rode the line in his special car, and everywhere he went he was likely to ask questions, always to the point. Nothing escaped him. Under him grew up a group of superintendents and foremen who were, like Vanderbilt himself, hard men but on the whole just, whose first idea was to run a railroad for the benefit of the New York Central & Hudson River Railroad Company.

Notable among the supers was George H. Burrows, a large and tall Yankee who liked to wear a silk hat even when he was crawling under a locomotive to see what was the matter with it. Burrows was probably as literal-minded a man as ever walked. Central's orders were orders. The Central could do no wrong. He once fired an engine driver who ran his locomotive at 16 miles an hour over a piece of track where Burrows had stipulated 15 miles an hour. If a freight engineer complained of being given too long a train, Burrows automatically added a few more cars to the next train the man took out. One time a man he had discharged was reinstated by the general superintendent at Albany. Burrows fired him again and continued to fire him until Albany at last gave up.

Less of a character, but just as able a man, was another divisional super, John M. Toucey, a Connecticut Yankee and a very thoughtful man. It was due largely to Toucey that the Central was one of the first lines to adopt the air brake, the automatic coupler, and the vestibule car. Together with William Buchanan, the Central's superintendent of motive power, Toucey devised one of the earliest of interlocking switch systems. It was probably

Toucey, too, who because of his invariable kindness to employees managed to hold a large majority of Central men at work during the great and bloody strikes of 1877, as related elsewhere in this book.

The Commodore did not turn his face to the wall until January 4, 1877, when he died quietly at eighty-three. Almost to the end he continued to enjoy his tremendous breakfasts, which were composed of from four to six eggs, two or three lamb chops, a good mess of toast, and nigh a quart of coffee. He never drank much liquor; now and then a glass of champagne on special occasions. Almost to the last, too, he exhibited a keen interest in his properties which amounted, according to newspaper reports at the time of his death, to $75,000,000, by all odds the biggest personal fortune in the United States up to that time.

On the death of the Commodore his son William H. Vanderbilt took charge. Contrary to the folklore concerning sons of wealthy self-made men —who are all supposed to be wasters and incompetents—the second Vanderbilt turned out to be a remarkably able railroad man himself. The Commodore, of course, had given his son more than a head start in the business, but the younger man knew how to carry on. He also had some ideas of his own. He entered with gusto into the savage battle of rate wars and low passenger fares staged by almost all of the roads that reached Chicago from the East, and more than held his own. It was during one of these wars that he made the remark that has ever since been quoted against all railroads, against all wealthy men, even against all industry and commerce. Asked by a newspaper reporter if the New York Central's limited train could operate at a profit on the New York-Chicago fare of $15, Vanderbilt said no, that it couldn't, and added that the Central had been forced to the step by the Pennsylvania, which had set the pace and the fare. "Otherwise," concluded Vanderbilt, "we would abandon it."

"But," asked the reporter, one of several interviewing the magnate, "don't you run it for the public benefit?"

"The public," remarked Mr. Vanderbilt in the now classic sentence, "be damned."

The Chicago Daily News printed the line verbatim, as turned in by free-lance reporter Clarence Dresser. It was an unfortunate remark to be made, especially by a Vanderbilt and at a time when much of the United States considered railroads to be public enemy No. 1. The press picked up the News' report and blew it up to twice normal size, and professed to see in it an expression of opinion and policy of the head of the New York Central.* Although the stock market did not break, in regard to Central's stock, the road suffered much calumny from the incident.

* From this time until his death, the newspapers credited Vanderbilt with an aggressive instinct he never possessed, according to Wayne Andrews, who wrote The Vanderbilt Legend (1941). In reality, says Mr. Andrews, compromise rather than battle was the second Vanderbilt's favorite policy. "He cringed from rows that the old Commodore would have hugely enjoyed."

Part of one of the Illinois Central's ads of the period 1860-61.

Under this print of an American coach interior The London Illustrated News, April 10, 1852, commented on "the attention paid to the comfort of travelers by the railway companies of America."

Mr. W. H. Vanderbilt and his men continued to run the various lines of the Central system in a manner pleasing to stockholders and not insufferable to the general public. In 1882 Vanderbilt picked up for $7,000,000 or so a new road, the New York, Chicago & St. Louis, soon to be known, for any one of a score of reasons, as the Nickel Plate. The Plate, which seems to have been built with the idea of being a nuisance that the Central would be happy to purchase, paralleled Vanderbilt's Lake Shore pretty much from Buffalo to Cleveland, then dipped south into Indiana, and finally reached Chicago. By buying it, Vanderbilt proved it had fulfilled its purpose.

More competition threatened from the East. This was the New York, West Shore & Buffalo, promoted by General E. L. Winslow, Horace Porter, and others, including George Pullman, the sleeping-car man, whom the Vanderbilts had treated rather scurvily, or so he thought, by dropping his fine sleeping and dining cars in favor of the product of Mr. Wagner's Palace Car Company. As a starter, the new railroad company put out an issue of $50,000,000 in stock. It was going to be a long and hard haul to Buffalo.

With its eastern end at Weehawken, New Jersey, just across the Hudson from New York, the new threat to the Central ran north up the west shore of the river to a point near Albany, turned west to parallel the Central's line all the way to Utica, then took a direct route to Syracuse, and so on to Buffalo. It did reach Buffalo, and on the very day it did so and started to accept through freight to New York, the New York Central slashed its own freight rates to the bone.

It wasn't long in coming. At first the West Shore's pay car began to be a little late making the rounds. West Shore employees started to file attachments and liens on West Shore property, in lieu of wages due them. In June of 1884 a realistic court declared the road bankrupt, having discovered that the receipts were coming in at the rate of $3,000,000 a year, hardly enough to pay interest on the West Shore's first mortgage bonds. A year later the West Shore went into the hands of the New York Central —hands, it turned out, that were far from palsied.

Far from palsied indeed. The second Mr. Vanderbilt next gave more than merely token aid to a line called the South Pennsylvania, which for some years had been struggling to get somewhere and become a competitor to the monopoly of the Pennsylvania Railroad. This encouragement of the competing line caused a great deal of excitement in Philadelphia, headquarters of the Pennsy. But only for a time. Just what happened to lay the storm isn't wholly known yet, but the results were clear: The New York Central suddenly dropped all aid to the South Pennsylvania. The Pennsylvania railroad, which may well have been giving aid to the West Shore that it might become a threat to the Central, did so no longer. It is generally known that the compromise came about on the yacht owned by J. P. Morgan the elder, a ship named the *Corsair*. Stockholders in the two nuisance lines, the said South Pennsylvania and the said West Shore, suffered fearfully from the operation performed on the two lines. As for Mr. Morgan, he received, for his surgery, according to his official biographer Carl Hovey, somewhere between one and three millions of dollars.

Vanderbilt's next purchase was no nuisance road, but a pretty fair system that had operated under various names and finally as the Cleveland, Cincinnati, Chicago & St. Louis, usually known as the Big Four, as it is to this day, which with its affiliates, put together and managed with consummate ability by Melville E. Ingalls, gave the Vanderbilt lines a fine road from Chicago into southern Illinois.

The next addition to the Central was the Rome, Watertown & Ogdensburg, a road that had been taken over in 1883 by a State of Mainer named Charles Parsons, who was a railroader from way back. Parsons soon bought the Utica & Black River and merged it with the Rome. He extended his line to connect with the Grand Trunk, giving access to Montreal, built his own line from Syracuse to Oswego and planned to continue on to Buffalo. This, of course, would never do. The New York Central sent surveying parties to work on a projected line into Watertown, a line that if built would compete with the Rome road. In 1891 Charles Parsons saw the light. He leased his homemade road to the Central, and the Central's surveyors left their stakes to rot where they had been driven.

A number of small roads remained to be picked up here and there, but the last big deal of the Central in the nineteenth century was to acquire— for all practical purposes—the Boston & Albany, whose title described exactly its route, with no fuss about it. A little later, in an ill-advised moment, the Central painted its own name on the rolling stock of the proud old Yankee road. A roar instantly went up that could be and was heard in the innermost sanctum of New York Central officials. Yankees fumed in print and on the platform. Yankee poets composed feverish strophes along the style of tear-her-tattered-ensign-down. Newspapers of Boston and way points were aghast, then furious. The foreigners of New York had breached the redoubt, but the embattled Yankees were not done fighting.

The New York Central had learned a good deal about public relations since the second Vanderbilt had uttered his famous cry. The highly offensive legend, "New York Central," was immediately removed from the locomotives and cars that ran into New England, and the old reliable "Boston & Albany" reappeared. All became quiet along the Charles and the Connecticut. It was a graceful gesture on the part of the Central, and little enough to pay for the continued good will of the strange Yankees. The line is still, in the matter of nomenclature, the Boston & Albany, and only in the retentive minds of a few codfish eaters are the dreadful days of the great insult remembered.

A sense of the value both of good publicity and of polished public relations had been steadily growing on the Central for a number of years, or ever since George Henry Daniels joined its payroll. Daniels was a short, rotund man who wore a white goatee and probably was, says Freeman Hubbard, the greatest railroad publicity man of the last century. He was possessed, says Mr. Hubbard, of the glamor of railroading and had a genius for communicating it to the public. A graduate of the Wabash Railroad, often cited as a notable school that turned out notable railroad men, Daniels had a big hand in thinking up and naming the Central's two celebrated trains, the *Empire State Express* and the *Twentieth-Century Limited*.

It was Daniels, too, who suggested that a really swift locomotive, a special job, be built just for the purpose of publicizing the *Empire State Express*. This was built in the West Albany shops of the company under the direction of the remarkable William Buchanan, previously mentioned. She was a high-wheeled Atlantic-type engine. On September 14, 1891, she performed the feat that has been reported in print thousands of times—she ran from New York to East Buffalo at the unprecedented rate of 61.4 miles an hour. This was all very well, but it wasn't enough to satisfy Daniels. The Central boys went to work and turned out *Number 999*, which Daniels wanted to be a feature at the coming World's Fair in Chicago, set for 1893.

On May 10th of that year, with Charlie Hogan at the throttle, *999* picked up the *Empire State Express* at Syracuse for the last lap of the run to Buffalo, and on a straight, level piece of track west of Batavia, he reputedly drove her for one mile at the rate of 112.5 miles an hour. Nothing that rolled, agree all railroad historians, had ever gone so fast.* And you may be sure Daniels saw that the newspapers heard of the miraculous performance.

Daniels wasn't done. He went to work on the Postmaster General of the United States, and out came a dandy two-cent stamp, picturing the *Empire State Express* in two colors and running, as was obvious from a look at the smoke, at the rate of 112.5 miles an hour. This was a feat that advertising and publicity men still speak of with awe. To follow up this stupendous opening, Daniels arranged to have *999* and a complete *Empire State Express* on view at the Columbian Exposition, which was the World's Fair of Ninety-Three. In the realm of railroad public relations, *999* was doubtless the greatest thing of its time.

Daniels went on from there. On New York Central trains all passengers, literate and otherwise, were soon presented with copies of Elbert Hubbard's *A Message to Garcia*, one of the most graceful and inaccurate essays

---

* Toy makers were quick to add to *999*'s glory. Such was the number on the locomotive of my first train-on-a-track, as miniature railroad sets were called in those days; and on the tender was the legend *Empire State Express*. Until I was a sizable youth, that specific locomotive and that specific train of the New York Central were the only ones I could have named, other than the *Airline* on the Boston & Maine, and the *Montreal Express* on the Grand Trunk.

imaginable. He took charge of the system's dining car and station restaurant service and immediately improved both its fare and its service. In 1902 another of Daniel's ideas became the *Twentieth-Century Limited*, New York to Chicago in 20 hours, like a bat out of hell, in specially built cars with extra-fine service, scooping up water from tanks between the tracks on the fly, the tracks cleared everywhere for this beauty of the rails. But the *Century* was no scoop, for there had been collusion. Railroad ethics had changed. On the very day the *Century* went into service, the Pennsylvania sent out its own idea of a 20-hour train to Chicago, in every way equal to the *Century* except in the felicity of its name.

Daniels also had opportunity to glorify the building of a new Grand Central Station in New York, the third of its name, which comprised eighteen city blocks and required seven years to build, being opened for business in 1910.

Another able man, having some claim to the title The Father of Modern High-Speed Trains, Dr. Plimmon H. Dudley (1843–1924), was for forty-three years the New York Central's consulting engineer on rails. "Dr. Dudley," said a Central president, A. H. Smith, "contributed at least as much as any other man to the development of American railroads. Perhaps it would not be an overstatement to say that he did more than any other one man to confer upon humanity the boon of rapid, safe and economical transportation."

A bearded six-footer having deep-set gray eyes, Dudley was the first engineer to realize the need for radical improvement in track to permit the railroad industry to develop still further. His best-known invention, the track indicator to record train-retarding and often dangerous irregularities in track, was the progenitor of the Sperry Rail Detector Car, without which present-day railroad operation as we know it would not be possible.

The Central built a special car to house Dudley's inventions. It included a housekeeping apartment, even a grand piano, for the doctor and his wife. This was the only home the Dudleys knew for four decades. In it the railmaster designed a new type of rail that increased rail strength 66 per cent by adding only 23 per cent weight. As a result of this, heavier rolling stock was built; and the world's first heavy, high-speed train, the *Empire State Express*, in 1891 began blazing the trail for today's fleets of passenger railiners and hotshot freights. Dudley's rail design became the basis for rail now in use all over the country. That, combined with Dudley's other work, is largely credited with reducing the number of broken rails on the New York Central from one in 600 to one in 142,000 over a thirteen-year period. The fruits of his inventions and research were made available not only to the Central but to all American railroads.

To return to the second Vanderbilt, he died in 1885, leaving an estate estimated at double that left by the Commodore. With his death the family's active interest in operation of the New York Central, though not in its stocks and bonds, declined. But the road did not suffer. Under continuous able management it has prospered as have few other roads, in the United States or elsewhere. It operates today in eleven states and two provinces of Canada, has 11,008 miles of road, 24,983 miles of track, and employs 87,392 men and women.

Doubtless the Central's locomotive and rolling stock have been improved steadily. It is a very "modern" railroad. The only fault some of us grumblers find with it, in 1947, is that it has made of that formerly glamorous train, that smoking, snorting, flashing *Century*, an all-Diesel affair, swift enough, to be sure, but now muttering and coughing along its way, sounding no whistle but a foghorn bleat like a poor dumb animal trying to give vent to some emotion. When steam left the *Century*, or any other train, something else went along too.

CHAPTER VIII

The Art of Colonization

The attention of the enterprising and industrious is directed to the Garden Spot of the West. There is no portion of the world where all the conditions of climate and soil so admirably combine. . . .
—Colonization poster of the Illinois Central, 1860.

A S THE century came to its halfway mark, editorial writers and other reflective Americans looked at the progress made by the railroads and found it better than good. They termed it amazing, and so it was. When 1850 began, there were more than nine thousand miles of railroads in operation, an increase of almost fivefold in one decade. Not even the most hidebound of the cocked-hat men, the-old-days-were-better men, and the paid propagandists for canals and stagecoach lines—not even they could stand up any longer and say that the steam roads were a passing fancy.

American railroads were not only doing things to geography; they were changing society, some said for the better, some thought the worse. Who, asked Charles Francis Adams, perhaps our greatest philosopher of railroads, who did not remember the quiet, the dullness of country towns before, say, 1840, and the staidness of the inhabitants? There had lived in these towns, in all or most of them, a class of men, solid, complacent, men of property but of few ideas—legitimate descendents of the English broadacred squires. These were the American gentry—the men who went up to the General Court (legislature), who served on the Governor's Council. They were men who could remember Governor Hancock and General Knox, and bore a certain trace of their manners. Their thinking, their beliefs, had undergone no perceptible change since the administration of John Quincy Adams.

By 1850 or thereabout, this class of men was extinct. The railroads had abolished them and their dress and manners and their habits and ways of thought. In many cases the railroads had abolished the very houses they had dwelt in. To take the place of this hereditary gentry, so Charles F. Adams observed, had come a race of hereditary businessmen, the men who would direct things during the latter half of the century. It was the railroad, more than any other one influence, that had brought them into being.

Adams was right. Of all the businessmen of the nineteenth century, none was more effective in changing the lives and times of their fellows than the men who built and operated the railroads. In 1850 all but a few hundred miles of their nine thousand miles of road were laid in the Atlantic and Gulf seaboard and adjoining states. Now they turned their eyes farther west. Out there in the Mississippi Valley a vast empire, said to be a land of plenty by land speculators and writers of immigrant guidebooks, only a few miles of weary track touched the eastern edge of the rich and limitless prairie, and over these few miles intermittently passed a train of cars, sometimes hauled by a consumptive locomotive, again by horses or oxen. Often no train ran at all, and groundhogs burrowed between the ties that squatters had not stolen to use as fuel in their sod huts. These rails were the relics of the boom-born railroads that died virtually at birth. One traveler in Illinois came upon a locomotive, alone and rusting, on a few yards of track set in the midst of a prairie—all else had departed, the rails and ties appropriated by squatters, the promoters of the line gone with last year's snows.

Illinois, it will be recalled, had gone wildly into the internal improvements business in 1837, when the state voted a truly gigantic program by which the state should build canals, highways, and railroads. The program went bust in the Panic of '37, and the state repudiated its many obligations. During the next dozen years able and aggressive men fought like mad wolves to get a railroad charter from the state, among them Illinois' two senators, Stephen A. Douglas, the Little Giant, and Sidney Breese, who was probably the first man to propose a central railroad in the state. Breese was also something of a character, and in a day of few beards he allowed his white hair to tumble down over his shoulders and peered out of a forest of splendid whiskers.

In 1851 the state granted a charter to a new corporation, the Illinois Central Railroad Company; and with it, if its charter terms were met, went a land grant of 2,595,000 federal acres, the first large land grant to a railroad in our history. The company included a number of prominent or able men, among them David A. Neal, president of the Eastern Railroad in Massachusetts; John F. A. Sanford, noted fur trader and Indian agent; Morris Ketchum, pioneer locomotive manufacturer; and Robert Rantoul, Massachusetts senator.

The charter was to prove a highly successful arrangement, both for the state and for the company. It was a partnership. No railroad was ever more a child of the state than the Illinois Central, and certainly no railroad ever did more for its parent than this one, nor with such speed. In six years the Central turned a lot of great open spaces into a busy and, on the whole, prosperous commonwealth, perhaps the most striking metamorphosis accomplished by a railroad anywhere.

It was not all to be easy sailing. The railroad agreed to build approximately 700 miles of road in six years. It agreed to pay the state seven per cent of its gross, not its net, income—unquestionably the best bargain a state ever made with a railroad. The company must finance itself from the sale of its granted lands, something the directors thought should be simple enough; they would merely issue bonds secured by mortgage on the two and a half million acres of the grant.

It was anything but simple. To begin with, the State of Ililnois in its official capacity was already notorious as a dead-beat, having repudiated its obligations of 1837. It had even failed to pay interest on its huge debt, and although the state and the railroad were two different parties, nevertheless the very name of "Illinois" worked immeasurable difficulties for the company in its early years.

Then, the railroad elected as its first president Robert Schuyler, son of a Continental Army general, nephew of Alexander Hamilton, and president of the New York & New Haven Railroad. Schuyler was presently under suspicion in New York, and soon confessed to an immense embezzlement of NY & NH funds that stunned even Wall Street and all right-thinking men. Although by the time the defalcation became known, Schuyler had resigned his position with the Illinois Central, his brief and nominal connection with the road proved to be a bad handicap in the selling of the road's stock and bonds.

Fortunately for the Illinois line, one of its vice-presidents was David Neal, who had made his pile in ships out of Salem, Massachusetts, a man who had the confidence of American men of capital. Neal took over the helm and after many discouraging rebuffs managed to get a loan of $5,-000,000 from a British syndicate, and he also succeeded in selling some of the original issues of stocks and bonds to prominent Americans. Among the British takers-of-chance were Richard Cobden, statesman; Sir Joseph Paxton; and the great William Gladstone, for all of whom towns along the IC's right-of-way were named. James C. Fargo, the express man; Abram Hewitt (Peter Cooper's son-in-law); Wendell Phillips, abolitionist; and Mrs. Harriet Beecher Stowe, novelist, were among the Americans to invest in the new undertaking.

While negotiations for loans went forward, surveying for the Illinois Central got under way, and in March of 1852 grading was begun with a gang of 700 men on the line from Chicago to Calumet (now Kensington). This wasn't exactly as the Central's directors had planned it. Because of an interlocking directorate with the Michigan Central, the Illinois line had originally planned for its first construction the laying of rails direct to the Indiana boundary where it could connect with the Michigan Central. Back of this plan was a complicated affair of fears, jealousies, and competition.

In 1851 two Michigan railroads were desperately trying to get tracks into Chicago, which had no rail connections with the east. They were the Central and the Southern, and with the former, as said, the Illinois Central had personal and financial relations. So, the Illinois road proposed to build its first track from Chicago direct to the Indiana line and permit the Michigan Central to run its trains into Chicago over IC rails.

It didn't work that way. As soon as the plan became known, Chicago fairly exploded in wrath. Its boosters, as wary and as vehement as they came, saw in this action the elimination of one line of track and one station from their home town. This was bad enough, for Chicago, never overly modest, felt that each railroad that came into its precincts should arrive over its own steel and in its own depot. Chicago wanted—and it got—lots of railroad depots. Worse, Chicago also feared that the point at which the Illinois road proposed to meet the Michigan Central might develop into a rival city; and that an east-west traffic artery, south of and not touching Chicago, could well develop. Such things were not only unspeakable, they were unthinkable, and the boosters of the city by the lake flew to action.

Protest meetings without difficulty raised $10,000 to fight the Illinois Central's blackguard plan. Stephen A. Douglas, whose own land interests were involved, was retained by the city to thwart the move. So bitter and determined was the opposition that the IC's directors dropped the idea and set their crews to building southward where, at Calumet, they could manage by a short stub line, a connection with the Michigan Central.

Now thoroughly aroused, the Chicago boosters extended the hand of welcome to the other Michigan road, the Southern, and granted it permission to build to their city. On February 20, 1852, the first train of the Michigan Southern, the first train from the east, rolled into Chicago while fire bells rang, cannon boomed, and the town's manifest destiny became more apparent then ever.

The Illinois Central's construction went ahead fast: in March its rails formed the junction with the Michigan Central fourteen miles south of the Lake; and in May the first Michigan Central train entered Chicago over the IC's tracks.

A tragic and senseless result of the fight between the Michigan lines, the Illinois road, and the city of Chicago came to fruition within a year, at Grand Crossing. Here was where the rails of the Illinois Central must cross those of the Michigan Southern. By right of prior construction the Southern prohibited a grade crossing; if the Illinois Central wanted to cross the Southern's rails, then let it build an overpass.

Roswell B. Mason, construction chief of the Illinois road, was no man to be treated so churlishly, nor was he much inclined to sit around and wait for the law, an abstract matter he held to be all right in its place but not to be consulted when it came to laying down a railroad. One dark night in April of 1852, the Michigan Southern's lone guard at Grand Crossing was kidnapped, and by daylight the Illinois rails had been thrown across the Southern's in as pretty a grade crossing as you would care to see. It was also a fit crossing to start the tradition of grade crossings that has continued down to the present day—that of sudden death.

It is said that neither the Illinois Central nor the Michigan Southern paid any attention to the other's operating schedule, if any such schedules existed, but shot their trains over Grand Crossing without warning or signal of any kind. Well, it happened one day in 1853; two trains met fair at the crossing. Fire and smoke rolled up from the debris. Men cried and women screamed, and 18 dead and 40 maimed passengers and crew members were taken to Chicago. The incident made a noise. Mobs gathered, the mayor spoke, and the newspapers commented on "Murder at the Grade Crossing." Some sort of agreement seems to have been made by which all trains were to come to full stop before crossing any intersection of tracks.

To carry out the terms of its charter the Illinois Central could hardly afford much delay. The charter provided that 50 miles of road should be completed and in operation within two years after the company was organized, that its main line should be ready in four years, and the branch line in six years. The main line was to run from the Wisconsin border down through the center of the state to a point at or near Cairo, where the Ohio enters the Mississippi. The so-called branch was to take off from the main line "at a point not north of the parallel of 39½ degrees north latitude, and running on the most eligible route into the City of Chicago." * This point later turned out to be Centralia; and the total amount of railroad to be constructed approximated 700 miles, much longer than any other road then in operation in the country.

Roswell Mason, chief engineer, turned out to be an extremely able and resourceful man, as the affair at Grand Crossing might indicate. Although his road had no mountains to cross, like the Erie and the Baltimore & Ohio, and although the whole terrain was level compared to that in the eastern states, the Illinois Central was faced with a truly gigantic problem in the matter of supply—supply of virtually all of the materials needed to build a railroad, and also of laborers to swing the picks and tamp the ties. It should be borne in mind that when the road began construction there was no rail connection whatever with the East, or anywhere else, and even the arrival of the two Michigan roads in Chicago did little to aid the business of supply. Most of the rails had to come from England by way of New York, the Erie Canal, and the Great Lakes, although some went around by New Orleans.

Labor was the biggest problem of all. In 1851 railroad building in all of the settled states was in a boom and the various roads were bidding against one another for the increasing supply of Irish and German immigrants. Chief Engineer Mason of the Illinois Central soon discovered that neither Chicago nor St. Louis nor New Orleans could furnish the labor he must have. He hired agents in New York to secure and forward

---

* Charter of the Illinois Central Railroad Company, and other documents, Chicago, 1878.

men to Illinois. He put advertisements in newspapers. And finally in the spring of 1853 he became desperate. He had no more than 3,000 men at work; his directors, fearing always lest the provisions of the charter not be met, were riding Mason hard; to keep up the pace necessary he knew he must have another 3,000 men.

Mason sat down and composed a poster of which he had thousands printed and distributed in and about New York City. It called for 3,000 laborers, offered wages of $1.25 a day, and guaranteed constant employment for two or more years. It also promised that good board could be obtained for $2 a week, but that men with families were preferred. The dodger went on to say that this was "a rare chance for persons to go West, being sure of permanent employment in a healthy climate, where land can be bought cheap, and for fertility is not to be surpassed in any part of the Union." As a clincher, the Illinois Central had made arrangements with other roads and lines for a special fare of $4.75, New York to Chicago, and this fact was given prominence in the broadside . . . Come on, ye tarriers, go see Mr. Phelps at 173 Broadway, corner of Courtlandt Street, then make your fortune in Illinois.

Mason's campaign brought results. He never had quite so many men as he wanted, but he did keep an average of 7,000 employed, and had at times as many as 10,000. A large majority of the early gangs were Irish, like those of the Erie, and they proved to be almost as turbulent a lot, drinking all the whiskey they could lay hands on, fighting townsmen and farmers, fighting among themselves, and meanwhile doing an immense amount of hard work. In time, Mason came to favor Germans, who were easier to handle, and he soon had the Dutch, as they were called, coming by the score, then by the hundred, many with their families.

Epidemics of ague and cholera slowed work on the road, for these distempers were loose and particularly virulent in Illinois during the period 1853–55. Labor agents for railroads elsewhere were quick to spread the story that working anywhere in Illinois was akin to suicide from the dread cholera. After a trip to the East coast, Mason reported it was the prevalent opinion there that a man could scarcely expect to live longer than six months on the Illinois prairie.

It was true that many did die from the disease. The gang working around Peru lost 130 of their number to cholera in two days. The disease was thought to come from various sources, including beef and butter and milk. Whiskey was believed, at least by the Irish, to bring immunity from cholera, and the lads spent every night possible in the traveling groggeries that followed the line of steel from the Wisconsin line to the mouth of the Ohio, and from Centralia north to the lake. Occasionally the liquor brought not only immunity from disease, but so filled the boys with the joy of living that they staged riots, at least four of which grew to such murderous size and enthusiasm that the militia had to be called out. Yet conditions were never so wild as they had been on the Erie, and although standard folklore in many parts of Illinois has it that the building of the IC called for "a murder a mile," nothing happened comparable to the Shin Hollow War during the laying of the Erie tracks.

Mason and the other men of the line coped successfully with all of the troubles, however, and on September 21, 1856, months before the time limit, the main line was done, the branch was done and connected, and the longest single railroad in the United States was in operation. A hundred, perhaps two hundred, local celebrations marked the progress of the IC rails. Picnics, with barbecues, and of course oratory, were held in this or that town on the day the first train was due. Ox teams jolted over the muddy roads for miles, bringing men and women and their children to see the Iron Horse and its train. On occasion, the train was late and the celebrants had to wait all day and much of the night, but they were rewarded when the big-stacked locomotive, drawing two long boxes on wheels, steamed into the settlement. Many a youngster remembered the sight to his dying day as the greatest thrill he had ever known. One passenger who rode such a train in southern Illinois said that people lined the track on either side and stood dumb with amazement, as if they had just come out between the shakes of fever and ague.

Farther east, the railroads had little difficulty in finding passengers and freight for their lines; they were built for the most part through country that was at least partially settled, and as soon as the rails were down customers were waiting. Not so in Illinois. The bad reputation the state had acquired by repudiating its early obligations caused immigrants to the West to believe it was not to be trusted, not a good place to settle. Nor had Illinois done anything to refurbish its soiled name. Neither did it show much interest in attracting new settlers.

It was different in adjoining states. Wisconsin had been one of the earliest to send agents into the eastern states and even to Europe to induce families to come and settle there. Minnesota soon followed suit, and now Iowa was bidding for immigrants to settle in its incomparable region. But the State of Illinois seemed not to care. Perhaps it was still suffering from the relapse that followed its fantastic orgy of internal improvements in 1837. In any case, here was the Illinois Central with its 700 miles of railroad and its more than two million acres of land for sale, and few customers for its freight and passenger cars. It quickly became apparent that if it were to survive, it must get people, thousands and thousands of them and soon, to buy land and settle along its tracks.

The colonization of a railroad's territory was a new thing. No rules had been made for it; there was no precedent. The IC directors must form their own plans and work out the business by trial and error. No one could advise them from experience, for such experience did not exist. It was a case of inventing a system, and a succession of IC land agents took up the task of selling the lands and of populating the line of the railroad with farmers, towns, and industries. One of the first moves was to get John W. Foster, a well-known geologist, to investigate the mineral resources of the region and to set down his findings in a pamphlet to which the company gave wide distribution. Among other things, Foster noted several large deposits of coal, and partly as a result of his pamphlet coal mining was presently under way in the Du Quoin and La Salle districts. And the railroad, ever ready to encourage its customers, began as early as 1858 to convert its wood-burning locomotives to coal-burners.

When Charles Du Puy became land agent of the company in 1854 he induced the road to go after settlers in a more aggressive manner than had been tried. An attractive poster was prepared in which IC lands were described in prose that fairly lilted and dripped with adjectives of great potency. The prices of IC lands, which were reasonable enough, and the terms easy, even for that day, were listed. One hundred thousand of the posters were mailed to a selected list of farmers in eastern and southern states, and others put up in postoffices.

Simultaneously with the posters, advertisements were inserted in the *Times* and the *Tribune* in New York, the *Enquirer* and the *Post* in Philadelphia, and the Boston *Traveler*. A bit later the newspaper campaign was expanded to include one Rhode Island and one Maine paper, three papers each in Vermont, New Hampshire, and Connecticut, five in Massachusetts, five more in upstate New York, two in New Jersey, and one in Missouri. Additional announcements of land prices and opportunities were made in several of the so-called "Emigrant Guides" that were flourishing.

The railroad's advertising was really expert for the time. It stressed the fact that the Illinois Central was bound by its charter to turn over seven cents of each dollar it took in to the state, which made it a semipublic institution. The papers carrying the advertisements, you may be certain, were asked to run "news stories" regarding the IC and its progress, and the editors appear to have been very kind in this respect. It is to be doubted, says Paul W. Gates, authority on this period of the IC railroad, that any other line, before the building of the first transcontinental, received so much publicity, both free and paid for, as the Illinois Central.*

Now Colonizer Du Puy stepped into a new field. He devised special placards to fit the panels of New York horsecars and had them inserted in the cars of the Second, the Third, and the Sixth Avenue lines. He also prepared one of the first of the fairyland pamphlets, a school of literature only distantly related to fact. This and subsequent "Improved" editions went into detail regarding Illinois Central lands, and stated, with no qualification whatever, that they were easy to plow, possessed of inexhaustible

* See his *The Illinois Central Railroad and Its Colonization Work*, Cambridge, 1934.

fertility, and capable of growing every crop known to agriculture since the times of ancient Egyptian farmers.

Pictures proved the astounding claims. True, they were not photographic but came out of the creative minds of artists, yet to many people the picture proved what the words said. One wood engraving shows what purports to be nothing more than a typical new farm on the Illinois Central. The farmhouse is snug, with a trace of sheer beauty in the gingerbread decorations under the eaves. Trees shade it—which must have surprised any person then living on the treeless prairie of so much of the state. Everything is neatly fenced, and well-behaved cattle graze or chew their cuds in the foreground. A horse, perhaps a stallion by his spirited stance, trots over the gently rolling land. Chickens are in the dooryard. A staunch plow rests beside a superbly fenced field of corn of gargantuan size. The rugged farmer himself is moving from house to barn, a splendid structure, and it is obvious that he has time from his labor for small things, for he seems to be gazing at a pretty birdhouse erected on a pole for his feathered friends. And, very important, in the distance, yet not too far, a handsome train of cars streaks across the fine open land, trailing a plume of smoke over the rustic and altogether charming scene. The cars are quite small in perspective and it is impossible to read the legend on their sides, but the reader could have been in no doubt as to the line shown.*

Although Land Agent Du Puy was patently a man of imagination, he must have lacked something, for after a year or so he was replaced by John Wilson, recently retired as federal land commissioner and a man of great vigor. Wilson continued to send out the fairyland pamphlets, and he also engaged, trained, and let loose a crew of agents who attended the county fairs in New York and New England, called on men of the cloth, sat in public meetings, and parroted the glowing phrases that had been pounded into them by John Corning, of Niagara Falls, a sort of chief agent and getter of freight and passengers for the IC.

The effect of the pamphlet barrage and the tours of the agents took hold almost immediately, and with particular force in New England. This region already had ties with Illinois, so the field was ripe. Princeton, Illinois, had been settled as early as 1831 by a frankly missionary group from around Northampton, Massachusetts, whose captain was named Cotton Mather. A little later a group from Gilmanton, New Hampshire, founded Metamora, Illinois. In 1837 Ira Hersey of Maine led a band of his fellow townsmen to found Rockton. Marshall Field of Conway, Massachusetts, landed in Chicago just when the Illinois Central was laying its first track. These Yankees and many another had been drawn West by way of the Erie Canal, and their letters home, combined with the revealed charms of

---

* This illustration is not from *Andersen's Fairy Tales,* but from *A Guide to the Illinois Central Railroad Lands,* Chicago, 1859.

the Illinois Central lands, piped so sweetly by the male sirens of John Corning's office, had brought them down out of their green but rocky hills and set them in motion.*

It was a sudden migration, this one of the 1850's, and of a size to alarm those who had no desire to leave. Prices of farm property in one Vermont county fell as much as 40 per cent in one year, due, it was said, solely to the migration to Illinois. *The New England Farmer* was doleful at the outlook in 1858. Upstate New York papers noted similar conditions. Both Maine and Massachusetts editors were discouraged. But nothing could stop the movement.

It had long been the custom of Yankees, gregarious people despite all folklore to the contrary, to migrate in groups, all usually from the same town or county. Out of Vermont soon came 200 families of the Vermont Emigration Association to settle New Rutland in Illinois. Another Yankee colony settled Boyleton. Fourteen Massachusetts families founded Rosemond. In New London, Connecticut, the Working Men's Settlement Association was organized in 1855, and a year later its vanguard was laying out the village of Lyman, Illinois. At about the same time an Ohio group moved to Champaign County; and the American Emigration Association of Louisville, Kentucky, sent an advance party to spy out the best lands on the Illinois Central.

Yes, they were coming, coming from the hill farms and the canebrakes to the magic country of Illinois, a land that the IC pamphlets liked to call The Garden State of the West. The railroad was generous in the matter of land for schools and churches and public buildings generally, and the character of the Yankee settlements was to be recognized by the Congregational churches that were built soon or at once in Monee, Kankakee, Clifton, Bulkley, Loda, Paxton, El Paso, Rutland, La Salle, Tonica, Nora, Galena, Dunleith, Amboy, Mendota, Bloomington, Hoyleton, Rosemond, and Sandoval.

In the meantime the company was making sporadic attempts to get immigrant settlers from Europe. Parke Godwin, son-in-law of William Cullen Bryant and editor of the *Harbinger*, organ of the disciples of Fourier, was hired to establish an "intelligence office" in New York, and John Corning's crew of Pied Pipers was put in his charge. Godwin turned out some fancy articles on IC land which were run in New York papers, and he also engaged four runners, one a German, to work on the arrivals from Europe. The company sent an educated Swede, Oscar Malmborg, who had worked in the IC land department, to the Scandinavian countries, but soon recalled him. A bit later, in 1860, when Swedes and Norwegians were coming in great numbers to Wisconsin and Minnesota, and few or

* In his *New England in the Life of the World*, (Boston, 1920) Howard A. Bridgman traces the westward trek of many a Yankee group.

none to Illinois, the company sent Malmborg again across the water.

Malmborg traveled extensively in Norway and Sweden, distributing pamphlets, writing pieces for the papers, giving talks. He reported to his company that the time was ripe; the peasant farmers, he said, were being slowly squeezed out of their possessions by the large landowners. He attended many fairs and did much talking to individuals. He also ran head-on into the opposition of anti-immigration groups.

It was not difficult to attack anyone from America who sought to get Europeans to leave their homes. Those deadfalls known as forwarding companies, mentioned in an earlier chapter, which got hold of immigrants and fleeced them by various methods were already notorious all over Europe. The distressing experiences of Swedes and Norwegians who had gone to America and been met on arrival by harpies of both sexes were now used against Malmborg. It was charged, and it was only too true, that runners employed by land and railroad companies had practiced fearful deception and knavery on the green immigrants, had beaten them out of their little money, even out of their very clothes and possessions, had shipped them into swamp hellholes, had robbed them at lodging houses, and gypped them on tickets.

This was powerful stuff. It put fear into the hearts of would-be immigrants, and Malmborg had to use all of his abilities to meet it. He appears to have been wholly honest and quite realistic in his dealings. He admitted the charges against only too many American runners and agents, but vowed that the Illinois Central's men took care of all immigrants planning to go to Illinois immediately upon their arrival and saw that they arrived at their destination in The Garden State of the West safe and sound. Nor is there anything in the record to indicate that the Illinois Central did not live up to the promises made by Agent Malmborg.

Malmborg's work soon showed results. With the outbreak of the Civil War immigration from other parts of the United States all but ceased, and it began from Scandinavia. Swedes came to settle Big Spring and Neoga; and at Paxton, Lutherans were given IC land on which to found Augustana College, later removed to Rock Island. But few Norwegians were attracted to the state; they much preferred Wisconsin and Minnesota, and many Swedes who did settle in Illinois later removed to one or the other of the preferred states.

Immigrant Germans were not overlooked. The company engaged Francis Hoffman, outstanding German of the state who had also served as its lieutenant governor, to head a German Land Company for the IC. Hoffman first made a trip to view IC lands in person, found them ideal, and then set about to catch some of the tide flowing out of Germany to Wisconsin and to deflect it to eastern Illinois. He took advertising space in German-language papers and hired runners in the port cities. He wrote pamphlets that he had printed and distributed in Germany itself. He brought special pressure to bear on the large German colony already settled in and around St. Louis. Many of these people were dissatisfied, and when Hoffman was done with them, they were content with nothing in Missouri but must move to Illinois. Hoffman plastered St. Louis with gaudy posters that told of the wonderful IC lands, so cheap, so fertile, so easy to work, and also offered free railroad transportation for bona fide settlers. The results were immediate and most gratifying—to the railroad. One group alone came and bought 2,300 acres.

Happy at the turn of affairs, Hoffman now turned his guns on Wisconsin, the New Germany of the West. With tactics similar to those he had used in St. Louis, Wisconsin Germans were made unhappy with conditions at home and filled with a burning desire to settle somewhere along the Illinois Central. In 1863 Germans from Wisconsin and elsewhere purchased almost 30,000 acres of Illinois Central lands, much of it going to individuals in 40-acre tracts. Through Hoffman's efforts almost alone, some two thousand German families were settled in the region between Centralia and Mattoon in the space of two years.

During the period 1855–61 almost one and a half million acres of the railroad lands were sold. In the decade ending in 1860, the population of the state had increased 101 per cent, to a total of 860,481. The Illinois Central was not alone responsible for this new population; other railroads in the state were doing something; so were land companies, so were the wild boosters of Chicago. Yet the Illinois Central, by its own efforts and by the example it set, was unquestionably the great factor in the swift settlement of the state.

The IC quickly discovered that merely settling people on its lands was not all there was to colonization. Squatters appeared, first by the hundred, then by the thousand, usually shiftless men who dug in on railroad land and refused to move except by force. In the wooded southern counties timber thieves became so bold and busy that a special corps of agents had to be detailed to keep them in bounds—or, rather, to try to keep them within bounds. These timber thieves were a dangerous nuisance. The squatters on agricultural land merely cultivated the soil—a little—and squatted. The timber robbers, however, duffed into the woods in reckless style, cutting and burning without any thought to the damage to the land or to their neighbors. Indeed, their neighbors scarce dared to leave their farms for more than a few days at a time, in fear they would return home to find, as many of them did, all the timber on their places gone.

The timber agents of the railroad were looked upon as minions of corporate wealth, and one of the agents, James Clark, reported that "the whole country is full of men cutting whatever they can find on anybody's land." Witnesses against the timber thieves were almost impossible to secure, for they feared the violent revenge certain to be paid them—a barn burned, fences destroyed, or even a shot in the back. A large number of state and county attorneys seem to have showed little interest in prosecution. Judges threw out cases on flimsy technicalities. The company's agents were beaten up, shot at, and otherwise warned to mind the company's business elsewhere.

Then, there was the matter of collecting payments for land sold to farmers. Many of these people were of little means when they bought and settled; they had relied on a quick and good crop to put them on their feet. Many also purchased far more land than they could possibly use. And, in spite of those glowing paragraphs in the railroad's land pamphlets, the prairie sod was really tough. It was hard to break, and there were early frosts, drought, cloudbursts, tornadoes, none of which had been so much as mentioned in the literature about The Garden State of the West.

A majority of farmers, then as now, were in no great rush about things, especially paying off mortgages; and they could and did find an endless number of reasons why they could not meet their payments. From the first the company seems to have been extremely lenient and to have gone to almost any end rather than to foreclose on a farmer. In certain bad years, however, thousands of acres of farm land were given up, either voluntarily or through cancellation by the company. In many instances, if a farmer had overbought, the company urged him to let part of his land revert to the company and to hold that part on which he had made payments.

The Illinois Central naturally had need of a large number of legal minds. Abraham Lincoln served the IC in a number of cases in the 1850's, and on one occasion presented the company with a bill for his fee of $2000. At that time George B. McClellan was vice-president in charge of operations. He looked at the bill with pretended astonishment. "Why, sir," he said to Attorney Lincoln, "this is as much as Daniel Webster himself would have charged. We cannot allow such a claim." Lincoln went away without his fee, but he sent in a new bill, this time for $5000, brought suit against the IC, and collected.

The Illinois Central was quick to do anything to aid and abet the prosperity of the people along its tracks. It spent considerable money to establish a state fair, and later county fairs. It also did a great deal of pioneering work in the promotion of agriculture, being the first railroad to interest itself in this matter and setting the style for later agricultural promotion by railroads.

It is true that in later years the Illinois Central became one of the targets for the enraged farmers of the Granger movement. No doubt it deserved some of the animosity directed against it in the 1870's. No doubt, too, that it suffered even more because of the arrogance and double-dealing of other railroads. Yet, this railroad, as perhaps none other, was the chief and the most successful promoter of the state that chartered it. It came into being in a region almost without population, and through its efforts it made Illinois the most talked-of state in the Union in the 1850's.

It was the IC, too, that pioneered the art of colonizing in relation to railroads. It planned and put into effect the many and various methods by which outlanders from other states and from Europe were induced to settle along its tracks. Later efforts of other roads to populate their lines appear to have added little or nothing basically new to the siren's charms, although many a railroad land department was less honest in its claims.

The officials of the IC in its early days appear to have been wise as well as shrewd men. The record shows that when this or that one of their policies ran counter to public opinion, they modified or abandoned it. They seem to have been men who believed firmly that the farmers and townsmen of Illinois must be happy and prosperous if the road was to be successful, and to these ends they bent their energies.

The State of Illinois did well by the bargain too. In seventy-five years following 1850, the Central had paid into state coffers approximately $65,000,000, which was the seven per cent of its gross revenues due as per charter. Ordinary railroad taxes during the period would have amounted to little more than half that sum. Meanwhile, too, the railroad grew and prospered; few other railroads have been so financially successful. It was a pretty good deal all around.

CHAPTER IX

Hoosiers Start a Railroad—The Monon

*Still we went ahead, crossed the Wabash, ran our engine off the track,
and got it on again. . . .*

—HORACE GREELEY, 1853.

T HE stock certificates of the New Albany & Salem Rail Road Company
were handsome and also rather chaste, when compared to the flamboy-
ance of most railroad printing of the day, which was the middle of last
century. There was, of course, a picture of a train of cars, for no symbol
of the nineteenth century was more potent than one of a locomotive with
its brigade of clattering boxes on wheels. The particular train of the New
Albany & Salem is just rounding a graceful curve of track, the 4-4-0 locomotive sending up from its stack a pleasing cloud of smoke that curls
back over the coaches and so on into the distance. The engine is hauling
five passenger cars. The tender is obviously piled high with cordwood.
The grade looks pretty good. The train is passing through a modest forest,
while far in the rear are high hills, almost mountains, of a size one does
not ordinarily think of in relation to Indiana. But then, Indiana has always
been a place for artists, either of brush or pen, and they are men who hold
license to see things with their own eyes and not as described by ordinary
people.

The New Albany & Salem was an Indiana railroad of purest genealogy
out of which was to grow the present Chicago, Indianapolis & Louisville,
commonly and with much greater felicity known as the Monon Route.
It sprang from the desire of Salem citizens to connect their village with
the nearby Ohio River at New Albany; and also, in the mind of at least one
Salemite, to connect the Ohio River with the Great Lakes. The founding
fathers believed, after a bit, that such a road would make both Salem and
New Albany vast cities of the Midwest by developing a traffic in freight
and passengers all along its entire length of nearly 300 miles. The belief
was typical of the time, a time when the very name of railroad was sheer
magic. There was nothing, absolutely nothing, that the steam cars could
not accomplish in the way of improving a region.

When the New Albany & Salem was incorporated in 1847, the former
place had a population of 8,181 and was the largest city in all Indiana.

Salem was a mere hamlet of 2,223 persons, and its citizens thought—oddly enough, perhaps—that by connecting their town with the great river port of New Albany, its own growth would be assured. This explains the fact that most if not all of the early stockholders were Salemites.

In all such groups there is always one leading spirit, and he who was to lead the New Albany & Salem through its first difficult years was James Brooks, a State of Mainer born in Orington who was thirty-seven years old when he incorporated the railroad. His business was running a store in Salem. It was he who intended the new road to run not only between the two towns of its corporate title, but on and on up through the middle of Indiana until the tracks came up short on the Lake Michigan shore, almost exactly 288 miles from New Albany.

Brooks and his fellow "commissioners," as they were called, managed to raise sufficient money to begin construction early in 1848. Brooks was elected president, and along with that job he appears to have been forced by circumstances into filling several other positions, one of which was the difficult work of persuading Hoosier farmers to allow right-of-way across their lands without asking damages ruinous to the new company. He seems to have been pretty good at this. His policy, which he defined in a number of letters, was that if the railroad damaged a man by building the road over his farm more than the farm was benefited by having the railroad there, he would pay such damage. But, however, if the so-called damage left the farm of more value than before the arrival of the rails, then, said Brooks in his best judicial manner, "we think he is not entitled to any damage as we leave him better off than we found him, notwithstanding we may use a few acres of his land in doing it." Brooks also believed, and his belief was virtually dogma, that iron rails almost automatically did a farm more good than harm.

Two years after beginning of construction the New Albany & Salem had completed 27 miles of road and was the third longest railway in the state, the two longer being the gigantic Madison & Indianapolis, with 88 miles of road, and the Indianapolis & Belfontaine with 28 miles. The mileage for the entire state totaled 212. The New Albany built its first track on ties laid four feet apart and connected by stringers imbedded in notches in the ties. The rails were simply bar iron, held in place by big spikes driven through the center and their heads countersunk in order not to project above the rails.

It was presently discovered that because the ends of the rails were connected by tongue and groove, there was not enough space to allow for the expansion caused by changes in temperature. The bars heaved and writhed, loosening the spikes. The spikes gave way, the bars spread, and locomotives were derailed. The T-rail was already being used on all of the better-financed roads which were publicizing the sinister menace inherent in bar rails in order to scare passenger traffic off such murderous contraptions. President Brooks was not slow to see the disadvantages of bar iron, and soon he was replacing his own tracks with T-rail made by the Crescent Iron Manufacturing Company of Wheeling, Virginia. This, he told his directors, would relieve the New Albany from the "bad name" of running on bar iron which, he said, "has had a very unfavorable influence upon our passenger business." He added that agents of competing roads had been able, by a series of gross and unspeakable misrepresentations, to alarm passengers and "keep them off our line."

President Brooks was a man of broad vision. He went ahead to get a sort of roving charter from the State of Indiana, a remarkable document that gave the New Albany & Salem the right to extend its line to "any other point or points" in the state. This charter, says the New Albany's historian, Frank P. Hargrave,* was probably unique in American railroad history. The road made the most of it, too, and by extension of its own line and the absorption of others, it at last reached the Great Lakes in 1854, connecting with the Michigan Central at Michigan City, Indiana, on the shore of Lake Michigan. The line had now reached the climax Brooks had planned for it: It started at New Albany, ran northwesterly to Salem, then almost directly north through Mitchell, Bloomington, Gosport, Green-castle, Crawfordsville, Lafayette, Monon (then called Bradford), and straight up through Starke and Laporte Counties to the lake.

Pioneer railroads such as the New Albany & Salem had to devise their methods of operation as they went along, and the primeval Hoosiers were equal to the task. Their first locomotives were flatteringly named for towns along the line, although after a few years classical mythology was given a trial and the iron horses appeared with *Apollo, Mercury,* and *Achilles* on their tenders or name boards. Then came a period when the engines were *Rover, Rusher, Samson, Tornado, Meteor,* and even *Rattler.* Each engineer was assigned a particular engine, which he ran so regularly as to feel a sense of ownership. It was common for an engineer to stay with his engine during all of the time required for a round trip, which might be as little as two or as much as six days.

Wood was, of course, the fuel used. The company figured it could run an average train about 28½ miles on one cord of four-foot wood; and the wood could be cut, delivered and piled in the tender for $1.41 a cord. Wood-up stations were established at regular intervals of from 20 to 25 miles, and here farmers delivered the wood in four-foot lengths. The wood-up at Lafayette was the largest on the line and remained in use until after 1870. It held one hundred cords. To cut the sticks once more for easy handling by firemen, the New Albany's ingenious mechanics de-

---

* See his *A Pioneer Indiana Railroad,* Indianapolis, 1932.

vised a flatcar with a stationary engine aboard, rigged to a circular saw. This was called *The Rooster*, and a picture of a cock appeared in full color on the car's sides. *The Rooster* was hauled up and down the line, its crew making little ones out of big ones. It became an institution.

The early locomotive stacks were not covered with any screen, and naturally gave forth a continuous shower of sparks, causing many fires in grass and forest, for which the company was held responsible. The sparks were also hard on both passengers and employees. Charles Bane, an old hogger of the New Albany, related that one could always tell a member of an engine crew of that day by the holes burned in the back of his vest.

Water for the locomotives was taken at likely places and was poured into the locomotive tank by a bucket brigade of engine and train crews. This system was followed by a pump worked by horse power, the horse being harnessed to a long pole and walking in a circle. Gravity water tanks gradually came into use as the company could afford their construction.

The first passenger cars cost $2,000 apiece and seated from fifty to sixty persons. The lamps burned lard oil, and were continuously smoking. The task of tending them was given to the trainboy, a sort of forerunner of the news butcher. One of the first trainboys on the New Albany was W. W. Garrott, 13 years old in 1856 when he made his first run. It was a dangerous job for a youngster. The cars were of various heights and were coupled together with three great links of chain, and it was necessary in getting from one coach to another to make a considerable leap. Young Garrot had to do this while carrying a basket of fruit and candy, or perhaps a bundle of newspapers. He was so sure-footed, however, that Conductor Rush Prosser permitted the lad to run regularly on his train. Another of Trainboy Garrott's duties was to supply drinking water to passengers. A barrel of ice water was carried in the baggage car and every hour or so Garrott had to fill a two-gallon can that had a long spout, and with this and two tin cups make his way through the train, cooling the throats of adults and of children, the latter never so thirsty as when traveling on the steam cars.

For a number of years one car served for baggage, mail, and express. The last car on the train was the Ladies' Car, and into this no male dared enter unless accompanied by a woman, who might or might not be a lady. All other males had to sit in the smoker, whether or not they smoked. All passenger cars were heated by round stoves fastened to the wall to prevent turning over in case of derailments, which apparently were many. The trainboys had to keep the stoves going and the woodboxes filled.

There were no wrecking cars in those days. Into a long box hung to the underside of each New Albany baggage car went chains, ropes, crowbars, hammers and such, for use in emergencies. Conductors were to open this "switch box" just before starting a run to make certain that no one had made off with the tools. The conductors were paid $83.33 a month, the brakemen $30. The scale for engineer and fireman was about the same. The trainboy got no regular wage, but Garrott recalled that he used to make as much as $40 a month in commission on sales. He did not mention any side-lines, so perhaps he was not working for a news agency but was on his own.

Like many another early road, the New Albany was often hard put to meet the payroll. At such times it was the custom to issue meal and lodging tickets. The regular paymaster was authorized to redeem these in cash when presented by anyone not an employee of the road but not when offered by employees.

The train crews on the New Albany were not slow in finding means to add to their wages. It soon became a custom for them to buy berries, eggs, and chestnuts along the way and sell them in the larger towns at a profit. The company did not object, at least not for many years, and the business of certain trainmen became so extensive as to call for newspaper comment. In 1857, for instance, the *Review* of Crawfordsville remarked it was time the Postmaster General of the United States added an extra car to make room for the mails that were being crowded out by heavy shipments of eggs and butter incident to the produce business being carried on by mail clerks and baggage men on the New Albany & Salem Railroad.

Operating schedules were set up in the early years but were seldom met. Horace Greeley wrote a vivid description about delays on this railroad in a letter to his paper in New York. He was on a speaking tour, this time on Temperance, and planned to leave on a certain train from Lafayette to get to Laporte, where another lecture was due. This was in October of 1853. Greeley went to what he thought was the New Albany & Salem Railroad station in Lafayette, and there he waited a long time only to learn that the train left from another depot, the one on Salem Street. He got to this depot just in time to see the smoke of the departing train. So, he remained overnight in Lafayette, and next day he caught the train. It was, one judges, quite a train:

I was in ample season (says Greeley), but the train that was to start at ten did not actually leave until noon, and then with a body entirely disproportionate to its head. Five cars closely packed with hogs, five ditto with wheat, two ditto with lumber, three or four with live stock and notions returning from the fair, and two or three cattle cars containing passengers, formed entirely too heavy a load for our asthmatic engine which had obviously seen its best days in the service of other roads before that from New Albany to Michigan City was constructed. Still, we went ahead, crossed the Wabash, passed the Tippecanoe Creek Battle ground, ran our engine partly off the track, and got it on again; and by three o'clock had reached Brookston, a station fourteen miles from Lafayette, with a fair prospect of traversing our ninety odd miles by the dawn of Monday morning.

Mr. Greeley's troubles were not over. They were merely beginning. The halt at Brookston seemed endless. The engine was in want of both wood and water, but neither was present. The locomotive was uncoupled and run ahead some five miles for water, still farther for wood, and two hours later returned to the stalled train and hitched on. The cheery call of "all aboard" gladdened the hearts of the passengers—though not for long. After a run of half a mile, the cock of the boiler blew out, letting off all water and steam.

The conductor, a hardy soul, one judges, a Spartan ready to meet any and all conditions imposed by life, considered the matter for a bit, then got aboard a handcar and started pumping back to Lafayette where, he said, he would get a locomotive that could haul the train and the disabled engine back to that village. Mr. Greeley did not want to return to Lafayette. He said so, aloud. He had seen, he remarked, enough of Lafayette, and now he must get on to Laporte. The engineer of the stalled train had an idea. He recollected that a pretty good locomotive was resting at Culvertown, forty-three miles ahead, and he proposed to take a handcar— there seemed to be plenty of handcars around Brookston—and go get it and run it back to Brookston.

Mr. Greeley had seen not only enough of Lafayette but of Brookston too. He grabbed his carpetbag and climbed aboard the handcar:

The full moon [reported the editor of the *New York Tribune*] was bright over the eastern woods as with the north star straight ahead, we bid adieu to the embryo city of Brookston. We were seven of us in the handcar, four propelling by twos, as if turning a heavy, two-handed grindstone . . . the car, about equal in size to a wheelbarrow and a half, just managed to hold us and give the propellors working room. To economize space, I sat a good part of the time facing backwards, with my feet dangling over the rear of the car, knocking here and there on a tie or a bridge timber, and often tickled through my boots by the coarse, rank weeds growing up at intervals between the ties and recently stiffened by the hard October frosts . . . We made our first five miles in twenty-five minutes, our first ten miles in an hour, but our propellors grew gradually weary. We stopped twice or thrice for oil, water, and perhaps one other liquor so that we were five hours in making forty-three miles, or from seven o'clock until midnight.

Excellent observer that he was, Greeley saw a good deal of the country on that ride. The night was clear and chilly. The course lay across the east end of that "Grand Prairie that stretched westerly from the banks of the Wabash across Indiana and Illinois to the Mississippi, and thence through Iowa and Nebraska, perhaps to Council Bluffs and the Rocky Mountains." The ground seemed nearly level, sometimes marshy, and for the most part, Greeley noted, clear of woods. But they frequently crossed belts of higher ground and Greeley noted occasional clumps of sturdy oaks

—isles of timber in the prairie sea. He saw four prairie fires, burning brightly but lazily. A flock of wild geese flew over, murmuring. The editor saw one great heron rise from beside the track and fly heavily over the marshes. The handcar frightened several wild animals, including one skunk and one opossum. Greeley took it all in, and at last came the climax. They reached Culvertown and found that the engine they had come for wasn't there. It had been taken north to Michigan City.

Well, that left Mr. Greeley still in the wilderness, still many miles from Laporte. Now that he had got his teeth into the matter, he resolved to go on at any cost. He waked everyone in Culvertown in an attempt to get a team to take him north. There were no teams. But the New Albany & Salem engineer who had bossed the handcar from Brookston liked Greeley's determination. He loaned Greeley the handcar and helped him to find two Culvertown men who agreed to pump the rig the remainder of the night. So Greeley and his two men struck out at one o'clock in the morning. At nine next morning Greeley was in Laporte, ready to speak that afternoon on the evils of dram taking.

Of the country he had passed through on what must have seemed an extremely long day and night, Greeley had an opinion. He reported that he had seen scarcely a hundred houses in that long ride, and they would have been dear at two hundred dollars each. He did see some fine timber, and "he who passes this way ten years hence will see a different state of things." There was a good future for the region, he thought. But he also remarked that the "financiering which conjured up the means of building the New Albany and Michigan City Railroad is worthy of a brazen monument." One wonders what President Brooks thought of such a remark.

If Mr. Greeley rode the New Albany & Salem on a free pass he must have indeed been irritated, just as the man who sees a show on a free pass and finds it bad is irritated. But it is probable the editor paid cash for his trip by train and handcar.

Free passes, of course, became one of the early evils of American railroads, and the New Albany & Salem had more than its share of difficulties and losses from this source, says Mr. Hargrave, the line's careful historian. The line issued passes in great numbers and for every reason that human ingenuity could think of. Whole families—and Hoosier families of the time were large—got passes in payment for the privilege of building a water tank or of piling wood on a farmer's land. All public officials, even those who had been in but were now out of office, expected free passes as a prerogative of their status. So did nearly all shippers of freight; and one such, who claimed he shipped as many hogs as any other men on the line, wanted a pass for that specific reason.

The knockdown on fares appears to have been discovered at an early date by the road's conductors and to have been followed intently and with such abandon that the company felt it necessary to issue an order that all passengers must purchase tickets before they boarded a train. Tickets for excursions were sold at a reduced rate, and excursions were one of the many ways in which the company sought to raise cash. Salem was the first town to which these trips were made. Later, the favorite excursion points were Bedford, Bloomington, Lafayette, and Michigan City on the lake. These trips were extremely popular, and the crowds grew so rapidly, the company could not always muster sufficient rolling stock to carry them all. It pressed coal cars into service, erecting over them a frame and covering it with green leaved branches of oak and other trees. Almost every political meeting called for a steam-car excursion, plus an ox barbecue.

Both the Adams and the American Express Companies were using the New Albany & Salem by 1853. They were allowed space not to exceed fifty-six square feet in the baggage car, and all express had to be in the care of an express-company agent, who was given passage at half fare. Mail service on the line was established in the same year, and the mails went into the baggage car along with the express—and the various products of the train crews engaging in farm produce as a side-line.

During the first six months of operation the government paid the company $5,759 for mail service, which came in mighty handy. Telegraphic service along the line was not available until 1859, when the railroad company made a contract with a concern that was soon to become a part of the Western Union. The New Albany & Salem was given exclusive control of the telegraph line for $9,000, though the Western Union reserved the right to do all of the paid business at four of the principal stations.

The New Albany & Salem managed to make a small yearly profit from the time it was opened until the end of 1856. But this paper profit was hardly a real net; the company owed a good deal of cash in back wages to its employes. President Brooks and his directors were worried enough, and with good right, when the panic of 1857 made its presence known. Brooks was retired and the road put in charge of a trustee. It seems a sad end for the man who thought up and largely built Indiana's first railroad from one end of the state to the other; yet, a survey of all early American railroads would probably show that few of the founding fathers of any line survived longer than the first bankruptcy and reorganization. When the real builders, such as Brooks was, had served their purpose, then the bankers, the financiers, stepped in and took over. It seemed almost an immutable law.

The reorganized New Albany & Salem became the Chicago, New Albany & Louisville, and it appears to have done little better under its new name and trusteeship. Even the Civil War, which saved at least temporarily so many ailing railroads, failed to help this one. In 1870 it was thrown into involuntary receivership. In 1897 another reorganization changed the style of the road to Chicago, Indianapolis & Louisville, the official title it still retains, although it is popularly known as the Monon Route. Just where this name came from is doubtful. Historian Hargrave says that some hold it to be a Potawatomi Indian word meaning "to carry." Another source has it "swiftly moving," a phrase that might make Horace Greeley's shade shake with amusement.

It is more than possible that a part of one of America's great books was written on a Monon train. In 1874 General Lew Wallace was living in Crawfordsville, a Monon town, engaged in writing *Ben Hur*, and though he finished the novel in Santa Fé, where he was serving as territorial governor of New Mexico, he often related that he had composed portions of the book while riding the cars between Crawfordsville and Indianapolis. Specifically, he related that he composed Tirza's song, "Wait Not," while on "a belated train" between those two cities.

Until someone can prove differently, let part of the glory of General Wallace and *Ben Hur* shine upon the honorable rails of the Monon Route. Anton Anderson, assistant chief operating officer of the Monon in 1946, told me he would like to believe that *Ben Hur* was written in part in a Monon coach, and that there is an even or better chance that it was. "General Wallace," he admits, "may have ridden horseback from Crawfordsville to Colfax, then taken a train on either one or the other lines which are now the New York Central and the Pennsylvania to Indianapolis. Or, again, he may have taken the Monon to Lafayette or Greencastle, then one of the other lines to Indianapolis. We do know that he used to come often over the Monon to Shelby, where he did a lot of fishing and hunting along the Kankakee River."

In any case, the original notes of both General Wallace's *Ben Hur* and his earlier *The Fair God* are in the gallant old soldier's library in Crawfordsville, a Monon town, I repeat, and may be seen by interested visitors. There may be no great mountains along the Monon, yet those pencilled notes for *Ben Hur* constitute sections of one of the mountains in our literature, for it was General Wallace's great book that was the first novel to break through the rustic and village opposition to popular fiction. *Ben Hur* rode that gilded chariot right through the front door to enter the homes of Hard-Shell Baptists and Methodists, and to an eager welcome. Hundreds of thousands of back-country Americans learned the charms of fiction through *Ben Hur*. (*Uncle Tom's Cabin* doesn't count, because it was not considered a novel at all but a Christian tract dictated by a Northern Congregational God.) For this reason, if for no other, Carl Van Doren has set *Ben Hur* down as an epochal work, a book that did something to change the thinking of many Americans. General Wallace lived most of his life in Crawfordsville. He worked there, died there. Let some now forgotten coach of the Monon stand as shelter for the traveling author of *Ben Hur*. And let the Monon name a locomotive for him.

CHAPTER X

War Comes to a "Neutral" Line

*They pointed to Napoleon's dismal experience in Russia, and sneered
at the Union which would not learn from disasters of the past. They
could not recognize the improved appliance of the age—the railroad.*
—CHARLES FRANCIS ADAMS, 1871.

U P TO the time when the struggle had been hopelessly and obviously
lost, the eminent military observers and other pomposities of Europe
had been banking on the South to win the War Between the States. After
Gettysburg, true, a few of them began to hedge a bit, yet mostly they continued to believe in the ultimate success of Confederate arms, even when
Sherman and his bummers were going through Georgia like the hounds of
hell. The news of Appomattox must have left them a bit deflated, if de-
flation is possible in the windy precincts of experts who attempt to comment on a war in a country few of them have ever seen and even fewer
know anything about.

In exercising their gifts of prophecy on the result of the great American
struggle, the European military men did not recognize, and therefore took
no count of, one of the improved and protean appliances of the age,
namely, the railroad. They observed the vastness of the region which the
North must subdue. They mentioned the power of a people acting on the
defensive in their own home. They cited the impossibility for the Union
to sustain its armies in hostile territory. They pointed to Napoleon's tragic
experience in Russia, and wondered, in print, why the Union high command would not learn from the disasters of the past.

But they never, as Charles Francis Adams, our great philosopher of
railroads, pointed out—they never took into consideration the new element of the railroad in war. So, as Mr. Adams put it, "the world saw a
powerful enemy's existence depending on a frail thread of railroad iron,
with the effectual destruction of which perished all hope of resistance.
It saw Sherman's three hundred miles of rear, and the base and supplies
of eighty thousand fighting men three days' journey by railway from the
sound of strife. It saw two whole army corps, numbering 18,000 men,
moved, with all their munitions and a portion of their artillery, thirteen
hundred miles around the circumference of a vast theater of war, from

121

Virginia to Tennessee, in the moment of danger, and this too in the apparently incredibly brief space of only seven days."

The American Civil War was the first real railroad war; and it is the opinion of many historians, including so careful a one as Robert S. Henry, that the superior use which the North was able to make of its own railroads and those of the Southern and Border states which came into its possession did "as much, certainly, as any one thing to settle the issue of the struggle."

General William Tecumseh Sherman himself said that his final campaign in the South would have been wholly impossible without the railroads. In speaking of this campaign Mr. Henry has written that "the problem was to keep General Sherman's great army of 100,000 men and 35,000 animals supplied and in fighting trim as it advanced into the heart of the enemy's country, in a campaign of 196 days. The means of supply was a single-track railroad, extending 473 miles from Louisville to Nashville, to Chattanooga and on to Atlanta. This campaign, which resulted in the fall of Atlanta, was the final deciding fact of the Confederate war."

One of the railroads that played a large part in that campaign, and in many another during the war, was the new and struggling Louisville & Nashville, destined to occupy, in the first years of strife, the awkward position of a "neutral" line; and because of its anomalous stand, to be wrecked and wrecked again by both contending armies. Railroading on the L&N during the war years must indeed have been a discouraging, almost a hopeless task, a nightmare to its employees ever after.

There had been a civil war within the directorate of the L&N just before the big Civil War started, and John M. Helm, its Kentucky-born, pro-slavery president, had been ousted, while into his place went the wealthy and arrogant yet quite realistic James Guthrie, a man of ability who had served as Secretary of the United States Treasury in Franklin Pierce's administration. Guthrie was also a native of Kentucky, and in 1860, when he was made president of the L&N, its stockholders and directors were virtually all natives of either Kentucky or Tennessee.

When the shooting started in April of '61, the L&N was operating 269 miles of track in the two states, with 30 locomotives, 28 passenger and baggage cars, 297 freight cars, and six cabooses.* For three months prior to the outbreak of hostilities, the line had been doing a huge business, all it could handle and more, in carrying southward an immense amount of supplies which the seven states that had seceded on February 1 had laid in, in case of emergency. When war came, President Guthrie, by what eloquence one may only guess, persuaded his Tennessee as well as his Ken-

---

* According to Kincaid Herr, author of *The Louisville and Nashville Railroad*, 1850–1942 (Louisville, 1943), one of the most complete histories inspired by any American railroad.

tucky directors that the railroad should remain, like the state of Kentucky, neutral.

The outbreak of actual war at first had only a happy effect on the L&N. The flow of provisions into Dixie continued without respite, and L&N cars became so hard worked that the company put a temporary embargo on freight of all kinds. Presently the people of Louisville were alarmed to see so many of their good hams and eggs and chickens and so much other food going out of their region and into the Deep South. They first made formal protest to the railroad, and when that seemed to have no effect, the citizens gathered, went out south of the city and tore up several miles of track, and blew up culverts and bridges. For a period in 1861, the company was obliged to send armed guards ahead to protect its rails and trains in home territory.

In May the Union government issued an order forbidding the carrying of provisions and munitions into the Confederacy, and for a time the contraband freight fell off, though it never ceased, and presently it started to grow again, bigger than ever. Because comparatively strict supervision was exercised at the terminal in Louisville, shippers toted their provisions and such by wagon to some flag station along the line and there put them into freight cars.

The Confederate blockade was more strict than that of the North, where, says Mr. Herr, the L&N's able historian, a flexible permit system was supplemented by an outright closing of one eye to the provisions of the embargo. This, says Mr. Herr, tended to reduce Southern sympathies in Kentucky; and such sympathy as remained was further alienated when Governor Isham Harris of Tennessee ordered seizure of all L&N rolling stock in that state.

Worse blows, much worse, were on the way. Late in 1861 the Memphis branch of the road, together with the main stem between the Tennessee state line and Lebanon Junction, was seized by Gen. Simon Bolivar Buckner, C. S. A., and thus the road lost about half of its remaining rolling stock and motive power. A part of the seized trackage was quickly recovered when Home Guards, under command of Gen. William T. Sherman, went out and cleared the track as far south as Elizabethtown, Kentucky, though in their retreat the Rebels worked havoc on L&N bridges. Buckner's forces fell back as far as Green River and there demolished the largest bridge on the entire L&N system, thus leaving a real gap in the line.

All L&N lines south of Elizabethtown remained in the Confederate hands until early in 1862, when Gen. Don Carlos Buell began his advance toward Nashville. On February 15th the Union forces entered that city, but found that the Rebels had thoroughly wrecked the L&N south of Bowling Green. Even depots and warehouses had been looted and burned. Ordinarily, Southern cavalry had little inclination for the hard work of destroying a railroad. Being, as they believed, the flower of the Confederate Army, it little behooved them to get down from their chargers and apply muscle and sweat to the lowly job of heating and twisting rails into knots.* But the gang that went to work on the L&N seem to have done a pretty fair job of wrecking. At South Tunnel, Tennessee, the longest bore on the line, they rolled several freight cars into the tunnel and set them afire. The supporting timbers caught fire, and the heat generated caused great quantities of shale rock and earth to fall into the tunnel, filling it 12 feet deep for more than 800 feet.

The L&N repair crews surely were hard and willing workers, for the line was operating all the way from Louisville to Nashville again by April. But there was to be no respite; for now the swift and hardy Gen. John Hunt Morgan and his raiders began operating against the railroad. At Gallatin, Tennessee, Morgan's men effectively sabotaged the line, and a few weeks later struck again near Cave City, Kentucky, where they destroyed a train of 37 freight cars, leaving the line with virtually no boxcars of its own. The Union Government had begun to sense what the L&N could mean in waging war, so it ordered rolling stock from other roads delivered to the L&N. The L&N gauge was 5 feet, that of the Northern roads either 4 feet 9 inches, or 4 feet 8½ inches. So a temporary track was laid from the canal at Louisville, where the cars were delivered, to the L&N depot at 10th and Broadway, where men set about revamping the gauge.

After their first brief successes, and a short hiatus, General Morgan's men struck again—at Lebanon, at Gallatin, and at Tunnel Hill for a second time. They ripped up rails, burned the ties, blasted bridges and culverts; and this time they cut the telegraph wires and removed long sections of them. Presently, too, Gen. Kirby Smith and Gen. Braxton Bragg and their men in gray advanced upon Louisville itself, getting as far as Munfordville where they were temporarily stopped, but not before they had destroyed the long bridge across Green River—the same Green River, incidentally, that gave its name to an excellent sour-mash whiskey that was revered by North and South alike.

On came Bragg's Rebels. Late in September they occupied Shepherdsville, and there put in three days' hard work wrecking the L&N bridge over Salt River, a terrible blow to the line. But there wasn't much left to the L&N's territory, anyway; President Guthrie released all employees from their duties, and they were organized into home-guard companies to defend Louisville. The L&N's annual report, made at this time, sounds a querulous note in regard to the Union forces. "The presence in Louisville

---

* More than one writer on the Civil War has thought that one of the weak links in the Confederate Army was that practically everybody wanted to ride a horse and to be armed with nothing more deadly than saber and horse pistol. But it was the infantry that *won* wars

of the whole of Buell's army," it says, "would seem to be sufficient to protect at least 18 miles of our road."

Yet General Buell's army did get to Louisville and General Bragg's didn't, and the former struck out at once to clear the tracks again, while soldiers and L&N employees, back again at the old stand, worked wonders in relaying track and building bridges. The great structure across Green River was rebuilt before the end of 1862, and trains were using it. Engineering forces of the Union Army turned to help the much battered L&N, and were of great aid in constructing trestles that permitted the Lebanon branch to resume operation. The tide had begun to turn, so far as the L&N was concerned. Buell went on to take Shepherdsville, then to hit Bragg a hard blow at the battle of Perryville, near Danville, Kentucky. The Confederates withdrew from the Blue Grass State.

Working like Trojans, the L&N crews tore into the work of reconstruction and repair. They put up temporary bridges, patched rails, and threw together boards and logs to make something like depots. Even so, the L&N locomotive engineers had to be careful, for many miles of the track had no ballast at all, and at best the road was rough. There was a great scarcity of almost everything, including wood for locomotive fuel. For a period the line used coal, for the first time; and it also hired from the Union government some 500 Negroes who had been conscripted. These Negroes went to work cutting cordwood for the big-stacked locomotives of the L&N.

Though the main theater of war had moved elsewhere, troubles were still in store for the railroad. On Christmas Day, 1862, and without any warning, General Morgan appeared again, this time with four thousand men. He had left Alexandria three days before. Except for two pieces of light artillery, all his force was on horseback. In the troops were some 400 men without any arms. Morgan said he would "soon get them guns from the Yankees." Even as it was, a goodly portion of Morgan's command was armed with Colt's revolvers captured from Northern soldiers. Each Morgan raider carried his own ammunition, two extra horseshoes, twelve horseshoe nails, and blankets for horse and man.

Morgan's advance guard entered Glasgow, Kentucky, at dusk on Christmas Eve, to find a part of the Second Michigan Cavalry just riding into the public square on return from a foraging expedition. Morgan's men let go a yell and charged. A brisk, brief fight followed. The Yankees were driven off, leaving one dead and two wounded. Twenty were taken prisoner —and thus were twenty-three of Morgan's 400 unarmed men given something to fight with.

The Rebel forces also captured a huge supply of turkeys the Yankees had planned to eat on the morrow. Cooking the big birds, the Rebels started north on Christmas morning, munching drumsticks as they rode. Ten miles out of Glasgow they were attacked by a superior Union force, but they rallied and continued on. Later that day they fell upon the heavy train of a sutler. Crossing Green River, they camped not far from Upton, and here they broke out the sutler's stores and had a wonderful feast. Now they were fair astride the L&N again. Filled with fine victuals, the men went to work with great gusto, pulling up track, burning bridges and trestles, and destroyed the stockade forts that the small Union forces had been using for protection of the L&N. Then the Rebels went away and the patient crews of the railroad resumed what must have by then seemed the interminable job of cleaning up after soldiers.

The repair crews had hardly got the 35-mile stretch in working order, before unseasonable freshets took out a score of small bridges and otherwise threw the line into such condition that not even a handcar could operate over it. One wonders what the operating superintendent, and what the various section bosses said when Nature boiled up so outrageously and undid the work of many hundreds of men during many weeks. But perhaps by that time L&N employees were immune to any and every devilment that might befall their line.

This time, however, the worst really was over. General Morgan paid his respects once more, on July 4, 1863, by wrecking the L&N yards and other facilities at Lebanon, Kentucky, just before he was captured on his raid into Ohio; and there were small attacks by guerrilla bands until the very end of the war. But the Northern railroads were now in the care of a very able man, Gen. Daniel McCallum, who at once provided armed guards for all L&N trains and established small forts and details all along the line. It was high time something like this was done. The L&N, at best a Border-State railroad, with no native or inherent sympathy for the North, and with only loathing for Abolition, had served the North well, moving troops and munitions and supplies forward, and bringing the wounded and ill back by the thousands. Possibly, in view of its great help in Sherman's final campaign, as well as the continuous aid it had given to other Northern commands, the L&N could be rated as a major factor in winning the war, so far as transportation was concerned.

The operating genius who kept this much-battered railroad working was the L&N's "engineer and superintendent of machinery and road department," a native German, Albert Fink. Fink, inventor of the bridge truss that bears his name, had come from Germany to the United States to work for the Baltimore & Ohio, from which he went to the L&N. The latter road's historian credits Fink with keeping the line running in spite of conditions no other railroader had ever met and mastered. His annual reports to the company are marvels of good reporting and they tell, as nothing else could, the difficulties faced by the L&N in the war years.

On June 30, 1862, Fink told his directors that "during the past 12 months the Road has been operated its entire length for seven months and 12 days. The Main Stem, and the Memphis, Lebanon and Bardstown branches were at various times in the possession of the Confederate forces, with the exception of some 20 miles of road north and 20 miles south of Bowling Green. For a period of two weeks trains could not even venture to leave Louisville." He went on to say that many L&N bridges had been twice wrecked during the year, a few of them three times. And he gave a vivid picture of the southern portion of the road as he had found it.

"All the repair hands who lived along the line," said Superintendent Fink, "had been driven off, and to supply their places was difficult, and required time. This country being destitute of everything—as desolate as though it had never been inhabited—it was almost impossible to obtain boarding and lodging for the hands, even after the men had been procured. All water stations between Nashville and Sinking Creek had been burned, and temporary ones, such as could be built in one day, had to be put in their places. The pumps, being unprotected against frost, had to be worked by hand, and no reliable man could be found to take charge of them. Most of the firewood had been burned by the Confederates, and there was not labor enough in the country to supply at once the necessary quantities which forced us to haul wood a great distance to keep the trains running. . . ."

Even after the Confederates had been driven back from the line, the raids by guerrillas continued. "These bands," said Mr. Fink in his report, "devote themselves to the destruction of cars, depots, bridges, and to stealing and plundering. On the 20th of February a train of 22 cars, loaded with Government mules, fell into the hands of guerrillas at Woodburn. They burned the cars with the mules in them, and started the locomotive, under a full head of steam, down the track. A collision with the passenger train coming in the opposite direction, and then due at the station, was only prevented by accident.

"On the 19th of March a passenger train was thrown from the track one and a half miles from Richland, by guerrillas who, after firing several volleys into the cars, commenced the work of plundering the passengers, and paroling the officers and soldiers aboard. But the bridge guard at Richland, having heard the firing, soon came to the rescue, and driving off the rebels, saved the train."

What the guerrillas apparently wanted to see was a good head-on collision. On June 13th, Mr. Fink continued, "a freight train going south fell into the hands of one of these bands at Elizabethtown, 42 miles from Louisville. They set fire to the cars and started the whole train, all in a blaze, down the road. Two miles south of the town it met a freight train coming north, but was fortunately discovered in time to prevent a serious collision."

In closing his report for this year Superintendent Fink spoke of the everlasting loyalty of L&N employees. He mentioned the great personal

danger many of them had been exposed to, and remarked they deserved
not only the thanks of the company, but also the thanks of their country
"in whose service this Road has been almost exclusively operated since
the beginning of the war."

Incidentally, Albert Fink went on to become one of the titans of railroading. After the war the L&N made him vice-president in charge of
operations. In 1874 he published *The Fink Report on the Cost of Transportation,* still regarded as the foundation stone of American writing on
railroad economics. He so managed the L&N that in the panic of 1873 it
was one of the few roads to escape bankruptcy and one of the fewer to
continue payment of interest on its funded debt. He was ready to retire
in 1877, but at the urgent request of several large trunk lines, he organized
the Trunk Line Association in an effort to settle the disastrous rate war
then in progress. This group brought some sort of order to the rate situation and continued to be effective until disbanded on formation of the
federal Interstate Commerce Commission.

It was also largely Fink's ability to keep the road in operation that
made the L&N the only Southern railroad to escape military seizure by
the Union government during the war. Apparently General McCallum
thought Fink and his men were doing as well or better with the harassed
line than military railroaders could.

Perhaps this is as good place as any to bring up the name of Daniel
Craig McCallum, which was never mentioned in any of the school histories of my time or of my father's time and which appears to be still, in
1947, virtually unknown to Americans who are not specialists in the War
Between the States. More than most general officers, McCallum was
responsible for the Union victory.

When the war broke out McCallum was 46 years old. He had been born
in Scotland, coming to the United States at an early age and teaching himself the rudiments of architecture and civil engineering. In 1859 he had
originated and patented what he called an Inflexible Arched Truss Bridge.
For two years he had served as general superintendent of the New York
& Erie Railroad. In 1861 he was president of the McCallum Bridge Company, specializing in railroad bridges. Early in 1862 Secretary of War
Stanton appointed him military director and superintendent of railroads
in the United States, giving him extraordinary war powers to seize and
operate all railroads and equipment necessary for successful prosecution of
the war. It was the first job of its kind, here or elsewhere, and to live up to
that job, even to conceive of such a job in that day, called for a good deal
of imagination and ability.

Commissioned a mere colonel, McCallum started with a seven-mile section of a haywire railroad in Virginia, and during the next three years
gradually took over 2,105 miles of road, and bossed 17,000 men who built

or rebuilt 641 miles of road or track and 26 miles of bridges, and operated 419 locomotives and some 600 cars.

Presently Secretary Stanton appointed another man to work in the railroad world, under the overall command of McCallum. This was Herman Haupt, an odd person of great energy, many fine qualities, and perhaps a few dubious ones. Haupt was a graduate of West Point who had served as a college professor and also as general manager of the Pennsylvania Railroad. When the war broke out he was still chief engineer and general factotum of the concern that for many years past had been drilling the Hoosac tunnel, long a political football in Massachusetts. Haupt was a man who made wonderful friends or terrible enemies of all who knew him. Seemingly, people could not be neutral about him.

As Colonel Haupt, however, he took hold of the chaotic railroad situation in Virginia and, with the backing and constant aid of General McCallum, accomplished marvels in the business of swift and ingenious repair. Haupt's greatest trial was the bullet-headed generals, as Nathaniel Hawthorne called them, all of whom wanted cars at one and the same time. Haupt told them off in right rugged style, paying no more attention to the biggest brass than he would have to the lowliest soldier. On a number of occasions, interference of military men with the railroads brought the Union armies close to disaster, but Secretary of War Stanton backed both McCallum and Haupt to the limit.

One of McCallum's greatest problems was to prevent Union commanders from using his freight cars as permanent warehouses and his passenger cars as permanent barracks or hospitals. McCallum knew, yet he had a dreadful time driving it into the heads of Union commanders, that the surest method to block a railroad and to render it useless was not to unload cars promptly on arrival, and turn them back whence they came. McCallum constantly pounded on the need to free cars as quickly as possible, and his strictures on eminent Union generals in this regard were quite blistering. He charged that more than one line in his care was carrying no more than one fifth of its capacity, simply because of unloaded cars at the front.

By the time of Sherman's Atlanta campaign, McCallum's efforts had taken effect, and every day for two hundred days, an average of 160 cars rolled over the single track of the L&N and connecting lines to supply Sherman's men. Judging by this record, the hoary tradition that Sherman's army lived entirely off the country does not stand up very well.

McCallum, who became a brigadier, then a major general, appeared to those who knew him well as of a cheerful and genial disposition, a man who seldom lost his temper even when the military commanders were at their bullet-headed worst. He was a powerfully built man and believed in strict discipline. He may also have been the sole major general of the Union Army who wrote verse, and shortly after the drums had ceased to beat, a group of his poems appeared in a volume entitled *The Water-Mill*. But no matter how powerful his frame, the strain of battling Union generals as well as Confederate armies took a heavy toll of General McCallum. He died after a year or so of ill health, in 1878, aged only sixty-three. It is a melancholy thing that the name of this man, who labored so well and so effectively for the Union cause, is never mentioned in our school history books, and in few other histories.

It is not my intention to narrate the history of the L&N since the end of the great war of the states. That has been done ably, as previously noted, by Mr. Herr. I should dislike to leave the subject, however, without noting that the gallant old road survived in fine shape all of the difficulties of peace, and of the wars to come. During the seventies the line suffered much from the fact that many connecting lines folded up; yet its trains continued to run, and soon the system was being expanded by purchase and new construction. It reached deep into Dixie, and presently had arrived at New Orleans. It survived a period when typically lawless natives occupied themselves with wrecking L&N property and trains, and when other natives enjoyed holding up its express and mail runs. It survived the buccaneering era of railroad buzzards, holding fast to its corporate title and becoming known, with good reason, as The Old Reliable. At the beginning of World War II the L&N operated almost 5,000 miles of road, and even though a majority of its capital stock was owned by the Atlantic Coast Lines, it was still very much an individual railroad, wearing no visible collar of Wall Street, as much an institution in its territory as, say, the Boston & Maine in New England, or the Burlington in Nebraska. It is a distinguished record for a road whose infancy was such as to have turned almost anything into a juvenile delinquent.

Harper's Weekly, Nov. 13, 1886

Immigrant cars of this type did much to help settle the West and thus create new business for the railroads.

"Four remarkably handsome drawing-room cars have been built lately for the Boston & Albany Railroad by the Wason Manufacturing Co., of Springfield, Mass.," the Railroad Gazette announced October 21, 1887, under this picture. The cars were finished in richly-carved mahogany, with metal work of statuary bronze, and were lit by electricity.

CHAPTER XI

The Big Junction

Player with railroads and the nation's freight handler. . . .
—CARL SANDBURG, 1916.

THERE is no other city in the United States so obviously the creation of railroads as Chicago. Whether one arrives by plane, train, bus, boat, or even on foot, the fact of the railroad is at once apparent, or is *felt*. The city is rated, and properly enough, both smoky and grimy; so is every other large city I was ever in, even New York, but it isn't merely locomotive smoke alone that tells the visitor to Chicago he has reached the great center of the rails. The whole atmosphere of the town is that of a gigantic railroad junction. It is brisk, and hurried, with the special hurry, nervous and staccato, one thinks of in relation to changing cars, of downing a doughnut and a cup of depot coffee between trains, while the station announcer waits, watch in hand, to call the next train for Boston, New Orleans, Houston, Seattle, and all way points.

No other city on earth has so many great railroad stations as Chicago. Step out of the Palmer House, the Morrison, the Stevens, any Loop hotel for a stroll in any direction and presently you come upon a railroad station of almost every sort of architecture you could imagine. There is the old Dearborn Street Station, with its gigantic shed, the whole affair hideous, quite dirty, breeding nostalgia for the days when all locomotives had diamond stacks and all conductors wore immense moustaches and fine cutaway coats. There is the rather severe Union Station, broodhouse of two trans-continentals, with its bookstore for literates and a fine Harvey eating room. There is the imposing Chicago & North Western with its ramps to the glossy and towering News building beside the river; the comparatively remote Illinois Central facing the Field Museum, and the Randolph Street Station of the Chicago, South Shore & South Bend, with its effect of catacombs and subterranean life; and the LaSalle Street and the copycat-named Grand Central. Each has a flavor all its own, each is quite wonderful with the sights, the smells, and the sounds inherent in the most exciting places Americans have built to date.*

---

* Few outlanders are able to name Chicago stations and the lines which use them. For the sake of the record, as of 1947, the lineup was as follows: Central Station—Illinois Central,

I am convinced it is its many railroad stations that make Chicago so exciting a city, for railroad stations are alive, throbbing, dynamic, charged with the urgency of life. Airports, even the largest, are dull indeed compared to a steamcar depot; and bus stations are no better. For one thing, they don't smell right; there is no excitement in the fumes of gasoline, even high-test gasoline; and when and if the railroads go wholly over to Diesel, then railroad stations will lose much in the coal gases that no longer will remind the traveler of far places beyond the city limits. For another thing, Diesels don't sound right, for the snorting of motors contains none of the magic of a locomotive with its nervous breathing; nor is the bray of an air horn any substitute for the melody of steam through a reed or the music of hammer on brass. And finally, at least to my mind, the sleekest plane ever made and the shiniest bus on the road are rather dull objects compared to a locomotive drowsing at the head of a long string of passenger cars.

Little wonder Chicago and its galaxy of railroad depots stands alone as the champion railroad junction of the country, and hence America's most exciting city.

It is in Chicago, and nowhere else, that the man from any corner of the Republic sees indications of roads he never rode on and perhaps never heard of. These are strange engines in the yards or pounding into or out of town, engines whose tenders carry names unknown in Maine or Florida or Oregon. Watch a bit and you'll see the Monon Route, the Alton, the Santa Fe, the Baltimore & Ohio, the Wabash, the Corn Belt Route, the Pere Marquette, the Soo Line, the Nickel Plate, the Chicago, Aurora & Elgin, and others.

Another thing that used to mark Chicago as the great rail center was the string of horse-drawn omnibuses that met, as the saying was, all the trains. These were visible signs of a concession known as the Parmalee Transfer Company, something of a monopoly, which moved most of the millions of travelers who changed cars in Chicago every year, and, because it was Chicago, also changed stations. The old Parmalee rigs are gone, though the company carries on with taxicabs and most tickets through Chicago still contain a small coupon marked "Parmalee Transfer," good for a ride from the Dearborn to the Union, or other depots.

Unsuspected to the common traveler is an underground Chicago of railroads, sixty-two miles of track beneath the city, much of it 40 feet down.

Michigan Central, Big Four; Dearborn Station—Santa Fe, Chicago & Eastern Illinois, Monon Route, Erie, Grand Trunk, Wabash; Grand Central Station—Baltimore & Ohio, Chicago Great Western, Soo Line, Pere Marquette; LaSalle Street Station—Rock Island, New York Central, Nickel Plate; Union Station—Alton, Burlington, Milwaukee Road, Pennsylvania; Chicago & North Western Station—Chicago & North Western Lines; the Chicago, North Shore & Milwaukee Railroad Station; and the Chicago, South Shore & South Bend Railroad Station.

This is the Chicago Tunnel Railway, and over its tracks 150 electric loco-motives and more than 3,000 cars deliver coal and other freight to the basements of Loop buildings, and take away ashes and more freight. It connects all of the freight terminals in town with all of the major build-ings.

The Chicago switching district embraces an area a little larger than Rhode Island, a conveniently sized state for comparisons, and contains nearly 8,000 miles of track. Some 600 freight trains enter or leave this switching district every day, Sundays included.

A total stranger might wonder how Chicago came to be such a center of the rails. The answer, if it had to be given in one word, would naturally be *location*. Yet, Chicago might not have become a tremendous railroad town so soon had it not been for a prophet and genius of the first mark.

So far as the early days of railroads in the eastern states were concerned, no really great genius of rails appeared. The pioneer roads all the way from Maine to Georgia were projected and built by all sorts of men, some of them able, some dismally unfit, but among them none—if Poor of the Grand Trunk be excepted—of whom one could say: Here was a true prophet and great genius of railroads. It remained for Chicago to present the first great railroad man. He was William Butler Ogden, who had been born in 1805 in Delaware County, New York, and in 1947 is all but for-gotten.

Before he arrived in Chicago in 1835, Ogden had been a strong advocate of the Erie Railroad, and although the next decade was to see him make a small fortune out of real estate, and another fortune because he loaned Cyrus McCormick $25,000 to make some kind of reaping machine, he never lost his interest in transportation. Off and on for ten years he dis-cussed with other Chicago business men the idea of building a railroad from that city into the West, perhaps even to the Mississippi River. Chi-cago, however, was not greatly interested. Most of its leading citizens were, in fact, against a railroad. One to the lead mines around Galena had been proposed, even chartered, but had been killed by the panic of 1837. Since that time, Chicago had come to believe its prosperity rested on Great Lakes shipping, plus the network of plank roads that had been built out of the city in every direction.

The plank-road idea seemed to almost everybody but Ogden to be the highway direct to Chicago's certain and glittering future. These roads were merely planks nailed to timbers on the ground. By the beginning of 1848 an average of 200 big wagons daily bumped into the city, and the road companies were rolling in wealth from the tolls. The shrewdest minds in the city held that the plank road constituted a revolution in transportation and that Chicago was growing great and wealthy because the plank-road spokes of her wheel ran north, south and west.

The plank roads developed professional teamsters, rough lads skilled in hogging the planks and crowding non-professional drivers off into the prairie mud. But many a farmer drove his own team into town, and the business grew so famously that Chicago set up a camp for them on the lake shore at the foot of Randolph Street. This great traffic was good for Chicago merchants, hotelkeepers and parasites. Whores carrying red lanterns prowled the vast tent camp at night. Gamblers came, too, and pickpockets, bunco steerers and assorted thugs. Somehow, because of legitimate business or by vice and thievery, every farmer and teamster managed to leave a good deal of cash in Chicago.

Thus Ogden could find little encouragement for his idea of a railroad. To quiet his continuous babble, Chicago's merchants at last told him a railroad would be the ruination of the city. It was a retail town, they said, and the farmers must come to town to trade. If they could ship their produce on a railroad, they would not come to the city at all. Other towns would grow up along the rails, too, and farmers would trade at the place nearest home. No, it wouldn't do. Everyone, or nearly everyone was getting rich as it was. Conditions must not be disturbed.

Ogden, as sharp and dynamic a character as ever went into the West, decided to leave his fellow citizens to their smug ideas of prosperity and plank roads. He took his cause direct to the farmers who lived out along the planks. In horse and buggy he drove across the flatlands to stop at every farm house and talk about the Galena & Chicago Union railroad, a moribund corporation he had revived for the sake of its charter, and to learn how they felt about a railroad. They felt pretty good about a railroad. Ogden next called meetings in log schoolhouses and barns for the purposes of selling stock. The farmers bought the stock, taking the cash out of sugar bowls and mattresses to pay a little down on a share. Within a short time Ogden had $250,000 on his subscription books. As soon as he had counted up his pot he acted swiftly, putting gangs to work building a railroad.

Chicago still didn't want a railroad cluttering up its waterfront. Its merchants and boss pimps defeated an ordinance which would have permitted the Galena & Chicago Union to have a depot within the city limits. Nevertheless, building and equipping the Galena went ahead. The rails, the locomotive, the cars, everything was secondhand, but workable. In November of 1848 Ogden and his board of directors rode out to the end of the line on the banks of the Des Plaines river, almost ten miles, and returned with a carload of wheat—the first of a host of such carloads. Within a week Chicago's drowsing merchants were startled to learn that no less than thirty carloads more of wheat were at the Des Plaines depot, waiting the little Galena & Chicago Union's freight train. They quickly killed their anti-railroad-depot ordinance; of a sudden it occurred to them that henceforth they could sell not only to Chicagoans and nearby farmers but to all the Northwest. They were beginning to see the vision Ogden had held before their eyes for a decade past, and it looked bright.

The first year of operation showed the new railroad to have earned better than $2,000 a month. Farmers along the line were elated with their first dividend checks. Ogden was running the road and running it well. He drove the rails still westward, reaching Elgin in 1850, Cherry Valley in 1852, Freeport a year later. In that year, too, Ogden became an active director in a new railroad east of Chicago, the Pittsburgh, Fort Wayne & Chicago, closely allied with the Pennsylvania. But Ogden's face was turned to the West. He pushed the Galena rails west and north until they came in contact with the Madison & Beloit, in Wisconsin. Ogden took over the M&B, extended it and later, after the financial troubles of '57, reorganized it into the Chicago & North Western, into which the Galena was also merged. Ogden now had the makings of a great railroad. He became president in 1859 and continued in that office for the next decade, meanwhile being elected the first president of the Union Pacific because of his great prestige in the railroad world and with the public.

As soon as Ogden had shown the dullard Chicago merchants that a railroad could do more for the town than any number of plank roads, they rejoiced exceedingly and called him a great man. His startling success with the Galena had also permeated the eastern centers of capital, which before then would not listen to such mad ideas as a railroad west of the Lakes. The Illinois Central, as related elsewhere in this book, began to build from one end of the state to the other. From Michigan, the two lines called the Central and the Southern were reaching for Chicago and were soon to get there. A good portion of the early construction of these lines was financed from New England. And with this new capital came John Murray Forbes of Boston.

Forbes was probably the only railroad man whom Ralph Waldo Emerson could and did characterize as a man of remarkable force, modesty, and all-round goodness. "How little," cried Emerson, referring to Forbes, "how little this man suspects, with his sympathy for men and his respect for lettered and scientific people, that he is not likely, in any company, to meet a man superior to himself." * That was a good deal to say, in the era of Vanderbilt and Drew and Gould and Fisk, of a railroad man. When he had taken hold of the Michigan Central and driven its rails to Chicago, Forbes looked to the West. He bought the tiny bankrupt outfit known as the Aurora Branch Railroad, called it the Chicago & Aurora, and extended it by purchasing several small, new, and penniless lines and arrived by these, in 1855, at the banks of the Mississippi in two places—at Quincy, Illinois, and at a spot just opposite Burlington, Iowa. The pattern of Forbes' new road, forged from odds and ends, now took its new and enduring name, the Chicago, Burlington & Quincy.

But Forbes wasn't done. With able associates, James F. Joy, late of

---

* Emerson, *Letters and Social Aims,* Boston, 1876.

Durham, New Hampshire, and John W. Brooks of Stow, Massachusetts, the Burlington raised more money and bought into the unfinished Hannibal & St. Joseph, in Missouri, which had laid only 35 miles of line in ten years, despite a land grant of half a million acres. Forbes and company completed the H&StJ, then tied it to the Burlington by a road from West Quincy to Palmyra, Missouri. Next, through working with the Burlington & Missouri River railroad, the Forbes road reached Omaha and thus made connection with the Union and Central Pacific system to the West Coast. From then to the present day the Burlington, or "The Q" as it is sometimes known to railroad men, has been one of the great systems of the country.

It is probably true, as contemporaries seem to have agreed, that the force of John Murray Forbes' personality was such as to imbue the Chicago, Burlington & Quincy with a character and a stability that "distinguished it sharply from other railroads of the era." Forbes was one of the few men of the time who thought of railroads in their relation to the public interest. The Burlington was fortunate, too, in its second president, Charles Elliott Perkins, a native of Ohio, who came up through the Burlington ranks to take the helm when Forbes dropped it, in 1881, and for the next two decades to run the line with great force and ability and, incidentally, to leave his mark on the West by his successful efforts to introduce alfalfa as a crop in Iowa and Nebraska.

With the Illinois Central, the two Michigan roads, the North Western, and the Burlington all touching Chicago, the city on the Lake began to take on the pattern of the railroad center of the United States; and civic leaders became imbued with the idea that they had believed in Chicago's future in the railroad world all along. I doubt that William Butler Ogden cared much one way or the other, just so long as the rails continued to reach out and civilize new territory. And they were reaching out too.

One of these lines was the Chicago, Rock Island & Pacific, which made something of a construction record under Henry Farnum by building, in less than two years, the 180 miles of road between Chicago and Rock Island, and then spanned the Mississippi with the first railroad bridge across that stream. It is interesting to note that the vice-president of the Missouri & Mississippi Railroad, which became a part of the Rock Island system, was William B. Ogden.

Another line in the pattern to make Chicago the colossus of rails was the present Alton, which, completed in 1854, got through to the city on the lake from St. Louis by connecting at Joliet with the Rock Island. Still another grew out of the two streaks of rust that had been the state-built Northern Cross Railroad, 50 miles of haywire between Meredosia, Illinois, and Springfield. N. H. Ridgeley of Springfield, with his associates James Dunlap and Joel Mattison, bought this wreck, which had cost the State of Illinois $406,233, for $20,000. The new owners laid new rails, built a few bridges, and purchased three locomotives and a few cars, then set up as a railroad. Things went pretty well, so the road was continued on across the state to the Indiana border where it met the Lake Erie, Wabash & St. Louis, then building westward. A little later these roads were merged into the Wabash System, with a line into Chicago.

What was to become another great rail system, a transcontinental, entered or left Chicago—either is correct—when the Chicago, Milwaukee & St. Paul Railway company was incorporated in 1872. Into this system went probably more predecessor lines than has been the case in any other railroad. Among the components, to name only a few, were the Milwaukee & Mississippi, the Milwaukee & Watertown, the Racine, Janesville & Mississippi, the Milwaukee & Northern, the Ontanagon & Brule River, the Wisconsin Union, the Menominee Branch, the Chicago & Pacific; and, as nearly as I can make out, around fifteen other midwestern lines.

Both the Pennsylvania and the New York Central, as noted earlier in this book, were early arrivals at the rising railroad metropolis, where for the next fifty years one or more railroad depots were continuously in the process of being constructed or rebuilt or enlarged; the work was nevei done. For the next fifty years, too, this or that railroad was seeking entrance to the magic spot at the foot of Lake Michigan.

With every new line to touch it, the city's population took a new leap. Cyrus McCormick saw early that it was to be a great railroad center. Armour, then Morris, then Swift picked Chicago as the place to get, kill, pack, and ship hogs and cattle. Montgomery Ward thought he could sell things to farmers by mail and that presently more mail trains would go out of Chicago in different directions than from any other place in the country. Ward drove his stakes by the lake. A few years later George Pullman saw the trend and moved his already huge industry from Detroit to Chicago. This city, indeed, was the place to make things and to ship them.

And where, a few years before, Chicago had fought against construction of even one railroad depot, it now wanted every railroad in the United States to come to Chicago and also to build there its own depot and terminal facilities. A goodly number of them did build depots, as has been said, and still use them in 1947. Many and widely separated depots were also a good thing for local business; and soon Parmalee was building his little feed and livery stable into a mighty monopoly of transportation from station to station, hauling travelers by the million every year.

The story of Frank Parmalee is in the best Horatio Alger tradition, although Parmalee was well on his way to success before the Master had penned his first Rags to Riches narrative. He was born Franklin Parmalee in Byron, Genesee County, New York, in 1816, and did not let go of life until eighty-eight years later. His folks were impecunious farmers, an occupation young Frank made up his mind not to follow. When he was twelve he left the farm and went to work as a relay boy for a stage concern, continuing in one capacity or another for stage companies until 1837, when he shipped as purser aboard a steamer on the General Reed Line, between Erie, Pennsylvania, and Chicago.

For the next sixteen years the young man rode the Great Lakes, saving his money for the day when he might find something really interesting. This proved to be the new city of Chicago, which was beginning to show signs of becoming a railroad town. In company with Liberty Bigelow and David Gage, Parmalee formed a concern to transfer travelers from dock to railroad station or hotel. This was in 1853. Two years later Frank Parmalee & Company obtained a charter for the first street railway in Chicago and operated as the City Omnibus Line between Lake Street Bridge and Archer Road.

Meanwhile, however, Parmalee had been building up the transfer business, adding more horses and rigs every little while, and advertising—and meaning it—that his agents were to be found at all railroad and boat routes running out of the city. He must have chosen these agents with some care, for they got the trade and held it through the years until the name of Parmalee and Chicago city transportation were synonymous. Frank Parmalee also set about to improve on the old coach style of horse-drawn rigs. He and his men devised a rear-loading type, with seats running lengthwise, and a baggage rack on top, plus three auxiliary seats behind the driver. These carriages were unique and as distinctive, in their design and a very special tint of green paint, as they were luxurious. To draw them were two horses to the rig, the finest, swore Frank Parmalee, a man who knew animals, the finest horses barring none owned by any concern in the country.

To top off this elegant equipage, the Parmalee drivers were not only good horsemen but genial and polite. They were all dressed in uniform clothing, which changed with the years but was always pretty fine, something to remember. At one gorgeous period, the Parmalee men appeared in long square-cut coats, the fronts of which were set off by two long rows of bright brass buttons; and a helmet for a hat. At another time, the square coats gave way to important looking swallow-tails, and the helmets were displaced by a sort of soldier cap with long peak and low crown. At any old time during a period of about sixty-five years, or until about the time of World War I, Parmalee men were easily visible, and became drab only when drabness became the style.

To keep his horseflesh the best possible, Parmalee early established a farm for the breeding and conditioning of these animals. The finest mares and studs in the land were purchased for the Parmalee stable-farm. The great fire of 1871 destroyed a number of the Parmalee animals, as well as the headquarters of the company, then at State and Randolph streets. A year later came a terrible horse epidemic, which killed a majority of the animals in Chicago and the region generally. Parmalee was so hard hit by this disaster, and the fact he could not buy animals elsewhere, that he was forced to hitch fourteen yoke of oxen to as many drays and carriages. Incidentally, at the peak of the company's career in the horse-and-buggy age, it required 1,200 animals to keep Parmalee rigs moving.

Frank Parmalee kept a close eye on the railroads. He got to know their officials. When a new line entered Chicago, Parmalee was ready to have one of his genial agents get aboard the trains just outside the city in order to aid passengers in planning their movements from station to station, or to hotel or dock. Parmalee agents knew all the answers, too. They were neatly dressed in uniform style, and were an agreeable contrast to the bunco steerers of various rackets who had been operating on American travelers since the earliest coaching days. A Parmalee agent was known to be honest. He was instructed to advise the passenger in the passenger's best interests, no matter if Parmalee lost a fare in the process. It wasn't long before Parmalee men were considered as worthy the trust of the traveler as were conductors or policemen.

In 1885 Frank Parmalee bought out his partners, and he ran the business with a sure hand until 1903, when he sold out to a Chicago syndicate composed of Marshall Field, John J. Mitchell, Frank Lowden, John C. Shaffer, and others. In 1929, to bring matters down to date, the company was sold to its present owners and the name later changed to Parmalee Transportation Company. By July 1921 the last of the Parmalee horses had been sold, and the company was completely motorized.

Parmalee employes of the present day are conscious of the long and honorable history of their company. They like to recall that Abraham Lincoln always took a Parmalee bus from the IC station to his hotel when he came to town from Springfield. Nearly all great Americans, at least nearly all of them who ever passed through or stopped at Chicago, were riders in Parmalee carriages or cars. And foreigners, too. Perhaps the heaviest single strain on the Parmalee rigs was occasioned whenever Sarah Bernhardt came to town; her baggage ran to forty trunks, big ones, trunks to call for two stout Parmalee men apiece. Incidentally, it is also recalled that U. S. Grant, even when he was President of the United States, never carried more than two modest trunks.*

Chicago prospered from the railroads in many ways, and one of them was the fact that all travelers had to change cars—and usually stations—when they got there. No passenger trains ran *through* Chicago. A freight train was different! Freights carried no human beings, except a few bums and hoboes who didn't count, and hence there was no good reason to halt

---

* Much of the author's information regarding Parmalee has come in letters from W. A. Scheeder, general manager of the company in 1947, who went to some effort to collect the facts for me. I am amazed that a company with so long a history as Parmalee's has never been made the subject of a monograph or pamphlet. Another old and honorable firm, the Chicago & North Western Railroad, is as bare of historical writing as it is filled with historical material.

freight trains at Chicago. But travelers and tourists spent money, just as the plank-road teamsters had done in the days when the Chicago & Galena Union was the city's only railroad and not wanted at that. As the years went by, styles changed, but basically Chicago remained the same, and it built many hotels and even more flophouses and saw to it that no traveler passed through Cook County without stopping to change cars, and stations, and to get a whiff of the bracing lake air.

During the years some thoughtful member of the traveling public stood up now and again to ask of the railroads why Chicago remained as a sort of boundary between East and West, why no passenger, except on a very special train, could get through without changing cars. The reply, which in time became standardized and immutable, was that the idea was "impracticable." Aye, and so had been air brakes on freight trains before old Alonzo Coffin clubbed the roads over their heads with Mr. Westinghouse's new invention. So had been automatic couplers. So, by the gods and except on the Alton road, had been Pullman sleeping cars.

There was more in the reply of "impracticable" than merely the reason cited; in it, many a man came to believe, was evidence of that creeping paralysis of the Railroad Mind which had been setting in, ever so gradually, since the 1890's. This mind had come in large to defend automatically the status quo, so far as innovation was concerned. It had remained unshaken almost while buses took away so much of its passenger traffic, and while motor trucks took large bites of first, its short-haul freight traffic, then its long-distance freight. Yes, and while airlines did the same thing.*

So the matter rested until 1946, when the Chesapeake & Ohio Railway Company prepared and inserted in leading newspapers and magazines a startling proposal. This paid advertisement began by saying that a hog could travel across the country without changing trains, but a human being couldn't. It went on to mention Chicago as "an invisible barrier down the middle of the United States which you cannot cross without inconvenience, lost time, and trouble." It indicated also that the situation in St. Louis and New Orleans was comparable.

The announcement stated that 500,000 persons, which with excellent psychology it termed "victims," had during 1945 been forced to make double Pullman reservations, pack and transfer their baggage, and wait around for connections, all because of this "phantom Chinese wall which splits America in half." Canada isn't split down its middle; there is no barrier such as Chicago at Toronto or Winnipeg. If American railroads

---

* From about 1925 to 1940 was a sad time for us old-fashioned likers of railroads and loathers of automobiles. During that period I did much traveling, east and west, and never once by bus if a railroad touched where I was going, nor by plane. But it was patent to me, as I occupied almost alone an entire Pullman or coach, that railroads, in spite of a few notable efforts of certain lines, were letting business get away without a struggle.

want to do away with the Chicago barrier, they can readily do so by cooperating to provide through service. Yet, to date, read the announcement, "the Chesapeake & Ohio and the Nickel Plate alone have made a public offer to do so."

At about the same time as the C&O announcement, Robert R. Young, chairman of that company's board, together with a few other railroad men and industrialists, made a bid for that part of the Pullman Company's business having to do with the ownership and operation of its sleeping and parlor cars. The government had long since told the Pullman people they were a horrid monopoly and must sell either their business of manufacturing cars or their business of operating them. Pullman chose to sell the latter. The sale to a group of railroads, made in 1945, was approved by the government in 1947.

Of even greater interest than the Chesapeake & Ohio's proposal about Chicago was a letter sent in 1946 to a selected list of Americans by Chairman Young of the C&O. In it, with no fumbling for words, he stated flatly that if the railroads were to continue prosperous they must acquire "a new state of mind." Their present state of mind, he intimated, is best understood by knowing that only a few years ago a number of roads agreed *not* to install air-conditioning. And where, asked Mr. Young, would the automobile business be if it had conspired not to install starters? Mr. Young went on to charge—and to the echoing cheers of millions of his fellow citizens—that the American railroad industry spends less to promote its offerings to the public than any one of the larger automobile makers. He charged that although he had tried, he has been unable to find another road, except the C&O's Nickel Plate subsidiary, to cooperate in sleeping-car service through Chicago and St. Louis. "Unless such steps are taken," he concluded, "and by which road or roads doesn't matter, for the others will follow, we shall not see the development of more convenient and attractive rail travel in this country, which we all know is possible."

Whatever may have instigated Mr. Young's outburst, it brought almost immediate results. At least two Western roads and two Eastern lines presently announced they were prepared to book Pullman passengers through Chicago without change. Many other roads soon followed.

Robert Young is more than a forced draft under the railroad boiler. His performance among the steam carriers has been such as to remind more than one observer of the style and ability of the late Commodore Vanderbilt. Although he does not have the Commodore's whiskers, and weighs but 135 pounds, he has become, at the tender age of fifty, one of the great figures in railroading.

A native of the Texas Panhandle, son of a well-heeled cattleman, he left college in his freshman year, married, and went to work for Du Pont at 28 cents an hour. By 1929 he was financial adviser to John J. Raskob, one of Du Pont's top men, who fired the youngster because of his "pessimistic" outlook. Seems Young told Raskob that a depression was about due.

Young made his first million during the dismal years of the early 1930's, then with friends bought control in several properties, among them the Chesapeake & Ohio, the Pere Marquette, and the Nickel Plate railroads. He worked wonders with these carriers, and early in 1947 began buying into Commodore Vanderbilt's old empire, the New York Central. Presently he announced that he had control of that road, even though he owned but 5 per cent of its stock.

In the meantime, Young lived high in the manner of industrial barons of the late nineteenth century, with a mansion at Newport, another at Palm Beach, and other homes. Unusual in such a mogul, he is a competent writer, and the concise and direct and grammatical copy put out under the names of his various railroads is his own composition. He would have made a great pamphleteer in ebullient eighteenth-century days, for his stuff hits hard, nor is it without both grace and humor. He has even written verse, some in blank form, and many a poet has made a reputation on a lesser product.

Whatever Young manages to do with the railroad empire that seems now in his hands—and may well include the Missouri Pacific—his berserker rage at the "antediluvian railroads," his fulminations against the works of the Interstate Commerce Commission, against the Association of American Railroads, out of which group he has taken his lines, and against the bankers, who he says are revolting, have surely had no little effect on the railroad system of the entire country. Perhaps he is a true historical business character in the making.

CHAPTER XII

The Rebel Route's Abraham Lincoln

Colonel Falkner started the railroad and was also author of the White Rose of Memphis. . . .

—Gulf, Mobile & Northern News.

A S THESE trains thunder into their terminal at the north or draw their freighted commerce to the shores of the southern sea, they realize the life dream of the silent sleeper in the Tippah Hills, whose sculptured figure, mute, inscrutable, stands guard in the quiet graveyard over the destinies of this creature of his vision." By which gifted prose an inspired writer meant to say that William C. Falkner was buried in Ripley, Mississippi, not far from the tracks of the present Gulf, Mobile & Ohio Railroad*.

Such lilting periods are proper for the subject, who was a soldier of the Old South passionately fond of oratory and who also was probably the only railroad president to write a popular novel, such as Colonel Falkner's *The White Rose of Memphis* unquestionably was. It is without hyperbole and with every right that the Gulf, Mobile & Ohio called itself The Rebel Route. No other Southern road has a better Confederate ancestry. And what is more, no other Southern railroad operates, as does The Rebel Route in 1946, two trains named *The Abraham Lincoln* and *The Ann Rutledge*. How such an unthinkable, such an incredible condition came about is quite a story, and it discovers railroads in the benign character of catalyst of the Blue and the Gray.

Like most other railroads of mature age, The Rebel Route is composed of a number of antecedents, the most colorful of which was the oddly named Ripley, Ship Island & Kentucky, two thirds of which title were and always remained pure oratory. This line was the child of good Colonel Falkner. Another and more important antecedent was the Mobile & Ohio, which in time actually did reach the Ohio River. This latter line, organized in 1848 by Mobile businessmen under the leadership of M. J. D. Baldwin, was projected and built for the purpose of getting north to the junction of

---

* "Life of Colonel Falkner, A Glorious Word Picture of the Founder by One Who Has Studied His Life," by Edmund Winston, in *GM&N News*, Mobile, Ala., Nov. 27, 1925.

the Ohio with the Mississippi River in order to divert freight and passengers—which otherwise would go to the Gulf by way of river steamers, to the port of Mobile. When the Civil War broke out, the line had got to Columbus, Kentucky. And there it stopped. For the next four years the M&O was battered and wrecked almost its entire length as opposing armies used or abused it according to the situation. Rails, trestles, bridges, depots were pulled up, torn down, or dynamited. Even the road's shops at Mobile were destroyed.

Next came the notorious era of the carpetbaggers, when the impoverished South was overrun by a horde of Northerners made up of a few able and decent men and a multitude of adventurous thugs and catchpoles. Somehow, the M&O survived, and its determined directors put it together as best they could and resumed operation with such rolling stock as could be collected and repaired. Then came the panic of 1873, which resulted in a receivership, and for the next several years the carrier knew hard times indeed. It continued to add a few miles of track each year, however, and in 1883 it at last arrived at its objective, the Ohio River at North Cairo, Illinois. Three years later it took over the narrow-gauge St. Louis & Cairo and widened it. The route now reached from St. Louis to Mobile and had some 650 miles of track.

The other main stem of what was to become The Rebel Route did not get under way until 1872. In that year its founder, the aforementioned Colonel William C. Falkner, was forty-seven years old. He had' served with distinction in the Rebel army, and with the end of the fighting returned to Ripley, Mississippi, to practice law. He got to thinking that Ripley, a mere backwoods hamlet to which freight had to be hauled by team, ought to have better contact with the world. Falkner did not have much capital, but he did possess eloquence, which in the South of that day was rated higher than capital, and he had an idea—a railroad from Ripley to tap the Memphis & Charleston at Middleton, Tennessee, twenty miles north. He put all of his own meager capital into the plan and applied to the state for a charter for the Ripley, Ship Island & Kentucky; and also for the $4,000 per mile subsidy which the State of Mississippi had agreed to pay to railroads built within its borders. Charter in hand, Colonel Falkner went out on tour of the countryside to raise additional cash from farmers and villagers along the proposed route.

Colonel Falkner was very successful. He must have had a winning personality, as well as the reputation of a Southern military hero, for he got his fellow Mississippians, nearly all of them made poor by the war, to supply cash and other aid in plenty. Some cleared the right-of-way. Others furnished lumber and ties and timbers. Many turned out to lay the rails. Much of this was donated labor. Among those paying cash for stock were the Harris, the Hines, and other well-to-do families, but the heaviest stockholder of all came to be R. J. Thurmond. a well-heeled and hotheaded person who wanted to become the Commodore Vanderbilt of Southern rails.

The twenty miles of railroad were completed within twelve months, but when Falkner went to collect his $4,000 per mile subsidy from the state, he discovered that the subsidy applied only to standard-gauge roads, while his own was narrow-gauge. Now, Falkner was neither a lawyer nor a Southerner for nothing. He appeared before the Mississippi Legislature and there waxed so eloquent about the little Ripley, Ship Island & Kentucky that the dazed and charmed servants of the state granted the cash immediately.

Now encouraged, Falkner began to extend the line southward, building toward Pontotoc. In those days, as in more recent times, all Southern states made a practice of leasing their convicts, generally to railroad and highway contractors and logging operators. A large gang of these felons was used to build the extension of Falkner's road, which by now, in the flush of enthusiasm of the subsidy, had become the Gulf & Chicago, indicating the rosy hopes of its owners.

In the convict deals with the state, the state held the contractor responsible for every prisoner. So the contractor hired as tough and brutal a crew of guards as could be found. While the guards stood with rifles ready, the overseer walked up and down the right-of-way where the poor devils were at work, a big bull whip in hand, cracking it with vicious snaps to remind them of his presence. If one of them faltered under the hot sun, the long whip cut the air to some purpose and a convict lost a piece of ear or was otherwise marked for life. Every foot of the way between Ripley and Pontotoc, some forty miles, said a local commentator, was marked with blood and brutality.

It was much cheaper to shoot dead on the spot any convict who made a break for liberty than to chase him. The guards were trigger-quick, and many prisoners died before they could reach the comparative safety of the pine woods close to the tracks. One such victim lies buried beside the rails near the little station of Gayle. His name isn't known, but he was a Frenchman of France who, so folklore has it, had been railroaded to prison by some ambitious prosecuting attorney for a crime he did not commit. Folklore leans that way. In any case, after a stretch of work under the contractor's whips and guns, the Frenchman decided anything else was to be preferred. He made a break for the woods and was shot down and buried where he fell. A kindly section foreman, John Walls, is said to have erected the small wooden cross that now marks the grave and enclosed the spot with a low picket fence. It has been cared for from that day to this by the railroad, and is often pointed out to travelers as The Frenchman's Grave, one of the sights of The Rebel Route.

Falkner's carrier was busy and prosperous almost from the first, and its sixty-odd miles of steel were kept warm and polished by the wheels of freights and passenger trains pulled by the *Dollie* and the *Tanglefoot*, which had to speed up as fast as possible in order to get over the slight grades. Colonel Falkner was a man who knew that good will meant much, and so long as he ran the road it had the best will in the world from people along the route. In 1889 the Mobile & Ohio, which had been building a new line west of its original stem, took over the Falkner road and made connections at Pontotoc. In that year, too, Colonel Falkner was elected to the Mississippi Legislature in a typical rough-and-tumble campaign against R. J. Thurmond who, as related, was a heavy stockholder in the Falkner railroad. On November 6, 1889, Falkner had just verified the election returns and was standing in the street, talking, when Thurmond appeared with a revolver in hand. The Colonel extended his arm. Thurmond fired, the bullet entering Falkner's mouth and coming out at the back of his head.

Colonel Falkner was the second member of the railroad's board of directors to die of gunfire. Six months previously General William Wirt Adams, postmaster at Jackson, Mississippi, and active in the Falkner road, engaged in a street duel with John Martin, arrogant and fire-eating editor of the *New Mississippian*. Both men were excellent shots and both died in the street, then and there.

What sort of a funeral Adams received at Jackson I do not know, but the people of Ripley turned out to do their old hero proud, and a bit later they erected the imposing monument on his grave at Ripley. At its top, in white marble, stands the old gentleman, frock-coated, wonderfully bearded, one hand in pocket, the other arm extended as if to point to the rails he is facing, a tribute to one of the most colorful railroaders of his place and time.*

The early Rebel Route train crews were, properly enough, spirited men, and the company had some difficulty preventing its engineers from racing the trains of the New Orleans & North Eastern, whose tracks paralleled those of the Rebel Route for many miles through the cotton fields around Meridian, Mississippi. But the racing influence did not quite die, for John Luther Jones, the immortal Casey, got his start railroading on The Rebel Route, and much later, on April 30, 1900, to be exact, he drove an Illinois Central locomotive straight into legend and into the most celebrated of railroad ballads.†

---

* The Falkner literary line did not die with the Colonel. Two of his great-grandsons, William and John Faulkner(sic), are novelists, the former rated particularly high among the literati.

† "The Casey Jones angle of the GM&O," writes Freeman Hubbard in a letter to the author, "has never been adequately handled. Not only did Casey learn railroading on a predecessor of the road, but his only surviving son, Charles, also began on the GM&O and his only daughter, Helen, is the wife of a GM&O employee today (1947). The oldest GM&O engineer in seniority is Casey's brother-in-law, Joseph C. Brady. Casey lies buried in Jackson, Tenn.,

Another ex-Rebel Route employee who became somewhat famous was Wilson W. Brown, a corporal in the Andrews Raiders. Incongruously enough in one who had worked for the Mobile road, Brown served in the Union Army and volunteered for the raiding party that stole the Confederate locomotive, *The General*, and took part in the celebrated flight of that engine that has gone into many books and into the movies.*

The modern Rebel Route, so modern that it is still expanding in 1947 and also improving its equipment, stems from 1920, when a young Tennessean, Isaac Burton Tigrett, took over as temporary president, a position he has held ever since. Tigrett was a country boy, a Baptist preacher's son, who grew up near Jackson, Tennessee, and still makes his home there. In 1911, through his connections with the small Union Bank & Trust Company of Jackson, he became treasurer of a tinpot railroad, grandiosely named the Birmingham & Northwestern, which got neither to Birmingham, nor anywhere near it, nor into any region that in wildest imaginative flight could be termed "Northwest."

To be more exact, the B&N was almost fifty miles of light and uncertain rails between Jackson and Dyersburg, Tennessee. It possessed two second-hand locomotives and a few wobbly coaches and boxcars. Its engineers hesitated to run faster than 20 miles an hour because of the crooked road-bed and the all-round insecurity of both bed and rails. The trains were as often off the track as on. One passenger who considered riding the B&N the experience of a lifetime, and said so in a remark often quoted to this day, was the lion tamer of a small circus that was moved from Jackson to Dyersburg, by nobody but the B&N, in the elapsed time of exactly 21 hours—or at a rate of approximately one mile every 26 minutes. "I have been sticking my head in a cat's mouth for ten years," said the circus man, "and I'll stick it in there and leave it, before I'll ever ride this goddam railroad again." †

Treasurer Tigrett was made president of the B&N in 1912. He improved its equipment and service beyond recognition. He also became a director of the Gulf, Mobile & Northern, and when that carrier was turned back to its directors after Federal operation during World War I, Tigrett, 26 years old, was appointed temporary president. In this position he began acquiring rail lines to expand what he was pleased to call The Rebel Route. He first picked up his old friend the Birmingham & Northwestern and merged it. In 1925 he added the 25-mile Memphis & Meridian. Next came

---

really the unofficial capital of the GM&O, for in that town lives President Tigrett, the genius of the line. Near his office, in a boarding house, lives Mrs. Casey Jones, widow of the famous engineer."

* For a clear, accurate and exciting account of the Andrews Raid see Freeman Hubbard's *Railroad Avenue*, cited elsewhere in this book.

† The incident is vouched for by Robert Talley, in an article in the *Memphis Commercial Appeal*, June 17, 1945.

the Jackson & Eaton, all of 15 miles, but which gave him a chance to extend its track to Jackson, Mississippi, where connection was made with the New Orleans & Great Northern. Tigrett still wanted a route into New Orleans. He got it in 1929, when his Rebel Route acquired the New Orleans & Great Northern on a 99-year lease, gaining entrance to the city by way of Slidell, Louisiana. In 1935 he gave the South its first stream-liner, *The Rebel,* and the world its first train hostess, Miss Kathryn Sullivan.

In 1940 the GM&N made its greatest single expansion, up to then, by taking over the bankrupt Mobile & Ohio. Out of the merger came the Gulf, Mobile & Ohio. The system now linked St. Louis with both Mobile and New Orleans, and embraced almost 2,000 miles of road. Then, in 1946, The Rebel Route acquired the ancient and honorable but seriously ailing Chicago & Alton, a line dating from 1847 and over which Mr. Pullman, as related elsewhere in this book, operated his first sleeping car and first diner.

The merger of the Alton and GM&O presents a most striking case of a blending of the Blue and the Gray. "The Alton Route" has been painted on The Rebel streamliners that operate between St. Louis and points south. North of St. Louis the Alton will carry on. Two of the Alton's best trains are *The Abraham Lincoln* and *The Ann Rutledge.* Lincoln is buried in a town on the Alton, even though the traveler cannot see the tomb from the train. The Rebel Route's streamliners, *The Rebel* and *The Little Rebel,* still run to Montgomery and Mobile, both once temporary capitals of the Confederate States of America.

It looks like a task, this harmonizing traditions of the North and the South, but those who know President Ike Tigrett believe he is wholly capable of accomplishing the feat. He has long been an admirer of Lincoln and even went so far as to make the GM&O slogan "The Alton Route," rather than "The Rebel Route" which had been used for many years.

One hopes that President Tigrett can integrate the traditions of the Blue and the Gray, the latter remaining particularly strong in the GM&O's southern territory.

Although it was a Southern line that bought a Northern line, and the GM&O is retaining its corporate title—merely adding "The Alton Route" as its slogan—I wonder how sleeps old Colonel William Falkner, C. S. A., there in Ripley, beside the track—that "pulsating, hurrying high-way of commerce and travel," as one of the Colonel's biographers has it. I wonder if the Colonel will not stir restlessly "every time the roar of a passing train resounds in the hills beyond, every time the shrill blast of its whistles echoes o'er the intervening vales," even though as "these vehicles of commerce pass northward and southward, they perpetuate the memory of this man whose genius and hard work made their existence in these hills possible."

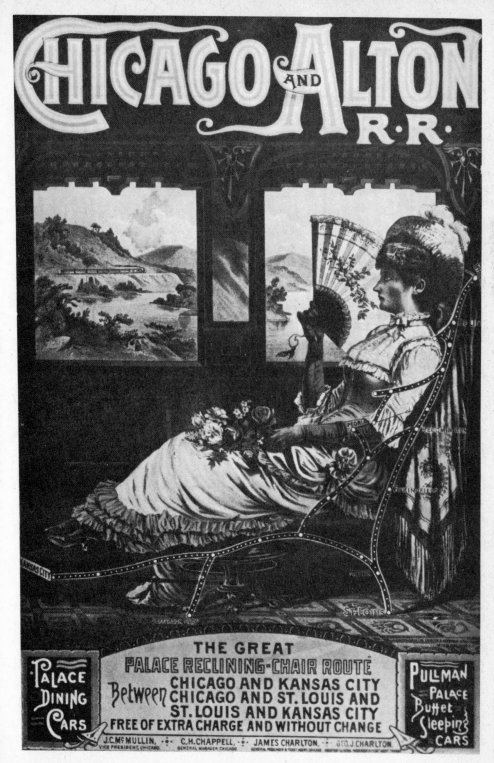

Poster of the 1880's advertising the road on which the first Pullman car ran, a road recently taken over by the GM&O. Note that the drawing of the seat is a map of the route.

New York & Erie Rail Road

RATES OF CHARGES,

For FREIGHT, between the City of New York and the Depots in

MIDDLETOWN, NEW HAMPTON, GOSHEN & CHESTER.

1845.

NAMES OF ARTICLES.		New York to or from		
		MIDDLETN.	N. HAMP'N.	GOSHEN
Ale, Beer, Porter, Vinegar and domestic spirits (in wood) per 100 lbs.				
Apples and Pears in Barrels or Baskets,				
Bacon, Hams or other smoked Meats, in casks or boxes,				
Beans, Peas, Clover, Timothy, Flax or other kinds of seed,				
Beef and Pork (salt) Fish of all kinds,				
Beef and Pork (fresh) Lard and tallow,				
Boots, Hats, Boots, Carriages, Cartas,				
Boots and shoes, in boxes, (by mens unt12½ lbs per cubic ft.)				
Cotton (in bales) Hops, Wooden ware,				
Chair Rail bedstead Stuff bench handles, (turned stuff,				
Crockery Queensware, dried fruit, Cabinet ware,				
Dry Goods, and Medicines, Segars and sugar boxes,				
Flour and Meal, in barrels,				
Feathers, Furs, lasts in boxes, (by mens unt 20 lbs per cub. ft.)				
Furniture, empty casks and boxes (by mens'nt 12½ lbs per cub ft.)				
Fresh Fish, Lamb, Veal, Mutton,				
Glassware, China, Brooms, Umbrellas, Whips,				
Grain of all kinds, Hay (if pressed) Salt				
Groceries (and Cotton in bales of all kinds,				
Hardware and Cutlery, Painted and Dry Stuffs,				
Molasses, Sugars in casks, Dried Fish, Rice,				
Nails, Spikes, bolts and bar Iron,				
Oranges, Lemons and Pine Apples in boxes- Melons,				
Potatoes, Turnips, Beets and similar vegetables,				
Oysters, Clams, and other shell fish,				
Poultry, Eggs, Game, Honey, Venison,				
Pork, Lard, in barrels- Dry Hides, Hair, Pelts,				
Wines and Foreign Spirits, in wood, Window Glass,				
Wool, woolen or Cotton baiting, Twine, wicking,				

NAMES OF ARTICLES.			New York to or from		
			MIDDLETN.	N. HAMP'N.	GOSHEN	CHESTER
Calves, less than 3 months old		per head			
do do Move than 3 mo. and less than 12 mo. old					
do do In lots of 10 or more					
Cows and other cattle except Oxen,	In lots of 20 or more				
do do In lots of 20 or more					
Oxen, weighing less than 1200 lbs each	In lots of 16 or more				
do do weighing more than 1500 lbs. each.	In lots of 12 or more				
Sheep (special bargains for large droves)	In lots of 20 or more				
Lambs	In lots of 20 or more				
Hogs live, weighing not more than 150	In lots of 30 or more				
Butter in firkins,	In lots of 20 or more	per firkin, each.			
Flour and Meal in barrels,		per barrel,			
Pork, Beef or Fish, salted in barrels	In lots of 20 or more	per barrel,			
do do do	In lots of 20 or more	per barrel,			
Salt barrels,	In lots of 20 or more	per barrel,			
do in sacks of 240 lbs.		per sack,			
do in bags of 145 lbs.	In lots of 50 or more	per bag,			
Oysters and Clams in barrels,	In lots of 50 or more,	per barrel,			

☞ For rates of charges on articles not specified, and for other particulars, see table of rates published July 1st, 1843.

Passengers to New York can procure Tickets at the following rates: From MIDDLETOWN $1 75; NEW HAMPTON $1 62 1-2; GOSHEN $1 50; CHESTER $1 40.

Merchants, Grocers, and others receiving Freight regularly by the Rail Road, the charges on which amount to One Hundred Dollars or more per annum, can procure a commutation Ticket for $10 per quarter, giving the person named thereon, the free use of the Road.

Farmers wishing twenty Gallons of Milk per day, may commute.

Farmers or others going to market with their own produce, the charges on which amount to five dollars or more, run procure a free Ticket to return, and if the charges amount to ten dollars, free tickets both ways will be given.

Families and **Parties** can procure tickets to New York and return the same day, as follows : for both ways, from Middletown $2 50; New Hampton $2 37½; Goshen $2 25; Chester $2 00, but the tickets cannot be used on any other day, without the payment of the difference between this and the regular rates for single tickets.

Families or **Parties** paying one fare or more tickets to any Depot or Station upon the Line of the Road, may return the same day free, or if the tickets are for the Evening Train they may return by the next morning train on the same conditions.

The above provisions in relation to passages free or by commutation, have been made with a desire to meet the business wants of the citizens of Orange County, and is hoped that the usefulness of the road will be promoted thereby. A general reduction of the present low rates charged upon the road, it is feared, would prove injurious to both stockholders and the public. During the close of navigation below the Highlands, the full rates will be charged. No departure from the above terms.

June 1845.

Erie freight rate table — 1845

I feel certain that Colonel Falkner would not like the removal of "The Rebel Route" from the cars, but I trust that replacing that brave slogan with "The Alton Route" will somewhat alleviate the pain. It surely will, if the Colonel reflects well on the name, in which case he might even like it. It was the pro-slavery element of Alton, Illinois, that lynched Elijah R. Lovejoy, in his time the leading Abolitionist in all the North.

CHAPTER XIII

Land—*Uncle Sam's Alternate Sections*

Well, sir, it is a great quantity of land; and unless some grant of the kind proposed be made, it will never command ten cents.
—The Hon. W. R. KING, in Congress, 1850.

A BILL granting a large expanse of land to something called the St. Croix & Bayfield Railroad Company was before Congress when, on the memorable 27th of January, 1871, the Hon. James Proctor Knott of Kentucky arose in the House to offer, as he said, a few remarks pertinent to the subject. No fellow member was electrified, none sat up in his seat when Mr. Knott was granted the floor for ten minutes. Mr. Knott spoke rarely. His fellow Congressmen considered him a sluggish, not to say a downright lazy person, and his entrance into the debate occasioned not a ripple of interest either on the floor or in the galleries.

Sluggish or not, it seems patent that on this occasion Mr. Knott's mind was slightly fogged, for when he got to his feet and opened his mouth he firmly believed he was speaking against a land-grant bill for a company that proposed its terminus be at a place called Duluth. That he was doing no such thing, but instead was speaking against a bill that the people of Duluth really wanted killed, had no effect whatever on the eloquence that was to pour out of the classically vocal Kentuckian.

"Years ago," began the Hon. J. Proctor Knott, in what ten minutes later was to be, and remain, the most celebrated speech ever delivered in the House. "Years ago, when I first heard that there was somewhere in the vast *terra incognita,* somewhere in the bleak regions of the great North-west, a stream of water known to the nomadic inhabitants of the neighbor-hood as the River St. Croix, I became satisfied that the construction of a railroad from that raging torrent to some point in the civilized world was essential to the happiness and prosperity of the American people. . . . I felt instinctively that the boundless resources of that prolific region of sand and shrubbery would never be fully developed without a railroad con-structed and equipped at the expense of the government, and perhaps not then. I had an abiding presentiment that, some day or other, the people of this whole country, irrespective of party affiliations, would rise in their majesty and demand an outlet for the enormous agricultural productions of those vast and fertile pine-barrens, drained in the rainy season by the surging waters of the turbid St. Croix. . . ."

The honorable gentlemen of the House began to sit up in their seats and to feel that, surprisingly enough in view of its source, something was in store for them. It was. Had they been mistaken about Mr. Knott all these years, they wondered? Had they been sitting on a log only to find it an alligator? The gentleman from Kentucky cleared his throat, and shifted the weight of his body to the other foot.

"Duluth!" he cried, "Duluth! The word fell on my ear with a peculiar and indescribable charm, like the gentle murmur of a low fountain stealing forth in the midst of roses, or the soft, sweet accents of an angel's whisper in the bright, joyous dream of sleeping innocence. Duluth! 'Twas the name for which my soul had panted for years, as the hart panteth for the water-brooks. But where, sirs, was Duluth? Never in all my limited reading had my vision been gladdened by seeing the celestial word in print. And I felt a profounder humiliation in my ignorance that its dulcet syllables had never before ravished my delighted ear. I rushed to the library and examined all of the maps I could find. I discovered in one of them a delicate, hair-like line, diverging from the Mississippi near a place called Prescott, which I supposed was intended to represent the River St. Croix, but I could nowhere find Duluth.

"Nevertheless, I was confident it existed somewhere, and that its discovery would constitute the crowning glory of the present century, if not of all modern times. I knew it was bound to exist, in the very nature of things; that the symmetry and perfection of our planetary system would be incomplete without it; that the elements of material nature would long since have resolved themselves back into original chaos if there had been such a hiatus in creation as would have resulted from leaving out Duluth. In fact, sir, I was overwhelmed with the conviction that Duluth not only existed somewhere, but that, wherever it was, it was a great and glorious place. I was convinced that the greatest calamity that ever befell the benighted nations of the ancient world was in their having passed away without a knowledge of the actual existence of Duluth; that their fabled Atlantis, never seen save by the hallowed vision of inspired poesy, was, in fact, but another name for Duluth; that the golden orchard of the Hesperides was but a poetical synonym for the beer-gardens in the vicinity of Duluth."

The assembled members of the House were now at the full alert, hearkening while a new and unsuspected master of oratory, and of satire, spoke on with ease and assurance. Mr. Knott well knew that his classical asides were charming his fellows, and now that he was really wound up, he gave them some more of the same.

"I was certain," he continued, "that Herodotus had died a miserable death because in all his travels and with all his geographical research he had never heard of Duluth. I knew that if the immortal spirit of Homer could look down from another heaven than that created by his own celestial genius upon the long lines of pilgrims from every nation of the earth to the gushing fountain of poesy opened by the touch of his magic wand . . . he would weep tears of bitter anguish that, instead of lavishing all the stores of his mighty genius upon the fall of Ilion, it had not been his blessed lot to crystallize in deathless song the rising glories of Duluth. Yet, sir, had it not been for this map, kindly furnished me by the legislature of Minnesota, I might have gone down to my obscure and humble grave in an agony of despair because I could nowhere find Duluth . . .

"But thanks to the beneficence of that band of ministering angels who have their bright abodes in the far-off capital of Minnesota, just as the agony of my anxiety was about to culminate in the frenzy of despair, this blessed map was placed in my hands; and as I unfolded it a resplendent scene of ineffable glory opened before me, such as I imagine burst upon the enraptured vision of the wandering peri through the opening gates of paradise. There, for the first time, my enchanted eye rested upon the ravishing word 'Duluth'."

Now that he had the undivided attention of House and gallery, Mr. Knott fully warmed to the subject. In the next five minutes of his deathless peroration he did more to blast land jobbers, whether camouflaged as railroad companies or whatever, than any other Congressman before or since. Gulping a glass of what may have been pure District of Columbia water, he went on to satirize in masterly style the maps and methods of land promoters masquerading as railroads.

"If the gentlemen will examine it," said Mr. Knott of Kentucky, as he flourished a huge map, "they will find Duluth not only in its center, but represented in the center of a series of concentric circles one hundred miles apart, and some of them as much as four thousand miles in diameter, embracing alike in their tremendous sweep the fragrant savannas of the sunlit South and the eternal solitudes of snow that mantle the ice-bound North. . . . The fact is, sir, Duluth is preeminently a central place. . . .

"I find by reference to this map that Duluth is situated somewhere near the western end of Lake Superior, but as there is no dot or other mark indicating its exact location I am unable to say whether it is actually confined to any particular spot. . . . I cannot really tell whether it is one of those airy exhalations of the speculator's brain, which I am told are ever flitting in the form of towns and cities along those lines of railroad, built with government subsidies, luring the unwary settler as the mirage in the desert lures the famishing traveler on, and ever on, until it fades away in the darkening horizon, or whether it is a real, bona fide, substantial city, all staked off, with the lots marked with their owners' names. But, however it may be, I am satisfied that Duluth is there, or thereabout, for I see it stated here on this map that it is exactly thirty-nine hundred and ninety miles from Liverpool. . . ."

Bemused, entranced with this suddenly revealed Webster in the House, the members were now trying to control their laughter sufficiently to hear more of Mr. Knott's observations. They came, flowing sonorously:

"Then, sir, there is the climate of Duluth, unquestionably the most salubrious and delightful to be found anywhere on the Lord's earth. Now, I have always been under the impression that in the region around Lake Superior it was cold enough for at least nine months in the year to freeze the smokestack off a locomotive. But I see it represented on this map that Duluth is situated exactly half way between the latitudes of Paris and Venice, so that gentlemen who have inhaled the exhilarating air of the one or basked in the golden sunlight of the other may see at a glance that Duluth must be a place of untold delights, a terrestrial paradise. . . .

"As to the commercial resources of Duluth, sir, they are simply illimitable and inexhaustible, as is shown on this map. I see it stated here that there is a vast scope of territory, embracing an area of over two million square miles, rich in every element of material wealth and commercial prosperity, all tributary to Duluth. . . . Look at it, sir, do you not see from these broad, brown lines drawn around this immense territory that the enterprising inhabitants of Duluth intend some day to inclose it all in one vast corral, so that its commerce will be bound to go there whether it would or not? And here, sir, I find on the map, that within convenient distance are the Piegan Indians, which, of all the many accessories to the glory of Duluth, I consider by far the most inestimable. For, sir, I have been told that when the smallpox breaks out among the women and childen of that famous tribe, as it sometimes does, they afford the finest subjects in the world for the strategical experiments of any enterprising military hero who desires to improve himself in the noble art of war. . . ."

Then Mr. Knott of Kentucky sat down, immortal from that day to this.*

The St. Croix & Bayfield Railroad Company did not get its land grant. The great days of the land grants, legitimate and otherwise, were almost at an end, anyway. Too many crafty men had formed too many dubious railroad companies, and the gigantic scandal of the building of the Union Pacific was still fresh in the public mind. By their own brassy or devious methods railroad promoters had killed that golden goose, the American eagle; henceforth, the federal government moved gradually away from the position it had held up to 1871, which was to encourage and assist

---

* Mr. Knott came to realize this fact long before his death in 1911, for when he was guest of honor at a banquet given by Duluth citizens in 1890, he remarked that "Possibly the mention of your city's name may bring my own to the recollection of millions long after I shall have mouldered into dust, and everything else pertaining to my existence faded from the memory of man."

"internal improvements" by grants of land and sometimes even of loans in cash.

The typical plan of railroad promoters of the era was first to organize a company whose title included two or more of the principal towns of regions through which it was allegedly to pass, or possibly merely the two terminal cities. The more enthusiastic or brazen promoters were given to no restraint at all; as soon as not they were ready to capitalize a concern whose style was, say, the Sauk Center & Pacific Shore Railway Company. Next came a charter involving land grants of alternate sections along the line of the proposed road. Next the railroad boys would incorporate a land company, owned by directors of the railroad, to develop and peddle the lands. With the proceeds of the land sales, to which cash subsidies from federal, state, or even city sources often were added, plus the sale of mortgage bonds in Europe, actual construction of the railroad was begun. Construction, however, was not done by the railroad company, but by a separate concern, also owned by the railroad's directors, which commonly paid off handsomely, although the grade was made and the rails laid at stupendous cost to the holders of the railroad's stocks and bonds. A considerable number of American railroads were financed by methods that cost the railroad's directors not a penny of their own in actual cash.

Elsewhere in this book is an account of the colonization of the lands of the Illinois Central railroad, one of the most intelligent jobs ever done. All Western railroads faced the problem of getting people settled along their lines, and many of them did not hesitate this side of fantasy in their inducements. The Winona & St. Peter, later a part of the Chicago & North Western, appears to have rung every change from fear to greed to get settlers. The W&StP had a grant of 1,160,000 acres in Minnesota. In 1878 it was offering these at rates from $2 to $8, on "long credit," or 12½ per cent discount for cash. In its message to prospective settlers the railroad company stressed the fact that "the vicissitudes constantly recurring in all branches of industry and trade periodically plunge an immense population into abject poverty." About the only way to protect oneself from this ghastly menace was to buy lands along the rails—soon to be laid—of the Winona & St. Peter. "The purchaser of these lands derives his title in direct line from the United States Government, through the State of Minnesota and the Railroad Company. His title is absolutely indisputable." This indicates that titles of all other kinds of land were probably disputable, no matter how come by.

The W&StP lands, it was admitted, were rolling prairie, yet "in no sense monotonous." As to crops, why there was scarcely anything that could not be grown here—even something called Chinese sugar cane. Fuel? Seems there were "immense stands of hardwood in the region." Health?

In some of the vaguest figures this author has ever tried to study, the Winona & St. Peter advertising genius propounded a table listing "deaths in proportion to population." This showed that whereas one in 46 died in Great Britain, one in 50 in Sweden, and one in 108 in Wisconsin, only one in 127 died in Minnesota. I do not know what these comparisons mean, but the table struck me as being terribly important.

If you didn't believe all this, and much more, then, said the W&StP Railroad, go ask the happy and prosperous settlers along the railroad. Ask S. D. Pumpelly of Morse, Minnesota, who formerly lived in desolate McLean County, Illinois. Ask J. F. Metcalf, also of Morse, who formerly eked out a bare existence in the wilds of Michigan. Ask James Abernathy, now of Rock Lake, who previously froze in Canada. Ask C. T. Bellingham, of Marshall, who theretofore had labored, practically in vain, to make a living in eastern Minnesota, a country hardly to be compared with that along the Winona & St. Peter.

In the 1870's the competition to get settlers on railroad lands rose sometimes to internecine warfare between railroads themselves. One sample of this unseemly strife was an attack on the Northern Pacific and was probably the work of the combined forces of the Kansas-Pacific, the Missouri-Kansas, the Union Pacific, and the Missouri-Kansas-Texas lines.

The NP had a tremendous amount of land to sell, and its colonization department was quite aggressive through much of its career. In 1872 George Sheppard, European agent for the NP, engaged the Rev. George Rodgers, a pastor of Stalbridge, Dorsetshire, England, to organize a group of settlers who were to be "good and prosperous persons." Taking a small party in advance, the Rev. Mr. Rodgers came to Minnesota, and so to Clay County. He and his people liked the look of the region and, having been empowered by the larger group to choose the place of settlement, they selected land at Hawley and called it Yeovil Colony. Then they returned to England to fetch the settlers.

The Yeovil colonists, eighty strong, arrived in Minnesota in March, 1873. It would seem a rather bad time of year to bring settlers to that northern clime, and indeed, a number of the Yeovilians did find the place disappointing. Perhaps their disappointment was engendered in part by a pamphlet, *Advice from an Old Yeovilian*—no publisher or author named —which declared in so many words that the region along the Northern Pacific Railroad was no place for civilized people to live. It indicated the climate to be something that only savages could put up with. It more than intimated that nothing would grow there. Moreover, the land itself was of no value and never would be.

This pamphlet was said by Northern Pacific men to be the work of the unspeakable Union Pacific and the Southwestern lines already mentioned —slimy railroads given to libeling their betters. No doubt it had an effect, but at least fifty of the Yeovilian families took land on NP acres and two months later "were settled and tranquil, happy farmers." Later that year the NP announced that the Furness Colony, some 200 persons, had arrived from England and taken up lands along the NP in Wadena, Perham, and Audubon, Minnesota. Still more Furness Colony families came in 1874.

The Wisconsin Central railroad had settled on the idea of German immigrants; and Charles Colby, president of the road, engaged Kent K. Kennan and sent him to Germany as agent. Kennan was a very wise man, and somehow got himself appointed State Land Agent for Wisconsin and presented the interests of the state as a whole, rather than just the Wisconsin Central Railroad. He used pamphlets, pocket maps, and advertisements in German papers. Kent found that because of the solid and reliable and semiofficial character of the pamphlets, they had far more weight with intelligent Germans than "the exaggerated statements of most of the other American states." In 1880, the Wisconsin Central people received a letter from some German in Dresden, who said that: "The State of Wisconsin with us stands higher, even though other states are sending us large quantities of pamphlets. . . . Wisconsin is the pearl of all. She will no doubt be the favorite with Germans for the coming year."

In Medford, Wisconsin, the state and the railroad erected a large receiving depot, and here immigrants were put up for a period of two weeks, free of charge, each family being furnished with a large cooking stove and plenty of fuel. By these and other methods the lands of the Wisconsin Central, and no doubt of other railroads in the state, were soon settled, a majority of them by Germans.

Getting back to land grants: Gradually, as knowledge of how railroads were being financed permeated to the general public, the whole affair of railroad promotion, both the honest and the otherwise, was lumped together to make a gigantic and national scandal which has ever since been a milepost in many American history books, many of which have showed maps displaying thick, sinister lines of black indicating the proportion of the public domain that had been granted to railroads. Historians, revolted at the exposés of the sharp railroad promoters, wrote angry texts that for the past sixty years have been accepted as gospel in our schools and colleges. Because the historians were angry, and because also they really did have reason for anger, many a textbook has been unfair to the railroads and to the administrations that made the land grants.* Only in more recent

* Of twenty-four American history textbooks examined by Robert S. Henry, of the Association of American Railroads, only one gave correct figures as to the areas of land grants to railroad companies; nearly all of the others were guilty of exaggeration in varying degree, while several gave no figures at all but were contented to refer to the size of the grants as "staggering" or "enormous" or even "breath-taking." See Mr. Henry's "The Railroad Land Grant Legend in American History Texts," in *Mississippi Valley Historical Review*, Sept. 1945.

years have a few writers come around to the position that, looking at the matter from the perspective of today, it was the government rather than the railroads that got the best of the deal.

The figure usually accepted as representing all public lands granted to railroads is that quoted in Donaldson's *Public Lands,* published in 1884, and is 155,504,994 acres. The amount, however, was substantially short of this acreage, chiefly because of non-completion of a number of projected roads, and is officially given by the United States General Land Office, in its annual report of 1943, as 131,350,534 acres. This, true enough, is a staggering, even a "breath-taking" lot of land; and how much was it worth when it was granted?

As far back as 1850 William R. King, later Vice-President of the United States, stood up in the Senate to consider a grant of land to the Illinois Central. "We are met by the objection," he said, "that this is an immense grant—that it is a great quantity of land. Well, sir, it is a great quantity; but it will be there for five hundred years; and unless some mode of the kind proposed be adopted, it will never command ten cents." The senator was looking at the land involved not as an absolute quantity but as a portion of the public domain which could never be of much value to civilization until it had the facilities of communication.

Another thing: The total length of railroads built on or with land grants was 18,738 miles, or about eight per cent of the whole. The other 92 per cent was constructed without the aid of any federal land, thus indicating that private enterprise was pretty much on its own during the great period of railroad construction activity. Nor was the federal government of so much aid in direct financing of railroads as is generally supposed. It did make a loan to six of the companies chartered to build the Pacific railroads. These loans totaled $64,623,512. For many years, or during the period when the sparsely settled country could supply but little traffic, the roads were unable to pay the six per cent interest called for by these loans; but when final settlement was made, in 1898–99, the government collected no less than $63,023,512 of principal, and a thumping $104,722,978 in interest. In other words, the government loaned approximately $65 million and collected approximately $167 million. It was what Prof. Hugo R. Meyer of Harvard college termed, for the government, a not less than brilliant transaction.*

There were several patterns in the land grants to railroads:

Grants of alternate sections of land in primary strips embracing the area within six miles on either side of the proposed railroad, with indemnity limits outside thereof extending 15 to 20 miles from the railroad.

* In his "The Settlement with the Pacific Railways," in *Quarterly Journal of Economics,* July, 1899.

Grants of alternate sections of land in primary strips embracing the area within ten miles on either side of the proposed railroad, some without indemnity limits, others with indemnity limits outside thereof, extending 20 to 30 miles from the railroad.

Grants of alternate sections of land in primary strips embracing the area within 40 miles on either side of the proposed railroad, with indemnity limits outside thereof extending 50, and in some cases 60, miles from the railroad. (This pattern applied only to territories.)

In no case did a railroad receive more than six sections of land to the mile of road. (A section is 640 acres.) The indemnity lands, also called the "in lieu" lands, were given to the railroad in place of lands that would have been in the primary strip except for the fact that they had previously been granted to others than the railroad. Hence, the "in lieu" or indemnity limits.

The propaganda possibilities inherent in maps showing land granted to railroads must have been recognized by politicians at an early date. But not until 1884, however, was such a map used for political purposes. In that year the Democratic party issued a campaign poster that was meant to dynamite the Republicans. It showed what purported to be a map of lands granted to railroads, which was captioned, in bold and accusing type, "How The Public Domain has been Squandered by Republican Congresses." The map was truly wonderful—when viewed by honest Democrats, and terrible to Republicans. Whoever looked at it saw a devastating picture of western United States, a land all but wiped out by the wide streaks of black ink that purported to be the acreage "given by Republican Congresses to Railroad Corporations."

It was a ghastly thing to consider. There, plain in front of the dazed eye was a Wisconsin as dark in all except a few southern counties and a brief strip in the east and north central portions, as midnight. Both Michigan and Minnesota appeared almost as dark. But it was Iowa that revealed as no other state the savage greed of the Railroad Power and its hirelings, the Republican congresses. Iowa was practically blotted out, as black as the lowest pit in hell itself, nothing showing white except for little wisps along the northern and southern borders.

Following with his eye, the sovereign voter of 1884 traced the slimy black trail westward. South Dakota had pretty much escaped the tracks of the Monster, but North Dakota was better than half black. Montana was smeared with a mighty span of ink, at least two-thirds of Washington was in a like condition. The entire Panhandle of Idaho was in deep shadow. Oregon was crossed and recrossed with black bands. California, Arizona, and New Mexico showed the marks of the Beast in varying degree. And across Nevada, Wyoming, Nebraska, Colorado, and Kansas the trail led eastward, to mar the otherwise handsome states of Missouri, Illinois, Arkansas, Louisiana, Mississippi, Alabama, and Florida.

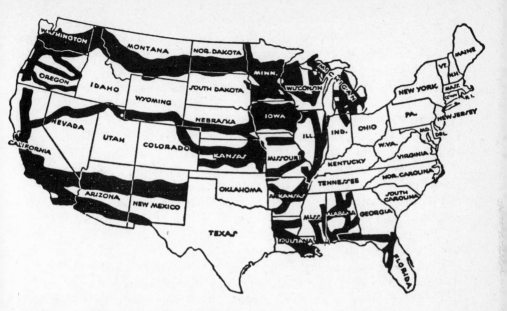

This map originally drawn to show the extreme outer limits of areas within which some land might be granted to railroads, is frequently reproduced in American History texts with captions describing it as showing lands actually granted—thereby exaggerating by approximately four times the area received by railroads.

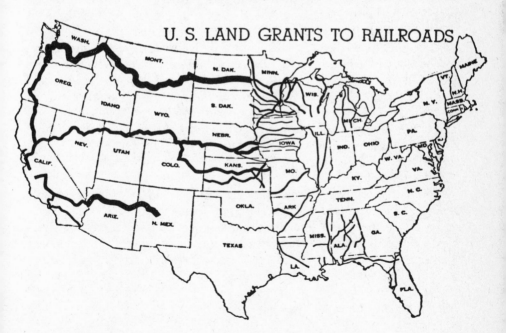

The Federal Government granted lands to railroads in alternate sections, retaining the sections between. It is impossible to present this "checkerboard" pattern on so small a map, but the shaded areas show the approximate locations of the land grants, and are in proportion to the amounts actually received by railroads.

This map, which, remember, was made for political purposes, has had a strange and influential history. It has been reproduced in many a school textbook since 1884 and is largely responsible, charges Mr. Henry of the Association of American Railroads, for the erroneous ideas most Americans hold today in regard to land grants. The map in question really represents wagon-road and river-improvement grants, as well as those to railroads; and it also shows the full area of the indemnity limits of both completed and uncompleted grants, but without any explanation. The shaded portions, remarks Mr. Henry, represent approximately four times the number of acres actually granted to railroad companies.

Thus was another myth conjured up and perpetuated. It will be as hard to kill, if killed it ever is, as the myth that our Founding Fathers at Plymouth and Jamestown lived in log cabins.*(This piece of folklore, which was not perpetrated until 1849, and not embellished with pictures until two decades later, nevertheless is now firmly entrenched in American mythology and will probably last as long as the Republic.)

That more than one railroad company grossly and cynically abused the terms of federal land grants is too well known to call for more than passing mention. Among others, the Southern Pacific was notorious in this respect, so notorious that only by able management during the past two decades or so has it dispelled the public antagonism it so well earned in earlier days. It was the overreaching greed of the SP directorate that brought about what has been termed one of the most challenging problems in American history—the Oregon & California Railroad revested land grant.

What today are known as the O&C lands in Oregon were originally composed of three land grants, one to the O&C Railroad, made in 1866, to aid in building a railroad from Portland to the California line; another in 1869 to aid in developing a military wagon road from Coos Bay to Roseburg, both in Oregon; and a third in 1870 to aid construction of a railroad from Portland to Astoria. The total amount granted was some 4,300,000 acres, a great deal of it covered with marvelous timber of unusual size and thickness of stand.

Neither the original railroads nor the wagon-road company were able to carry out the terms of their grants. Their identities disappeared in bankruptcy proceedings and into the scene stepped the experienced and forward men of the Southern Pacific, to take over the grants. An important clause provided that the O&C lands be sold to actual settlers in quarter-section, or 160-acre lots, at no more than $2.50 an acre. The SP paid no attention to this clause, and soon vast areas were being bought by speculating land companies and by logging concerns.

---

* Incidentally, the great transcontinental land grant railroads—the Northern Pacific, Central Pacific, and Union Pacific, all were bankrupt before 1890. Jim Hill drove his Great Northern rails to the West Coast without the aid of a land grant. I am not sure what this proves.

By the turn of the century public dissatisfaction grew into a strong campaign to remove all O&C lands from the railroad company's administration, to repossess, in short, the entire grant. Bitter battles in the Oregon Legislature and in Congress, and litigation that at last reached the Supreme Court resulted, in 1915, in a revestment of the lands, and title to approximately three million acres was restored to the federal government. For the next 20 years the O&C lands remained something of a burden on both state and federal governments. The lands had to be protected against fire, always a costly process, but they returned little income from the sale of timber. Then, in 1937, the Department of the Interior initiated a piece of new legislation (50 Stat. 874) which laid the foundation for a new forest policy in regard to the lands. The measure provides for conservation of land, water, forest, and forage on a permanent basis; and seeks, through the practice of sustained-yield logging, to guarantee perpetual forests that will support industrial communities indefinitely.

Since then, the administration and use of O&C lands has been a bright spot in the world of lumbering and forestry. The lands are not only paying their way but are also providing substantial revenues to the counties and repaying the original investment and costs of administration and litigation before 1937. After more than half a century of scandal and disgrace, the O&C lands have come into their own and are a source of steady and probably permanent income to the state that once seemed to have been robbed in a particularly cynical manner.

No discussion, no matter how brief, of railroad federal land grants would be fair unless the matter of reduced rates to the government be mentioned, for it is in this that Uncle Sam proved himself a Yankee bargainer of the first class. In most land grants to railroads, the same phraseology was used that had applied to the earlier canal and wagon-road grants, namely, that the railroad "should be and remain a public highway for the use of the government of the United States, free from toll or other charge upon the transportation of any property or troops of the United States." This meant free hauling.

The clause, of course, set up an impossible condition, recognized as such by both government and the railroads. It was adjusted by the Supreme Court and the United States Court of Claims which provided that government men and property be carried for 50 per cent of the normal commercial rates; and later, by several acts of Congress, was extended to those few land-grant roads whose grants did not contain the toll-free provision. And by what are known as the equalization agreements, even roads that had never received a land grant undertook to handle government traffic at the same rates applying to the land grant lines.

In 1940 Congress eliminated the 50-per cent reductions on the government's civilian passenger and freight traffic; but the low rates were continued, and remained in effect, for the carrying of Army and Navy freight and personnel. One gets an idea of what this meant in cash from the report of a congressional committee made in 1945. "It is possible," says this report, "that the railroads have contributed over $900 million in payment of the lands that were transferred to them under the Land Grant Acts. This is double the amount received for the lands sold by the railroads plus the estimated value of such lands still under railroad ownership. Former Commissioner Eastman estimated that the total value of the lands at the time they were granted . . . was not more than $126 million." *

Thus Uncle Sam did not do so badly. If anyone got a bargain in the railroad land-grant deals, it seems to have been the federal government. Since October 1, 1946, all land-grant deductions have been discontinued.

---

* Committee on Interstate and Foreign Commerce, House of Representatives Report No. 393, 79 Cong., 1 Sess., March 26, 1946, pp. 1–2.

New York City, Fourth Avenue at 126th Street, showing the New York & Harlem Railroad,
as seen by a staff artist in Frank Leslie's Illustrated Newspaper of Feb 15, 1873

Harper's Weekly, July 17, 1875

Railroad building on the great plains.
Northern Pacific contributed its share to the 40,000 miles of new railroad built in the 1870's.

CHAPTER XIV

The First Transcontinental

There is more poetry in the rush of a single railroad train across the continent than in all the gory story of burning Troy . . .
—JOAQUIN MILLER.

WHO thought of it first is beyond knowing. One of the earliest to propose the idea in print did not even sign his name. In the *Emigrant*, a weekly paper published at Ann Arbor, Michigan, he suggested that a steam railroad be built from New York City by way of the Great Lakes and the Platte Valley to the Oregon country. That was in 1832, when few Americans had gone overland to the Pacific and even fewer had seen a locomotive.

The idea was never quite extinguished thereafter. Almost at once Dr. Hartwell Carver, grandson of the Jonathan Carver who had explored a good deal in the field and even more in his fertile imagination, memorialized Congress to construct a highway of iron rails between New York and San Francisco. Four years later Lewis Gaylord Clarke said the idea had been his; and Clarke was followed by many others, including the Rev. Samuel Parker, Governor Lilburn Boggs of Missouri, and John Plumbe of Iowa. In 1847 Plumbe was honored at a meeting as the "Original Projector of the Great Oregon Railroad." Then, there was Asa Whitney.

All of the proposers except Whitney seem to have given up in the face of a tremendous lethargy on the part of Congress and the public. Whitney did not waver. A Yankee of North Groton, Massachusetts, his resemblance to Napoleon Bonaparte was so great as often to cause him embarassment, yet he had little of that noted man's characteristics except high intelligence. In 1844 he proposed to Congress his plan for a transcontinental railroad from Lake Michigan to the Pacific via the South Pass of the Rockies. Because of his failure to make demands leading to his own profit, he was generally believed by the stout American materialists of the period to be contemplating some vast and secret speculation by which he would be enriched at the expense of the Government and the public. Altruism was so rare in 1844, apparently, that few men believed it existed at all.

For the next five years Whitney carried on an astonishing publicizing program in the press, with the result that the transcontinental-railroad idea remained constantly in the public eye, nor was it permitted ever to languish again. When Whitney died in 1872, one such railroad had been completed and others were building.

And now to another fanatic, Crazy Judah, the man who began at the far end of the idea and actually started to lay transcontinental rails eastward. He was born Theodore Dehone Judah, the son of an Episcopal clergyman of Bridgeport, Connecticut, in 1826. After schooling at Rensselaer he went to work in the engineering department of the New Haven, Hartford & Springfield Railroad, leaving to build bridges on the Connecticut Valley Railway. Later, he planned and built the Niagara Gorge Railroad, a wonder of its day. In 1854 he was engaged by C. L. Wilson of Sacramento, California, to go west to become chief engineer for a projected railroad that was to run from the California capital into the placer mining country of the Sierra foothills.

Judah was twenty-eight when he arrived at Sacramento, an industrious, competent, opinionated and humorless person who already had large plans in his head for a railroad from ocean to ocean. Not a rail had been laid anywhere in California when he set the course the Sacramento Valley line was to take. His report and preliminary survey for it was in the hands of his employers fifteen days after he arrived. It was to run between Sacramento and Folsom, a distance of 21 miles. By February 1855 it was completed and in operation.

The railroad cut a full day between Sacramento and the mines and for a brief period, or until the placers started to peter out, did a thumping big business, though it was never to grow. When it was in operation, Judah engaged to explore the passes of the Sierras for a proposed wagon-road company planned to tap the growing silver towns of Nevada. He made the survey, but forgot that it was to be a mere wagon road. Instead, he returned to his base fired with enthusiasm for what he said was a practical passage of the mountains for iron rails—rails that would run on and on to the Atlantic shore.

Judah's employers were not interested in rails. They set him down as a fanatic, which he assuredly was. He now went about to rouse all California to the need for a transcontinental railroad. Getting interest was not difficult. Nearly everybody in the state had come from Back East. All felt isolated from their old homes. Most were as avid as Judah for the railroad. He kept up his drumming from platform and in the press, and in September of 1859 managed to stage a Pacific Railroad Convention in San Francisco. The meeting heard Judah speak and knew they had found their Moses. A month later he was on his way to Washington and Congress, there to lay his plan before the wise men.

Judah, as his best biographer remarks,* was a singularly well-posted

* See *The Big Four*, by Oscar Lewis, cited elsewhere in this book.

mad man. Loaded to the brim with facts, as voluble on his pet subject as any congressman was on Patriotism or The Log Cabin, the young engineer captured the imagination of both House and Senate, then went on to charm and hypnotize newspaper editors as well. Aided by Congressman John A. Logan, Judah was allowed to use a room in the Capitol and here he established what he was pleased to call The Pacific Railroad Museum. Here, too, he held forth from early morning until late hours, dispensing information about the road on which he said America's future greatness rested. He was eloquent, too.

Had it not been for the issue of slavery, Judah likely would have got a Pacific Railroad Act through Congress in 1859. But slavery was the big, almost the sole thing. Like all else, Judah's bill was shoved ahead to the next session. Returning to San Francisco, Judah turned in his expense account to the Pacific Railroad Convention. It contained but one item: "For printing bill and circulars $40.00." He himself had paid for his voyage, his living expenses, and charged nothing for many months of his time. Genuine fanatics are that way.

Back now in California, his enthusiasm stronger than ever, Judah thought he would make another survey through the mountains so he could say: "Here are the actual maps, the profiles, the estimates of my route." He struck into the hills at once, and presently near the mining town of Dutch Flat he found the pass he wanted. Without more ado, he spread out a sheet of paper on the counter of Dr. Strong's Dutch Flat drugstore and then and there wrote "The Articles of Association of the Central Pacific Railroad of California." This was the genesis of the western half of what was to be the first transcontinental. Incidentally, Judah managed to sell Dr. Strong a batch of stock before he left the drugstore.

The next thing was capital. Although he tried, he could not interest San Francisco money, so he returned to Sacramento and called a meeting, which about a dozen men attended, among them a wholesale grocer, Leland Stanford; a drygoods merchant named Charley Crocker; and partners in a local hardware store, Mark Hopkins and Collis P. Huntington.

Judah knew that these small-town merchants would not be taken by any plan to build a railroad across the nation. What they wanted was something that could be built quickly at small cost and would return big money immediately. So Judah eliminated all except the purely local features of his immense plan. He told his dozen that by building a railroad through the mountains they could get and hold a monopoly of the traffic with the burgeoning silver cities of Nevada.

Here was an idea his hearers could grasp—grasp and hold lovingly. Nevada, they knew, was fairly acrawl with men seeking fortunes. It was the Forty-nine Rush all over again. Tons of freight were leaving Sacramento in wagons every day, all for the new camps. Rates were extremely high. To this picture Judah added the pleasant news that the Government would be certain to grant land to such an enterprise.

Judah spoke well that night, and before the meeting adjourned the minimum amount of cash required for incorporation had been promised. Only Collis Huntington held out. "In later life," says Oscar Lewis, "four of Judah's listeners that evening accepted easily the roles of men of vision, who had perceived a matchless opportunity and grasped it with courage. It was a role none of them deserved." Mr. Lewis refers, of course, to the Big Four, namely Crocker, Huntington, Stanford and Hopkins, all good business men but wholly blind to the tremendous vision that stirred Theodore Judah.

There was to be no stalling. With a few assistants Judah at once set about running the line of the Central Pacific, beginning in the muddy streets of Sacramento itself. By June his survey had crossed the foothills, and he followed the receding snow line up the western slope of the Sierras. In the fall he quit this work and went again around the Horn to Washington. He reopened his quaint Pacific Railroad Museum, which now displayed sketches of Donner Pass made by his wife, and also the Central Pacific brand-new stock certificates. Throughout the winter months he lobbied for the Pacific Railroad Bill, and after war broke out in April, he found the going easier.

Easier, but not yet too simple. Not until July 1, 1862, did President Lincoln sign the Pacific Railroad Act. Judah then sent a telegram to his Sacramento associates: "We have drawn the elephant. Now let us see if we can harness him up."

The act designated two companies to build and operate a railroad between Sacramento and the Missouri River, and a telegraph line on the same route. The act incorporated the happily named Union Pacific Railroad Company, authorizing a capital of $100,000,000. The Central Pacific was already incorporated. The former was to build an Iowa branch to the main line, and to construct the main line from the 100th meridian in the Territory of Nebraska (thus dodging any states'-rights troubles) to the California line. The Central Pacific was to build that portion of the road which lay within the state of California. Whichever of the two companies should first reach the California line was to build westward or eastward, as the case might be, until it met the other.

Land grants of ten alternate sections per mile of public domain on both sides of the line over the entire distance were made; and the Federal Government agreed to lend the companies, in five per cent bonds, amounts ranging from $16,000 to $48,000 per mile, depending on the terrain.

Judah returned to Sacramento, no longer a tiresome monomaniac but a man of consequence. On January 8, 1863, seven speeches were delivered and one shovelful of earth turned on the levee at Sacramento, as the Central Pacific started construction. Judah made none of the speeches, which were mere echoes of what he had been saying for years. Now he was to be in charge of actual construction.

Not for long, however. By terms of the Government act the bonds were not to become available until 40 miles of the line had been completed. It soon developed that Judah and the Huntington group viewed these first 40 miles from poles apart. Huntington and his crowd considered this section as a deplorable hurdle that must be surmounted before the subsidy would come into the coffers, Judah thought that the first 40 miles should be built rapidly but well. The others wanted only speed and the cheapest sort of construction. On this difference the two parties broke, and it was apparent to Judah that he could not work with these men to whom the dollar was everything. The Big Four and their associates were happy to buy him out for $100,000. He took ship for the East Coast where, it is more than possible, he planned to approach the Vanderbilt group for cash with which to buy out the Big Four. But yellow fever laid hands on him during the voyage. He died a week after landing in New York.

To the Big Four went the glory, and the cash, for building the Central Pacific. Not until sixty years after his death was Judah commemorated, and it was then the *employees* of the Southern Pacific, heir to the CP, who paid for the modest monument to the engineer and prophet that stands in Sacramento. And in popular literature, only Oscar Lewis has done him justice.

–At the Union Pacific's end of the line, construction work started on December 2, 1863, at Omaha. Or, rather, ground was broken at the small and dismal settlement, while George Francis Train, a notable eccentric, made the principal speech. Labor was scarce, however, what with the North at war; and cash for stock came in in driblets. A year and a half after incorporation of the Union Pacific not a foot of grade had been opened.

But contracts had been let; and Peter A. Dey, chief engineer for the road, did not like the look of the business. On December 7, 1864, he sent his resignation to General John A. Dix, the Union Pacific president. Mr. Dey was as direct as he was honest. "I do not," he wrote, "approve of the contract for building the first hundred miles from Omaha west, and I do not care to have my name so connected with the railroad that I shall appear to endorse the contract."

Engineer Dey himself had estimated the cost of the first 100 miles at $30,000 per mile. His estimate was overruled and the actual contract let at $60,000 per mile. The difference would be sheer profit to a contracting outfit named Crédit Mobilier, of which more presently.

To replace Mr. Dey the Union Pacific virtually drafted from the Army General Grenville M. Dodge, probably the best qualified man in the country to tackle its biggest railroad job. Born in a farmhouse in small Danvers, Massachusetts, in 1831, he had taken an engineering course at Norwich College, in Vermont, and by 1851 was surveying in Illinois. Peter Dey was then laying a line through Iowa for the Mississippi & Missouri Railroad. He engaged young Dodge as chief assistant. Planting his home in Council Bluffs, Dodge ranged the Midwest with surveying parties, traded with the Indians, and did some freighting. For almost a decade he received a practical education for what was to be his greatest work.

One incident of these years that was to have a strong influence on his future happened in 1859, when Abraham Lincoln, the Illinois lawyer, found Dodge sitting on the stoop of the Pacific House in Council Bluffs, and, says Dodge, "sat down beside me, and by his kindly ways soon drew from me all I knew about the country west, and the results of my reconnaissances. . . . He got all the secrets that were later to go to my employers." *

On the outbreak of war, Dodge became colonel of the 4th Iowa Infantry and, although he was not anointed, having never been near West Point, he rose to major general of volunteers, was wounded at Pea Ridge and again in front of Atlanta, and was highly commended by General Grant for his uncanny skill in reconstructing and equipping railroads for use of the Army. As soon as he took over UP's construction, things began to happen.

The financial condition of the company had been improved—and perhaps "improved" is an understatement. In 1863 Thomas C. Durant, an official of the UP, together with several associates, formed a concern whose charter gave it almost unlimited powers. This was Crédit Mobilier, named by the same George F. Train who got around so much, and it was to become notorious if not downright loathsome. Briefly, the Crédit Mobilier was formed of stockholders of the UP, as a separate company, for the purpose of letting contracts for construction, for purchasing supplies and selling them to the railroad at what might be termed fancy prices.

Notorious or not, the trick concern provided immediate and lush funds for General Dodge's many surveying parties and his swiftly growing construction gangs. By the middle of September, 1866, 180 miles of track had been laid, an average of more than a mile a day since Dodge took charge. The first division point was established at Grand Island, Nebraska, and on the last day of the year the base was at North Platte, at Milepost 293.

Much of the UP's track was to be laid by the Casement Brothers, Daniel and General Jack, small, wiry, tough men as genial as they were ruthless and competent. With almost incredible speed the Casements assembled more than a thousand men and several hundred teams. The gangs

---

* See General Dodge's *How We Built the Union Pacific Railway*, Government Printing Office, 1910.

were composed of ex-Union and ex-Confederate soldiers, hundreds of Irishmen from New York, ex-convicts from everywhere, and a scattering of plains mule skinners, mountain men, and dubious bushwackers. They had hardly turned up a mile of sod before a whole raft of gamblers, sellers of grog, and female harpies had set up shop near the railhead.

A majority of the graders and tracklayers were ex-soldiers, and the company armed them one and all with carbines, rifles, and revolvers. The Indians wanted no rails across the buffalo country. But General W. T. Sherman did not think the savages would trouble a great deal. "No particular danger need be apprehended from the Indians," he said in what turned out to be short of true prophecy. "So large a number of workmen distributed along the line will introduce enough whisky to kill all the Indians within 300 miles of the road." There was a plenty of whisky, to be sure, but the Indians did not get enough of it to lay their fears. Across Nebraska, then across much of Wyoming, as far as Bitter Creek, the construction crews often had to drop their tools and pick up guns. The Army supplied partial protection, but the troopers were too few. As General George Crook tartly remarked, it was difficult to surround three Indians with one soldier.

The Central Pacific had little trouble with the savages. For one thing, they had to treat mostly with the Diggers and the Snakes, neither tribe of which was to be compared with the warlike Sioux of the plains. And Collis Huntington made a most remarkable treaty when the CP entered the country of the Paiutes and Shoshones. "We gave the old chiefs a pass each, good on the passenger cars," he related, "and we told our men to let the common Indians ride on the freight cars whenever they saw fit." It worked like Big Medicine.

The difficulties of the Central Pacific were largely centered in terrain and climate; the Sierras had to be crossed before the desert was reached. Samuel Montague, a most competent man, had succeeded Judah as chief engineer. Charles Crocker, who added "& Company" to his name, set up as general contractor to grade and lay tracks. Crocker, one of the Big Four, normally weighed 250 pounds and alternated between periods of extreme activity and something near sloth. But he was a roaring bull most of the time, boastful, tactless, vain, of a wonderful profanity.

Although the gold rush of '49 and after had brought thousands of men to California, it had long since been ebbing and there was nowhere nearly sufficient labor in the state for Central Pacific purposes. Crocker attempted to bring in a mass of peons from Mexico, but it could not be arranged. He now thought of the Chinese. Thousands of them were in California, working the old placer mines, growing vegetables, operating laundries, working as house servants. Almost nobody believed that the Chinese, who averaged around 110 pounds, were strong or tough enough to stand the Sierra climate and do the heavy work necessary. Crocker hired fifty and hauled them to the end of track. They established a neat and efficient camp with great speed, cooked a supper of rice, then went to sleep with a nonchalance that astonished the Caucasians. When the sun came up, the Chinese were up too and already at their picks and shovels. Twelve hours later Crocker was wiring Sacramento for more Chinese.

The second, the third, and the other gangs were just as good. All doubt vanished. Within six months more than two thousand Orientals were swarming over the right-of-way, blue-jeaned, basket-hatted, pig-tailed, demons for work. Still more were imported direct from Canton. By mid-1866 some six thousand of them were at work on the CP, many drilling away at Summit Tunnel, a quarter-mile bore through the solid granite backbone of the range. This tunnel was a year in the making, even with the aid of the new if eccentric explosive, called nitroglycerine, manufactured on the spot by one Swanson, a Swedish chemist.

A heap of work had to be done above the 6,000-foot level. Snow fell in vast quantities in early October and continued almost without remission for six months. Fifteen feet of it often covered the grade. Five locomotives were used with one snowplow to buck the 30-foot drifts. At times, all work had to cease except that in the bores. Avalanches became frequent, and on at least four occasions an entire camp, buildings and men, went hurtling into a canyon, to be buried until spring.

In June of 1868 the tracks reached from Sacramento to the state line, and immediately heavy freights were rolling down the eastern slope with supplies and equipment to build across the Nevada desert. By that time the Union Pacific rails had reached and passed the summit of the Rockies at Sherman, Wyoming. The race was on. Each outfit wanted to build as many miles as possible, for each mile meant a rich subsidy in land and bonds. So eager were the opposing companies that the UP's engineers were surveying ahead almost to the California border, while CP men were choosing a route hundreds of miles east of Ogden, Utah. Building continued until the graded lines paralleled each other for long distances.

The Chinese and Irish crews looked at each other, then rolled boulders at each other. They set off blasts to destroy the opposing grade. Now and then crew members did a little shooting with guns. The point of joining the rails, however, had to be fought out in Washington, and it was finally selected as Promontory Point, six miles west of Ogden.*

The driving of the Last Spike, connecting the UP and the CP tracks, occurred on May 10, 1869, and was accompanied by a truly stupendous celebration at the shack town of Promontory, where oratory and whisky flowed in about equal amounts. Photographs of the event are probably the best known railroad pictures extant; and among railroad verse, like-

---

* This historic spot has also been called Promontory Summit, Promontory Mountain, and simply Promontory.

wise best known is the doggerel composed for the occasion by Francis Bret
Harte, a writer then resident in San Francisco, which will be found, by
anyone who oddly enough has never read it, in Harte's *Collected Poems*
(1871).

Completing the first transcontinental railroad in the brief space of five
years told Americans—if they needed to be told—that they were a race
of builders and doers without peer. General Dodge, the Casements and
their Irish, even Charley Crocker and his coolies, one and all were the
heroes of a day. "There is more poetry in the rush of a single railroad train
across the continent," wrote Joaquin Miller, "than in all the gory story
of burning Troy."

Then—of course—came the scandals. Americans do not build a railroad from Omaha to the Pacific in five years, making grade and laying
track under almost impossible conditions, meanwhile fighting savage tribes
and prehensile politicians, without at least a trace of corruption. The
scandal of the Union Pacific came into the open in December of 1867,
when the fancy building company known as Crédit Mobilier declared its
first dividend. This turned out to be approximately 100 per cent which,
even in that era of rubbery business ethics, was considered more than
decent.

Then, too, there had been litigation within Crédit Mobilier between one
group represented by the Ames brothers, Oakes and Oliver, and the
group led by Thomas C. Durant. The litigation brought out the fact that
Oakes Ames, representative in Congress from Massachusetts, had been
distributing Crédit Mobilier stock among influential members of Congress.
"Where it would do us the most good," said Mr. Ames simply.

Congressional investigating committees went to work. Oakes Ames himself called the roll of corruption, implicating Democrats and Republicans,
including James Garfield, Schuyler Colfax, and many lesser lights. The
Republican machine turned upon Ames and impeached him, as a warning,
says Claude Bowers, "to corrupt politicians against turning state's evidence." * It was one of the greatest and most lasting upheavals Congress
had known. Scores of reputations were tarnished. Years later Senator
George Hoar summed up pretty well the opinion of the public. Said he:
"When the greatest railroad in the world, binding together the continent
and uniting two great seas which wash our shores, was finished, I have
seen our national triumph and exaltation turned to bitterness and shame
by the unanimous reports of three committees of Congress that every
step of that mighty enterprise had been taken in fraud."

Oakes Ames was made goat-in-chief for the whole rotten business, and
it is only fair to point out that more recent and cooler historical opinion

---

* See his melancholy if absorbing *The Tragic Era*, Boston, 1929.

has cleared him of the charge of being consciously corrupt. He had been both selfish and highly unethical, but these were qualities so common they should not, in that gilt era, have raised an eyebrow, had not thieves fallen out and Congress needed a figure to hold up to loathing and scorn.

As for the Central Pacific contracts, they were almost as scandalous as the Crédit Mobilier and are used to this very day to harass the Central Pacific's heir, the Southern Pacific; but at the time, the United States was not equal to two scandals of such magnitude as Crédit Mobilier. Nothing quite approaching it was to be seen until, fifty years later, Mr. Harding ushered in normalcy and an administration beside which Crédit Mobilier appeared like a company of saints dedicated to poverty.

By the time the Union Pacific scandals were dying away, James J. Hill of St. Paul, Minnesota, was starting to build a transcontinental without benefit of Government land or other subsidy.

CHAPTER XV

Jim Hill's Empire

Mr. Hill's judgment has never been seriously at fault in any of his undertakings.
—The Strategy of Great Railroads, 1904.

FIRST of all came the blizzards. Then came the droughts, then the grasshoppers, and hard on the leaping legs of the parasites came the greatest curse of all—James Jerome Hill, Jim Hill, the Little Giant, the Devil's Curse of the northern plains, the prince of the Great Northern, king of the NP, emperor of the Burlington—the man who *made* the Pacific Northwest, the Empire Builder, the man who wrecked Minnesota, wrecked the Dakotas, Montana, and all Puget Sound, the Prophet of Northern Wheat, the Evil One of Homesteaders—aye, Jim Hill, the barbed-wired, shaggy-headed, one-eyed old sonofabitch of Western railroading.

In his lifetime Jim Hill was each and all of those things, a legend while he lived, a legend still in death (and death came thirty years ago), a legend so powerful, so varied, and so insistent in its countless inconsistencies, and the measured critical writing on the man so meager, that it seems improbable a fair estimate of Hill and his work will ever be set down on paper. What old Corneal Vanderbilt had been to the tight little kingdom of New York, Jim Hill was to a vast empire that ranged unbroken from the Great Lakes to Puget Sound, from the Canadian border to Missouri and Colorado, and on across the Pacific to China and Japan.

Jim Hill was vindictive: Because the mayor of a small Minnesota town objected mildly to all-night switching in his village, Hill tore down the station and set it up more than a mile away. Jim Hill was loyal: When he had used his own, not his stockholders' money, to speculate in Minnesota ore lands, and the speculation turned out to be a magnificently wonderful investment, he let his stockholders who had risked nothing into the deal, to their enrichment by millions of dollars in dividends. Jim Hill was down to earth: He would grab the shovel from the hands of one of his laborers to spell him off, meanwhile shoveling snow from the Great Northern tracks as though he were a steam-driven plow. He had delusions of grandeur: He built a castle in St. Paul and considered himself as *the* builder of empires, on a plane with Genghis Khan and Napoleon.

Only one thing seems certain about Jim Hill: He assuredly was *the*
genius and *the* Titan of Western railroading. He was in a class all by himself. "Good" or "bad," Hill stood alone.

When he was eighteen years old in 1856, Hill arrived in the settlement
on the Mississippi that was beginning to dislike its early name of Pig's
Eye and was calling itself St. Paul. He had been born in Ontario of parents
who wanted him to become a doctor. The loss of one eye from the acci-
dental discharge of an arrow seemed to prevent a career of medicine, and,
anyway, young Hill thought he'd like to be a trader in the Orient, like
Marco Polo. He struck out to approach the Orient from a Pacific American port, his first thought being to join one of the brigades of trappers who
ranged the country between the Mississippi and the West Coast of America. From San Francisco or Portland, he believed, he might get passage
on a ship across the great ocean.

St. Paul was then a jumping-off place for trappers, but young Hill
arrived there just a few days too late to join the last brigade of the year,
a fact that probably changed the entire course of his life. He had to wait
a year before another brigade would set out. But twelve months could not
pass a youth of Hill's energy and find him the same man. In the intervening time, he had so firmly taken root in the community that he never
more talked of trapping his way west. St. Paul was to be his base of operations for the next sixty years.

Hill's first job was clerk for an outfit that operated packet steamers on
the big river. He saw the first shipments of Minnesota grains go down-
stream. With his own hands he cut the first stencil for the first label on the
first flour made in Minnesota.* He noted the increasing numbers of immigrants. With his quick and also reflective and analytical mind, he came
to believe he was stationed at one of the great crossroads of Western trade.
Through his urging, his employers enlarged their activities to include general trading in groceries and farm implements. One of young Hill's many
duties, one he relished, was fixing freight and passenger rates for his company, work that he did most competently and the experience of which was
to stand him in good stead in later years.

Hill tried to enlist for the Civil War, but though he could see more
with his one eye than most men could with two, he was rejected and immediately threw his energy into organizing the First Minnesota Volunteers. The demands of war had a tremendous effect on the growing of
wheat in Minnesota, and Hill did not ignore the implications. In 1865 he
set up for himself as a forwarding agent and general transportation man.
He pressed and sold hay. He acted as warehouseman. He learned how to

---

* The stencil was a fake, too. It said: "Muskingum Mills, Troy, Ohio, The Genuine." In
that day Minnesota flour was unknown, and Ohio was a great wheat state.

buy and sell goods to the best advantage, how to choose the cheapest methods of moving goods, and how best they could be stored in a warehouse.

In about 1866 Hill began to act for the St. Paul & Pacific Railroad, a sort of political football that had never got anywhere but managed somehow to keep a few trains moving. Among other things he contracted to supply the railroad with fuel. Fuel was then wood, and Hill thought it very poor fuel for a railroad. Coal, he was sure, was much better. So, with the characteristic thoroughness that marked him throughout life, Hill made a survey of all available sources of coal, and started shipments of it coming to St. Paul. With Chauncey W. Griggs, a Connecticut Yankee who was making his mark in wholesale groceries, he formed Hill, Griggs & Company, a fuel, freighting, merchandising, and warehouse concern which soon had virtually a monopoly of the fuel business in the city and nearby region.

Hill also had his one eye on the Red River of the North, a large and muddy stream that rose in Dakota Territory to flow north into Lake Winnipeg, in Manitoba. At Winnipeg, then called Fort Garry, was an important post of the venerable yet aggressive Hudson's Bay Company. This hoary concern was fighting to maintain its monopoly of the Canadian fur trade. It could not consistently carry the freight of the independent traders, whom it was trying to put out of business; and Norman Kittson, agent at St. Paul for the British company, suggested to Hill that he might find a way to transport the independent traders. Hill did so, operating a boat on the Red River to such effect that the Hudson's Bay Company's boats found Hill's competition dangerous. Kittson next suggested that he and Hill combine. They did so, forming the Red River Transportation Company. Out of this line Hill was to make the foundation of his fortune.

In 1870 Hill went up the Red River into Canada to investigate the causes of the rebellion led by Louis Riel, the brilliant, vain, and flighty French-Indian who had raised a mob and captured the fur company's post of Fort Garry. On this trip Hill met for the first time Donald A. Smith, governor of the Hudson's Bay Company. The two men met, it has often been told, on a snow-covered prairie in dog sleds, 150 miles from the nearest house. Few meetings of two men have been more portentous; none of greater importance to both the United States and Canada.

On this and subsequent trips Hill did a lot of traveling between St. Paul and Dakota and Fort Garry, much of it on horseback. He saw the rich black soil and the vast expanses of a virgin region. He had also watched the steady decay of the St. Paul & Pacific Railroad. If he could but lay hands on that haywire pike, he believed, he could extend it into Dakota and on to Fort Garry and make it a paying line. Just then along came the panic of 1873 to add the final touches needed to ripen the St. Paul and Pacific for Hill's ready hands. The road had been grossly overcapitalized from the start, and poorly built. It was now in terrible physical condition, and its financial condition was beyond repair. The Northern Pacific Railroad had been taking steps toward buying it when the panic put the NP into receivership. Hill saw his chance.

Hill went first to Kittson, his St. Paul friend and ally. Kittson had a little money, and so had Hill, but they needed more, much, much more. Hill and Kittson approached Donald Smith, the Hudson's Bay man, and laid out Hill's plan for getting the StP&P. Smith said he would advance some cash, and he also talked George Stephen, president of the Bank of Montreal, into joining the deal. Hill had thoroughly investigated the ailing road, and knew more about it than any of its officials. In 1878 the four men bought the distressed line for approximately one-fifth of its worth, as estimated by Hill. And now Hill, barely forty, set out to perform wonders with the dismal remains of the grandiosely named St. Paul & Pacific.

For very little cash and a lot of credit, Hill laid hands on rails, rolling stock, locomotives, and laborers. Directing the job in person, much of the time at the railhead or in advance of it, Hill drove his construction crews at a furious rate, laying one mile of track every working day, sometimes a mile and a half of it. When he had reached the Canadian border, he reorganized the road into the St. Paul, Minneapolis & Manitoba. The Canadian Pacific, building west in the Dominion, ran a line down from Winnipeg and the two roads met at Pembina. It was destined to be a busy line.

The organization of Hill's new railroad could not have happened at a more opportune time. Two thumping great harvests followed. What had been a trickle of immigrants from Norway and Sweden now rose to full flood. There were homesteads for the taking; or Hill would sell some of the Minnesota land grant that went with the railroad for from $2.50 to $5 an acre. From the first day of its operation the St. Paul, Minneapolis & Manitoba was a highly profitable carrier. Nor was Pembina, or even Winnipeg, Hill's idea for an end of his line. He told friends, as early as 1879, that he was going to push his railroad across the continent to reach Puget Sound. A few of those who knew him best probably believed him. The others jeered.

Jim Hill didn't give a good goddam whether they cheered or jeered. This thickset man, with massive head, graying beard and long gray hair, and one eye—this already grim old lion as he was characterized when still but forty, was of the general aggressive type of American magnate, frontier type, but he was also more. Where most pioneering businessmen worked for today, Hill worked for the future. Hill projected an idea ahead of him, often far ahead, and worked up to it. He had a superb imagination, and brains in plenty. It turned out, a little later, that as a financier he was fit to talk turkey even to J. P. Morgan the elder, and lose neither his shirt nor his pants. His knowledge of the country through which he proposed to lay rails was encyclopedic. How he carried it all in his head was the despair of his enemies, and often of his own employees and associates.

George Westinghouse

Thousands of brakemen were killed or maimed coupling with link and pin.

"Braking in Hard Weather," 1888. The hand-brake was another curse of the trainman's life.

Maj. E. H. Janney: ad. of coupler in The American Engineer (Sept. '93), and print showing device on car.

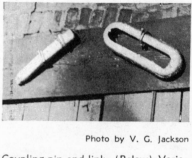

Photo by V. G. Jackson

Coupling pin and link. (Below) Variations: 1, solid-head pin; 2, eye-head flat pin; 3, bent-head pin; 4, crooked link.

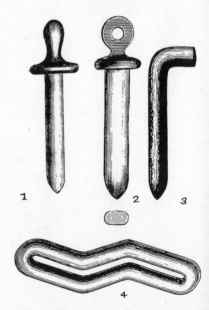

The Airbrake Fanatic, Lorenzo Coffin.

For another thing, Hill insisted that his railroad should be the best possible to build. He often delayed adopting a route until he himself had inspected the grades and curves, but once he had accepted the line of the right-of-way, his roadbed must be perfect. By locomotive, by handcar, passenger coach, caboose, or on horseback, Hill was continuously going over his line, built or projected, seeing everything, asking questions, arguing with his engineers, even with his track foremen, demanding a change here, another there. No cheap bridges for him, either. His model for a railroad bridge was the one he had put across the Mississippi at St. Paul-Minneapolis, a monstrous solid thing of thick granite, fit for a couple of centuries, he said. He wanted the best steel, the biggest and most powerful locomotives.

An aside at this point is necessary to indicate briefly the part played by Jim Hill in the Canadian Pacific Railway, a part of his life that has been obscured by his greater achievements in the American Northwest. Hill's friends Smith and Stephen were leading spirits in building the great Canadian transcontinental. They invited Hill to join the syndicate that underwrote the project. This he did, and he also gave excellent advice as to the route selected and the policies of construction. But Hill's greatest contribution to the CPR was his recommendation of William Cornelius Van Horne to be its manager. Hill knew Van Horne as the austere young American who had done marvels in managing the Chicago, Milwaukee & St. Paul Railroad; and now in 1881 he told his CPR associates that Van Horne was the man for them. They engaged him, and Van Horne went ahead to drive the CP rails through to the Pacific shore in one of the great construction epics of North America. Incidentally, Smith, Stephen, and Van Horne all received either baronetcies or knighthoods for their work with the Canadian Pacific. Hill continued to serve as a CPR director until 1883 when, it becoming apparent that the CP and Hill's American lines were competitors in a way, he resigned.

Getting back to the St. Paul, Minneapolis & Manitoba, some of that line's stockholders were aghast when Hill announced he was going to push it through to the Pacific coast. No other company had ever attempted to do such a thing without a subsidy from the government, in lands and sometimes with loans as well. The Union Pacific, the Central Pacific, and the Northern Pacific all had been given millions of acres of public lands. Hill could get no grant—other than the Minnesota land grant which would be of no aid to him in building across Dakota, Montana, Idaho and Washington. And even if by some quirk he did manage to lay his rails to Puget Sound, how then could he hope to compete with the old subsidized lines? The majestic railroad Hill planned to make out of the StPM&M was labeled Hill's Folly.

Hill's Folly moved swiftly westward into Dakota, putting out short feeder branches as it went, for Hill had studied the country at first hand and he knew, as no other did, where a branch might blossom at once because of traffic; and presently the line started on the long haul across Montana, running well north of the Northern Pacific but an encroachment, to the minds of Northern Pacific officials, wherever it went. This unhappy road, now rejuvenated somewhat and in charge of Henry Villard, a cultured man of high imagination and real ability, was carrying on construction at both ends of its line, east and west. Hill ignored it, other than to set his own rates uncommonly low in territory where he could compete with the NP. He had designs on the Villard road, true enough, but he was content to run his own line for the present and to let time and the sheriff catch up with the NP. Hill knew that road to be overcapitalized, and in many portions poorly built. To his good friend, Charles Elliott Perkins of the friendly Burlington, Hill wrote to the effect that the NP ran through a stretch of worthless country, that its bad grades and high interest charges and operating expenses in general were such as to ruin it.

On went the Manitoba, alias Hill's Folly, reaching Great Falls, Montana, in 1887, and that town was glad to grant Hill a strip through its fine park, for it had seen what Hill could do to a stubborn community. He had just built his railroad in a graceful arc around Fort Benton, a town that had rejected his demands for a right-of-way, and left it a full mile from the tracks.

Hill always protected his rear, for there he saw to it that a defense of grain elevators went up and that more and still more immigrants, chiefly from northern Europe, came to settle and plow and harvest, and use the grain elevators and the Manitoba's low freight rates to market. Hill would haul a healthy immigrant half way across the United States for $10, if he'd agree to settle along Hill rails; or, if it were an entire family, complete with household effects and perhaps even a few animals, he'd rent 'em a freight car for little more—just so long as they settled along the Manitoba.

Nor did Hill, despite much loose writing to the contrary, gouge his new settlers with high rates once he had them on the land. He wrote his partners again and again that it was to their best advantage to give low rates and to do all possible to develop the country and increase traffic as they pushed the rails ever westward.

While the Manitoba continued its way steadily through Montana, the Northern Pacific was going the way Hill had predicted. Villard was soon ousted in the midst of a typical railroad scandal of the period. Then came the panic year of 1893—incidentally, the year in which Hill's Folly, called the Great Northern since 1890, reached Puget Sound at Everett, Washington—and the NP failed again. It was a tough year for Pacific railroads. The Santa Fe went into the hands of a receiver. So did the Union Pacific. Of all the rails that reached the West Shore, only Hill's Great Northern survived intact. And now Hill was ready to take care of the troublesome NP. With Edward Tuck and his old associate of the Bank of Montreal, now Lord Mount Stephen, Hill made an agreement with NP bond-holders to take over that railroad. But a Great Northern stockholder objected, citing a Minnesota law that prohibited unification of parallel and competing railroads. An injunction was granted and the agreement halted.

There was, however, no legal barrier to Hill and his associates buying into the NP as individuals. This they did, and henceforth the NP was, for all practical purposes, a second track for the Great Northern. What had been first the St. Paul & Pacific, then the St. Paul, Minneapolis & Manitoba, then Hill's Folly, was now the Great Northern and, with the Northern Pacific was coming to be known simply as the Hill Lines. The Hill Lines were due for further expansion.

During all of this battle for rights-of-way, of titans jousting, of big-time financing and immense strategy, Jim Hill still had time to permit play of his minor likes and passions. I think several incidents are revealing of his character and of his insatiable and immediate interest in anything per-taining to his railroads. One glimpse of Hill in action comes from Lee Howard. Mr. Howard, later a celebrated pilot on the Yukon, and still rugged in 1946, told me of working in a Hill track gang in Dakota, in the late 70's. "During a sizable blizzard," Mr. Howard recalls, "Jim Hill came out in his special car to where a crew of us were trying to clear the line. He didn't stay in his car, either. He grabbed my shovel and started tossing snow, telling me to go back to his car and I'd find a pot of coffee there. I did, and spent half an hour drinking coffee and resting. Mr. Hill spelled off first one man, then another. My, but he was tough! He must have shoveled snow two or three hours that day.

"It has been told of Jim Hill that he knew all of his superintendents and chief foremen by name. Hell, he even knew the first names of all of the older shovel-stiffs! He cussed us impartially when things went wrong, or when we weren't working fast enough to suit him. He was obviously a man who was used to having his own way. When he didn't, he got hot under his collar, and I'm telling you he wore a powerfully big collar."

One of the remembered great snows of the prairies came in 1897. At that time, and among many other things, Hill had the contract to carry the mails between Ortonville, Minnesota, and Ellendale, North Dakota. The railroad was paralyzed by six feet of brand-new snow. The story goes that the Post Office Department wired Hill, after several days of no mail at Ellendale, saying they were going to fine him $5,000 for breach of contract. Hill wired back: "Gladly pay you ten thousand dollars if you will get this line open and keep it that way."

Of Jim Hill's vindictiveness many a town has a story to tell. One of the best of the authenticated stories, and perhaps as typical as any in the lot, concerns Wayzata, on the shores of Lake Minnetonka, celebrated by Longfellow, and comes from Mrs. Thelma Jones, a resident of the town. "In the days before malarial control," says Mrs. Jones,* "many rich Southern families, particularly from New Orleans and St. Louis, came north to Lake Minnetonka, with their colored servants, to escape the fever season. For these people large wooden hotels sprang up all around the lake. Two of these hotels, the Gleason House and the Minnetonka House, were right in the village of Wayzata, and almost upon the water's edge. Almost, but not quite, for between them and the beach ran the Great Northern tracks.

"The through trains would go past at quite a clip, whistling. Added to that was a good deal of switching of cars, some of it at night, right between the aristocratic guests and the beautiful lake. Hotel guests were annoyed by the noise and the obstruction of their view, and the townspeople also became incensed.

"Sometime in the nineties, the Wayzata mayor, E. B. Sanders, who perhaps not incidentally owned the Gleason House, brought some sort of injunction against the railroad, and it was fined. Jim Hill was pretty mad about it, and he is said to have vowed to wipe Wayzata off the map. He immediately had the Wayzata station taken down and moved to Holdridge, a mile or so to the east.

"Many of the villagers lined up to watch the first train that was to pass them by. She went through with the bell ringing and the whistle blowing derisively, and with the big stack throwing smoke and cinders over everything, including the water tank, which caught fire. From that day on, for about fifteen years, according to oldtimers here—although one insists it was longer, lasting until Hill's death in 1916—Wayzatans had to take livery service, at fifty cents a head, to ride to Holdridge to catch the train. The livery service did very well because, of course, all freight for Wayzata was also put off at Holdridge.

"It was pressure brought by influential families, including the Pillsburys, the Peavys, and Lorings—who had estates in the neighborhood—that ultimately got Jim Hill, or his son Louis, to restore service at Wayzata, and when this was finally done, the GN put up one of the finest small stations along its line."

The Wayzata business was Jim Hill at his worst. Just as typical was his loyalty and honesty. Mrs. Anne McDonnell, assistant librarian of the Montana State Historical Society, relates † that when Johnny Grant, famous pioneer character, sold his Montana property for $20,000 and retired to a farm near Winnipeg, Manitoba, about 1868, he thought it was too much money to have around his place. He gave it to young Jim Hill,

---

* In letters to the author, 1946.
† In a letter to the author, 1946.

then carrying on the Red River Transportation Company, to take care of. Hill invested it so well in his own enterprises that when Johnny came to need some of his $20,000, Hill returned it to him, not only in full, but in more than triple—and some say even more than that.

None of these small matters, however, deflected Hill in the least from his great consuming passion—to build a railroad system that should embrace the northwestern United States, yes, and perhaps the Middle West states as well. With the NP at last where he wanted it, and his own GN at last on Puget Sound, he turned his attention to getting a through line to Chicago and St. Louis—for a very good reason: Hill knew that for at least several years the Great Northern's eastbound business would be lumber, or nothing. Lumber was about all the Pacific Northwest had to offer. Hill knew that the treeless Midwest was potentially the greatest lumber market in the country. Very well, then, he would supply the lumber and deliver it so cheaply that even the near-at-hand Southern pine people could not compete with the Northwest product in the Midwest market.

Lumber, then, would be Hill's traffic eastward. But it would not do to haul empty cars back to the Northwest. In Jim Hill's sight nothing was quite so loathsome as an empty Great Northern freight car. So, he must plot his strategy so that his westbound cars should be filled to the very roofs and bulging at the sides. The Orient, as related, had always appealed to Hill's imagination, and now he sent agents to Japan and China to investigate trade conditions. These men he instructed to get a manifest of every ship that cleared a Japanese or a Chinese port; to learn where all imports came from, what they were; and where all exports went to. At the same time Hill sent agents into New England, into the Atlantic states, into the South, with orders to find out what could be made or grown in those parts that would be welcome in the Orient.

While these investigations were going forward very quietly, Hill set out to get the railroad he wanted to complete his empire of rails. This turned out to be no less than the Chicago, Burlington & Quincy. The Burlington was based on the Great Lakes and extended to the Rocky Mountains. It was particularly strong on the Mississippi and the Missouri. Its mileage in Nebraska alone was sufficient for a trunk line from New York to Salt Lake City; and if its Iowa mileage were added, the line would extend to Los Angeles or Puget Sound. One arm of the Burlington connected Chicago and Denver; another, reaching out from St. Louis and Kansas, passed diagonally through Nebraska, into the Black Hills of Dakota and Wyoming, crossed the Crow Reservation in Montana and made a connection with the Northern Pacific near Billings. If Hill could get control of the Burlington, he would have direct contact with the cotton-hauling roads entering St. Louis and Kansas City, with the smelters of Denver and the Black Hills, with the great packing houses of Omaha, Kansas City, and

Chicago; and, most important of all, he would have a direct line into the heart of the lumber-consuming region of the prairie states.*

With J. P. Morgan as his ally, Hill set out to buy the Burlington from under the nose of Edward Henry Harriman, then head of the Union Pacific. Harriman wanted the Burlington for himself, and though he was astute, swift, and ruthless, the Hill-Morgan forces outgeneralled him and got control of the CB&Q. Harriman, however, was not done. After trying vainly to get at least a third of the Burlington stock for himself, he determined on the bold plan of snatching control of the Northern Pacific from Hill. So quietly and swiftly did Harriman buy that he had a majority of all NP stock before such ordinarily lynx-eyed men as Hill and Morgan knew what was up.

Yet, Harriman still did not own a majority of NP common; and presently he feared, with very good reason, that Hill was going to call a meeting and have his stockholders vote to retire the NP preferred stock, and thus outwit Harriman. To prevent such a calamity, Harriman ordered his men to buy 40,000 shares of NP common, regardless of price. They failed to do so. Hill and Morgan retained control. They also made a sort of temporary and strictly regional peace with Harriman.

Hill now controlled the great system of the Burlington. And now the far-seeing strategy of the Great Northern's Little Giant becomes plain: Hill's agents in the Orient and elsewhere had been working to some purpose. Japanese industrialists crossed the Pacific to meet Mr. Hill, and Mr. Hill prevailed on them to try a shipment of American cotton to mix with the short-staple article that Japanese mills had been getting from India. Hill said he would deliver the American cotton to Japan free of carrying charges, if they did not find it good. They took Hill at his word. They found the American cotton very good indeed, and from then on Great Northern cars carried a steadily increasing amount of Southern cotton over Burlington and GN rails to Seattle for shipment to Japan. It proved to be a huge business. So did the American export of New England cotton goods to China. Minnesota flour went across the Pacific. So did metals from Colorado. Thus did Jim Hill's imagination build a trade route from New Orleans and Boston to the Orient.

Hill kept his rates, not as high as the traffic would stand, but as low as the Great Northern-Northern Pacific-Burlington could stand. He liked to say that if the people of a single province of China could be induced to eat an ounce of American flour a day, it would require some 70 million bushels of Midwest wheat annually. Hill lines carried the flour dirt-cheap to Seattle where, through arrangements and inducements made by Hill, the

---

* The late Frederick Weyerhaeuser, whose position in the lumber industry was as great as Hill's in the railroad world, used to say that he would rather have the lumber trade of Iowa alone than of any other three states combined. The Burlington then had some 1,400 miles of track in Iowa.

Nippon Yusen Kaisha sent its ships to take the product across the ocean. Meanwhile, Hill's line laid Puget Sound and North Idaho lumber down at sidings of the American Midwest at prices which encouraged the building of the rugged houses and barns and silos and fences that still mark that region.

Another of Hill's dreams was to populate the great and so-called wasteland between the Great Lakes and Puget Sound—to populate it with farmers and ranchers until there should scarcely be an unused acre in the region. To this end he imported the finest cattle possible, animals which combined qualities of both beef and milk production, and gave them away free to farmers along the Hill lines. He advocated diversified farming. He instigated and supported dry-farming congresses. He set up prizes for the best exhibits of grain grown on dry farms within 25 miles of his railroad. To Europe he sent scores of agents armed with wonderful photographic slides depicting Western farming, to be thrown on screens to amaze and seduce Scotsmen, Englishmen, Norwegians, and Swedes.

The effects of Hill's variegated campaigns were startling. In 1909 homesteaders took up more than one million acres in Montana alone. In 1910 still more homesteaders settled on 4,750,000 Montana acres. Between 1910 and 1922, 42 per cent of the entire area of the state was settled by homesteaders, virtually all of them induced to come there by the enthusiasm and perseverance of Hill (who died in 1916) and his inspired agents.

The tragedy of all this, according to many authorities,* was that at least 80 per cent of the area settled was unfit for crop agriculture, even though the wheat acreage increased from 258,000 acres in 1909 to 3,417,-000 acres ten years later. This, so it turned out, was the mere laying of groundwork for the disaster that followed. Deep plowing of the land brought erosion. The wind, which in Montana and the Dakotas, never stops blowing, blew the soil out of and disaster into the region. Thousands of small personal tragedies followed. A couple of lines of statistics largely explain the tragedies: From 1900 to 1916 the grasslands of Montana yielded an annual average of more than 25 bushels of wheat to the plowed acre. In 1919 the yield was 2.4 bushels per plowed acre. . . . The honyockers, the come-lately homesteaders, gave up and moved away. It was the one portion of Jim Hill's magnificent dream that did not pan out as he had planned it.

In the meantime, the Hill-Harriman war had broken out again, this time in the Far West. Jim Hill seems to have been the aggressor. Perhaps he

* Including Joseph Kinsey Howard, whose affectionate yet hardboiled and realistic *Montana, High, Wide, and Handsome,* New Haven, 1943, is a fine and moving account of what happened to Montana homesteads and homesteaders.

did not enjoy contemplating the fact that Harriman, through his Union Pacific and Southern Pacific, naturally enough considered Oregon as his private preserve. In 1905, while attending the Lewis and Clark Exposition in Portland, Jim Hill took occasion to announce, rather casually, that he intended to "help in the development of this great state."

Now, when Jim Hill planned to help with development anywhere, it behooved any other developers to watch out. Harriman soon learned that Hill already had completed surveys down the North Bank of the Columbia River to occupy the water-level route across the Cascade Mountains which the NP had once planned to use but had been deflected to the South Bank by some eccentricity of Henry Villard. Hill now set crews to grading and laying track.

Harriman met the threat to his empire with gusto, organizing a couple of trick paper-railroads to conflict with the Hill locations all the way. Much of this portion of the war was fought in the courts, although the opposing crews in the field made it something of a personal matter by carrying on fist fights, night raids on one another, and several attempts at dynamiting equipment. It was during this battle that Harriman was stricken with appendicitis and had to go to the hospital for an operation. Just as soon as he could sit upright in bed and hold a telephone in his hand, he called Jim Hill long distance to say that he, E. H. Harriman, was feeling fit as a fiddle and would soon be back at the front. Aye, they had warriors in those days. . . .

Hill won the North Bank fight, and his new line, later called the Spokane, Portland & Seattle, went into joint operation by the Great Northern and Northern Pacific. In 1908, Hill trains started rolling to Portland. Nor was Hill quite finished with his urge to "develop this great state." Into the Central Oregon country, one day soon, went a genial sportsman, one John F. Sampson, who carried more poles and reels and trout flies than had ever before been seen on the Deschutes River, a notable trout stream. Sampson appeared to be carrying a lot of cash, too, and so taken was he with this sportsman's paradise that he bought options on wild lands and ranches all over the place. Then he suddenly disappeared.

In Portland at this time lived William Nelson who owned controlling interest in a nonexistent railroad called the Oregon Trunk. A little surveying had been done for this road, long before, up the east bank of the Deschutes River. Otherwise it existed wholly on paper and was wholly moribund when Nelson was surprised to be approached by the mysterious sportsman, Mr. Sampson, and all but stunned, a few days later, when Mr. Sampson and he met in a city park and Sampson paid him $150,000 in good legal tender for his stock in the Oregon Trunk. It was an event, in Mr. Nelson's otherwise comparatively unexciting career; he afterward related everything as being either before or after Mr. Sampson's appearance in his life.

Right on the heels of this astounding transaction, the stranger appeared again, this time under his right name, which was John F. Stevens. He was none other than the former chief engineer of the Panama Canal, the same engineer who had discovered, or rediscovered, a fine lost pass through the Rockies for his present employer, Mr. Hill, for whom he acted as agent and chief engineer.* Stevens now announced that Mr. Hill was about to construct a railroad from the Columbia River up the Deschutes River and to an unknown town of Central Oregon called Bend. Bend happened to be 165 miles from the Columbia and situated in a region marked by some of the greatest open spaces known to man—practically unlimited stretches of sagebrush desert hedged with a truly wonderful stand of Ponderosa pine. A few Indians and even fewer white people lived in the region.

But Mr. Harriman knew very well that Bend was not the terminus Mr. Hill had in mind for his seemingly weird Oregon railroad. Hill, he was certain, meant to build to Bend, right enough, and so on in a direct line to San Francisco. It would not do to leave Central Oregon alone with Mr. Hill for a moment. To parallel Hill's Oregon Trunk, Harriman moved a gigantic crew into the neighborhood and they proceeded to make grade and lay track up the west bank of the Deschutes, calling their line the Deschutes Railroad.

George W. Boschke, he who had built the famous sea wall at Galveston, Texas, was in charge of the Harriman forces. Porter Brothers were building the Hill line. And now while much of the West watched with increasing excitement, the two great men of Western railroading engaged in what proved to be the last of the formidable railroad-construction wars.

Oldtimers in Central Oregon still cherish memories of the Deschutes railroad war. All supplies, even hay, had to be packed in for the huge crews working for each company. In the narrow Deschutes canyon, a cleft in high hills of rock, the gangs carried on war by exploding dynamite charges to interfere with the opposing faction. Men were killed, some by boulders that mysteriously started rolling. A crisis came at Mile 75, when Engineer Boschke received a telegram, purportedly from Galveston: "The sea wall has broken." Boschke ignored it for the fake it was, saying that he had built the sea wall to stand and stand he knew it did.

A mixup in titles and surveys and court orders and one thing and another came to a head at the ranch of a man named Smith, who managed to prove his claim to the land, then sold a right-of-way to Harriman. As there was no other route to get to Bend from this point, other than over the Smith place, Hill decided to arbitrate matters, and a truce was made by which Hill agreed to build no farther than Bend and to permit Harri-

---

* He is remembered in a statue to be seen from GN trains going through Marias Pass, at Summit. Montana.

man to use his line on which to run Harriman trains from Metolius, a small collection of huts 42 miles from Bend.

The truce, however, applied only to Central Oregon. In the western part of the state, where the Harriman Southern Pacific had long dominated affairs, Hill now bought several electric lines to compete with the SP. He bought an ocean terminal near Astoria, at the mouth of the Columbia, installed two big steamers on the San Francisco run, and put on a boat train to carry passengers from Portland to the docks, making good enough time to compete successfully with the SP rails to California. Harriman built several extension feeder lines in western Oregon, and laid plans for a new SP main line from Weed, California, to Portland by way of Klamath Falls. This line was completed after Harriman's death in 1909, just as a Great Northern extension was completed from Bend to San Francisco after Hill's death, six years later in 1915. So was the war of the Western giants continued long after they had ceased to be interested in rails.

Almost to the day of his death Jim Hill continued active. His temper did not improve with the years, and associates found him increasingly difficult to get along with. On one occasion he tore a telephone from its roots and heaved it through a window. On another, he fired an inoffensive Great Northern clerk who, when asked by Hill, replied that his name was Spittles. It *was* Spittles, too, and Hill fired him because of it.

In matters of art Hill showed a taste that is not usually associated with self-made industrialists. He filled his St. Paul home with paintings, not of alleged Old Masters and fading academicians so favored by most millionaires, but with French moderns, and this at a time when few others except, perhaps, Gertrude Stein could see and comprehend the new trend in painting and unerringly pick the masters of it. Hill put up a fine library building in St. Paul and endowed it generously. He wrote a book or two. He held ideas about civilization that were similar to and antedated those of Frederick Jackson Turner, author of *The Frontier in American History,* one of the most influential books in American literature. "Population without the Prairie," said Hill. "is a mob, and the Prairie without Population is a desert."

Well, Jim Hill did his damnedest to bring the mob to the prairie. Judge Thomas Burke, one of Seattle's great figures, summed up Hill's contributions as of 1905. "Twenty-five years ago," he said, "Mr. Hill found the Northwest, between Minnesota and Puget Sound, practically a wild, uninhabited, and inaccessible country. A considerable portion of it used to be set down in the old geographies as a part of the Great American Desert. Yet, largely owing to his superior knowledge of the real character and capabilities of the new land, and through his wonderful energy and ability in providing for it, even in advance of population, the most judiciously planned, the most economically constructed, and the most wisely managed line that has ever served a new country, that region has, in less than fifteen years, given four new states to the Union with an aggregate population of more than one million five hundred thousand people."

That is no bombast, no hyperbole. Even though the wind and the plow removed many of those people from the region, others came, and Hill's empire across the northern boundary still stands, with a future as great as anything Hill imagined. Judge Burke might also have mentioned the unquestioned fact of Hill's contributions to the art and science of operating a railroad through a sparsely settled country. Probably no other railroad man on the American scene ever had the imagination and ability combined in Jim Hill. Some prideful Westerners have called him the first Titan of railroading. Perhaps he was. I think both Commodore Vanderbilt and William B. Ogden deserve the name of Titan, too, as we in the United States apply it to our outstanding figures of industry and commerce. But I also believe that Hill was the greatest of the Titans, and also the last of the line.

The Great Northern's Number 1 train, the *Empire Builder,* is named for Hill, and no train of steamcars has a name more solidly founded on fact. When Number 1 whistles for Sauk Center or Whitefish or Bonners Ferry or Snohomish, for two thousand miles across the top of the United States, the echoes scarcely find a swampy nook or a mountain valley that Jim Hill himself did not know at first hand. No other empire builder ever knew his empire so well, so minutely as the shaggy-headed, one-eyed lad from Ontario.

I think there are today qualities of Jim Hill to be felt along the line of the Great Northern, I mean in the land and the climate and the very towns and stations of this striking, handsome, harsh, desolate, wild, and often bitter region. Little forlorn Malta, an angry sun beating down, baking the falsefronts, roasting the soil, dust rolling up from behind the *Empire Builder* . . . Havre at night, snapping from intense cold, while engines are being changed, coyotes howling just outside the town limits . . . The fabulous glittering hill that is Butte at night, seen from the NP's *North Coast Limited* as it comes out of the high pass—Butte the exterminator of vegetation, and away to the south the gigantic stack that is Anaconda, Tallest Stack on Earth, spewing forth its yellow fumes. . . . Bonners Ferry in the Idaho Panhandle, still fragrant with white pine sawdust of a mill whose soul is now gone but whose skeleton stands stark in the moonlight, banked by ten feet of snow. . . . The tumultuous Kootenai River, boiling white over the rocks, vivid green in the pools. . . . East Portal, then the long thundering bore through the Cascade Range, and the emergence into the dripping, fog-ridden silence of the towering firs, the most sombre and melancholy forest on earth; and soon the lights of Puget Sound and of ships leaving for the Orient.

Seventy years ago, in his imagination, Jim Hill hitched these Pacific shore docks to the cornfields of Iowa, to the cotton fields of the South, and to the spindles of Amoskeag in Manchester on the Merrimac. Seventy years ago Hill dreamed it. Fifty years ago it was done. I can think of no other single American who had quite so much influence on quite so large a region.

Commodore Cornelius
Vanderbilt

James J. Hill

Union Pacific photo

Edward H. Harriman

"The Public Be Damned!" Muckraking cartoon from Puck (Oct. 18, 1882) attacking William H. Vanderbilt, New York Central president.

The Brave Engineer was one of the epic figures of the 19th century. The Police Gazette's caption said: "A Fast Life! How the Railroad Engineer Kills Time and Space, and Couples Cares and Pleasures in his Swift Pursuit of a Living."

CHAPTER XVI

Locating the Route

The real winning of the West belongs to the railroads.
— EDWARD GILLETTE, Locating Engineer, 1925.

IN 1879 when he was twenty-five years old, Edward Gillette arrived in the village of Sante Fé, territorial capital of New Mexico, as an assistant topographer of the United States Survey west of the 100th meridian. He was dead broke, and found that neither his chief nor any other member of his party had come. He also discovered that food and lodging was on a strictly cash basis. The situation was bad from a personal viewpoint, but hardly one for intervention of the state, so it was with considerable hesitancy that the young man made a call on the territorial governor, General Lew Wallace.

General Wallace was not then nearly so well known as he was to become a bit later, for when Gillette met him, the whiskered veteran of the Rebellion was just putting the finishing touches to his book which he completed in what he described as a "vile old chamber" in the fort at Santa Fé, a "gloomy den indeed." In 1879 the General also had a feuding cattle war on his hands, yet he had time for the young tenderfoot with the Yankee accent. General Wallace told the hotel proprietor to let Gillette have what cash and credit he wanted, and otherwise smoothed the way for the young man. Gillette never forgot it, and in his old age he wrote with warmth of Wallace, saying that no stranger had ever been so kind to him.

Gillette, born in New Haven, was fairly fresh out of Sheffield Scientific School at Yale, where one of his classmates had been John Hays Hammond, soon to be a world figure. Gillette himself was to become something of a figure in the American West as a locating engineer. He was one of those restless Yankees who in the latter half of last century seemed determined to locate, build, and operate all of the railroads West of the Mississippi. He also belonged to a smaller, a more exclusive class than that of the railroad presidents and general managers, in that he was one of the leading scouts in the advance toward the Pacific of the steel rails. Landlookers, timber cruisers, railroad locating engineers, they all are members of the same club, men who can and do work silently, almost secretively, and to no applause.

It was Gillette's first trip to the West, and he found the West inclined to live up to the reputation accorded it in the novels of Mr. Beadle's Dime Library. On his way through Missouri on a railroad train a wild crew of political supporters and their candidate for Congress got aboard and turned the cars into a campaign arena. The candidate was ordered to make a speech, but before he was finished the order was changed to a request for a song. So, like all good politicians, he sang. The place was bedlam. Whiskey had come aboard in gallons and now it flowed, while the gang staggered from car to car, several of them drawing guns and shooting holes through the tops of the coaches. At way stations, those members of the political group who could still walk, got off the cars and compelled Negroes to sing and dance, supporting the performance by shooting into the ground to accelerate matters.

El Moro, Colorado, was the end of the line in 1879. Gillette boarded a stage, to find the driver enjoying a terrific hangover. Said he had been to a Mexican dance the night before and thought that now, just before leaving, would be a good time for a pickup. He threw down three more tumblers of straight whiskey, cracked his whip, and away they went. Gillette was the only passenger, and the driver gave him a ride he never forgot. He kept the horses at a reckless gait, and the stage careened sickeningly along narrow canyon roads, leaped across ditches, and shook like palsy. Gillette wondered at the driver's desire for speed until the man, soggy with booze, broke down enough to remark he was getting out of Colorado pronto, that at the dance he had killed or badly wounded a couple of Mexicans—he didn't know which it was—and he thought it might be a good idea to leave the country "until the affair blew over."

On they went, taking the sharp canyon curves on two wheels. When they met a Mexican on a pony, the driver let go a yell, lashed his team, and bore down on the little brown man and horse, throwing the man and delighting the sadistic driver. Then the stage gave a mighty lurch, and Gillette looked down to see one wheel rolling away through the brush. He leaped and landed plumb in a bunch of cactus. When he had climbed out of the prickly things, he saw that the three-wheeled stage had been forced to halt. He found the driver hanging over the pole, completely oblivious and badly injured. Gillette managed to get the fourth wheel put back, then took the reins and drove on to Fort Union. Here he tried lodging in a shack that passed for a hotel, but soon found the bed fairly crawling. He got up, took his own blankets, and went out onto the prairie where he lay down for the night, being disturbed only once and that by a polecat. When he got up next morning he suffered from an acute attack of homesickness. New Haven was never like this.

The trip from Fort Union to Santa Fé was made without incident, and the kindness of General Wallace put a new face on the Wild West, even though young Gillette could not have known that he was to spend the rest of his long life in taming that same Wild West, locating the lines of railroads in Arizona, Colorado, Nebraska, the Dakotas, Wyoming, Montana, and finally Alaska. "The winning of the west," he said in his old age, "has been ascribed to the early trappers, explorers, stockmen, and settlers, but the real winning of the West belongs to the railroads." He was right, and for the next forty years he helped to prove it.

For little more than a year Gillette received a wonderful course in surveying in rough country, the scene being the Leadville, Twin Lakes, and Gunnison regions of Colorado, and the object being to verify and correct former government surveys. Most of the work was above the 10,000-foot level, and some reached 14,000 feet. Gillette soon discovered that a man could not move so fast nor so far on such heights as in the valleys. It was smoky much of the time, too, from continuous forest fires. In the Silver City district where, as related elsewhere in this book the Santa Fe and the Denver & Rio Grande were contesting the right-of-way, Gillette's government party was immediately under suspicion by the latter road's men being minions of the Santa Fe. Despite their denials an armed guard was set to watch their camp.

At Leadville, Gillette's party found intense activity, and miners there tried to seduce them to remain and take up the business of surveying mine claims. They refused, although Gillette remarked that the miners offered to pay them more for two days' work than the government paid them for a month's. But the railroads finally got Gillette. In 1881 he joined the main survey party of the Sevier Valley line, a subsidiary of the Denver & Rio Grande, and started work where the 39th degree of latitude crosses Green River. A band of Ute Indians told the party they had better forget the railroad and to skin out of there before Ute braves set upon them. The surveyors paid them no heed.

Gillette's party was ordered to survey one route west from Green River to Salina Canyon, which was to be the main line to San Francisco, and a branch line from Green River to Salt Lake City by way of Soldier Canyon. Although Gillette was not chief engineer, he had done more preliminary map work on the survey than anyone else in the party; and he was surprised that Soldier Canyon rather than Price Canyon was to be the route. He boldly asked his chief why, and got the answer that one Sam Gilson, a noted character of the region, had said that Price Canyon was so crooked a bird couldn't fly through it. Gillette got out his maps and demonstrated to his chief that Price Canyon was not only an easier grade but also a shorter route than the other. The chief must have been a little put out at this forwardness. He at once appropriated the maps and also thought the matter over. Meanwhile Gillette, a man who kept up with the times, had been reading to good purpose in the copy of Wellington's already classic *The Economic Theory of the Location of Railways* that he carried in his blanket roll; and he argued for Wellington's theories in connection with the Price Canyon route.* Gillette's chief changed his mind. The line went through Price Canyon, says Gillette proudly, on a two and one-half per cent grade instead of the four per cent grade in Soldier Canyon.

Unlike many a gentile, Edward Gillette had a good word to say for the Mormons. He told that they bid so close on grading jobs that no other contractor could compete with them, and they worked together like true brothers and sisters. He visited one of their grading camps and was amazed to see the order and cleanliness that was maintained under the most difficult conditions. He noted that the men were particular to wash and to comb their hair before each meal. The Mormon women did the cooking and waited on table. What was more, the grading was always completed within the time limits stipulated in the contract and was all done in a most satisfactory manner.

A bit later, while surveying for an extension through the San Pete Valley, the Mormons of the town of Moroni objected strenuously to the road being laid through their village. The matter was referred to President John Taylor of the Latter-day Saints, a man of the greatest influence who had been wounded seriously when the Prophet was murdered at Carthage jail. Taylor instructed the bishop at Moroni to give the railroad one of the village streets for the right-of-way and also the tithing yard on which to build a depot. Gillette often dined with Mormons in their own homes, and on one occasion, when he was asked to do so, even said grace at table, doubtless in the best Congregational manner that had been observed in his native Connecticut.

Gillette's work must have been quite satisfactory, perhaps even better than that, for he was presently made chief draftsman for the Denver & Rio Grande, and helped to plot the company's line through to San Francisco, by way of Walker Pass and the San Joaquin Valley. There were other extensions of the road, too, and thirty-six parties were kept busy in the field. One troubled route was that from Salt Lake City to Ogden, which the Utah Central attempted to block by laying spur tracks from their main line to the nearby mountains, thus to force the Denver & Rio Grande to make many crossings. Gillette and his party met this difficulty by locating "on the opposite side of the Utah Central, crossing some arms of Great Salt Lake and affording us a straighter and better location for the road."

Late in 1885 Gillette left the D&RG to take charge of a locating party for the Burlington & Missouri River Railroad, a subsidiary of the Chicago, Burlington & Quincy and, except for an interim in Alaska

---

* This bible of railroad engineers, then a standard monograph and still rated as valuable, was published in 1877, the work of Arthur Mellen Wellington, native of Waltham, Mass., who began locating railroad routes in the sixties and later became one of the owners and editors of *Engineering News*.

and a few years in private practice, he spent the rest of his life with the Burlington.

During the next several decades Gillette often reflected that most people first see a railroad as a big crew of laborers who are making right-of-way, laying steel, getting drunk and raising hell generally. Only now and then did observant folk understand the significance of a small party of earnest men who had come through the region, long before the track gangs, with surveying instruments, who worked swiftly and silently, said little or nothing to anybody, then passed on, leaving no trace of their coming other than for a few stakes, driven here and there with no system apparent to the layman. These were the men who said where the tracks were to go, and they had it in their ability or their incompetence either to aid the road to success or to condemn it to failure. It has always seemed to me that the locating engineers of railroads have never had their due, or anything approaching it, in the literature of the rails.

It is likely that Edward Gillette was well above average in this field, and he entered it at a great period. Eighty-four was the start of a great heyday of railroad construction in the West. All of the lines, both the dinkies and the big ones, were searching out routes and laying steel with furious speed and greed. Civil engineers, as more than one railroad president came to learn, could make or break a line with almost no effort. "I'm tired of building monuments to engineers," said old Collis Huntington, a man of direct speech, when some engineer or other of the Central Pacific made an error that would have bankrupted a weaker line.

Railroads could be and were built where a mountain goat couldn't climb and often with no thought of the future, for, as Wellington remarked, a company could be bled to death through operating expenses from bad location, expenses which came "from a gentle but unceasing ooze from every pore which attracts no attention, albeit resulting in a loss vastly larger than any possible loss from bad construction." Gillette never forgot this admonition of the master. He considered every curve and grade in the light of operation and must have been pretty successful at it, in view of his long record with one line. He also had to contend with the matter of speed in locating, for in that period of great rivalry, railroads were anything but polite to each other. They fought each other with thugs and guns, and they raced to see which could get its tracks laid first into ripe territory. Gillette's first job with the Burlington was one of these.

The order was to locate a line from Aurora to Hastings, Nebraska. He was given maps and profiles of several surveys made by railroad engineers and told to go ahead and select the best route but to do it as speedily as possible; a right-of-way agent was to follow closely on his heels to buy the land over which the route was located.

Well, Chief of Party Gillette, on his first Burlington job, looked over

the maps of previous surveys. He found that all of the lines deviated
from a direct route for the purpose of following a stream named Blue
River. It was flat country, also thickly populated when compared to the
Utah region he had been working in. He didn't like the meandering lines
indicated. He drew on his map a straight line between Aurora and Hastings, then got a horse and rode out along the section lines, noting where
his line would run. He found it to miss most of the barns and farmhouses,
and to be for the most part on good level ground, crossing nothing but
small drainage. After riding along this line for some 12 miles he returned
to his party and started in to locate the right-of-way.

One gets an idea of what was meant by "as soon as possible" by learning that the first 12 miles was located in 48 hours, and that the third day
after locating work was begun, the Burlington agent was dickering with
farmers and buying rights to cross their lands. The Aurora-Hastings line,
as located by Gillette, turned out to be two miles shorter than any of the
surveys, and also of much less grade. He felt pretty good that his first job
should turn out so well, especially considering the speed with which it was
done.

The personnel of a railroad-locating party favored by Gillette consisted
of the chief, a transitman, head chainman, rear chainman, back flagman,
stake marker, stake driver, levelman, rodman, topographer, and assistant,
draftsman, cook, two line teamsters and a supply teamster. Where there
was much timber, he took along a few axmen; and in rough country employed a pack train of three packers and about twenty animals. In game
country, he also carried a hunter to supply the table. "And a dog," he
added. "A camp without a dog is the same as a home without children."

What was he like, this Yankee engineer who was to locate so much railroad in the American West? F. T. Darrow, long-time chief engineer of the
Burlington Lines, knew him well and found him able as well as affable.
"I recall him, Gillette," Mr. Darrow told me, "as of medium height and
inclined to stoutness, though he was agile even in his age. He was, of
course, tanned like leather, had brown hair and wore a clipped mustache.
He had a dry sense of humor that is supposed to be and probably is
Yankee. He could even take a joke on himself and enjoy it. His manner
of working was to pick the best men he could find, and then to rely on them
for all details. He was always ready to discuss the work in hand with any
of his party."

There were hard and dangerous times in the business, and in January of
'86 Gillette had a narrow escape from death in a blizzard, saving himself
only by the most prodigious courage. The party was locating the line
north of Broken Bow. Not only the weather was bitter. So were the times;
the cheapest fuel was corn bought from the widely scattered farmers
at ten cents a bushel. The region was so wild that when the party arrived

at Rankin's ranch on the middle fork of Loup River, the cowhands there could not believe that a railroad was about to penetrate so remote a spot.

With spring came grass fires; the pests came with the warmer days, and Gillette says they were quite terrible. The horses suffered most, even when they were covered with grain sacks. Once, when he clapped his hand to a horse's nose, Gillette killed fourteen great horseflies, big as bees.

Gillette pushed on, heading for the entrance of the Black Hills in South Dakota. He found some difficulty crossing Pine Ridge to Crawford because of steep grades, but beyond Crawford, where the line touched that of the Chicago & North Western, the going was fine and dandy into Dakota and on to the TOT ranch, which became the town of Edgemont. When they reached the Cheyenne River, the party surveyed a branch line through the middle of the Black Hills to Deadwood, already a fabulous place. A few members of the party were taken with the urge to dig for gold, but none seems to have become addicted to three other items for which the region celebrated itself—rum, robbery, and Indian women of purchasable virtue. They found plenty of wild game to supply their table, but often had trouble getting good water.

The Sioux had not yet given up their desire to be left alone in their own lands. A number of smaller uprisings had led to the tragic and bloody climax at Wounded Knee. Gillette and his party came upon ranch after ranch that was wholly deserted, the cows and chickens left to shift for themselves. The ranchers had fled to Custer. But no Indians came, even though the railroad party went fully armed with rifles and made quite a display wherever they camped, the guns stacked military-fashion.

The rails were following hard on the heels of the locators. On January 27, 1888, the steel had reached Alliance, Nebraska. And now Gillette had an opportunity to see what had been going on in his wake. He made a trip in the cars from Alliance to Lincoln, and was all but dazed at the changes. Towns, says he, with courthouses, schools, churches and stores had sprung up. Where he had scarcely yesterday sighted a level along some desolate river bank, now stood what looked to him like a city. It was wonderful, he thought, and he permitted himself to reflect with pride that it was the railroad that had done this. The world had never seen such transformation in so brief a space of time, all thanks to the Burlington, and, of course, to the Union Pacific and the Chicago & North Western.

With hardly a breathing spell Gillette took out another party to locate the Burlington between Greeley Center and Ord. The Union Pacific had by now come to look at the Burlington as an invading and dangerous enemy; and Gillette was warned to use as much secrecy as possible when running new locations. He adopted a plan by which he and his party would arrive at a certain spot on an agreed day, locate the line that day, and next day supply a cross-section party with profiles of the line and the land agent with maps and notes sufficient to permit him to purchase right-of-way intelligently. All of this happened in two days. On the third day there would heave in, as if dumped down from the sky, a crew of several hundred laborers together with horses and wagons. Construction started when they arrived.

Many of the routes selected so hurriedly no doubt had to be abandoned later, but so greedy were the roads to tap rich territory that they thought the best thing to do first was to get there; and to consider revamping the line later. Yet, a surprisingly large percentage of Gillette's original locations were never improved upon.

When not hurried Gillette surveyed with care. He liked to run preliminary lines over every possible route between two points, then by personal comparison to select the best. Other conditions being equal, he took the route with the easiest grade. Distance, he thought, was of secondary importance compared to a light grade. Indeed, he often sought distance in order to lighten a grade. In general he avoided shallow cuts, on account of snow, and took the sunny side of a valley where he could.

In time, Gillette came to believe that railroads, all railroads, made a mistake when they let a construction job at a rate too low to permit a decent profit to the contractor. It had been done, time and again, on the Denver & Rio Grande, on the Burlington, on the Chicago & North Western. Gillette took pains to check these jobs and to note what the results had been. In every case, he says, where a contractor lost money, the railroad suffered even more, and for many reasons. For one thing, the stores and farmers were usually left holding the bag for the provisions they had supplied. Often the men didn't even get their wages. And when the rate of contract became obviously too low, and the contractors realized they had made a bad bargain, they were inclined to do shoddy work. Worse than all of these were the countless enemies of the railroad left in the wake of a contractor's failure. Farmers and others held the railroad itself responsible. Often a generation had to pass before old sores were healed.

After doing considerable surveying in the Black Hills, Gillette led his party into Wyoming and so on at last into Montana and to what proved to be farthest west for the Burlington, in the Billings region.

Occasionally he liked to look back to see if the tracks were following him and his men. They were. The steel got to Edgemont, South Dakota, in October of 1889, and crossed into Wyoming on the 30th, passing the state line at 9:45 of a morning. One John Smith drove the first spike in Wyoming; the first Burlington train was flagged by W. Hartsell; and John Barry, engineer, and Fireman M. J. Fearing were aboard Locomotive No. 191, the first to cross the line. The conductor was C. E. Shepard. Gillette obviously, and rightly, felt that these "firsts" were just as important to history as the golden-spike-driving ceremonies indulged in by silk-hatted officials of railroads who did not know a fishplate from a bolt, or the meaning of a green flag.

A happy surprise was in store for Gillette. While locating the route across Wyoming he was notified by the head office that Gillette was to be the name of a town on the line between Edgemont and Sheridan. Along with this news came a raise in pay and an official letter expressing appreciation for his saving the company "five miles of line, considerable grading, and the necessity for 30 bridges," all of which a preliminary survey had indicated. The town of Gillette became a county seat almost by the time the rails arrived, which was on August 12, 1891.

Meanwhile, of course, Gillette and party had kept well in advance of the steel. He took the route into Sheridan at an elevation of 3,732 feet, in the fall of 1890, and the rails reached town two years later. He went ahead to locate a line to Buffalo, but this was abandoned when a sizable cattle war broke out. This was the notorious Johnson County War, celebrated in all annals of the Old West, brought on by the nesters (farmers) who wanted fences and the cattlemen who wanted the open range. It was reason enough to start a war. The nesters combined with rustlers to make life hard for the cattle kings and were so able at it that in the spring of 1892 the cattlemen raised a small army of sharp-shooting men, some of them rather careless with guns, chartered a special train to take them to Casper, then started a long march overland to attack the town of Buffalo, which was held to be headquarters of the farmer-rustler combine.

Buffalo, hearing of the approach of the army, spread the alarm, one of its merchants, Robert Foote, becoming a sort of Western Paul Revere in the process. Foote mounted a black horse and galloped up and down the main stem, his white beard flying in the wind, calling on all good and brave citizens to muster at his store. Here he passed out free guns and ammunition, and tobacco. The Home Defenders Corps was organized at once and went to drilling. Ranchers and their families drove in from the surrounding country to swell the defending force that was to repel the minions of the hated cattle kings.

The cattle kings' army never reached Buffalo. They did kill a couple of Buffalo spies on the way, drank no little rum, then surrendered in a body to Colonel Van Horne and the United States army at Fort McKinney.

Gillette paid the Johnson County War little heed. He kept the line moving west, and on October 3, 1894, the rails following him made connection with the Northern Pacific at Huntley, Montana, thus establishing a through route to the Pacific coast at Portland and Puget Sound.

By this time Locating Engineer Gillette felt the need of having some personal headquarters. He settled not in Gillette but in nearby Sheridan, which thirty-five years later he still held to be the finest spot in the United States, due in part to God, who had given the region such wonderful soil, such gorgeous mountains, such wonderful hunting and fishing, and due also in part to the Chicago, Burlington & Quincy Railroad. Look, he cried again and again during three decades, look at what the rails did for the Sheridan country. Before they arrived, the one bank in Sheridan all but owned all of the ranches roundabout, holding mortgages that would soon become due. But what happened instead? Within thirty days after the Burlington tracks had come into town, those same ranchers had paid off $30,000 in loans, and the community "has been prosperous ever since."

Such was the faith this man had in the railroad, the railroad whose manner of coming he pioneered. No wonder he was a good locating engineer.

In 1899 Gillette, who was then locating the Burlington from Toluca, Montana, to Cody, Wyoming, was asked by the Secretary of War to explore and locate an all-American railroad route in Alaska. This he did with his usual ability and dispatch, then returned to his beloved Wyoming and more locating work for the Burlington and other Lines. By then the great days of railroad expansion were beginning to come to a close, to be followed only too swiftly by the abandonment of branch lines here and there. After he retired, Edward Gillette reflected a good deal on railroads and, although he never changed his opinion that they had been the great civilizing force in North America, he was not uncritical of their shortcomings. He looked at a railroad as "a commonsense business affair in which the employees are the clerks, the public the customers, and transportation the goods to be sold." He thought that many managers of railroads would be better suited to their work if they possessed a certain few qualifications of department-store officials. He seemed to feel, as he looked back over the years, that the railroads had done a superb job of construction, and even of operation, but had failed quite miserably to give sufficient attention to their relations with the public. He died, aged 82, in 1936, at his home in Sheridan, one of the last of the old-school locating engineers, and doubtless one of the best.

Looking for Trouble

A sample of the "lascivious" material contained in "The Paris Package," a side-line of news butchers who sold the Package to gulls for one dollar, "not to be opened until you got off the cars."

Train Boy: Rock candy, rock candy, sir?"

Crusty Old Party: "No, no, go away. I haven't any teeth."

Train Boy: "Gum drops, sir?"

"All aboard!" Typical scene in a railroad lunch room in the period before dining cars became popular.

CHAPTER XVII

The Saga of Stampede Pass

The whole extent of today's work was 5½ feet by hand drills.
—Diary of Captain Sidney Bennett, at Stampede Pass, April 2, 1886.

TO THE pioneers who traveled on foot and in oxcart, the Cascade Range was known simply, and hopefully, as the Last Mountains. In their name for these difficult peaks was the glimmer of optimism that was so needed to bolster flagging spirits, which were already sorely tried by the great plains and the Rockies; if they could but get over these, the last mountains, they would at last gain their promised land in the Oregon country.

To surmount the Cascades the pioneers needed all of the hope they could muster. As they made their halting way across Idaho and into eastern Oregon, they saw the Cascades looming up ahead, glittering in the sun, handsome yet grim enough, the last test before coming to their new Canaan. As they continued westward, they soon found that these mountains had a mirage quality about them. They seemed near, but were still far indeed. And, once in the very foothills, the main peaks appeared to recede at every step. Canyon wound into canyon, each worse than the former. On they plodded, reaching a sort of plateau at last, only to find that the summit mocked them still; still miles away, still miles up. It was a heartbreaking experience, and it broke both the heart and the body of hundreds.

The Cascade Mountains range from British Columbia through Washington and Oregon into California and, next to the Rockies, are the highest and most extensive in the United States. They parallel the coast line at an average distance of 75 miles inland. Rainier is their highest peak, at 14,408 feet, and nine other mountains reach above the 10,000-foot level. Perhaps nowhere else in the nation does a range have so much influence on the territory it divides into two regions as here in Washington and Oregon; west of this range the climate is mild and damp, the forest dominated by Douglas fir; to the east the climate is severe and dry, the forests of pine. It is not too much to say that the Cascades make two very different regions of the Northwest.

If the Cascades presented a heartbreaking trial to the pioneers, they also presented one of the greatest problems ever faced by the builders of railroads. The Northern Pacific's men were the first to tackle it; between 1873 and 1884 NP engineers considered first one then another of the supposed passes of the Cascades. They cruised here, then there, and argued the advantages or otherwise of three notches in the tall barrier—those that came to be known as the Snoqualmie, the Stampede, and the Natchess passes.

Growing towns on the coast were much interested in which pass was to be selected and became noisy in their championing hullabaloo. Seattle wanted the railroad to come through Snoqualmie Pass. Tacoma hoped for the Natchess Pass, and so did Yakima, on the eastern side of the range. But V. G. Bogue, chief assistant engineer of the railroad, on whom the final decision largely rested, chose the Stampede route, lying between the other two.*

While the engineers were surveying and arguing, the rails were creeping westward from the western end of Lake Superior. By 1885 they had reached Yakima in eastern Washington, and then were started up the Yakima River, toward Ellensburg, into the foothills. At this time, too, it was discovered that the grade through the Stampede pass was going to call for a tunnel, probably about two miles long, at an elevation above the sea of a little more than 2,800 feet. The Northern Pacific advertised for bids to build the tunnel. Twelve were received, and these were opened on January 21, 1886. The bid of Nelson Bennett was found to be the lowest.

The figures quoted by the other eleven bidders were practically double those submitted by Bennett. They were high because the bidders were given pause by stipulations that the job must be completed within 28 months or the bidder forfeit $100,000 plus 10 per cent of the contract price. And they feared the time element of the job—with good reason; they knew that getting men, machinery, and supplies to the tunnel site would call for almost superhuman effort. There was no track to roll on; everything would have to go overland, as the saying is. Overland in the Cascades was a method to make any man shudder who had seen the terrain.

Bennett himself must have been a little wary of the time limit, for he submitted two bids—one within the 28-months limit, the other bid at $100,000 less and the assurance that the work would be "prosecuted with unabated vigor" if the company would release him from the limit of time. But the company accepted his first bid, the one stipulating 28 months, and Bennett girded his loins.

Nelson Bennett was the proper man to bore a tunnel high in the moun-

---

* Where the name came from isn't to be known with any certainty. One old account, dating perhaps from the 1850's, when George B. McClellan and crew were surveying here, has it that it comes from a "stampede" of trail cutters who didn't like either the country or their foreman. and left the job in a hurry.

tains. More than that, he was the proper man to get equipment and supplies to a place where he could bore that tunnel—for it was the preparation that turned out to be the heroic part of conquering Stampede Pass, the clearing of the way and the getting machinery overland to where it could be used in boring. One contemporary, who knew at first hand the difficulties Bennett would face, wrote that not one man in a thousand would undertake the task of boring the Stampede Tunnel before track had reached anywhere near its east portal.

Bennett was perhaps one man in ten thousand. In 1886 he was 43 years old, built, as one who knew him recalls, like an ox—five feet seven inches tall; and almost that wide across his shoulders. He gave the impression of being shorter than he was, but also the impression, which was no illusion, of great strength. He wore a vast mustache and a goatee, both graying in 1886. Born in 1843 in Ontario, Canada, he had come to the States in 1864 to work as a brakeman on the Dixon Air Line, later a part of the Chicago & North Western Railroad. He soon went west and into mining. In 1871 he arrived in Salt Lake City, dressed in buckskins and broke. Mining hadn't paid very well. He set up as a small contractor and worked at sinking shafts for other miners. He took the first wagon train into the rough Challis country of Idaho. He became acquainted with Washington Dunn, then building a part of the Utah & Northern Railroad. With him he formed the contracting firm of Washington Dunn & Company.

Dunn died in 1883. Bennett now organized his own concern and contracted to build 134 miles of the Northern Pacific between Pasco and Ellensburg, Washington. During this period he got a hard blow when $18,000 in cash to meet the payroll was lost in transit by the Northern Pacific Express Company. Although he got the money back after a court action lasting two years, he was hard put to keep his crew paid at the time. Then the Northern Pacific failed. Almost alone of all the NP contractors, Bennett kept his job going, using all of his powers of cajolery to stave off creditors and to keep his crew from rioting and leaving. When the NP reorganized, Bennett was promptly paid and met all of his obligations, which at one time had threatened to lay him low. Then, in 1886, his low bid brought him the Stampede Tunnel job.

On the day he got the contract Bennett telegraphed to his general superintendent, a brother, known as Captain Sidney J. Bennett, at Yakima, to clear the way to the tunnel site for the machinery and supplies that would presently arrive at Yakima, the end of NP track.

Captain Bennett lost no time, for he well understood the meaning of 28 months as it applied to doing anything in the middle of the Cascades. On February 1st, eleven days after the contract was signed, the first wagon-load of stuff left Yakima for the tunnel site. And with it began the epic

part of the building of the Stampede, an epic that can hardly be compre-
hended by anyone who has not been over the ground.

It is probably futile to attempt to describe the mountainous jungle
through which Captain Bennett had to move his equipment. From Yakima
to the east portal was 82 miles, to the west portal 87 miles—and such miles.
In altitude the material moved from 500 feet above sea level to 2,800 feet,
It moved over ridges, into and out of canyons, across rushing streams.
Always it moved through the thickest coniferous forest imaginable, that
reached out a million limbs to slow all that moved through the trees. Six
of the precious 28 months was used up merely in getting ready to bore the
tunnel.

Captain Bennett's advance force reached the east portal early in February. Hand-drilling began on the 13th. On March 1st a gang was hand-
drilling at the west portal. Meanwhile, the main body of equipment and
material was moving steadily off the end-of-track at Yakima and onto
Captain Bennett's overland mountain road. Included in it were five
donkey engines, two water wheels, five air compressors, four big exhaust
fans, two complete electric arc-light plants, four miles of pipe, two ma-
chine-shop outfits, 36 air-drilling machines, several tons of drills, and two
locomotives, the *Sadie* and the *Ceta,* named for Nelson Bennett's young
daughters.* Included, too, were two sawmill outfits, 60 dump cars, several
miles of steel rail, and ton upon ton of food and other supplies.

Captain Sidney Bennett's overland road started out on the ground, but
soon went to plank. All of the plank had to be brought forward from sawmills in the rear. The little mills whined all day and all night to furnish
the stuff, and Bennett's men were there ready to catch the planks as they
fell from the saw and hustle them up into the foothills. Here they were
laid end to end on mud so deep that a wagon would sink above its hubs
in it.

The motive power was at first straight horse-team, but as the grade
stiffened, not enough horses could be hitched together to move the heavily
laden wagons. Here, block and tackle was rigged, and one end fastened to
the tongue of a wagon. Men guided the wheels by the tongue, while horses
put all their might onto the rope beyond the blocks. Fifteen of the eighty-
odd miles were made by this method alone, at the rate of about one mile
per day per wagon. When the foothills had been surmounted, new conditions faced the road builders. The gorges were packed with snow so deep
that sleds had to be improvised on which to place and skid the wagons.
Often canyons from 500 to a thousand feet deep called for a perilous route
hanging to a mountainside.

It required a small army to keep the wagons moving. Many bridges had

---

* Few American locomotives or trains have ever been given feminine names. Only two
American passenger trains today bear the names of specific women: The Alton's *Ann Rutledge* and the Norfolk & Western's *Pocahontas.*

to be built. Camps or way stations were established every 12 miles from the base of supplies to the tunnel—which was about the distance a team could make in a day. These were ragcamps, tents where men and beasts were fed, where blacksmiths pounded out repairs that seemed endless. But even these stations were too far apart at times, for besides the 15 mile area mentioned above there is record of loads that moved but one mile in 12 hours, of many loads that progressed only six miles a day.

There was weather, too. On February 9th, Captain Sidney and party reached what was to become the east portal. Before they could get to the face of the tunnel they had to shovel a road 800 feet through snow that was six to eight feet deep. On March 15th no less than 36 inches of new snow came down. On the 21st it rained for 24 hours solid. Always the wind blew, in great gusts down the canyons, steadily and with terrific force on the ridges.

Approximately 100 wagons were moving from the end of track to the tunnel much of the time between February and July merely to set the scene for the job itself. It was hellish work. Men grumbled, men talked, men quit. Captain Sidney, and often Nelson Bennett harangued or bullied them into staying a while longer. At least one attempt at a strike brought Bennett to the fore, and somehow by mere force of character he kept them working—if not content.

When finally a crew and equipment got to the east portal, it was found to be right behind a huge fall of water that came over a cliff 170 feet above. Captain Sidney sent a crew up there to dam and turn the torrent, while another gang cut through 150 feet of solid ice ten feet deep to get to the face. Then they began to drill by hand.

Captain Sidney was a slave-driver of the old school, and his men were slaves of the old school. It made a perfect combination to drive a tunnel in fast time. On March 27th, the Captain had at last, and long ahead of the main supply of equipment, got a crew to work on the actual bore. By March 31st he "commenced timbering at east end; put in 12 setts." On April 1st, according to the report written in his own hand, he had 60 men working inside the east portal. On the next day he commenced running the heading at the west end. "The extent of today's work was 5½ feet by hand drills." On April 6th the rock uncovered at the west end was harder stuff, "blue trapite." On May 1st heavy snows were slowing work at the east end. But June 19th was a great day: "Two Ingersoll drills started in east end, the first machinery to be started." On July 24th the gang at the east end finally boiled up and over. They "struck for nine hours as a day's work." The trouble lasted two days, Captain Sidney noted, "but did not prevail." The strike must have been more serious than the Captain's report indicated, for a sheriff was called to "prevent disorder and injury to persons or property." The sheriff shot one man for what Captain Sidney said was "an attempt to escape arrest on a criminal charge."

More snows came down upon the gangs in the hills. Floods almost washed them back down the mountain. There were many bad and a few terrible accidents. There was discontent with the monotonous if healthy and plentiful food, discontent with living conditions. Men came and men went. A few left only to return because they could not face the long hike to more civilized parts.

Making his headquarters in Tacoma, Nelson Bennett constantly read in the papers what an utter fool he had been to contract to build the Stampede Tunnel in the space of 28 months. It bothered him not at all, for he was often at the scene of action and there he goaded and bullied and cajoled his men into greater and greater efforts. He watched, approvingly, while his crews shoveled off 20 feet of snow to get to a ground foundation at the east portal—tier upon tier of men, throwing the shovels of snow ever higher until some of the banks reared up forty feet and more. He watched while they set up a small sawmill, cut down trees, and sawed the trees into lumber to build bunkhouses and stables and machine shop and warehouses. He watched, and no doubt muttered, while another gang built a 1,600-foot haul for a waste dump. And perhaps he swore a little when he found that his men had to make 10,000 yards of rock excavation before a place for the railroad approach to the east end could be leveled. But that he ever doubted the job would be finished ahead of time was not in his makeup.

The terms of Bennett's contract called for a tunnel approximately two miles long. It was to be 16½ feet wide in the clear; 22 feet high from the bottom to the apex of the arch; and to be completed 28 months after January 21, 1886. The character of the rock for nearly the full length of the bore was of the basaltic trap species. The strata varied in thickness from six inches to four or five feet. The method of boring was the upward heading process extended from the top of the arch downward eight feet, and inward 30 feet ahead of the bench or bottom work. The entire tunnel was timbered along the sides and overhead, as the work progressed. The timbering of the heading or upper section rested upon the bench, and as that was removed timbers were placed under those above. Some engineers have claimed that this method is the most expensive and rapid process there is for working a tunnel through rock. Nelson Bennett had to have speed, no matter the cost.

The wages ranged from $2.50 to $5.00 per ten-hour shift. Board and lodging at the Bennett camps was 75 cents a day. When, after several weeks work, Bennett discovered that the progress being made was not up to the average he had figured was necessary to complete the job on time, he added the impetus of a bonus: For every foot gained over the necessary average of 13 feet six inches per day, he agreed to pay each laborer 25 cents extra, and 50 cents extra to each driller or other skilled man. There was an immediate spurt, one that appears to have held, with a few small fluctuations, to the end.

Yet, the troubles continued. In August of 1886 a monstrous and ill-timed blast blew one man to bits and injured several others. In September smoke and fumes from blasting became so bad that work had to be halted and the entire fan system revamped. In that month, too, five more days were lost because blasting shots had caused the breaking of rock above the grade of the tunnel. In October cracking and falling of rock caused more delays. In November a large crew had to be hurriedly put to work building snow sheds over the dump tracks; and a sizable landslide stopped all work at the east end for a week. In December, snow changed to rain, the rain to a prolonged cloudburst, and the east end of the tunnel was flooded. Work had to stop again.

January, 1887, started off well and the month ended with an overall gain of 24 feet; but May wiped out the gain and resulted in an overall loss of 146 feet—caused by floods in the east end again. So it went. Delayed or premature blasts took the lives of a dozen men. Perhaps a hundred more had to be sent to hospitals on account of injury. But illness did not amount to much; Bennett fed his men well and most plentifully, and for the most part they stayed tough and rugged. As time went on, and the softies were weeded out, a rivalry was built up between the east and west end crews. This of course resulted in gains above the average, and on May 3, 1888, the two gangs were so near each other that the partition was blasted open and communication established between men who had known of and heard each other for two years but had never met. On May 14th, the bore was completed—only seven days ahead of the deadline of the contract. On the 22nd the first regular scheduled train went through. Nelson Bennett had won. He had completed what a contemporary expert on tunnels said was the longest mountain railroad tunnel on the continent, excepting the Hoosac, and "in the shortest comparative time and under the greatest difficulties, of any in the world."

Unquestionably Captain Sidney Bennett was a good man for the time, which is to say a slave driver of the first quality. He had to be, if he was to work for his brother Nelson. An incident about the latter is more indicative of the character of the man who built the tunnel at Stampede than the reams of eulogy that appeared about him in the papers. The incident happened in Tacoma, Nelson Bennett's headquarters. He was dining there in a hotel, when outside in the street a man set up a soapbox, gathered a crowd and began to harangue them on the vile conditions and low wages being paid for work at Stampede. Bennett finished his soup, while through the big dining-room windows came now and then an echo of the man on the box. ". . . Fellow workers, Nelson Bennett is committing both robbery and murder . . . men dying like flies . . . victims of speed and greed . . . unite . . . nothing to lose but your chains." The squat, powerful man put down his napkin, excused himself from his guests, and went out into the street. He elbowed his way through the massed proletariat, and without a word reached up and plucked the speaker from his box. He then proceeded to shake the man until he was all of a blur. "What you say is all a lie!" Bennett bellowed in the voice of a Bashan bull. "Begone!" The street meeting was over; and Mr. Bennett returned to his table for the second course.*

It took men such as Bennett to build the railroad tunnels of the day when America was in a hurry to conquer the continent. No other kind could have built them so fast or so well. Probably no other kind could have built them at all, then.

---

* This incident was related to the author by a middle-aged woman who as a young girl had been the guest of Mr. and Mrs. Bennett at dinner that evening.

CHAPTER XVIII

Out in the Wild and Woolly

Meanwhile San Francisco and Chicago spring up like a very palace of Aladdin, and the center of population is transferred. . . .
—CHARLES FRANCIS ADAMS, 1871.

T HE Wild West of the dime novels of the eighties and nineties was pretty much the Southwest, just as it is today, the big-hat, two-gun, high-heeled country of the movies, the place where they shoot just a little quicker, yell a little louder, where the dawn comes up early and stays all day and kodachrome photography means something. Locating Engineer Edward Gillette, as related, saw a bit of this Wild West in the days he worked for the Denver & Rio Grande, but he soon moved out of gunshot and into the comparatively civilized wastes of Iowa, South Dakota, and Wyoming.

Into the Wild West of the dime novels and movies, during the last third of the last century, moved a number of railroads, two of which probably had as rooting, tooting, shooting a time of it as any line of steel rails in the United States, the much publicized Union Pacific not excepted. One was the present Missouri-Kansas-Texas Lines, more or less affectionately called the Katy; the other and much larger, the Atchison, Topeka & Santa Fe.

The Santa Fe was the vision of a capable Pennsylvanian, Cyrus Kurtz Holliday, born in 1826 and educated at Allegheny College in Meadville, who moved to Kansas in 1854 and set up as a lawyer. It was the era of Bloody Kansas. Holliday allied himself with the Free State Party and, thinking it was time Kansas had a capital, he led a group of men up the Kansas river and staked out what is now Topeka. Five years later he appeared before the Wyandotte constitutional convention and with great eloquence and no little lobbying succeeded in having his town proclaimed the territorial capital.

While supporting the Free Soldiers and also boosting for his new city, Holliday dreamed up a railroad that was to start at his town and follow the old pack-and-cattle trail to Santa Fé. He secured a state charter, in 1859, for what he modestly named the Atchison & Topeka Railroad. He was president. Nothing much happened for a while. Holliday drafted and got through Congress a land-grant bill for his road, three million acres in alternate sections in Kansas which was to become the property of the company on condition that the line was built to the Colorado border within ten years.

With the land grant settled, Holliday's credit went up and he was able to get contractors to start work. Twenty-eight miles of road were laid in 1869 to connect Topeka and Burlingame. Two years later the end of track had reached a town that rose up out of the prairie simultaneously with arrival of the rails. This was fabulous Dodge City, which became so riotous at once as to call for a lockup. Lumber being scarce, a well was dug down 15 feet into the ground and into it were lowered the more recalcitrant drunks to sober off. It was typical of the rough-and-ready style of the time and place.

Onward went the rails and near the end of 1872 they arrived at the Colorado line, thus putting the land grant in the bag. There had to be farmers to settle on these lands, so A. E. Touzalin, land commissioner, freight and passenger agent, and general factotum of the A&T, doubtless taking a few leaves from the Illinois Central's book of colonization, set out to populate the lands of the Atchison & Topeka. He prepared some pretty enthusiastic posters and pamphlets which he sent to all parts of the United States and much of Europe. He placed sizable advertising contracts and organized an army of agents. He also engaged one C. B. Schmidt, an ex-newspaperman of Saxony who was out to see the world, and made him immigration agent. Schmidt was a man of action. He packed his valise and promptly set out for Russia with the idea of bringing back the prosperous sect called Mennonites, descendents of German-speaking agriculturists who had moved to Russia in 1786.*

When the Czar's agents learned that Schmidt was in the realm for the purpose of enticing Mennonites to America, they were not pleased. The police were put on Schmidt's trail. But he was a slippery and a quick-moving phantom. By fast drives at night, and lying low in the daytime, he managed to keep out of their clutches and got safely out of Russia after having spilled a good deal of his Atchison & Topeka brand of poison. In 1875 the first detachment of Mennonites arrived in Kansas, bringing, it

---

* To Philistines all Mennonites are alike, but not to Mennonites. The followers of Memmo Simons (1492–1559), a prophet who broke away from the Anabaptists, are represented in the United States today by at least sixteen sects and are listed by an authority, Elmer T. Clark (*The Small Sects in America*, 1937) as follows: Mennonite church, Hutterian Brethren, Conservative Amish Mennonites, Old Order Amish Mennonites, Church of God in Christ Mennonite, Old Order Mennonites Wisler, Reformed Mennonites, Mennonite Brethren in Christ, Mennonite Church of North America, Krimmer Brueder Gemeinde, Mennonite Kleine Gemeinde, Central Conference of Mennonites, Conference of the Defenseless Mennonites, Stauffer Mennonites, and five unaffiliated Mennonite congregations. Their many schisms have been occasioned by such cosmic differences of opinion as regulations about marriage, preaching in English, four-part singing, and the cut of a preacher's coat. They are generally able farmers, law-abiding, and given to minding their own business and that of the Lord.

was said, $2,200,000 in gold with them, sewed into their coats and dresses. Attired in native garb, this group of men, women and children called in a body on the governor at Topeka, making one of the most spectacular incidents in the state's history. The governor of Kansas said a few well-chosen words, which were translated—I hope—by Immigration Agent Schmidt. Then, after their leading men had looked over the A&T lands and made their selections, the entire group moved on to the soil and went at once to work with a zeal that amazed and pleased the railroad's officials.

The Mennonites arrived at just the right time, for they had barely missed a great trouble. The year before, indeed, had been one of dreadful trials in Kansas. Grasshoppers in a volume seldom if ever before seen made a raid on the region. For three days the flight of the insects was so great as to spread a haze over the sun. When they landed they began to eat. They ate the crops, they ate the leaves off the trees, they invaded homes and went to work on everything therein. So thick were the hoppers that for several days neither horse nor man could stand up to them and work. Trains on the A&T were slowed, then stalled where they stood by the thick slimy pulp of crushed bodies on the rails.

The Mennonites missed that one, and they had time to get set before the next blow. This came in a series of droughts in 1879 and 1880, an early warning of the dustbowl to come half a century later. All crops withered and disappeared. Farm animals died. Hundreds of settlers left the country and had to be carried free by the A&T. Those who decided to remain and stick it out were furnished with free seed, by the railroad, when the rains came again. But the grasshoppers and the droughts had put a severe strain on the little railroad. It might have gone to the wall except for the expert financing of Joseph and Thomas Nickerson, Boston bankers, and the old firm of Kidder, Peabody & Company.

Thomas Nickerson became president of the road in 1874, the grasshopper year, the third Yankee to hold that office in five years. His handling of the carrier's finances during this critical period was very able. He also gave free rein to his new and young chief engineer, a native of Vermont named Albert Alonzo Robinson, who had got his degree at the University of Michigan and along with the degree packed enough ability for half a dozen ordinary engineers.

Now Nickerson reached out to steal a general manager from the Burlington Route. This was William Barstow Strong, a human dynamo who had been born in small Brownington, Vermont, in 1837, and had worked his way up from station agent to superintendent of the Burlington.*

---

* Strong was a boyhood friend and classmate, in Brownington Academy, of the author's maternal grandfather, Edward Amherst Stewart, who visited Mr. Strong in his Santa Fe days and wrote a travelogue of his trip over the line in 1881. Mr. Strong's success, he wrote, was unquestionably due to certain *Yankee* characteristics such as "industry, perseverance, determination and ambition, plus the necessary foundation of native ability, guided by high moral purpose and shaped by unflinching integrity under all temptations."

Strong wore a long square-cut beard, and out of his bold face peered a pair of extremely bright and searching eyes. Some said of Strong that he appeared as if he were looking for trouble. This was not so; he was merely ready to meet it.

The reorganized Atchison, Topeka & Santa Fe now started to live up to its new corporate title. The road pushed westward into Colorado, then north to Pueblo to connect with the Denver & Rio Grande, bringing new traffic from the growing city of Denver and the mines. To get out of Colorado and so on to the third name declared in its title the road, now managed by Strong, needed possession of Raton Pass. It seemed the logical, the only way, to lay the rails south. It would be a difficult task in any event, and what made it worse was that the Denver & Rio Grande also planned to build through the Raton.

The lawful rights in the affair of Raton Pass appear to have been somewhat ambiguous, that is, except to attorneys of the Santa Fe *and* attorneys of the Rio Grande roads. Both lines began to build toward it, and meanwhile General Manager Strong of the Santa Fe made a trip into New Mexico to obtain necessary legislation for his line to build into that Territory. Here he ran smack into the hard fact of the aggressive Southern Pacific, which planned to keep New Mexico for its own and which, only a few days before Strong's arrival, had got a law passed providing that a majority of any board of directors of a railroad operating in the region must be residents of the Territory, and that 10 per cent of the cost of construction must be in evidence before work was started. The law would make construction of the Santa Fe in New Mexico Territory impossible.

Strong looked into the business. He discovered in no time at all that the Southern Pacific agents had neglected to insert in their inspired measure a clause repealing an older law. The old law was still in force and it permitted incorporation without any of the fancy trimmings suggested by the Southern Pacific. Strong's whiskers fairly vibrated. He immediately incorporated the New Mexico & Southern Pacific Railroad Company to build from Raton Pass to the Arizona border. And just to indicate how an effete Easterner liked to have his railroads, Strong got the Territorial legislature to pass an act exempting railroads from taxes for six years.

Hurrying back to headquarters, Strong urged that surveys through Raton Pass and on to Santa Fé be started at once. The company told him to go ahead. He sent for young Albert Robinson and instructed him to put the line through the pass, even if force were necessary. Getting aboard a Denver & Rio Grande train at Pueblo to go to El Moro, nearest railroad point to the pass, Robinson noticed that Chief Engineer J. A. McMurtie of the Rio Grande was in the smoker. Each, of course, guessed the other's business. On reaching El Moro, strictly a synthetic creation of the Rio Grande, McMurtie got off and began to recruit and arm a force to take and hold the pass. Robinson mounted a horse and rode as fast as he could on to Trinidad, an old settlement that had been by-passed by the Rio Grande.

Trinidad citizens had no liking for any railroad that ignored their town, and Robinson had no trouble in collecting a small but enthusiastic army who provided themselves with rifles and shovels and followed him to the north entrance to the pass. Here they arrived in the four o'clock dark of a morning. There are a score of versions as to what happened next.

The Denver & Rio Grande forces arrived not much later, some say a mere half hour, and there ensued a lot of loud talk between McMurtie and Robinson. Another tale has it that McMurtie and his gang arrived first, then made camp and went to bed, while Robinson and his crew worked throughout the night driving surveyors' stakes. In either case, there was no shooting, and the Santa Fe held the pass and built through it, the first train going over on December 7, 1878, by means of a switchback. During the next year Robinson ran a 2,000-foot tunnel through the summit and reduced the maximum grade from 316 feet to the mile to 185 feet.

The Raton Pass affair did not end the war between the two roads, and now came a more serious encounter, the battle for the Grand Canyon of the Arkansas, a narrow rift 3,000 feet deep through the granite of the Rockies west of Pueblo. The Rio Grande planned to put its tracks through this canyon in order to get to the great mining region around Leadville. The ebullient Strong wanted the Santa Fe to tap that rich country, and in the spring of 1878 he began making arrangements for a secret grab of the canyon. The Rio Grande, which happened to be in possession of all telegraph wires in Colorado, learned of Strong's intent. They moved to checkmate him.

When Strong ordered an engineer, William R. Morley, to go to Canyon City and organize a force to hold the canyon against the Rio Grande minions, General William Jackson Palmer, head of that line, made certain that no train was available to take Morley from Pueblo to Canyon City. Morley struck out on horseback, just as Robinson had done in the Raton affair, to cover the 63 miles. After Robinson had left Pueblo, Palmer loaded a Rio Grande train with a hundred or so armed men and sent them on their way to take possession of the canyon. Story has it that Morley's horse petered out somewhere along the way, and the Rio Grande crew beat him to Canyon City. If so, it didn't help them much. Morley quickly raised a gang of his own, went at once to the mouth of the canyon, and so to work. A few of his crew actually wielded picks and shovels; the rest took up their stations behind boulders, standing watch with ready rifles lest the hated Palmer gang show up. They did show up, presently, but after looking the situation over decided to withdraw. The first round thus went to the Santa Fe. Strong was so happy with Engineer Morley's work that he presented him with "a repeating rifle elaborately mounted with gold."

General Palmer of the Rio Grande had been an able commander of

Federal troops in the Civil War, and he was no man to give in easily to a crowd of Santa Fe bullies. He directed his chief engineer, McMurtie, no doubt still stinging from the Raton affair, to move in force upon the canyon. McMurtie picked up a crew of laborers and riflemen, advanced to a spot nearer to the canyon than the Santa Fe camp, then erected two or three rude forts, and started construction, the forts fairly bristling with Winchesters. General Palmer also moved by way of the courts, getting an injunction to stop the Santa Fe work. Strong had the injunction transferred to a Federal court, alleging that the Santa Fe could not get justice or anything like it from Colorado judges. Judge Hallet, a Federal jurist, ordered both carriers to cease and desist until the matter could be settled by the United States Supreme Court. But General Palmer was discouraged. In October of 1878 he leased the Rio Grande to the Santa Fe.

It would appear from the record that the Santa Fe now set out deliberately to wreck the Rio Grande, using various methods one of which was to raise freight rates out of Denver to prohibitive levels. General Palmer, again aroused, claimed the lease agreement had been broken by the Santa Fe's actions and declared the Rio Grande to be again in possession of its property. He sent armed detachments into the canyon to wait until the Supreme Court's action was known, and from a local judge got an order restoring the Rio Grande to its original owners. Copies of this order were placed in the hands of sheriffs in the several counties concerned and were to be served on Santa Fe employees at 6 o'clock on the morning of June 9, 1879. The sheriffs were backed by an unusual number of armed deputies.

A notable Rio Grande partisan was A. C. Hunt, ex-governor of Colorado, and on this morning he staged a spectacular raid. With the knowledge, and probably too with the best wishes of General Palmer, he loaded a train with 200 armed men at El Moro and started north up the line to Pueblo, stopping at every depot and taking captive such agents as declared their loyalty to the Santa Fe. At Cuchara there was shooting, and two Santa Fe men were killed and two more wounded. At Pueblo the Santa Fe had prepared for possible trouble by hiring Bat Masterson, the celebrated or notorious marshal of Dodge City, and a gang of shooting men to defend Santa Fe property. When word of the coming of Raider Hunt reached him, Masterson posted his forces around the roundhouse and prepared to give battle. But there was no battle; the Rio Grande men, knowing the venality of Masterson's crowd, attempted no assault. Under a flag of truce Treasurer R. F. Weitbrec bought them off.

Yet one stronghold remained in Santa Fe hands, the dispatchers' office at Pueblo. In early evening the Hunt raiders charged and took it after a good deal of shooting. No one was hit. Hunt now led his wild marksmen on to Canyon City where several Santa Fe men had fled with four locomotives. Canyon City fell without a shot. The Rio Grande was again in possession of its railroad.

The bridge disaster at Ashtabula, Ohio, in 1876, in which 83 persons met death in the second worst train wreck of the 19th century.

Back in the 1870's, Cunard liners docked at East Boston beside the gleaming rails of the Eastern Railroad of Massachusetts (now part of the Boston & Maine). The Cunard steamship seen behind the trim diamond-stacked Six-spot is the Batavia.

Strong now moved to the courts again, and got an order restoring the road to the Santa Fe. Guerrilla warfare broke out. Santa Fe train crews, operating on the Rio Grande, were set upon and beaten. Their families were threatened. Violence flared at roundhouses and depots. At last came the Supreme Court's decision: It restored the property to the Rio Grande. The Santa Fe wasn't quite ready to give up, and for the next several months both sides maintained small armies in the field, spying on each other, committing acts of sabotage, kidnaping public officials, cutting telegraph wires, and diverting Colorado very much. It could not go on forever, however, and peace was signed in Boston in February of 1880. The Rio Grande retained its line and the right to the canyon.

Incidentally, the shooting war between the two roads served to develop some excellent marksmen among employees. One of them was Charles Watlington, a freight conductor of the Santa Fe. On one occasion when his train had been stalled by a washout near Cimarron, Kansas, Conductor Watlington hurried down the track ahead to meet and warn an eastbound train, then about due. Pretty soon, sure enough, there she came, Number 4, batting along in the dark and rain. Watlington waved his red lantern, but Number 4's engineer couldn't see it. He just highballed right by, heading straight into destruction of the stalled freight and washout. Suddenly, Conductor Watlington recalled his recent training in the Santa Fe-Rio Grande war. He reached around into his hip pocket, drew out his single-action Colt .44, and let go, shooting out the air hose between the last two passenger cars and stopping the train.

With the Colorado situation settled, the Santa Fe resumed construction of its line into New Mexico, following the odd Rio Grande river much of the way. This stream, according to railroad employees of the period, moved around considerably. One week it might be on the east side of the tracks, next week on the west side. But the rails moved on, at last reaching Santa Fé, by stub line, then Albuquerque. It must have occurred to Santa Fe officials, at about this time, that they ought to have a line through to the Pacific Coast. New Mexico, thinly populated and with little agriculture and no industry, could not feed the engines. Strong and his directors looked around for a method to get to California independently of the powerful Southern Pacific. Presently they thought they had found it in the St. Louis & San Francisco Railroad.

In 1881 the Santa Fe purchased a half interest in a charter owned by the StL&SF which would permit it to build into California. The Santa Fe also raised more than sixteen million dollars to do the building. But, and so quietly that the Santa Fe never suspected it, the St. Louis & San Francisco had been bought by Jay Gould and Collis Huntington, chief owners of the Texas & Pacific and Southern Pacific lines, neither of which wanted the Santa Fe to build anywhere. The move effectively blocked the Santa Fe at the Colorado River. After a deal of wrangling and threats, the three larger concerns compromised matters in a highly complicated settlement by which the Santa Fe was permitted access to the Pacific Coast and San Francisco over a combination of its own and leased lines.

The Santa Fe's next move was eastward. It acquired the Chicago & St. Louis Railroad between Chicago and Streator, Illinois, then built a line from Streator to the Missouri River, making connections with its own steel.

In little more than ten years William B. Strong had expanded the Santa Fe from 2,200 to 7,000 miles, and it now operated from the Great Lakes to the West Coast, and to the Gulf of Mexico. There had been, however, a reckless policy in the payment of dividends, and within a year the company went into receivership, a common enough occurrence in the history of most railroads, large or small. The next four years were marked by what appears to have been extremely bad management. The receivership failed, and an examination of the books indicated what so able and conservative a historian as John Moody termed "gross irregularities, dishonest management, and manipulation of accounts." *

Into this mass of corruption and wreckage, in 1896, went Edward R. Ripley, late of Dorchester, Massachusetts, and even later of the Burlington and the Milwaukee railroads. For the next twenty-four years Ripley ran the Santa Fe like one inspired. Under his direction the system grew to 11,291 miles and became one of the most profitable roads in the nation. One of Ripley's most important contributions was a fixed policy of promotion from the ranks. He also introduced a pension and insurance system for employees and, in fact, did everything possible toward building up a company morale which, a quarter of a century after Ripley's death, is one of the outstanding characteristics of the Santa Fe System.

Most travelers rightly think of Fred Harvey in connection with the Santa Fe; and Fred Harvey must be mentioned here.

In the 1870's the worst food served in the United States was unquestionably that put before travelers in the quick-lunch restaurants of depots. For the most part these dismal places were operated on the theory that speed and not food was what counted. Dining cars were still rather esoteric things, especially so in the West. Many Western lines did not possess a single diner. The practice on long trips was to stop the train ten minutes at some station, at or near noon, again around supper time, when the passengers would be told they had time for a meal, while a fellow stood on the depot platform and rang a bell, shouting what he thought were enticements to come and get it. Like a herd of buffaloes the travelers then stampeded into the quick-lunch, and there greasy and strident viragos

---

* *The Railroad Builders*, New Haven, 1919.

called waitresses shoved soggy doughnuts and groggy coffee at them across the counter.

So very bad were a majority of railroad restaurants that they became a notable subject for gagsters and cartoonists. A whole literature and a comic art grew up around the depot quick-lunch, showing it as a madhouse where maniacal travelers fought each other for the privilege of buying ptomaine poison, at high prices, while at the door stood a stern, blue-coated railway conductor, watch in hand, to hurry them to even greater bursts of gustatory speed. The picture was not far from the truth, and especially fitted actual conditions in the American West.

In those days few railroads gave much thought to the comfort of their passengers; if they delivered them at their destination not too far behind schedule, and in one piece, that was sufficient. So far as food was concerned, the railroads did not consider that a part of their job, or their business. Then, in about 1876, Frederick Henry Harvey, half-Scot, half-English, came to Charles F. Morse, superintendent of the Santa Fe Railroad, with an idea. Harvey had been operating eating houses in small Kansas towns and had done very well. He told Morse that if the Santa Fe would help him with space and supplies, he, Harvey, would open a depot eating house that would amaze everybody and be a credit to the railroad. Morse had imagination. He said to go ahead. Harvey took over a room in the Topeka station, scrubbed it thoroughly, painted it, got brand new tableclothes, napkins, and silver, and stocked up with good food. Harvey himself saw that the food was well cooked and served. The place quickly caught on. Both the Santa Fe and Fred Harvey knew they had something.

With financial aid from the railroad, Harvey next took over a rundown hotel in Florence, Kansas, population 100, stocked it with elegant walnut furniture, its dining room with silver from England and linen from Ireland, and hired the head chef away from the great Palmer House in Chicago. The Florence House soon became famous as the best place to eat in all Kansas; and travelers soon were planning to break their long journeys by an overnight stop at Harvey's place in Florence. Fred Harvey's idea was working. When he died in 1901 he and the Santa Fe owned and operated fifteen hotels, forty-seven restaurants, and thirty dining cars.*

Fred Harvey and his waitresses, known as Harvey Girls, have been credited by more than one observer with civilizing the Southwest in the matter of decent food. The Harvey Girls made such a record, both in the business of food and of matrimony, that not long ago they became the subject of a movie, the true accolade of fame in the United States. Harvey got his girls by running classified ads in Midwest and Eastern papers, asking for "Young women of good character, attractive and intelligent, 18 to 30," to work in his eating places. The good character requirement

---

* See *Santa Fe, the Railroad that Built an Empire,* .By James Marshall, New York, 1945

meant what it said; the Girls had to be morally decent, or at least very cir-
cumspect. They lived in Harvey dormitories, each of which was in charge
of a matron, and there was no helling-around at night; ten o'clock was
their curfew. They dressed in a standard uniform which included black
shoes and hose, black dress with an Elsie collar, and a black bow. The
only hair adornment permitted was a white ribbon. Their starting wage
was $17.50 a month, very good for the time, plus tips and room and board.

The Harvey Girls seem to have been pretty decent, intelligent, and
attractive women. On the whole they married soon, and well, their favorite
mates being Santa Fe engineers, conductors, and station agents, although
a few of them appear to have fallen for the breezy charms of drummers.
It is estimated that at least 5,000 of them married railroadmen, chiefly
Santa Fe employees, so thus they retained an indirect relationship with
the railroad. Elbert Hubbard, one of the most graceful and inaccurate
reporters ever in practice, related in one of his essays that more than
4,000 babies had been christened Fred or Harvey, or both. Yet there
can be no doubt that Harvey and his Girls influenced their time, and incidentally made a whopping success of the Harvey system.

On Fred Harvey's death the business was carried on by a son; and another son took over in 1928 and is still in charge. In 1943 the Harvey
system served some 30 million meals.

Getting back to Kansas, a few months after the Atchison & Topeka
came into being in 1869, another line that was to have an exciting youth
was organized as the Missouri, Kansas & Texas Railway, whose operating
heads were Levi Parsons and George Denison, respectively president and
vice-president. The road was born for the purposes of getting a land grant
that the Federal government promised to the first line to lay rails to the
important outpost of Fort Gibson, deep in Indian Territory, to connect
it with the great supply depot of Fort Leavenworth, Kansas. Land grants
were very popular in that day, and the financial backers of the MK&T,
better known then and now as the Katy, were men possessed of plenty of
vision, among them August Belmont, J. Pierpont Morgan the elder, Levi
P. Morton, and John D. Rockefeller, men who knew what could be done
with a good, sound land grant.

Two other railroad groups wanted a land grant. One was the Kansas &
Neosho Valley, the other the Leavenworth, Lawrence & Fort Gibson. The
government indicated it didn't care much which road got the grant; it
should go to the first to enter the Territory. The three-sided race began
in May of 1870. The LL&FG soon got into financial difficulties and quit,
and the Katy and the Kansas & Neosho Valley were left to fight it out.

Apparently both sides used every trick they could think up, and along
with the tricks went no little violence. Long before its end of steel got
anywhere near the Territorial border, Levi Parsons of the Katy shipped

a gang of men and a wagonload of rails overland to the state line and sought to gain the prize then and there by laying a section of track, all by itself, into the Territory. A determined mob of goons from the Kansas & Neosho Valley arrived on their heels and a bloody but indecisive battle was fought with ax handles, picks and shovels. The Katy's slicker attempt was so scandalous that President U. S. Grant of the United States had to step in with an executive order to halt it.

Both crews now returned to their railheads and went to work with new frenzy. No pretense of laying down a good solid railroad was made; the ties went down flat on the prairie soil, and plump went the rails on top of the ties. Laborers and their bosses worked around the clock, eating now and again, putting down steel by the light of bonfires, sometimes under the bright Kansas moon. On June 6, 1870, the Katy's gang paused a moment to look up at a sight that cheered them—hundreds of silent and blanketed Indians watching the proceedings. The rails had crossed the border into the Territory. At noon, according to Katy legend, a diamond-stacked locomotive snorted down the last length of bouncy, wavy track, stopped at the end, and whistled. The place was just south of present-day Chetopa, Kansas. When the Katy's officials in Sedalia, and in New York and Cleveland got the news, they must have felt certain the land grant would soon be in Katy hands.

As for the Kansas & Neosho Valley crowd, they also had crossed the line at almost the same hour. Through a stupendous error of the engineering staff, however, they had not arrived in the territory of the Five Nations, as stipulated in the land grant deal, but in the Quapaw Indian Reservation, where no railroad had any rights.

Nor was the Katy any better off, for the courts held that Congress had exceeded its authority in promising land that belonged to the Five Nations. Nobody got free land.

What Katy officials thought of this failure of the government to meet its promise is not divulged by the Katy's anonymous and lively official historian.* Seemingly, they simply decided to keep on building southward. They did not reach Fort Gibson, chiefly because the Cherokees became more surly with every mile of track, but headed for what is now Muskogee and kept on going to cross the Red River at present-day Denison.

Named for a Katy vice-president, Denison came into being on Christmas Day, 1872, when Engineer Pat Tobin drove a bedecked locomotive across the brand-new Katy bridge, the whistle open, and came to a stop in front of a scattering of false-front saloons and boarding houses, the latter containing one chambermaid to each room. Three months later Denison had a population, such as it was, of 3,000 "Every third building is a drinking saloon with gambling appurtenances," said a contemporary.

---

* *The Opening of the Great Southwest,* St. Louis, 1945.

"Robberies are of frequent occurrence in these gambling hells, but in the primitive hotels where passengers from the M. K. & T. Ry. await transfer by stage to Sherman, they are as safe from robbery or outrage as in any first-class hotel." Maybe so, but the better element in Denison felt the need for a tough peace officer and they imported a celebrated character, "Red" Hall, who arrived carrying both a Winchester and a Colt and proceeded with little fuss to work wonders with Denison's riffraff, who were practically without number, shooting, arresting, or merely driving them out of town.

Back on the main line in Kansas, meantime, another wild town had begun to boom. This was Parsons, named for the Katy president, a junction point where brothels and keno joints were opened and doing business before the first legitimate settlers arrived. In Muskogee, one man was shot, killed, and buried before either a street had been laid out or the first train had come, and three more died with their boots on as soon as the first cars hove in. These bad men of the Katy towns soon became known as "terminuses," an awkward name, too, because they liked to hang around the end of steel. They were given to all of the customary practices of thugs and parasites, and also liked to tamper with switches to derail trains. Soon, Katy trainmen went to work armed, and they showed they could be just as tough as the terminuses. In time, President Grant sent the Tenth Cavalry into Indian Territory where the troopers rode herd so fiercely that a majority of the terminuses left the region.

The Katy was the first railroad to enter Texas from the north, and it made the most of it. It got out and plastered the West with gaudy posters that sloganed "Gateway to Texas" and showed a cowboy riding a longhorn steer, just ahead of a Katy locomotive, across the new Red River bridge. Another poster, heavy with the humor of the period, shouted "Check my Trunk to Denison" and depicted, of course, an elephant waving his trunk toward the new bridge.

The Katy steel gangs kept busy. Working often with armed sentinels on watch for hostile Indians, or even worse white men, they laid tracks from Denison to Wichita Falls, then from Denison to Greenville, and on to Waco. Later, by construction and consolidation of other roads, the Katy at last arrived at tidewater on the Gulf of Mexico at Galveston.

At the northern end of the road, Sedalia, the Katy expanded to St. Louis by purchase of the Missouri, Kansas & Eastern, which a group of St. Louis men had built to tap the Katy's Sedalia railhead. By almost superhuman effort a name was synthesized from the MK&E's title to fit a divisional point. Hence Mokane, still on the map of Missouri. The Katy continued to build and to buy railroads with unusual good judgment right down to 1931, when it acquired the 105-mile Beaver, Meade & Englewood from Forgan to Keyes, Oklahoma, and the system today embraces 3,294 miles of road.

Throughout three-quarters of a century the Katy lines have never been long out of the news. Its tough towns of Parsons and Denison were great stuff for Sunday supplement two-gun stories for more than a generation. Then the James and Younger crowd operated on a number of Katy trains. Then the Daltons picked a Katy town, Coffeyville, Kansas, for what turned out to be their valedictory, and four of them were shot dead and tossed into a single grave near the Katy tracks. Other gangs came into being along the Katy road, operated a while, and disappeared; and in August of 1923 the last great raid was made on a Katy train by the Al Spencer gang, which staged an old-fashioned holdup and rifled the mailcar of $21,000. A bit later Spencer was shot with his boots on in a rousing battle with officers, and the rest of the mob was brought to jail by the combined efforts of J. K. Ellis, Katy's chief detective, and Federal and local authorities.

The Katy itself has never been stodgy, and nothing could be more indicative of its early policies than The Great Train Wreck which it planned and carried out on the otherwise dull and gloomy 15th of September, 1896, an event, says Kenneth Foree, unique in Texas history.* The affair was a child of the brain of W. G. Crush, general passenger agent of the Katy, who found business dull enough in the sombre and depression months of 1896.

William George Crush must have been a natural showman, one fit to sit with Phineas Taylor Barnum. He told Katy officials that if they'd just give him a modest consignment of rolling stock and two old locomotives, he would stage a Monster Wreck—Crush talked in capitals at times—that would cause 20,000 persons to buy tickets on Katy trains. Now, 20,-000 tickets was a heap of tickets in Texas in 1896, and Mr. Crush was given the green light. He selected a spot near the town of West, between Waco and Hillsboro, for the occasion. He papered Kansas, Missouri, Indian Territory and much of Texas with eye-bugging posters that described in circus language the immensity of the collision and wreck that would occur on September 15, when the Katy turned loose two complete and wild passenger trains to fly at each other's heads and be demolished BY THE IMPACT.

Mr. Crush thoughtfully added a list of the many excursion trains that would carry the fortunate to the scene of chaos. He filled newspapers with stories that said the town of Crush was even then being built simply to

---

* My account of this happening is largely drawn from Mr. Foree's story of it in the *Dallas Morning News* of Nov. 13, 1925; and from brief notes in the *Katy Employees Magazine*.

accommodate the multitude that would come. The *Dallas News* reported that 500 men were working to lay a 2,100-foot station platform at Crush, laying pipes to connect five tank cars of water with 100 faucets; that Leo Wolfson of Dallas would be in charge of a dozen gigantic lemonade stands in the deliberately chosen prohibition precinct; and that F. E. Miller, commissary chief of the day, was preparing to have a huge dining salon open at Crush.

At the Denison shops, meanwhile, Master Mechanic C. T. McElvaney supervised the conditioning and decorating of two aging locomotives which soon appeared, glorious as two rainbows, to tour the Katy lines as ballyhoo. The thing grew to fever pitch. Even politics was forgotten as the gargantuan dream of William George Crush took form and substance. It *was* gargantuan, too, for in that sparsely settled region, on September 15th, seven long specials pulled out of Dallas and Fort Worth carrying 2,000 persons at $2 a head. These were only a fraction, for when the *Dallas News* man arrived at Crush around ten in the morning, he found 10,000 people there ahead of him. During the next two hours or so, more special trains arrived at the rate of one every twelve minutes until more than 30,000 persons milled around in the wide shallow valley. They brought thousands of baskets of fried chicken and other picnic fare, and even though the district was nominally dry, no little beer put in an appearance and was consumed, along with nobody knows how many gallons of moonshine.

At four in the afternoon the two elegant locomotives were set nose to nose at the point where the collision was to take place, while photographers pictured the scene. Then they backed up to the tops of the opposite hills, each pushing a train of six ancient wooden coaches. And there they stood for almost an hour, a mile apart, each belching smoke and cinders, while Crush and a posse of 200 special constables attempted to get the crowd— "the biggest crowd in Texas history"—far enough from the collision point for safety. It proved a herculean task, but by five o'clock it was thought to have been accomplished. Crush, master of ceremonies and enjoying it hugely, raised his hat in signal. The engineers opened their throttles, tied down the whistle cords, and leaped. So did the two locomotives. Let an eloquent if unknown reporter of the *Dallas Morning News* of 1896 tell it:

"The rumble of the two trains, faint and far off at first, but growing nearer and more distinct with each flitting second, was like the gathering of a cyclone. Nearer and nearer they came, whistles blowing and the torpedoes, which had been placed on the track, exploding like the rattle of musketry. Every eye was strained. Every nerve on edge. They rolled down at a frightful speed (sixty miles an hour each) and hundreds who had come miles to see found their hearts growing faint and were compelled to turn away." But not all of them, though, for the brave man of the *Morning News* kept his eye on the main event.

"Words bend and break in attempt to describe it," he continued. "It is a scene that will haunt many a man . . . A crash, a sound of timbers torn and rent, then a shower of splinters. Then followed a swift silence. Then the boilers exploded and the air was filled with flying missiles from the size of a postage stamp to half a drive wheel falling indiscriminately on the just and the unjust, the rich and poor, great and small."

It was a Roman, nay, a Texan holiday. The two engines went right through each other. A pair of heavy trucks weighing a ton blew over the Texas landscape for 300 yards. A smokestack landed a quarter of a mile away. Theodore Millenberger, farmer, appalled, tumbled out of a tree to break his leg. A chunk of good oak timber laid Photographer Louis Bergstrom flat. A Mrs. Overstreet fell like a plummet when a hunk of wreckage broke her skull. A flying bolt went clean through the leg of Roy Kendrick. Another photographer, J. C. Deane, got a bolt and washer that gouged out one eye, then buried itself in his brain. Ernest Darnall died that night because a brake chain had torn away a goodly part of his head.

It had been a wonderful holiday indeed. After rendering such first aid as was possible to the injured, the crowd loaded the dead and the wounded into the cars, guzzled its last beer and moonshine, then went home satisfied it had witnessed the greatest event in Texas since Sheriff Pat Garrett shot and killed the eminent sadist and moron, William H. Bonney, in 1881.

CHAPTER XIX

Up in the Cold and Icy

Hitting a moose (Alces americana) is too dangerous a sport for well-trained engineers, such as ours. . . .
—WINGATE CRAM, President, Bangor & Aroostook Railroad.

IF THE Katy and the Santa Fe have been favored from the first by "western" influences and western difficulties, there is another road that has been conditioned by climate and geography and has had its share of deviltry to contend with. Snow comes down eleven feet deep over its rails and in spots mounts into drifts that reach up to the telephone wires. The temperature hits fifty and more under the zero mark, and it can be read at midnight by the glow of dancing lights crackling in the northern sky. A train left standing more than a few moments is frozen hard to the rails. Moose often get in the way of locomotives. Such things are a part of the life and times of the Bangor & Aroostook Railroad in Maine, most northerly road in the eastern United States, locally known as the Pulp & Potato Route.

Bangor is a city on the Penobscot River, in its day the lumber capital of America, which Henry Thoreau likened to a star on the edge of night, a rambunctious town feeding on the dark wilderness that surrounded it on every side.

Aroostook is a county of Maine. It is also more than a county. It is a region, an empire, a state of mind, for *the* Aroostook, as it is known in Maine, was the last frontier in eastern United States and the material and spiritual effects of the frontier are still to be seen there, and felt.

The Aroostook is that vast northern section of Maine where the people speak of Quebec City and Montreal as south, and south they are although few Americans realize that in this region a part of Canada is south of the United States. Aroostook is almost as large as the State of Massachusetts, and even today contains some of the wildest country east of the Mississippi. Still sparsely populated, it lives largely from its potatoes and its pulp and paper, and from the city slickers who go there by the thousand to hunt and fish. It is big enough for all who come, and each season the outlanders, most of whom claim to be veritable Dan'l Boones, get lost in large numbers in the northern Maine woods. It is this region that the

222

Bangor & Aroostook serves, a Class 1 road operating some 900 miles of main line and branches and employing around fourteen hundred persons.

There were two reasons why the Aroostook, alone in all New England, remained frontier country up to little more than fifty years ago. For one thing it was the most remote section of New England. For the other, its sovereignty was in doubt until 1842, when the Webster-Ashburton Treaty was signed by the United States and Great Britain. During the 1830's it was a battle ground. Both American and Canadian lumbermen were claiming, and cutting, the immense forests of spruce and pine along the St. John River. The business went from local-feud proportions into the realm of international "incidents." Lumberjacks finally took to shooting at one another. American flags were hoisted by Yankees, and cut down by Canadians. There were beatings, raids, arrests, imprisonments. The United States at last moved troops into the Aroostook and built log bastions they named Fort Kent and Fort Fairfield. The wild Maine loggers were not satisfied; they forced the governor of the Pine Tree State to call out the militia and arm them with cannon. The lads, dressed in special and very handsome uniforms, marched and drilled and made military noises. It had begun to look quite dangerous when General Winfield Scott, incidentally as able, as competent and as decently patriotic an American as ever lived, entered the affair with such good sense and diplomacy that Mr. Daniel Webster and Lord Ashburton were able to draw up a treaty that set the boundary and made peace, even though die-hard Canadians held to the last that Canada had been robbed of millions of acres of fine woods, as I do not doubt for a moment was the case.

Settlement of the Aroostook was started in large part by men who had seen the region first as soldiers in the Aroostook War, but the settling was no boom, and isolated logging camps outnumbered any other kind of community for the next forty years. In time, the New Brunswick Railroad discreetly touched here and there on Aroostook borders, but the Aroostook had no rail connection with the rest of Maine and the United States in general, until the 1890's when a group of men headed by Franklin W. Cram of Bangor and Albert Burleigh of Aroostook organized the Bangor & Aroostook Railroad Company. By then the echo of the Aroostook War had died away, for this railroad was probably the first in Maine whose charter did not begin with the avowed purpose: *"For the protection of the Northeastern frontier. . . ."*

Cram and Burleigh and their associates were genuine railroad builders, not promoters interested chiefly in stock issues and land grants. As soon as they got their charter, they hired all local labor available and brought in several thousand pick-and-shovel men from Boston. There was no delay. On went the grade from Brownsville up through the deep woods of Piscataquis County, on into the spruce of the Millinockets, over the Aroostook plateau to Caribou in the heart of the soon-to-be potato country, then branches to Ashland and Fort Fairfield.

Meanwhile, the company acquired the small Bangor & Piscataquis, between Old Town and Greenville, and the even smaller Bangor & Katahdin Iron Works Railway. In 1899 it extended its main line from Caribou to Ashland, and also bought two more little roads, the Patten & Sherman and the Aroostook Northern. Within eight years after its incorporation the road had main line or branches into a good part of the budding empire. It was budding but it was far from being in bloom; those 8,000 square miles contained less than 50,000 people.*

Perhaps no better example of the manner in which industry and agriculture follows the rails could be had than in the Aroostook. Potato production increased fivefold in eight years. Starch factories tripled in number. A big paper concern, the Great Northern, built its huge mills and the city of Millinocket, and presently was turning out 150,000 tons of newsprint a year. The starch factories soon declined in importance as the Bangor & Aroostook opened new markets for eating, or table potatoes, which have been coming out of the region on BAR trains in increasing quantity for the past forty-five years.

In 1907 the BAR got an extremely able man as executive vice-president. He was Percy R. Todd, who had started railroading in 1878 on the Ogdensburg & Lake Champlain, served successively on the West Shore, the Canada Atlantic, and the New Haven, and resigned from the latter road in protest against its financial policy, which, he said, correctly enough, would lead it into insolvency. When Todd took hold of the BAR it was a good railroad. He made it into a much better one. He went after new industries and got them—mostly more pulp and paper mills to use the tremendous resources of spruce that still covered so much of the Aroostook and bordering Piscataquis and Penobscot counties. He gave much attention to the growing and shipping of potatoes, and although his railroad was a monopoly in its region, Todd appears to have been anything but the arrogant railroad baron so familiar in the literature of the day. He consulted with the spud growers about trains, dates, and times. He built loading sidings where the growers said they would be most convenient. He went out of his way to encourage experiments with new varieties of potatoes.

And sure enough, Todd's railroad hauled more potatoes year by year, and more pulp and paper. Lumberjacks kicked out windows of BAR trains and made life strenuous for the train crews. The red-shirted boys fell off

---
* The Bangor & Aroostook continued to expand, modestly, for another decade by way of the following subsidiaries: Fish River Railroad, Ashland to Fort Kent (1902); Northern Maine Seaport Railroad, South Lagrange to Searsport (1904); Schoodic Stream Railroad, main line to East Millinocket (1906); Medford Extension, South Lagrange to Packard via Medford (1907); St. John River Extension, Van Buren to St. Francis (1909-'10); Washburn Extension, Squa Pan to Stockholm, with branch from Mapleton to Presque Isle (1909-'10), and the extension to Van Buren Bridge (1915).

trains, staggered in front of moving locomotives, and all but wrecked smoking cars. But these were the lads who produced one half of the BAR's total tonnage, and they were always given consideration, even though they caused no end of trouble. "I've made the run to Bangor," a retired conductor of the line told me, "with three hundred jacks in the cars, some sleeping under the seats, others fighting, others singing, all of them smelling to high heaven. After we got steam heat in the cars, it wasn't so bad. I used to have the brakemen turn it on full blast when the jacks were numerous and noisy. We'd keep the windows and doors closed, the heat would mount—seventy, eighty, even ninety degrees—and the combination of liquor and heat would generally turn the trick. By the time we got to Northern Maine Junction the cars would be quiet enough, except for snores."

Todd, who became president, added the several extensions to the line that have already been noted, but expanded only after he had given each district a hard-boiled study. Every additional length of rail had to be warranted by conditions. In 1915 the last link in the system was completed by a bridge across the St. John River that connected the BAR with the Canadian National Railways.

President Todd knew every man on the line by name, a majority of them, then as now, natives of the region. Boomers never have amounted to much on the road. Homeguards held the jobs and passed them on to their sons. There has, indeed, always been something more than a formal *esprit de corps* on the BAR. By family, by marriage, and by place of birth its employees have been tied to one another and to the railroad. The outlander riding it for the first time is sure to be struck by the easy ways of its employees. They are rattling good railroaders, too.

For six months of the year railroading on the BAR calls for men who are more or less impervious to cold and snow. A look at the map of Maine tells why. From Bangor the line runs north to Fort Kent and Van Buren, Canadian-border towns, both well north of Quebec and Montreal. It also runs south from Bangor to Searsport on the coast, a cold enough territory in winter for most people, but it is the northern division that calls for fortitude. The Government weather bureau at Fort Kent keeps the snow record, and for one recent winter it went as follows: 35.5 inches in November, 34.5 in December, 29.5 in January, an even 23 in February, a mere 9.5 in March. That totals 132 inches, or 11 feet in a fairly severe but not a record season.

Such snow calls for more than a broom. Snowplows are useless in drifts 30 feet deep and more. Almost every winter sees a thousand or even twelve hundred men who shovel and sweat and freeze to keep the tracks clear. They work in tiers on the BAR, like an open pit mine, with the men on the top tier of snow out of sight of the men working close to the rails.

In many cases the top tier has been on a level with the telegraph and telephone wires. All this is hard and cruel work, and it shows up on the balance sheet too. Shoveling snow, wholly apart from locomotives with snowplows, cost the road $59,356 for the first three months of 1933. The same period in 1934 cost $105,003. It makes quite an item for a small railroad that owns only sixty-five locomotives and sixty-nine passenger cars and whose total operating income runs to little more than one million dollars.

Even if there were no passenger trains, the BAR would have to keep its tracks open. It is during the winter months that the world's greatest potato crop moves to market. Forty thousand big boxcars have to roll out of the spud empire when the demand is best, and that happens to be just when the snow is deepest. In former days each of these cars housed what was locally known as a "potato bug," a man who rode the car to Boston or New York and kept a fire going in a stove. Hundreds of young men of the Aroostook have served time as potato bugs, but the job gradually disappeared with the advent of refrigerator cars that are preheated on the warehouse sidings, then loaded and a small charcoal fire lighted to keep the temperature even for the entire haul.

It is a picture for some artist, a mile-long siding of smoking cars at Presque Isle or Houlton—brown and green and red boxes standing out with cameo clearness against the stark white of snowbanks, overhead the flat, steel-gray, and bitter Aroostook sky of December. I think the city eaters of Aroostook potatoes would see more on their plate than a portion of food, could they have a glance at one of those immense and frosty freights standing on a siding, a locomotive at each end, ready for the long haul to market.

The grade out of the Aroostook is an easy one, with no high mountain passes; but it doesn't do to let a 200-car train stand for more than a few minutes. Sometimes they do have to stand, and then the trains has to be broken up and started by sections. No locomotive yet made could move a complete Aroostook train that has had time to freeze to the rails.

Winter also presents a problem of water. In really severe weather hot coal fires burn day and night to keep the BAR's 24-foot tanks in liquid condition. Every switch, every siding has to be shoveled out scores of times each winter, and so often do the railroad depots themselves, which are commonly banked with snow higher than the eaves. Down at Northern Maine Junction, where the BAR connects with the Maine Central, a potato train pulling in is another sight not soon to be forgotten, the locomotive plated sheer all over with ice, every one of the two hundred cars smoking like Dewey's fleet, yet all covered with ice. But there seems no way out of it; forty thousand carloads, or 27 million bushels of potatoes must be moved during the bitterest months of the year. That is why the commonest operating injury to BAR employees is frostbite. They are tough men, too, well weathered.

Courtesy GM&O News

Col. William C. Falkner who founded the predecessor of the Gulf, Mobile & Ohio.

Phoebe Snow, a press-agent creation of 1904, symbolizing the daintiness of Lackawanna travel, attained pin-up girl popularity.

From The American Railway, 1888

Tramps riding a freight get the bum's rush from a brakeman, while a fellow "shack" hastens to the scene of trouble, according to A. B. Frost, one of the best-known pen artists of his time.

Miss Eva Evans who was to have married John Sontag had he not died of wounds in a gun battle with a huge posse.

Christopher Evans. Picture taken by his daughter Eva after his release from prison.

Courtesy of Mrs. Eva Evans McCullough

John Sontag, wounded and captured. He died later in Visalia jail — weighted, said the attending physician, with more lead than he had ever before seen in a human being.

Spring brings trials of its own. The snows melt and the deep frost comes out of the ground so quickly, and with such surging force, that mile upon mile of track is twisted out of alignment. Track crews are multiplied each spring and set to work relaying the steel across blocks of wood, to remain thus until the earth has settled back to normal. By then, come the black flies and mosquitoes, to which BAR employees are almost but not quite immune. They are not immune to forest fire. Maine's tall old pines are gone, but the railroad runs through interminable forests of second growth, mostly spruce, and every little while all hands have to drop everything and to turn out and fight with water and axes and shovels and grub hoes to keep the very ties from burning up.

The forests, as related, are the sources of the railroad's second largest income—the hauling of pulp and paper. Pulp logs are carried to the big mill at Millinocket and East Millinocket, and to Madawasca, and paper comes away, a total of a million tons of forest products every year.

It is worthy of note that all but two of the Bangor & Aroostook's officials are New England Yankees, most of them State of Mainers by birth. Of its board of directors, as of recent date, four were natives of and lived in Bangor; others made their homes in their native towns of Presque Isle, Fort Fairfield, Limestone, and Caribou, all in Aroostook County. Thus the carrier does not have to contend with the sinister forces so often charged to absentee ownership and direction. The line probably has less bickering and trouble with its public than any road of comparative size in the country.

For the past decade and more the BAR has had as its president Wingate Cram, son of one of the founders, without any doubt one of the most remarkable men in all New England. Mr. Cram went to work as a water boy in 1900, direct from four years at Harvard, and after serving in a number of jobs for thirty-six years arrived at the top. Much of his early life on the railroad was spent in the woods, buying lands from hundreds of Frenchmen, from Scotch-Irish Canadians, from Yankees; running lines, helping to plot what are now towns with busy industrial enterprises.

Built like a moose, and not, as somebody remarked in print, like a silo, Cram is a lusty, jovial yet shrewd character whose roars can be heard above the wildest Aroostook storm. Of saturnine countenance, his wit and humor belie his face, for he is of great good humor, although members of the bar report that when badgered, at some railroad hearing or trial, his retorts come like lightning and often are barbed. "Mr. Cram as a witness," an eminent and opposing counsel once said with studied understatement, "requires special handling."

Railroader Cram must have taken more out of college than most big men of commerce and industry do. He is a really educated person with a sound familiarity with the classics, both ancient and modern. He reads everything, without glasses, and his knowledge both of Maine and of the United States is little short of startling. This knowledge is not confined to railroading, but includes such items as the specific wording of treaties with foreign powers, the varieties of caribou, the humor of the late Colonel Robert G. Ingersoll, the comparative architectural abilities of Charles Bulfinch and Stanford White, and the various cycles of the American drama from the time of "Bertha, the Beautiful Sewing-Machine Girl" to the latest tragedy of incest under New England elms.

All public heroes make Mr. Cram slightly ill, but his special loathing is reserved for unduly pious statesmen. Of a prominent and holy Maine politician of recent vintage he once remarked: "He is an esthete of the worst sort. Likes crackers and water and things like that." Mr. Cram's outspoken ambition for many years has been to own a live elephant. "It hasn't seemed practicable in Bangor, where I live," he remarked to this writer not long ago, "to own and harbor a pachyderm, but by God one of these days I am going to buy me one."

Cram's letters are celebrated for many reasons, and not so long ago one of them became public property. Maine's fish and game commissioner sent a protest to President Cram saying that he had received reports that locomotive engineers of the BAR had run down a number of moose, just for the hell of it, and he wondered if it were not possible to put a stop to the practice. President Cram gave the matter his consideration, then dictated a reply to the commissioner. "My dear sir," he wrote, "I have read with interest and no little pleasure your game warden's account of how our engineers have been stalking moose, and leaping at them with their iron horses. But this report, I fear, smells of nature faking of the worst sort. Hitting a moose (*Alces americana*) is too dangerous a sport for well-trained engineers, such as ours, who are a conservative lot and do not consider it fun to run into *anything* which may be on the rails. Of course, one of them may occasionally run a rabbit to earth or point a grouse with his 500,000-pound monster, but they never use them for big game. . . ."

It is doubtful if any other president of a Class 1 road knows its territory and people as well as Cram knows his. He is a two-legged geography of the woods, the lakes, rivers, streams, and brooks of Maine and the Maritime Provinces, who will stop a board meeting to discuss hunting and fishing. He is the Great Menace to bait fishermen, whom he abuses vocally and in print whenever he thinks of the subject. "A horse thief," he remarked to the author, "is a gentleman compared to the saurian who will use bait on trout and salmon." Cram himself throws a dry fly 75 feet, which is better than merely good for a railroad president.

Along the BAR line Cram knows three generations of hundreds of families—the countless McDonalds, McNeils, McDermotts. He knows which Cyr boy married which Michaud girl and how many children they have. He is privy to old family feuds and skeletons in closets. How many marriages, christenings, and funerals he has attended in the Aroostook is beyond knowing. He has bailed a number of Aroostook men out of jail, or has tried to save them from prison. Others he has aided in securing pardons or paroles. This is his own, his native land, and he obviously feels as much a part of it as any hunting guide at Madawaska or the First See-lect Man of Caribou. Somehow he manages to keep a table of vital statistics in his shaggy head that often surprises even a town clerk or a parish priest.

Under this perfectly natural coloring of being a common man, Wingate Cram cloaks some of the shrewdest brains in the railroad world. He is the road's best advertisement and public-relations counsel. It is a wonderfully good and successful railroad, the BAR. It continued to pay dividends throughout the drear 1920's, the grim 1930's. Its mortgage bonds are legal investments for savings banks in Maine and Massachusetts, and other careful states. Without ever attempting to lead the railroad procession, the line keeps pretty well up with the times. Its *Aroostook Flyer*, streamlined, air-conditioned, glossy, and with a modest amount of slick silver metal and pastel colors, is a handsome train, a surprising one to see gliding over the boundless Aroostook plains and through the Piscataquis forests. This train never gets within 300 miles of a large city. Its diners, in pre-war years, served a good dinner for 75 cents, and for $1.35 came a grilled steak with mushrooms, a generous salad, desert and coffee. The bar service, on which Mr. Cram prided himself—with a sardonic bow in memory of General Neal Dow, father of the Maine Prohibition Law—served, when I was last on the *Flyer*, a bonded rye or bourbon at 45 cents, and genuine Scotch at the same price, plus a long line of potables to suit the taste of any potato grower who had made or lost a small fortune on his last crop.

Long before other railroads had given much if any attention to getting, or rather to holding the passenger business that they had originally taken away from the stagecoach lines, the Bangor & Aroostook went after potential customers with an annual book. Entitled *In the Maine Woods*, with only a modest notice given to the railroads, these annuals are classics with sportsmen, tops in recreation publicity. Good photographs show beyond all doubt what hunters and anglers have been finding in the woods and streams. Canoe trips are routed, with approximate costs. Maine's fish and game laws, often rather complex, are kept up to date. So is the now more than 50-year record of kills of bear, deer, and moose, not counting those leaped at and destroyed by BAR locomotives.

The annual lists hotels and their rates, their distance from the rails or depots of the BAR. Coupled with the superb photographs throughout the fat book is a lively and informative text—the whole thing enough to make almost anyone restless to get out into the great silent places—along the Bangor & Aroostook Railroad.*

---

* I never asked, but I do not believe the annual *In the Maine Woods* is a heavy strain on the BAR treasury. It is filled with paid advertisements for everything from hotels and resorts to

Busses, automobiles, truck lines and airplanes came to the Aroostook just as they came elsewhere, and after thinking the matter over carefully, the BAR long ago bought a fleet of fine busses and put them into operation, both as feeders and along the lesser-used branch lines. The BAR bus drivers are dressed like full admirals and know how deep a snowdrift their machines can buck successfully.

But one thing these BAR Yankees have apparently never attempted, and that is immoderate expansion. They have, the record indicates, played their hand close to the table. The company's policy has been to plow its modest but almost continuous profits right back into equipment, rolling stock, and other improvements, not one of which could by any stretch of imagination be termed other than conservative. It is said of this railroad in Maine that it has never had a boom and will never have a bust. One more thing to be said for the BAR is that it has probably made the most possible of its territory, both in resources and friendship. This should set it high in the list of railroads of the nation.

---

plumbing supplies, fishing tackle, and "the P-V Hatchet, the One Hunters Prefer." This last a product of the old reliable Peavey Manufacturing Company, whose founder invented the tool that bears his name and is famous wherever lugs roll on the landings or heave in the river.

CHAPTER XX

The Carriers Are Harassed

The railroads have debauched and demoralized our courts and legislatures . . . have robbed the nation of an empire of domain . . . will cover the whole land with ruin and suffering. . . .
—EDWARD WINSLOW MARTIN, *The Granger Movement,* 1874.

FROM the first railroads had to meet opposition that was seldom if ever wholly disinterested. The attacks by the canal companies and the turnpike people have been mentioned, and also the rear-guard action of the stagecoach lines, of livery-stable keepers, even of farmers who sold grain for stage horses to eat. None of the opposition, of course, had any perceptible effect on the rails and the trains of cars. With steadily increasing self-assurance the carriers, up until about 1870, did pretty much as they pleased.

Almost from the first, too, the railroads had to undergo the harassments of politicians and their catchpoles, or to pay blackmail in one way or another. The method was almost sure-fire; the politico, usually a member of a state legislature, thought up some law or regulation that would be costly or awkward to the railroads in his state. He then put this into the form of a bill, talked loudly about it, about how it must pass if the sovereign people were to be protected against the monster railroad, and then waited for some hireling of the railroad to dissuade him by a method as old as man. There is record of as many as thirty-five bills that would harass railroads being introduced at one sitting of one legislature.

It did not take the railroad officials long to discover that the best way to prevent adverse legislation was to nip it before it had taken form, no matter how nebulous, in a bill. So, the free pass was invented, and for more than half a century the free pass was the most effective public-relations work any railroad could muster. Passes went to all members of the legislative arm in any given state; and also to governors, judges, sheriffs, constables, and of course to those in charge of assessing taxes. They went to United States senators and representatives. They went, in time, to bankers, merchants, journalists, all large shippers, to hotelkeepers and, of course, to all men of the cloth.

A typical example of the free pass in action concerns the redoubtable

J. F. Joy, general counsel and general factotum for the Michigan Central, who, on March 25, 1872, took occasion to write a letter to the then governor of Michigan. Mr. Joy wrote in reference to a bill then pending in the state legislature which would require wooden cattle guards at every grade crossing. In his opinion, said Mr. Joy, such guards at crossings would be "very dangerous to the public." The wood would soon decay, the expense to the railroads would be great, so great, indeed, as to be termed "an extraordinary burden"; and, anyway, no such silly requirements "exist in any other states." Then, in a postscript, Mr. Joy really got down to business. Wrote he, to the governor of Michigan: "I have directed Mr. Hurd to send return passes to your friends in the Legislature. They will have liberty to go home, therefore, when they have finished with their business." *

But not all the free passes on earth could dissipate the resentment felt by many of the clergy. No doubt they objected to Sunday operation of trains on the grounds it was against God; and perhaps, too, the more astute of them noticed that Sunday operation of trains had a depressing effect on attendance at holy services. They professed to see in the steam rail-carriers a force that might well wreck the nation by desecrating the Sabbath. In the earliest days of steam, the roads had no reason to operate on the Sabbath, as the Christian clergy insist on calling Sunday, hence the parsons were not alarmed. But by the middle forties business had increased to such an extent on the older lines that now and again a train was sent out on the first day of the week.

One of the first attacks on Sunday trains occurred on the Long Island Rail Road during the forties, although the actual reasons underlying the affair may have been something else. The farmers of Suffolk County had become bitter about the Long Island road. Their fields and woods were set on fire by sparks from the locomotives; the clatter of the wheels, together with the bells and whistles, frightened their horses, disturbed their stock, and caused the cows to withhold their milk. The smoke, moreover, sprayed their wives' washings with cinders and soot.†

Whether or not the parsons of Long Island agitated the attack is not clear from the record, but whoever led them, the Suffolk farmers banded into groups and tore up tracks, burned stations, and caused train wrecks by pulling track spikes. The road ceased Sunday operations, yet even this did not calm the wild farmers. Not until the line's officials awarded cash damages to those who claimed them was peace accomplished. The difficulties with the Suffolk farmers probably hastened the Long Island's bankruptcy, which occurred in 1850.

By 1850, too, the parsons, having watched the tendency to Sunday

---

* The letter is contained in *Michigan History Magazine,* Vol. VIII, page 395, Lansing, 1924.
† David Robinson George, *Growth of the Long Island Rail Road,* New York, 1934; a mimeographed ms.

operation with increasing unease, were coming out in full cry against the abomination. Groups were formed in various parts of Massachusetts, Connecticut, New York and Pennsylvania for the purpose of prohibiting Sunday operation by law.

Railroad officials adopted, at first, a sort of give-and-take attitude toward the growing chorus. A forerunner of the Boston & Maine thought up a truly magnificent piece of indirection, printing, in its Table of Arrangements (timetables) of 1850, the following order: "Persons purchasing tickets for Sunday trains will he required to sign a pledge they will use the tickets for no other purpose than attending church." Thus were hypocrites made in great number.

In towns where the religious groups were well organized and strongly led, little or no railroad work was attempted on Sunday. One such place was Altoona, Pennsylvania, which for a number of years was held up by preachers everywhere as a model of what a Christian city should be. The train that got into Altoona from Cincinnati late on a Saturday night simply remained there until Monday. "This is one city," gloated the Rev. S. G. Buckingham in a notable sermon, "where locomotives keep the Sabbath— where freight trains rest on the Lord's Day. . . ."

Yet Satan still held other towns and railroads in his sooty fingers. A writer of letters to the editor, in *The Independent* of October 2, 1851, put the finger on one deplorable case. "I am sorry," he wrote, "to find that the stockholders of the Saratoga Railroad still run their cars on the Sabbath. It is an odious and monstrous violation, not only of the laws of God, but of all the decencies of Christian society. And yet I have noticed ladies traveling in them, thundering into Saratoga on the Lord's Day! Women traveling in public conveyances on the Sabbath! There is something in this particularly degrading and shameful. It ought to be only the lowest of the sex that will stoop to such debasement."

In a majority of places the railroads of the early 1850's operated trains as and when they thought necessary, without reference to Holy Writ. No doubt some few of the rail officials were even truculent in the matter, and if so, they were ill-advised, for their truculence soon brought retaliation in the form of Sabbath Committees, well organized and well financed, which began to exert real pressure on the struggling railroads. One of the most active of these committees was that of New York. In 1858 it went after all of the roads that operated on Sunday within the state's borders, circularizing their officials and publishing their replies on the subject in pamphlets given wide distribution.

The New York Sabbath Committee probably thought it was being most reasonable about everything. One of its pamphlets has obviously a sweet and conciliatory tone, and it begins by first patting railroads on their backs. "As a civilizing power," it remarks, "the Railways can hardly be over-estimated. The snort of the iron horse as he rushes through the forest, or over the prairie, or along the valley, wakes the indolent to effort, and breaks in upon the stupor of helpless isolation. . . ."

This is all very well, but if such a power is not directed to the glory of God, what then? "The *moral* influence," continues the pamphlet with italics, "is a matter of immense moment. If it [the railroad] be made the channel for the distribution of a corrupt and debasing literature [*i.e.*, Sunday newspapers]; or the means of training a multitude in its service and along its lines in the habits of godlessness; or if it becomes the medium of invading the hours of *sacred repose* guaranteed by the laws of God and man—then will its pecuniary and commercial advantages furnish an inadequate offset to the injuries it will inflict on interests of infinitely higher concern." This was clear enough, but it was not all. "Valuable as the Locomotive may be," the pamphlet sums up with awful finality, "it is less valuable than the Decalogue; and if it cannot do its appointed work without running over 'the tables of stone,' it were better it never ran at all." *

There is no clear record of how the railroads met this new and concerted attack, other than to ignore it. Probably, when they used strategy, it was similar to that exhibited by an unnamed official of the New Haven road. He told the New York Sabbath Committee: "We send out a single train (with the mail) at 6 o'clock P.M. on Sunday, with a passenger car attached, and take only those persons who must go, on account of sickness and death, or other urgent matter." That last phrase, about "or other urgent matter," covering as it does just about anybody and everybody who wanted to take a Sunday ride on the cars, must have been invented by some primeval, yet able, public-relations counsel.

On the whole, the roads appear to have run trains when they thought best, and the holy men continued to harass them at every opportunity. The Sabbath agitation was pretty much laid aside during Civil-War years, but by 1872 it was back again, worse than ever before. Various Sabbath Committees or Alliances were rejuvenated, or organized anew, and they went furiously at the railroads, who were now also under attack by the so-called Granger Laws, of which more presently. Individual clergymen were alert to the railroad menace and were quick to spring in full cry into the pulpit and let fly. Typical of the time and attitude was the Rev. S. G. Buckingham of Springfield, Massachusetts, who sought to prevent the horror of a Sunday excursion in 1872. The target was the Vermont & Massachusetts Railroad, which had announced that a special train would be run from Greenfield to Boston and return on the Sabbath to take people to what was described and probably was a "sacred concert at the Coliseum."

---

* This remarkable preachment appears in the form and style of *Railroads and The Sabbath*, Second Document of the New York Sabbath Committee, New York, 1858.

The Rev. Mr. Buckingham was wholly out of patience with railroads, and in no mealy-mouthed fashion he said it was time Christians put a stop to Sunday travel on the steamcars. If railroads could not get their work done in six days, he said, then their managers were to blame, and the roads should discharge them and get new and presumably devout Christian managers. The good man really worked up a mighty head of steam on that otherwise quiet Sunday of June, 1872, and he gave the railroads everything he had in stock.* Into his long sermon he fetched God, Jesus Christ, the Pharisees, Jewish laws, David, and much else. And, like a good showman, he kept his most sensational suggestion till the end. "Labor," he cried, "labor would not be obliged to strike for shorter workdays if they would only guard the Sabbath and keep it holy as a day of rest." It must have left the railroad employees bemused, in those days of savage labor relations, to hear that merely by refusing to work on Sunday they could gain their ends without strikes.

Sporadic and gradually weakening attempts to halt Sunday railroad operation continued throughout the 1870's, but they had little overall influence. There was one road, however, that did not operate on Sunday simply because its president was fanatically opposed to Sabbath trains. That road was the St. Johnsbury & Lake Champlain in Vermont, locally and profanely known as the St. Jesus & Long Coming, and its head was Horace Fairbanks, one-time governor (1876–'78) of the Green Mountain State and a notable manufacturer of weighing scales. John S. Kendall relates how the St. J's superintendent often found it necessary to send out a work train or perhaps a snowplow on a Sunday, if Monday were to see regular trains moving. Knowing Fairbank's feeling in the matter, the super had the train or plow eased out of the town of St. Johnsbury as quietly as possible, neither bell nor whistle sounding, until it was well beyond danger of offending the ears of Horace Fairbanks. And Fairbanks had keen ears, for on several occasions he detected the noise that became sacrilegious at two seconds past midnight on Saturday; and when he did, there was hell to pay on the StJ&LC.†

Although the Sabbath agitation embarrassed and harassed railroads for half a century, the roads paid it decreasing heed and ran full tilt all trains that the traffic warranted. The agitation brought about no discernible reform, no general change in the attitude of the carriers toward the public. Campaigns against needless accidents, however, acted as constant pressure to improve operating safety, though the carriers appear to have often been reluctant to install or adopt new devices for preventing collisions, or even injury to employees. In short, by 1870, to pick an arbitrary date, railroads had become, as only too many orators of the day pointed out, a law unto

---

* "The Sabbath and the Railroads," A Sermon Preached in the South Congregational Church at Springfield, Mass., June 30, 1872.

† History of the St. Johnsbury & Lake Champlain Railroad, 1940.

themselves. They had bought United States senators and congressmen, just as they bought rails and locomotives—with cash. They owned whole legislatures, and often the state courts. They ran trains when and where and how they pleased. They charged what they would for freight and passengers. To call the roads of 1870 corrupt is none too strong a term.

The first real challenge to these powerful corporations grew out of a secret order, which, oddly enough in view of its subsequent accomplishments, was founded to improve the social and intellectual well-being of farmers. This was the Patrons of Husbandry, commonly known as the Grange, and it began as a mere hobby in the unusual mind of a fanatic named Oliver Hudson Kelley.

Born in 1826 in Boston, Kelley was kin to the Holmes and Sewall and other old Yankee families, but seems to have been unusually restless even for a Yankee in that restless period. After roving through the Midwest, working as newspaperman and telegrapher, he took a homestead in Sherburne County, Minnesota, and was soon contributing voluntary reports on farming conditions in that state to the Bureau of Agriculture. The Bureau found his reports and articles so competent that in 1866 it asked Kelley to make a tour of the South and to gather statistical and other information.

Kelley was much more than a collector of statistics. He had an excellent mind and was a keen observer of almost everything that passed before his eyes. One who knew him at the time described him as a man of dignified appearance, a full beard already turning white at forty, the high broad forehead usually thought to be associated with intellect, and the eager eyes of an enthusiast. Above all, Kelley was energetic. "An engine with too much steam on all the time," was the way a friend put it.

What the Southern farmers, plunged into desperate condition by the war and Reconstruction thought of this abnormally active Yankee isn't known; but Kelley looked at them not as a hostile Northerner might but as a fellow agriculturalist. He saw their plight and was deeply sympathetic. Worse than their physical plight, Kelley thought, was their antiquated thinking and the desolate apathy of their outlook. Kelley pondered the matter and came to the conclusion it was due in large part to lack of social opportunities, lack of chance to meet their fellows.

To think, for Kelley, was to act. By the time he had returned to Washington from his Southern trip he had in mind an organization of farmers, built along the lines of the Masonic order, to which Kelley belonged, which should serve to bind the farmers together for "purposes of social and intellectual advancement." He discussed the idea with his niece, Miss Carrie Hall of Boston, who told him the plan was good but that the farmer's women should be admitted to full membership. Only in that way, said Miss Hall, could the order accomplish its ends.

The engine in which Casey rode to his death on April 30, 1900.

John Luther Jones, better known as Casey Jones, shown here not long before he made his trip to the Promised Land. (Right) A recent picture of Casey's widow and railroading son Charles beside the memorial at Cayce, Ky., from which town our hero derived his nickname.

One of the most popular ballads of the 1890's was Gussie Davis' "In the Baggage Coach Ahead." The alert press agent of the New York Central managed to get his Empire State Express on the cover of the song.

Kelley went back to his homestead in Minnesota, and spent several months carrying on his farm and mulling over his idea. A year later he went back to Washington and entered the Post Office department as a clerk. He talked about his farmer group to other employees of the Post Office, Treasury, and Agriculture departments, and six men joined with him, on December 4, 1867, in framing and adopting a constitution which proclaimed them to be the National Grange of the Patrons of Husbandry.

The order embraced seven degrees, the four subordinate degrees for men being those of Laborer, Cultivator, Harvester, and Husbandman; and the corresponding degrees for women being Maid, Shepherdess, Gleaner, and Matron. The state grange was to confer the fifth, or Pomona (Hope) degree on masters and past-masters of subordinate granges and their wives if matrons who had taken the fifth degree. Members of the sixth degree were to constitute the National Council and after serving as such for one year might take the seventh and become masters of the Senate, which had control of the secret work of the order. The final degree was Demeter or Ceres (Faith).

Kelley, logically enough, was made secretary of the high-sounding order that had no other members than the original incorporators, and not a penny in the treasury. He organized Potomac No. 1 in Washington, and in February of 1868 resigned his clerkship in the Post Office and struck out into the open spaces, his eyes gleaming with the fire of the true missionary.

It was hard going. Traveling always on something less than a shoestring, Kelley worked his way to Fredonia, New York, where he set up what proved to be the first permanent grange. Then he swept on into the Midwest, dispensing charters for local granges to pay his expenses. Michigan, Illinois, Wisconsin, Minnesota, Iowa, one after the other the farmers fell before Kelley's charm and forceful argument. Working like a demon, and often without enough cash to buy postage stamps, he spent his evenings either talking or in writing letters, as well as composing pieces for agricultural papers. He said little about any political possibilities of the new order, but stressed always its social and intellectual benefits.

There was also the mystery of the order, with its quaint names of officers, and the sense of tribalism that went with it. But the more astute among the farmers were quick to see that here was something they could use to battle the aggressions of corporations, especially railroads, which they held to be responsible for the bad economic plight of the farmers. Certainly such men as Ignatius Donnelly of Nininger, Minnesota, saw the possibilities of a united front of farmers, and to the grange he lent his strong personality and really great oratorical powers.

With the Midwest organized in good shape, and with field men at work in distant California and Oregon, Kelley moved into the South, and there in spite of his Yankee manners and accent, founded grange after grange.

By the middle of 1874 there were more than 20,000 locals in the order, with a total of more than one and one-half million members. Even before then, the grange had begun to feel its muscle.

The spectacular and sudden growth of the Patrons of Husbandry was based in large part on one thing: The farmers' fear and hate of the railroads. This fear and hate was intense because of the arrogant and short-sighted attitudes of the carriers, all the way from their boards of directors to the lowliest employees. The roads shielded themselves behind the famous Dartmouth College Decision, which asserted the private character of business corporations so far as their management was concerned—the same attitude represented by the celebrated the-public-be-damned statement of a railroad executive—and denied the right of the public, the states, or of the federal government to regulate or in any way interfere with their operations.

Unquestionably there was also a quite general disregard, on the part of railroad officials and employees, of the convenience of the public. The poison had seeped all the way down the line. Discourtesy seems to have been thought the proper way to treat the public. The purchase of law-makers and enforcers by the roads was well known. The free pass became a fighting word. Worst of all was the habit of the carriers to make and change rates when they would and with no advance notice to shippers.

The period from the end of the Civil War to 1873 was one of great prosperity for the manufacturing interests and the railroads, but not for the farmers of the West and South. The acreage put to crops had expanded faster than had population. Fluctuation of currency values, high tariffs, and generally low prices for agricultural products all worked to the disadvantage of rural folk. Mortgages increased on the farms. No longer could the farmer pull up stakes and hit further west; there was still some of the West left but the choicest lands had been taken, too many of them, the farmer came to believe, by the railroads that were accursed of God.

So, home-grown orators went through the rural regions and told them there was no hope for them except to organize and fight the Leviathan of aggressive capitalism in all of its many and dreadful forms—banks, warehouse concerns, brokers, merchants, railroads, especially railroads, by far the worst of a bad lot. And when midwest farmers came to one winter and discovered it was cheaper to burn their 15-cent corn than to buy fuel, although that same corn sold in the East at one dollar, why, it did seem the time had come to rear up on their hind legs.

In dim schoolhouses and grange halls, and in even dimmer barns, lighted by smoking lanterns, the men of the soil and their women gathered to listen to the drums and brass of their secular prophets, while frost snapped in the rafters and winds that came out of the Rockies, far to the West, rattled the doors and windows. Aye, and a new wind was rising, a wind of the same sort that had blown Daniel Shays into horrifying prominence right after the Revolution; but now the wind was of infinitely greater power. It blew through Muscatine and Union counties in Iowa, in October of 1872, when Dudley W. Adams, a master of the grange, gave voice.

"What we want in agriculture," cried he, and his shadow thrown on the walls by flickering lanterns from Montgomery Ward & Company, was, symbolically perhaps, gigantic, "what we want in agriculture is a new Declaration of Independence. We have heard enough, ten times enough, about the hardened hand of honest toil, the supreme glory of the sweating brow, and how magnificent is the suit of coarse homespun which covers a form bent with overwork. . . ."

And on the benches, spellbound with the sheer music of Master Adams' words, the forms of both incompetent and lazy bucolics and of intelligent and hard-working farmers, sat straighter, chins stood out as the chins of their forefathers had stood out at Bunker Hill, at the Alamo, at Antietam, and eyes saw a splendid vision of rural power in the fantastic great shadows of the gesticulating orator.

"I tell you," Master Adams went on, "I tell you, my brother tillers of the soil, there is something in this world worth living for besides hard work. We have heard enough of this professional blarney about the honest farmer, the backbone of the nation. We have been too much alone. We need to get together to rub off the rough corners and polish down into symmetry. We want to exchange views and above all we want to *learn to think*. . . ."

The farmers of 1872 were beginning to think. They read again from the Preamble to the Patrons of Husbandry: *"The soil is the source from whence we derive all that constitutes wealth. . . ."* They looked again at the brightly colored lithograph on the wall of the grange halls. It showed eight men in individual poses. "I pray for all," says the parson, one hand pointed upward. "I trade for all," says the merchant, patently a rich fellow. "I plead for all," says the black-coated lawyer. "I legislate for all," says a statesman who looks uncommonly like James Abram Garfield. "I prescribe for all," says a physician dressed in a coat of mauve colored plush. "I fight for all," says the soldier, drawing his sword. "I carry for all," says a bearded and none-too-honest appearing ogre at whose back is a diamond-stacked locomotive, clouds of smoke arising from it. And in the center of this stupendous lithograph is a gigantic figure, the Farmer, with spade in soil, and around him fruits and vegetables of monstrous size and gorgeous color, without end. Says he, and his voice is strong and clear: "And I PAY for all."

Forward went the campaign, rising to the ferocity of a religious war. Pamphlets and books were hurriedly composed, printed and sold by subscription to farmers, many of whom had never bought a book before. One of the most popular was Edward W. Martin's rousing tome, *History*

of the Grange Movement; or, the Farmers' War Against Monopolies,
which was as direct as it was prejudiced. It was the Railroad Monopolies,
cried Mr. Martin, that by their unscrupulous course had saddled burdens
on the farmers, that had wrecked the financial system of the country, that
had debauched and demoralized the courts and legislatures, that had
robbed the nation of a domain sufficient to constitute an empire, and had
generally trampled upon individual and public rights and liberties, openly
boasting they were too powerful to be made amenable to the laws.

It was as damning and inclusive an indictment as had ever been compounded outside holy church, and you may be certain Author Martin had
a remedy for the wickedness. "The Grange," he said, "seeks to array the
agricultural class, nearly one half of our whole population, as a compact
body against these evils." Shall we stand idle, he demanded, and thus form,
around enormously powerful and rich corporations, a timid, weak, and
hopeless public?

"No," said the grangers, first of Illinois, then of Iowa, Wisconsin, Minnesota, Indiana, and so on and on, to include Vermont and Mississippi
and Oregon and Kentucky and Alabama, until the "No" welled up in massive chorus from forty-two states and territories. The granges as such did
not emit the "No." The granges were merely the meeting and breeding
grounds from which came the railroad laws that were to trouble the carriers, in one form or another, from that day to this. The laws were proposed, introduced, and supported by farmers—all grangers—who called
themselves by various names, such as Producers Convention, Anti-Monop-
oly Party, Railroad Committee.

Written in haste and often under great emotional stress, most of the
so-called granger laws were probably as unfair as they were unworkable.
Several were downright preposterous. Illinois passed an act providing that
freight charges should be based wholly on the distance traversed and attempted to force all rates to the lowest competitive rates of the year previous. Minnesota fixed schedules for both freight and passengers, and
provided for a railroad commission. Iowa and Wisconsin tried to establish
maximum rates by direct legislative action and created commissions to
collect information about the carriers. Many other states followed the
lead of these bellwethers.

At last railroad officials awoke to the storm that had seemed to beat
down on them without warning. There had been warnings enough, but they
had not been heeded. So now the embattled roads threw up their defenses
and counterattacked. On the whole they flatly refused to take the new laws
seriously. They violated them at once, were convicted in one of the lower
courts, then appealed. But their attitude toward the farmers, and in fact
toward all the public, took a decided and sudden change. Right away their
employees became courteous, even conciliatory. Complaints were an-

swered. Companies let it be known they were ready to settle all differences of opinion by arbitration with the newly formed railroad commissions. Alleged overcharges and other abuses were investigated by the roads themselves, or in cooperation with the commissions.

The carriers also did considerable "educational" work; they had able men explain the fallacies of much of the proposed or actual legislation to the farmers. They said that the new laws would not only prevent extension of the rails, but would hamper operations of lines in use. And in Wisconsin, where a notorious act called the Potter Law had gone into effect, the roads of that state cut service to one train a day on many lines, and set to rolling all of the antiquated cars and locomotives they could assemble. "A Potter Law," said the railroads, "calls for Potter cars, Potter rails, Potter time."

Badgered and met at last by the first competent opposition they had ever known, the carriers closed ranks, forgot their internecine wars of rates and rights-of-way, and fought back. They hired expensive counsel to hamstring the new laws. When they pretended to obey the laws, they managed by ingenious and subtle methods to show that the laws worked a greater hardship on the public than on the roads. And constantly they increased their efforts to conciliate the general public. By every legal means, and some of doubtful legality, they fought a thumping good battle from 1870 to 1876, and in some few of the states for a couple of years more.

Virtually all of the granger laws were soon repealed, or otherwise became inoperative; and by 1876 the Grange itself was on the decline. Comparative prosperity had meanwhile come to the farmer, and he no longer saw red when he looked at a train of steam cars. Then, the grangers of a number of states had been beguiled into starting co-op stores and co-op manufacturing enterprises. Many of the stores soon failed, and then the Iowa grange's great experiment in manufacturing farm machinery blew up in an expensive crash that cost the farmer-stockholders a lot of cash. The Grange itself did not go out of business. It has remained to this day the one great bond between farmers all over the country.

As for the so-called granger laws, even though they were largely repealed before they were even tried, they set a new style for the railroads. They led to decisions of the United States Supreme Court that established the rights of the states to control rail carriers, and thus laid the ground for later legislation, including the Interstate Commerce Act of 1887.* When the smoke had cleared, even a few railroad officials admitted the need for the granger laws. A. B. Stickney, president of the Chicago & Great Western, upheld the grangers and remarked that the evils which most railroad men laid to the laws were really the result of bad management on the part

---

* So says, among many others, Solon J. Buck, in his *The Granger Movement*, a standard authority.

of the roads themselves. Charles Francis Adams clearly set forth the abuses in railway management and said the granger laws had perhaps been necessary for the purpose of bringing about a better understanding of the obligations of railroad corporations to the public.

Oliver Kelley, genius of the Patrons of Husbandry, must have been amazed, and perhaps not wholly pleased, at the odd turn his little fraternal lodge had taken, with its modest ideas of social and intellectual improvement. He resigned as general secretary in 1878 and went to Florida, where he founded the town of Carrabelle. He soon returned to Washington, however, and in 1905 was pensioned by the order he had helped to found. He died in 1913.

When the tremendous reform movement of the grangers had spent its force, many of the Grange members, while retaining membership in the order, went into other groups that were openly political and carried on the fight against railroads, and much else, to the end of the century. These grangers, ex or otherwise, became the Agricultural Wheel, the Farmers Alliance, the Greenbackers, the Farmers Union, the Brothers of Freedom, the Farmers Mutual Benefit Association, the Cooperative Union of America, and at last, with ebullient Ignatius Donnelly trumpeting their platform, the Populist Party. One of the many demands of the Populists was not regulation of the railroads, but their ownership and operation by the government. Never since Kelley started his little social group have the railroads been free from one reform group or another; and it has probably been a good thing, not only for the public but for the carriers too.

The Interstate Commerce Commission was set up by the Interstate Commerce Act of 1887. Perhaps it is significant that agitation for a regulatory body such as this was started in 1870—exactly when the grangers were starting to feel their oats. No matter what or who was responsible for it, the ICC grew into a sort of police officer and judge so far as the carriers are concerned. Its first duties were to attempt regulation of freight and passenger rates. This proved dreadfully difficult, in the face of highly competent railroad lawyers, and for several years most of the ICC's orders were set aside on some legal count or other. The Commission persevered, however, and in 1906 it was given the power to set maximum rates above which railroads could not go. Four years later it was given power to suspend rates for investigation and decision of their reasonableness. And by 1920 its powers included the right to fix minimum rates below which the carriers could not go. In 1935 the ICC began to fix rates and regulations for motor carriers operating for hire.

Another of the ICC's duties is to investigate and to grant or to deny the request of any railroad for abandonment of portions of its line. These requests are, naturally enough, more often than not to abandon branch lines, many of which never paid operating expenses after the first few years. During the past two decades the Commission has granted permission to abandon something more than 22,000 miles. Yet, in many cases it has also denied permission. The trend, in the mid-forties, seems toward more abandonment rather than less.

The Interstate Commerce Commission has been staffed by men of more than average ability, and of no little moral courage. One of the ICC's important and generally unknown—so far as the public is concerned—duties is to prescribe the forms of all accounts, records, and memoranda to be kept by the railroads; and also to inspect them. The accounting system includes thirty-seven accounts, or classifications, into which all items of operating revenue fall, and 165 classifications for the great variety of items of operating expenses. It is the ICC that has the last word in permitting or denying a railroad the right to change any of its classifications.

As is to be expected of such a regulatory body, the ICC has been roundly criticized, and as often damned, by both public and the carriers. Yet, a fair overall consideration of its work during the past sixty years must convince the layman that the Commission has been one of the most useful, and needed, controls in our system of government. The Interstate Commerce Act, first major regulatory legislation of the Federal government, established the pattern for almost all subsequent regulation of business: the delegation of power to a small committee to be composed of competent, experienced, informed administrators. The railroads did not want the ICC, or any other regulatory body, and perhaps they would not have had to accept one, had they handled all of their business as well as they did the matter of Time. In the matter of Time, indeed, the railroads inaugurated a reform that was at last adopted by the government and accepted by the public. The railroad's system of Time has worked so well that it is difficult today to understand how we got along without it.

CHAPTER XXI

Times of Trouble

Finally, having found nothing more to get out of the stockholders, the railroads have commenced raiding their own employees.
—Chicago Daily News, July 26, 1877.

IN THEIR more than one hundred years of existence the carriers have been remarkably free from industrial strife. This may be due in part to their quasi-public nature. It may be due in no small measure to the general attitude and practice of the rail unions, the Brotherhoods, which have usually been blessed with capable managers, if not leaders, who for the most part lacked any urge for Utopia. And the very nature of railroad men assuredly has had something to do with it. They are well above the average intelligence of wage earners. They are steady. They are well disciplined by training, if not by heritage, and conservative in their outlook on almost everything.

But on the outstanding occasions when they did feel the need to strike, the railroad boys staged two of the most violent and bloody industrial upheavals the United States has ever seen. They struck with the courage of desperation in the middle of the most savage era of labor exploitation in our history. Into their strikes they put everything they had, even their lives in considerable number, and though they technically lost their two great struggles, they really gained much in the end. The first and greatest of all railroad strikes came in 1877.

The seventies was a jungle period for railroad workers. Employed by corporations which in large part had been making huge profits from actual operation of the lines, and even greater profits from the popular custom of watering their stocks, any pinch in business that affected ever so slightly the income from operation and from stocks and bonds was made up for, if possible, by shoddy operating practices, shoddy equipment, shoddy and murderous bridges and trestles, and the reduction of wages.

The Panic of 1873 put a slight crimp in railroad income. The roads cut wages. Unemployment was prevalent in all industries, and railroad employees took the cut with only minor and ineffectual protests. So for the most part did all other industrial workers.

Times grew worse. The farmers, through their new Patrons of Husbandry, started a war of laws against the carriers. In Chicago, the packing-house and other lines of labor staged a gigantic demonstration during which, on a bitter day in December of 1873, some 20,000 men and women paraded. Three weeks later, in Tompkins Square, Manhattan, New Yorkers witnessed what all right-thinking people believed to be a fore-runner of Revolution. A vast crowd gathered there and was being ha-rangued by speakers when mounted and foot police charged with drawn clubs. The crowd started a mad stampede while clubs rose and fell and blood ran along the sidewalks.*

Times got no better, and for the next two years the jobless outnumbered those working in most lines of business and industry. Yet the railroads continued to pay dividends. The New York Central paid 8 per cent in 1874, 10 per cent in 1875. The Pennsylvania paid almost as much. And in spite of its many difficulties the Central Pacific managed to return 8 per cent on its stock. Yet, in June of 1877 the Pennsylvania put into effect a wage cut of 10 per cent. Other lines, including the Erie, the Michi-gan Southern, the Lake Shore, and the New York Central announced a similar reduction for July 1st.

There was a little, but wholly insufficient, organized opposition to the cuts. This came from the Brotherhood of Locomotive Engineers, which had been organized in 1863 as the Brotherhood of the Footboard. In April, the Engineers had protested the coming wage cut with small strikes on the Boston & Albany and the Philadelphia & Reading. Both had been quickly abortive. And Franklin Benjamin Gowen, president of the Reading, who only recently had ably prosecuted and adequately hanged the leaders of the Molly McGuire terrorists, issued an order calling on all Reading engineers to drop their membership in the Brotherhood, or be discharged. The other two rail Brotherhoods of the time, the Conductors and the Fire-men & Enginemen, were weak and almost wholly devoted to the ritualism of a fraternal order. They did not protest the pay cuts.†

Although it was the Pennsylvania road that first announced a wage reduction in 1877, what proved to be spark for the tinder was struck by the management of the Baltimore & Ohio. It merely announced a 10-per-cent wage cut, effective July 16th, on all wages of more than $1 a day. The B&O could have foreseen no difficulties; similar cuts had been an-nounced, or put into effect, on most of the larger lines. The B&O firemen and brakemen, however, immediately presented a protest to the company.

---

* Samuel Gompers, later head of the American Federation of Labor but a mere cigarmaker in 1873, barely saved his head in the Tompkins Square riot by diving down a cellarway.

† The Brotherhood of the Footboard (Locomotive Engineers) resulted from the meeting of a few men in Marshall, Mich., at which W. D. Robinson outlined the plan of organization. The Order of Railway Conductors dates from 1868, the Brotherhood of Locomotive Firemen & Enginemen from 1873. In 1883 brakemen meeting in a caboose sidetracked at Oneonta, N. Y., founded the Brotherhood of Railroad Trainmen.

The company was polite enough, yet firm, and the cut went into force on the 16th.

On the morning of that day some forty firemen and brakemen on B&O freight trains being prepared to leave Baltimore refused to work. Their places were promptly filled from the large reservoir of the jobless.

At Martinsburg, West Virginia, on the morning of the 16th, the B&O firemen at this important junction climbed down from their cabs and refused to work unless the wage cut was restored. Arrested by the mayor and police, the firemen were quickly freed by a large crowd of fellow citizens who also prevented new men from taking their places. While this was going on, B&O freight brakemen at Martinsburg had been discussing matters. They joined the striking firemen. Passenger trains were not molested, but no freight was permitted to roll through the town. The strikers stopped them. Two days later, seventy trains totaling 1,200 freight cars, many of them loaded, blocked the tracks at Martinsburg.

These events were indeed shocking to B&O officials in Baltimore, but they were prepared to act; they sent a request to Governor Matthews of West Virginia, asking him to call out the militia. The governor mustered the two companies stationed in Martinsburg. The B&O sent its transportation boss, a Colonel Sharp, to the seat of trouble.

In the Martinsburg militia were many relatives and friends of the strikers. They refused to shoot or even to interfere. Governor Matthews, a man of low boiling point, called out the Wheeling militia, took his place at the head of the column, and away they marched toward seething Martinsburg. The whole region was beginning to boil, and at Grafton, hardly halfway to the scene, the governor changed his mind about being in command and left his troops. Everywhere along the route, he had learned, a great majority of the people were on the side of the strikers.

The trouble now spread swiftly. Out came the B&O employees in Grafton, then in Keyser, then in Wheeling itself. Urged by the B&O management, Governor Matthews petitioned Rutherford Hayes, President of the United States, to send federal troops. So on the 19th part of a regiment of regulars arrived at Martinsburg. Scabbing employees of the B&O proceeded to make up two trains, one to run east, the other west; and managed to complete the job while the troops drove off the strikers with bayonets and finally arrested one of their leaders, Dick Zepp.

Running through towns and a countryside now fully aroused and in almost complete sympathy with the strikers, the two trains, guarded from locomotive to last car by regular soldiers, reached their destinations to the echo of jeers, bricks, stones, and stovewood. On the next day the company and the troops moved a total of thirteen trains out of Martinsburg. The strikers held a meeting at Grafton, swore to stick out the strike, and offered to negotiate with the company. The B&O refused to meet the strikers' committee, but saw fit to announce that all faithful B&O employees would

The New York Illustrated News, April 4, 1863

"Beanpole" bridge built by the Union Army in 1863 on what is now the Richmond, Fredericksburg & Potomac Railroad.

One of the world's highest railroad bridges carries the Sunset Limited of the Southern Pacific (Texas-Louisiana Lines) over the Pecos River. A cantilever type built in 1944, it is 1,390½ feet long and towers 321 feet above the stream.

be rewarded by having their names placed first on the list for promotion and, what was more and what must have seemed arrogantly preposterous to men striking for a subsistence wage, each faithful employee would be presented with a fine medal. It was one hell of a time to be talking about medals. . . .

As the strike continued to spread along the line of the B&O, the company demanded more troops. Governor John Carroll of Maryland called out the Fifth Regiment of the Maryland National Guard, and a part of the Sixth, both of Baltimore, and sent them marching to get aboard a train at Camden Junction, on the outskirts of the city. The Fifth made it to the train, although followed every step by a hostile crowd which, on arrival at Camden Junction, drove the engine crew from the waiting train and left the regiment stranded.

Three companies of the Sixth Regiment started for the Junction but immediately ran into serious trouble. A mob of some 2,000 people turned suddenly into savages, in the manner mobs have a way of doing, and started to club the marching men, while those who could not get near enough for clubbing heaved missiles. The hard-pressed soldiers fired into the mob, killing ten and wounding nigh forty more. They reached the Junction with no serious casualties of their own but on arrival there were unable to go farther because an immense crowd blocked the tracks solidly. Federal troops now came from Washington and for the next several days artillery, Gatling guns, and infantry stood guard at Camden Junction. Already, thirteen citizens were dead, and the hospitals filled with more than a hundred wounded men.

On the 26th, a committee of the strikers called on Governor Carroll of Maryland with an offer of arbitration. The B&O management refused to discuss the matter and, with steadily increasing numbers of federal troops, began to break the strike, division by division. By the first day of August, the strike on the B&O had been thoroughly broken.

The spark from the B&O had meanwhile set fire to ready material elsewhere, especially in Pittsburgh. The Pennsylvania Railroad, it will be recalled, had been among the first to announce the wage cut. What was more, the Pennsylvania had also announced, to its employees, that henceforth freight trains would be doubled in length and pulled by two locomotives. Employees grumbled, but for eighteen days continued to perform their duties. Then, on July 19th when news of the B&O strike reached the Steel City, Pennsylvania employees left their engines and their trains where they stood and walked away.

Following the standard pattern, the company called for troops, and the troops, local militia, simply looked on while strikers met all incoming trains and either by threats or appeal "pulled" the crews. Now came a thousand soldiers, with a battery of artillery, from Philadelphia, and started a march out Liberty Street to disperse the strikers and sympathizers congregated there. Somebody heaved a few rocks. The troops fired two volleys, and twenty men died, while among the two score wounded were a woman and three children. The scene was set for one of America's greatest riots of all time. . . .

The smoke of the first gunfire was still hanging on the air when crowds began to gather on street corners all over town and to move in the direction of the railroad station and yards. The troops retreated to the Pennsylvania's roundhouse, which was quickly surrounded by 15,000 maddened men and women, some of whom were armed. Three soldiers attempting to flee the roundhouse were shot dead as they ran; and the city of Pittsburgh fairly blew up with violence.

Mobs rushed hardware stores and looted them of guns and ammunition. They rushed food shops and tumbled out with bread and cakes and other table fare. Thugs found conditions to their liking and so did the nameless city scum that ever crawls from under the pavement and comes to the surface at such times. Fire alarms both real and false filled the streets with clanging apparatus. The pious timid flocked to the churches while their pastors asked for help from Jehovah.

Down near the roundhouse, a determined mob took a gondola piled high with coke, saturated it with oil, set it on fire, and then rammed it head-on against one side of the roundhouse. Out came the desperate militia, shooting right and left, shooting their way through the tremendous crowd, which was now wholly berserk from the accumulation of violence. The crowd gave way here and there, as components of it went down before the bullets, first one or two, then half a dozen, until an even twenty lay still or writhed their lives away on the smoking ties. The wounded were hauled off the cinders beside the tracks and laid out in rows on warehouse platforms.

The troops lost three dead, and few of them escaped without bruises or cuts from bricks and stones and track spikes. But they managed to shoot and club their way through the mobs and got away, to the comparative peace of nearby Sharpsburg.

As for unhappy Pittsburgh, chaos was taking over. While the battle of the roundhouse was being fought to its bloody finish, fire broke out in the long lines of freight cars outside the Union depot. It must have been encouraged, for it spread from car to car, from track to track, with incredible speed. It spread to 104 locomotives, standing in the yards and shops. It spread to the Union Depot and Hotel. It spread to the Pennsylvania's office and to nearby buildings. Smoke rolled up into a night sky that was brilliant from such a fire as Pittsburgh had never seen before. It roared and grew, and mearwhile the mobs cheered for joy to contemplate the cost of this conflagration to the damned and double-damned and god-damned Pennsylvania Railroad. It was wonderful. Wonderful, too, was the looting of freight cars that went on while the fires were getting under way.

The Coal & Iron Police were brought into action. So was an army of 3,000 regulars in command of General Winfield Scott Hancock, one of the true fighting generals of the Civil War. General Hancock found Pittsburgh quiet, and terribly tired, but he found plenty of work for his troops to do in other places—in Altoona, in Easton, Johnstown, Bethlehem, and in Reading, where the soldiers became embroiled in a riot that ended with the death of ten civilians and as many more wounded.

By now at least 10,000 troops of one kind or another were posted along the Pennsylvania's line between Pittsburgh and Blairsville. Directed by Governor John F. Hartranft, a flying squadron moved west out of Harrisburg to open the railroad's divisions, one after the other, a gondola car mounting a Gatling gun running ahead of the locomotive. By July 30 the Pennsylvania announced that all of its lines were open and running again.

The battered and bankrupt Erie was having troubles other than financial. On July 20th at Hornellsville, in protest against the wage cut, Erie freight firemen and brakemen walked off the job and under the leadership of one Barney Donahue began to organize effectively for the emergency. They stopped freight trains, greased rails, tore up tracks, closed saloons. On came the militia to arrest strike leader Donahue and his committeemen, but to engage in no shooting.

Firemen of the Lake Shore road at Buffalo walked out, and the troops marched in, among them 1,600 militia, 1,800 members of the Grand Army of the Republic, and a citizens volunteer force. Eight strikers or sympathizers were shot and killed. A number of soldiers were wounded in the street fighting.

From Buffalo, news of the rioting traveled east, and presently employees of the New York Central struck at Rochester, at Syracuse and Albany. William H. Vanderbilt, head of the line, when interviewed by the press, professed not to know of any strike of his employees. Said he hadn't even received any demand from his men who, he asserted with a fairly benign cast of countenance, were not on strike at all. The mobs who were rioting in many towns served only by the New York Central, he said, were not Central employees but unemployed who wanted the good jobs of the men who worked for Vanderbilt.

All of this was reported in the press with a straight face, even though men who had worked but were no longer working for Vanderbilt were sitting in strike meetings and picketing freight yards. Negotiations between Central strikers and the company went ahead, and within a week things on the Central were smooth again. And the 10-per-cent wage cut remained in force. But Vanderbilt performed handsomely, compared to other railroad managements. He announced that the pay of his men would be increased "the moment the business of the country will justify it"—a statement that even then had become banal and meaningless; but Vanderbilt also *did* something and it was a truly masterful stroke of public relations. He said that the sum of $100,000 was to be divided, immediately and proportionately, according to their positions, among the loyal men of the New York Central & Hudson River Railroad. And it was, too, and promptly.

From Buffalo, the strike flashed into Chicago and began there with walkouts in the Michigan Central yards. Sailors on lake boats tied up in the city went out in sympathy. Workers in other railroad yards struck. Within twenty-four hours something very near a general strike was clutching at Chicago. Police clashed with a mob at the Chicago, Burlington & Quincy roundhouse, wounding seven, killing three. The Board of Trade enlisted 5,000 men as police deputies, and armed them. Several companies of militia were called out. On July 26th, at the Halstead Street viaduct, soldiers and mounted police rushed a monstrous mob and killed an even dozen, making several hundred arrests. A call for regulars was dispatched to Washington, and from there telegraphed to General Phil Sheridan, just then campaigning against the Sioux, who responded by sending several companies of infantry to the frightened city. There were more street fighting, more dead, and more wounded before July 28th, when order was partially restored and a freight train, a sort of sample to test conditions and the first train to move anywhere in the region for more than a week, was sent east under military guard.

The strike in Chicago had begun, as it had elsewhere, as an unorganized uprising. In Chicago it was quickly taken over by the Workingmen's Party, an allegedly radical group formed the year before, and fanned by professional agitators. The same was true in St. Louis, where mass meetings were staged ostensibly to air the wrongs of the railroad workers but turned out to be educational forums in the interests of a Red Dawn. St. Louis police raided the Workingmen's Party hall, arrested several speakers and clapped them into jail, with bail set at $3,000 a head. In San Francisco, a coincident upheaval was staged around striking railroad men and turned into the familiar and special California pattern—race riots directed against the Chinese who had been imported in droves to build the Central Pacific, then turned loose to shift as they could.

The little local strike that began in the B&O yards at Baltimore had spread across the United States, for there were minor troubles in Boston and Providence, both in connection with discontented rail workers. All of the sporadic strikes had been defeated, all the defeats had been bitter, and bloody. More than one hundred men had died. At least five times as many had been wounded. Yet, railroad workers had gained something, a spirit of union and solidarity they had not known before.

As they ruminated in switchhouse and caboose, in yard shack and Brotherhood hall, and discussed their defeats, they realized that defeat had come largely because of a refusal of all of the workers to act together. From this point on, according to many writers on the period, the Brotherhoods forgot the ritual and hocus-pocus of what had been their purely fraternal organizations, and turned their unions toward the goal of collective bargaining. If this was so, then it was enough, for out of the 1877 troubles came the most successful labor unions in the country.*

For seventeen years after 1877, strikes or walkouts of railroad employees occurred here and there, but except for locomotive engineers of the Chicago, Burlington & Quincy, who staged a bitter and effective battle in 1888, the disturbances were of little importance, other than for training both employees and managements in the techniques of industrial struggle and warfare.

The Brotherhoods had been gaining strength steadily, but they were altogether too exclusive and conservative for Eugene Victor Debs, an ex-fireman on the Terre Haute & Indianapolis, who had become grand secretary of the Brotherhood of Locomotive Firemen. In 1893 Debs joined with others in establishing a labor group of the vertical or industrial type, the American Railway Union, of which he was chosen president.

Both eloquent and brilliant, as well as honest, Debs within a year had organized workers of the Great Northern Railroad and of several other lines into the new group; and in April of 1894 the ARU staged a strike for higher wages on the GN. Eighteen days later the men returned to work with most of their demands satisfied. So spectacular a success had an immediate effect. Railroad employees of most of the lines fanning out from Chicago began to join the new union. If an industrial union such as this could bring Jim Hill to terms so quickly, then let the old craft unions go.

Recruiting for the ARU went ahead at a gratifying rate, and by early June it could muster 150,000 members, of whom some 4,000 were strictly speaking not railroad workers at all but employees of the Pullman Company, manufacturers and operators of sleeping and chair cars. The ARU was criticized, by members who were railroad employees, for taking Pullman employees into the organization. Debs maintained that all workers having to do with railroads, even if not directly, should belong to one big union capable of backing the demands of any portion of its membership.

There were several reasons why Pullman employees wanted a strong

---

* For a careful and detailed consideration of the strikes of 1877, see *American Labor Struggles*, by Samuel Yellen, New York, 1936.

organization to represent them. One was a dislike of the manner in which the town of Pullman, Illinois, was run. Pullman the town had long been the pride of George Mortimer Pullman. He founded it in 1880 with the idea of making it the finest industrial community in the United States. And it did look pretty good to visitors. One of my own grandfathers saw it in 1881 and was impressed. Wrote he to his newspaper: "Pullman is located in a beautiful spot on the southern shore of Lake Michigan, and it is a magnificent affair. You might think it a paradise, with its macadamized walks and streets decorated with flowers, its fine structures with marble fronts and the general air of elegance that pervades the place. The outlay is simply enormous." *

Pullman struck many a visitor the same way, but Pullman employees, after a decade, discovered the marble fronts to be inedible and the general air of elegance poor clothing for their wives and children. Wages, in 1893, were cut to the bone. Rents of Pullman tenements, none of them built of marble, had remained at predepression levels. The company exercised a maddening paternal attitude. It viewed all labor-union groups with great hostility. The blacklist was used against employees who found fault with Pullman the town, or Pullman the company, or the teachers and preachers employed in Pullman schools and churches. Worst of all was a final cut in wages that brought employees' incomes to such a level that many of them could not even keep up with their rents of Pullman-owned tenements.

Early in May of 1894, following a long winter of slim rations, Pullman employees sent a committee to wait upon the company and demand a restoration of the wage levels of a year before. The company explained that it was operating solely for the reason of giving its employees work, that no thought of a wage increase could be considered, nor could rents be reduced. Knowing that the company had paid 8 per cent on its stock in 1893, the employees were not greatly impressed. On the day following the employees' committee's futile efforts, however, work in the plant was resumed as usual. Then the news raced through the works that the company had discharged the three members of the grievance committee. That night an impromptu mass meeting was held, and next day 2,500 employees walked off the job. By night virtually all of the force was out. A central strike committee was elected to notify the company of three demands: reinstatement without prejudice of the discharged committee members, lowering of rents, restoration of the wage cuts. The company refused even to consider the demands and promptly put up notices saying that the Pullman works would be closed indefinitely.

The strike was on. The American Railway Union assessed its members three cents a day each to support the strikers. The Pullman company pre-

---

* Edward Amherst Stewart, "A Trip in the West, No. 14," in *The Express & Standard,* Newport, Vt., December 1881.

pared to starve its employees into submission. On June 12 a convention of the ARU was held in Chicago at which a majority of delegates favored a sympathetic strike and a boycott of Pullman cars. Debs counselled patience. On the 13th the ARU sent a committee to meet with Pullman Company officials, who declined. Pullman also let it be known that it would not submit the matter to arbitration. On the 26th the ARU ordered its members to operate no trains of which Pullman cars were a part. The battle was on, and it was going to be one of the greatest battles ever fought by American labor and American managements.

The General Managers' Association, a voluntary group of twenty-four representatives of as many railroads in the Chicago area, allied itself with Pullman and took command of the fight against the ARU. The GMA was, naturally enough, well-heeled in the matter of cash and it also contained many men of great force and unlimited energy who were also ruthless. They simply had to be ruthless or they would not have been representing American railroads in labor troubles in 1894; they were products not of the philosophy of Mr. Emerson but of Mr. Spencer. The Association's first move was to issue a public statement protesting the boycott against Pullman as unfair and not in the public interest. It added, too, that members of the Association would "act unitedly" to defeat the American Railway Union.

Members of the ARU were also acting in a united manner. Two days after the boycott began, Pullman-car traffic out of Chicago had almost wholly stopped. A few days later Pullman cars were being sidetracked at the far western end of the Northern Pacific, and all along the Southern Pacific. The thing was working, working beautifully, and as the news came in from the remote reaches of the West, the ARU boys were jubilant.

Acting swiftly, too, the General Managers group asked the United States marshal at Chicago for special deputies, and within a few days 3,600 men had been deputized and armed. These men served both as United States officers of the law and as railroad employees, being paid by the several roads. Violence entered the affair at the same time the deputies went to work, and freight cars in the yards started to burn. The ARU claimed this arson to have been the work of agents provocateurs paid by the railroads. The General Managers charged it was the work of "anarchistic members" of the American Railway Union.

The General Managers called for federal troops, and on the Fourth of July four companies of the Fifteenth Infantry moved in and set up camp on the lake front. A week later more than 2,000 regulars were in the city, under command of General Nelson A. Miles, who established his headquarters nowhere but in the Pullman Building.

Governor John P. Altgeld of Illinois was incensed. He had not asked for federal troops, and now he sat him down and said so in a sharp note to

Stephen Grover Cleveland, President of the United States. The President
dismissed Altgeld's note briefly.

Guarded by federal troops, strikebreakers on July 5th moved a train
of Swift's meats out of the Union Stock Yards, while a huge crowd
gathered and at last had to be dispersed by cavalry charges. The mayor of
Chicago asked Governor Altgeld for militia, and five regiments were mustered and ordered into service.

Street fighting started in earnest on the 6th, when two men were killed.
On the 7th as a company of national guardsmen were moving a train at
Loomis and 49th streets, they came into conflict with a gigantic crowd.
The troops fired, and twenty persons were killed on the spot or died of
wounds. It was getting bloody now, for keeps, but the strikers were
holding well. On the day of the riot thirteen of the twenty-four railroads of the Chicago area had ceased to run any trains at all, and the
others operated only mail and passenger service, with no Pullman cars
attached.

In the meantime, federal or state troops, or both, had been ordered into
service in Michigan, Iowa, and California. The situation seemed so grave
to President Cleveland that on the 9th he issued an extraordinary procla-
mation, effective at noon on the 9th, warning all persons of Illinois against
assembling in crowds; and next day extended the warning to North Dakota, Montana, Idaho, Washington, Wyoming, Colorado, and California.
Sympathetic walkouts of engineers, telegraph operators, switchmen and
car cleaners took place in widely separated places. Although the railroad
Brotherhoods were officially against the boycott, Lodge 233 of the Firemen, Chicago, turned in its charter to the Brotherhood and joined the
ARU in a body.

The next move of the General Managers was a telling one; they prevailed on the attorney general of the United States to issue a series of injunctions which, when divested of their legal verbiage, prevented any form
of picketing. The ARU ignored the injunctions. Debs and three other
officers of the ARU were indicted on charges of having interrupted interstate commerce, obstructed the mails, and intimidated citizens in the free
exercise and enjoyment of their rights and privileges. Of which, doubtless,
they were quite guilty. Debs and his officers were arrested, then released
on bail.

Debs now attempted to stage a general strike in Chicago, but except for
the Cigarmakers and Bakers, there was no response. The ARU, seeing the
end just ahead, proposed to the General Managers to call off the strike and
boycott if the Managers would agree that all members of the ARU, except
those convicted of crimes, would be reinstated in their former jobs without
discrimination. The GM did not reply. Debs went on with plans for continuing the strike. He was arrested again, this time for contempt of court.
Indictments were issued against 190 other ARU members, and police

arrested 515 others and charged them with offenses ranging from murder to intimidation.

The strike and boycott were being broken, steadily, surely. It started to give way between July 14th and 21st, when the movement of trains out of Chicago took a surge upward. On the 20th federal troops were withdrawn from the city, and some of them dispatched to handle ARU troubles elsewhere. Almost simultaneously the Pullman Company announced that its shops would resume as soon as a working force could be assembled. By August 2nd, there was no boycott of Pullman cars anywhere in the United States. The Debs Rebellion, as newspapers were calling it, looked to have been a complete and abject failure.

Debs remained, where he was, in jail. With his counsel, Clarence Darrow, he asked repeatedly to be put upon trial, and on February 9, 1895, it was actually begun, but halted when a juryman was taken ill. It was postponed a number of times and at last dropped from the records. "Both sides," Darrow remarked later, "recognized that Debs had been sent to jail because he had led a great fight to benefit the toilers and the poor. It was purely a part of the world class-struggle for which no individual can be blamed."

The ARU strike and boycott changed nothing, for the moment, at Pullman, Illinois, although it unquestionably caused Pullman officials to know that their employees were not nearly so happy and contented as they had believed.

The struggle caused the railroad Brotherhoods to feel more certain than ever, if that were possible, that their own form of labor organization was the only sort fit for railroaders.

The fight showed most patently how injunctions could be used successfully against labor groups. And it made of Eugene Debs a national, perhaps a world-known, figure. Debs went on from there convinced that Socialism was the answer to the world's woes, went on even to prison and to repeated nominations for the Presidency of his country.

Perhaps the most sinister thing to come out of the Debs Rebellion was a hangover piece of revenge that probably caused more heartaches and distress than all of the beatings and killings that went on during the strike itself. This was the blacklist instituted by the General Managers Association. Not all railroad companies belonging to the General Managers took part in the blacklist. The Rock Island road and a few others, says Freeman Hubbard, who has been studying the subject for many years, were ready to forget and forgive.* The Rock Island, indeed, immediately rehired more than 4,000 of its 4,500 employees who had joined the strike and boycott. But the Rock Island was a notable exception. Most lines re-

---

* See his *Railroad Avenue,* previously cited.

fused absolutely to verify the railroad experience of their former employees who had joined the ARU and who, after the strike, were trying to get jobs on lines that had not been affected by the Debs Rebellion. One such employee sued his former employer and won; he got damages as well as a service letter. Whereupon the General Managers got an unholy idea: Any of their erstwhile employees requesting a service letter, or clearance, got it. The letter, says Mr. Hubbard, set forth the man's record and closed with the conventional "Left our service of his own accord." But there was more in the letter than met the casual eye.

What did not meet the casual eye was a watermark in the fabric of the paper. There were two kinds of paper, two kinds of watermarks, although both watermarks were in the form of a crane, that long-legged bird of the creeks. To the ex-employee who may have gone on strike with the ARU but was neither a leader, an agitator, nor a saboteur, went a clearance on paper watermarked with a crane who stood erect with his head up. To the ex-employee who had taken an active part in the strike went a clearance on paper watermarked with a crane whose neck was "broken," the head hanging listlessly. Some men who have seen this watermark describe it as "the crane in a feeding position."

It was a very clever and diabolical method, both of protection against incompetent or trouble-making employees, and of sheer revenge. The method is credited with adding to the ranks of the boomer-railroaders, the men who never worked more than a year, often no more than a few months, for one road, before going on to another. Charles Anthony Roach, oldtime railroad man known as "Silent Slim," now of Portland, Oregon, had one of the clearance letters of the "broken-neck" kind—though he did not know it then. It failed, of course, to get him a job on the Louisville & Nashville, or on other roads to which he showed it. So, he started to booming and around a hobo jungle fire in Springfield, Illinois, met another veteran railroad man to whom Slim related his experience. This man asked to see Slim's clearance letter. He held it up to the light of the jungle fire and called attention to the frog-catcher with its "broken neck." It was then the affair became clear to Silent Slim.

Mr. Hubbard has interviewed many oldtimers who had "broken-necked" letters, but none had saved his copy.

The "broken-neck" fraternity, the blacklisted men, naturally set about to find some method of beating the damning watermark. It didn't take very long. There was a jerk-line road, the Missouri & Northern Arkansas, whose owner, president, general manager, and operating superintendent was a benevolent old gentleman. A boomer could get on there without any sort of clearance, work a few weeks, then get a clearance on M&NA paper that would cover not only his actual length of service on the M&NA but also, if he asked for it, cover those months when the ARU was striking. Harry K. McClintock, now of San Pedro, California, got his clearance that way. He says the road was known as the "Clickety-Bang" and was a tower of comfort to the men on the General Managers' blacklist.

Another way of beating the blacklist was to get a clearance, done in proper style and on the proper letterhead, from any one of several underground printing outfits that made phony clearance papers a profitable sideline. These cost all the way from $1 up to $25, and were worth it. The boomer would choose some road whose company records were known to have been destroyed by fire or otherwise, such as the Fort Worth & Denver City, and could be certain that no one could check on his claim. Another popular road, *after* 1917, was the Colorado Midland, which was torn up at that time and its rails sent to France. Still another was the abandoned Kansas City Northwestern.

But as time went on, the old hates waned, then died, and membership in the ARU ceased to be a factor in not getting a job. By then, the boomer railroader was passing, anyway. His golden era, veterans say, had passed by the end of World War I.

Most railroad men believe that the crane with the broken neck was the first use of a blacklist by watermark, by railroads. Yet before he could have heard of the crane device, one oldtime conductor had told about another such device. In his curious and otherwise not very interesting book, *Without Due Process; A Typical Tale of Life on the Rail*, S. E. Farnham, longtime employee of the Soo Railroad, described in detail the blacklisting watermark of an unnamed railway. "Stamped within the fibre of the paper," says he, "was a figure of a man walking away from a train, holding a grip upon which could be seen the letters B.O.R. meaning By Official Request."

Conductor Farnham said that he himself had never been the victim of a blacklist, but he knew it existed on many lines previous to 1893, a full year before the ARU strike, and he damned it both in secular and biblical language.

The so-called Big Four Brotherhoods, the Engineers, Firemen, Conductors and Trainmen were little affected by the ARU and its strike. The last of the Big Four, the Trainmen, was founded in 1883. It was followed by the Order of Railroad Telegraphers, organized in 1886 at Cedar Rapids, Iowa; by the Brotherhood of Maintenance of Way Employees, founded in 1887, it is said, by a small group who met under an oak tree at Demopolis, Alabama; by the Brotherhood of Railway Carmen, dating from 1891; by the Switchmen's Union of North America, 1894; by the fearfully named Brotherhood of Railway and Steamship Clerks, Freight Handlers, Express and Station Employees, 1898; and by the Brotherhood of Railroad Signalmen, 1901.

Against continuous yet weakening opposition by railroad managements, these unions carried on a campaign for recognition as collective bargaining agencies. This bore fruit during federal operation of the carriers (1918–'20) in the national agreements signed by the unions and the United States Railroad Administration. Other rail groups were being organized in this period, such as the Order of Sleeping Car Conductors, the Brotherhood of Dining Car Conductors, the Railroad Yardmasters of America, and the American Train Dispatchers Association.

Negro rail workers began to organize first in 1912, with the Association of Colored Railway Trainmen and Locomotive Firemen, and a little later formed the Association of Train Porters, Brakemen and Switchmen, the Brotherhood of Dining Car Employees, the National Association of Brakemen-Porters, and the Brotherhood of Sleeping Car Porters.

The vast and complicated subject of labor relations between railroad managements and the unions was first recognized in 1888 when Congress provided for special emergency investigating boards in case of disputes. This act was followed, in subsequent years, by further legislation, culminating in 1934 in an act providing for a National Mediation Board of three members, with powers to mediate in disputes and also to hold elections for determining who should be the representative of any class of rail employees. The same act created a National Railroad Adjustment Board of 18 representatives of the railroads and a like number from the unions, which has exclusive jurisdiction concerning grievances, interpretations and applications of working agreements. In case of deadlock, appointment of a referee is provided for.

The rail unions and rail managements, as intimated, have on the whole and over the years run their joint business of labor relations in a highly intelligent manner, beneficial to themselves and to the public. For half a century after the Debs Rebellion of 1894 nothing that could by any means be termed a general strike occurred in the American railroad system. Then, in 1946, after long rumblings of trouble to which few paid any heed, the whole elaborate and complicated machinery for settling differences broke down, and a strike began.

Only two of the Brotherhoods struck, yet so dependent are the rails on the coordinated efforts of specialized workers, that the effects of the strike were immediately appalling. The greatest transportation system in the world stopped dead, almost in its wheel tracks. The big terminal stations of the cities glutted with crowds that were bewildered or frantic, while across the land, at desolate junctions and forlorn flagstops, men and women waited anxiously for trains that did not come—for the first time, probably, since 1894. It was incredible. . . .

Freight and express and mail started to pile up so quickly that the piles were mountains within a few hours. The telegraph and the telephone wires swiftly clogged because they could not begin to carry the messages of regrets and demand and explanation incident to the stalled wheels of the

There's a tunnel at each end of the Cumberland River railroad bridge in Kentucky, one at Somerset, the other at Burnside. The Southern's Royal Palm has just emerged from the Somerset bore and is heading toward the other one, enroute to Florida, on what used to be called "The Rat-Hole Division."

Frank Leslie's Illustrated Newspaper, Feb. 17, 1872

Chinese labor gangs with white overseers were used by the Union Pacific to break snow blockades of the 'Seventies, when passengers were marooned for as long as three weeks in temperatures sometimes 30° below zero. A mail train, doubleheaded by engines with great diamond stacks, nearly buried near Ogden, Utah, in 1872.

nation. Coffins and their contents lay on baggage trucks, while six-foot excavations waited in distant church yards. Fruits spoiled in sidetracked express cars. Weddings were postponed, and so, perhaps, were matings not blessed by legal bonds. Prisoners on their way to penitentiaries had a few more hours of comparative freedom; other prisoners, waiting in condemned cells, lived a few more hours beyond their allotted time because the man with the satchel containing a hemp rope found his train cancelled. . . . Throughout forty-eight states, and penetrating to the remote counties, the arteries of rails ceased to throb with the life-giving steam and Diesel.

The strike was over almost by the time its paralyzing effects had been felt, yet it had lasted long enough to let America know, for all its vaunted highways and automobiles, for all its planes and its inland waterways, that the railroad was still the medium upon which much of the United States depended for transportation of itself and to carry its goods. Perhaps some day, as so many glib prophets of the Brave New World had been saying for two decades, perhaps some day grass would grow high between rusting rails, but not yet . . . not in any foreseeable time. In the United States, in 1946, the American railroad system was still the most important piece of machinery in the country.

CHAPTER XXII

Through the Dark Ages—And After

How wonderful it was to think back to the link-and-pin days, and to realize that all these developments had happened in the span of my lifetime.
—CHAUNCEY DEL FRENCH, veteran railroader, in 1938.

IT IS all but impossible to comprehend fully the crudity of railroading a century ago. The little old woodcuts of the dinky, wide-open engines pulling their coachlike cars look odd and perhaps a bit romantic, but they fail to give little more than an intimation of the difficulties of operation. In old accounts, too, one may read quaint items; how a train of cars was known as a "brigade," the conductor as a "captain," and how on occasion all male passengers were obliged to get off to push the consumptive engine over some slight rise of ground. Yet, a picture of railroading in those and slightly later days from the viewpoint of one of the train crew, is a rare thing. There are perhaps several reasons for the rarity of such accounts. Literacy in the United States of the mid-nineteenth century was not nearly so common as now, nor in any case were many railroad operating men much given to the pen and memoirs. And the danger to railroad men in those days can scarcely be visualized today; a good many of them were either killed on the job, or so badly injured and frightened that they went into some comparatively safe line of business, such as steepleclimbing.

Among the rather few railroad men who began work even before steam had completely supplanted horses and mules as motive power on the rails and continued on through the early days of steam, and so on to the times of air brakes and big locomotives of the 1890's, was Charles H. Frisbie, who closed his career as a bewhiskered patriarch of all the engineers of the Burlington System after a full half-century, most of it spent on the head end of trains.

The stouthearted and indestructible Frisbie was born in 1822 in Cortland County, New York, where his father was a farmer and also kept an inn, one of the old-time kind, from above whose door a swinging sign still moved with the wind. The nearest thing to a railroad in the United States was the turnpike road, elevated and leveled by a turnpike company, at each end of which was a toll gate. No wagon or foot traveler passed over a turnpike without paying toll.

Droves of cattle and sheep from western New York passed the Frisbie inn, walking two hundred, even three hundred miles to their fate in the metropolis, making four or five miles a day, while the drovers, many of them given to the dramcup, stopped at every inn for refreshment. Most travelers of the time used one or another of the many competing stage-coach lines, and among Frisbie's earliest memories were the four-horse coaches stopping at his father's inn. Even with the Erie Canal a-building, it seemed to all that the stagecoach was immutable, the one and only method for making long journeys by land. Yet, it was only a few years later that Peter Wells of Port Jervis, New York, wrote their obituary:

> The good times when our fathers rode
> In safety by the stage,
> Have passed before the onward march
> Of this progressive age;
> And now no goodly coach-and-four
> Draws up beside the stage-house door.
>
> How rang the laugh, the jest, the joke,
> As altogether rode,
> Coached up in friendly jollity
> Like boys of one abode;
> The weary miles seemed shorter then,
> As thus we rode o'er hill and glen.
>
> Full half the pleasure by the way
> Was appetite and fare—
> *This* gathered from mine host's full board,
> *That* from the mountain air.
> O! then we went life's flowery way.
> They ended with our staging days.
>
> O, that was music! when at morn,
> As, winding around by yon old hill,
> The driver blew his sounding horn,
> And echo answered from the hill.
> No echoing horn and prancing team
> Is heard amid this age of steam.
>
> But drawn beneath some sheltering shed
> The old stage-coach neglected stands;
> Its curtains flapping in the wind—
> The ghost of ruin's waving hands;
> While on the wheels the gathering rust
> Proclaims the mortal "dust to dust."
>
> While in the fields their scattered bones,
> Or on the common turned to die:

Their trips all o'er—their routes all run—
The wheelers and the leaders lie;
The driver's pride and labor gone,
And he like one who stands alone.

One can believe that Charlie Frisbie never mourned the old stagecoach. When he was but fifteen years old, in 1837, he went to work as an "engineer" in a construction crew laying track for the Syracuse & Utica Rail Road Company. In other words, he drove a pair of mules that hauled cars on the rails, which were built of wood. At that period many of the railroads being built planned to use mule or horse power, and many of them did, for a time. Frisbie describes the track laid for the Syracuse & Utica as having a base of eight-inch beams, which came direct from the sawmill. These were sunk into the ground—mudsills, he calls them—in parallel tiers, even with the surface. Then came the crossties, split out of white oak with cavities to fit an eight-inch wooden rail. On top of the rail was fastened a strap of bar iron, one inch thick by two and one-half inches wide. Over these rolled the first mule-drawn construction trains. There wasn't a steam locomotive in the region.

But a year or so later young Frisbie was fireman on a brand new locomotive, the *Wyoming*, which had been built in the state prison at Auburn. The Syracuse & Utica acquired also two other engines, the *Phoenix* and the *Varrum*. This road, one of the several components of what was to be the New York Central, also had a kind of genius in Milt Alcott, who worked in the roundhouse and who, says Frisbie, built the first efficient locomotive headlight in the United States. To make a good reflector, Alcott melted down sixteen silver dollars and added the metal to some regular babbitt. It worked fine, much better than the older models which were made of wood and shaped like a sun bonnet, with a mere piece of tin for reflector.

Just how long Frisbie worked for the Syracuse & Utica isn't clear from his narrative.* It was probably about two years, for early in the 1840's he was firing the locomotive *Jersey City* on the New Jersey Central, happy as a lark, says he, with his job and his $20 a month. He had got the job on asking for it, "three minutes after" he had arrived, a strange country youth, in Jersey City. In that day, the road operated both Baldwin and Rogers locomotives between Jersey City and New Brunswick, and English makes between New Brunswick and Trenton.

Now we get as realistic a picture of engine-driving of the period as could be found. None of the locomotives had whistles. In order to signal to apply brakes, says Frisbie, the engineer raised the safety valve which made a

---

* "Sketch of the Life and Experience of Charles H. Frisbie, For Forty-Seven Years a Locomotive Engineer," included as an appendix in *The Burlington Strike*, by C. H. Salmons, Aurora, Ill., 1889.

noise "similar to the one you make when you drive a snooping cat out of mischief, and not much louder." Each night, when they had put the train away, the engine crew drove to a sidetrack to take water, which had to be pumped from a deep well. The locomotive was run directly over the well, the drivers propped up off the rails, then connected with the pump. The locomotive gear was put in motion, slowly, which operated the pump, and the tank filled.

The tanks of the time were very small, and Frisbie remarks they would serve to run a three-car train about ten miles before refilling was necessary. When the tank was filled, the engine crew still had some work to do and you must follow closely to comprehend the business: They backed the locomotive to the engine house, ran it onto the turntable, disconnected the tender, ran the engine off the table, pushed the tender to a short sidetrack, ran the engine back over the table, pushed the tender onto the table, turned it the rest of the way around and backed it into the house, then turned the engine and backed it up to the tender, and at last filled the tender with wood, which was of the best Norway pine and, says Frisbie, the finest wood he ever saw for generating steam. There was plenty of it, ready to toss into the fire-box, to be had at one dollar and fifty cents a cord.* The crew could then go home.

In those times three men rode the engine, the engineer, first fireman, and second fireman or wood passer, who had to stand between the engine and tender. One brakeman always stood on the platform of the first car, ready to give the signal for brakes. The coaches were all four-wheeled, hung on thorough braces, and twelve passengers was a carful. Before Bergen Hill, west of Jersey City, was tunneled, the little trains often had to have the help of horses to get over the grade; but when the tunneling was done, says Frisbie, the Jersey Central cars were made larger. Every car was lettered, every seat had a number, and your ticket carried both car and seat number. For some reason he does not make clear, the end doors of the passenger cars were kept locked and travelers boarded them through the side door.

Frisbie rather liked Jersey. He said the principal production of the state was Jersey lightning, or cider brandy, and buckwheat cakes, both of which were excellent. But Jersey schools were not so good. Most of the Jersey Central employees simply made their marks, when they signed for their pay. Frisbie served three years as second or first fireman, then got to running extra as engineer. By this time the locomotives were improving and growing larger. He drove a Rogers machine that was considered a monster. It had six-foot double drivers, a cylinder with a 13-inch bore, a 22-inch stroke. Driving was dangerous in the many Jersey fogs, for there

---

* Good board in Jersey City then was $1.50 a week; cigars, the kind Frisbie smoked, two for one cent.

were three draw bridges on the route, one each over the Raritan, the Passaic and the Hackensack, and the draws were often open. Frisbie managed to miss an open draw, but one of his colleagues didn't. Although this engineer was alert and sighted the open draw a full quarter of a mile away, the braking system of the time was so poor that try as he and the brakemen did, the locomotive and baggage car went into the river. Indeed, at that time, and for many years to come, a locomotive engineeer had to operate in the knowledge that he might well encounter an open and unguarded drawbridge either by day or by night. He might also expect to find another train out of its scheduled running order at any old place along the line.

In the matter of braking trains, the brakemen were supposed to be on the alert at all times. As late as 1858 one important paragraph in the "Rules and Regulations for Operating the Pittsburgh, Ft. Wayne & Chicago Rail Road" stated: "Passenger train brakemen will generally ride upon the platforms of the cars while the train is in motion; but during inclement weather they may stand at the door inside of the cars, ready to apply the brakes in case of alarm, and to stop the train at the stations; they will supply the cars with *fuel* for the *stoves* in *winter*, from the wood boxes on the line . . ."

It seems surprising today that so many railroad men and passengers survived the early days of the steamcars. A difference of at least five minutes appears to have been expected in the watches of the engineer and conductor. Head-on and rear-end collisions grew steadily in number and fatality through the late forties and all through the fifties. Open switches were extremely common. Rolling stock was at best brittle and highly inflammable. Rails cracked and broke in great number. Worst of all, perhaps, was the poor construction of trestles and bridges, scores of which buckled and went down without warning and to the death or injury of almost everybody aboard, with the engine crew almost certain to get theirs for keeps.

Frisbie, now an engineer of a few months' experience, had survived the perils of the Jersey Central without a scratch. Hearing that a new outfit from Boston was building the Michigan Central, he quit his job, packed his valise and headed for Detroit. He got a job at once, being given the locomotive *Mayflower*, a name Frisbie was not particularly happy about. A Lake Erie steamer of that name had recently sunk for the third time, and this time stayed down.

Although he remarks that *perhaps* there is nothing in a name, still, Frisbie felt it was needlessly defying Fate to name a locomotive *Mayflower*, and sure enough the *Mayflower* was a bad rig. While he was driving her across a switch at Dexter, Michigan, one of the cross bars that held the rails in place broke. The Mayflower went down onto the frozen ground and ice, and started up the village street. After making some fifty feet on the ice, she turned upside down, pinning Frisbie by the left leg. Steam started blowing on his leg. It also quickly thawed the ice underneath, releasing the engineer's leg. He got out of it with a badly scalded foot but no broken bones.

He still didn't like the *Mayflower*. Every railroad, says he, has at least one engine on which bad luck rides oftener than on any other. On the Michigan Central it was the *Mayflower*. Frisbie took her out again, and this time, three miles out of Marshall, he ran plumb into a big steer on the track. The locomotive and every car of the train were derailed. The *Mayflower* rolled over twice, then lay on her back, fifty feet from the rails, headed in the opposite direction. The fireman was so badly injured he presently died. Frisbie himself was seriously hurt, his face and hands scalded, collar bone and right arm broken. He was laid up a year, and although he returned to work for the Michigan Central, he never drove the *Mayflower* again.

The Michigan Central treated Frisbie pretty fine. Paid his doctor's bill, he says, and full wages for the twelve months he was off. And now he was ready to stick by the company through a period of much violence and of great danger to the Central's operating crews. This was the war, reported elsewhere in this book, that the farmers of Michigan waged against the Michigan Central because that road would not pay the same ridiculous sums for farm stock killed on the rails that they had become accustomed to by the previous management, the State of Michigan.

For most of 1850, and much of the following year, Frisbie ran his locomotive through what must have been hell enough. The enraged farmers loosened rails, opened switches, set fires, rolled boulders onto the tracks, and at last took to throwing stones and shooting guns at train crews. Many an engineer and fireman quit the Central, but not Frisbie. He took out a train any time they asked him to, and he ran the gauntlet of the stones and bullets, ducking down, says he, "behind the driving wheel guards to be kept from being shot." Again, at night, a crew of the farmer-thugs would run a handcar just ahead of a train, to delay it. And in Detroit, firebugs burned the Central's freight house. The gang was finally broken up by home-grown detectives.

Frisbie remarks of the Central officials and boss men that they were all able and decent, except for an unnamed master mechanic who took the place of the beloved S. T. Newhall, who had died. To resist this man, who was the worst sort of tyrant, says Frisbie, the Michigan Central's engineers organized the Brotherhood of the Foot Board which, as related elsewhere, became the Brotherhood of Locomotive Engineers.

Engineer Frisbie was no boomer, but he had one more move to make. Soon after the Michigan Central trouble had been settled, he went to the Burlington road, and there he remained, so far as I have been able to learn, to the end of his active days, making his home in Aurora and raising one son who became a locomotive engineer on the Santa Fe. Charles Frisbie, obscure in his day, and obscure still, was one of the many Americans, as necessarily courageous as any professional soldier, who saw railroads through their days of great hazard, days when neither life nor accident insurance companies were anxious for the trade of train crews. Perhaps these men were just as much heroes as have been our soldiers.

By the time Charles Frisbie was a bearded hogger on the main line of the Burlington, another man who was to spend his life railroading was getting his first job, that of a call boy on the Hannibal & St. Joseph. He was Henry Clay French, almost fourteen, and he doubtless earned the $15 a month the railroad paid him. What he most wanted to be was a brakeman, for he had been captivated by watching the catfooted men who ran along the tops of swaying freight cars and twisted the brake wheels. But you had to come a long way out of the depths before they'd let you brake a train, and the depths of railroading were the call-boy jobs, who, call book in hand, chased around the town to find and notify this or that employee that he was wanted for a run.

In those days, railroaders when off duty and in spite of what became known as Rule G were as likely to be found in a saloon as anywhere else, and call boys came to know all the bars and dives and also which were the preferred drinking places of the men they sought. When he found his man, it was the duty of the call boy to have him read the order in the book, then to sign his name. In that day before telephones, call boys who were also good detectives were important persons to any railroad; they had to know the habits, the places and the hours when a man was more likely to be discussing politics in the Western Cafe than in the Prairie Belle.

Young French didn't remain a call boy long. Fascinated by the erratic and continuous clicking of the telegraph instruments, he learned the Morse alphabet, then spent his spare time translating the clicks into words and sentences. Less than a year after he had started work, he was serving as a relief telegraph operator at O'Fallon, on the North Missouri Railroad, then at St. Charles. He had begun to think seriously of following telegraphy instead of railroading, when one day he had a chance to serve as relief baggageman on the St. Charles accommodation train. Those few days riding the baggage car, he said in his old age, spoiled a good telegraph operator. Henceforth, although he often took over a key, he had little liking for any work not connected with the operation of trains. As soon as he could ditch his job at St. Charles, he went to work as a switchman for the Hannibal & St. Joe in the Kansas City yards.

Although this was 1875, a period when aging Charles Frisbie considered railroads to be reaching their apex of perfection, it was in reality a time when the roads had hardly begun to adopt the many improvements that were being urged upon them, more or less vainly, by all sorts of inventors, some of them good inventors. It was also an era of great danger for railroad men, one which in retrospect seems unnecessarily ruthless and callous. It was something more than imagination that caused young French's sister, when he told her he was now a switchman, to lay aside a nice clean sheet.

Yard switchmen had to couple and uncouple many cars every day. The link and pin coupling was still in use. To use it, the link was first fastened with a pin to one car, then another pin was cocked at a slight angle on the other car. As the two cars came together, the switchman guided the link into its slot, and the impact usually shook down the cocked pin, thus completing the operation. If the pin did not shake down, the operator stepped between the cars and pounded it down with a spare pin. In his age, French looked back on these days with a full realization of their danger. Wary feet, he said, an alert mind, and chilled nerve were needed every instant.*

Uncoupling was even worse, for this was often done while the cars were in motion, and the switchman had his choice of running along between the cars and pulling out the pin, or of lying on the beam that held the coupling slot. In his first season at switching in the Hannibal & St. Joe yards, an average of four men were either killed or maimed each week. Hardly a thing was thought of it—except perhaps by the insurance companies and a few fanatics such as Lorenzo Coffin.

None of the switch frogs were blocked as they are today. A foot that strayed into a frog might be cut off by a wheel before it could be jerked out. Rail ends of all switches were open, making the same sort of trap as the frogs. Freight cars were anything but safe. Handholds—those brackets which are used for getting on and off and climbing over cars—were not dependable, and inspection had not even been thought of. Some of the handholds were wired, some patched with nails. All brakes were, of course, set by hand, and when a brake-chain snapped, a man had about an even chance of being thrown under the wheels. Young Harry French survived the Hannibal & St. Joe yards, but not his good friend Jack Foster. One night when Foster was making a coupling, his body was caught between two boxcars, and French's dim lantern was bright enough to show a rib protruding through Foster's skin while blood gushed out, black blood. Foster died right there on the cinders.

Foster's death didn't quite cure French of being a switchman for good, but it did make him quit the yards at Kansas City. He drew his time and headed for Topeka, where he got a job braking on the Santa Fe between Topeka and Newton. This was in 1876. The rush to find the gold in the Black Hills of the Dakotas was on, and the Santa Fe was swamped

---

* In his memoirs, a forthright job, as told to his son Chauncey Del French, in *Railroad Man,* published in 1938.

with passenger business. Many railroad employees quit and joined the stampede, but French wasn't tempted. He now was a brakeman, one of those catfooted men who ran over the cars and lived dangerously and gloriously. Times were stirring. When the gold seekers were leaving the region, immigrants from Europe were coming in to take homesteads, and capacity stock trains rolled up out of the Southwest, filled with cattle for Kansas City and Chicago.

Another thing besides haywire equipment that made railroading dangerous at the time were the herds of longhorns and buffalo, which often started to "drift" in the face of a blizzard, and when they drifted nothing could stop them. Running into the teeth of a storm, when no view of the track was possible, many an engineer on the Santa Fe plowed into a herd before he saw the animals. By then the entire train might be surrounded by thousands of either longhorns or buffalo, and there the train stayed until the animals moved on.

French was supposed to be drawing $40 a month, but it wasn't long before he found the Santa Fe was three months in arrears with the company payroll. Employees could get meal tickets at eating houses, but rent and grocery bills had to be put off for weeks and occasionally for months. French thinks this manner of doing business was quite common with Western railroads of the day, and in any case there seemed to be nothing to be done about it.

On an extra run to Dodge City, the first time he had seen that fabulous town, French discovered it to live up to its reputation. After a rather wild supper in a joint where he was one of the few men not carrying a gun, French went out to look over the false-front village. Attracted by the noise of a dance hall, he was standing around outside, in the street, when two horsemen rode up. Out of the shadows of the dance hall just then stepped a man, a gun in each hand. He killed both horsemen as they sat in their saddles, one shot each. The killer was Bat Masterson. French never forgot it, for Masterson, already quite a figure, went on to become a great legend in all of the West.*

Although neither the Santa Fe nor most other roads were in a hurry to adopt new inventions, the Santa Fe held in high esteem a gadget known as a Dutch clock. This device, perhaps the most unpopular one with railroad men of the day, was set up in the caboose and it noted and recorded on a tape the speed at which the train traveled. The rule was that freights should maintain a speed of eighteen miles an hour, no more, no less. The Dutch clock soon brought reprimands to all freight conductors who tried to make up time for the breakdowns of equipment that were forever happening.

---

* In my time I've met only too many men who "knew Bat Masterson," and have reason to believe 95 per cent of them liars. But in this category I do not place Henry Clay French. French was patently an honest raconteur, not given to romancing.

After considerable discussion of the Dutch clock, the boys figured out a method of handling the menace. On the first sidetrack out of the terminal, the crew would uncouple the caboose, then uncouple the engine, bring it back to the rear on the main line, set it in behind the caboose, then use it to slam the caboose into the standing train at a speed of exactly 18 miles an hour. This, it has been discovered, so affected the Dutch clock's insides that thereafter it continued to clock 18 miles an hour regardless of the speed developed. This fixing the Dutch clock was considered fine sport, and always left the train crew with a sense of immoderate satisfaction.

Another menace was the rule that trainmen were held responsible for flat wheels on cars in their charge. Although the rule was never enforced to the limit, it was enforced sufficiently to create much resentment when the company deducted small amounts from the pay envelopes to pay for damage caused by brakes being set too tight, thus skidding the wheels and flattening them in spots. French says that this flat-wheel rule, common to nearly all of the roads, was finally broken by the Brotherhoods, who supported a lawsuit staged by a trainman who had been fined. The suit proved to the satisfaction of a court that the trainman had paid for a set of damaged wheels, and that the railroad had then retreaded and used them. The court, French relates with joy, ordered the railroad company to pay the trainmen for "rent" of the wheels. Whether this actually happened, or is merely a fine piece of folklore, doesn't matter; the flatwheel rule was discarded.

After a couple of years on the Santa Fe, French became restless. He says that he quit because of a row with one of his superiors, but he probably quit because he was setting out, all unknown to him, to be something of a boomer, a traveling railroad man. From the Santa Fe he moved to the Lawrence, Leavenworth & Galveston, known popularly as the Lazy, Lousy & Greasy, where he was to remain, surprisingly enough, for seven years, working as brakeman on both freights and passenger trains, and as baggageman. The latter job turned out to be wonderful. It seemed that almost everybody who rode a passenger train in Kansas took along quite a bit of baggage—and rifles, dogs, saddles, bed rolls, and trunks were not allowed in the coaches. Extra fees were charged for this baggage, and all of the money went to the baggageman. The inanimate objects were fine, but the dogs created a number of problems and it was here, remarks French, that he gained a life-long aversion to man's best friend except his mother.

On the strength of his monstrous income of wages plus fees, French married and built a house. In 1881 when he was twenty-one, the LL&G made him a freight conductor, and he had his name and office inscribed in beautiful Gothic letters on a shaving mug in the barber shop at Ottawa. This was pretty big-time stuff, he felt, and he also liked bossing the stock trains. On one of these he rode into his first head-on collision. It happened between Lenexa and Rosedale, Kansas, when the stock train was running under orders to make all speed possible, Dutch clock or no Dutch clock. The opposing train was a regular run of the Missouri, Fort Scott & Gulf which on French's orders showed as "canceled." The two trains came together in a blinding snowstorm and with terrific force.

By the time French got to his feet, the train was afire, and a car of oil on the other train immediately blew up. Many of the stock cars were ditched, and out of them tore and tumbled hundreds of bewildered longhorns, mad with fright, bellowing, threshing, plunging. The cowboys came out of the caboose and went to work with dispatch and what French considered great courage. They went into the burning cars and when they found a trapped animal, they shot him dead, then went on to kill others or to free them from the flames. The oil car continued to burn, sending fire high into the immense snowstorm that seemed otherwise to shut in the wreck from all else. The noise of burning and dying cattle was dreadful. So was the stench.

The poor animals who were freed stood around, mooing and pawing, being held in check by the cowboys who kept them herded in pretty fair shape until dawn, when they quieted with daylight and an end of the storm. Several of the train crew members were injured, but none seriously. There was, of course, an investigation as to the cause of the collision. French's orders cleared him and his crew. He does not say who was to blame.

Hunnewell was the toughest town along the line, and it was here that railroadmen learned to keep their lighted lanterns out of sight of villagers and visiting cowboys. These apes liked to come out of the saloons that faced the tracks and shoot out the headlight, the caboose tail lights, and any lanterns they happened to see in the hands of brakemen or conductors. When they were to remain overnight in this lovely town, French's engine crew always put away the locomotive in total darkness, rather than risk a volley.

It was in Hunnewell that a gigantic stranger climbed atop the caboose just as French's freight was pulling out. French was in the cupola when he sighted the man, a huge and surly-looking fellow. When French attempted to collect a fare—passengers were officially permitted to travel on freights in those days—the man drew a gun and remarked that *that* was his fare. Meanwhile, the rear brakeman had seen the man. He came up from behind and swung a mighty blow with a short brake club. The big fellow went down without a grunt, and they bound him hand and foot. Arrived at Wellington, they turned the groggy gunman over to the sheriff and learned that he was a man wanted by authorities to the extent of a $2,000 reward. The club-wielding brakie got the money, and immediately, much to French's disgust, quit railroading for farming on a homestead near Burden, Kansas.

Photo by Illinois Central

Even in modern times, clearing away snowdrifts is a battle, whether the job is done by hand as on the Illinois Central near Remson, Iowa, in February, 1936, or with a rotary plow as on the Milwaukee Road near Hyak, Wash., ten years later.

Photo by The Seattle Times

(Top): Clerks sorting letters in the original Fast Mail. (From The American Railway, 1889).

(Bottom): Picking up the mail at high speed. The Empire State Express snapped by William Hallenbeck of Hudson, N. Y., for Railroad Magazine.

When the law didn't move fast enough in Kansas of the eighties, the lay public was likely to do something about it. Once at Winfield, near an overhead bridge, French's engineer whistled for a stop, and stopped. Hanging down from the bridge, in the glare of the headlight, was a rope, a man at its end. French called the coroner, who remarked that the dead man had been very careless about where he got his riding horses. "I've been expecting this for quite a spell," the coroner said mildly as he cut down the stiff and stowed it away in his buggy.

Now came one of those periods that come, it is said, to every railroader, and perhaps to every man no matter his occupation. French ran into a series of wrecks, one piled almost atop the other. He had five wrecks in five weeks, drawing demerits, being fired, then hired again. It looked like a jinx. The way to cure a jinx is to make a change. French applied for a job as fireman and got it.

Firing a locomotive in the early eighties carried an element of no little personal danger. This was in part due to one of the fireman's duties, that of oiling the valves while running. When the hogger gave the order, the fireman took his tallow pot, opened his window that led out to the running board and climbed out there. Then, clinging to the handrail that ran along the boiler, he crept down to the steam chest, the locomotive meanwhile bounding along, the air flow sliding past like a hurricane. When the engineer figured the fireman was set and ready, he shut off the throttle for an instant and during that instant the fireman poured oil into the vent in the steam chest. It was from this operation that the fireman got the name that still clings to him—tallow pot.

The locomotives of the period left a great deal to be desired in safety. Side rods, French remarks, had a bad habit of coming loose and wiping the side of the engine. Nor were boilers very good, and they were seldom inspected. Yet French found the work invigorating, even exciting. He held the job until restlessness again came upon him, and, in 1883, he quit to join what appears to have been a sizable trek of railroad men to Oregon. In that new country a heap of railroad construction was under way. Raised as he was on romantic stories about the building of the Union and the Central Pacific railroads, French thought he'd prefer a job following the end of steel to one of operating trains.

After some switching and braking work for the Oregon Railroad & Navigation Company, French got the job he wanted—conductor of a gravel train with the construction crew on the Astoria & Coast Railroad. The laborers were Chinese, hundreds of them, and French soon discovered that the old hard-boiled system of labor relations used on the first transcontinental was still in force. The boss of the Chinese crews was Dick Harding, a veteran of the Central Pacific. Harding was a disciplinarian who did not look for trouble but appears to have been quite capable of meeting it if it came. Trouble was brewing, too, brewing out of dissatisfaction that Chinese rations had been delayed and the Chinese were forced to eat American food, a dreadful insult both to Chinese palates and esthetics.

So, one day the mutiny broke suddenly. One minute, French remembered, the Chinese were peacefully loading gravel cars, and the next, they ganged up as if by command and went for Dick Harding, swinging shovels, waving long knives. Harding backed up to the nearest flatcar, selected a pick, tapped the end of it on a tie to remove the iron part of the tool, then whaled into the China boys with astonishing energy and fury. The circle around him quickly widened, and Harding followed up, beating the men over their heads, their rears, anywhere he could hit them. Bones snapped, blood flowed, and the mutiny was broken. Harding threw away his pick handle and detailed men to tote the wounded back to camp for first-aid attention.

Chinese were in the tradition of railroad building in the West. So were Indians. But French found that the day when grading and track crews went armed had passed. Still, there was some excitement after he left the Astoria & Coast and went to work with a similar crew on the Oregon Railroad & Navigation road in the Inland Empire of Washington. The construction camp was at Prosser Falls, a town of ten houses and one store, right on the edge of an Indian reservation. Near Prosser Falls was a ranch owned by one Kenny. Kenny said he had been promised that a town was to be platted on his place by the railroad, and a station erected. When this proved to be inaccurate and when, further and worse, Kenny learned that the railroad town at this spot was to be called Prosser, and not Kennyville, his choler rose.

Now Kenny was no man to be run down by a village named Prosser. He engaged six Indians, all known among their people as extremely bad Indians, to take up station on his ranch and there engage in target practice across the right-of-way. Bullets zipped not too high over the heads of the steel gang, and the crew quit. The target practice continued sporadically for ten days or so. Then, C. S. Prowell, construction boss, invited Kenny and his gang into a saloon for a conference. Much free liquor flowed, and the conference ran on and on. When it was done, and Kenny and his brigade staggered out, the rails were already laid across his land.

The construction work now continued without more interference. When the rails had reached Yakima, a federal commission arrived to inspect the work done, and French drew assignment as conductor on the special train. He found the Pullman car to be pretty well taken up by a long bar, and just before the train was to pull out, Conductor French got some special running orders from the trainmaster. "Tell your engineer to take it easy for the first two hours," he said. "Kill all the time you can until we hit the new track. We want the liquor to get going in good shape before we reach it."

French told the hogger, and they started out. Running slowly and stopping every little while, the train made its way, while genial bartenders worked promptly on all requests, which were many, for railroad inspection commissions were made up in large part of men with notable thirsts. The jaunt was wholly successful. "By the time we reached the new line," remarks French, "most of the government inspectors didn't know whether they were on a train or a boat. And," he adds, "the line was accepted as perfect."

Harry French was still booming, still restless, looking for the railroad that ran through green fields where the clover was tall and sweet, the road all men look for and none find. He worked for the OR&N as fireman, as engineer, conductor, telegrapher. These were still the days when a man could change jobs as well as companies. He even did a stretch on the Oregon Pacific, that dream of a strange man, T. Egenden Hogg, who planned a road to reach from Yaquina Bay on the Oregon coast to the Island of Manhattan, New York. It was one of the last of the fantastic enterprises with which the West had been filled for forty years.

To hold the franchise he had obtained, Hogg moved equipment up into the high reaches of the Cascade range where he vowed his road should cross through what he said was Hogg Pass. Up into these timbered heights, on pack horses, Hogg moved ties and steel and food and a handcar; and finally a boxcar in sections, also on horseback. The crew laid a few lengths of rail in the otherwise wholly primeval forest—rails that started nowhere, went nowhere—and thereafter once a year, for several years, the boxcar was moved over the track by mulepower.

Hogg's railroad never crossed the mountains, and today a highway crosses the Hogg grade, a monument to those who were perhaps the only men to build a brief stretch of isolated railroad high in a mountain pass. French didn't work in the Pass, but on the more level stretches of the road between Corvallis and the ocean. He said that Rule G, the famous railroad regulation regarding intoxicating liquor, had never even been heard of on Hogg's Oregon Pacific. Everyone employed, he says, even the officials, drank steadily and copiously. So thirsty were these men that at the western terminus of the line a character named "One-Legged" Jack Slavens anchored a monstrous barge in Yaquina Bay and there sold rum twenty-four hours a day, seven days a week, and was never lonesome.

Paydays on the Oregon Pacific were quite irregular, and one day Conductor French suddenly became tired of the whole thing. With his own train on the sidetrack in Albany, Oregon, he walked away and left it there, steam up and everything, and without telling anyone or trying to get his back pay, he jumped a Southern Pacific train into Portland, and so on to a new job with the Oregon Railroad & Navigation Company, which presently became a part of the Union Pacific.

Yes, sir, a man could still move around a bit, and for the next twenty-two years Harry French moved around. It was 1887 when he walked off his Oregon Pacific train at Albany. In the same year he worked as telegrapher for the Oregon Railroad & Navigation road and for the Northern Pacific, and closed the year as a brakeman-conductor for the former line. In 1894 he jumped back to the Santa Fe and went to switching, but quickly changed to the Kansas City Belt Line where he remained for almost three years. He left the Midwest in 1897 to return to the Pacific Northwest, where he served both as brakeman and conductor on the Northern Pacific. In 1904 he took a turn as conductor on the Seattle-Tacoma Interurban, an electric line. During the first part of 1905 he worked switching for the Oregon Railroad & Navigation, and the latter part as conductor on the Tacoma & Eastern, later a part of the Milwaukee Road. Here he remained for almost three years, when he went to work as conductor on a logging railroad, that of the St. Paul & Tacoma Lumber Company of Tacoma, Wash. He quickly left that one, and before the year was out had a new and worse job with the Eastern Railway & Lumber Company of Centralia, Washington, a haywire road. It was in 1909 that French at last found the perfect, or almost the perfect railroad. This turned out to be the Union Pacific, and here in the UP's Seattle yards, he worked as switchman and finally as yardmaster, for twenty-one years, being retired for age in 1930.

There were no tallow pots when Harry French quit railroading. The old man never ceased to marvel at the swift and steady progress railroading had made in his time. He loved to watch the huge UP locomotives and to compare them with the pots he had fired back in Kansas in the 1870's. He noted with keen interest every step the road made to increase safety for its employees and its passengers. He was critical, too, and though he mellowed, and though he came to think the Union Pacific represented the best in railroading, he did not lose his perspective. The UP *could* do wrong, and occasionally did. On one point, however, French never faltered: The life of a railroad man is the finest life there is.

The working years of the two men whose stories make up this chapter covered the whole of American railroading from the days of wooden rails to the days of the streamliners, or almost one hundred years. Their lives, even their working days, overlapped in the eighties. Charlie Frisbie began railroading before locomotives had cabs. When Harry French quit railroading, Diesel engines were beginning to replace steam, and many were prophesying the passing of railroads altogether.

CHAPTER XXIII

Moments of Disaster

A mighty crash of timber,
The sound of hissing steam,
The groans and cries of anguish,
A woman's stifled scream.
The dead and dying mingled
With broken beams and bars,
An awful human carnage—
A dreadful wreck of cars.
—The Chatsworth Wreck, 1887.

THE drama that is virtually inherent in the operation of trains on steel rails has for its climactic third acts the horrifying scenes of disasters, chiefly those of collisions and derailments. No tragedies of American life have so fastened themselves on our imagination. Not even the swift and almost certain death that accompanies the Icarian accidents of the air lines—the great bird plummeting to the earth, or crashing headlong into a mountain, and followed by explosive flames—has caught the imagination sufficiently to dim the vision of two locomotives arriving at full tilt at the same spot at the same moment; nor to dim the picture of the spread rail or the decayed bridge waiting for the Fast Mail.

One hundred years ago most of the pictures showing railroads in action were fulsomely optimistic. They depicted brave little engines puffing along through ideal scenery, hauling cars filled with happy travelers all in holiday mood, while from the countryside cows and horses observed them in the moods given to cows and horses, the former chewing her cud, the latter snorting and showing off. But all of this idealizing of the railroad soon passed. Beginning in the late 1840's and continuing almost to the end of the century, the most popular illustrations in any magazine were the often ghastly, and always dramatic, accidents to trains of steamcars.

Disasters on the rails grew into a national scandal in the fifties. They showed a little though not much decline during the Civil War, when in any case they were thrown into deep shadow by the other and greater tragedy that was vast and continuous. With railroad expansion in the seventies, accidents increased in proportion and possibly in deadly effects.

275

Throughout the eighties, when the roads began cautiously to adopt the air brake, the rate of accidents dropped, though far too many persons were killed or injured to produce any great faith in traveling safety. When at last in the nineties the railroads were forced by federal law into adoption of the air brake, real progress in rail safety began.

Almost every region of the East and South has its self-styled "America's worst railroad disaster," but only Nashville, Tennessee, has a right to such claim. There, on July 9, 1918, when two trains came together, 99 persons were killed, 171 injured. It was and remains America's greatest railroad wreck from the viewpoint of casualties, according to Freeman H. Hubbard, unquestionably an authority on the subject, who states that the Nashville disaster was caused by a lack of proper running orders.

What effect, if any, the Nashville accident had on the operation of American railroads is not to be known. It no doubt had a most chastening effect on the Nashville, Chattanooga & St. Louis Railway, which was responsible. Probably most bad wrecks have had an influence on officials of the lines on which they occurred, and on other lines as well. One accident that had more than local or momentary influence occurred in 1853 at Norwalk, Connecticut, when an engineer failed to note a low-ball signal set against him at an open drawbridge. Forty were killed and 80 injured, and suits for damages all but wrecked the New York & New Haven. The telling effect of the Norwalk horror, however, was that it jolted Connecticut into creating a state railroad commission armed with all powers for regulation.

Another disaster that resulted in immediate efforts to improve safety on the rails was the tragedy at Angola, New York, on December 19, 1867. Angola was a mere station of the Lake Shore & Michigan Southern, now a part of the New York Central, 22 miles west of Buffalo, where Big Sisters Creek was spanned by a truss bridge 40 feet above the water and 100 feet long. The eastern bank of the creek was flat and low, the western bank a high and sheer bluff, making the railroad approach from west to east a sharp down grade.

The *New York Express*, due in Buffalo at 1:30 P.M., with Charles Carscadin, who had the reputation of being a careful man, at the throttle, was running two hours late passing Angola, not an express stop, and the *Express* went by at fair speed. Just beyond the little depot the rear coach of the six-car train loosened an axle as it crossed a frog in a switch, throwing the wheels an inch or more out of their proper position. The coach began to jolt, alarming the passengers so that many of them moved into the car just ahead.

Up in the cab Carscadin did not at once discover anything was wrong. The crippled car dragged along until it reached the bridge over the creek. By that time it had worked itself off the rails, also pulling off the coach ahead of it, and both bounded along the wooden flooring of the ancient bridge. By now and with pretty good reason the passengers were terrified. Just then came a fearful crash, and the rear car broke loose and went plunging off the bridge to fall into the frozen creek below, north of the tracks. The next car bumped on a bit farther or until it was almost at the other end of the bridge, then its coupling snapped and it too went over the edge, falling south of the tracks.

Not until the rest of the train had gone some distance did the engineer know that trouble was in the rear. He backed up to the span, and train crew and passengers looked down to the creek on a dreadful scene, a mass of debris, already beginning to smoke and flame, in which some fifty persons moved and screamed or lay still. The two pot-bellied stoves, red hot when the crash came, set about their work of cremating the wreck and its victims. The dry splintered wood of the coaches made excellent fuel, and before the lucky ones on the bridge could get pails and break the creek ice for water, the flames were roaring high. Indeed, before the bucket brigade could get into action, what had been the rear car of the train, together with most of its occupants, had been consumed in fire. The other car started to burn, too, but the bucket men extinguished the fire before it had reached the injured.

Forty-nine died in a few minutes in the holocaust beneath the bridge. Forty more were injured. Nor had they died or been injured wholly in vain.

The accident happened on Thursday. The official investigation did not begin until Monday. In the meantime, according to a part of the testimony, the management of the Lake Shore & Michigan Southern had not been inactive. John S. Taggart, telegraph operator at the Angola station, testified that when he heard the crash of the derailed cars, he hurried to the bridge, saw what had happened, then started back to the depot to wire for help.

"On my way back," he said, "I passed the frog where the rear car had been derailed. Mr. Barnes, the section boss, was there. I asked him if the frog was all right. He said it had been all right before the train went over it. He stood there gazing at the frog, and I noticed the wing rail was twisted, spikes being partly drawn out, and the rail turned over sidewise. One side of the rail was nicked as if something had cut into it. The space between the bottom of the rail was an inch or more. This was where the car had left the frog and struck the line of rail.

"At that time," continued Mr. Taggart, "nothing in the way of repairing the rail had been done, but later, after I had picked up a lot of cushions and other things that had fallen from the coaches and loaded them onto a wagon where there were some dead men, I heard Roadmaster Washburne say: *'Take out that rail and put in a new one.'* " The italics are mine, but I hope that Mr. Taggart emphasized the sentence that told of tampering with evidence.

Their was much other testimony, too, and it resulted in a moral if not an official agreement that the derailment had been caused by the use of an extremely dangerous makeshift known as "compromise cars." Compromise cars were occasioned by the fact that the gage of the New York Central was 4 feet 8½ inches; the gage of the Lake Shore was 4 feet 10 inches. To obviate a change in one or the other of the gages, the connecting and cooperating lines hit on the compromise cars, the wheels of which were wide enough to run on and cover completely the rails of the Central, but would not cover the Lake Shore rails by three-quarters of an inch. In other words, any lateral motion that threw the wheels three-quarters of an inch off center, while running on Lake Shore track, would be sufficient to derail a compromise car. The rear car of the derailed train was a compromise car. The rails were of the Lake Shore. The imperfect frog on the switch at Angola station showed how shoddy a thing was a compromise car. Presently they were relegated to the boneyard.

Another catastrophe of far-reaching results was that which happened on the Eastern Railroad of Massachusetts and was known as long as it remained in public consciousness as the Revere Disaster. It had its groundwork in the "conservatism" that amounted to pigheadedness in the pure and unsullied Yankee mind of Jeremiah Prescott, superintendent of the Eastern. Mr. Prescott was a man who patently wanted no truck with any of the so-called improvements, not even with the telegraph, which at the time Superintendent Prescott became notorious, had been in use by other railroads than his own for two decades, being first introduced into train operation, in fact, by another Yankee, Charles Minot, on the Erie. Perhaps it will give the unbelieving outlander a better comprehension of the mind of Superintendent Prescott to know that a few years previous to the Revere Disaster, his method of dispatching trains was such that on at least one occasion an Eastern freight train waited all night at Salem for an extra passenger train, which in turn spent the night at Ipswich, waiting for the freight.

Nor had Superintendent Prescott's ideas undergone any radical change by 1871. On Saturday, August 26th, that year, passenger traffic out of Boston was immense. The city sweltered in the dog days. People lay under the elms on the Common, sticky and motionless. In the dismal purlieus of the South End, kids turned on fire hydrants, while adults tried to find relief on fire escapes. No vagrant breeze found its way even through the handsome open windows on Beacon Hill. The Bostonians who could afford it were trying to get out of town to one of the brisk and salty places along the North Shore or in Maine.

The Eastern Railroad ran along the North Shore to Portland, Maine's major city; and due to the overbuilding and amalgamations of previous years, the Eastern now owned two almost parallel lines between Everett, a suburb of Boston, and Lynn, which was on the way to Portland. One of these short parallel lines was called the Saugus branch, the other was known as the main line and ran through Revere. The junction, or Y, as we have said, was at Everett.

On this particular sweltering Saturday, when so many Bostonians were trying to get away, the Eastern's staff in the terminal was hard pressed. They turned their energies to getting trains made up and started; and once off, it would seem, they lost all interest in what became of the trains. Between halfpast six and eight o'clock that evening, four trains were scheduled to leave, two to depart at 6:30 and seven and take the Saugus branch —a main-line local at seven, and the *Portland Express,* the swift "candy" train, by the main line at eight. In the obvious confusion prevailing under Superintendent Prescott at the terminal, all of the four trains were late in leaving, and the second Saugus branch train became sandwiched between the local and the *Portland Express.*

All four trains ran to Everett Junction over the same rails, and there the first and third were to take the branch, the second and fourth the main stem. It is important to know that a prime Eastern rule was that no northbound train might enter the Saugus branch at Everett Junction before any southbound train then due should have arrived and passed off the branch. It so happened, that evening, that a southbound Branch train out of Lynn was delayed an hour and a half by some mechanical trouble. So, when the first northbound out of Boston reached Everett, there it stopped and there it waited. So did the second train, and the third train, for although it seems incredible, there was no side track at Everett by which a train for the main line could pass a train waiting to get onto the Saugus branch.

The main factors of the tragedy had now been compounded, but the several hundred people in the stalled trains only knew that the Eastern was living up to its reputation of running its trains when and how it wished. In one of the coaches, and unworried by the shortcomings of railroads, sat the venerable Rev. Ezra Stiles Gannett, grandson of the late Ezra Stiles, president of Yale College, and in his own right one of the shining lights of New England Unitarianism. The Rev. Dr. Gannett, Harvard 1820, and now seventy years old, was on his way to Lynn where on the morrow he was to preach.

There they stood at Everett Junction, the three trains, one of them for an hour and forty minutes, another for an hour and ten minutes, the last for just under an hour—time enough and more for any and all of them to have run to Lynn. But rules were rules and there was to be no monkeying with such frivolous things as the magnetic telegraph. Charles Francis Adams, Massachusetts railroad commissioner, said it for all time. "A simple message," he commented later, "to the branch trains to meet and pass at any given point other than that in the schedule would have solved the difficulty; but no!—*there* were the rules, and all of the rolling stock of the road might gather at Everett in solemn procession, but, until the locomotive at Lynn could be repaired, the law of the Medes and the Persians was plain: and in this case it read that the telegraph was a new-fangled and unreliable auxiliary." *

At 8:10 the delayed train from Lynn arrived at Saugus, and after no little see-sawing the two Saugus branch trains were released and went on their way, with the main line local leaving between them. Back in the Boston terminal, at a little past eight, when the *Portland Express* was about to leave, Superintendent Prescott suddenly noticed that the train from Lynn had not arrived. Thus he knew very well there were three trains stalled at Everett. All the precaution he took was to say, orally, to the engineer of the departing *Portland Express* to "watch out" for trains ahead of him—just as though engineers were not in that very habit.

The engineer of the *Portland Express* pulled out of Boston with no knowledge that the main-line local had left Everett Junction only about five minutes ahead of the *Express*. Nor did the train crew of the local know that they had little more than left the Junction when the Portland train pounded over the frogs and so onto the main line. The night was particularly dark, and a light fog had drifted in from sea. At Revere the local stopped to let off passengers, and there it stood the few tragic minutes necessary to take up the slack between it and the oncoming *Express*.

The local's rear equipment exhibited two red-globed lanterns that had no reflectors, no lights to gleam far in the dark and mist of an August night along the shore. The *Portland Express* plowed into the local an instant after the engineer saw the two pitiful blobs of dim red almost under his nose.

Twenty-nine died that night. Fifty-seven were injured. This was bad enough, but the number of dead, which included the Reverend Mr. Gannett, somehow enraged New England as other and deadlier railroad accidents had not done. Perhaps it was because it happened so near Boston, and since the end of the Civil War, Boston's yeasty agitators of one kind and another had been attempting to find a Cause comparable to Abolition. Temperance had been tried. So had Rights for Women, and while both made fairly good causes, neither had just the right flavor of battle. The Revere Disaster did, and for the next several years the railroads of New England, and to a lesser extent those of the United States, were to hear and sometimes to feel the resonant echoes of the Revere Disaster.

Right after the accident many mass meetings were held, some in Boston, others in Lynn, Swampscott, Portsmouth, Portland, Worcester, and elsewhere. And a champion, full-blown and terrible in his wrath against the railroads, sprang up. He was Wendell Phillips, the former and fiery abolitionist and all-around reformer, perhaps the most fanatical man in all

---

* See his *Notes on Railroad Accidents,* New York, 1879.

New England and certainly one of the best orators of a day when oratory counted much.

First, at an "indignation" mass meeting in Swampscott, then at later meetings, Phillips, no man of moderation, said the Revere Disaster was "deliberate murder." He said a great deal more, too, and the more he talked the more vitriolic he became.

Commissioner of Railroads Adams did some investigating, and among other things asked Superintendent Prescott whether use of the telegraph might not have prevented the accident. No, Prescott replied calmly, he didn't think so. The telegraph might work under certain conditions, but speaking for himself, he preferred not to rely on such a thing for the operation of trains. One of the conductors involved in the wreck testified that he had more than once complained to Superintendent Prescott, and also to President Browne of the Eastern, that it was impossible to make a quick stop with hand brakes. They had always told him to "do the best you can." Meanwhile Westinghouse's brakes were being gradually adopted by other roads for passenger trains.

Although Adams was deep and thorough in his investigation of the Revere accident, and completely fearless in making his findings known, he did not think Wendell Phillips had contributed anything to the improvement of railroad safety. Adams remarked that to judge by the tenor of public comment, it might fairly be supposed that railroad officials were in the custom of plotting to bring about disasters, and to take a fiendish delight in them. On the contrary, he said, and next to the immediate sufferers in accidents and their families, it was the unfortunate railroad men concerned to whom wrecks were the greatest tragedy, for an employee who was implicated in a wreck lived thereafter under a stigma, no matter if he were in no way to blame for what happened.

Newspapers of New England quickly took up the cry sounded by Phillips. Pamphlets attacking the road and its management appeared. The affair at Revere forced the resignation of President Browne of the Eastern. Prescott, for reasons that are not now understandable, remained another year with the road, but he was put under the charge of a new general manager, Charles F. Hatch, brought from the Lake Shore & Michigan Southern, a man who had long been used to running trains by telegraph. With him, to the Eastern, Hatch brought an expert dispatcher. Henceforth, all Eastern trains moved on telegraphic orders, while all other New England roads that had not done so adopted the system.

The Revere accident cost the Eastern something like half a million dollars in damages, and for the next decade the road was under almost continual attack by pamphleteers and also on the verge of bankruptcy. The road fought back by hiring cynical and sardonic Benjamin F. Butler as its chief spokesman and counsel. Possibly it was an unwise move, for Butler's reputation was full of cracks, and journalists and pamphleteers found a

number of things to say about him. Charles W. Felt, a Granger in the unlikely Granger town of Salem, rode hard on old Butler, charging that
Butler had acted in deals to swindle the Eastern while he was on the Eastern payroll. For fourteen years after 1871, the Eastern never knew peace;
and in 1884 it lost its identity by lease to its up-and-coming rival, the
Boston & Maine. Probably a great deal of its troubles had stemmed from
the state of mind that made the Revere Disaster not only possible but
assured.

It was chance rather than an archaic method of operation that brought
New England its next bad railroad disaster, a wreck that sorely tried the
faith of many devout Yankee Christians. This was because the wreck
occurred to an excursion train that was returning to their homes in Connecticut towns more than a thousand earnest pilgrims who had been to
hear the great Dwight L. Moody and his songster, Ira D. Sankey, perform
at Hartford.

This Moody and Sankey revival, like many of the others staged by these
two talented men, was being held in an old skating rink in Connecticut's
capital city. The night of January 14, 1878, had seen a wonderful feast
of Gospel, when Moody, his great voice reaching to the farthest corners,
had electrified the audience with his message of God's fatherly love, rather
than of the hell fire to which the Yankees had been condemned since the
days of the Mathers. Speaking colloquially, using short, rugged words, he
addressed his hearers in man-to-man fashion, though not in the cheap style
used so effectively on lower-grade customers by other evangelists of the
time and since. And the clear-voiced Sankey, all 220 pounds of him, his
long side whiskers flying with every motion of his head, sat down to the
little reed organ, and gave forth in a sonorous baritone of no great range
but of great effectiveness, with the hymns that left his audience feeling
they had looked across Jordan and seen the Gates.

The great meeting did not break up until almost 11 o'clock. Waiting at
the Hartford terminal was a double-header, ten-car special of the Connecticut Western Railroad, steam up and Conductor Tom Elmore ready to
see the gospelers aboard and to deliver them to their homes in Winsted,
Canaan and other towns of Litchfield County. When every car was full,
Elmore gave the high ball. About half-past eleven the heavy train reached
the Tariffville bridge that spanned the Farmington River. It wasn't a new
bridge, and Conductor Elmore, if nobody else, had thought it rather shaky
when the special had crossed it that afternoon on the way to Hartford.
Shaky it must have been, for the two locomotives had little more than
arrived on the span before it started to give way, at first a slow and sicken-
ing collapse, followed an instant later by a tremendous crash. Both locomotives went down onto and through the ice of the river, dragging four
of the coaches after them. Seventeen died, forty-three were sent to hospitals.

Seeing the world from the rolling deck of a freight train.

Harper's Weekly, Aug. 14, 1877

Bloodshed and violence marked the great railroad strike of 1877. Rioters burned the Pittsburgh Union Depot, among other railroad property.

"King Debs." One of the milder attacks on Eugene V. Debs during the American Railway Union strike of 1894 was this cartoon by W. A. Rogers in Harper's Weekly on July 14th. Debs was president of the ARU.

Evidence at the investigation indicated that on the bridge was a long stretch of rail with no ties beneath it, thus causing the rail to sag and derail the leading locomotive, which crashed into one of the bridge supports and caused the bridge to give way. Evidence also indicated that the railroad had been more than careful in having the tracks patrolled by section crews that day, and that the crews had found all ties in place. Many years afterward John F. Jones, superintendent of the Western Connecticut, related that the ties on the bridge had surely been tampered with and insisted that three separate investigations right after the tragedy had come to that conclusion. Mr. Jones added that the wreck on the Tariffville bridge had resulted in new laws in most states providing that railroads should "bolt guard rails to the ends of ties to prevent them from crawling or being displaced."

It was long past time that railroads had done something to improve the quality of the bridges; two years before the Tariffville tragedy there had occurred what the newspapers were still referring to as the Ashtabula Catastrophe. This had happened to the *Pacific Express* of the Lake Shore & Michigan Southern on December 29, 1876, an eleven-car train, westbound and double-headed by two fine locomotives, the *Columbia* and the *Socrates*. Pulling out of Ashtabula, Ohio, in early evening, the *Express* slowed to cross the 165-foot span that crossed high over Ashtabula creek. In the lead engine, the *Socrates*, Engineer Dan McGuire suddenly noted that his locomotive seemed to be "running up hill." He couldn't know what the matter was, but he acted quickly, opening the throttle, and the *Socrates* leaped ahead, breaking the drawbar that coupled it to the *Columbia*.

The bridge was giving way. As the *Socrates* gained the far side, the *Columbia* sank to the accompaniment of the groans and wails of timber collapsing. The *Columbia* and eleven cars crashed onto and through the frozen creek. Flames soon consumed the wreckage. Thirty-four died, many more were badly injured. Nobody was to blame. It was just another railroad bridge giving way, and although the public was shocked and horrified, for the moment, no one was surprised.

Then came the Tariffville accident, to be followed by an almost continuous series of bridge disasters great and small, among them one on the Central Vermont, at two o'clock of a bitter February morning in 1887, when something happened to the *Montreal Express* and it keeled off a bridge across the White River, killing thirty-eight, injuring forty. But the monster bridge wreck of them all was still to happen, and happen it did in the same year, out in Illinois, and this one went into balladry.

The bridge involved was little more than a culvert on the Toledo, Peoria & Western, less than three miles from the town of Chatsworth. The TP&W Railroad was a notable collection of locomotives held together with haywire and rolling stock which was inadequately described as "obsolete." The company was having a difficult time meeting its payroll, and among its efforts in this direction was a series of cheap excursions from Illinois to Niagara Falls. The excursion of August 10th was a double-header with fifteen cars, all crammed with sight-seers. Battling along in the night, it struck a short low span which had been eaten away and weakened by grass fires along the tracks. The lead locomotive got across. The other engine and fifteen cars went down with the bridge and piled one atop the other. The usual flames leaped up. Eighty-four died, and some unknown song writer composed a long and quite dreadful ballad on the occasion.*

There was, however, a steady if slow improvement made in railroad bridges, and before the end of the century bridge disasters were the exception rather than the rule. Derailments, of course, continued, just as they do to this day, and also collisions. Collisions were and are usually attributable to some failure of a human being. Such failures are taken into consideration by railroads and every effort made to prevent them, but now and then some factor wholly new to the business puts in an appearance, with terrible results. It is safe to say that no one connected with American railroads in 1918 ever in his wildest moments thought of kidney pills in relation to disaster on the rails.

The tragedy happened just before dawn of the clear and star-flecked night of June 22nd. The second section of a train hauling the Hagenbeck-Wallace circus left Michigan City, Indiana, with orders to detour onto the Gary & Western road at Ivanhoe. The train had fourteen flatcars, seven stock or animal cars, four sleepers and a caboose. All cars were of wood, the sleepers being rebuilt old Pullmans with three tiers of berths, dimly lighted by lanterns hung above the center aisles. Although it was three o'clock in the morning, Charles Dollmer, circus manager, was still working over the show's books. The berths were filled with performers and roustabouts, all getting the sleep they would need to make them alert for the show in Hammond next day. Miss Rose Borland, the featured equestrienne who was said to receive $25,000 a season for her work on the backs of Hagenbeck-Wallace's wonderful horses, had a berth to herself. So did Hercules Navarro, The Strongest Man Since Sandow; and Joe Coyle, boss clown, whose wife and two babies were in an upper. Another of the sleeping cars was crammed double with the pretty and agile members of Hagenbeck-Wallace's ballet of "100 Dancing Girls, Count Them."

Just east of tiny Ivanhoe, doubtless named by some Hoosier lover of the Waverly Novels, Conductor R. W. Johnson of the circus train thought he caught the aroma of an overheated journal. He signaled the engineer to stop, and the train halted a few feet from the crossing of the Elgin, Joliet & Eastern. Flagman Trimm promptly got off and went back to protect the rear of his train.

In the meantime what had been a troop train, but was now empty of

* See chapter on songs.

soldiers, had cleared Michigan City 27 minutes after the circus had pulled out of there. The margin was large enough for almost any contingency that a railroad man could have conjured up. The night was quite clear. All signal lights were showing. Jogging along at around 30 miles an hour, the trooper passed, some two miles east of Ivanhoe, an automatic signal set at caution. It did not even slow its pace. Soon it came abreast of and passed another automatic signal, this one shining bright crimson. On it pounded, and Flagman Trimm could hardly believe his eyes. Here he was, well back from his own train, watching a big headlight coming swiftly at him. He knew it must have already passed a caution signal. Now he saw it pass a red signal.

I can idly put myself in Flagman Trimm's place and wonder what I would have thought to see that dazzling beam coming straight and true down the track toward me, and to feel the tremble of the ties and the ground, to hear the singing of the rails, to know that close behind me, and I now and inexplicably their last and only protector, was a cargo of humanity and another cargo of strange beasts from the outlands of the earth. Being in Flagman Trimm's place, I should have been a railroad man and thus have taken in the full horror of it, indeed the hideous knowledge that it simply could not happen, that it must be some form of insane hallucination that had suddenly taken charge of all my faculties.

It must have been a terrible moment in Flagman Trimm's life. There he stood, helpless now except for his own efforts. He put them into use at once. He swung his bright red lantern as he had never swung it before—swung it wildly in great arcs, swung it desperately and, at last, hopelessly. This mad and possibly illusionary train came pounding on, relentless, certain, never slackening. In a last effort as the trooper passed him, Trimm hurled a flaming red fusee plumb into the cab of the locomotive. An instant later the mad train plowed like a battering ram into the rear of the circus extra.

It was a mighty crash, a clap of sudden thunder that woke all in sleeping Ivanhoe. It also woke almost everybody in the circus train, but not all, for a few were crushed as they slept and never knew what had happened. Close on the crash came the flames from the swinging lanterns in the cars. The heap of matchwood started to burn at once, while the dark was made more dreadful by the fearful noises of the beasts of the far corners of the earth who were here assembled on Indiana soil. Higher pitched than the roars of the animals were the cries that came from the telescoped and splintered sleeping cars. The girls of the ballet—One hundred Beauties— were dying horribly and too slowly in the licking flames, many of them already mangled beyond knowing . . .

Pretty and dainty Rose Borland never cried. She was beyond crying and probably never roused. But Hercules the Strong Man roused. He could lift a ton, said his billing, but he was no match for Engine Number 8485 as operated by Alonzo Sargent, for Hercules crumpled like so much card-board. He was crushed completely to pulp from the waist down, and when they found him his great arm muscles could barely twitch as he begged one of the rescuers to kill him . . .

Joe Coyle, the famous clown, survived, though his wife and two babies died in the berth above him. Nor were they alone, for a dozen of the lovely ballet girls died where they lay sleeping. The Rooney Family of bareback riders was wiped out. So were the Famous Meyers, animal trainers, the Cotterell Family, horsemen and horsewomen par excellence, and three old-time joeys, veteran clowns.

As the flames rose higher from the burning wood and flesh, dawn came to Indiana to find disaster and chaos spread on the tracks at Ivanhoe and in the fields. The grass and cinders were strewed with the gauds and tinsels of the world of the circus—spangles, shreds of tights and ballet dresses, tin crescents, stars, *fleurs-de-lis,* and the ridiculous great shoes and pantaloons of the clowns, funny no longer, but rather and peculiarly tragic in their present situation.

Ivanhoe turned out to give such succor as it could. The tracks from Gary were cleared, and a hastily assembled special brought doctors and nurses. Another came loaded from Hammond. But no water was handy, and the great mass of debris burned on and on while brave men tried desperately and often futilely to save those who were trapped in the jumble. The survivors were put aboard a train and taken to Hammond, where many were hospitalized and the others filed past a gilt circus wagon set up in an open lot where Manager Dollmer checked the living against the names on the circus payroll. Sixty-eight had died, one way or another, by being crushed, suffocated, or burned. One hundred and twenty-seven others went to hospital. There was no show that day in Hammond.

Five days later investigators met in Hammond to determine responsibility for the wreck. Conductor Johnson of the circus extra testified that his train was stopped to fix a hotbox when he saw the engine of the troop train coming headlong. He had seen his flagman, the trusty Trimm, give the washout, the emergency stop signal, by swinging a red lantern. Trimm himself took the stand to relate his story.

The chief witness, of course, was Engineer Alonzo K. Sargent of the troop train. He testified that he had had little or no sleep for twenty-four hours prior to the wreck. He said he had eaten a couple of heavy meals before going on the fatal trip. He said the wind had been high that night, and he had closed the cab window to make the place comfortable.

The questioning of Engineer Sargent continued. He said he had taken "some kidney pills" just before he started the run. Doctors testified that most, if not all, kidney pills contained a narcotic that "tended to produce unavoidable drowsiness." The investigation was at last getting somewhere. Filled with the drug, Engineer Sargent, a railroad man of long experience, had put his hand on the throttle to pull out of Michigan City and had kept it there. He admitted he had then dozed and had been dozing when he ran past the caution signal. He was still dozing when he passed the automatic red signal. He had never seen Flagman Trimm with his waving lantern. Even the thrown fusee had failed to wake him. The first warning of danger he got, he vowed, was when he saw the tail lights of the stalled circus train. Meanwhile, Sargent's fireman, a new employee, had either not seen the automatic signals or had not recognized their import. He had continued to shovel coal, as a good fireman should, and kept the steam well up in the gauge, while Engineer Sargent, his kidneys at last eased by the soothing effect of drugs, had slumbered long enough to perpetrate the greatest circus train disaster in the annals of the three-ring sawdust world.

What effect, if any, the Ivanhoe wreck had on the matter of kidney pills and railroads I do not know. There was, however, a wreck in my home territory, forty years ago, that was popularly, and possibly rightly, held to have been the reason for changing the names of many a depot in New England. On the 15th of September, 1907, a freight and a passenger train crashed together at 4:26 A.M. in a dense fog, near West Canaan, New Hampshire, killing twenty-five persons. Investigation disclosed that the accident had been "due to an error in a dispatcher's order." It was said at the time, and is still generally believed in the region, that the error mentioned concerned a mistaken use of "Canaan" instead of "West Canaan." I am not sure this is true, but that is the way it reached the public and such is the belief today.

In any case, not long after the West Canaan affair, the Boston & Maine Railroad, on which the wreck occurred, started to change the names of many of its stations. Between 1907 and 1917 West Lebanon, New Hampshire, became Westboro. North Haverhill became Blackmount. Fatal West Canaan was changed to Pattee. East Andover became Halcyon, South Newbery became Conicut, and North Stratford was made Coös. Charles E. Fisher, president of the Railway and Locomotive Society, who lives in Boston, tells me that the changing of names affected eleven stations bearing the word "East," eight stations with "North" in their names, nine with "West," and ten with "South." The villages, of course, still function under their own proud and venerable names. Only the signs on the depots were changed.

By the time of the West Canaan wreck, of course, railroads had long since mended their free and easy manner of the operation of trains, and were on the way, though not yet arrived, to the point they were to achieve in the second decade of the twentieth century and to maintain to the present day—that of the safest mode of travel we have.

Two of the greatest single advances made for safety on the rails were forced upon the carriers by the federal government—the general adoption of the air brake and the automatic coupler. And for twenty years before the government was ready to act, the voice of a monomaniac and fanatic was almost the sole voice raised against the needless killing and maiming of railroad employees, and incidentally of passengers.

CHAPTER XXIV

The Airbrake Fanatic

I discovered it was taken as a matter of course *that railroad men of necessity be maimed and killed.*
—LORENZO COFFIN, 1913.

MONOMANIACS are often bores. I have attracted more than my share of them, I believe, and not one of them of my acquaintance ever got anywhere with his big idea, yet they pestered me and anyone else who would listen, or couldn't help himself, until even religious fanatics, who are of course in a class by themselves, would have been almost welcome. But not quite, for I enjoyed, for the first ten or a dozen sessions, hearing of a lost cave in the Cascade Mountains of Oregon that was dripping with diamonds; and of learning over and over again, and at some cost in drink, from one "Silent" Smith, a relic of the Indian wars, that George Armstrong Custer still lived—in 1926. And I have looked, until my eyes blurred, at charts and statistics that proved beyond all doubt that Douglas fir cones, set on sticks around house and barn, would deflect bolts of lightning and make them harmless, all "because of essences released from the cones at the approach of a thunderstorm."

These men were pure monomaniacs. They had each brooded so long on his pet subject that he had come to believe it of cosmic importance, that all else should be put aside until the Big Thing had been accomplished, or proved. That they and their ideas quickly became unpopular with those to whom they talked only worked as a martyrizing influence and gave them a determination not to quit until their notions had been firmly impressed upon all their fellows.

But occasionally there has been a monomaniac who was of great benefit, and no better example could be found than Lorenzo Coffin, the bearded and forgotten fanatic whose one-track mind and grim determination were of incalculable aid in bringing to success the two greatest railroad inventions since the steam locomotive. I mean the air brake of George Westinghouse and the automatic coupler of Eli Hamilton Janney. Westinghouse merely invented the one, and Janney the other. But if you are of the opinion that the railroads of the United States fell over themselves to adopt the brake and the coupler, it is only natural, no matter how mistaken, for popular history has room only for the foremost names.

Coffin, Westinghouse and Janney all served in the Civil War, the first two with the Union, the latter with the Confederacy. Janney's coupler was patented in 1868, and perfected in a patent of 1873, which remains to this day the basic invention of the automatic coupler. Before Janney's device —and on many a railroad for thirty and more years after—cars were connected with link and pin, a crude affair that did hold the cars together but also accounted for the majority of maimed or dead trainmen. This was so because with link and pin the brakeman had to stand between the cars being coupled in order to steer the link into the socket, then to drop the pin that held them in place.

This link and pin coupling was the dread of all men who ever had to couple cars; and there are old railroaders living today whose memories are filled with remembered incidents when a comrade lost a finger, or a hand, or his life, in that instant when two cars came together. Amputated fingers or hand told all railroad men that this or that man, no matter his present job, had once been a brakeman on a link-and-pin road.

Janney whittled out of wood his first model for an automatic coupler. Six years later he managed to get the Pennsylvania to test it. The Pennsylvania found it good and in 1876–77 made it standard equipment for its cars. But not until 1882, when the Master Car-Builders Association at last adopted the device, did Janney and the company he had formed begin to prosper. Even then, and for another decade, there were far more link-and-pins than automatics on American railroads. The maiming and the slaughter of trainmen continued.

When he was twenty-two years old, in 1869, George Westinghouse, an up-state New Yorker, patented his air brake. He had already invented and secured patents on a water meter, a car-replacer and a railroad frog. His air brake, however, was of revolutionary importance, even though few railroad officials knew it. Coincident with this invention, the Westinghouse Air Brake Company was incorporated in Pennsylvania to manufacture the device. The man proved to be as good in business as he was an inventor, for he went on to purchase signal and interlocking switch patents which he combined with his own inventions until he had acquired a complete signal system for railroads, then organized the Union Switch & Signal Company.

The man was dynamic, and one who knew him well, Nikola Tesla, also something of a genius, gave an excellent picture of him. "A powerful frame," wrote Tesla of his friend, "with every joint in working order, an eye as clear as crystal, a quick and springy step—he presented a rare example of health and strength. Like a lion in the forest, he breathed deep and with delight the smoky air of his factories. Always smiling and polite, he stood in marked contrast to the rough and ready men I met. And yet no fiercer adversary than Westinghouse could have been found when he was aroused. An athlete in ordinary life, he was transformed into a giant when confronted with difficulties which seemed insurmountable. He enjoyed the struggle and never lost confidence. When others gave up in despair, he triumphed. Had he been transferred to another planet with everything against him he would have worked out his salvation."

Yet such an indomitable man, with such an invention as his air brake, discovered that a majority of American railroads of the 1870's were not interested in adopting his method for stopping trains. True, a few roads cautiously put air brakes on some of their equipment, but as a general thing the invention, like the automatic coupler of Janney, was going begging when Lorenzo Coffin turned from a prosperous farmer into a fanatic.

Coffin's younger days had no bearing on the achievements of his old age. He was older than either Westinghouse or Janney, having been born in 1823 on a New Hampshire farm. He attended college at Oberlin, Ohio, a place that somehow has sent out a large number of influential men and women. Coffin taught school a while, then in 1861 went off as chaplain in the 32nd Iowa Infantry to serve throughout the war. After his discharge he went to Iowa and to farming, near Fort Dodge.

It was in 1874 that Coffin's life took a new turn. In those days travel in the Midwest was rather informal. You might buy a ticket and ride as a formal passenger on a freight train, if no passenger cars were due at the moment. Coffin was riding a freight, which soon stopped at some way station to pick up a couple of boxcars. In doing the switching and coupling necessary, one of the brakemen lost the two remaining fingers on his right hand in the by-then familiar link-and-pin accident. He had lost the other fingers in a like accident the year before.

Talking with the train crew, Coffin learned that relatively few brakemen of long experience possessed all of their fingers because of the highly dangerous operation of the link-and-pin process. He learned also that many more brakemen lost not their hands but their lives in falling from moving trains while twisting at the old hand brakes.

The accident he had seen and the knowledge he had gained produced a powerful effect on Coffin. Less and less he tended his fine farm. He brooded much. Had not an automatic coupler, one that precluded the brakeman standing between moving cars, been invented and was even then being manufactured? Had not this man Westinghouse devised an air brake that was even then being used on the passenger trains of a few Eastern lines?

More and more Coffin rode about the Middle West on freight trains, always talking with the crews. They told him that the new brake and the new coupler were not being widely adopted because of the cost. Coffin vowed there and then that he was going to do something about it, that he had found his real life's work. So he became a fanatic, a monomaniac.

"My first job," said Coffin years later, "was to arouse the public to this awful wrong, this butchering of these faithful men who were serving the people at such fearful risk of life and limb. Why, I had discovered that it was taken as a *matter of course* that railroad men of necessity be maimed and killed."

Lorenzo Coffin did a great deal of traveling in the late 1870's—all to a good purpose. He wasn't going anywhere; he was getting an arsenal of facts that he could use as a battering ram—an arsenal of facts about how railroad employees were being needlessly butchered, chiefly through operation of links-and-pins and hand brakes. He gave little if any thought to the traveling public. Then, when he had a mass of facts gathered, he set out to remedy the conditions responsible. He wanted all the railroads to adopt Mr. Westinghouse's air brake and to install Mr. Janney's automatic coupler.

The railroads, however, were immune to suggestions, to pleading, even to laws. They had begun buying the influence of United States senators and congressmen, just as they bought rails and rolling stock. They operated trains when and where they pleased. They charged what they would for freight and passengers. They said, when asked, that the many and terrible accidents on their lines were "unfortunate" and laid the whole dreary business to Acts of God.

It is true that during the seventies, the Grangers had somewhat tamed the railroads, had made them a bit more amenable to the influence of public opinion. Yet they were still powerful and at times arrogant, capable of handling and defeating all efforts of state and federal governments to control them in the least. Lorenzo Coffin, a long, bewhiskered farmer from Iowa, set out to tackle these giants singlehanded, and presently he had become only too well known as The Air Brake Fanatic.

Railroad officials got to know Coffin as a bore, a gadfly, and when he tried to see them in person he found them "gone to Europe," a sort of effective euphemism of the day comparable to "in conference." Snubbed, often bodily thrown out of offices, Coffin turned to the press. He wrote pieces for the daily papers, whose editors tossed them into waste baskets. Just another wild-eyed fanatic. The only outlets Coffin could find for his protests were the small religious, family, and farm periodicals; and into these dismally printed mediums he poured his eloquence.

In direct and appealing language, using quaint asides and scriptural allusions, Coffin attacked both the emotions and the reason. He described in some detail the tragedies brought to countless families—in 1881 they numbered some 30,000—by loss of their breadwinners who had been killed or maimed for life because of accidents with hand brakes and coupling pins. He took pains to describe these lethal devices and showed how great numbers of men had fallen to their deaths or been crushed to a bloody pulp in their operation. He pictured a long freight weaving through a Colorado pass in a storm, the cars heaving and rocking like ships in a rough sea, while a blizzard complete with wind beat upon their tops, and the poor brakemen—God save them on a night like this!—their heads against the storm, turned and twisted the wheels of the brakes—and 'twas a miracle if one of them did not fall to his death.

Needless, cried old Coffin, all needless tragedy! He said that Mr. Westinghouse had invented a brake that would do away with all or much of this murder, but that because of the cost, the railroads would not install it. Coffin was right, too. Lyman Abbott said as much in the authoritative pages of *Harper's New Monthly Magazine.* "The radical cause of their neglect," he wrote of railroad officials in relation to their failure to adopt the automatic coupler and the air brake, "is probably the fact that the lives of railroad employees are inexpensive. The railroad corporation is held responsible for all accidents, occasioned by its negligence, to its passengers, but a rule of law, which certainly in this instance works with apparent injustice, renders them exempt from damages in the case of injuries to employees." And then, with the use of italics, one of the most influential clergyman-journalists of his day summed up the matter in almost the very words Lorenzo Coffin was using in the Midwest. *"So long,"* wrote Mr. Abbott, *"so long as brakes cost more than trainmen we may expect the present sacrificial method of car coupling to be continued."* *

It was something, in the 1870's, to have the Rev. Lyman Abbott on your side, but even Mr. Abbott's strictures failed to make any detectable dent in the hides of railroad officials. Throughout the rest of the decade Coffin's voice was a lonely one, yet it was persistent and, in Iowa at least, he was making progress. In 1883, when he was sixty, that state made him its first railroad commissioner. He at once wrote and sent out thousands of letters, not form letters but real ones, to railroad officials, to common men and women, to newspapers, lodges, societies, Granges, labor unions. He asked for moral support, for help of any kind, to club the recalcitrant roads into adopting the two simple devices that would vastly reduce injury and fatality to railroad employees. He still gave no thought to the traveling public.

Commissioner Coffin, with an almost empty title, invited himself to conventions of railroad officials and equipment builders, and here he was as welcome as leprosy. But he attended, when they did not stop him by force, and once there he stood up and accused the railroads of committing murder and mayhem. Always he closed his arguments by pointing out that safe brakes and safe couplers had been long since invented and were ready; all that was needed was their application.

---

* See his "The American Railroad," *Harpers New Monthly Magazine,* New York, Vol. XLIX, 1874.

Although at this period, as related, both automatic couplers and air brakes were already in limited use on passenger trains of some lines, these were the exception; and air brakes were not used at all on freights. Nor had the lines, as Coffin soon discovered to his amazement, any intention of generally adopting either the air brake or the automatic coupler. Cost too much to install and maintain, they argued.

Coffin argued back at them. "But I note," he shouted, "that the Chicago & Alton and most other lines continue to pay their eight per cent dividends regularly."

The tall old fanatic now took a new tack. By almost superhuman efforts he prevailed on the Master Car-Builders Association to agree to a test of air brakes on a long freight train. Nearly everybody considered this a futile effort; the new invention might be used on short, light trains, but not on heavy freights. It simply would not work.

Coffin continued to hound the Master Car-Builders until they set a date for the tests. The first of these came in 1886—seventeen years after Westinghouse's first patent. It proved disappointing, and after the second day of the tests, Coffin was the only state railroad commissioner present. The others had gone home, declaring they had wasted their time in listening to a crazy fanatic. The trials were repeated in May, 1887, and this time Coffin had prevailed on Westinghouse himself to attend. The tests again failed, and again Coffin heard himself denounced. But Westinghouse had watched the trials. He had seen what his invention lacked in the matter of stopping a heavy train of freight cars. He returned to Pittsburgh, took off his coat and went to work in his shops to perfect a brake that would stop a 50-car freight dead in its tracks, or almost.

Later in that summer of 1887 came the third test—famed now in railroad history as the Burlington Trials because they were held on a long grade of track of the Chicago, Burlington & Quincy, eight miles west of Burlington, Iowa. Both Westinghouse and Coffin were present. According to an eyewitness, the two men, the inventor and the fanatic, watched closely while "an immense train was hurled down the steep grade into Burlington at 40 miles an hour." At a given signal the air brakes were applied, and "the train came to a standstill *within 500 feet* and with hardly a jar." It was wonderful, that stopping to the hissing of compressed air!

Lorenzo Coffin, aged and weatherbeaten, stood close by the tracks and bystanders saw tears of joy stream from his eyes and run shamelessly down his lined leathery face. "I am," he cried, choking with emotion, "I am the happiest man in all Creation!"

It was an epochal day in American railroad history. Never before had a long, heavy train of cars been stopped by air, quickly and without harm to men or equipment. Coffin, still naïve in regard to railroads of the time, thought his work was done. It was really just beginning. Not yet were the

Photo from Joseph Lavelle collection

This stack on a Rogers consolidation engine was the Great Northern's answer to the tunnel smoke hazard in 1902. A more modern device, used by the Southern Railway, is the Rhodes, Guffey & Sheehan tunnel mask.

Photo from H. G. Monroe

One of the Hill Lines was the Northern Pacific, and its pride for many years was its Transcontinental Express, pictured by an artist, c. 1890.

roads ready to adopt the air brake, or, for that matter, the automatic coupler.

Soon after the third and successful test, Coffin drafted the first railroad safety appliance law ever written. It required that all trains operating in Iowa should be equipped with air brakes and automatic couplers. The act was promptly made into state law; and the law was promptly disregarded by the railroads operating in Iowa. They had no intention of adopting the new devices.

Then, in the spring of 1888, the Interstate Commerce Commission began to function. The Commission's first act was to invite the state railroad commissioners of the nation to a meeting in Washington to discuss various problems having to do with railroading, but chiefly the matter of traffic rates. By now Coffin was no longer a commissioner. But he sat down and rewrote his state safety appliance law to fit the entire United States. This he put into his valise and took a train of cars for Washington.

The big gathering was called to order. On the first day Coffin, who had no right to be there, got up. He stood straight and tall in spite of his years. The old fire burned brightly. He told the assembled experts, before they could stop him, more about railroad accidents than they had ever guessed, or wanted to hear. He piled horror upon horror, and interspersed the bloody statistics with pitiful tales of the aftermath of accidents. "These are cold and awful facts," he cried, his voice shaking. On and on he went, now picturing a sad-eyed widow sitting by the window looking down at the yards, waiting for a brakeman husband who would never return; now describing fatherless children forced to leave school to work in support of their mother. He painted these scenes in a manner to make his listeners squirm, and left many of them wet-eyed. He was eloquent, this old man from the back-country, and he knew what he was talking about.

Coffin's unbidden address to this first meeting of railroad commissioners was superb. It had a lasting influence on many in the audience, including the Interstate Commerce Commissioners themselves. The meeting laid aside Coffin's proposed national act. The time wasn't quite ripe. Coffin went back to his farm, not to brood or to weep but to prepare for the next attack. He raised a little money from his own resources, then returned to Washington where he was to remain for four years, living a Spartan life in cheap boarding houses because he could afford no better fare. But he happened to be a true fanatic—that kind of man who never counts the odds against him and his Idea.

The Idea was an act, a law, that would cover every mile of every railroad in every state, a truly vast conception in its day. This law would be made to apply to all roads and would impose on all of them what Coffin said—nay, what he vowed to God—was the absolute necessity of air brakes and automatic couplers, on freights and passenger trains alike. He soon learned that most senators and congressmen felt that air brakes and such were very fine in the abstract but were not to be introduced into serious legislation on a national scale. The railroads did not want brakes or anything else forced upon them. All of the Southern lines made it plain they wanted no part of the newfangled devices with or without law. Most of the Northern roads were either apathetic or hostile, Coffin found, although the Vanderbilt lines, he said, "never fought me, but often gave me *private* encouragement."

Coffin continued his lobbying, year after year. He rewrote his national law again and again, and at last he got a pretty fair bill through the House, then hovered over it until it had passed the Senate; and on March 2, 1893, often called "the greatest day in railroad history," President Benjamin Harrison gave it his approval. The President also gave the pen with which he signed the bill to Coffin, who until the end of his long life cherished it as witness to his triumph in a struggle that had lasted almost two decades.

The Railroad Safety Appliance Act brought immediate and striking improvement. It reduced the rate of accidents to employees by a whopping 60 per cent. The passenger accident rate fell to almost nothing, for Coffin's work was to benefit passengers almost as much as it did railroad employees. The act had another influence. Once the more progressive roads discovered the happy effects of safety on their business, they went wholeheartedly for anything new and better. Train speeds continued to increase, and railroad safety became almost proverbial.

Coffin lived well into the present century and witnessed the steady improvement and safety of travel by train. His main work was done yet, being a fanatic, he still must have something to live for.* This turned out to be a battle with The Demon of rum as it afflicted railroad employees. Apparently Coffin was not greatly interested in what farmers and steel workers and actors and steamboatmen did with booze, or what it did to them. He merely set out to save railroad workers from the stuff that has the sting of an adder and, he had been long convinced, was second only to hand brakes and link-and-pin as a cause of accident and disaster.

It seems probable that Coffin's new field was a wide one that needed

---

* When a part of this chapter appeared as a magazine article, Robert S. Henry of the Association of American Railroads wrote me that "the automatic coupler and the freight air brake owe much less to the earnest efforts of Mr. Coffin than they do to the sound engineering of George Westinghouse, Major Janney, and the testing committee of the Master Car-Builders Association, and to the railroad managements all over the country which adopted them long before there was a requirement of federal law on the subject. Final and *complete adoption was brought about by statutory enactment* [my italics—Author] but most substantial progress was made by numerous railroads voluntarily and without the requirement of law." I do not doubt the good will of Westinghouse, Janney and the Car-Builders, but remain quite unshaken in my opinion that so far as complete or even general adoption was concerned, Coffin had more influence than them all. This opinion is not colored from prejudice, but comes from considerable original research into the subject and is bolstered by what railroadmen of the eighties and nineties have told me, men who used link-and-pin and hand brakes.

working. If old-timers are to be believed, then railroad employees of late last century and early this one were given in no small numbers to drink. Rule G, prohibiting use of intoxicants while on duty, put a number of them out of railroading, it is true, but a large number of them survived Rule G and continued to railroad and to drink more than was good for them. In any case, old Coffin's answer to it was the Railroad Temperance Association, which he founded and maintained at his own expense. Wherever the old man went his pockets were filled with little white buttons which he gave to such trainmen and other employees who "had given me their word to abstain from the use of those beverages which destroy man· hood and render the individual unfitted for the performance of his duties." He distributed more than 250,000 of these buttons in person. He also helped to found in Chicago the Home for Aged and Disabled Railroad Men. In 1907 he campaigned for the governorship of Iowa on the Prohibition ticket.

Thus was Coffin a true fanatic to the last, one of the most useful fanatics this country has produced, the man Westinghouse and Janney needed to give their inventions real and widespread use, and much sooner than otherwise might have been the case. It is a commentary on something or other that we Americans will erect monuments to Grant, to Lee, Houston, Dewey, the Unknown Soldier—killers to a man—but few of us know that Lorenzo Coffin, a saver of countless lives, ever lived. He died, January 15, 1915, aged ninety-two, a genial and kindly patriarch who had known more success than most fanatics, before or since.

Long before Coffin's death, American railroads had learned that the safety of their own employees, as well as the safety of passengers, paid dividends both in cash and in good will. The happy results of the adoption of air brakes and automatic couplers were, as I have mentioned, apparent almost at once; and from this point down to the present day, few if any industries have been so prompt as the railroads to install any machine, gadget, or practice that seemed to promise safer operation.

One of the greatest single advances was perfection of the automatic block signal, the idea of which is to keep trains apart by a certain block or interval of space. A block may be a fraction of a mile or even several miles, depending on density of traffic. Manually-operated blocks were in use as early as 1864, but manually-operated blocks depended wholly on the reliability of a man or men. Hence, only too often the signals failed to be set or were set incorrectly, and accidents resulted. Then, in 1871, William Robinson devised a block signal system operated by an electric current in the rails which would automatically set a signal on contact of the rails and the wheels of an approaching locomotive. It was the foundation for the development of the efficient automatic blocks in use today, signals whereby each train moving along a track maintains its own protection and, further, retains control of the signal so long as it occupies any part of the track which that signal is guarding.* In 1946 more than 110,000 miles of lines in the United States were protected by automatic blocks.

Another important automatic device had its start in 1880, when the first of many patents was granted on an invention to stop a train physically that ran past a stop signal. The 1880 gadget was a contact device that broke a glass tube on the locomotive, which, in turn, applied brakes to the train. The idea was perfect in theory but it would not do, for it was soon discovered that icicles hanging from tunnels would break the tube, nor would the tube system manipulate the brakes in the several ways necessary if trains of varying characteristics were to be stopped without damage.

Yet, the inventors kept at the idea, so many of them that when the New Haven road offered a rich cash prize for a practical automatic train control device, no less than 3,300 inventors submitted their gadgets. None proved to work successfully. Neither the inventors nor the railroads, however, were discouraged. By the early 1920's, four different types of automatic stops were being improved, and one type was being tried on portions of the Chicago & Eastern Illinois, the Rock Island, and the Chesapeake & Ohio. All of these systems depended on a contact between a shoe on the engine and a ramp beside the track.

At about this time, a special committee of the railroads, working with the signal companies, decided to make a trial installation of a different kind of device, an intermittent-induction type operated by magnets laid between the ties. "This," says Robert Henry, "reflects the conditions in the track circuit to which they are attached . . . If that condition is such as to cause a signal to go to *stop*, the magnet buried in the ballast will set up electric currents, by induction, in the receiving apparatus of any engine which might pass over it. The receiving apparatus on the locomotive, in turn, sets in motion a series of electrical controls, which apply the air brakes and stop the train." † Good as it was, this system was soon improved by what is called continuous induction, designed to provide continuous information to the engineer on the changing state of things along the track ahead. "To accomplish such a result," says Mr. Henry, "the apparatus responds not only to what the signals ahead may say, but also to any breaks or obstructions which may develop within a block even after the train has passed the signal and entered upon it." For instance, should another engine be shunting cars within the block, or should a rail be broken, the receiving apparatus in the approaching locomotive acts immediately and automatically to bring the control into force.

In logical sequence came centralized traffic control, an intricate system using electric currents by which an operator in a room at a terminal or

---

* See Robert S. Henry, *This Fascinating Railroad Business*, cited elsewhere.
† *Op. cit.*

division point has complete control of all switches and signals over an extended piece of track. It does away with train orders, does away with time lost by trains waiting on sidings, and permits a single-track line to operate up to 75 per cent of double-track capacity. It also permits closer meets between opposing trains and quicker run-arounds of a slow train by faster ones. It also and obviously operates to the increased safety of all who ride or operate trains.

Communication between the rear and the head ends of long trains, and between the train and railroad offices, was first done successfully in 1938 on the Bessemer & Lake Erie with a device installed by the Union Switch & Signal Company and known as inductive train communication. This ITC, it seems, is technically neither telephone nor radio. It uses the rails, the ground and existing wires adjacent to the tracks for transmission. Beginning in 1940, the Pennsylvania and several other roads began installing ITC, and the system is still being improved, to the betterment of safety and to the specific joy of freight conductors of mile-long trains.

For many years track circuits have been used to operate warning signals and gates at grade crossings. Not so familiar to the public are other devices that depend on electric current, such as the slide-detector fences that set signals at both ends of a block should a rock or snow slide disturb the current. At many a railroad bridge a high-water indicator will set signals at either end of the structure calling for caution or a stop.

Such are a few of the more spectacular devices that have been perfected and installed after many years of trial and error. In the meantime, too, the carriers have constantly improved rails, improved rolling stock down to the last bolt and bearing, and in short done everything possible to lessen the danger of mechanical failure. In 1913, the Association of American Railroads and the National Safety Council joined hands in an organized effort to lessen human failure; this joint effort has never flagged and has brought results so good that the campaign is virtually a part of the American railroad system.

One of the newest gadgets to make railroading safer and more efficient is the hotbox alarm, described by S. Kip Farrington, Jr., in his *Railroading from The Rear End* (New York, 1946) as being installed on all passenger rolling stock and locomotives of the New York Central. A hotbox, as most everyone should know, is an overheated "journal," or axle bearing. On a fast passenger train hotboxes can be a serious danger. The new hotbox alarm employs two indicators—smoke for observation, and a rich and unpleasant odor—and consists of two containers placed in cavities made for the purpose. Each container holds a different liquid and has a small hole sealed with fusible metal, which melts when a temperature dangerous to the journal has been reached. Then, the two liquids vaporize and escape, that from one container sending forth a penetrating odor which will reach into the cars, that from the other producing a dense white smoke.

If the railroads have been quick to adopt new devices and practices ever since air brakes and automatic couplers proved their worth, the rail Brotherhoods have not lagged. Each of these big unions has supported a committee or department whose duty has been to consider any measure that sought to protect railroad workers from death or injury.

It would please old Lorenzo Coffin, could he know the steady advance of safety along the rails of the nation since his death in 1915. Because of them, railroads are the safest means of travel we have, even during the rush and overloading and undermanned years of World War II, when derailments and collisions appeared to be taking a higher toll than had been the case for three decades past. Accidents, true enough, were worse and came more often in the war years, yet the fatality and injury rate to passengers did not rise. A passenger in a modern railroad coach or Pullman is about as safe as he is anywhere else, and much safer than in certain other places, such as his own automobile or the bathroom of his own home.

CHAPTER XXV

The Rise of the Railway Express

Daniel Niles has commenced running an Express in connection with the Boston & Portland Railroad. He flatters himself that he is favorably known and solicits a share of the public patronage. Any packages left for him before 4 o'clock at 11 Elm Street will meet with his attention.

—Boston Advertiser, 1842.

THE sixteen-foot monument to William Frederick Harnden in Mount Auburn cemetery, Cambridge, Massachusetts, is probably deserved. Its legend states that Harnden was "Founder of The Express Business in America." Harnden died in 1845. The shaft was erected in 1856 by the combined effort of the express companies then in operation in the United States. If they credited Harnden as the Founder, then founder he was.

William Harnden was a native of Reading, Massachusetts. Weighing exactly one hundred pounds, and generally in poor health, he was one of those true monomaniacs who stick to an idea no matter the odds against them. When railroads at last got under way out of Boston, Harnden took a job as conductor on the Boston & Worcester. His working hours commonly ran to sixteen per day, and after three years, during which his health steadily became worse, he resigned. While looking around for something to do he made a trip to New York, where James Hale of Boston was building up a good business as a sort of informal express company for the Providence steamboat line. Bankers and merchants of Manhattan found Hale's service of use in sending packages of banknotes, bonds, and such to Boston.

Hale advised Harnden to set up as an express messenger between the two cities, carrying the packages himself. Ought to be a place for such a service, he said. Harnden consulted the steamboat company which granted him special rates between New York and Providence and even gave him what amounted to being an exclusive franchise. On the railroad between Providence and Worcester, however, the brothers Earle, B. D. and L. B., had been operating Earle's Express ever since the road opened in 1834, and Harnden could not obtain anything in the nature of an exclusive right. His relations with the Earles must have been harmonious, for the two concerns used the same trains, and a bit later, after Harnden got under way, the Earles rented office space from him in Providence.

In February of 1839 Harnden was ready, and being a consistent believer in the power of newspapers, he inserted paid notices in the Boston and New York newspapers at once. In these advertisements Harnden used the word "express" in the meaning we use it today.* He also made it a point to carry news dispatches or copies of newspapers for editors, doing this without charge and thus creating much goodwill in the inky sanctums. By late March the *Boston Transcript* was showing its appreciation by an editorial which spoke of Harnden's "honesty and fidelity" and went on to recommend "with much pleasure" his Express Service.

Although his friend Hale, in New York, worked hard to get all the business he could for Harnden, the amount at first was rather small. For several months a valise served to carry everything entrusted to the Harnden Express Company. Harnden was, in fact, about to give it up when the Cunard Line of Atlantic steamers went into operation between Boston and Liverpool. Business picked up immediately, chiefly through packages for New York and Philadelphia, which Harnden, with his brother Adolphus (now a member of the firm), could deliver much more quickly than if the stuff were left for transfer to the Boston & Providence road and the New York boat from Providence by the usual routine.

Harnden now added a messenger, Luke Damon, to make the run from Boston to New York and return by way of Stonington, Connecticut, and opened a formal office at 2 Wall Street, Manhattan. On January 13, 1840, he suffered a tragedy. Brother Adolphus, carrying many letters and some $40,000 in packages, went down on the steamer *Lexington*, on the way to Providence, which burned and sank with a loss of 121 lives, the worst disaster in a generation. But the company continued, with the blessing of the Merchants' Bank of Boston, then the largest in New England, which did not press to collect from Harnden a sizable portion of the money lost in the disaster and thus probably permitted him to remain in business.

Presently Harnden sent Dexter Brigham, a new partner, to England to establish a transatlantic express line and foreign-exchange business. Harnden went after business on the New York and Albany boats, and here he ran into the fact that the captains and pursers on the boats were making a good deal of money, on the side, by carrying letters and packages. Harnden could find no way to overcome this opposition until he made the acquaintance of Henry Wells, who appears to have had some influence with Daniel Drew, the sharp and cold-blooded riverboat magnate of the day. Wells, a Vermont Yankee, got Harnden an exclusive franchise for express on the New York-Albany boats; and Harnden appointed Wells his agent in Albany.

---

* See Alvin Harlow's *Old Waybills*, the best general account of American express companies in print; New York, 1934.

The Harnden Express Company now had a profitable triangle trade, between New York, Albany and Boston. Wells turned out to be an aggressive and competent agent. He urged Harnden to expand his service to the westward, to Buffalo, Cincinnati, even beyond, but the man wasn't interested. He apparently took little heed of the steady movement west of both old-stock Americans and new immigrants. Besides, competition was raising its head in many places, chiefly around Boston.

Typical of the new express lines following in the wake of the founder was Daniel Niles, for 20 years a stagecoach driver, who in January of 1842 took space in the Boston papers to announce that he had "commenced running an Express in connection with the Boston & Portland Railroad," and that he "solicits a share of the public patronage." He added that "he flatters himself that he is favorably known" and planned to leave Boston for Dover, New Hampshire, every day on the five-o'clock train. Any packages left for him before four o'clock at 11 Elm Street would meet with his attention.

Then, there was another outfit, Burke & Company's Express, which made its first messenger trip about a year after Harnden began. One of the partners was P. B. Burke, of whom history knows nothing, and the other was Alvin Adams, soon, though neither he nor Harnden knew it, to be one of the giants of the express business. Adams, a native of Andover, Vermont, had gone broke as a produce merchant. He watched closely the expanding business of Harnden and decided there was room for another company. Burke seems to have dropped out of the concern almost at once, and for a year or so Adams was the whole of Adams & Company. In a stovepipe hat he lugged letters and small packages between Boston and Worcester, and also executed errands and small business for his customers.

Alvin Adams was alert and determined. He was also a genial sort, and he like Harnden knew the value of the friendship of the press. He took pains to bring the latest New York papers to Boston editors, without charge and as quickly as possible, and he never thought of charging an editor for carrying a dispatch or even a personal letter. Adams also was expanding his business, first to New York by way of steamers from Stonington, then to Philadelphia. At the Boston end he hired one Sam Woodward, old-time stagecoach driver, to pick up and deliver packages. Woodward, a sort of shrewd and kindly Quincy-Adams-Sawyer type of person, proved to be a fine getter of business; and it was said, after a little, that no Boston firm dared leave any bundles lying around for fear old Sam Woodward would pick them up and ship them to New York.

Meanwhile, and though he never showed any interest in invading the West, Harnden was doing a good deal to encourage immigration to the United States. Perhaps it was he who invented the system whereby new Irish and German immigrants in this country could pay the fare of kinsmen to Harnden's company, which would then attend to all details of bringing them over from Europe. Harnden was honest, too, in contrast to many of the so-called forwarding companies, and in time his offices were usually filled with brand-new immigrants waiting transportation to Western states. Harnden got out posters and cards advertising this feature of his business, and appears to have been one of the few American agencies which did not set about to trim the new arrivals.

Then, in 1845, Harnden, worn out by illness, died, and the business was carried on by others until Adams & Company bought and converted it, with a number of other small concerns, into the Adams Express Company, destined for a long life.

Before Harnden died, his able Albany agent, Henry Wells, had gone into partnership with George E. Pomeroy to start an express service between Albany and Buffalo. To make the trip Wells, who acted as messenger during the early period, rode on the Mohawk & Hudson, the Utica & Schenectady, the Syracuse & Utica, the Auburn & Syracuse, the Auburn & Rochester, and the Tonawanda railroads, plus three intervening jumps by stage. The one-way trip occupied four nights and three days. Thaddeus Pomeroy soon joined the firm as a messenger. The three men proved to be a fine combination, energetic and with plenty of imagination. Among many other innovations they carried the first fresh oysters from New York to Buffalo and thus created a sensation, said Wells in later years, beyond description.

Pomeroy & Company also contributed much to the reduction of charges of the United States Post Office for carrying letters, a feat of the first importance. The Post Office had been uneasy about the new express companies for some time, or since 1840, when it became known that in the express pouch carried by Adolphus Harnden, a victim of the *Lexington* disaster, as related, were 148 letters. Postmasters in all parts of the Eastern states were beginning to grumble that the express men were taking away their life's blood. In 1841 the Post Office set investigators at work. They soon found that it was indeed true: the express concerns were carrying letters by the piece, by the package, and in great bundles. What was more, there were a lot of companies. Working out of Boston alone, in addition to Harnden, Niles, Adams, and the Earles, were Davenport to Taunton, Hatch to New Bedford and Martha's Vineyard, Kingsley to Fall River, Leonard to Worcester, Gray to Lowell, Gillis to Nashua, Dow to Haverhill, and Conant & Walker to Portsmouth, New Hampshire. A character known as Colonel Favor was the sole owner and staff of Favor's Eastport Express, operating between Boston and points in Eastern Maine and in New Brunswick. Benjamin P. Cheney, who had been driving stage, was about to start Cheney & Company's Express to Burlington, Vermont, which he built into one of the biggest outfits in New England and Eastern Canada.

The Postmaster General was worried not only because of the increasing

Refrigerator cars, called "reefers," consume millions of tons of ice a year. An icing job in the Maywood yards of the NYNH&H.

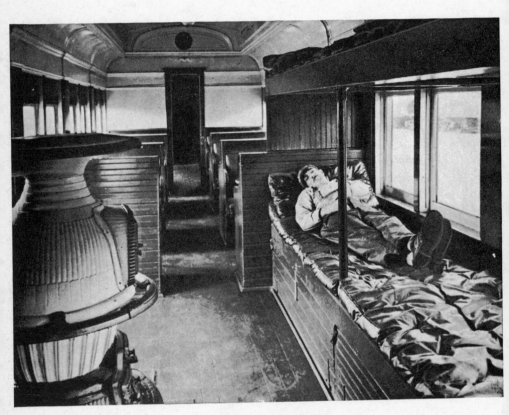

Interior of a work-train car.

number of express companies; he discovered without too much effort that business men and the public generally were in sympathy with the express men. It isn't difficult to understand why. In 1840 the United States charged from 6 to 25 cents for carrying a one-sheet letter, depending on distance, and the service was so slow and uncertain as to be the butt of comedians in print and variety hall. The Harnden and Adams companies would take a letter from New York to Boston for 12½ cents, half the rate of the Post Office. Pomeroy & Company had been doing a big business in letters, and early in 1843 this concern announced it would carry a letter anywhere in the country at a flat rate of six cents. Or, if you bought Pomeroy & Company stamps at 20 for $1, the rate was five cents.

It was time, said the Post Office Department, to put a stop to this "violation of law." It began to arrest Pomeroy & Company's messengers on the route between Albany and Buffalo, taking them off the trains and putting them into jail. Juries promptly acquitted them, despite their patent guilt. Pomeroy, to obviate the delays due to arrest of their young men, mounted them on fast horses and thus established the first Pony Express, its riders galloping across much of New York state, occasionally pursued by mounted government agents. The messengers were usually warned by citizens when the hated agents were nigh, and were guided across country to evade them. The business men of Rochester, to show how they stood in the matter, publicly offered outright aid of $6,000 a year to Pomeroy & Company if their agents would make daily trips to New York City. Proponents of the express companies argued that it was wrong for the government to seek to monopolize the carriage of mail. The Post Office countered by considering the taking over of all the express companies in business.

The government had to bow to public sentiment. In 1845 a bill was passed lowering postage rates to 5 cents for 300 miles, 10 cents to anywhere in the Union except the Pacific Coast states. At the same time the one-sheet rule was dropped. A letter was now an envelope and contents weighing not over one ounce. Pomeroy & Company presently retired from mail-carrying and became Livingston, Wells & Company, still very much in the express business. This concern bought out smaller express firms in its area, and managed to keep affairs pretty much of a monopoly.

The agent for Livingston, Wells at Buffalo was William G. Fargo, a native of Onondaga County, New York, who had previously worked for the Auburn & Syracuse railroad. Fargo was a young man of considerable vision, just the man to team with Wells, and on April 1, 1845, sure enough, Wells, Fargo and Dan Dunning organized the Western Express to handle business west of Buffalo. A year later Wells sold his interest in this firm to William A. Livingston, which became Livingston & Fargo, and went to live in Manhattan, there to manage Wells & Company.

The many small railroads between the Hudson and Lake Erie were rapidly being forged into the New York Central, and almost immediately an express company organized by John Butterfield, ex-stage driver, began to operate over the Central. Wells & Company had been paying Mr. Vanderbilt $100 a day for the privilege of having its express trunks and messenger ride from New York to Albany, and the new firm had to pay the same. This was obviously good for the Central and ruinous for the express companies. Being astute men, the Messrs. Wells, Livingston, Fargo, and Butterfield merged their outfits into two companies which, in turn, were made owners of another new concern, the American Express Company. This merger occurred in 1850.

Adams & Company had also been growing, chiefly in the south. They also paid well for a franchise on the New York & New Haven railroad. They took over the express line being operated out of Indianapolis by George W. Cass. They opened a service from Philadelphia to Pittsburgh via rail and canal; and presently had extended this end of the line to reach and pass Cincinnati, Louisville, and Cairo, to St. Louis. They also purchased privileges over the Baltimore & Ohio Railroad. Long before the railroads got there, they established agents in New Orleans. By 1854, Adams' service touched Charleston, Atlanta, Montgomery, Chattanooga, Memphis, Mobile. By 1859, Adams was operating out of Galveston and Houston. And on the Adams' board of directors sat Johnston Livingston, a director also in the American Express, Adams Express's great rival.

South went the Adams' tentacles, and West went those of the American. Chiefly through the alertness and imagination of the several Fargo brothers, all engaged with the American Express, that firm captured the Midwest while Adams was working south. The American service followed the Michigan Central as it crept into Chicago. It went on to occupy the Illinois Central, and the Chicago, Burlington & Quincy. Charles Fargo organized a line of Great Lakes steamers which the American soon took over. Presently an American agent had an office in Milwaukee, another in St. Paul.

Competition resulted in better services. Adams set out to buy the finest horses to draw its wagons, which were painted a beautiful blue and often decorated with landscape paintings. The American chose bright red for its wagons and its color scheme generally. Express offices were enlarged and decorated in what the word of the era said was elegant taste. Uniforms appeared on certain employees. The trunks of messengers were prettied up. The collect-on-delivery shipment was invented. So was the use of waybills, in order to keep track of a package from the time of its acceptance to that of delivery.

Competition also had set off an epic fight to get and keep the fabulous business incident to the great gold strike in California. Adams got there first. Late in '49 Alvin Adams organized a new concern, Adams & Company of California, and put one of his partners, D. H. Haskell, late of Boston, in charge. Haskell opened offices in San Francisco on December

1st, and started express lines to Sacramento, and to Stockton, thus to cover both the northern and the southern diggings. For the next two and a half years Adams & Company worked up a tremendous business between the States and California, using the Panama, the Nicaragua and Cape Horn routes, steadily expanding its routes in California and into the Oregon country. It had competition, of course, but Adams managed to do more business than all of the small concerns put together.

In the middle of 1852 the up-and-coming American Express organized a subsidiary to act as its western ally, calling it Wells, Fargo & Company. The first thing Wells Fargo did was to open an ocean express service between New York and San Francisco, via Panama, and set the rate at 40 cents a pound, or 20 cents under the monopoly rate charged by Adams. It also built a gaudy office building in San Francisco, and began at once to buy out the small concerns whose routes it wanted. Both concerns now concentrated on speed, which resulted on one memorable occasion in a race to deliver to Portland, Oregon, copies of a presidential message to Congress. There were no railroads, so the message must go by horseback. Bill Lowden, special rider for Adams, covered much of the ground, and did so well that the Wells Fargo men gave up the contest at Shasta. Adams & Company were said to have spent $2,000 on this race and figured the publicity was well worth the cost.

Races between the two firms to get the latest Eastern newspapers from the San Francisco docks to interior towns kept up the rivalry for business, and were followed with great interest by miners and others. Both outfits went into the letter-carrying trade, and Adams got out special 25-cent postage stamps. The Post Office Department cracked down in 1853 with an order that all letters carried by express must also carry United States postage. The order was obeyed to a certain extent, but the express companies, and particularly Wells Fargo, continued for many years to be the main reliance of pioneers for mail service in the remoter parts of the region.

Both concerns made a business of buying gold dust. Both operated banks. Adams & Company appear to have been rather careless in many things, including the losing of considerable quantities of gold dust. There were other banking firms, too, and in 1855 one of them, Page, Bacon & Company, underwent a run, started it was said because one of its drafts in the East had been dishonored. After paying out some $600,000, Page Bacon closed their doors. Public confidence, which had been undergoing pressure because of a number of small bank failures, was getting lower by the day, and runs now started on Adams, on Wells Fargo and other big banks. All closed their doors, and the city of San Francisco went into a panic. Almost 200 business houses, with liabilities of $8,000,000, were forced to suspend. Adams and many another concern went into bankruptcy. Wells, Fargo & Company continued to pay all of their obligations. When the smoke had cleared from the panic, they were the dominant express company on the Pacific Coast, and so they remained until they lost their identity in merger with the American Express many years later.

The original Adams & Company was still in business in the East and South. Just before the shot was fired at Sumter in 1861, a new concern, the Southern Express Company, suddenly took over all of the Adams business in seven Southern states in what Alvin F. Harlow calls "one of the deepest and foggiest of all the mysteries" in the history of American express companies. The Southern served the Confederate Army faithfully throughout the war, while in the North, Adams & Company all but had a monopoly of serving the Army and other government agencies. For the next four years messengers for both companies often traveled in cars piled high with coffins that were occupied. As the Northern armies gradually overran the South, the Adams company took over the routes given up by the Southern; and in 1866 it turned back these routes to the Southern.

Adams and Southern continued to work in close harmony after the war, so much so that certain stockholders in Adams believed that the Southern Company was merely a dummy, that high-up Adams men were getting a large income, undercover, from Southern. The affair finally broke out in a lawsuit, which failed but did bring to light some mighty odd business deals between Adams and Southern men. The Southern continued its identity until taken over in 1918 by American Railway Express.

During the last half of the century, Adams, American, and Wells Fargo often had to put down competitors, some of them operated by the railroads. The United States Express Company, a creature of the American, was first organized to operate on the Erie railroad. Then the Erie formed its own express, but later was happy to turn it back to the United States concern which, through new stockholders and officials later became stiff competition to the American in some areas. The National Express built up a big business with Montreal at its northern end, and was taken over and operated as a subsidy by American. The Eastern Express was formed of a number of tiny concerns to control business in Maine and much of New Hampshire before it was taken over by what in time came to be called the Express Trust. In the Far West Wells Fargo fought road agents and Ben Holladay's Overland Mail & Express Company. Their agents killed a good many of the road gentry, and Wells Fargo at last bought out Holladay, and also took over the bumptious Pacific Express.

For the most part the moguls of the express business became wealthy in a very short time, but nearly all of them continued to live without undue ostentation. It was said that by the 1870's express had made a hundred millionaires. Only one of them appears to have gone in for show. He was John Hoey who started as a clerk with Adams and rose to become general manager. Hoey built an atrocious mansion on Long Island, along with 130 acres of landscaped grounds, and went in for as vulgar a display of new wealth as the times could boast, thus causing many ordinarily unthinking people to believe there must be some money in the express business. Hoey the showoff, indeed, may have been an influence in the steadily mounting cry for regulation of the express companies.

Regulation was coming, too. As early as the 1880's a demand arose for a parcel post, operated by the government, to break the monopoly of the four great express concerns. The agitation never ceased for 30 years. The new Interstate Commerce Commission looked closely into the affairs of the express companies, then charged that they were guilty of double collections, exorbitant rates, unreasonable delays through indirect routings, excessive rates of insurance, and discrimination between shippers. Newspapers and magazines took up the cry. Cartoonists made the Express Trust of their pictures a fat, drooling ogre fit for the company of the fat drooling ogres of Steel, Meat, Sugar, and Railroads. In Congress, Senators Platt and Depew fought nobly against any regulation at all, but the pressure was becoming too great, and in 1913 government parcel post went into effect. At the same time Congress ordered express rates lowered. The stock values of all express companies declined.

The great and gouging days were over. In 1914 the United States Express folded up, the American taking part of its routes, Wells Fargo the remainder. When America entered the war in 1917, the government took over the railroads and began to seize and use express cars for hauling troop baggage and other materials of war. A year later the government merged the existing express concerns into one company, which presently became known as the American Railway Express Company. Into it went the Adams, American, Southern, and Wells Fargo. The office buildings of the American in New York and of Wells Fargo in Portland, Oregon, were excepted in the deal.

The merged company ceased to exist in 1929 when it was bought by 86 railroads, which reorganized it into the form in which it is known today, the Railway Express Agency. As of 1940, the Agency maintained service on some 12,000 trains a day, operating over 213,000 miles of railway line, plus 45,000 miles of air lines, and 20,000 miles of water lines. It employed 57,000 persons, had 23,000 offices, and operated 13,000 motor trucks, the largest single fleet in the country.

The Express Agency's services are as protean as ever they were in the great free and easy days. It accepts almost everything from fresh human blood for plasma, to hives of bees. It will redeem an article in pawn and return it to its now solvent owner. It will transport cobras, bulls, corpses. Race horses are one of its specialties. Tropical fruits and flowers and baby chickens come in great seasonable loads.

Railway Express Agency messengers, many of whom began work for one of the several older concerns, have acquitted themselves superbly in their dangerous and important duties. No class of men had more troubles and dangers to contend with than the messengers from the end of the

Civil War right down to the present, for holdups of trains more often than not were for the primary purpose of robbing the express cars. In defending their cars, the messengers have died by the score.* Even more have died in wrecks, the express car usually being well ahead in the train and liable to disaster in head-on collisions and derailments. Yet, there is something about the life of an express messenger that seems to hold the boys to their cars. It is to be doubted that there is another concern in the United States with proportionately as many veteran employees as will be found in the Railway Express Agency.

* A number of messengers are mentioned in Chapter XXXII.

CHAPTER XXVI

The Fast Mail

You are instructed to test by actual experience and upon such railroad route as you may select at Chicago, the plans proposed by you for simplifying the Mail Service.
—MONTGOMERY BLAIR, United States Postmaster General, to GEORGE B. ARMSTRONG, July 1, 1864.

T HE credit of conceiving and then of founding the Railway Mail Service belongs to George B. Armstrong, long an employee of the Post Office, who was assistant postmaster in Chicago in 1864, when he got his big idea. Before Armstrong, however, a clerk named W. A. Davis, in the Post Office at St. Joseph, Missouri, had come up with a suggestion that by sorting letters and other matter on the cars running between Quincy, Illinois, and St. Joseph, the overland mail for the West, made up in the latter city, could be greatly speeded.

Davis was given permission in 1862 to try his scheme. It was found to work pretty well and was still being used when Armstrong proposed a wide adaption of it two years later. Armstrong was fortunate that he made his proposal at a time when a highly intelligent man was Postmaster General, namely Montgomery Blair. On the first day of July, 1864, in reply to letters from Armstrong, Blair instructed that energetic man to test by actual experience "and upon such railroad route as you may select at Chicago, the plans proposed by you for simplifying the mail service." Up to this time, except as noted, the railroads had carried mail but the mails were locked in pouches.

Blair's encouragement was all Armstrong needed. He went immediately to the Chicago & North Western and arranged to try out his plan on the Galena Division. The railroad company took the drawings supplied by Armstrong and from them remodeled two or three old cars into the first railway mail cars. On August 28 one of these, in charge of mail clerks Leonard and Bradley, and accompanied by Armstrong himself and several newspapermen, started on the run from Chicago to Clinton, Iowa.

It is interesting to know that among the newspapermen on this occasion was Mr. Joseph Medill, of the *Chicago Tribune,* a paper as sure of its opinions in 1864, apparently, as it is today. Mr. Medill had said in his paper, in ridicule of Armstrong's idea, that the government would be obliged to employ a small army of men, just to follow each mail car in order to pick up the thousands of letters that would blow out of the car doors. Mr. Medill, indeed, vowed that the one and only way to transfer mail from one point to another on the steam cars was by locked mail pouch. All else, said he, was foolish. He and many another man of 1864 could not even conceive of such a thing as sorting letters while the cars were moving.

The experimental run on the C&NW was an unqualified success. So were subsequent runs. In December, Armstrong was given a newly created job, that of special agent of the Railway Mail Service, and told to put his plan into overall operation. His second mail-sorting run was between New York and Washington, which proved highly satisfactory to all concerned; and then he installed cars and the new service on the Rock Island, on the Burlington, the Alton, the Illinois Central, the Hannibal & St. Joseph, and the Erie, in quick succession, as fast as he could have cars remodeled or built to his specifications.

No further expansion was made for almost two years. This halting progress, says the historian of the Railway Mail Service, James E. White,* was due to the savage opposition of the heads of the great eastern distributing centers, by which he meant the postmasters of Boston, New York, Philadelphia, and Washington, who thought that the sorting of mail on the cars would somehow reduce the importance of their terminals. It is the same kind of opposition that most new ideas must meet.

There was little or no opposition in the West. Out there the railroad managers and the postmasters of Chicago and other cities welcomed the experiment of the traveling Post Office, novel though it was. The roads were quick to remodel cars for its use. The postmasters worked closely with Armstrong to detail their best men to act as clerks and the clerks, in turn, seem to have been on their mettle to prove that the system would improve mail delivery and speed it. And the mails *were* speeded, by hours in some cases, by whole days in others. News of the successful operation got around. By 1868 New England and other parts of the cautious East had given up their opposition and were glad to have the new service.

In 1869 Armstrong's ability was officially recognized. He was made the first general superintendent of Railway Mail Service and set out to devise and put into effect an overall and systematic practice for handling the mails. Up to this time there had been nothing approaching a system to cover all of the runs. Each division, and often each mail clerk, had its or his own method of sorting and distributing mail. Now Armstrong, assisted

---

* A long-time superintendent of the service, Mr. White wrote *A Life Span and Reminiscences of Railway Mail Service,* published in Philadelphia in 1910. A frontispiece shows him with Custer mustaches and goatee, keen eyes, a frock coat, and in its lapel the rosette of the Loyal Legion, fraternal group of Union veteran officers of the Civil War.

ably by his successor at Chicago, George S. Bangs, recommended to the Postmaster General that the United States be divided into six divisions, with headquarters in each at a central transportation point. The plan was approved. Five men designated as assistant superintendents were appointed and assigned, one to each of the first five divisions named in the list. The sixth embraced the vast and sparsely settled region west of the Rockies, including many star routes, and was left in charge of numerous special agents.

On the death of Armstrong in 1871 Bangs took charge of the Railway Mail Service. For the next five years he ran it with a strong hand and an unusual amount of intelligence. Under Bangs the miles of railroad upon which mail was carried and sorted nearly doubled. More important was the morale that he built up among the clerks and other employees. He believed that any change in the national administration should have no effect on the trained and specialized employees of the government, such as those in his department, that they should be certain of their jobs so long as their behavior and efficiency were good. He made promotions from the ranks and could not be bullied into employing political catchpoles. Indeed, Bangs probably had as much to do with starting the civil-service reform movement as any other man.

Bangs had one more good idea—a fast mail train, to carry nothing but mail and to make the run from New York to Chicago in twenty-four hours. In 1874 he made such a proposal to the Post Office. It was approved, but no appropriation for it was made. So Bangs went to old Commodore Vanderbilt and asked if the New York Central would build twenty special cars for such a train and operate on the fast schedule indicated. Old Vanderbilt, better known for his shrewdness than for his public spirit, was less than interested. Bangs did not give up. He went to the Commodore's son, William H. Vanderbilt, and talked him into building the needed cars and agreeing to operate the train. In return, said Bangs, the New York Central should carry all matter originating at or coming into the New York Post Office which could best be delivered to destination by the Central. The railroad company should have the right to demand a weighing of mail matter at will, and was to be paid by weight.

When the old Commodore learned of the deal made by his son he did not attempt to countermand it, but merely remarked to William H., "If you want to do this, then go ahead, but I *know* the Post Office Department, and so will you, within a year." And so William H. did, and one can wonder if the Commodore could have resisted rubbing it in a little bit. But the business started out well. The New York Central built the special cars, beauties, and arranged its schedules to permit clear tracks for the *Fast Mail* all the way to Chicago.

The train was manned by the best clerks the service could muster. Sacks of different colors were provided to help speed the sorting and distributing process. From its first trip the *Fast Mail*, running over tracks of the New York Central and its affiliated Lake Shore & Michigan Southern was a success. So, too, was the *Limited Mail* established almost simultaneously over the Pennsylvania Railroad from Philadelphia to the West. Both trains were speeding the mails when Congress, despite efforts of the Post Office Department, passed an act reducing "the already inadequate compensation" to the lines carrying mail. The Messrs. Vanderbilt and Scott of the Central and the Pennsylvania immediately ordered discontinuance of their mail trains. Old Commodore Vanderbilt had been right.

As for General Superintendent Bangs, he was so mortified at the action of Congress that he resigned his position, a wholly disheartened man. Yet, his *Fast Mail* had been sound and it was shortly revived through the efforts of Bangs' successor, Theodore Newton Vail, who was presently to depart for the field of the telephone and telegraph. Vail managed to get new appropriations from Congress and in 1877 the Fast Mails between the East Coast and Chicago were resumed. A bit later the *Fast Mail* idea was extended, with runs from Chicago west to connect with the Union Pacific, which took over and carried the mails to the Pacific Coast on regular passenger and mail trains.

From the first the *Fast Mail* had taken the fancy of the general public. A song was written around it, and then came plays, perhaps a dozen of them, all having to do with fast mail trains. The thought of a special train, devoted wholly to written and printed communications of one kind and another, was cherished by the people. The picking up of mail pouches from the stanchions of way stations, while the cars fled past, was dramatic. The sorting of letters while the cars thundered on through the night seemed wonderful—and it *was* wonderful. Railway mail clerks became interesting if not quite romantic figures, and within a short time at least one private school was established to teach the art of the railway mail clerk, properly enough by correspondence.

A serious hazard to all railway mail clerks was the accidents and wrecks, in only too many of which the clerks played the part of victims. In almost every wreck, the postal car, being up forward, was derailed or smashed, and often burned. From 1876 to 1905, there were 9,355 accidents to trains carrying postal cars. In these collisions and derailments a total of 207 clerks were killed, 1,516 others seriously injured, and 3,764 more slightly injured. That adds up to 5,280 casualties, or more than one casualty to every two accidents.

A one-time Postmaster General, Thomas L. James, took occasion to stress to the public the dangers of the railway mail clerk's calling. But, he said, in his eloquent plea, the danger was but one reason why the postal clerks should be paid better wages. No other government position, he said, called for so many requirements. The railway mail clerk must be possessed of "more than ordinary intelligence, and a retentive memory. His work is constant, and his only recreation, study. He must not only be proficient in his immediate work, but he must have a general knowledge of the entire country, all forty-eight states, so that the correspondence he handles shall reach its destination at the earliest possible moment.

"He must know no night and no day," cried Mr. James. "He must be impervious to heat and cold. Rushing along at the rate of forty or fifty miles an hour, in charge of that which is sacred—the correspondence of the people—catching his meals as he may; at home only semi-occasionally, the wonder is that men competent to discharge the duties of so high a calling can be found for so small a competence, and for so uncertain a tenure of official life. They have not only to take the extrahazardous risks of their toilsome duties, but they are at the mercy of the practical politicians who believe that to the victor belong the spoils."

Perhaps Mr. James should wonder why men could be found of such quality and who would put up with the vagaries and dangers of the life. But it would seem clear enough that the reason was the same as that which caught other men and made them into railroaders—namely, the magic of the railroad, the sights, the sounds, the movement, the changing scene, the very smells of the railroad. No matter what the reason, the magic of the railroad was sufficient to attract and to hold men by ties that became, in time, closer than those of blood.

The role of the railway postal worker has improved steadily since the time when Postmaster General James spoke up for him. In the end, civil service reached him in fact as well as in name. So did the Railway Mail Association, a sort of union and benefit society founded in 1891 which has contributed much to the advancement of members of the service. Beginning as an independent group, the Association soon ran head-on into opposition by the Post Office Department, which issued a gag order prohibiting employees of the United States from joining any association the purpose of which was "to solicit an increase of pay or to influence or attempt to influence in their interest," any legislation.

The postal clerks ignored the order, and the Post Office set about intimidating them by espionage and discipline, sometimes removing the more outspoken clerks "for the good of the service." It was even charged that Post Office inspectors opened private mail of workers suspected of being active in the movement.* Then, in 1912, the American Federation of Labor entered wholeheartedly into the battle, and late that year Congress passed the so-called Lloyd-LaFollette bill, establishing the right of government workers to organize for their own benefit. In 1917 the Railway Mail Association was issued a charter by the Federation.

---

* See a pamphlet, *The Railway Mail Association and the Railway Postal Clerk*, 1891–1946, published by the Association, 1946.

The postal clerk's salary grew better, not much, but better. A pension plan, one of the best in the country, was put into effect. The railway postal cars improved. In 1936 a speed differential was established for clerks on fast trains, and since then a number of new regulations and salary adjustments have made the lot of the railway postal clerk compare favorably with that of any other public-service employee. Moreover, he still rides the *Fast Mail*, and perhaps that is the chief reason why the rifts in his ranks caused by retirements are readily filled. The magic of the moving train has not been wholly dissipated by the mail that goes by air.

Backbone of the railroad industry is coal. We see here the Norfolk & Western freight classification yard at Williamson, W. Va., and (below) a locomotive fireman taking on a tender load of "black diamonds."

Filling the sand dome of a Norfolk & Western locomotive. Clean, dry sand increases driving-wheel grip on wet rails by as much as 25 percent.

CHAPTER XXVII

The Story of the Sleeping Car

To the train on the Chicago, Alton & St. Louis Railroad, which passed up at noon today, was attached one of Pullman's improved and beautiful sleeping carriages . . . We are informed by Mr. Pullman himself that these cars will hereafter be run on this line . . .
—Daily Illinois State Register, Springfield, Ill., May 26, 1865.

YEARS before there was any railroad in the country extensive enough to call for travel at night, inventive minds were at work on the notion of a sleeping car. In 1829 there appeared in Boston one R. F. Morgan of Stockbridge, Massachusetts, a man of many ideas regarding railroads. Three years previously he had surveyed, partly on his own and partly aided by funds from friends, a route for a railroad to run from Albany, New York, to Springfield, Massachusetts. As a surveyor he was pretty good, for his route turned out years later to be almost precisely that adopted by the Boston & Albany line.

Morgan also turned his attention to wheels for railroad cars, and presently designed such a free wheeling job that he claimed friction was reduced almost to nothing. It was this wheel idea that took him to Boston in 1829. There in Fanueil Hall he exhibited the wheel under auspices of the new and locally organized Rail Road Association. He also exhibited what was probably the first special design for a sleeping car. 'Twas a fearful thing to behold, this Morgan's Rail Road Carriage, a double-decker so big that the reporter of the *American Traveller* of Boston termed it a land barge.

The upper level was to be a sort of promenade deck, complete with benches and covered with awning, and also containing what Morgan said was a "captain's office." The lower level was inclosed and contained five "births," a spelling the *Traveller* did not take the trouble to correct. And because in those days decor was an absolute necessity, a cupola rose beautifully from the stern of the top deck and was surmounted by an American flag. Apparently Morgan did not patent his land barge, but soon dropped it and went on to other things.

The idea of a sleeping car, with experiments in 1836–37 on the Cumberland Valley R.R., continued to bemuse the minds of the countless Americans who were thinking up things for the new railroads, and in 1838 a plan for a sleeping car was actually patented by one Charles McGraw. Nothing seems to have come from Mr. McGraw's patent, although in the same year the *Baltimore Chronicle* reported that "cars intended for night travel" between that city and Philadelphia had gone into use. They were truly wonderful, said the *Chronicle,* for you could "go to rest in a pleasant berth, sleep as soundly as in your own bed at home, and on awakening next morning find yourself at the end of your journey, and in time to take your passage to New York if you are bent there." One need not be a cynic to doubt the basic accuracy of that statement.

It is doubtful, judging from a contemporary account, that sleeping cars had improved very much by 1843, when the New York & Erie railroad had two built and put into use. They were named the *Erie* and the *Ontario,* but they were known as the *Diamond Cars* because their windows were in that shape. The frames of the seats were stationary, the cushions loose. Two iron rods could be slid from under one seat and fitted into holes in the frame of the other seat, then the seat cushions moved onto the bars, and the back cushions moved down flat, the whole making a sort of couch. Incidentally, the cushions were of horsehair cloth, to which only the thickest clothing was impervious. There were no pillows or bedclothes, and travelers went to bed boots, saddles and all. But the Erie's diamond cars were found too heavy for use, and soon became boarding houses for track crews.*

The idea of the sleeping car, however, was sound and many men were pondering it. In the latter part of the 1850 decade at least three of them got down to actual work. It matters little who was first, for in the end it was George Pullman who came to build and operate the sleeping cars of the nation.

In 1858 the depot master of the New York Central station at Palatine Bridge, New York, went to Commodore Vanderbilt with designs of a sleeping car. He was Webster Wagner, a former wagonmaker, born in 1817. The plans looked good to the Commodore and he aided Wagner with money to build four cars. They were well made, and had a single tier of berths, and bedding closets at each end of the car. They were put into use on the Central immediately and within a few months were extremely popular, even though Wagner did have a time of it to get his patrons to take off at least their boots before they retired.

Now Wagner, still aided by Vanderbilt, organized the New York Central

---

* Though they were not successful, the Erie's diamond cars of 1843 played a part 36 years later. When the Pullman company brought suit in 1879 for infringement against the Wagner Sleeping Car Company, it was "so nonplussed at revelations made in regard to the Erie sleeping cars of 1843, that a halt was called in the proceedings and both Pullman and Wagner concluded it would not do to stand a legal test of their rights, so they compromised and agreed to share in the profits of an invention which was old long before either of the claimants had thought of making it his own."

Sleeping Car Company to build and operate cars exclusively for that road. In 1865 Wagner evolved a drawing-room car—a sort of parlor car—that was dolled up fit to kill with mirrors, polished woods, fine upholstery. This too was a quick success, and now Wagner reorganized to become the Wagner Palace Car Company, out of which he and his associates made fortunes, though not without tangling with George Pullman, of which more later.

While Wagner was getting under way, G. B. Gates, an official of the Lake Shore Railroad, began to make his own sleepers for use on the Lake Shore. In 1869 when the Lake Shore was taken over by the New York Central, Wagner absorbed the Gates Sleeping Car Company.

Meanwhile, too, Edward Collings Knight, who already had made his pile in sugar and other ventures, thought up a sleeping car and was presently building them for the Baltimore & Ohio and the Camden & Amboy roads. Knight's sleepers, naturally known to all punsters as "Knights," were even more elegant than those made by Wagner. Knight apparently built the best car he could conceive of, using only the finest materials. His cars had berths only on one side, and were three high, two of them double-berths, one single-berth.

Then came T. T. Woodruff, master car builder of the Terre Haute & Alton, who built a series of sleepers that had twelve sections, six on a side; and incorporated a car building company capitalized at $100,000. A little later, and at the unlikely spot of Bangor, Maine, a short-lived concern called the Flower Sleeping Car Company was formed and began putting out a car with the seats down the middle, thus leaving an aisle on each side. In this type of car two berths could be made up into a double bed, if wanted, and one of the claims made for the Flower car was that there was a much freer circulation of air than in other cars.

And now came the celebrated, or at least notorious, Colonel William D'Alton Mann, to design, at first only for the European trade, then for American lines also, the elegant and ingenious Mann's Boudoir Car. It was Mann who really gave Europe the sleeper, and he organized the Compagnie Internationale des Wagons-Lits to supply the demand for them. The Mann job was divided into compartments, or boudoirs as that esthete liked to call them, each entered directly from the side, and "connected by a private door permitting the passage of the attendant to and through the several compartments." Each compartment contained four seats, which by night could be made into beds, although the Mann Boudoirs designed for and operated in the United States had compartments for two persons. They were pretty elegant, too, but their smaller passenger capacity called for a higher rate per passenger than was charged in other sleepers.

"Knights" or "Palace cars" or "Boudoirs," it was all the same to George Mortimer Pullman, the genius of the bed on wheels, who was to take over or break all of his competitors inside of 30 years.

When Pullman arrived in Chicago in 1855 he was twenty-four years old. Chicago itself was even younger, but it was lusty and growing like mad. Already it had started to dredge its river in an effort to turn the swamp that was Michigan, Wabash, and State streets—where frogs and mosquitoes sang—into something like solid land. The streets had to be raised, and the buildings too, among them the Tremont House, Chicago's skyscraper, four stories tall, all of brick. Pullman had registered at the Tremont, and now he heard talk that the hotel's proprietors saw no way other than to tear down their hotel and rebuild it. You could not move so big a brick building.

Pullman had learned something about brick buildings. In small Albion, New York, where for ten years he had been working with a brother at cabinet making, it had been found necessary to widen the Erie Canal, which passed through the village. Pullman studied the matter, and took first one, then several contracts for moving Albion's brick houses back to where the new banks of the canal would be. He carried out these contracts successfully.

Now in Chicago he went to the Tremont's owners and told them he could move their hotel, colossus though it was, without so much as breaking a pane of glass or tipping the froth off a beer in the refectory. The Tremont men were skeptical, but they told the young man to go ahead. He did. Within a few hours Pullman had assembled twelve hundred workers and some five thousand jackscrews. He put them all in the basement, had them get set, then on a signal each man gave four screws a half turn. Slowly, gently, so gradually that life in the hotel went on uninterrupted, the big brick building went up inch by inch until the desired level was reached. Not a chambermaid blinked an eye, nor dropped any crockery.

Raising the Tremont had been an easy task for young Pullman, but it made quite a noise in the newspapers and he became a noted citizen of the bustling metropolis scarcely before he had shaken the mud of upstate New York off his shoes. Many more raising jobs came his way. He took them all, did them well, and started to accumulate some capital. Like many another man of the period, as we have seen, Pullman had been giving thought to a sleeping car. He was now in a city that fully intended, quite consciously, to become the railroad center of the United States. Many lines already were branching out from the foot of the lake—the Illinois Central, the Burlington, the Chicago & North Western, the Alton. To the Chicago & Alton went young Pullman with his sleeping-car idea. Mildly interested, that road gave him two day coaches which constituted exactly one-sixth of the road's rolling stock and told him to see what he could do with them, with his own money, of course.

The two coaches that were to become the first Pullman cars were 44 feet long, flat-roofed, with the roof a little more than 6 feet from the floor of the car. There were 14 windows to a side, each window containing but one pane of glass and that one foot square. Pullman hired Leonard Seibert, a mechanic of the Alton road, to help him remodel the cars during the summer of 1858. Seibert recalled in later years, when he had become something of a historical character by reason of his work on the first Pullmans, that he and Pullman went ahead with no blueprints or drawn plans of any sort. Pullman outlined his ideas, the two men made measurements, cut material to fit, then put the pieces together.

Young Pullman's idea of what constituted a bed may be gleaned by knowing that he and Seibert put ten sleeping sections into each of the cars, plus a linen locker and two washrooms, which must have left the bunks little if any more than six feet in length. Pullman wanted to use hickory for the seats and berths, but had to accept cherry wood instead. But into these two cars went Pullman's own idea of an upper berth that could be closed when not in use and also serve to hold the bedding for both upper and lower beds; it was here that Pullman made his first great contribution to the sleeping car.

The upper berth that disappeared during the day was really a radical innovation, brilliant and practical compared to other sleeping cars of the time the bunks of which were permanently placed. But not yet had Pullman arrived at his hinged upper berth. In these first two Pullmans iron rods ran from floor to ceiling. The upper berth was suspended from the ceiling by ropes and pulleys attached to each of the four corners. During the day the berth was pulled up snug to the roof, and by night was let down about halfway between roof and floor. Curtains were used in front and between the berths. The cars had a wood stove at each end. Lighting was still by candle. There were blankets and pillows, but no sheets.

On the night of September 1, 1858, the first run of one of these primeval Pullmans was made from Bloomington to Chicago. In charge of the sleeper was twenty-two-year-old J. L. Barnes, hired by George Pullman himself, who was also aboard, as the first Pullman conductor. Conductor Barnes wore some sort of badge, but no uniform. The car was filled, every berth taken, all men. Bloomington had no way of knowing what was afoot that night, and no crowd came down to see the first Pullman start its journey. "We moved out of the station," recalled Conductor Barnes many years after, "in solitary grandeur. I remember on that first night I had to compel the passengers to take their boots off before they got into the berths. They wanted to keep them on—seemed afraid to take them off."

The first month found business just so-so; but it started to pick up and within a short time the two Pullmans were proving so popular on the Chicago & Alton that a third car was converted. The idea did not spread, however, and George Pullman dropped the scheme and went to Colorado, scene of a mining boom, where for the next four years he conducted a store and continued to work on plans for a better sleeping car.

He saved his money and in 1863 returned to Chicago with the one idea of making a sleeping car that would be worthy the name.

Talking a boyhood friend, Ben Field of Albion, New York, into a partnership, Pullman and Field applied for and in 1864 were granted two patents, one for the hinged upper berth (No. 42,182), one for hinging the back and seat cushions so that the back could be placed on the seat and the seat cushion extended to meet that of the opposite seat (No. 49,992). Both devices remain unchanged in principle to this day.

Now, indeed, George Pullman had what was needed, but if he had not also possessed great staying powers and salesmanship approaching genius, he might well have given up. It was to be hard going for a while, or until the death of President Lincoln dropped into Pullman's lap a wondrous opportunity of which Pullman made the most. First, of course, Pullman & Field had to incorporate the new ideas into material form. In a shed belonging to the Alton Railroad, on the site now occupied by the Union Station in Chicago, Pullman and Field with artisans took almost a year to build the finest sleeping car ever seen up to that time. Fully equipped, it cost Pullman and his partner all of their capital, or a little more than twenty thousand dollars.

Up to the building of this sleeper, which was named the *Pioneer*, not more than $5,000 had ever been expended on a railway car of any kind. To begin with, the *Pioneer* was a foot wider and two and one-half feet higher than any other car then in service. It rested on improved trucks with springs reinforced by blocks of solid rubber. Every bit of space was utilized, and no iron rods from floor to ceiling marred the beauty of the interior; those upper berth hinges worked to perfection, making by day a clear, uncluttered view from end to end.

The woodwork, the upholstery, and the hangings were magnificent. Much hand carving went into the seats and panels. There was a plush carpet, many mirrors. At one stride, said a historian of the company, an advance of fifty years had been effected.

Whether or not George Pullman knew that the dimensions of his *Pioneer* were too large to permit its passage through many of the stations and bridges of the Chicago & Alton, or of any other railroad of the day for that matter, is not now known. Quite probably he did, and if he did, he must have had a deep faith indeed in his new sleeping car to believe that railroads would change their depot platforms and their bridges just for the sake of drawing it over their lines.

Tradition has it that Mrs. Lincoln, on a visit to Illinois early in 1865, saw and inspected Mr. Pullman's *Pioneer*, and was enchanted. She did not forget its beauty, and when the funeral train to carry the President from Washington to Springfield was being prepared, the widow is said to have requested that the *Pioneer* be attached to it at Chicago for her own use on the remainder of the journey. The request of a President's widow is not to be refused, and the Chicago & Alton, over whose tracks the train would proceed to Springfield, set crews to work hurriedly narrowing the platforms of their way stations and widening the sides of their bridges.

Slowly the funeral train crawled north and west from Washington. Baltimore, Philadelphia, New York, each must pay its homage, at each the body of the tall, gaunt man must lie in state while hundreds of thousands looked upon the lined face, or at least saw the enormous coffin. At Albany sixty thousand persons crowded the draped streets, and four thousand an hour passed by the open casket. Moving out of the city the train ran under arches made of evergreens and flowers. At every stop thirty-six young women, representing the thirty-six states, dressed in white, with black rosettes on their shoulders, sang or recited tributes, and left morbid mottoes in the hearse car. All through the night bonfires lighted the tracks at way stations and much of the way in between, while cannon, many dating back to the War of 1812, thundered a bass to the turning wheels. Buffalo, Cleveland, then south to Columbus, to Milford, Urbana, Conners, Piqua, Richmond and Indianapolis, at last into Illinois and so to Chicago.

The Alton's line was ready to take the funeral train, couple on the *Pioneer* and proceed to the end of the journey. On May 2nd it pulled out of Chicago under special orders the like of which had not been seen before nor since. The Alton's tracks were, of course, cleared. A pilot engine ran ten minutes ahead of the train, and the pilot could not pass any station unless a white flag by day, or red and white lanterns at night, were displayed. All telegraph stations were kept open continuously. A guard armed with flag and lantern stood at each crossing. The train slowed down as it passed every station, no matter how unimportant, and always the engine's bell was tolled. It tolled through Fort Wayne Junction, through Bridgeport, Summit, Joy's, Lemont, Lockport, Joliet, Stewart's Grove, and finally through Sherman, Sangamon and into Springfield.*

Whether or not tradition is right in attributing the quick success of Pullman's new and elegant sleeping car to the whim of Mrs. Lincoln is of little moment, but from this time forward there was no doubt but that George Mortimer Pullman had an idea and ability to be reckoned with. Not long after the Lincoln train, General U. S. Grant rode the Pullman *Pioneer* from Detroit to his old home of Galena, and the Chicago & North Western made the depot platform and the bridge alterations necessary for its passage.

By this time Pullman had engaged a small crew of expert workmen and had set them to building more cars like the *Pioneer*. And presently the rising young industrialist proposed to the Chicago & Alton, which had given him his first and to date only encouragement, that he build and oper-

---

* A dramatic yet realistic account of the funeral train appears in Lloyd Lewis's *Myths After Lincoln*, New York, 1929.

ate sleeping cars for them. The company liked the idea and in this agreement was the genesis of the whole Pullman business.

Pullman's *Pioneer* had cost $20,000 to build. His second, third and perhaps a dozen more cost $24,000 each. They were by far the finest things on wheels in the United States and Pullman intended the public should pay more for riding in them than in the common variety of sleepers. Organizing the Pullman Palace Car Company in 1867, he placed several of his cars on the Michigan Central and charged 50 cents more per night than the Central charged in its own sleepers. There was no argument. The public was glad to pay the premium, and the other sleepers went begging. Pullman put other cars on the Burlington, then on the Great Western (Grand Trunk). He established his works for a time in Palmyra, New York, but soon moved to Detroit, which for the next decade was the home of the Pullman Palace Cars.

In 1867, too, Pullman made and tried out on the Great Western what he called a Hotel Car. This was a combination sleeping and eating car—berths, with a kitchen in one end of the car, and removable tables set between the seats at mealtimes. This may not have been the first car in which meals were cooked for passengers, but it was unquestionably the finest, for Pullman would have nothing shoddy. Pullman was always an excellent publicist, and this first hotel car was introduced with fanfare and an excursion from Chicago to New York, taking seven days for the trip. Loaded with notables, and marking inauguration of a standard-gauge track between the two big cities that permitted the same cars to pass over the entire trackage, it was heralded as a great event. Pullman sleepers were in the train too, you may be sure, and the party made stops all along the way. Newspapers made much of it, even printing the menu of the hotel car, which, incidentally, offered sugar-cured ham at 40 cents, beefsteak with potatoes at 60 cents, a welsh rarebit at half a dollar.

The hotel-car idea was half way to the diner, and a year later Pullman himself designed his first diner which he named *Delmonico*, after the eminent restaurateur, and put into service on the Chicago & Alton, the guinea-pig route for all of Pullman's experiments. The dining car caught on quickly. Pullman built and also operated diners on a number of lines, while for others he simply built the cars and left them to the individual lines to operate.

Even with high prices of food, and waiters subsidized by the public with tips, few if any railroads ever made money on their dining cars. The opposite has rather been the case. Many a road, faced with strong competition for passengers, has sought to attract trade by serving excellent meals at comparatively low rates. And in 1946, one road, the Pere Marquette, announced that on June 10th it would take an extraordinary, almost a revolutionary step; on that day it would prohibit tipping in its dining cars. "No dagger glances from waiters will follow this step," said a Pere Marquette announcement, "since the company has arranged to compensate workers for any loss incurred."

In 1869 the plains, the mountains, and the Great American Desert were spanned by rails. Pullman was ready for the opportunity, and at once he set his men to building a whole train of special hotel, drawing-room, and sleeping cars, more magnificent even than anything he had conceived before, and at the same time promoted the idea of a first transcontinental trip by steam train, in the same cars, without change, from Boston to San Francisco. The trip was made in 1870, and it was no less than a stroke of genius on Pullman's part.* When it was done, Pullman was perhaps the foremost industrial name in the United States, and railroads tumbled over themselves to get contracts with Mr. Pullman to operate his wondrous cars on their lines. Even the Pennsylvania, which had made considerable effort with its own sleeping and dining cars, abandoned its service and came to Pullman.

One should not lose sight of the fact that Pullman did not offer only fine cars to the railroads. His cars, indeed, were the simplest part of the deal. Pullman undertook to operate them, and it was in this department that he revealed even more ability than in his manufacture. There were no precedents to go on. George Pullman had to lay his plans as he went along, then to change them by the trial-and-error method, always costly but usually sure. Slowly he evolved the conception of a system by which passengers might be carried in comfort to almost any part of the nation in cars of uniform construction, equipped for day and night travel, and served and protected by trained employees of Pullman, not of the railroads, whose sole function was to provide for the passenger's safety, comfort, and convenience.

It was a gigantic task, this building a company, a big business, on a new conception, and Pullman, together with his brother, whom he made general superintendent, and advisers, whom he chose with shrewdness, were just the men to do it. And Pullman was not long in being assured of adequate capital. One of his big stockholders was Marshall Field, the Chicago merchant who in time became what many thought was dictator to Pullman.

Business of the Pullman Palace Car Company continued to increase through bad years and good, and in 1881 Pullman built a feudal and what many contemporaries held to be the finest "company town" in the country. This was Pullman, on the outskirts of Chicago, which for sixteen years continued to be a separate municipality. That Pullman's rents were too high, the public services too costly, and the wages too low, was made all too apparent in 1894 and after, when a strike and an investigation took

---

* This monumental journey seems so important and amusing I have devoted a separate chapter to it. See Chapter 30.

the headlines of the nation. But it was in Pullman that 20,000 men worked and made Pullman cars to roll up and down and across a continent.

George Pullman believed in fine cars and also in monopoly. When a competitor showed himself troublesome, Pullman either bought him out, at Pullman's price, or broke him. Knight, Woodruff, Flower, Mann, they all went down before Pullman; and in 1881 Pullman went after the Wagner company, charging infringement of patents to the tune of one million dollars; and again in 1888 he sued Wagner for infringement of patent on the vestibule just put into use by Pullman. Court battles in both cases were extensive. Wagner was probably in the wrong, or at least so the courts found, and Pullman presently took over the last of his competitors.

Webster Wagner himself was cremated in one of his own sleepers, in an accident due to a rear-end collision, at Spuyten Duyvil, New York, January 13, 1882.

No matter what you might say about George Pullman, he and his men were always just a little in advance of their competitors. Pullman adopted kerosene lamps ahead of almost everyone. He introduced to America the brilliant Pintsch light from Europe, for many years thereafter the standard illumination in all railroad passenger cars. When the electric light was ready, Pullman adopted it, just as he did a succession of constantly improving generators. Pullman probably was the first to introduce bed linen to the rails, linen changed every day, and for many years this service proved no end of trouble. The company hung large placards in every car: "Please Take Off Your Boots Before Retiring," and printed the same request on all its tickets.

Pullman washrooms and toilets grew in elegance and ingenuity. Horsehair seats gave way to plush, then to leather, then to synthetic materials. Any inventor of gadgets or designer of new furnishings went to Pullman with them, and anyone who had something really new and good to offer was given a hearing.

The first Pullman conductor, J. L. Barnes, who rode those first candlelit sleepers on the Alton, was the progenitor of thousands of Pullman conductors, many if not all of whom have been successful as combined railroad men, hotel clerks, physicians, diplomats, mathematicians and, in a pinch, bouncers. One of them, Gardner Stratton, who retired in 1945 after more than half a century for Pullman, saw a good deal of the United States through Pullman windows. He ran on the Great Northern, the Louisville & Nashville, the Pennsylvania, the Central of Georgia, Atlantic Coast Lines, Union Pacific, Chicago & North Western, the Monon Route, New York Central, Chicago & Alton, Chicago, Burlington & Quincy, Los Angeles & Salt Lake, Rock Island, Frisco Lines, Southern Pacific, Denver & Rio Grande Western, Santa Fe, Michigan Central, Pere Marquette, and the Soo Line.

Yes, Pullman conductors got around some. Veteran Stratton recalls one run on the Great Northern when his train was stuck for more than two days in mighty snow drifts near Glacier, Montana. Food got low, and all hands were rationed, but nobody went actually hungry. The snows were so packed, Stratton tells, that when the big rotary plow struck them, it seemed to bounce back, again and again.

Gamblers on the Western lines used to give Pullman conductors trouble in former times, says Stratton, but they have been scarce in the past ten years or so. At one time the Pullman company supplied its conductors with small cards, the size of calling cards, on which was printed in script: "It is dangerous to play cards with strangers." Stratton used to pack a few of these in his pocket, and if a situation seemed to warrant it because he knew professional gamblers were involved in the game, he would quietly hand a card to the suckers.

One strongly enforced rule of the Pullman Company was that if death came to a passenger, the corpse was to be put off at the *next* station, no matter whether the town possessed an undertaker or not. One time an ill man, a stretcher case, was put aboard Stratton's car at a flagstop in Montana. The man was accompanied by a sad-eyed woman. The couple were given a stateroom. Stratton noticed the man looked as if he had not long to live, and in about half an hour Stratton went into the room and spoke to him. The man said nothing, though his eyes were open and staring. Feeling his pulse, the conductor realized he had a dead man in his stateroom.

Well, Stratton knew the rule about the *next* station which, in this case, was a forlorn place with a couple of houses and a water tank. He looked at the sad-eyed woman. "Her face was too much for me," he related. "I pretended the man wasn't dead and didn't die until just before we pulled into the next divisional point, Whitefish, where I knew there was an under-taker."

Stratton is of the opinion that a Pullman conductor's work is primarily much the same as that of a head clerk or manager of a hotel. Good porters lessen his work; shoddy or inexperienced porters can make the job almost unbearable. Only a very small part of the traveling public, says Stratton, are difficult to handle. The few trouble-makers are probably congenital, he believes, and neither an excellent porter nor a good conductor has any effect on them.

I have good reason to remember one Pullman conductor. He is F. W. Colson of Chicago. A few years ago, in Washington, D. C., I boarded the Pennsylvania's *Liberty Limited,* having given my large suitcase to a Union Station redcap. When, at about five minutes before departure the boy had not arrived with my baggage, I went to the Pullman Conductor, Mr. Colson—wholly a stranger to me—and told him the situation. He tried to be cheerful about it, but I knew as well as he that we would probably take off without my suitcase. Sure enough, we did.

My suitcase not only contained clothing and so forth, all of which could have been replaced if lost, but in it were some 20,000 words in notes I had made hurriedly for the purpose of writing a book. No carbon of these notes existed. I had been three weeks, working day and into the night, to make them—interviews with soldiers and sailors and Army nurses. If the notes were lost, then lost too was the book I had contracted to write. I was pretty low.

The *Liberty Limited* pulled smoothly out of Washington's station and away we went. No redcap, no suitcase. I walked forward through the long train, asking each Pullman porter if he had a piece of baggage not accounted for. None had. Then I started through one of the diners and met a Pullman attendant (not a porter) who was staggering under the weight of my big suitcase. I was staggered, too, and with joy.

It turned out that Pullman Conductor Colson, a most alert man, had been watching the depot platform, and just as our train was about to leave, he saw a redcap trying to put a huge suitcase aboard a train on the next track, a train, incidentally, heading for St. Louis, not Chicago. Colson took a chance. He shouted to the redcap to give *him* the baggage, and this the boy did just as our train started moving. Colson took it aboard far ahead on our train, then started it back for my car by the attendant. I do not say that Conductor Colson's quick thinking and action saved for posterity a gorgeous piece of Literature with a capital letter; but it did save for a hard-working writer the fruits of three weeks' continuous labor, and the book did appear. And you may be sure I wrote a note of deep appreciation to the Pullman Company, as soon as we got to Chicago.

As I remarked a while back, the name of the first Pullman conductor is known. It is unfortunate that the name of the first Pullman porter isn't. He was the progenitor of a class of men who are unique and who deserve special treatment.

CHAPTER XXVIII

The Life of the Pullman Porter

To Porter John W. Blair, for gallant and faithful discharge of duty in the Year 1894, on Limited Train No. 4, in Forest Fires, Sept. 1.
—Citation by the St. Paul & Duluth Railroad Company.

ONE October evening in 1937 a stunning blonde about thirty years old engaged a Pullman compartment on a Great Northern train leaving Portland, Oregon, for Seattle. She was tall and graceful, modishly dressed in dark blue, right up to her earrings; and the porter on her car, a man we will call Johnson for that was not his name, still thinks she was the handsomest woman he has ever seen. Nor was her luggage, he recalls, met with every day. It was handmade to the last stitch and rivet.

An hour or so later, as the train was leaving Kelso, Washington, the lady rang for Porter Johnson and then handed him a letter in a pale blue envelope. "I want you to be sure," she said with emphasis, "to mail this at Aberdeen—and nowhere else." She gave him a quarter.

Porter Johnson told the woman, truthfully, that the train did not go to or even near Aberdeen, a seacoast town. She appeared stunned for a moment, and a look of desperation hardened her face. She was obviously, the porter now came to see, in a highly nervous state. Her small hand shook. "This letter," she said, "simply *must* be mailed in Aberdeen— and nowhere else—by tomorrow morning." Saying which, she put a twenty-dollar bill in Porter Johnson's hand. "Can't you arrange it somehow?" she pleaded. "It's almost a matter—a matter of life or death." Porter Johnson, who like most of his craft was and is a man of quick thinking and practically unlimited resources, considered hard for a moment, then told the blonde that he thought he could handle the matter. At Centralia, as the porter knew, his Great Northern train (a pooled train with the NP and the UP) would stop briefly for water and exchange of passengers, mail, and express. Centralia was a junction point from which a Northern Pacific local would depart for Aberdeen as soon as the Great Northern main-line train had discharged its passengers. The porter knew that the two-car local did not carry a Pullman or porter.

At the exact moment Jim Hill's train of cars came to a stop that rainy night in Centralia, Porter Johnson hit the long platform and when he hit

he was running like the wind. He dashed forward almost the full length
of his train, crossed over to the NP tracks and peered through the gloom
at the local's conductor. Luck had it he was a man with whom Johnson
had run in the past. Johnson handed him the pale blue letter and a one-
dollar bill—a five would have looked suspicious—and told the conductor
about mailing it in Aberdeen. Then he hurried back to his own train and
car.

So far as Porter Johnson knows, the letter was mailed late that night
in Aberdeen, and today, he says, he would give at least half of that
twenty-dollar bill to know what it was all about. He has never since seen
the lady in blue.

Things like the lady and the letter happen often in the lives of the nine
thousand Pullman porters who ride up and down and across the country
every day and night of the year. Small adventure comes to them in plenty,
over the clicking rails, and sometimes they have really big moments—
like finding $75,000 in jewelry scattered around in a car, or opening the
door of a drawing room at command of federal officers who want to talk
to the occupant, an inoffensive little man who, it turns out, has murder on
his hands and fifty thousand dollars in his suitcase.

But Pullman porters are the tightest-lipped of all men, and the traveling public knows little more of their lives and work than it does of the
people of Mars. Strange bits of drama flit past their terribly keen if
guarded vision. One of them told me it is like getting a ten-second flash
of every movie ever filmed. And they have lives of their own. People
who accept the porter as something that comes with the car, a fixture as
impersonal as the berths, seem not to suspect that the porter has his special likes, his pet peeves, his worries, joys, and triumphs.

It is regrettable, as has been said, that the name of the first Pullman
porter isn't known. The great Chicago fire of 1871 destroyed all of the
early records of the Pullman company, and not even the year the first
porter took over is certain, though it probably was 1867 and it is also
probable that the porter was a well trained ex-slave. It may well have
been a Negro from Georgia or the Carolinas, for those states have long
been the favorite recruiting grounds of the Pullman company. More
porters come from those three states than from any other region.

The Pullman porter is selected with discrimination and is also carefully trained. Many families now have their third generation of porters
on the road, for the occupation tends to become hereditary and Pullman
employees stand high in any Negro community. Applicants are usually
vouched for by old and trusted porters, and the company then scans
their records. The next step is training. The rookie porter is sent to
school in one of the larger railroad centers where the Pullman Company
has a car sidetracked for a schoolroom. Here in charge of a veteran the

rookie learns the proper method of folding and putting away blankets, of making berths. He is taught that a sheet, towel, or pillow slip once unfolded cannot be used again; it may be clean, yet technically it is soiled and must go to the laundry. He goes through the motions of making up and making down the beds. He is shown how the heating, lighting, and air-conditioning controls operate. He is taught how to wake passengers—no noise, not even a knock on the edge of the berth, but merely a gentle shake of the curtains from the outside. Meanwhile, from the wise old heads who instruct him, the rookie learns a good deal about the habits of passengers whom he will meet.

Now comes an actual trip, though still under the eye of an experienced porter. The rookie will doubtless make several of these trial trips, and then, one night, he makes the trip out alone. If all goes well, or even pretty well, he is on his way to being a Pullman porter, and once he is such, he is more often than not set in the occupation he will follow the rest of his life. Few Pullman porters are discharged. Most are retired for age after from 20 to 40 years of service. Most new openings are made when ambitious porters leave to go to college or into business for themselves.

It is still a firmly entrenched notion of American travelers that Pullman porters are paid almost nothing in wages. Thirty years ago this notion had a basis of fact; base pay was around $20 a month. In 1937 things started to improve when the Brotherhood of Sleeping Car Porters got the company to agree to a scale ranging from a minimum of $89.50 per month to $127.50 for a porter running-in-charge, that is, one who acts as porter and also as Pullman conductor of his car. Since 1937 the rates have been increased again.

For the first ten years the porter buys his own uniforms, after which the company pays for them. The porter buys the polish used on passengers' shoes. For meals he ordinarily takes with him at least one lunch put up at home, eating this with coffee in the diner. On long runs he eats at odd times in the diner, paying approximately one-half the regular tariff.

What a porter receives in tips is pretty much a matter between God and himself. Half the time the porter doesn't know what his tips amount to. He just knows they are good, medium, or bad. Porters will lie with clear conscience about tips. It isn't hard to understand why. A ten-year-service man who by his good work has made a certain run worth, say, a monthly average of $100 in tips, isn't prone to be bragging about it. He more probably will appear altogether discouraged about the whole business and swear that his tips never run to more than $45 a month. He doesn't want some eleven-year-service man, who thus ranks him, bumping him off his well-tilled run.

It works the other way, too. Given a run that proves poor in tips, an up-and-coming man will try to do something about it. Returning to a Pullman dormitory fresh from his run, he'll reach deep into his pocket and come up with a great handful of change—halves, quarters (and silver dollars west of Chicago)—and let the boys feast their eyes. He will brag to heaven that he makes eight runs a month and that the take is never less than $12 a run. It's his bunco game to get rid of a poor run, to tempt some senior porter to bump him. The gag is seldom successful, I am told, unless played for a long time by a consummate actor.

It is patently impossible to say what an average porter's tips amount to in a year. It is known that in many parts of the South tips run to no more than $20 a month. There are certain overnight runs in New England worth no more than $45 a month in summer, $35 in winter. The run into Upper Michigan is no better. And in former days the Nickel Plate road had such a poor reputation for tips that porters tell how they requested to be put on the Extra List, rather than to run Regular on the Plate.

At the other end of the line is the unquestioned $200 and better averaged monthly (in normal times) by the star veterans on the *Twentieth-Century Limited*, the *Broadway Limited*, the Santa Fe *Chief* and several other extra-fare trains. These are the 24-carat runs, held for many years by the same men. Twenty years on the *Century* is not unusual for a porter.

Porters appear to have different and strongly held opinions about tipping, but seem in agreement on certain things. For instance: They can usually gauge a man's tip before they get it. Of women travelers they can tell nothing at all until the tip is in hand. The ladies are highly erratic tippers; on the whole they tip better than men, and often give tips that are all out of proportion to the service rendered. All foreigners are poor tippers, the English worst of the lot. New England natives haven't a very high reputation for tips, although regular trippers on the New Haven are said to be consistent tippers and the amount adds up well in a year. Prosperous show folk are excellent tippers and they also demand more attention than anyone else. The late George Cohan was a legendary tipper. So is Jack Dempsey, the ex-fighter. The late Calvin Coolidge was a consistent tipper, and his tip never varied. It was always fifteen cents.

More than one porter has been remembered in the will of some much-traveled man. Diamond Jim Brady left $2,500 to a favorite porter. A wealthy Chicagoan left $3,000 for the purpose of putting the son of a porter through medical college. Not long ago a group of Hollywood people chipped in to buy their favorite Pullman maid a colossal automobile.

Possibly the pet aversions of all Pullman porters are professional baseball players, most of whom, so one intelligent porter has said, are vulgar and uncouth yahoos. "They tear up the linen," he relates, "destroy pillows in their adolescent horseplay, and abuse every piece of equipment aboard. Cattle cars would be too good for a majority of professional ballplayers."

The favorites of porters are the professional traveling men, the so-called drummers. They know good service and how to appreciate it. They are usually reasonable in all things and make little trouble. Their tips aren't

the largest, but the porter can always bank on a tip and know it will be the regulation amount. Among the drummers, however, as among other classes of travelers, is the pseudo-sophisticated male who addresses all porters as "George," which he seems to believe is an extremely witty reminder of George Mortimer Pullman.*

A porter's life is no life of ease. It calls for a rugged constitution. Hours are irregular. Wakefulness and sleep come in batches. Meals are usually eaten hurriedly. Making down a berth is not play. There is much baggage to handle. And when all of the passengers have departed, the porter has much work to do. He also works under rigid discipline, and often has to contend with impossible people. There is the man, or woman, who goes to bed in a berth smoking a cigarette; the loudmouthed male who wants to sit talking in the washroom until two in the morning; the fellow—called a "whitewasher"—who spreads a coat of lather over the men's wash basins and leaves it there; the old woman, of either sex, who rings and rings the bell at every hour of the day and night, to say that the car is too warm, too cold, or too drafty, despite the fact that today's Pullmans are for the most part air-conditioned and the temperatures kept steady by automatic control. Worst of all, perhaps, is the fellow who whistles, as if for a dog, to attract the porter's attention.

Yet the Pullman porter has an interesting life, not to say a colorful, or even a romantic one. Young colored boys and many older ones look at the porter as tops in everything desirable in the Negro world. He is the most traveled of his race. He knows the ways of the world. He is a knight of the road. In time, if he has the ability as well as the ambition, he leaves the sleeping car for better things. If he stays on, his children are likely to have better things, anyway.

In riding a Pullman for twenty years or more, a lot can happen to a porter and his charges. Porters have assisted at births, deaths, even marriages. They have been in wrecks and in holdups. A few have become heroes. There was Oscar J. Daniels, the only porter for whom a Pullman car was named.

On June 16, 1925, Porter Daniels was in charge of the *Sirocco,* a sleeper assigned to one of the Eastern lines. When the train was derailed by a washout, the *Sirocco* fell parallel with and close to the engine. The door nearest the locomotive was blown open and a cloud of scalding steam billowed into the Pullman. Passengers screamed. Porter Daniels ran through the hot vapor and slammed the door shut. Then he fell unconscious. He

* The late George M. Dulany (white), a midwest lumberman, did a good deal to eliminate "George" as a generic name for porters. He accomplished this by the wide publicity accorded his Society for the Prevention of Calling Pullman Porters George, a no-dues lodge Mr. Dulany carried on for many years at his own expense and to his vast enjoyment. He told me once that he had "converted" more than 10,000 Americans to his contention that Pullman porters should be addressed as Porter and not as George. Today, only congenital hicks use "George."

died from his terrible burns, but his passengers' lives had been saved.

There was heroic John W. Blair on ill-fated No. 4 of the St. Paul & Duluth, in charge of the chair car. The day was September 1, 1894, the day Hinckley and other towns of eastern Minnesota were destroyed in one of the greatest forest fires of all time.

Heading south from Duluth, Number 4 soon ran into a land covered with smoke and alight with flame. As it approached Hinckley village, Engineer Jim Root saw the town was going up in billows of fire. He stopped, took aboard scores of fleeing citizens, then reversed the lever and the train started backing toward Skunk Lake, a mudhole six miles to the rear.

It was a run through hell. Flames lined the tracks. Ties started to smolder, then to burn. Paint on the outside of the coaches began to run; and presently the inside paint was running too. Porter Blair calmed the panic-stricken passengers. He stood by the water tank wetting towels and passing them to his charges to wrap around their heads. The coach lamps, which had been lighted, now began to blow up from explosions, apparently of gas generated by the forest fire, which also broke almost every window in the train. Blair talked to the few children, dampened their heads, had them lie flat on the floor. A big man, evidently a religious fanatic, tore into the car, his eyes popping. "We are all going to heaven together," he shouted. Blair grabbed and held him, telling him to be quiet, that all would be well.

Just before the train arrived at Skunk Lake, the cars themselves started to burn fiercely, and Blair took down the fire extinguisher—a plain water affair—and sprayed passengers lying on the floor, putting out fires that were burning women's hair off their heads. When the train at last stopped, Blair, assisted by several passengers and train crew, saw that the women and kids were put off first, then he got down, his clothes afire, his hair and eyebrows singed, and crawled into the scum of Skunk Lake along with some three hundred others. Four hundred and eighteen Minnesotans died that terrible afternoon, though not all of their bodies could be identified.

It is good to report that Negro Porter Blair's noble efforts were not forgotten. A little later, in St. Paul, survivors of the fire and other people staged a party at which Blair was honored by the presentation of a handsome badge "of beautiful design, the face being engraved with the picture of a burning train." To Blair also went a fine gold watch, presented by "The St. Paul & Duluth R. R. Co. for gallant and faithful discharge of duty on Limited Train No. 4, in Forest Fires, Sept. 1, 1894." *

A porter on the Union Pacific had a hand in the taking of Roy Gardiner, the notorious outlaw. All porters keep an eye out for thieves and for pro-

---

* See *Memorials of the Minnesota Forest Fires in the Year 1894,* by the Rev. William Wilkinson, Minneapolis, 1895.

fessional gamblers. Small adventures are common. They always just happen and are never expected. There is more of the quality of certainty about finding things, valuable things, left behind by heedless passengers. It is a fact that passengers will and do leave almost everything one could think of behind them in the Pullman cars. In company with a Pullman inspector I once got aboard a Santa Fe *Chief* in the Chicago yards right after the passengers had left. In the train we found the following: one new and expensive mink coat, lady's; two golf bags complete with clubs; one costly cowhide bag; four powder compacts, one quite expensive; one small diamond ring; two pairs of cuff links; one quart bottle nearly full of bonded rye; and fourteen copies of *Variety,* a weekly periodical of the world of show business.

Lost and found goods are turned in at the nearest Pullman office. The company prides itself on its record of finding owners. A sample of this service occurred in the spring of 1939, when a porter at the end of his run in Chicago found a platinum watch set with diamonds in the ladies' room of his car. Through its markings, plus a lot of hard work and the assistance of the jeweler who had made it, the watch was returned three weeks later to its owner, who apparently had never missed it.

One day in 1923 Porter J. T. McArthur, on an Ohio run, discovered enough stuff in his car to jolt him out of his usual self-control. Going through the sleeper at the end of the run, he found: one pearl necklace, one diamond necklace, one bar pin with 14 diamonds, one set of earrings, green, with pearls, one set of gold and pearl cuff links, one wrist watch, platinum, and three platinum rings. The stuff was valued later by an expert at $75,000. Porter McArthur thought for sure he had stumbled onto a batch of goods so "hot" that the thieves did not dare to leave the train with it. Scooped up and taken to the Pullman office at high speed, they were retrieved next day by the rightful owner who, of course, was a woman. Said she had simply forgotten them.

On a June day in 1929 Porter Pierson found a chamois bag in a drawing room. It held $400,000 worth of jewelry, said to have been the largest find ever made in a Pullman. The owner, a woman, was located. She said she thought she had left the bag in the stateroom of a ship from Europe. Anyway, she gave Pierson a $100 reward.

The list of sizable finds seems endless. Every day in the week, the Pullman company estimates, passengers leave goods to the total value of $5,000 in Pullman cars. Every effort is made to find the owners. Unclaimed goods are held for two years, then returned to the finders. Incidentally, immediate dismissal follows discovery that a porter has not reported an article found.

In the folklore that has grown up around porters is the belief that they have an elaborate sign language by which they communicate with each other as their trains pass in opposite directions. The only bit of sign language one reporter was able to unearth has to do with the hotel guidebook that appears in a rack at the men's end of a sleeper. The male reader will have seen it often, a fat volume with a bright red cover. Well, if this book is held up to a window, flat against the glass, when two trains are passing, it means that a Pullman inspector, or spotter, is somewhere about, and the porter so warned had best see that his car is in fine condition.

Porters never lack for topics of conversation. Much of the talk takes place in the Pullman dormitories maintained by the company in all of the large terminals. Here in the barracks, between runs, porters discuss the ups and downs and exciting moments of life aboard a sleeping car. The talkfests are known in the trade as the Baker Heater League, so-called from the now obsolete type of heating apparatus once used in Pullmans.

In talk among themselves porters refer to a "boxcar," by which they mean the new type of all-room Pullmans. An observation car is a "buggy." A "tin can" is a buffet car. A "battleship" is the oldline 16-section sleeper. Like mariners with ships, porters have favorite cars, and then there are jinx cars, bad luck for anyone. And, being Negroes and having a sense of humor, perhaps to alleviate their status as partial citizens of the United States, they are keen for funny happenings to porters.

There was that night when Porter Johnnie Jones, running on the Pennsylvania out of New York, collected all of the shoes in his car and took them into the next Pullman where he might shine them and also talk with Porter Jackson, during the lonely morning hours. This was, of course, strictly against the rules, but the two porters did have a right good visit and did an excellent job of shining. When Porter Jones, loaded with shoes, started to return to his own car, it wasn't there. Sudden emergency orders had cut out his car and held it for inclusion in a second section of the same train. It was quite embarrassing for Porter Jones, to say nothing of his shoeless passengers. The colored boys still mention it now and then in the Pullman dormitories.

Another favorite story of the Baker Heater League concerns a Porter Johnson, who in 1908 was in charge of a car on the Northern Pacific running between St. Paul and Seattle. Johnson left St. Paul on November 5, in the sleeper *Umpyna*, deadheading to Butte, where he arrived on the 7th and learned he was to remain there overnight. So, well content with the layover, he ate his supper, made up a berth in the empty *Umpyna*, and went to bed about eleven o'clock.

Sometime in the night Porter Johnson awoke to find that his car was in motion. This did not immediately worry him, for he believed, naturally enough from long experience, that for some reason or other the yard crew was shifting his car to another track. But he put up the shade and looked out. It was still dark, but he came to the conclusion he was moving pretty fast, far too fast for yard switching, and he also saw what looked to be a small depot flash past.

"I lighted my lantern," said Porter Johnson in his report to the Pullman company, "and began to ascertain the situation of things. Went to front end of car and found nothing in front of me, no signals nor anything. So I says to myself, 'This is queer railroading,' and went to the other end of the car and found standard car *Kooskia* hooked onto me. I went through the *Kooskia*, and found no porter or anybody else aboard, and kept on to the rear vestibule and found it same as front of my car *Umpyna*. Then I turned white . . ."

Porter Johnson thought it was time he did something. His two-car, engineless train was doing, he calculated, about 75 miles an hour. He grabbed the brakes and began turning the ratchet. It didn't seem to do any good at all. "So," he reported later, "I then ran to front end of my car and saw men piling ties and putting a rail across the track in order to ditch me, not knowing anybody was aboard. But me and my two cars was too slick for that game and broke the rail in two pieces and shoved the ties ahead near two miles, knocking down all the switches. The Butte & Anaconda freight had just pulled in below Durant, and they threw open their switch, which put me on their road and at the same time administering to me an upgrade. While otherwise I would have kept on the NP down grade to four miles beyond Durant, and as Number 2 *Northcoast Limited* was late, saved me from slapping them square in the mouth. So I am still alive but am awful scared. Cause of the runaway, brakes being released by some unknown person in the yards. They telegraphed all along the line to look out for runaway cars, but I was beating all telegraphic communications time."

Porter Johnson and the runaway at Butte is from the record. There is no record, only folklore, concerning the most terrific Pullman porter who ever made down a berth. He was Daddy Joe. No living porter claims ever to have seen him, but a few of the older veterans vow they once knew somebody who had seen Daddy Joe in the flesh. He was so tall, this dusky Daddy Joe, and so strong, that he commonly stood in the car aisle, on the floor, and let down an upper with each hand; then he made down both uppers and lowers simultaneously. And when Daddy Joe was really in a hurry, the thud and clatter of uppers sounded like a giant walking downstairs.

Once, on the Yazoo & Mississippi Valley Railroad, Daddy Joe's sleeping car and all the train were surrounded by the rising waters of the river. There was panic in the Pullman, with passengers screaming and trying to get out the doors in order to drown in the open rather than in the car. Daddy Joe rose nobly to the emergency. He stood up tall on his long legs and delivered such a powerful oration that the passengers were soothed. They took their seats again. The waters fell and the train proceeded to Memphis, arriving four hours and thirty minutes late, which was the exact time consumed by Daddy Joe's sermon.

Once, on the Central Pacific, it was just as tough. Hostile Indians attacked the train at a water tank. Daddy Joe climbed on top of his car—a notable infringement of Pullman regulations—and there harangued the redskins in their own tongue, dazing them into inaction by the sonorous periods of his great voice, which was like thunder. Then Daddy Joe came down. He tossed a pretty brown Pullman blanket to each of the seven chiefs and subchiefs in the attacking party, gave them his blessing, and the train rolled on in safety to Salt Lake City.

The boys don't talk about him much any more, but they used to, and Daddy Joe came down through the years and on every railroad in the country performed his wondrous feats. Sometimes, it appears, he was known as Daddy Henry, but Joe or Henry, he was always master of the situation and never failed to bring his charges unscathed through fire, hurricane, high water, Indians, and robbers. "We don't get no tips till the end of the run," Daddy Joe always said. It is a piece of revealing folklore because it always has the porter bending his every energy, even risking his life to save his passengers. And always at the end is the worldly-wise payoff—the part about tips.

Among porters, as among passengers, there long ago grew up the legend that the marvellous names of Pullman cars were thought up by Florence Pullman, daughter of the founder of the company. Rumors, then newspaper items, appeared to say that Miss Pullman received one hundred dollars (sometimes it was one thousand dollars) for each name she selected. This pleasant story has been repeatedly denied by the company which no longer pays it any heed when it reappears, as it does every little while. The Pullman Company, indeed, has stated with brutal frankness that Miss Pullman never named so much as one car.

From almost the beginning Pullman cars were named by a committee of company officials. At first it was thought that Pullmans, like ships, should have feminine names, and many were so christened. Then place names became quite a factor. Great men also must be honored, especially railroad officials, soldiers, sailors, statesmen. Then came a line of mountains and rivers and capes. The sometimes difficult classical names of ancient times were not in use until Pullman acquired the Wagner Palace Car Company, its chief competitor, and discovered that some three hundred of the Wagner cars bore names duplicated in the Pullmans. There must be new names, and at once.

Richmond Dean, a vice-president of the Pullman, had an inspiration. Taking a corps of clerks, he moved in a body to the Chicago Public Library and there delved into the history and the mythology of Greece and

Photo by H. C. Dorer, Sunday Call, Newark, N. J.

Service-track stop for a commuter engine. The fireman puts six thousand gallons of water around the splash-plates of a Jersey Central tank.

The celebrated Starucca Viaduct, built in 1848 with the idea that the Erie would be in business for a long time, still carries Erie trains over Starucca creek, between Lanesboro and Susquehanna, Pa. In its day this was one of the marvels of railroading.

Rome. Within twenty-four hours, some of the most beautiful, and also some of the biggest mouthfuls, of names were ready for the newly acquired cars—names ranging from *Circe* and *Sibyl* to *Archimedes* and *Belisarius*.

In later years the company found it convenient to adopt names in a series, so that the name would denote a certain type of car. This plan has been continued. Compartment and drawing room cars have been named for poets, dramatists, and authors. The *Lake, Camp*, and *Fort* cars are all of one sort—ten sections, drawing room and two compartments. The *Saints* and *Macs* contain twelve sections and a drawing room. There is a series of ten-sections-plus-two-drawing-room cars named *Point Alexander, Point Bonita* and so on. The parlor cars of the *Congressional Limited*, running on the Pennsylvania between New York and Washington, were named after signers of the Declaration, and prominent members of the Continental Congress and the Constitutional Convention—*Caesar Rodney, Charles Carroll, Roger Sherman, et al.* The *President* series is another type of compartment and drawing-room car with special interior finish.

In recent years cars have been named for cities and landmarks along a specific railroad; and there is the *Silver* series, such as *Silver Star, Silver Bay, Silver Peak,* and *Silver Stream*, made for the Santa Fe railroad's *California Limited*. The Southern Pacific has a series named *Sunset Beach, Sunset Cape, Sunset Heights,* and so on.

"Certain rules," says a Pullman statement sternly, "have been adopted by the committee on nomenclature regarding the naming of type cars with the object of indicating, without reference to book or catalog, the character of the car." This is all very well, but I for one prefer to think of Miss Florence Pullman, a copy of Shelley in one hand, gazing out the window at the glistening waters of Lake Michigan, a faraway look in her eyes, earning an honest dollar by applying the name of some Aegean god to a new car that is waiting, shining yet nameless, on the factory sidetracks in Pullman, Illinois.

CHAPTER XXIX

Spotters

The cardinal principles of my detective system are: That crime can and must be detected by the pure and honest heart obtaining a controlling power over that of the criminal.

—ALLAN PINKERTON, 1880.

THE reason railroad companies engaged spotters to observe the practices of conductors on passenger trains was impressed most strongly on the mind of Henry Clay French when he became conductor on a branch line of the Oregon Railroad & Navigation Company, in the 1890's. The nineties, I should judge from what I have heard from old railroaders, was a lush period for conductors, perhaps the lushest since the invention of the ticket and the punch.

Conductor French's run was the line from Arlington to Heppner, Oregon, forty-five miles through vast open spaces, mostly sheep and cattle country. He had been railroading elsewhere for twenty years, as call boy, brakeman, fireman, switchman, even a little conductoring, but his experiences on the Heppner Branch were something new in his life. His first month's turn-in ran to more than five thousand dollars and it created a sensation at OR&N headquarters. No such sum had ever been turned in by a conductor on the Heppner line.

French, who had no idea of the furore his first month's receipts were to make, thought it odd that almost no tickets were sold by local agents in Arlington, in Heppner, or in any of the way stations. The fare over the branch was $2.25, all of it, of course, belonging to the railroad company. French had made no more than a couple of runs before he discovered that the previous conductors on this branch had been selling tickets direct to passengers at the fire-sale rate of $1.50, thus giving the passenger a sizable if dubious bonus of seventy-five cents. Little of the remainder went to the company.

French soon discovered, too, that his engineer was conducting a profitable side-line by permitting farmers, sheep-herders and cattle ranch hands to ride in the cab in response to a dollar or so. Conductor French held that a railroad man in good standing with one of the Brotherhoods was entitled to ride free in a locomotive, anytime, anywhere, but he stopped the

340

Heppner Branch hogger from accepting other passengers. This made the engineer a French enemy.

Another crew of enemies made by Conductor French's odd practice of selling tickets and demanding full fares were the station agents along the line. They had never been accustomed to selling many tickets, but after a month or so of the French regime, potential passengers, knowing they could do nothing with French, started to buy their tickets at the stations, all of which made a good deal more work for the agents. The agents were not in favor of more work, and they cursed French and his methods of conducting passenger service.

French held the run for a little more than two years and the passenger receipts retained the new high they had reached during his first month. And then, in 1893, French was discharged by the railroad for "the theft of thirty-six cents." He believed this was brought about by a detective or spotter—whether this man was of the railroad, private agency, or police variety I do not know—who "had an old grudge against French." Of the particular run on which he was alleged to have stolen the thirty-six cents, French remarks that "Not even the fact that I was able to prove my paid fares and tickets showed five more passengers than the report against me claimed, saved me from the frame-up. At the end of the hearing I was discharged."

The case against Conductor French must have contained some elements of weakness, for he closed his career of half a century on the rails by working twenty-one consecutive years for the Union Pacific, the road that took over the OR&N, including its celebrated Heppner Branch.

French's experience on the Heppner line would indicate that the knocking-down of fares by conductors had become quite a business by the early Nineties. The son of another oldtime conductor tells me that his father salted down $25,000 by knocking-down before he was fifty, then retired to live the rest of his life in comparative ease. Let's call him Conductor Smith, which is nothing like his real name. He began braking on the Chicago & North Western in Minnesota in 1880, and later moved to Nebraska and served as conductor on the Fremont, Elkhorn & Missouri Valley line. In that day and place there were few ticket offices in any but the largest stations. Travelers had long had the habit of buying their tickets on the train. Mostly they paid in gold or silver, and much of this metal remained in the hands of Conductor Smith, who was an excellent judge of how much cash the company expected him to turn in.

In those days, many a general manager and division superintendent of a railroad had at some time or another acted as conductor. They had knocked down fares in their time, and they expected the same of the conductors under them. Knocking-down, says my informant, was not considered to be a crime, nor even something reprehensible. The conductors told each other, varying an old piece of folklore, that they never failed to toss all cash into the air and that that part of it which stuck to the bellcord belonged to the company.

Spotters, says Conductor Smith's son, were never a menace, not even a bother to his father. Spotters rode the trains on occasion, but usually Smith was tipped off in advance and knew how to conduct himself with a spotter in the car. He was never detected once, or at least was never reprimanded, and so he worked steadily and industriously at knocking-down until he had accumulated the sum he wanted; then he left railroading for good.

When knocking-down began will never be known. Back in the primeval days of the New York & Erie, the Boston & Lowell, and the New York & Hudson River, some captains, as they were then called, probably discovered there was little or no danger in selling the right to ride on the cars to a passenger with no ticket and putting the cash into the deep pockets of their long frock or cutaway coats. The practice, like all good things, soon spread, and in time the railroads had to take steps.

The spotter was the logical answer, a man in plain clothes, known to nobody except the big boss in the head office, who rode the cars and either attempted to seduce the conductor into selling a fare for which no report would be made, or trying to observe how the conductor did business with other passengers. From that day to this, spotters have been figures on company payrolls, shadowy figures, perhaps, but present all the time, doing their best, and perhaps their worst, to get evidence against the men who took the tickets and commanded the passenger trains.

In time, a number of private detective agencies began to supply spotters to railroads. Often no one on the road knew who the spotter was, nor what he looked like, for his reports were made direct to his chief detective, who in turn sent them to the railroad company. But a considerable number of railroads hired and supervised their own spotters.

By the very nature of his work, the life of a spotter on any one railroad —or division—was not very long. Conductors who knocked down fares were likely to be both sharp and alert, and they quickly became suspicious of any genial stranger who appeared to be riding their cars a good deal. One spotter who apparently fooled conductors of Midwestern lines for twenty-eight years was a Swede who rode the Rock Island, the Burlington, the Great Northern, the Milwaukee, and probably other roads, and posed as a farmer who had a fine farm to sell and wanted to talk about it to everybody he met, passenger or railroad man.

This Scandinavian went by the name of Peter Anderson. He was a fine-looking man who had kindly and naïve blue eyes and a long and fatherly beard, almost white. His accent was wonderful, and gave people the idea they were talking with a stout rustic soul, the essence of simplicity and the salt of the earth, the kind of immigrant who was taming the prairies and making them to bloom with wheat and corn and barley and rye. He told simple stories, using quaint turns of speech that folks, even railroad conductors, found entrancing. There was many a conductor called upon the carpet at divisional headquarters and many a one who was discharged who never once suspected his downfall had been engineered by good old Peter Anderson, the homesteader from Anoka, Minnesota, and from Calliope, Iowa, and from Alma, Wisconsin.

A railroad brakeman friend of mine used to speak occasionally, and with more amusement than bitterness, of a spotter who rode the trains of the Great Northern some twenty-five years ago. By some means or other this spotter, who was known to the train crews only as "Pinkie," the rather obvious nickname for an operative of a famous private detective agency, was recognized for what he was by the railroad crews long before Pinkie himself or his employers knew he was a marked man.

So far as my friend knew, Pinkie never got any evidence against the train crews, and presently he left that particular GN run and was never seen again.

At least one old-time spotter once felt the urge to tell the public about his work. He was Clarence E. Ray, who said he had been a spotter for fifteen years, running on Northern, Western, and Southern lines. "A new system," Spotter Ray wrote in 1916, "is to have a Negro spotter board the train at some point where the railroad does not have a ticket office, and pay a cash fare. The Negro's money looks pretty good to the conductor who is inclined to graft a bit on occasion. A con isn't nearly so likely to suspect a Negro as he is a white man."

Spotter Ray told of once riding a train on a branch line in Tennessee where there had been a circus. He counted some four hundred Negroes in the cars, and later learned that the conductor had turned in only ten fares. On a higher level, Ray himself once boarded a solid Pullman train in New Mexico and paid cash fare for the long trip to Chicago. It was discovered later that no record had been turned in of the railroad fare, of the Pullman fare, or even of the dining-car receipts.*

It was the custom of many spotters to join one or several of the larger fraternal orders, such as Elks, Eagles, Moose or Woodmen, which also have many members who are railroad men, and trade upon their membership to gain the confidence of trainmen in order to get evidence against their "brothers." Lodge membership could also work the other way. Spotter Ray tells of working in conjunction with a spotter named McKenzie, a big Englishman who had seen better days and had taken the job only to keep his family from starving.

"We traveled together on a Southern road out of Chicago," Ray relates,

---

* In his booklet, *The Railroad Spotter*, St. Paul, 1916, which is extremely hard to come by, Author Ray is very cagey about mentioning railroads by name; but in it he does tell a good deal about spotters' methods and no little of their undependability.

"but I soon noted that trainmen who had accepted a cash fare from me without issuing a receipt, would later come back and hand me a receipt with a smile. I began to wonder what was up, and after at least half a dozen similar occurrences like this, I discovered that McKenzie was an important official in one of the larger fraternal organizations. He tipped off every lodge brother who was inclined to burn his fingers on our money. Poor Old Mac was a loyal lodge brother but a darned poor spotter."

Ray knew two spotters who played the business from both ends. These men, whose working names were Riley and Johnson, were sent to Denver to check a certain line out of that city. After several trips as spotters, they observed to themselves that the pickings on this line were particularly juicy. The conductors and brakemen had worked up a really big business. So, Spotters Riley and Johnson exposed themselves to the train crews with whom they rode, and from that point all hands worked together to graft every penny possible from the passenger traffic. It must have been even better pickings than the Heppner Branch of the OR&N, for Riley told that he alone had cleaned up $6,000 in cash fares during the two months he had been employed on the job—as a spotter.

Among the spotters who Ray says were "famous" at the end of the century and early in this one, were LaRue, Bennett, Hanson, Nowrey, Slipski, Westland, and Marrs. There were two other noted spotters, Tilley and Lloyd, who Ray believed belonged to just about every fraternal group in the United States.

In discussing the methods used by spotters in his own active period, which must have been from around 1900 to 1915, Ray reported that "Spotter Marrs always posed as a land agent and caught trainmen in bunches of twenty at a time . . . Bates is a short and gray man who poses as a booze agent. Plummer carries a side line of art goods. . . . Tilley handles a line of teas and coffees out of Chicago. Beach is a good-looking, light-haired boy who poses as a high-school kid."

Perhaps it was defensive, maybe it was merely true, but Ray was of the opinion that railroad spotters numbered many strictly honest men in their ranks, and a few terrible crooks. On the whole, he thought, spotters were much as any other group of men. Of the honesty or otherwise of railroad men, and particularly of railroad passenger conductors, he has almost nothing to say except in regard to one named railroad and one anonymous railroad. "The Northern Pacific trainmen," he says, "strike me as the most loyal and best disciplined of any I have ever met, and I have ridden on many lines. Those of a certain Southern railroad strike me as the worst employees I have ever seen on a railroad."

In spite of Spotter Ray, at some time or another there must have been a conductor on the Northern Pacific who knocked down fares, or at least was suspected of doing so, for there was once a woman spotter who rode the red coaches of the NP in Montana, her wiles set to catch the suspected conductor. Whether or not she ever got the goods on a con, I don't know. I don't even know her name, although she was "Pretty Kitty" to the members of the train crew with whom she took several rides between Butte and Spokane.

Pretty Kitty really was pretty, I am told. Blue-eyed, blonde, long-haired, long-lashed, and shapely in the manner of the late Lillian Russell, much in vogue at the time, she was quite an eyeful in Montana. She also seemed fantastically naïve for a business woman who said she sold corsets and other intimate things to the merchants of Butte and Spokane and way points. She was always forgetting to buy a ticket before she boarded a train. She hardly knew how to get a drink of water or a meal, or even to find the toilet on a train. Always she asked the conductor or a brakeman where or what, and how and when, and they found her, after a fashion, quite charming.

On the second or third trip with a crew, one of whose members I came to know, Pretty Kitty suggested to the conductor that she thought he ought to let her ride for half fare, seeing how she was so petite and young —hardly more than a schoolgirl, she said roguishly with what she thought was a fetching smile. "And I don't need any of your old tickets or receipts," she said, just to make everything clear. Then she tried to hand the conductor approximately half the regular fare. But that churl insisted on full fare and then and there he gave her a receipt, and went about his business.

The head brakeman, a handsome chap who could and did tell Kitty all about the scenery along the way, made an impression on the girl. And on one of her trips, she agreed to meet him that night for dinner in Spokane. To the old Coeur d'Alene Hotel they went, then the finest place in town, and there they ate, and drank. The brakeman declared, long after, that he did not make any advances, honorable or otherwise, to Pretty Kitty. He said, however, that Pretty Kitty made advances to him. She had fallen, she said after the fifth or sixth drink, madly in love with the handsome brakeman. This was all right with him, for he had taken her to dinner with a purpose other than the one that might have been suspected in a young brakeman, or in several other kinds of men, for that matter. Before the effect of the excellent Coeur d'Alene liquor had evaporated, Pretty Kitty had confessed that she was a spotter—she called it "being a spy"—for a detective agency who had wanted to see how a woman spotter would work out on a railroad.

"She broke down and wept and wept," the brakeman told me. "She swore she would resign her job and never again would become a spotter or any kind of a dick. She said she had never done anything like it before and didn't like the work. She said she never would have taken it on, except she wanted to show the detective agency that a woman could be a spotter as well as a man."

If the agency's desire was merely to learn how a female spotter would work out, they presently found out. After a month or so of riding the cars, during which she never once detected any knocking-down, Pretty Kitty reported back to her agency headquarters in Chicago where, she soon confessed, she was in a condition best described, perhaps, as delicate. What she did about her condition is not a part of the saga as it came to me. All I know is that the handsome brakie, who may have been responsible, did not marry her. I have often wondered if the detective agency ever tried another woman as pretty as Kitty in the role of spotter.

In the late 1920's this shot of a three-level railway crossing was made at Richmond, Va., with trains of the Chesapeake & Ohio (top), Seaboard Air Line (middle) and Southern Railway.

The Milwaukee Journal

The big gauge in front of the Milwaukee Road engineer is the speed recorder, its hand pointing to 100 miles an hour. This photo was made in the cab of one of the Hiawatha's engines on a regular run in 1938. The engineer's left hand rests on the throttle lever. His other hand is near the reverse-gear lever, just below which is the independent (engine) brake valve, and still further below, the automatic brake valve. To the right of the throttle level is the windshield. Between the throttle lever and the speed recorder are two airbrake gauges. Left of the speed recorder is the water-glass drain valve. Below the speed recorder is a Spree lamp, to the left of which is the speed-recorder oil cup. Below the lamp is the steam cylinder cock operating valve. At the middle extreme left of the photograph is the double-faced steam gauge.

CHAPTER XXX

First Transcontinental Trip

When I hear the Iron Horse make the hills echo with his snort of thunder . . . it seems to me as if the earth had got a race now worthy to inhabit it.

—THOREAU, *Walden.*

RAILROADS were not only building Chicago into a vast city and taking settlers into the back country by the hundred thousand. They were also serving as a superb course in education in the facts of life pertaining to the United States of America. A specific example of the railroad at work as educator is to be discovered, from long dusty files of a little newspaper, in the Boston Board of Trade's remarkable excursion.

Somewhere between the classic journey of Lewis & Clark and the first coast-to-coast flight of a plane, we have lost sight of this first transcontinental trip of a railroad train pulled by a steam locomotive. It was made in the summer of 1870 and it was more than a ten-day wonder, for it set a style, or rather a goal, that lasted until well into the next century; no man was accounted a traveled American unless he had crossed the Great Plains and the Rockies in a train of steamcars.

This first coast-to-coast trip behind the Iron Horse began at Boston on May 23rd, and one of the several happy slogans conjured up for the occasion was "From Faneuil Hall to the Golden Gate." This was no misnomer, for the party took with them a bottle of water from the hallowed tides of Massachusetts Bay and seven days later poured it into San Francisco Harbor.

The group was made up of members of the Boston Board of Trade, together with several wives and a few children, one of the latter being down on the list as "Master F. H. Rindge," who later founded a famous technical school in his native Cambridge. They numbered one hundred and twenty-nine in all. The party was headed by the Hon. Alexander H. Rice, soon to be governor of the Bay State, and contained family names of great potency in the professional, literary, and mercantile circles of Boston—names like Brooks, Dana, Guild, Houghton, Kittredge, Longley, McIntire, Peabody, and Warren.

Notable publicity over a period of weeks had churned The Hub into a frenzy of interest. Fifty thousand people visited the train during the two days it lay in Boston, and on the day of departure what was described as a vast multitude was on hand at the depot to see the truly splendid procession of cars that had been built especially for this trip. It was billed as the *Pullman Hotel Express* and it was likely as fine an advertisement for his company as shrewd George Pullman ever thought up. Mr. Pullman himself was present, to ride as far as Chicago and his brother Albert, general superintendent, was to stay with the party throughout the trip. Bostonians had gazed in awe or envy at eight "of the most elegant cars ever drawn over an American railway." They cheered mightily now as the train pulled majestically out of the Boston & Albany station on the first lap of the journey, while the locomotive engineer sounded his whistle in long sonorous blasts, a practice he kept up as far as Worcester.

It is fortunate that the *Pullman Hotel Express* party included, just as Lewis & Clark's party did, a competent observer who made note of all worthy things along the way and set them down for contemporaries and for posterity, not in this case in notebooks but in all the authority of type and printers' ink. The observer was W. R. Steele, journalist, and in the baggage car of this extraordinary train was a "brand-new quarto-medium Gordon printing press" on which during the trip he printed twelve issues of the first paper ever written, composed, printed and published on the rolling wheels of a steam railroad train. It was the *Trans-Continental.** Its gorgeous masthead, unquestionably drawn by a gifted man of Pullman, reveals a train steaming across an infinite plain, heading for distant high mountains, each beautiful car plainly marked "Pullman Pacific Car Company," while sitting moodily on a rock ledge in the foreground is an Indian, feathered and blanketed, contemplating no doubt the end of the bison.

Editor Steele was patently a man alive to the importance of the event he was to chronicle. Words all but failed him when, in composing his first issue, he felt need to impale the moment of departure. Yet, words did not quite fail him, and he compared the "all aboard to San Francisco" of his train conductor to the "yes" spoken by Helen of Troy, to the "nod of a Belgian peasant to Napoleon," to the first transatlantic cablegram, and went on from there to liken the links binding the two American shores to the "Massive links in the Campo Santo at Pisa." Classicism was not dead in Boston, and Boston was riding the rails.

Local dignitaries greeted the special along the way. All were struck by the magnificence of Mr. Pullman's art. Let us see how it looked to Editor Steele as he rolled westward. There were eight carriages, he says, the first in line being the baggage car. But such a baggage car! It contained five

---

* Very few copies seem to have survived. I used the file now in the Rare Book Room of the New York Public Library.

large ice closets and a refrigerator, and also that shiny new quarto-medium Gordon printing press. Next came a very handsome smoking car divided into four rooms. Here in one was ye ed's office, complete with black walnut cases for type; another was a sumptuously appointed wine room; and a smoking room with euchre tables and a beautifully furnished hair-dressing and shaving saloon. Now followed two hotel cars bearing names famous in the Bay State—the *Revere* and the *Arlington;* the two Palace Sleeping and Drawing-Room Cars, one named with a slightly Mormon flavor *Palmyra,* the other *Marquette;* and lastly the "commissary and dining cars" *St. Cloud* and *St. Charles.*

Everyone who saw it must have noticed that the entire train was "equipped with every desirable accessory that may tend in the least to promote the ease of the passengers," and these accessories appear to have been elaborate hangings, costly upholstery, artistic gilding, and beautifully finished woodwork. And perhaps because it was a Boston party, there were two well-stocked libraries aboard, replete, said Mr. Steele, a man of taste, with choice works of history, poetry, and fiction. To cap everything there were "two of the improved Burdett Organs." There must have been other music, too, for a roguish item in the first issue of the rolling newspaper said: "Wanted—In the Revere Car, a Tenor and a Bass." Apparently some of the Apleys were getting into voice.

The first untoward incident seems to have occurred at the crossing of the Grand Trunk Railway near Detroit, where a madman leaped upon the platform of the *St. Cloud* while the train was moving, and pulled the bellcord. He then grabbed a brake and started to turn it furiously. Presently he bounded to the top of the car. The train stopped. The man, throwing off coat and vest, started to declaim in the wildest manner imaginable, shouting that he was in command of a Fenian army, and everybody had better take to the woods. It required four men to catch and get the mad one into a straightjacket, and so back to the asylum from which he had escaped. Fenians were much in the news just then, and in his telegraphic dispatches that day Editor Steele ran an item dated at St. Albans, Vermont, which said that "O'Neill crossed the line into Canada last night with two columns. They now occupy the same camp as last year. Over 1,000 Fenians passed through Rutland last evening. . . ."

At Chicago the Board of Trade and an immense concourse of people greeted the special. Speeches were made, then Chicago bid Godspeed to the party as it left over the Galena Division of the Chicago & North Western. General Superintendent George L. Dunlap rode as far as Sterling. But one of the Boston group had been left behind, a Mr. Sterne Morse. It was at this point that Editor Steele first revealed his revolting capacity as a punster by remarking, with use of italics, that "one gentleman was left a-*stern* in Chicago, and filled with re-*morse* is now chasing our train in a special engine."

The party marveled at the steam-powered drawbridge over the Mississippi, a mile wide. It found Iowa a pleasant and prosperous land.

At Omaha the party was shown "through the extensive work shops of the railroad company."

On the way from Omaha to Cheyenne, Editor Steele noted that Columbus, population 800, was George Francis Train's geographical center of the United States and that Train—a noted eccentric of the day—planned to move the national capital to Columbus when he was elected president of the United States.

A brief stop at Cheyenne, where only three years before there had been but one house, brought more dignitaries and speeches; then on to Ogden. The village of Sherman was noted as being 8,235 feet above the sea, named "in honor of Gen. Sherman the tallest general in the service." This station was 519 miles from Omaha, 1,225 miles from Sacramento. The party stood on the car platforms at Sherman and could see Pike's Peak, 165 miles to the South.

Laramie City, Creston, Point of Rocks, Bryan—"the country around here is barren and uninviting"—Carter's Station, Wasatch, and Echo City unveiled themselves one after the other; dust rolled up in clouds, the sun beat down, and the ladies thrilled that they were seeing what in their school geographies of a slightly earlier day had been labeled Great American Desert. Then the special hove into Ogden, which "presented the usual appearance of Mormon towns, the houses being widely scattered, with the gardens and orchards filling up the intervening spaces."

The members of the excursion had been avid to see herds of bison, and along the North Fork of the Platte the train had passed "small groups" of this animal, and also of antelope. They also noted that the Boys in Blue were on the job, for in this region were many posts of the army.

The Mormons knew how to make the desert bloom, how to organize a country. Even the Bostonians, probably as well informed as any gentiles in the land, were astonished at the great work accomplished in so short a time by the Latter-day Saints. Suddenly the reader of today is brought smack into the presence of one of the really great characters in American history:

Yesterday, by invitation of Mr. A. B. Pullman, the following gentlemen dined on board our train: President Brigham Young, Daniel H. Wells, George A. Smith; and Apostles John Taylor, Orson Pratt, Sen. Wilfred Woodruff, George Q. Cannon, Brigham Young, Jr., and Bishop J. C. Little.

One wonders if the Bostonians realized what a personage they dined that day in Salt Lake City? Did they then consider Young merely as a freak, a shrewd if eccentric opportunist? Did he seem to them a comic, perhaps a slightly obscene character? Did they realize that here was a man beside whom the great Webster was a pygmy, beside whom Sumner was a shadow? One cannot tell what their thoughts were when the man with the strange cut to his beard came into their train. But they found him gregarious, and informative. Direct, too. He told his hosts that he then had sixteen wives and forty-nine living children; that he was sixty-nine years old; that he had attended school but eleven days in his life.

President Young invited the party to the Tabernacle and here, if not before, Boston was more than impressed, both by the size and magnificence of the building and even more by the "remarkable address" he delivered with ease and sureness. The Prophet, indeed, produced an effect that is apparent still in the fading pages of Mr. Steele's newspaper. One feels that the Boston men felt finally, and perhaps uneasily, that they had met and heard one of the great forces of the Western United States.

Filled with a new respect for the abilities of Mormons, the passengers of the *Pullman Hotel Express* pulled out for the long haul to the Pacific, while talk turned to the wonders of transportation and communication. Out here in the region of vast spaces, where Boston seemed so far away, the magic of the telegraph was really brought home. One of the party had sent a wire to The Hub to learn if his family were well, and 'we had scarce run 47 miles farther when the reply was received. . . ." It set Editor Steele to pondering that this wonderful agent should be so strong a channel between the train and friends at home, that it could transmit information in the twinkling of an eye. Perhaps, he brooded, the same or a similar principle might be expanded and applied to locomotion, annihilating distance and almost outrunning time. An equal advance in science to that of the past century would render such a thing possible, he believed, within a few years. . . . Aye, Mr. Steele, travel and observation stimulate the mind, take it far from State Street and Back Bay, lift it immeasurably higher than Beacon Hill, send it wafting into regions unknown even to the higher faculty members of Harvard college. . . .

At last, the special pounded over the hump at Summit, then down through the American River Canyon to Sacramento, and San Francisco. Editor Steele rose to the occasion of entering California. When, he asked, as if anybody cared, when is a cow real estate? and answered; when she is turned into a field. . . . A day later the bottle of Massachusetts Bay water was emptied into San Francisco Bay, with all of the amenities proper for such an occasion.

The Boston Board of Trade party was now taken in hand by masters of entertaining—wined, dined, praised, taken to Stockton for a trip over the Mother Lode, another through Yosemite, then wined and dined again. In 1870, even as now, the sunny state of California had a notable yeasty effect on many people, and the front page of the Boston party's newspaper, dated at San Francisco on June 25th, reveals this influence at work in a heady manner. The entire page is devoted to a poem, or at least words that more or less rhyme, dedicated, you may be certain, to California. In three cantos and 26 stanzas, running to a total of 104 lines, the poet, who signs himself J. F. H., and who could have been either J. F. Hunnewell or J. F. Huestis, both of Boston, reaches for the stars and beyond them to God, to tell of the wonders of these new Elysian Fields.

Then, on this June 25th, punctually to the minute, "our beloved train, which had been tastefully decorated" while the party was junketing up and down the state, left Oakland on the return trip.

Although the return trip was of necessity over the same rails, the party saw many new things, Indians for one, friendly Utes and Shoshones, and enormous swarms of crickets that often impeded the wheels of the special. They saw at Bitter Creek a thorough and complete specimen of an ox driver of the plains, garbed in fancy buckskin and wielding with great dexterity a blacksnake whip 18 feet long. At Cheyenne a desert rat called Buckskin Joe entertained the group with tales of his prowess as hunter, trader, trapper, and exterminator of Indians. Joe said he was waiting for the eastbound express to take him back to his old home in New York, much to the surprise of his audience who, of course, supposed Joe had been born, fully clothed in buckskin, right there on the Great American Desert.

At half-past six on July 2nd, six weeks to a day from its departure, the *Pullman Hotel Express* pulled into Boston. No doubt most of the travelers were glad to be off wheels and home again; but the trip had been a tremendous experience for them all. They were wiser people for their journey, certainly better Americans. Editor Steele, on the whole an alert and competent reporter and a reflective man as well, summed up when he arrived back on Tremont street. "Thank God!" he cried, "that we have a Massachusetts, a Maine, and a California, and for all the noble Commonwealths of the sisterhood of states . . . it shall not be our fault if the glorious promise of the future in fame and progress be not fulfilled." That was it. The Union, the glorious Union, and she was flying with her own wings, flying high and handsome, Destiny in her talons.

The men and women of Boston had now seen the Indian in his own habitat. They had seen and talked with Mormons, with prospectors, cowhands, homesteaders, with farmers of the West, with lumberjacks, with trappers. They had seen the great fertile acres of the Midwest, the illimitable grasslands, the deserts, the strange rock forms of Wyoming, the mighty cliffs of the Rockies and the Sierras, and the wild blue of the Pacific. It was all America, all United States, warp and woof, good and bad. Mr. Thoreau, the Walden man, had remarked that he could travel far in Concord, a town six miles square, which was all very well, but not everybody could or even wanted to hole-up and look down their noses at all else. The men and women of the Boston Board of Trade's journey would never be quite the same again. They had seen a sequoia that was vastly bigger and taller than Bunker Hill Monument. They had crossed rivers to make the Charles seem the drippings of an eaves spout. More important than all else, they had seen at first hand how many miles stretched across America from Boston to San Francisco and how those miles had been caught and tamed by the rails and the telegraph wires— not only caught and tamed, but bound together. No, henceforth the words "United States of America" would mean something new, something infinitely greater.

Well, the great journey was over. As for the magnificent cars of the *Pullman Hotel Express,* they were to be taken West again for operation over the division between Omaha and Ogden, to run as a special sort of regular excursion train, and with a fine Car of Observation attached.

A Pacific footnote to the story of the Boston excursion appeared in a contemporary issue of the San Francisco *Bulletin.* "Some of our improvident people," it remarked, "have indulged in stale witticisms over the economizing disposition evinced by the Boston party." In other words, the Yankees had seemed mighty stingy to the easy-come-and-go people of the West Coast. "Yet," continued the *Bulletin,* getting tarter by the moment, "these are the people who give larger sums of money for educational and charitable purposes, in the ratio of population, than any other people on earth." Then it tore into the San Franciscans who were so careless of their own nickels and dimes, few of whom, said the *Bulletin,* had a hundred dollars to their names. They had better emulate the Yankee than to try to keep alive the highly questionable "prosperity" that stemmed from the wild and now obsolete old days of the mining camps. Economy in detail is and should be respectable, said the paper, and it was high time, and past, for the West Coast to deflate its preposterous notions about dimes, nickels, and pennies.

So, if the Yankees learned a good deal on their long journey, they may also have left a few ideas in their wake. As good Editor Steele remarked: "Hurrah for the railroad!"

CHAPTER XXXI

Time and the Railroads

The sun is no longer boss of the job. People, 55,000,000 of them, must eat, sleep and work as well as travel by railroad time. . . .
Indianapolis Sentinel, 1883.

UNTIL noon of the 18th of November, 1883, which was a Sunday, the matter of time on American railroads, and indeed in all American life, was pretty much chaos. The city of Buffalo was a fair example. On its ornate railroad station were three clocks, one operating on New York City time, used by the New York Central; one set to Columbus, Ohio, time, favored by the Michigan Southern and other railroads of the region, and the third set to local Buffalo time. In Pittsburgh the situation was even worse, for the railroads touching there used a total of six time standards.

Then, at noon on this 18th day of November, the clocks used by railroads in the United States were reset to fit the four time standards that had been agreed upon only after years of effort, much of which had to be expended in beating down the opposition of traditionalists, obscurantists, and of interests that would lose, or thought they would lose, something by adoption of the time standards. It was a victory of the first importance, this agreement among the many railroads of the country, and it came, not from government, which indeed opposed it, but from the General Time Convention, fathered and sponsored by American railroads.

In days before the steamcars time, as regulated by clocks, meant comparatively little in the United States. It was pretty much the same with stagecoach lines. But with the advent of railroads the subject became of interest, at least to railroad men. Little by little the roads worked out the idea of regular schedules of trains. At first no timetables were issued for the traveling public. Only operating crews and station agents were given the crude, handwritten sheets which, incidentally, were more hopeful than accurate.

After a bit the B&O, the Boston & Lowell, the Erie, and other of the early lines, boldly posted sheets of timetables, which were called "arrangements of trains," in their stations, and some effort was made to operate the trains accordingly. As the rails spread and lengthened, trains ran through cities and neighborhoods whose citizens had their own ideas of what the right time was and refused to have any truck with the alleged time of any other community. Generally speaking, each of the larger cities had its own local time, regulated by the sun, which was adopted by most but not always all of the smaller towns in the region.

The railroads naturally ran all of their trains by the local time of the road's terminal. In the case of the New York Central this meant that its trains, leaving Manhattan by terminal time, arrived at Buffalo fifteen minutes late by Buffalo time. In the latitude of Chicago, it was known, the passage of the sun across the meridian varied one minute for every thirteen miles, or one second for every 1,140 feet of longitude. Railroads had long since ceased to think in terms of hours only, but were holding their schedules to minutes. The Pennsylvania used Philadelphia time in the East, which was 5 minutes slower than New York City's, but 5 minutes faster than Baltimore time. The B&O system was very complicated. It used Baltimore time for trains running out of Baltimore, Columbus time for trains in Ohio, Vincennes time for trains west of Cincinnati. When solar time was noon in Chicago, it was 12:31 in Pittsburgh, 12:24 in Cleveland, 12:13 in Cincinnati, 12:09 in Louisville, 12:07 in Indianapolis, 11:50 in St. Louis, 11:48 in Dubuque, 11:41 in St. Paul, 11:27 in Omaha. There were at least 27 local times in Michigan, 38 in Wisconsin, 27 in Illinois, and 23 in Indiana.* A careful traveler, going from Eastport, Maine, to San Francisco, changed his stem-winder 20 times during the trip.

In Kansas City, and to a certain extent in Boston, each of the leading jewelers set up his own standard time and defended it with the same emotional intensity generally expended only in defending a religion. Each jeweler's customers became partisans, loud and insistent. The situation in Kansas City became so bad, what with everybody missing trains and one thing and another, that the town at last adopted a time-ball system.

In every city and town the multiplicity of time standards confused and bewildered passengers, shippers, and railway employees. Only too often errors and mistakes turned out disastrously, for railroads were now running fast trains on tight schedules; a minute or two might mean the difference between smooth operation and a collision.

One of the earliest, and perhaps the first, Americans, to propose to do something about the hundreds of local time standards in the United States was Prof. C. F. Dowd, principal of Temple Grove Seminary for Young Ladies at Saratoga Springs, New York. By means of letters and pamphlets to railroad executives, urging adoption of four or more time belts, he created considerable interest. By 1873 his plans had made such progress

---

* According to Carlton J. Corliss, in his *The Day of Two Noons,* an authoritative pamphlet, Chicago, 1941.

that he had received letters from a majority of the railroad executives agreeing to his proposal. The Panic of '73 just then put the roads into many troubles, and the matter was temporarily dropped.

But the idea was far from dead. In 1872 a large number of railroad superintendents had met in St. Louis to arrange summer passenger schedules. They formed a permanent organization which became successively the Time-Table Convention, the General Time Convention, the American Railway Association, and lastly the Association of American Railroads.

The time now was ripe for some man who could iron out the still-remaining objections of certain roads to time standards, and who could take the plans of Prof. Dowd and other pioneers and merge them into a practical system to fit the entire country, coast to coast. He appeared promptly. He was William Frederick Allen, former resident engineer of the Camden & Amboy Railroad, but since 1872 a member of the staff of the *Official Guide of the Railways and Steam Navigation Lines*. He was elected secretary of the first General Time Convention (1876), and went at the job with vigor and imagination. In 1881 he began to draw up his plans for time standards, and early in 1883 submitted them to the Convention.

Allen's plan differed from previous plans in that they had assumed adoption of meridians an even hour apart, while Allen adapted his to the territory in question. In other words, he applied his knowledge of geography, economics, large cities, and general habits to the idea, and came out with a practical rather than a theoretical plan. On October 11, 1883, the General Time Convention adopted Allen's plan, and noon of November 18th was selected as the moment it should go into effect.

The Allen plan provided for five time zones—Intercolonial, Eastern, Central, Mountain, and Pacific. The four United States zones were based on the 75th, 90th, 105th and 120th meridians west of Greenwich. The four American time belts are approximately on the longitudes of Philadelphia, Memphis, Denver, and Fresno.

There were to be no mobs to rise and protest the change when November 18th arrived, as there had been in olden days in Europe when the Gregorian calendar supplanted the Julian and eleven whole days dropped out of sight. But you may be sure there was some opposition before the day. Up in Bangor, Maine, Mayor Dogberry was aroused as no other Maine man had been since Neal Dow fastened Prohibition on the Pine Tree State. Just what prompted Dogberry to his fury isn't to be known. He vetoed a city ordinance that provided Bangor should adopt Eastern Standard Time, and with great feeling shouted that "It is unconstitutional, being an attempt to change the immutable laws of God Almighty and hard on the workingman by changing day into night." He went even further and threatened to have his constables prevent the sextons from ringing the church bells on the new and unspeakable time.

Columbus and Fort Wayne also delayed adopting the new standard

Photo at left by G. W. Clark, at right from Sue Morehead

Various types of train-order cranes are now used,
such as one at Comus, Minn., on the Milwaukee Road.
At the right, Sue Morehead, Southern Pacific operator
at Stockham, Ariz., hands up a "flimsy."

Great Northern Railway photo

A 13½-ton shovel loads cars at the Mahoning pit, world's largest open-pit mine, at Hibbing, Minnesota.

because of its alleged bad effects on the honest workingman. The Indian-apolis *Sentinel* didn't like it any better. Said the *Sentinel's* editor:

> The sun is no longer boss of the job. People—55,000,000 of them—must eat, sleep and work as well as travel by railroad time. It is a revolt, a rebellion. The sun will be requested to rise and set by railroad time. The planets must, in the future, make their circuits by such timetables as railroad magnates arrange . . . People will have to marry by railroad time, and die by rail-road time. Ministers will be required to preach by railroad time—in fact, the Railroad Convention has taken charge of the time business and the people may as well set about adjusting their affairs in accordance with its decree . . . We presume the sun, moon, and stars will make an attempt to ignore the orders of the Railroad Convention, but they, too, will have to give in at last.

Aye, the preachers would have to preach by railroad time, and many of them, still loathing the roads because they operated on the Sabbath, let fly with all they had. One Boston parson told his flock to ignore the whole matter, for "it is a lie," and continue their Christian ways on Christian time. His words echoed from the West and South. In Des Moines a man of Full Gospel cried aloud that the hosts of Hell were attempting to take over the universe and damned the steam cars as vehicles of the pride that goeth before the fall. In intellectual Tennessee, a Rev. Mr. Watson defied the Louisville & Nashville Railroad to hamper the sun and pounded his dollar watch into pulp with a claw-hammer, right on the pulpit. For some obscure reason, it seemed, the coming time standards had made all watches worthless, though many a gaping primate must have winced to see Mr. Watson belabor his shiny Waterbury.

Newspapers on the whole were in favor of the new standards, though many of them liked to treat the matter with a light, not to say facetious, hand. A St. Louis editor remarked that it would make little difference to such Western cities as North Platte and Dodge City, except "for a man who is about to be hanged." And added that such a man "would be good for another hour of life if he can induce the sheriff to stage the act by Mountain instead of Central Time." Mr. Bennett's *Herald* in New York found various reasons to rejoice. "The man who goes to church in New York on November 18th, it said, "will hug himself with delight to find that the noon service has been curtailed to the extent of nearly four minutes, while every old maid on Beacon Hill, in Boston, will rejoice to discover that she is younger by almost 16 minutes."

Out in the Northwest, Harvey Scott of *The Morning Oregonian* wrote in Portland that the new time standards would be a good thing, and re-marked, possibly in error, that the railroads of New England had already put the change into effect and had suffered no ill consequences. The *Rich-mond Dispatch* welcomed the new standards but thought the railroads had made an error in not adopting 24-hour time, thus doing away with the need of using A.M. and P.M. The *Detroit Evening Journal* actually adopted 24-hour time, coming out with front page notations saying that this was the 14 o'clock edition, the 16 o'clock edition, and so on. And the Cleveland, Mt. Vernon & Delaware Railroad, now part of the Pennsylvania System, printed 24-hour timetables. A few months later, however, this road fell in line with the others.

Monkeying with time was bound to bring complications here and there, and one such case occurred in Iowa and involved the question of whether a fire-insurance policy that expired at noon of a certain day should be governed by solar or Standard time. If sun time governed, then the policy was surely in force when the fire broke out; otherwise, the policy became null and void 2½ minutes before the fire started. The Supreme Court held that it was presumed the parties to the contract intended sun time and decided in favor of the policyholder.

The change, welcome though it was, put something of a strain on all railroads, for the adjustment called for extreme care and watchfulness lest disasters due to collisions occur. Specific orders were issued on every division. Train crews were instructed as to what change to make in their watches. A typical order was that issued by Superintendent Rowland of the Louisville & Nashville. "Should any train or engine be caught between telegraph stations at 10 A.M. on Sunday, November 18," it read, "they will stop at precisely 10 o'clock wherever they may be and stand still and securely protect their trains or engines in the rear and front until 10:18 A.M., and then turn their watches back to precisely 10 o'clock, new standard time, and then proceed on card rights or on any special orders they may have in their possession for the movement of their trains to the first telegraph station where they will stop and compare watches with the clock and be sure they have the correct new standard time before leaving . . ."

On the 18th, as the minutes ticked away in the morning, a reporter for the *Chicago Tribune* found an unusual blanket of solemnity in the West Side Union Depot, which served the Pennsylvania, Burlington, Pan Handle, and Alton railroads. He sensed that all present felt something of an extraordinary nature was about to happen. At quarter to noon, Chicago local time, conductors, engineers and other employees began dropping into the lobby, each with timepiece in hand. Depot Master Cropsey had his fine chronometer under a strong magnifying glass to mark the exact second. When the big clock on the wall, by which the running of the trains in the depot was regulated, stood fair at noon, it was stopped. Telegraph instruments were then connected with the pendulum of the clock in the observatory at Allegheny, Pennsylvania. Each movement of the pendulum was faithfully repeated by the ticking instruments, and at exactly 9 minutes 32 seconds after 12, Chicago time, "the movement of the pendulum stopped, indicating that it was 12 noon by 90th meridian time. The feat was successfully accomplished, and a general murmur of satisfaction ran through the room."

New timetables had been prepared by all railroads, and now they were released to the public. Although there appear to have been no collisions, due to the change, or any other trouble or obstacle in the operating end of the roads, there were, of course, a large number of those persons who don't read the newspapers, or fail to understand what they have read. On November 19, these luckless persons were having a time of it. "Full many a being," remarked the *New York Herald* with no little satisfaction, "dashed into a railway depot with fire in his eye and dyspepsia in his aspect only to find that he had run himself out of breath without reason, and had minutes to spare."

The traveling public, and shippers too, quickly fell in with the new time-belt plan, and naturally found it good. But Uncle Sam wasn't ready to admit the change was beneficial. A few days before November 18th the Attorney General of the United States issued an order that no government department had a right to adopt railroad time until authorized by Congress. The railroads went right ahead with the plan, and the Attorney General, according to a good and perhaps apocryphal story, went to the Washington depot late in the afternoon of the 18th to take a train for Philadelphia. He was greatly astonished, it was reported, to find he was exactly 8 minutes and 20 seconds too late.

Congress did not get around to doing anything about standard time for thirty-five years. On March 19, 1918, it passed what was known as the Standard Time Act, which gave sanction of the federal government to the four-zone system instituted by the railroads a full generation before. It also gave the Interstate Commerce Commission power to define by order the boundaries of each time zone. Since then, the ICC has made several changes in the times zones, one of the last being to transfer Michigan and western Ohio from the Central to the Eastern zone. Once, too, the city of Chicago thought it ought to be in the Eastern zone and passed an edict to that effect. It quickly brought chaotic conditions and was dropped by general acclaim.

The conception and final adoption of standard time in the United States was an eventful, possibly a momentous, day. Mention of it has seldom if ever been made in our history books, and most Americans seem to be of the general if somewhat fuzzy idea that the time zones were invented either by Benjamin Franklin or George Washington. The plan itself was the work of many men. The man who made it effective, William F. Allen, who died in 1915, has at last been memorialized. In the waiting room of the Union Station in Washington you will see a bronze tablet to his memory. He deserves it.

CHAPTER XXXII

The Little Fellers

Next station is Bridgton Junction. Change cars for Sebago, Bridgton, and Harrison. . . .

Booklet of the Bridgton & Harrison Railroad.

THE chariot wheels of imperial Rome were set exactly 4 feet 8½ inches apart. When these wheels had rolled over conquered England for a period, and rutted it well, the native troglodytes, even then a race of traditionalists, saw no good reason to change, hence the wagon roads of England remained of the same measure after the Romans had gone. And when the time arrived for iron rails, they, too, were spaced like the chariot wheels.

The thing went further than that. Because English locomotives, often with the men to run them, were imported for several of the early American railroads, rails in the United States were laid to fit the engines in the old chariot measure. But not all the rails. The New York & Erie set up in business with a 6-foot gauge, and many another road, as has been related elsewhere in this book, chose a gauge different from England's. By the time construction work was ready to start on our first transcontinental, the Union-Central Pacific, American lines were a welter of odd gauges.

It was then President Lincoln and his advisors recommended a 5-foot gauge for the government-subsidized transcontinental. The recommendation was ignored, however, and away across the prairies and mountains went steel laid to what Romans of antiquity said was the proper distance between wheels. During the next two decades, other American railroads were built or changed to that measure, and by the middle of 1886 it was declared to be Standard Gauge.

There were still mavericks at large, however. During the same two decades that witnessed the standardization of the gauge of most American railroads, the mavericks were at work building some 5,000 miles of narrow-gauge—rails set 3 feet 6 inches apart, or 3 feet, and a few as narrow as 2 feet. In 1876 there were 81 narrow-gauge roads in operation in 26 states. Pennsylvania had 11, California 8, Utah 6, Ohio 5; 4 each in Colorado, Massachusetts, New York, Iowa, Nevada, and Illinois; 3 in Mississippi, 3 in Texas, and the others scattered over 15 other states.

The first of the common-carrier two-footers, incidentally, was the 8-mile Billerica & Bedford, in Massachusetts; and the last two-footer was assuredly the Bridgton & Harrison, in Maine, which went out of business as recently as 1941.

The Billerica & Bedford itself was a cómplete failure as a railroad, but it was important historically because it fathered a large system of 24-inch-gauge track in different parts of the country, notably in Maine. The two-footer was a child in the mind of George E. Mansfield, a Yankee of Hyde Park, Massachusetts, who, while on a trip through Wales rode on and was captivated by a two-foot-gauge line that was doing a grand job hauling passengers and freight. Shortly after his return home, Mansfield learned of a projected railroad from North Billerica, on the Boston & Lowell, to Bedford, some eight miles distant. Being, unquestionably, a fanatic on the subject, he went at once to the promoters and talked them into the idea of building the new road as a two-footer. More economical, he said. The promoters not only listened to Mansfield, but put him in charge.

Construction of the B&B started in 1876, with Mansfield acting as a sort of general factotum. He bought two engines designed by M. M. Forney, one-piece jobs that comprised both locomotive and tender and, what was more—and was almost too much for the public to see—the headlight, cowcatcher and cab were on the front end. The engine seemed to be running backward and thus it shocked the esthetic morals if that is the term, of many people to whom status quo meant a great deal. The Forney engines worked well enough, even excellently, but the B&B was doomed from its inception because of lack of capital. Its contractors were obliged to resort to the courts to collect monies due them for construction, long before the line was completed. It did get finished, all eight miles of it, and it did operate after a fashion. In 1878 the sheriff caught up and sold it at public auction.

But the B&B rails and rolling stock were to carry on elsewhere. Up in Franklin County, Maine, the people of several villages had been wanting a railroad. Hearing of the B&B and its "economical cost of construction and operation," a committee of Maine townsmen visited that unfortunate road just as the auctioneer was about ready to call for bids. Seemingly quite unconcerned that, economical or not, it had never paid a dividend nor yet earned its keep, the Maine men got an option on its equipment, then went home to raise the cash.

Raising money in Maine was never a simple or easy task, and although the good townspeople of Rangeley, Strong, Phillips, and other places felt the sore need of a railroad, they were not exactly forward in putting up money for it. A Railroad Aid Society was organized. It put on picnics, dances, home-talent plays and harvest dinners, while orators whooped up the subject. In March 1879, the Society announced that it had recorded $60,000 in promises of subscriptions, of which $3,000 had been paid in actual cash.

So, on the little cash and the more in promises, the Sandy River Railroad was formed in 1879 to build from Farmington, on the Maine Central, through Strong to Phillips, eighteen miles. Grading began almost at once. The two B&B engines, renamed *Dawn* and *Echo*, arrived and were set on the ground to await the tracks. The tracks went down and forward slowly, so haltingly that the orators again took to the field and called upon every able-bodied man and boy to give a day's work, or more, to the railroad. They turned out, too, in numbers. October came on, and with it winter in that part of Maine. The volunteers, dressed like loggers against the bitter weather, worked with great good will. They dropped ties, distributed spikes and plates. They unloaded steel and brought it forward for the professionals to complete the tracklaying.

In early November a flurry of snow quickly turned into a young blizzard. A full foot of snow came down. It was simply ignored. On went the rails. A week later, the volunteers were still going strong, and to permit longer workdays they built great bonfires and hung lanterns on the spruces of the right-of-way. On November 20th, the two locomotives set up a mighty blowing of whistles, the countryside was awakened, and all hurried to the new bridge that led into Phillips, a town now on a railroad. It was a wonderful morning to have a locomotive and a train of cars heave in.

A year or so later began a long period of extension of the two-footers in this region, all of them hooked to the original Sandy River Railroad. In 1883 stockholders of the Sandy River organized the Franklin & Megantic, to build from Strong to Kingfield, fifteen miles. In 1894 the Kingfield & Dead River was formed to carry the rails on to Bigelow. Meanwhile, another manifestation called the Phillips & Rangeley was chartered to run between those towns. Separate branch lines were built and named the Madrid * and the Eustis railroads.

Not one of these two-footers, so far as I can learn, ever paid many dividends. Yet they continued to operate for years. Their trains often required two or three days to cover the original course of the line, that between Farmington and Phillips, eighteen miles. Beavers enjoyed undermining the road wherever it came near any of the many sawmill ponds along the system. And once, according to H. T. Crittenden, an authority on two-footers, an engineer and fireman leaped from opposite sides of the cab, simultaneously, to get a shot at a herd of deer the train was passing through, and left the engine to run along untended until a brakeman could crawl over the tender and shut off the power.†

Somehow, the Little Fellers, as the standard-gauge Maine Central train crews called them, managed to carry on until 1908, when they were formed

---

* The givers of place names in the State of Maine went all over the world in their search. Towns or villages were named: Albion, Jerusalem, Naples, New Sweden, Norway, Orient, Rome, Paris, Verona.

† See Mr. Crittenden's exhaustive and excellent *The Two-Footers*, cited in the Bibliography.

into one system, the Sandy River & Rangeley Lakes, and a bit of capital pumped into them. For the next three years the system showed a small profit. In 1911 control was acquired by the Maine Central. Not long afterward the first effects of the automobile began to be felt. Pulpwood, always a heavy freight item for the road, went to trucking outfits. Passenger business fell off rapidly, and in 1931 steam passenger trains were replaced by gasoline-driven cars, usually the sign of abandonment. Rails were pulled up here and there and sold for junk. By the end of 1936 what was claimed to be the largest system of two-footers in the United States had vanished.

The aforementioned Bridgton & Harrison, the last two-foot passenger carrier to go out of existence, was opened in 1883 at a cost of more than $200,000. In active control was the same George E. Mansfield who had built the original two-footer, the B&B in Massachusetts, then built most of the varied lines of the Sandy River & Rangeley Lakes system, and from there had come to Bridgton, in southeastern Maine.

Like the others, the B&H was never to know great prosperity, but it carried on for some sixty years. To do so, it enlisted the aid of a literary gentleman of imagination who wrote a pamphlet describing the charms of B&H territory, a work of art that should not be permitted to die. I regret I do not know who this writer was, for he was a hard worker, a man who overlooked no rippling brook, no mountain crag, nor any dead hero who would add glory to the Bridgton & Harrison's mighty system of twenty-one miles of two-foot track. Hark while he sings:

"How do you get to Bridgton? The answer is as plain and easy as the route itself. You press the button at Portland, that is, buy an excursion ticket to Bridgton, and steam and the conductor do the rest. When the latter, soon after the train has passed famous Hiram Falls on the Saco river, cries, 'Next station is Bridgton Junction, change cars for Sebago, Bridgton, and Harrison,' you gather up your luggage, and presently you step upon the platform and into the cozy little cars of the odd, narrow-gauge railroad. 'All aboard!' And as you see the long train of the Maine Central disappear on its northern way, you are on your quiet journey to the eastward for a fifty minutes' ride to Bridgton.

"You need have no anxiety whatever, as the little engine, with its combined mail, baggage, and smoking car, and its one passenger car, climbs and descends heavy grades, dashes around astonishingly sharp curves—a rare topographical instance, by the way—or accelerates its speed on a straight, level section, for the conductor, in reply to your question, assures you that in all the many years of the road's existence no passenger has been killed or even injured. So, disarmed of all fear, you are free to take your ease in your comfortable seat. As in the case of most other railroads, some sections of the way are dull and uninteresting, while others are interesting and pleasing, their charms heightened by very contrast. On leaving the Junction a pretty view is afforded at the immediate left. This is picturesque Hiram Village, situated at the foot of Mt. Cutler, a small mountain rising abruptly on its western side, and the Saco river, flowing through its residential and business midst, on its clear, winding way to the sea. About a mile further on the train is following lively Hancock brook, whose swift waters dash and foam and eddy along at the right; and soon you skirt a pretty lakelet, Barker pond, on the same side, and very shortly, on the left, a larger and more beautiful sheet of water, Hancock pond, whose calm, slightly blue mirror is set in a sandy-white and woodland-green frame, the southern segment of whose border is touched by the iron rails. This lake is much sought by summer guests in the vicinity, who, besides the pleasure of sailing its waters, find therein a plenitude of pickerel, salmon, black bass and white perch, or seek not in vain the brook trout in its incoming and outgoing brooks. And here, while the train halts some minutes to water the iron horse, you may enjoy a pleasing view of the distant northwestern horizon of the White mountains, which, however, wear a blue rather than white tinge, and a nearer prospect of the game-suggestive, picnic-hinting hills.

"Next you pass through a portion of the town of Denmark, noted as the birthplace and boyhood home of two famous Americans, Major General Rufus Ingalls, Grant's West Point classmate and intimate friend, and Quartermaster General of the Army, and Gov. Hazen S. Pingree of Michigan. Here is a way station, known as Perleys Mills, with a quickly-dissolving glimpse of a rustic mill, a dwelling or two, and a narrow stretch of open, farming country. A few miles further, after passing a long and deep cut through granite ledges, you emerge from the forest into a typical down-East hamlet or village, with mills, store, post office and various industrial shops, church and schoolhouse, clusters of dwellings, and intersected by a wide stream—a pretty, rural neighborhood, bearing the uneuphonious name of Sandy creek. A brief halt, and the train continues on through a two-miles' stretch of meadows, fields and patches of forest, crossing several times sinuous Willet Creek, and lo! you now disembark at Bridgton, a station which, in architecture and with its aggregation of people and teams, is a composite picture of the rural and the metropolitan. The wished-for goal is reached. . . ."

The B&H was bought and again sold by the Maine Central, and during its latter years was owned by the Town of Bridgton. Application for abandonment was made in 1940; and after another year of running railroad-fan specials, it was junked.

Another Little Feller that outlived its time and was still operating in 1946, though with freight service only, is the East Tennessee & Western North Carolina, running 24 miles between Port Rayon, Tennessee, and Elk Park, North Carolina. In his charming and nostalgic book, *Slow Train* *to Yesterday,** Archie Robertson calls this line one of the most interesting and appealing in the country. Part of it is 3-foot gauge and part standard. Known locally as "Tweetsie," and dating from the 1860's, the ET&WNC wound up its passenger career, much like the B&H, by running special excursions for railroad fans. They came in considerable droves, too, but they were not enough to keep her running.

It was the Rocky Mountain region of Colorado where the narrow-gauge flourished as nowhere else, usually in its 3-foot form. Here were operated the dinky engines and cars of the Denver & Rio Grande Western, the Rio Grande Southern, the Florence & Cripple Creek, the Silverton Northern, the Crystal River & San Juan, and many more. In 1942, when there were but 1,400 miles of narrow-gauge remaining in the United States, 900 miles of it were in Colorado.

It was the expense and difficulty of standard construction that prompted much of the narrow-gauge in Colorado. The 162-mile main line of the still-operating Rio Grande Southern, for instance, connects towns scarcely 60 miles apart as the crow flies, which will give an idea of the terrain. That the RGS has survived and continues to give passenger service of a kind, even if with gasoline cars, indicates the kind of country in which it operates. It is a rugged and almost inaccessible region. The rails connect towns, many of them now ghostly enough, named Mancos, Lizard Head, Ophir, Telluride and Placerville. In its heyday this narrow-gauge operated luxury cars, described in the language of the period as elegant, for the miners, many of them new-born capitalists who loved the paneled wood interiors, the silver washstands and plumbing fixtures, and the shiny brass beds in the little staterooms.†

If there was reason enough for building railroads to the 3-foot gauge in such mountainous country as Colorado, no one now connected with the Sumpter Valley Railroad in Oregon remembers why that line was laid to the narrow measure. In fact, it had barely been completed when its officials contemplated a change to standard-gauge and ordered that all tie replacements should be made with that object in view, though the change was never accomplished and likely never will be, for in 1947 the company was hopefully awaiting permission from the Interstate Commerce Commission to abandon all trackage except that in its yards at South Baker.

The Sumpter Valley was thought up by David Eccles, energetic Mormon

---

* Boston, 1945.
† Described with gusto by Lucius Beebe, author of *Highball: A Pageant of Trains,* and other books about railroads, in the *New York Herald Tribune,* October 12, 1946. Mr. Beebe had just made a trip in these elegant if antique cars, which were put in service for a special run over the line.

businessman and industrialist from Utah, who was interested in getting a lot of gentile ponderosa pine in eastern Oregon and making it into lumber at Baker, a town on the Union Pacific. He acquired the timber, south and west of Baker, started construction of a sawmill, and in 1890 organized the railroad company. Most of the stockholders were members of the Church of Jesus Christ of Latter-day Saints, so the Sumpter Valley Railroad was immediately christened by local gentiles, and with typically delicate frontier wit, the Polygamy Central.

The original investment in the road was $1,654,000, quite a sum in its place and period, and it served to buy a lot of light rail, several second-hand 3-foot-gauge locomotives, a string of secondhand rolling stock, and to get the work under way. The first 22 miles to McEwen were completed in 1892. At this period the plan seems to have been to build on southward to Burns, and still on across the desert lands of southeastern Oregon to Lake-view, where the line would meet another narrow-gauge operating out of Reno, Nevada. The Sumpter Valley never got to Lakeview, or anywhere near it. In 1897 it reached the active and rowdy mining town of Sumpter, from which the valley takes its name, the early settlers of which were un-reconstructed Carolinians who sought to honor Fort Sumter and inci-dentally exposed in their orthography the state of learning in their native heath. Sumpter village was almost 30 miles out of Baker. The road con-tinued building, through Whitney, through Tipton and, at last, in 1910, arrived at what was to be the end of the line, Prairie City, a full 60 miles from the Baker roundhouse.

The secondhand locomotives, their tenders bravely painted "Sumpter Valley," had to be converted to wood, for slabs from local sawmills were to be their fuel for many years. U. S. Carpenter, veteran retired engineer of the line, recalls that five cords of slab and edgings would be put aboard the tender at Baker and usually more had to be picked up along the line before Prairie City was reached. When it got into the Blue Mountains, the road had one grade of 4.08 per cent, another of 3.10 per cent. In the last 12 miles, the road dropped 2,000 feet from Dixie Mountain to Prairie City, long since abandoned.

During World War I a notable wreck occurred between Sumpter and Larch station when the wooden brake beam on one of a string of stock cars loosened and dropped to the rails. Derailment of the stock cars fol-lowed, and they were strung out along the tracks on their sides, the steers bellowing like their fathers of Bashan and boiling against the car tops until they knocked off the roofs. Many were so badly injured they had to be killed; and the others took off into the valley. The train crew refused to turn cowboy, so a posse of buckaroos was engaged to hunt the cattle and return them, which they did—along with several more steers than were originally listed.

Mormon road or no, the Sumpter Valley toted beer into the mining camps along its tracks, and one happy day, when a runaway freight on Dixie Mountain strewed full kegs and sent them rolling all over the neighborhood, the word flashed to the mines and the miners downed their tools and went to work at salvage, much of which was done right on the spot, wherever a keg was corralled.

Although the Sumpter Valley was laid primarily to bring out fine pine lumber, and no little ore from the mines, passengers were a good business from the first. Hundreds of loggers had to be brought down to Baker from the camps periodically, for the alleged and standard reason of getting dental work done; and then had to be taken back, morose and shakey from their dentistry, into the timbered hills and distributed to the various camps. I rode the line once, many years ago, in company with several husky jacks who were patently on the verge of delirium tremens, and remember the diplomacy and all-around finesse with which the conductor and brakemen handled their jittery charges. In those days, I was told, as many as a hundred passengers, together with their bindles and bottles, might climb aboard the cars at Baker.

Then, there was Sumpter and its mines, which came into a delayed boom period with the arrival of the railroad. Prospecting, even some actual mining, had been done in the district as early as 1862, and had been followed by hundreds of Chinese working the old tailings. But things petered out and remained quiescent until the Sumpter Valley's rails came to town. A year or so later the settlement contained 3,000 persons, and holes in the hardrock were producing fairly rich ore under the names of Mammoth, Goldbug-Grizzly, Baby McKee, and Belle of Baker. Naturally, there was also a Bonanza. More than twelve miles of tunnels were in operation under the town. A dozen saloons and as many cathouses were operating above ground. Citizens got together and put up a Grand Opera House.

Seven miles from Sumpter was the fantastic incorporated town of Bourne, site of the alleged mining operations of something called the Sampson Company, Limited, of London, New York, and Bourne, one of Oregon's biggest and best swindles. Bourne grew rapidly like an evil weed, and its actual mining activities were put into shadow by the vast printing establishment operated by the Sampson Company, which put out two newspapers, one for local consumption, the other, with a gigantic mailing list covering much of the civilized world, for the edification of suckers wherever they might be. This big-circulation edition contained glowing accounts of gold strikes that never happened, scintillating accounts of ore mills that were never built, and of "fabulously rich" claims acquired by Sampson, Ltd. The whole affair seems to have been the dream of J. Wallace White, who made a fortune out of his Bourne printing presses before the thing blew up in 1906. The inhabitants started moving out, almost in a mass, leaving everything right where it was. In 1937 a cloudburst removed most of the buildings.

As for Sumpter, it began to peter out about 1916, and the next year a fire destroyed much of the town, despite efforts of some 200 men brought to the scene as fast as a special of the Sumpter Valley Railroad could take them. There was a little rebuilding, but Sumpter's great days were over.

The railroad's Daily-except-Sunday passenger train, known as the Stump Dodger, managed to carry on until 1937, when the use of passenger coaches was discontinued. It was possible, early in 1947, to buy a ticket for a ride in the caboose. Now and then some weatherbeaten prospector takes the train to Whitney, where he means to uncover any one of the two or three hundred "Lost" mines there, but the business is pretty small. During 1945, so the company's books show, the line carried a total of 32 passengers for a total of 1,488 passenger miles, and brought in a revenue of exactly $28.

Wood-burners went out of operation in 1939 when the road purchased two large Mallet-type locomotives from the Uintah Railroad in Utah. With these and a small Diesel, used for switching in the South Baker yards, the last narrow-gauge in the Pacific Northwest survives, hauling logs and lumber mostly, and a few sheep. When Earl Pomeroy, newspaperman of Portland, made a trip over the line in 1946, the road was operating six freight trains a week, three each way. Herbert M. Miles, general manager, told Pomeroy that several of the old wood-burners of the Sumpter Valley were bought by the Peruvian Government, and two more went to the White Pass & Yukon in the Far North, where at last report they were still running.

Perhaps the most significant and melancholy fact about the Sumpter Valley Railroad is the reason it wants to abandon its main line: it plans to replace its Mallets and rolling stock with a fleet of gasoline-driven trucks that will take to the highways.

For some reason or other, the narrow-gauge lines have always enjoyed a great popularity with railroad fans. They like to read about them, and they will travel halfway across the United States to make a trip on a narrow-gauge passenger train. Perhaps this is so simply because they are "little" railroads. Perhaps a contributing factor is that the narrow-gaugers are often more intimate, more personal, than the big standard-gauge lines; they have an individuality as friendly as it is quaint. They are not so big that one cannot appreciate their personality. In any case, narrow-gauge lines have been the subject of more writing than their importance would indicate on any grounds except just plain affection.

Writing in the old reliable *Railroad Magazine*, Linwood Moody, a fan of the narrow-gauge, told his readers to "Make 1941 a See-Our-Narrow-Gauges Year. Visit the little old roads that stand today as mutilated fragments of colorful history. Get photos and other souvenirs of them while you can, for the night is surely coming—a night in which no more such pictures can be taken. Right now, it is sunset on the narrow-gauge."

Double-decked coach developed for commuter traffic by the Long Island Railroad, only Class
1 road whose passenger revenue tops its freight revenue.

Two hundred of the 2,690 conductors' punch patterns used by the Pennsylvania Railroad today. Each passenger conductor in active service has an identifying punch, but some ticket collectors hold duplicates. No. 1 is assigned to six different collectors. The system varies somewhat on other roads.

CHAPTER XXXIII

Robbing the Steamcars

To add to the mood of change, came the realization that the long
financial panic was over. Times were better. Bankers and railroads
seemed not quite so hateful—and Jesse James not quite so heroic.
—LLOYD LEWIS, *Oscar Wilde Visits America* (1882).

ONLY a rash man would assert the name of the first train robber to
operate in the United States, but the first formal holdup of a train of
steam cars appears to have been accomplished on the 6th of October,
1866, by a crew of Hoosiers who thought it up, then put it into practice on
the Ohio & Mississippi Railway near Seymour, in Jackson County,
Indiana.

This first stickup was a simple job. A passenger train carrying an
express and baggage car pulled out of Seymour in early evening, heading
east, and almost immediately two masked men came into the express car
from the coach just behind. In those days it hadn't occurred to express-
men to lock their car's doors, so the entry was made without fuss. The
two men secured the messenger's keys, opened his safe, took out some
$13,000, then pulled the bellcord to signal the engineer to stop. Stop he
did, and the robbers dumped another safe, unopened, from the car, and
leaped after it into the darkness.

This was something new. The train crew hardly knew what was expected of them. They discussed the event wonderingly, then took the
train to the next station. Here an armed posse was recruited. They
pumped their way on a handcar back to the scene of the crime, to find
only the unopened safe, which had been too much for the robbers. Such
was the holdup. A bit later, and doubtless with good reason, John and
Simeon Reno, brothers of questionable habits, and Frank Sparks, no
better than he should be, were arrested, indicted for the crime, and admitted to bail. Their trial was postponed from time to time and was never
held.

Then, almost a year later, the same eastbound train was held up and
robbed, again near Seymour, in the same manner, by two imitative souls
named Walker Hammond and Michael Collins. It was believed that the
Reno boys, of whom there were four "bad" ones in all, were behind the

369

second holdup. Pinkerton detectives managed to lay hands on John Reno and this time he was sent to the pen, though on exactly what charges I do not know.

What by now was becoming known as the Reno Gang presently turned up in Iowa in the burglary business. Captured and put in jail, four of them escaped and worked their way back to God's country of Indiana, where they proceeded to hold up a richly laden train of the Jefferson, Madison & Indianapolis Railroad, taking $96,000 from two safes in the express car. This time murder was done, for the messenger, beaten and thrown from the moving train, died. In quick succession there were holdups on the Cincinnati, Hamilton & Dayton road, and on the Ohio & Mississippi Valley. Several alleged members of the Reno Gang were arrested and, before they could be tried, were taken by a party of vigilantes and hanged from a tree that was, appropriately enough, right beside a railroad track. And on a November night in 1868, more vigilantes called at the jail in New Albany, Indiana, where three Reno brothers and one Anderson were confined, awaiting trial, and after a stiff fight with the jailer, secured the four men and hanged them from the rafters of the jail. This was the end of the Reno Gang, and their reputation all but died with them. This seems odd to happen to the inventors of a new profession, for if the Renos were, as many contemporary writers claimed, the first to commit train robbery, they were the founders of a typically American institution that was to flourish for the next half century and from which Americans were to draw many of their most popular folk heroes of song and story.*

With the death of the last of the Reno Gang train robbery had a hiatus of almost two years. Then, in 1870, it was revived almost simultaneously in Kentucky, Tennessee, and Nevada. The first holdup was of a Mobile & Ohio train at Moscow, Kentucky, the second of a Nashville & Northwestern express car, the third of an N&N train near Union City, Tennessee. In the latter affair Expressman Morrell was shot through both lungs. The Pinkertons were called in, and this time William and Robert, two sons of old Allan, the founder, took the trail.

The wounded messenger gave descriptions of the robbers that seemed to fit twin brothers, Hilary and Levi Farrington, who had been absent from their homes near Gilman, Tennessee, for some time. The Pinkertons trailed the suspected pair to a tiny hamlet of three or four cabins on the banks of the Mississippi, a sort of Tobacco Road community, fairly crawling with queer characters of odd morals and a vast suspicion of all strangers. Arriving at this simian lair at nightfall, William Pinkerton and a companion approached the largest cabin in the place, which they could see was lighted by a single candle. Pinkerton didn't trouble to knock. He

---

* For a full account of the Reno boys see Alvin F. Harlow's grand book, *Old Waybills*, New York, 1934, on which my account rests heavily.

pushed open the door and walked in. Five men, one woman and a young girl leaped to their feet, the light went out, and the shooting commenced.

Two men escaped by the back door, two surrendered to Pinkerton, and the other man lay dead on the floor. If the Brothers Farrington had been among the party, they were the two men who had escaped. The Pinkertons did not let down; they soon caught Hilary Farrington in Missouri, and Levi in Illinois. This finished the Farrington Gang, which had barely got started anyway.

Nevada saw the next train holdup, on November 5, 1870. Why the event had been delayed so long is not to be rationally explained. For many years past bold road agents had been holding up Western stagecoaches, chiefly to get their hands into the fabulously rich strong boxes of Wells, Fargo & Company, but had not attempted the like on the Central Pacific Railroad, operating now for more than five years. It was long overdue, this first Nevada stickup of a train, which began at Truckee when six men boarded an eastbound train at one o'clock in the morning. When the train stopped at Verdi two of the gang went forward and covered the engine crew. The others took over the express car which gave up a thumping good haul in cash and bullion, close to $40,000.

On the next night the same train was held up again, this time near Toana, 400 miles to the east, and to the tune of another $40,000 in cash and bullion. No arrests appear to have been made in connection with these robberies, although at least one of them was popularly laid at the door of Jack Davis, a leading gambler and business man of Virginia City, much revered for his charity to the poor.

That train robbery should break out in Nevada, long celebrated for its lawlessness, was no surprise. It was the next job that astonished the public: Into Messenger Halpine's express car on the Boston & Albany Railroad, one day in 1871, stepped John I. Filkins, a former express company employee. He wantonly shot Halpine twice, robbed the safe, and departed. The incident electrified all New England, which theretofore had got its banditry vicariously from Mr. Beadle's Dime Novel Library.

It was almost time for the great hero of the dime novel writers to appear, the hillbilly they were to magnify to twice his life-size, the thug they were to blow into folklore, even into the chaste pages of the *Dictionary of American Biography*—Jesse Woodson James.*

Perhaps, as folklore has it, Jesse James was "kind to his mother and to little children"—that is, all little children except those who happened to be on the trains that he and his goons wrecked in order to rob. Perhaps, too, as alleged by his apologists, Jesse's youth had been embittered by hardships incident to the Civil War. So had the youth of many another man who did not, however, use it to explain and justify a career of crime.

---

* Vol. IX, New York, 1932.

What is a certainty, and no folklore, is that James and his gang showed an indifference to human life that should put him, and possibly them, beyond the pale of consideration as human beings.

Frank and Jesse James were Missourians who had taken up bank robbery in a small way after the Civil War. In some or all of these affairs they were aided by Coleman Younger and on occasion by Younger's brothers, Bob, John and Jim, and other men. None of the gang had been arrested when on July 21, 1873, they made their first bid for national headlines by holding up a train on the Chicago, Rock Island & Pacific, near Adair, Iowa. Train holdups, of course, had been going on for many years. The James-Younger contribution to the technique was to wreck the train first.

As this particular Rock Island train sped across the hot summer prairie on that sultry evening, Engineer Rafferty, an excellent man, was at the throttle, his eye on the track, his heart glad that the grain harvest was to be good for the struggling farmers. The tall wheat and the towering corn fled by in the falling twilight, thousands of acres of it, waving in a soft prairie breeze. All seemed well ahead. The shining rails stretched out, true and level, beyond the beam of the great headlight. Then, came a curve and as they rounded it, Rafferty's fireman saw a rope suddenly tauten, then a rail slide out of place. He shouted warning. Rafferty threw his engine into reverse, but there wasn't time. Over keeled the locomotive on its side, crushing poor Rafferty to death. Half a dozen men piled out of the trackside hedge, subdued the train crew, and two of them went through the express safe. The others went through the coaches and sleepers and forced passengers to toss their cash and valuables into a grain sack one of the robbers carried. The total haul was small, estimated at around $4,000.

Nobody was arrested, but detectives thought that descriptions of the robbers fitted the James and Younger boys rather closely. The gang laid low until January, 1874, when they held up a stagecoach in Arkansas, and two weeks later five of them took over the depot at Gadeshill Station, on the Iron Mountain Railroad in Missouri, tying up the station agent and five loungers who were there to see the steamcars go by. When the steamcars arrived a few minutes later, they were flagged down, and the robbers went through the express safe and also through the passengers.

Soon the Pinkertons were on the case. In a gun battle with some of the Youngers, two Pinkertons were killed, and John Younger shot dead. The James brothers trapped another Pinkerton and killed him. The Pinkertons then made a deplorable mistake in the field of public relations: they heaved a sizable bomb through an open window of the James home in Missouri, thinking to kill Frank and Jesse. Both men happened to be away, but the bomb killed Archie Samuel, a half-brother, and blew off part of the right arm of Mrs. Samuel, the James' boy's mother. It was a most unfortunate affair for the detectives. The press heaped scorn upon them, calling them murderers, and made so great a noise that many persons who had no sympathy for the James gang became almost their partisans henceforth.

The robbing went on. In December of 1874 six men flagged down a Kansas Pacific train near Muncie, Kansas, just west of Kansas City, by piling the track high with ties. The train stopped and the usual proceedings went on, the gang taking some $30,000 in cash, bullion, and other valuables from the express car, then working over the passengers. Hard on this job the police of Kansas City arrested one Bud McDaniels who, when sufficiently sober, worked now and then as a railroad brakeman. Bud was packing considerable jewelry, quite a roll of bills, and two big guns. But he wouldn't talk. He escaped from a deputy while being taken to trial and was killed by a posse.

During the next year somebody, and likely the James-Younger crew, stuck up a stage in Texas, and held up a bank in West Virginia. It was surely the James and Youngers who flagged down a Missouri Pacific train on July 7, 1876, not far from Sedalia, shot the cars full of holes just for the hell of it, and robbed safe and passengers—the swag going into the inevitable grain sack, an item never absent from a formal job of the James and Youngers.

Still no arrests were made. It seems incredible that a gang could perform so often, and over so wide an area, for three years and still be almost intact. Even the Pinkertons, who in that day were tough and determined and on the whole able detectives, had been unable to cope with the gang. The explanation surely lies partly in the public attitude toward railroads in the 1870's. It was one largely of fear and hate combined. The roads had done a good deal, as I have attempted to show elsewhere, to bring about this state of affairs. Farmers who felt they had been cheated, either in land deals or in freight rates, were not prone to worrying much if other men preyed on the railroads. Still other men had lost their savings in wildcat railroad stocks and bonds. Many laboring men felt the roads were grinding them down—and in 1877 were to stage a strike and riots the like of which the country had not seen until then. So, the James and the Youngers and their men continued to ride and rob with what in retrospect seems to have been comparative ease and safety. They might have continued their profession for some years to come had they not attempted a raid on the First National Bank of Northfield, Minnesota, a place not to be trifled with.

Northfield was a sleepy college town and a trading center for farmers roundabout, but it harbored a large number of citizens who were prompt to defend their institutions and rights, dead shots, too, who had learned their fighting manners in the interminable Indian wars of the time and place. When Jesse James and seven of his crew rode into Northfield on the pleasant 7th of September, 1876, and went to work on the bank, a young medical student named Henry Wheeler was drowsing on the porch of the Dampier hotel, across the street. Stirred by the untoward noise, Wheeler got to his feet, went inside, then appeared at a window with an old Army carbine and let fly. In less than two minutes, the street was swarming with men, mostly armed, mostly shooting, and shooting very well. The gang had been unable to get into the vault, and now they started to get out of Northfield, firing in every direction. Calmly taking stances where they could do the best work, the embattled citizens shot three of the yahoos dead—Clell Miller, Bill Stiles, and Sam Wells. They also wounded Cole, Bob, and Jim Younger. Jesse and Frank James, by tactics that some said were more self-preservative than heroic, got away. The Youngers, too, managed to get out of town, while close behind them came a posse of the savagely efficient citizenry. These villagers ran the wounded Youngers to earth on Hanska Slough, in Brown County, took them in tow, and they were put away in the Minnesota penitentiary at Stillwater. Bob died there, Jim committed suicide behind the walls, and Cole was paroled in 1901, to travel with Frank James Wild West Show for a time, and to take to the lecture platform. He died, the last of the gang, in 1915, in bed and with his shoes removed.

Those seven minutes in Northfield were the hottest the James gang ever faced.* The affair wrecked the original gang, and Jesse and Frank lay low for three years, meanwhile, it is alleged, engaging in legitimate business. Yet they weren't quite done with the steamcars. They recruited a number of relatives and friends and on August 7, 1879, stopped and robbed a Chicago & Alton train near Glendale, Missouri. Although their haul wasn't large, and nothing spectacular happened during the holdup, this was the gang's feat that got into balladry.†

Two more train jobs remained. The first was of a Rock Island train, July 15, 1881, at Winston, Missouri, during which two members of the train crew were brutally and needlessly shot and killed; the next, seven weeks later, of a Chicago & Alton express at Blue Cut, Missouri, during which nobody was killed. It was the James Boys' last train robbery. On April 3rd, next, in 1882, Jesse was killed by the immortal little coward who shot Mister Howard—a thug named Robert Ford. Frank James gave himself up and reformed, if that is the word, dying in 1915 and leaving a widow who survived until July 6, 1944.

Once in a long while suspected train robbers were baited into a trap. A successful occasion of this sort was staged in 1888 on the Black Hills & Fort Pierre Railroad in South Dakota and was inspired by Alex McKenzie, paymaster for a logging outfit which had operations along the line. It was McKenzie's practice, once a month, to board a train at Lead, carrying

---

* Being in Northfield several years ago, I was politely shown holes and marks made by bullets during the battle, and had the honor of shaking hands with one of the citizens who participated. I regret I did not make note of his name.

† See Chapter XXXVIII, "Ballads of the Rails."

in one hand a cowhide bag containing anywhere from ten to twenty thousand dollars, in the other hand a rifle. No attempt had been made to hold him up, so he started out on the September trip as usual, riding in the tiny caboose which followed a string of flats, two box cars and a locomotive in charge of Engineer John Cominsky.

At Galena Junction the train stopped to cut out the two box cars and take them to Galena, on a stub line, leaving the rest of the train at the Junction. McKenzie and his rich bag of gold and silver usually waited in the caboose for the locomotive to return, hook on, and proceed to Brownsville and Elk Canyon. On this day, however, he had business in Galena and rode in on the locomotive. Looking back he was surprised to see several horsemen charge out of the woods and chase the train, shouting like so many Indians. McKenzie remarked on this, but Engineer Cominsky thought nothing of it. "Cowboys," he said, "are damned fools and like to show off by racing trains."

A bit later that day McKenzie discovered the telegraph line beside the tracks had been cut. He wondered if this fact had any connection with the horsemen, and said as much next day to Superintendent Blackstone of the railroad. Blackstone believed the two items to be more than coincidence, and just before McKenzie was due to make the next pay trip, a come-on story was put in the local newspaper. It related, with typical local pride, that the October payroll was to be $32,000 and it would go out to the logging camps on the 12th. Joe Koller, newspaperman of Lead, who knew participants in the affair, later told the story for the *Daily Argus-Leader* of Sioux Falls.

"This time," said Mr. Koller, "a combination express and smoker coach was coupled behind the engine. McKenzie seemed quite alone as he carried his valise aboard. The train pulled out as usual. On the outskirts of Lead it slowed for a switch, and there Deadwood Dick Bullock (the second of that name in these parts) and the late William A. Reimer, a young man of courage who later served as Lawrence County sheriff, climbed up the cab steps and settled down on the coal pile in the tender to await events.

"The attack came at a place later called Avalon. The engine, rounding a curve, rammed into a pile of ties. As it stopped it skidded off the spread rails. A shot heralded the cause of banditry in Jesse James style. Masked men pushed out of the trackside underbrush. At command the engineer and fireman jumped down and walked forward. Then gun thunder broke from the gangway and coal bin, and one of the masked men cried as a bullet from Bill Reimer's gun hit him.

"The bandits darted into the brush, and now began some fast shooting between them and the two guards. Bullets splattered against the locomotive and thudded into the coach, while Reimer and Bullock fired back. The bandits reached their horses and escaped—all but one, who was badly wounded and was taken in charge by the guards. They worked him over to such purpose that he divulged the names of his pals, and that night in Deadwood the rest of the gang was rounded up. All were convicted and sent to prison."

Before getting on to what were perhaps the most interesting train robbers in nineteenth-century America, it is necessary to mention Sam Bass, another Black Hills product, hero of the long, illiterate, hideous, and popular ballad that bears his name, if for no other reason than that Sam is one of the seven desperadoes to get into the *Dictionary of American Biography*. Sam, as the song relates, "come from Indiana" being born there on a most unfortunate day in 1851. He was not a scholarly fellow, admits one of his more infatuated biographers, and was unable to read or write at the time of his sudden death at the age of twenty-seven. He came to notoriety as a stage robber in the Black Hills, in 1877, committing the jobs for need of money to spend on race horses, faro banks, whores, and other necessities. In that same year he and four partners got into the big time by holding up a Union Pacific train at Big Springs, Nebraska, and cleaning the express car of more than $65,000, a good haul then or now.

Fleeing to Texas, Bass and his companions went immediately to work, staging a series of holdups on the Houston & Texas Central and the Texas & Pacific roads, none of which paid off very well in cash, one job being as low as $50. Turning to the field of banking, as had his betters, the James-Younger set, Bass was mortally wounded at Round Rock, Texas, by a member of the Texas Rangers, who thus contributed no little to the progress of civilization. Bass was properly buried at Round Rock, and the sentimental and gun-loving Texans put up a neat gravestone with a characteristic epitaph: "A Brave Man Reposes in Death Here. Why was he Not True?" The Sam Bass legend began at once and has grown steadily; and in the Lone Star state today one may, if one is not careful, be shown as many as one hundred and forty-six different revolvers, any and all of which are certified as being the gun last carried by the illiterate thug.*

I regret exceedingly that neither Christopher Evans nor John Sontag rate a sketch in the classic *Dictionary of American Biography*, for they belong there more than does Sam Bass and are as fitted for its pages as are Jesse James and Coleman Younger. Evans and Sontag had a deep and, to them—and to many others as well—a very proper motivation for their robberies on the Southern Pacific Railroad. That is, if they ever did any robbing at all. Theirs is a curious case. Neither was ever convicted of robbery, and although I believe they staged five very efficient stickups of SP trains, there is many a Californian to this day who will swear that the two men were hounded to prison or death merely because they opposed, or

---

* In his *Treasury of American Folklore,* New York, 1944, B. A. Botkin has an amusing summary of the fantastic legends about Bass.

agitated against, a powerful railroad corporation. Whatever else they were or weren't, Evans and Sontag were the nearest to being indestructible of any human beings I can think of, offhand or after long deliberation.

To comprehend the cold hate that appears to have motivated Chris Evans it is necessary to know a little about the Southern Pacific Railroad of the last quarter of the nineteenth century. That road's policy, according to a fairminded and even friendly historian,* was to create and maintain a monopoly of transportation in California, and more, to exact from that monopoly "the utmost possible profit." Doubtless such a policy was not unusual among railroads of the time, but in the case of the SP it appears to have been administered with a cynicism and often with a brutality that would be hard to match. Living down the reputation it acquired during this period has been one of the most difficult things the management of the road has had to contend with these past forty years.

In building and acquiring its lines southward from San Francisco in the 1870's, the SP was subsidized by land grants along each side of its right-of-way. It announced that as soon as these lands had been properly surveyed and the titles validated, it would sell them to farmers at $2.50 an acre. By this time immigrants already were squatting on the lands. Many had also begun legal proceedings to obtain titles of their own direct from the government. Probably most if not all of the settlers were prepared to buy from the railroad at the $2.50 an acre price announced. But when the SP at last received clear titles to the lands of the grant, it put prices up, well up, and advertised the properties at $10, $25, even $30 an acre.

Settlers up and down the San Joaquin Valley, through which the road ran to Los Angeles, were alarmed and naturally angry. They formed a number of Settlers' Rights Leagues, one of which in the Mussel Slough region of present Kings County, was led by John J. Doyle, a man of force and ability. Doyle attacked the railroad's title to the lands. Aided by the League, he took the fight through the federal courts in California, then appealed directly to the Interior Department in Washington. He was defeated at every turn. The railroad announced it would dispossess all "squatters" on its lands.

In May of 1880 came tragedy, blundering or planned, in either case dreadful. In a last attempt to stave off the blow that was about to fall, the settlers of Mussel Slough, led by Major Thomas McQuiddy, who had always counseled moderation, arranged a mass meeting and barbecue at the town of Hanford, which was to be addressed by David Smith Terry, celebrated as jurist, political figure of great and rash courage, and a duelist. On horseback and in buckboards the farmers and their families came in to town by the hundreds. On this particular day a United States Marshal, accompanied by a couple of deputies and also by one man who has been

* *Chapters in the History of the Southern Pacific*, by Stuart Daggett, New York, 1922.

called an agent provocateur of the Southern Pacific, arrived in the neighborhood and set about immediately to dispossess several farmers.

On the place of a man named Brewer the marshal and his men were met by a number of farmers. The alleged SP man, one Crow, started shooting. The farmers shot back. When the smoke had cleared five farmers and two officers lay dead. For this "murder" of the officers seventeen farmers were tried, found guilty, and sent to prison.

The Mussel Slough tragedy was only the most spectacular of the many incidents that followed hard on the railroad's removal of settlers from lands they believed, and with considerable right, to be their own; and as such it served as the rallying cry of the San Joaquin valley farmers— *Remember Mussel Slough!*

Contrary to folklore that has grown up around the affair, and has even been put into books, Chris Evans was not dispossessed of his land by the railroad. Close relatives of his wife, however, lost their farms after the Mussel Slough incident and this unquestionably fanned the resentment, felt by all farmers in the region against the SP, of Evans, a highly intelligent and determined man. Born in Canada, reared in Vermont, Evans was thirty-three years old in 1880. He had served as a scout with the Army fighting Indians in the Dakotas, and had walked much of the way over Union Pacific and Central Pacific tracks into California in 1873, all of which was pretty good training for what was ahead.

Now married, and with children arrived and on the way, Evans worked for the Bank of California, having charge of three warehouses where he checked and graded grain that the bank took from farmers in payment on mortgages. The warehouses were at Goshen, Pixley, and Alila. (Mark those names; they were soon to be in the news.) In this job the sympathetic and reflective man heard a-plenty from farmers regarding the highbinder methods of the Southern Pacific—enough to change his resentment to hatred.

The warehouse job did not pay Evans enough to support his growing family, so he moved to Modesto where he opened a livery stable. (Mark the name of Modesto.) The stable presently burned with all its contents, including twenty-two animals. Evans gave up trying to be a business man. Taking his family he moved to a small tract of land near Visalia.

Evans had become acquainted with John Sontag, a tall, rugged man from Mankato, Minnesota, a sort of boomer railroadman who had been badly injured while braking for the Southern Pacific. Sontag claimed that neglect of his injury in the railroad company's hospital at Sacramento had maimed him for life. True or not, it was a fact that company hospitals of all kinds in that era were far from healthy places. Sontag limped badly and was unable to perform the rugged work to which the SP assigned him. He was as bitter against the railroad for this reason as Evans was for the lost acres of his wife's family.

Big Boy. No steam locomotive in the world is larger than those of the Union Pacific's 4000 class.

Five of the Santa Fe's fleet of speedy air-conditioned railiners in the Chicago terminal yard.

Well, things began happening to the SP's trains on the cloudy evening of February 22, 1889. As Number 17 pulled out of Pixley, a village right handy to Mussell Slough, two masked men climbed over the coal in the locomotive tender and into the cab. Guns in hand they ordered the engineer to stop the train. He did, and he and the fireman were grounded under orders of the robbers, who now shouted to the man in the express car, Messenger Kelly, to throw out the safe. Kelly refused. "Very well," said the shorter of the two bandits. He placed a stick of dynamite under the car and a moment later it went off, lifting the car off the rails. Kelly was still game; he refused to toss out the safe or to unlock the doors. Whereupon the robbers announced they would shoot the engineer and fireman unless the safe was delivered. Out it came. The train crew had been milling around the stalled cars, and one of the robbers now shot and killed a trainman named Gabert, and wounded another man. The robbers told the train crew to take the train back to Pixley, which was done. When police came to the scene, perhaps half an hour later, the robbers had disappeared, along with perhaps $5,000 from the express safe.

Eyewitnesses agreed there were only two robbers, one short and stocky, who seemed to direct things, the other a large man about six feet tall. No identification was made, no suspicion was engendered. Chris Evans, grain inspector at Pixley, continued to grade the wheat and barley. Almost a year later, this time near Goshen, where Evans inspected grain, a holdup of southbound Number 19 was accomplished with virtually the same methods used at Pixley, except that no shooting occurred and that the safe contained $20,000. The railroad's detectives converged on the neighborhood from north and south but found never a clue, nor any sympathy from citizens who jeered them as hirelings of The Octopus. Then, on February 6, 1891, Number 17 was held up a second time, this job being done at Alila, just south of Pixley. There was no profit, for Messenger C. C. Haswell defied the robbers and replied with profane and obscene words to their demands to open the express car. Haswell also started shooting, blindly yet wickedly, through the grating of the express car's side doors. The robbers fled. Fireman Radcliffe died of wounds from bullets fired either by the messenger or by the robbers, nobody ever knew which.

But somebody had to be arrested and the cops, lacking a better, arrested the heroic Haswell and charged him with murdering the fireman. Haswell had to stand trial, too, even though he was speedily acquitted. And presently two more goats appeared. These were Bill and Gratton Dalton, of a gang already notorious in the Midwest. The two Daltons had been living for a while in the San Joaquin Valley, and now they were arrested, apparently on general principles, and Gratton was convicted of attempted robbery and of manslaughter on what would appear to have been the slimmest of evidence.

While Grat Dalton was still in jail, and Bill Dalton out on bail, the SP robbers struck again, this time near Modesto, a town a hundred miles north of the scene of the other robberies and incidentally the place to which Evans had removed and was even then operating a livery stable. (To be done with the Daltons, Gratton walked quietly and successfully out of his cell in one of the easiest deliveries of record, then went back to Kansas to die in the raid on Coffeyville, little more than a year later.) The Modesto attack, even to two dynamite attempts on the express car, was much like the others, only this time two SP detectives, Harris and Lawton, who were on the train, got into the battle. There was considerable shooting, during which Detective Harris received a bad wound. The bandits, one short, one tall, got away clean, though without any cash.

The Evans Livery Stable in Modesto burned at about this time, and Evans moved to Visalia, as related. Nearly a year went by with no holdups on the SP. What proved to be the next and last of the series took place at midnight, August 3, 1892, just west of Fresno, a town much nearer to Visalia, if that had any significance, than to Modesto. The train was old Number 17 again. The routine was basically the same—the two robbers climbing into the cab over the coal, the application of dynamite to the express car, defended with great courage by Messenger George D. Roberts until the explosions knocked him unconscious; then the moving of 125 pounds of silver coin into a buggy that was waiting in the road near the tracks, and the disappearance of the robbers.

It is not difficult to imagine that by this time the men of Wells, Fargo & Company, of the Southern Pacific, and to a lesser degree the police officers of the counties where the holdups had occurred, were one and all knowing the sneers and jeers of the public and feeling the heat applied by their own higher-ups. Combining forces, public, express, and railroad detectives and police started looking for suspects and arresting them. A kind of hysteria must have taken them, for within two days after the Fresno holdup, some fifty-odd men were in various jails in the San Joaquin Valley.

In Visalia at this time was one George Sontag, a dudish punk who seemed to have little if any occupation other than running off at the mouth. Much of his talk concerned the hellish Southern Pacific which, among many other derelictions, had treated his brother, John, in a most brutal manner. He liked to talk about it, did George. And George also said he had been a passenger on Number 17 when it had been held up near Fresno a few days previously. Detective Will Smith of the Southern Pacific took the garrulous fellow in hand for a questioning. Sontag became confused, and made contradictory statements regarding his brother John. Leaving George Sontag in the sheriff's office under guard, Detective Smith, accompanied by Deputy Sheriff Witty, went to Chris Evans' home on the outskirts of Visalia. As they were tying their team to a post in front of the place, the two officers saw John Sontag enter the Evans' home from the back door.

Smith and Witty walked up to the front porch. The door was open. Without knocking or making themselves known in any way, the officers stepped inside and into the living room, startling Eva Evans, sixteen, blond haired, brown-eyed and pretty elder daughter of Chris Evans. With more speed than finesse Smith went about his work. "I want to see John Sontag," he said. The girl replied that Sontag wasn't there; nor did she know that he was, for he had then barely entered the back door of the house. Then Detective Smith, patently no Chesterfield, remarked that the girl was "a damned little liar." *

As shocked as she was astonished, Eva Evans turned and ran out of the house, toward the barn, where her father was. She met him coming in and told him two strangers had walked unannounced into the house, and that one of them had called her a bad name. Evans was a man of sudden temper, and this time, perhaps, he had reason for his choler. He strode through the back door, noticed a revolver with which Eva had been shooting at a target a little while before, and picked it up. He put it into his pocket, then went into the living room.

Shooting began at once, with all three men engaged and with John Sontag presently taking a hand. Who fired first is beyond knowing. The results: Deputy Sheriff Witty down in the road in front of the house, badly hit; Detective Smith, mildly wounded and running toward town; and Evans and John Sontag getting into the officers' wagon and driving off.

Now began the greatest manhunt California had known. It was to last a year and a half. Some three thousand men were to engage in it, and it was to end only with the death of John Sontag, by then virtually weighted with lead, and the capture of Evans, minus an eye, an arm, and scarred and pitted by many bullets.

From the Evans home the two men drove toward the Sierras, a large posse of mounted men hot on the trail. A few miles out of town the outlaws drove into a meadow behind some haystacks and waited for the posse to gallop by, returned to the Evans home, enjoyed a substantial supper, then proceeded to load up the buggy with provisions for a long stay in the mountains. Just as they were about to leave, Deputy Sheriff Overall and two other officers came up. It was too dark to see much, but both sides started to shoot and Deputy Sheriff Oscar Beaver was killed. Evans and Sontag now drove away into the hills to eastward.

Meanwhile, George Sontag had been convicted, on almost no evidence at all, of having had a part in the last Southern Pacific robbery. He was sent to Folsom prison. At the instigation of her father, who was seldom long out of touch with his family, Eva Evans and other sympathizers planned a

---

* In his account of the case, the best I know of, C. G. Glasscock remarks that it is important to bear in mind the brutal approach of Detective Smith, if events immediately subsequent are to be judged fairly. See his *Bandits and the Southern Pacific*, New York, 1929.

prison delivery for George Sontag. Just how it was arranged isn't too clear, but anyway, on June 27, 1893, George Sontag and three other convicts who were working in the prison rock quarry suddenly picked guns out of thin air and started shooting at their guards. It looked good for a moment, but not longer. Guards shot them all down, killing all but Sontag who was merely crippled for life.

Meanwhile, too, Evans and Sontag were holding their own in fine shape. Once, possibly twice, they drove into Visalia at night, and once had to shoot their way through a cordon of cops around the Evans home. Mostly, though, the two men stayed in the hills, and here they lived very well, eating at logging camps. where no questions were asked, and with miners. The United States Government and the Southern Pacific Railroad hired marshals and police by the score. Two Indian trackers were brought into the chase. So was a pack of hounds. The woods came to be so filled with armed men that they took to shooting at each other, and at least eleven deputies were wounded by other deputies. The Southern Pacific and Wells, Fargo & Company combined to offer a $10,000 reward for the two men, dead or alive.

At a place called Young's Cabin, Evans and Sontag were almost taken by a posse but managed to shoot out of it. A bit later came a terrific battle at Stone Corral, where United States Marshal George Gard and a posse lay in wait for the outlaws. The officers were all hidden in a cabin. As soon as Evans and Sontag came into range, one of the more nervous deputies opened fire. The two outlaws dropped down behind a pile of straw and manure and there for the next several hours they remained, shooting and being shot at—and hit. Sontag received bullets through his right arm, two or three in his side and chest, and a number of flesh wounds. Evans' left arm was all but shot away, hanging in shreds. A charge of buckshot struck his head fair and took out his right eye. Another bullet caught him in the right shoulder. The outlaws' own shots had merely wounded one of the officers.

Marshal Gard and his men, knowing the two outlaws to be badly wounded, prepared to wait out the night. Sontag had become so weak he could not lift a hand; and as dusk fell, Evans started to creep away into the nearby woods. The officers detected the move and opened fire, and Evans managed to shoot back once. Then he disappeared. As for Sontag, he began to chill notably from loss of blood. Toward morning he revived a little and tried to kill himself, but he was so weak and the revolver so heavy the first bullet merely plowed his temple. The next shot went through his face, just back of the nose. He faded again and remembered nothing until the deputies stood over him. They took him to the Visalia jail * and there

---

* Information as to Sontag's last hours came to the author from Eva Evans McCullough herself, who was to have married him and who talked with him in the jailhouse just before he died.

he presently died weighted, said the attending physician, with more lead than he had ever seen in a human being before.

Up in the hills, Evans, as soon as he received the cover of night and the woods, plodded on. His clothing soaked with blood, both arms hanging by his sides, one of them mere strips of flesh and bone, and with three shots embedded in his head, Vermont's sole contribution to California banditry started a journey that was termed by a contemporary an "amazing instance of human endurance and will power." Stumbling through the dark of a mountain night, Evans somehow traveled six miles in deep woods to reach a cabin occupied by a Perkins family. From here, where he lay in bed, white from loss of blood, he sent a Perkins boy to Sheriff Kay in Visalia with word that he, Evans, was prepared to give up without more ado, with the understanding that the reward for his capture should go to his wife. Officers came to take him out. In jail his left arm was amputated, and a bit later he was tried and convicted of the murder of one of the posse near the Evans' home.

The trial was held in Fresno. Before he could be removed to prison, a gun was smuggled in to Evans. With it he forced the jailer to let him out; and then, with his accomplice, one Ed Morrell, Evans took to the hills again. The chase began all over. Handicapped with an artificial arm, and blind in one eye, the outlaw managed to keep out of the hands of the many posses. The officers patently had given up the idea they could take him by force. Instead, they sent a faked message to him to the effect that one of his children was seriously ill and was pleading to see her father. Evans came home at once and was there captured by a posse large enough to have stormed a fort.

While Evans was in jail, R. C. White, a playwright of San Francisco, wrote and produced a melodrama, *Evans & Sontag*. At the time no other explanation was needed to tell what the play was about. Evans and Sontag were as widely known—and incidentally more favorably—than even the names of the Big Four of the Southern Pacific. Playwright White offered Mrs. Chris Evans and daughter Eva 25 per cent of the net receipts if they would play parts in the show. They agreed.

Mrs. Evans disliked the business, even though her part was small. Eva took to the stage like a born trouper. And Eva sat them up in their seats. On a fine black horse she galloped on stage just as the two actors playing the parts of Evans and Sontag rushed from their hiding place in the woods to greet her. From this point on the play was pretty much one shot after another. The *San Francisco Examiner* featured its drama critic's report with headlines of studhorse size: "Like the Roar of Battle—The Evans and Sontag Drama at the National Theater a Perfect Volley of Musketry —Eva Evans Given a Genuinely Enthusiastic Reception and Proves to be an Actress."

"Of course, it was the rankest melodrama," Eva Evans McCullough told me fifty-four years later. "I can smile now, looking back at the blood and thunder of it. But I was not then conscious of the cheapness of the play. I was earning money for my father's court battle. That was what counted. We had to pay many lawyers."

But the lawyers could not save Chris Evans. In 1894 he was sentenced to Folsom prison for life. In 1911 he was paroled by Governor Hiram Johnson, no lover of the SP. Evans and family moved to Portland, Oregon, where he often sat sunning himself on a bench in the park blocks, often in company with Frank Coulter, a violin maker whom he had known in Modesto many years before. "Evans," the late Mr. Coulter told me, "was a soft-spoken and genial sort of man. It was hard for me to look at him, to hear him talk, and think that this was the man who had successfully defied the Southern Pacific and the State of California—at that time almost the same thing—for so many years, and took on the United States Government to boot. I came to know him well, but he never so much as intimated he had ever robbed a train."

When I met Eva Evans McCullough in 1947, I saw a good looking, genial and neat woman of seventy or so, as vibrant as most women half her age. Obviously she inherited the intellectual bent of her father, a man who read Darwin, Huxley, Shakespeare and Herbert Spencer—probably the only man ever credited with train robbery who had a working knowledge of those titans.

"Dad really did love good books," Mrs. McCullough said. "Even when the family had little more than shelter, clothing and food, there were books in our house. Dad read them, too, and I learned from him to love books. On only one occasion did I ever hear him use profanity, nor would he permit his children to use it.

"During his years in prison he wrote a book which he called *Eurasia*. It was not, as you might expect, a diatribe against the Southern Pacific. It was a plan for a wise and rational government, one of those Utopian republics. He outlined the political, educational and industrial arrangements. Women were to play an equal part with men in all things. The courts were to be simplified. Dad had ideas about prisons, not their abolishment by any means, nor to make them pleasant hotels for lazy or vicious persons; but to make them institutions of genuine reform. The little book was published by the *San Francisco Star*. It was far ahead of its time. Dad was an incurable idealist."

Chris Evans died in 1917, in Portland, Oregon, the last of the great train robbers—if robber he was—of the old school, and certainly the most unusual of them. He remains pretty much unknown except on the Pacific coast and to experts in the history of holding up the steam cars.

During the period of the many holdups of SP trains in California, a rather astonishing robber turned up in the effete East. He was Oliver C.

Perry. Although nearly all trains robberies have been committed by gangs of from two to ten men, Perry was a lone wolf and a most spectacular one. He was an Amsterdam, New York, boy, born in 1865, who went West and worked as cowboy and small-time robber, winding up in a cell in the Minnesota Penitentiary for pilfering a store. On his release he returned to his native state and in Troy, so the story goes, met an estimable young woman, one Amelia Haswell, who taught a Bible class. She worked hard to make Perry a good Christian, helping him to get a job on the New York Central as brakeman. Falling in love with the girl, and lacking sufficient money on which to marry, but characteristically not wanting to work for wages to earn it, Perry cooked up a plan to rob a train.

On September 30, 1891, a special express of ten cars pulled out of the Grand Central in Manhattan for Buffalo. At Albany, where a stop to change engines was made, Perry, a small man, got into the front vestibule of a richly-laden car in charge of Messenger E. A. Moore. He sawed through the door, stuck a gun in Moore's face, picked up a package containing "several thousand dollars in currency," then returned to the platform, where he reached down and cut the hose of the airbrake coupling. The train came to a stop and the robber leaped off, and away.

It had all been so easy. Five months later he did it again. This time he got aboard at Syracuse and took his stand on the head platform of the money car, in charge of Messenger Daniel McInerney. When the train pulled out, Perry strapped his valise and derby hat to the railing. He put on a mask. Then he strung a sort of patent rope ladder of his own devising to the top of the car, letting it hang down over one side. Now he swung out on the ladder, a truly precarious place, where he could peer through the side-door windows to watch the messenger and pick a good time to break in.

Here, indeed, was something new and ingenious in the business of robbing trains. Perry clung to the rope ladder on the outside of the express car while the train picked up speed. Thirty, forty, finally fifty miles an hour was being clicked off. The time was February, and Perry's hands got so cold he could hardly remove the gun from his pocket. The wind blew him away from the car a number of times, and he barely missed being scraped off by a bridge. He rubbed his hands vigorously, then managed to get out his gun and cock it, meanwhile watching through the windows to mark the movements of the messenger.

Near Weedsport Perry saw his chance. He opened the unlocked door, swung in neatly, his gun ready. Messenger McInerney reached for his own gun, and Perry fired. The bullet grazed the messenger, who then reached for the bellcord, yanking it before Perry could shoot him down. Perry hurriedly picked up some packages that looked valuable. Just then Conductor Haas, who had heard the air whistle sound faintly, climbed onto the rail of the platform of the express car and peered through the bellcord hole.

He could see a masked man, which was enough. Haas set the brakes. The train slowed down, and stopped. Haas stuck his head out to take a look ahead along the cars, and just then bullets began whistling. Perry ordered the conductor to signal the engineer to go ahead. He did.

At Port Byron a stop was made and the express car investigated. The messenger, though living, was badly hurt. There was no sign of the robber. Wiring ahead to Rochester for an ambulance to meet the train, it went on. It had to stop briefly at Lyons, and at Lyons, in the crowd at the depot, was a young man wearing gold-rimmed spectacles and carrying a valise strapped over one shoulder. One of the trainmen had noticed this young man at the Syracuse depot, and now he wondered how he had got to Lyons so quickly. He started to question him. Perry, for it was he, pulled a gun. He backed across the tracks until he came to a coal train, steam up, ready to leave. He uncoupled the locomotive, drove off the engine crew, then got into the cab and started on a journey such as railroad men swear no other train robber ever made.

Conductor Haas and a switchman had got hold of shotguns. They uncoupled the engine of the special, got aboard, and started in pursuit of the bandit engineer. The New York Central, even in 1892, was a four-track road, and the two engines sped along on different tracks. As Perry's locomotive began to lose ground, the other coming up fast, the bandit threw his engine into reverse, then poured a stream of bullets into the other engine as it passed him. Three or four times the two locomotives passed and repassed each other. Haas and the switchman got into action with their shotguns. Perry kept up an erratic fire until he saw his engine was almost out of steam. He stopped it, leaped off and ran.

Haas and his engine returned to Lyons, where the sheriff organized a posse and set out. They ran the bandit to earth not far from Newark. A bit later he pleaded guilty at Rochester and was sent up for 49 years to Auburn prison. Although he soon escaped, and was taken again, Perry never robbed another train. He died as recently as September 10, 1930, in the Dannemora State Prison for the Criminal Insane. His feat with a rope ladder and his escape in the stolen locomotive are generally held to have been unique in the annals of train robbery.

By the time Perry was safely put away, and Evans and Sontag had quit robbing trains, the profession of train robbery was on the downgrade. Well-made and extra heavy express cars doubtless had an effect in discouraging the practice. Train robberies dropped from 29 in 1900 to seven in 1905. Nor did they ever increase much again. There were, however, a few spectacular affairs after 1905, and two of the outstanding jobs occurred on the much-robbed Southern Pacific. On March 13, 1912, two men made the fatal mistake of holding up the *Sunset Express* on the San Antonio-El Paso run at a water stop called Dryden, in Texas. David A.

Trousdale was the Wells Fargo messenger aboard. He inveigled one of the two bandits into stooping over to pick up from the floor what Trousdale told him was a valuable package. As he did so, Trousdale picked up a heavy mallet that was used for cracking ice and let go a blow so mighty it killed the thug then and there.

The other thug was outside the car, on the track. Picking up the dead man's rifle, Trousdale waited until he saw a good chance, then drilled the second thug neatly through the head. It was noble work, work more likely to give parasites pause than any amount of moral suasion and pious words. Two murderous parasites dead in two minutes. The train crew, glad to be helpful, tossed the second body into the express car with the other, and the *Sunset Express* went on, a little late but still intact, and with Messenger Trousdale cleaning up the mussed-up car. One of the dead men proved to be Gil Fitzpatrick, said to have been the last of the Hole-in-the-Wall Gang, terrors in their day. The other was one Ed Welch.

Wells Fargo presented a gold watch, suitably inscribed, to Messenger Trousdale; and passengers contributed to purchase a gold watch fob, "with a diamond set in a Texas star" for the brave man. Twenty-three years afterward, thanks to the unremitting labor of the Rev. A. N. Eshman, minister of a church in Trousdale's old home town of Columbia, Tennessee, Congress considered the matter and awarded one thousand dollars to the messenger who had safeguarded registered mail valued at $66,000. In February of 1946, according to an interview with him in the *Erie Railroad Magazine,* Trousdale, still hale and rugged, had just retired after 43 years on the rails, all spent in the service of Railway Express and predecessor concerns.

I could wish that some ballad maker of the hillbilly school, which has celebrated in song nearly all of the thugs and parasites of the South and Southwest, would be inspired by the cold courage displayed by Dave Trousdale to give us a dozen or so strophes entitled "The Brave Wells Fargo Man," dedicated to him who so deftly exterminated two roaches at Dryden, Texas, in 1912.

Another lone robber of the Oliver Perry school, but of much later date, was the once well-publicized William J. Carlisle of Wyoming. He specialized in Union Pacific trains, holding up four of them and each time forced members of the train crew to pass the hat among the passengers for their cash and valuables. All of his robberies were committed in 1916, and in that year the law caught up and sent him to prison. But he was no businessman. His total loot amounted to less than a thousand dollars.

Worse than Carlisle as businessmen, but virtually sadistic in their one crime, were three brothers named D'Autremont who in 1923 stopped a Southern Pacific train at Siskiyou Pass in Oregon. Unquestionably influenced by having seen too many Western movies, these three punks shot and killed the engineer and one trainman, killed the messenger by heaving dynamite into his car, then fled without a penny. All three were taken and sent to the Oregon pen. Within six months of their incarceration some moron had composed a long ballad sentimentalizing them. I don't think it has survived, and am quite happy it didn't.

The track pan is the modern method of taking on water. Left: the scoop which is lowered into the pan beneath the locomotive. Right: periodically the pan must be cleaned of rocks.

Below: spray is flung out as the speeding New York Central freight takes on water.

Powered by a steam turbine instead of cylinders, pistons and driving rods, this Pennsylvania Railroad coal-burner is the first direct-drive steam turbine locomotive built in America. Engine and tender together weigh nearly a million pounds, cover 123 feet of track. (Below) The PRR Broadway Limited began running between New York and Chicago as a steam train in 1902 on a 20-hour schedule. Now electric-powered, it covers the 908 miles in 16 hours.

CHAPTER XXXIV

Riders of the Rods and the Blinds

Where the boxcars all are empty
And the sun shines every day;
Where there's the birds and the bees
And the cigaret trees;
Where the lemonade springs
And the blue bird sings
In the Big Rock Candy Mountains.
—Ballad by "HAYWIRE MAC"
McCLINTOCK, 1895.

TRAIN robbers made big headlines but they were never so costly to the railroads as tramps and bums. This was so not because the tramps and bums rode without paying fares, but because of their thefts of and damage to freight, and also because tramps and bums were likely to become clients of a whole army of shyster lawyers whose specialty was suing railroads on account of injuries to men who, to begin with, had no right to be where they were when injured.

Although from the very first days of steamcars there were men who preferred to ride on or in them without payment, and did so, the railroad tramp did not become an American institution until right after the Civil War. A decade later the tramp had entered literature, sometimes as a growing national problem, more often as a worthless if comic character. In the eighties he began to appear in American newspaper and periodical art and was soon portrayed as the Weary Willie vagabond, drawn with such gusty humor by Zim and Opper and presently made into a national character, Happy Hooligan, by the latter artist.

The tramp visualized by the periodical and newspaper artists was a nondescript male in fearful, tattered clothing, whose face was dark not with a full-grown beard, but with a black hedge somewhere between a poor shave and real whiskers. His nose, of course, was crimson, a badge of his habits. Over his shoulder was a stick, on the end of the stick a small bundle, tied up like a bag in a red bandanna handkerchief, in which were his entire possessions—food, extra clothing if any, and whatever else he saw fit to carry with him on his travels.

389

Nat Wills, the actor, put the literary and pictorial tramp into the theater in the classic pattern of American tramps; and the various creations of Zim and Opper—and of Frost in the "quality" magazines—plus the appearance of Wills in full make-up, served to conjure up the railroad tramp or bum or hobo as he looked to the mind of most Americans of the past sixty years or so.

Whether or not this railroad tramp was like the flesh-and-blood tramps who actually rode the rods, the blind baggage, and the boxcars and gondolas, I am not able to say, nor is anyone else. Doubtless, like most such creations, the stage and literary tramp possessed some of the characteristics of the real article. And it is more than possible that the real tramps, or at least the more degenerate among them, once the stage and literary species had been visualized, made conscious effort to look like the counterfeits of themselves, just as cowhands have tried to live up to the cowboys of the dime novels and the Western movies.

Tramps are often called hoboes or bums, but although all three are migrants, they are not the same thing. Ben L. Reitman, who tramped a good deal himself, remarked that a hobo works and wanders, a tramp dreams and wanders, and a bum drinks and wanders. Migratory workers, if they apply any of the terms to themselves, are more likely than not to say they are hoboes.

Josiah Flynt was one of the first Americans to make a close study of migrants by railroad. He traveled across the continent, working here and there, living in hobo jungles, and everywhere trying to get acquainted with the men who were always on the move. In the nineties, he estimated that the railroad tramp population was around 60,000 men. They were already recognized as a problem by the railroad companies, chiefly because of the damage and theft they did to shipments and in warehouses. Flynt also pointed out, and perhaps was the first to do so in a book of general circulation, the racket of shysters who sought out tramps injured on railroad property and through them brought "nuisance" suits against the carriers, a form of blackmail carried on to this day, though with less success than of old.

Train crews of the nineties also recognized the hobo, often as a source of income. Flynt found the rate for travel on the freights was more or less standardized at ten cents a hundred miles, or twenty cents "for an all-night ride." This rate may have held in the nineties and before, but early in the new century trainmen certainly upped the rates, for old-time hoboes have told me that shacks, or brakemen, charged them whatever they thought the case would bear, and kicked them off if they could not or would not meet the tariff. More recently the generally accepted rate collected from tramps by train freightmen has been "a dollar a division." The length of a division varies, but 100 miles is a fair average.

When occasion demanded it, hoboes used strategem to flag down a train that otherwise would not stop where the 'boes waited. The late Jerry Springer, long-time locomotive engineer on the Soo Line, told of such an incident one night in Wisconsin. "We left Weyerhaeuser on time," he related,* "but were held up at Ladysmith a little longer than usual. When we left, I pulled her open to make up for lost time. Just as we passed the station at Tony, the glare of the headlight picked up what looked to me like a railroad tie across the rails ahead. I slowed down, then came to a full stop and hollered to my fireman to get down and take the tie off the track.

"He jumped off and removed the obstruction. When he got back into the cab, he said to me, 'That wasn't a tie. It was an inch-board the length of a tie and placed on edge across the rails to look thick like a tie.' I gave the matter little thought until we got to Pennington and stopped for water. Then I noticed two hoboes who were riding on the blind. I was sure they hadn't got aboard at Ladysmith, our last stop. The fireman was going to put them off, but I told him to let them ride. Any two boes as smart as they were, I said, were entitled to ride blind the whole division, if they wanted to."

The "blind" referred to was the space between the baggage car and the locomotive. Baggage cars did not have a forward-end door, hence were blind. Riders there were comparatively safe except for the engine crew, who might take to throwing coal; but the engine crew, being concerned with what was ahead of, rather than behind the engine, were unlikely to be troublesome.

Although blind baggage was a favorite place for riding, it was while attempting to get aboard a blind that William Davies, the English tramp who became a writer of prose and poetry, lost part of a leg. The tragedy happened in Ontario, Canada, and though he does not cite the road, it was probably the Canadian Pacific. He and a companion were waiting for the train to start pulling out of a small station, to mount it before it could pick up speed. Now they ran for it. "The train was going faster and faster," Davies said, "and making a leap, my companion caught the handle-bar and sprang lightly on the step, after which my hand quickly took possession of this bar, and I ran with the train, prepared to follow his example.

"To my surprise, instead of at once taking his place on the platform, my companion stood thoughtlessly irresolute on the step, leaving me no room to make the attempt. But I still held to the bar, though the train was now going so fast that I found great difficulty in keeping step with it. I shouted to him to clear the step. This he proceeded to do, very deliberately, I thought, for the train was now going at a very rapid rate. My foot came short of the step, and I fell, and, still clinging to the handle-bar, was

---

* In a letter to his son, George T. Springer of Minneapolis, who permitted its use here.

dragged several yards before I relinquished my hold. And there I lay for several minutes, feeling a little shaken, whilst the train passed swiftly on into the darkness . . ."

Davies did not at first realize what had happened. When he attempted to get to get to his feet he saw that his right foot had been severed just above the ankle.*

Many hoboes preferred, in decent weather, to ride the deck—which was the top of a baggage car or coach. This was dangerous, for a wink of sleep might serve to send a man rolling off the heaving cars. Empty boxcars probably carried more tramps than any other accommodation; in these the tramps often did much damage by lighting fires, for warmth or cooking, on the bare floor. If all box and other cars were full, the boys might ride either the rods or the bumpers. The rods were the iron bars that were a part of the freight car frames. They permitted a space of some eighteen inches between the bars and the bottom of the car. A man not given to stoutness could lie flat across these rods and ride, certain death a foot or so beneath him, and dust and maddening noise all around. Then, too, there were brakemen who used a horrible method for removing the riders of rods. A brakie would tie a railroad spike to a heavy cord and suspend the spike just so it would strike the ties and bounce—bounce and bounce until it struck the hobo and, it was to be hoped, dislodged him. . .

The bumpers were the coupling gear between freight cars, better for night than for day travel when brakies ranged the tops of the cars and could spot a man in such an exposed place.

The more reflective hoboes occasionally applied the science of mathematics to their routes of travel, according to A-No.1, a far-ranging man who bummed his way, apparently, chiefly for the purpose of putting his experiences into print. A-No.1 was of the opinion that one of the busiest hobo junctions in the United States was Mattoon, Illinois, where the east-west tracks of the Big Four Route crossed the north-south line of the Illinois Central. Both main lines were double-tracked to handle the great volume of traffic. All trains stopped at Mattoon for varying lengths of time. Other than for the Lake Shore Division of the New York Central, the Chicago-St. Louis route of the Chicago & Alton, and the Chicago-Kansas City route of the Santa Fe, no other carrier in the country was so plagued with hoboes, says A-No. 1, as the two systems crossing at Mattoon.

The boys had the percentages all figured out. The chances of a bo being arrested for trespass on the Big Four stood at something like 107 to 1 in the bo's favor. This ratio was arrived at by multiplying 535, the mileage between Cleveland and St. Louis, by 2, the track count on this double-tracked line, and again by 20, the average run of daily trains, then dividing 21,400, the product obtained, by 200, a number representing the actual

---

* Davies, William H., *The Autobiography of a Super-Tramp*, London, 1908.

track mileage patrolled by each agent in the road's police department, each agent being assigned to guard 100 miles of the line.

The Illinois Central of the time, it seems, presented an even better break. You multiplied 363 (Chicago to Cairo mileage) by 2, again by 35, and divided the product of 25,410 by 100, giving the bo the better of the deal by 254 to 1. It is amusing to think of those genuine bums, dodgers of work, scorners of education, sitting around some jungle fire while the mulligan stewed, applying the science of numbers to their daily occupation of getting from where they were to somewhere else, free of charge.

This A-No.1 tramp seems to have got around a good deal. During the first decade and a half of the present century, a common sign seen on western railroad underpasses and bridges, on warehouses and even depots, was A-No.1, painted in huge letters, sometimes in red. Whether these moniker marks were left by the A-No.1 who wrote the paper-backs published in Erie, Pennsylvania, or whether a number of hoboes were using the same moniker, as was the case of "T-Bone Slim" of the wobblies, isn't to be known. The literary A-No.1 claimed to have traveled "500,000 miles for $7.61," and turned out at least an even dozen of atrociously written and printed books which were sold through the American News Company. He seems to have done for tramps what Thomas L. Jackson did for drummers ——I mean the Jackson of slow-train-through-Arkansas celebrity.

From around 1906 until 1923, men riding freights in the West found it advisable to carry a Little Red Card, showing membership in the Industrial Workers of the World. Somehow, a red card came in time to be the badge of the honest if migratory worker and trainmen were prone to be easy on such men, even to letting them ride free of charge. So, naturally, even the lowest of the bums tried to get and carry a wobbly card.

The 60,000 tramps estimated by Flynt in the nineties grew after the turn of the century to probably fifteen times that number. In 1921, for instance, 20,643 "undesirable persons" were removed during the one month of October from "trains and property" of one company, the Southern Pacific, according to Dan O'Connell, chief special agent for that carrier. In times of depression more than a million men were probably moving somewhere in the United States by other than orthodox tickets on railroads. Various hobo organizations flourished, then faded, and here and there a man, like Jeff Davis—said to be moving still, in 1946, though feebly—set himself up as King of the Hoboes and made an occupation of being king.

By the turn of the century the chief job of railroad detectives or police was to keep tramps off the trains and away from the railroad yards. Civil police were not greatly interested in how a migrant traveled. In fact, more often than not they arrested a tramp only to tell him he must "leave town on the next train." So the railroad bulls came into being. Their job was not simply to make arrests but primarily to keep to a minimum the number of men trespassing on company property, trains, or land. Hence railroad bulls endeavored to put fear into the hearts of all migrants who rode rods, blinds, bumpers, and decks. They accomplished this in various ways, by tossing tramps off moving trains, by shooting at and sometimes hitting them, by beating them up with fists or saps.

The more determined and aggressive railroad bulls quickly earned a reputation that unquestionably served to keep the more timid hoboes off their divisions. Nels Anderson, in one of his many books on migrants, related that for several years the railroad yards at Galesburg, Illinois, were known throughout the United States as a good place to keep away from, all because of a "bad" railroad bull there. At Green River, Wyoming, a private cop known as "Green River Slim" became a terror to hoboes and was given a wide berth.

I once knew a railroad detective named Hotchkiss who may or may not have been typical of the Western lines of twenty and more years ago. I think he was born cruel, or maybe he got that way from his work; and his work, which he performed most efficiently, was putting the fear of his railroad's police department ahead of the fear of even hell-fire and damnation into all hoboes, tramps and bums. Hotchkiss worked sometimes in the yards at Portland and Eugene, Oregon, and at Oakland, California. Occasionally he rode the freights, for he seemed to have a sort of roving commission. Wherever he was he must indeed have been a terror. He was a large man, but quick on his feet, and had an arm like a ham, except the arm was all muscle.

"The best way to keep tramps off trains or other railroad property," Hotchkiss told me, "is to beat up any unauthorized person you find in the yards. I might see a couple of men hanging around. They looked as if they were waiting for a freight to be made up. I'd go directly up to them and ask one of them a question. No matter what he answered, I'd cuff him across the face with a good slap. I'd ask the other guy a question. He'd start to back off. I'd follow him up and really hit him. Then I'd turn back to the first bo. If he wasn't already getting the hell out of there, I'd give him the billy—not hard enough to break anything, but hard enough so he'd remember.

"On the trains, I might talk a while with tramps riding the boxcars, and I'd never throw them off if we were highballing. I'd wait until we were down to twenty miles or so an hour, then force them to jump, or push them off. Some of them, of course would get right back on the same train, so I always made it a practice to work back on the cars. If I recognized any bum I had just thrown off, this time I whaled the hell out of him—if he didn't jump when he saw me coming."

Hotchkiss said that carrying a Little Red Card made no difference to him, unless the sight of it made him madder. He belonged to one of the railroad Brotherhoods, having once been an engineer, and still paid his dues. But he thought the IWW was a terrible danger to American institutions. "If a guy flashed a wobbly card on me," he said, "I'd snatch it and tear it up and toss the pieces off the train. I'll bet I've torn up a thousand red cards."

Hobo jungles made Hotchkiss see red. He blamed town and city authorities for permitting these camping places of itinerants and said that no chief of police should hold office who had not promised to eliminate hobo jungles in his area. Hotchkiss liked nothing better than to devastate a jungle. If hoboes were present in large number, he would take two or three other railroad bulls with him. First thing was to drive all the bums out of camp, not giving them time to pick up their bindles and suitcases, or even the food they were preparing. Then the bulls would shoot every cooking utensil full of holes and tear down any small shelter such as a homemade tent or shack. If there was washing hanging on a line, as was often the case, Hotchkiss tore it off and threw it on the jungle fire. I can imagine that many a traveling hobo looked at Hotchkiss as the Attila of the West Coast.

Far worse than railroad bulls, from the viewpoint of the honest if migratory worker, were the yeggs, the various kinds of crooks who were also riding the rods and living in the jungles. The depredations of these criminals put a blight on all men who traveled by freight, and it was not to be wondered at that the bulls made little attempt to separate the genuine workingmen from the parasites. In discussing the problem faced by railroad police, T. T. Kelihor, chief special agent of the Illinois Central, said that there were seemingly no property or other rights of his railroad that the modern (1922) hobo felt called upon to respect. Millions of dollars worth of railroad property and merchandise, he said, were being destroyed or stolen every year, both in transit and in warehouses. He added that the actual value of the merchandise stolen was only a small part of the loss of merchandise in trains.

"The average hobo," went on Chief Special Agent Kelihor, "realizes that he is not provided with means of carrying away a large amount of bulky goods. Consequently when hoboes enter a merchandise car, they break open a great many cases and dump or throw out the contents on the floor in searching for small, compact, valuable goods that they can carry off concealed about their persons. It often happens that they will not take more than $50 value in valuable articles, but they will destroy and damage $500 worth of goods by destroying the original containers and soiling the contents by trampling on them on the dirty floor of the car and otherwise damaging them." * Incidentally, it was at about this period that A. L. Green, of the freight-claims committee of the then American Railway As-

---

* Quoted in *The Hobo*, by Nels Anderson, Chicago, 1923.

sociation, declared that thefts and robberies suffered by American rail-roads during 1920 "amounted to at least $25,000,000."

Although no one knows how many men are riding about the country on freights, or in blind baggage, at any one time, it is not difficult to know in a general way the rise and fall of the population of hoboes, tramps and bums. Their number probably slowly decreased throughout the 1920's; then, after about 1930, it increased quickly and enormously, and this time to the number of males was added many thousands of girls and women. Before the 1930's were out, however, the number of railroad tramps had unquestionably fallen, and meanwhile the number of auto tramps had increased and they were being discussed in serious study and fiction as the new American problem. The railroad had helped to create the Weary Willie; the automobile was creating the Oakie and Arkie. . . . Then came the busy war years, when few men or women rode freights. Not until 1946 did the number of freight riders increase appreciably.

Women and girls rode the freights and the blinds both before and during the depression of the 1930's. One of the most experienced and articulate of them was known as Boxcar Bertha. She said there were at least one and a half million hoboes on the road in United States and Canada, and that perhaps a half of one per cent were women. In her ramblings Bertha met a number of men who called themselves kings or princes or champions of hoboes. One was Al Kaufman, a "stuttering, handsome Jew" who claimed to have traveled 300,000 miles on thirty cents and his nerve. Another she knew as Thomas Fitzgerald, a driedup man of fifty who had been in forty-eight states and fifty jails. Bertha met the celebrated Jeff Davis a number of times. She relates that he spent a good deal of his energy in denouncing all other hobo kings and getting his own name in the newspapers.

Occasionally Bertha met up with a brakeman who insisted on a little cash to ride over a division in the comfort of a boxcar. She said that only a minority of female tramps would "give themselves" to railroad men for the privilege of riding, and intimates that she herself either rode scot-free, or for small cash, never for her body. One is inclined to believe her, too, for she was anything but reticent regarding her amorous relations with men, many men.* She must have ridden thousands of miles in one hobo style or another. She became acquainted with many sisters of the road, and came to believe they were of four main groups: the unemployed, the antisocial or criminal, the over-sex-conscious group, and the rebels.

Tramps and hoboes and bums naturally enough built up an argot over the years. It is rather extensive and it will not be gone into here at any length. There are many books and a few pamphlets dealing with this argot, which is usually combined in part with the argot of the out-and-out crimi-

---

* See her *Sister of the Road,* as told to Dr. Ben L. Reitman, New York, 1937.

nal class. Probably the IWW or Wobblies contributed as much as anyone to the language.

The wobblies called their bedroll a *bindle* or *balloon,* and the man who carried one a *bindle stiff.* If a bindle stiff moves around a good deal, which is likely, then he is a *boomer.* His opposite is a *homeguard.* A peace officer is a *town-clown.* Whether it was a wob or the railroad men themselves who concocted slang terms for railroad objects and personnel, not even Henry Louis Mencken pretends to know.* Doubtless both sources contributed, and the result was *hog* for a large, usually a freight, locomotive; *crummy* for a caboose, *rattler* for a freight train, *reefer* for a refrigerator car, *drag* for a slow or heavy train of dead freight, *manifest* or *redball* for a fast freight train.

Other generally accepted terms include *hoghead* or *hogger* for an engineer, *con* for a conductor, *shack* for a brakeman, *gandy dancer* for a section hand, *snake* for a switchman. *Highball,* much older in lineage than the others mentioned is used as a verb, to make a fast run; as a noun it means the signal that the track is clear, get going.

Free-riders and railroad men also constructed more or less fancy names for the several railroads. The Chicago & Alton was the Carry-All; the Chicago, Burlington & Quincy, simply The Q; the Baltimore & Ohio, the Dope; the Missouri-Pacific, the Mop; the Southern Pacific, the Soup Line, and a part of it, in Arizona, the Gila Monster Route. It may have been a tramp, but it may have been some ribald farmer along the line who applied to the St. Johnsbury & Lake Champlain the immortal moniker of St. Jesus & Long Coming.

The Hobo Mecca of Meccas is right where it has been for almost a hundred years—the city of Chicago, the Big Junction, and specifically West Madison Street. This is natural, for Chicago is the great railroad hub of the United States, a city with some 3,000 miles of tracks within its corporate limits, a city from which fan out the lines of forty railroads. On West Madison are the slave markets, the employment offices, no longer so important as they used to be but their very presence there for many years set the tone of the district. The railroad yards of several roads are handy to West Madison, and many a man has lived fifty years and never once rode into or out of Chicago on a seat in a passenger car.

There is a West Madison kind of street in all Western cities, but no matter what its name, it is usually known as The Skid Road, a term of sound lineage out of Seattle, where in the early days the logging road of Henry Yesler, crossed at intervals with skids, came down the hill and so across the town to end at the waterfront and Yesler's sawmill. Bulls hauled the logs and the thoroughfare was a skid road.† Along Seattle's skid road

---

* Not skidrow, as certain writers, who don't know what they are talking about, would have you believe.

† See his superlative *The American Language,* New York, 1936.

went up the city's first saloons and cheap hotels, boarding houses, and employment offices, hence it became the district to which loggers, miners, harvest hands, and other itinerant workers flocked.

The skid roads of the West are rapidly changing, taking on new and often even worse features than they knew in olden days, but they still have the old flavor that is distinctive. Here, and never far from the railroad depot or the yards, are the Rooms Upstairs 25 Cents, the barber colleges, the cheap-john stores of all kinds, the slave markets, the burlesque houses, the medicine fakers, tattoo parlors, eating joints. There are also, of course, saloons and fancy houses. The skid-road district is where homeless men live, the men who ride the freights.

The skid road, as I have intimated, is and for some years has been in transition. Less and less do men come there and leave there on the drags and manifests. They come for the greater part, these days, by hitchhiking, or by stealing rides on the trucks of the burgeoning motor freight lines. In 1946 a railroad detective told me that the railroad tramp has certainly been fading, indeed was fading before the depression of the 1930's seemed to revive his numbers.

This railroad special agent doesn't think the railroad tramp will ever return, that is, not in the hordes that once rode the rods, the blinds, and the boxcars. The automobile, in one form or another, is taking him off the steamcars. It is one effect of the motor age that has been of considerable benefit to the railroads.

CHAPTER XXXV

News Butchers

Tobacco . . . candy . . . cigars . . . all the latest newspapers and magazines. . . .
—*The Erie Train Boy*, By HORATIO ALGER, JR.

MOST Americans of middle age can remember a day when the news agent on the train was a somewhat dazzling character. True, he was not so glamorous as the brassbound conductor, nor was he to be mentioned in company with the grimy if godlike personage who had his hand on the throttle of the locomotive. But the news agent had an appeal to the adolescent that was not to be denied.

A writer who never missed a chance to glorify American boys in all walks of life, namely Horatio Alger, Jr., early recognized the news agent as a fit subject for one of his interminable stories, and put him forthwith into *The Erie Train Boy*, a lad who, so it turned out, by hard work and attention to his customers, became wealthy and wound up in his middle years with a fortune and a gold-headed cane. How many lads of the late nineteenth century Alger's deathless work sent seeking news agent jobs isn't known, but at least two of them, William A. Brady and Thomas Alva Edison, made good and went on from there to success in other lines, although Brady's eventual occupation, that of show business, wasn't too distant in spirit from the business of news agentry.

I cannot learn who was the first peddler of newspapers, magazines, candy, fruit, and tobacco on an American railway train. Not even William A. Eichhorn, secretary of the American News Company, the colossus of news agencies, can tell me. Perhaps he was that Billy Skelly who sold his wares on the trains of the New York & Erie at an early date and in time controlled all sales on all Erie trains and finally sold out at a thumping big profit to the Union News Company, thus proving beyond doubt that Horatio Alger was right.

Neither is it certain when the train boy, newsboy, or news agent became the train news butcher. The titles mean the same thing and all appear to be still in use, and used interchangeably. But one thing is sure: news butchers have been singularly backward in discussing their profession in print. Only Edison, and to a much lesser degree William Brady, recalled their news butcher days in books, and both were quite uncommunicative regarding the tricks of the trade. Possibly, news butchers are like magicians and prefer their public to remain in the dark, anyway.

The newsboy was commonly a worldly character, once he had made a run or two on the cars. In the early period he was anywhere from twelve to eighteen years of age. He worked either pretty much on his own, that is, his job was a concession, and all he made from it was his own, or he worked on commission for some individual capitalist such as the aforementioned Skelly of the Erie. Working on commission has a tendency to make a lad hustle, as the phrase has it, and no young Americans of the latter part of last century were better known for their hustling qualities than the train newsboys. The most successful of them were good showmen as well as alert for every chance to turn an honest or even a partly honest dollar, or perhaps dime.

A successful train newsboy had to be quick-witted. Every day he met from one to one hundred people who would trim him in a deal if they could, and he quickly grew in shrewdness and often turned the tables by trimming the would-be trimmers and many an honest man as well. No few newsboys were brash, cocky, imitating the manners of the more vulgar drummers or traveling salesmen who were their steadiest customers. With their blue uniforms and brass buttons, which appeared early in the business, and the cap that said News Agent on it, the lads felt very important and looked down from vast sophisticated heights on all other boys their age, whom they considered bucolics, no matter where born and reared.

So, by around 1850 at the earliest, probably, the newsboy on the train was a figure of the American railroad, almost as conventionalized as the brave engineer, the jaunty brakeman, the dignified conductor, or the president with his plug hat and sideburns.

In my youth the train newsboy was something of a fabulous person, at least in Boston & Maine territory. He had the blue suit and cap with brass name plate. He smoked cigarettes before the rest of us had got through the cubeb period. He read the *Police Gazette,* which he also sold, and he was thought to know all about Sex. His voice, as I recall it, was commonly of high pitch and great power, but his enunciation was so swift as to be all but unintelligible, sounding like "candycigaretscigars" and "newspapersmagazines". . . . He waved at farm girls who stood beside barns and well sweeps, and winked at female passengers of all ages. All of these things set him apart from the rest of us, and so did his ability to make change quickly—indeed, so quickly that I never knew whether or not it was the correct change.

It was firmly believed in my group that train newsboys could drink all the soda pop they wanted, free of charge; and eat all of the candy and crackerjack they could hold. This, of course, was not true, but we believed it, and it added to the newsboy's glamour. Another thing was that he seemed to know almost all adult men who were on a train, and often called them by their first names. As if these privileges were not enough, the newsboy sometimes helped the conductor to pick up the ticket markers from the clips above the seats; and he was permitted to get on and off the train when it was moving into or out of a station. This he did nonchalantly, as if he were bored slightly at having to get off a train operating at less than 40 miles an hour.

I doubt that Thomas Alva Edison was a typical train newsboy, or that he went into the business because of any glamour he saw in it. What Al Edison wanted in 1859, when at the age of twelve he became a newsboy, was to make a lot of money and to be able to spend his off hours in the Detroit Free Library. Those were his stated ambitions, and there is no reason to doubt them. His first run was on a Grand Trunk train that left his home town of Port Huron, Michigan, at 7 A. M. and arrived at Detroit three hours later. It was an accommodation train, made up of a combination baggage car with smoker and two coaches, one of them reserved for ladies and their escorts. The baggage portion of the combination car was divided into three compartments, one for mail, one for trunks and suit cases, and one the smoker. Young Al kept his stock of goods in the smoker.

As soon as the train reached Detroit at ten, Edison hurried to the Free Library and there read books and magazines until six, when he boarded a train for the return trip to Port Huron, arriving there at half-past nine. His reading centered on chemistry. A chemist must have a laboratory, so young Edison set up one in a corner of the baggage car, making experiments between trips through the train with his newsboy wares.

Chemistry and news agentry were not enough for the lad. He next began buying butter and vegetables along the line and selling them in Detroit and Port Huron. He soon hired boys at both end points to help him. When the Grand Trunk put an express train on the division, Edison got the concession and installed a newsboy to work for him. He did the same on a Grand Trunk immigrant train, handling bread as well as tobacco and candy. In 1860, when he was thirteen, the young lad got a font of type and a handpress, set them up in the baggage car, and put out a newspaper, the *Weekly Herald*, which consisted of news items he received from depot telegraph operators at way stations and terminals. The little paper made a hit. Demand for it reached 800 copies, and turned a profit for the editor and publisher of $45 a month.

The youngster was now working twenty hours a day and thriving, yet disaster was near. When his train ran into a derailment and the baggage car took a terrible lurch, Edison's chemicals tipped over and started a brisk fire. Conductor Alex Stevenson put out the flames, cursed the chemist, and boxed him soundly on the ears. From this stemmed the beginning of Edison's deafness, which in time became total. A bit later a trainman grabbed him by the ears to pull him aboard a moving car, and doubtless was a contributing factor to the affliction.

Conductor Stevenson was so angry about the fire in the baggage car that he tossed the laboratory, the printing press, and Edison off the train at Mount Clemens, Michigan. Although he returned to his news agent job for a time, Edison wanted now to be a telegraph operator, and did so, promptly, and went on from there to his long life as inventor and perfector of inventions.

Perhaps a more typical train news butcher than Edison was William A. Brady, onetime manager of James J. Corbett and James J Jeffries, and a noted producer of plays. Brad was a butcher on the immigrant trains of the Central Pacific and Union ᵣacific Railroads in the 1870's. He has said that he was virtually a general store on two legs, for he carried reading matter, groceries, hardware, notions, tobacco, candy, bedding for the hard wooden bunks, guidebooks, and wholly useless souvenirs such as fancy little boxes filled with "mineral specimens."

"You could work off an awful lot of that kind of junk on prosperous drunks," Brady recalled, "and the prices charged were as much as you dared to ask over and above the news company's bookkeeping prices. The difference went into your own pocket." Brady did well at the job. He built up his run until it grossed $400 weekly, of which 20 per cent was his commission. His sales methods were spectacular. As he entered a coach for the first time on a run, he did so spouting lines from Shakespeare at the top of his lungs. His sporting instincts, however, cost him dear, and on at least one occasion he lost his entire stock to a kindly stranger who taught him the mysteries of stud poker.

It may have been young Brady who was newsboy on the immigrant train that carried Robert Louis Stevenson on his last lap across the United States. The Scot remarked that the lad from Ogden to Sacramento was a fine youngster who endeared himself to all the passengers. "You could hardly overpraise his services," he wrote. "All in the cars came to love him." Whoever he was, this newsboy was in great contrast to the one who rode the train out of Chicago, a young gangster who looked to Stevenson to be "a dark, bullying, contemptuous, insolent scoundrel," which seems like quite an order. Stevenson observed that in general the newsboy was quite a personage on American trains and in the West sold "soap, towels, tin washing basins, tin coffee pitchers, coffee, tea, sugar, and tinned eatables, mostly hash or beans and bacon."

Peddling drinking water was a source of income to news butchers on some lines in the 1880's. Harry F. Thomas, aged fifteen, discovered this fact when he became an agent on the Old Colony Railroad out of Taunton, Massachusetts, in 1889. He sold papers, magazines, tobacco and candy, but ". . . most of my sales were of drinking water, which I peddled up and down the train. About that time the railroads were beginning to install ice-water tanks in the cars, so that passengers could get water for themselves; but this train had no such modern convenience. I carried a carrier resembling a teakettle. On each side of the spout was a holder and in each holder a glass. The passengers drank from these two glasses. Sure, the glasses were washed once in a while, when the trainboy wasn't too busy selling his merchandise. . . ."

But June 1st, 1889, was Trainboy Thomas' really big day. He went through his train shouting: "Boston morning papers—all about the great flood in Johnstown. . . ." He sold out immediately, for even the semi-literate wanted to read about one of America's greatest disasters.

The train Thomas operated on ran between Taunton and New Bedford. It consisted of a small wood-burning locomotive, a wooden baggage car, and a couple of yellow-painted coaches. The coaches had open vestibules, a coal stove for heating, kerosene lamps for illumination, and stiff-backed seats. "To me," he says, "they were rolling palaces. I felt mighty puffed-up when I announced the station names from the back of the rear coach, just before we stopped. As soon as we got in motion again I would go to the baggage car where I stored my newspapers, etc., pick up my tray and slowly promenade through the two coaches, calling out my wares." *

Alexander F. Whitney, long-time president of the Brotherhood of Railroad Trainmen, worked as a news butcher for one day. That was on the Illinois Central running from Cherokee to Dubuque, when he was fifteen. What young Whitney wanted was to get to the latter place without buying a ticket. With his sole capital, four dollars, he laid in a stock of stuff at Cherokee, boarded a train without orders from anybody, without the train crew knowing who he was, and made the run to Dubuque, selling his merchandise on the way. At Dubuque, he got a job as brakeman and never returned to the world of news butchers.†

Collecting firsthand material about train butchers, as I have intimated, proved a difficult task, and only through the help of *Railroad Magazine* did I manage to get in touch with old-time members of the craft. Sam Golden, now of New York City, was one. He started riding the trains when he was thirteen, selling newspapers and such on the Fall Brook Railroad between Lyons, New York, and Williamsport, Pennsylvania. This line later became a part of the New York Central.

"In the spring," Mr. Golden told me, "the lumberjacks did a lot of riding, getting on the cars at stations between Corning and Williamsport, where the tracks followed Pinecreek, a log-driving steam. Most butchers sold jewelry, but I was considered too young for that.

"Most of my extra money came from tips. On a later run, to Niagara

---

* Quoted from Mr. Thomas' brief article, "Fifty Years on the Rail," in *Railroad Magazine.* He did not remain a butcher very long, but became a telegrapher.

† As related by John Austin in *Railroad Magazine,* July, 1931.

Falls, I used to do quite a business with souvenir postcards. When I was sixteen, I was promoted and awarded the platform sale of newspapers and periodicals in the Buffalo station. Here, when the *Empire State Express* was about to leave, I would make a little speech in each car to the effect that nothing would be sold after the train left the station. This tickled all of the old-time traveling men, who came to wait for my lecture. I called myself 'The Conductor of Literature.'

"The popular magazines of those days were *Harper's, Scribner's, Munseys,* and the comics *Puck* and *Judge.*"

One of the most successful writers of fiction in the United States, Ernest Haycox, began his business career as a news butcher, a career he found so altogether dismal and discouraging that he was soon driven to finding some other way of making a living. Mr. Haycox, a friend and neighbor of many years, believes that he was unquestionably one of the worst train butchers of record. "And I was probably given one of the worst runs in existence," he told me. "It was from Oakland to Sacramento, California, with now and then a trip to Mount Diablo. Either run was too short. Few passengers felt the need to buy anything from the butcher. I was little more than a silly intruder in the cars.

"I could sell a few newspapers, of course, and though the profit was small, the older butchers taught me how to increase the margin by the ancient and dishonorable method of shortchange. Say that the customer gave me a fifty-cent piece for a five-cent newspaper. I'd assume it was a quarter he had given me, and return him twenty cents in change, meanwhile, however, retaining a quarter in the palm of my hand. If the customer noted the discrepancy, why, I was quick to drop the quarter into his hand and say, 'Sorry!' But half the time, at least, the customer didn't notice, and I was twenty-five cents ahead. My moral being unquestionably suffered injury to a much greater extent.

"The runs I had were so bad that I could earn barely enough to pay for my meals and a room in a flophouse. After a while I discovered a place in San Francisco where I could buy three packages of gum for a nickel. These I would sell at five cents each, thus making a profit of a dime on the deal, for this was not news-company merchandise, but my own sideline.

"Then, there was crackerjack, which sold for ten cents a box. Quite often some kid would buy a box, and then his mother would prevent his eating but a little of it. My eagle eye, sharpened by want, never missed such a happening, and when mother and child had got off the cars, I was on hand to snatch the crackerjack. This I would inspect carefully and if the contents were less than half devoured, and the general appearance of the package still passable, I would later and in secret open eight or ten boxes of the stuff, take a little from each to fill the depleted package, seal all packages again, and return to the market with eleven instead of ten packages and the assurance of a dime clear profit. It was only by such shady practices that I could earn enough for my modest living expenses.

"Often the railroad company would run an excursion up into the hills where the Mount Diablo dam was under construction. The first such event · I attended was an Italian picnic. The news company seemed to think that this picnic would be a big killing. They loaded me up with six gigantic cans of ice cream, one thousand cones, and God alone knows what other stuff. The excursion train ran to nine cars, and every seat was taken by an Italian.

"Well, right after we pulled out I started my campaign by going through the train with salted peanuts. That was the style of merchandising the old-time butchers had taught me—first, get everybody in the train thirsty, then break out the soda pop and ice cream. So I went through with salted peanuts. I think I sold two five-cent bags in the entire train. Next I prepared a big tray of ice-cream cones and took them through. I did exactly that: I took them through the train and back again to my headquarters in the end of the first car. On that long, long day, and to that immense crowd of Italian folks, I sold four cones.

"It was on the same day I learned what my employers should have long since known—namely, that Italians traveling take with them sufficient food and drink to last not only all day, but to last two or three days, in case the train should be delayed for that length of time. The Italians in this particular train carried enormous stocks of bread, cheese, sausage, and wine, all so well garnished with garlic that after one trip through the cars, my tray of ice-cream cones, which I finally ate to prevent their complete disintegration, had a flavor I never shall forget.

"It was quite a picnic, on which I made a total profit, if that is the term, of forty cents. It convinced me I was not cut out for the glamorous job of train butcher. I presently resigned, and I am sure the news company never missed me. Yet, my few months at the job gave me a professional outlook in the matter of news butchering; and today, thirty years after, I never fail to note the butcher on any train I am riding and watch closely his technique. That, however, is as near as I care to be to one of the most difficult and hazardous occupations I can think of."

Living today (1947) in Purdy, Missouri, is an old-time railroad man who retired on pension in 1937 and who began his career in the early 1890's as a train butcher. He is Forrest O. Hayes, and I am indebted to him for much of what I have been able to learn about the art of the butcher of his era. Hayes lived in Punxsutawney, Pennsylvania, southern terminus of the old Buffalo, Rochester & Pittsburgh, now a part of the Baltimore & Ohio, and known locally in its day as the Bums, Robbers & Pickpockets. For his first run as a trainboy Hayes put on a brassbound cap that said

News Agent on it and mounted the train that ran from Punxsutawney to Bradford and return, some 104 miles each way.

"At that period," Mr. Hayes recalls, "all butchers in my region worked for the Union News Company, which had a warehouse and superintendent at Rochester, and from there came our supplies. Our stock consisted of newspapers, periodicals, books, candy, chewing gum, tobacco, and cigars. We also had a few side lines, which I shall take up presently.

"My leading numbers in the literary field were the paperbacks at twenty-five and fifty cents. Laura Jean Libbey and Bertha M. Clay * were far and away the best sellers at twenty-five cents. I found it difficult to keep in stock *A Mad Betrothal* and *Parted by Fate*. The leading fifty-cent author was Archibald Clavering Gunter and the favorites were *Mr. Barnes of New York* and *Mr. Potter of Texas*.

"The magazines we handled at that time were really good—no such trash as clutters the trains and the stands today. We sold *Century, Harper's, Lippincott's, McClure's, Everybody's*, and the *Argosy*. The humorous weeklies were quite popular, *Puck, Judge*, and *Life*. We butchers did not carry the *National Police Gazette*.† It was not supplied by our news company, and few butchers to my knowledge troubled to handle it as a side line.

"All graduate butchers of the day did have side lines, and my literary side line was composed of several books written, as I recall it, by one Albert Ross, and entitled with seductive care *Stolen Sweets, Thou Shalt Not*, and *His Private Character*. And we all carried the old stand-by, *The Decameron* of Boccaccio. All of these numbers were contraband in those days, and to be caught with them meant trouble and possibly discharge. For a time, too, we sold an alleged *Fanny Hill*, but this was an out-and-out fake, not so much as a suggestive line in it.

"For these supposedly off-color books we charged $2.50 to $3, and butchers were pretty good at holding the market that high. We unloaded them largely on lumberjacks up around Mt. Jewett, Pennsylvania, who would readily pay the prices we asked. I remember that at Bradford was a woman, known simply as Madame Stoddard, who operated places of entertainment for loggers, both at Bradford and at Johnsonburg, a paper-mill and tannery town. Her business required Madame to make a trip about once a week. She was quite a source of revenue to me. But she never purchased any of the off-color books. She wouldn't even look at them.

---

* The original Bertha M. Clay appears to have been an English writer, Charlotte Mary Brame, but the pseudonym was appropriated and used by various American publishers as a stock name, much in the same manner as "Nicholas Carter" and "Noname."

† Many train butchers did carry the *Gazette*, however, for on November 19, 1883, *The Morning Oregonian* of Portland carried a statement by Henry Villard, president of the Northern Pacific, saying that sale of the celebrated "sporting" journal had been prohibited on trains of the railroad.

But how she did love Laura Jean Libbey and Bertha M. Clay. Usually she bought ten or twelve of those titles at a time.

"The Union News supplied us butchers with some pretty bad cigars, real stinkeroos. (I never sold a package of cigarettes, or had a call for one.) I hated to sell such rank cigars to deadheading railroad men or to drummers or station crews along the way. For them I carried a good line of cigars, a Roig and a Lawrence Barrett, and never made any profit on them at all. It was a good-will gesture. I also sold a good deal of chewing tobacco.

"The drummers did not buy an awful lot from me, but I remember them with gratitude. They were always jolly, telling stories and buying our papers. They were careful not to tear or crease the papers, but would give them back to us to resell as slick as they had been when they came from the press. Incidentally, I think the American traveling man, by and large, is the salt of the earth. Both as train butcher and later as conductor for many years, I got to know them well and to like them immensely.

"The drummers liked to kid us old-time train butchers, calling us Train Robbers, naming us Jesse, Frank, and Cole, and we enjoyed it too.

"Among our confectionery lines were glass pistols filled with hard candy or gum drops. All of our candy was packaged. A little box of lemon drops sold for five cents and contained more paper packing than candy.

"My run between Bradford and Punxsutawney tapped a rich and virgin territory. The south end was busy with coke and coal, then began the timber region that finally terminated in the oil fields around Bradford. Tanneries, paper mills, pulp mills, sawmills, and glass works dotted the district. The Swedes who worked in the tanneries bought almost nothing from us butchers. Nor did the coal miners, who were Welsh, English and Irish, and were pretty hard up in the Nineties, being unorganized and exploited. But the native-born American lumberjack was a real spender, perhaps the best of them all, especially when he had taken on a load of Bradford liquor. He had to be handled carefully or a riot would ensue.

"The farmers, whether native stock or German, were poor spenders. Many were well-to-do and had got that way through thrift, not from buying stuff from train butchers. The New York State farmers on the New York Central were also notoriously thrifty. For a time I had the run from Rochester to Syracuse and many a round-trip *grossed* less than one dollar in sales. I stayed on the Central no longer than it took to get a transfer."

Newsboy Hayes transferred to the Altoona office of Union News and worked out of there on various runs. By now he was a veteran, wise to the ways of travelers and the world, and he was doing very well. A boyhood chum of about his own age, Johnny J. Jones, son of a miner, did not want to work in the mines. He pestered Hayes to get him a job as train butcher.

"Pretty soon," recalls Mr. Hayes, "an opening appeared, and I asked my boss, B. H. Billman, to give Johnny a chance. Billman sent him out on the Bald Eagle Valley run, between.Tyrone and Lock Haven. Jonesy's first run was a terror. First thing he lost his fine new cap, which cost him $2.50. Next day he lost the lock off his trunk, another dollar gone. He was pretty discouraged, but we persuaded him to try it again. He did so and became a whizz. I've never known another person with so pleasing a personality as Jonesy, and he used it to good advantage. The first decent cheap watch had just made its appearance. I think it was a Waterbury, not the famous Waterbury Dollar Watch, but one ahead of it. Anyway, Jonesy sold from two to five of them almost every day, and within a few weeks he was outselling every other butch from the Altoona office.

"When Mr. Billman was transferred to Williamsport, he took Johnny with him and put him on the best run, that between Williamsport and Erie, on the Philadelphia & Erie Railroad. This was a long run through lumber regions and oil fields. Jonesy became rich on that run and quit it only to put his savings into a scenic railway concession, which did well, then to go into the outdoor show business. The Johnny J. Jones Exposition Shows have been tops in the carnival world ever since.

"For a while I had a job selling Union News sandwiches in the Altoona station. These consisted of two thin slices of bread between which reposed a piece of ham the thickness of a safety-razor blade. They cost ten cents each. I could sell from 125 to 200 every night, earning for myself from $2.50 to $4, which was good wages for the period.

"I forgot to mention that a favorite stunt of butchers of my day was to have always on hand a big supply of pennies and the large two-cent pieces then current. Our system, in selling a paper to a Pullman passenger, was to start doling out pennies in change for a twenty-five or fifty-cent piece. When the customer saw all that copper rolling out, he often said to keep the change—and we did.

"Occasionally, there was an excursion to the great Kinzua Viaduct, two or three miles north of Mt. Jewett, a structure 2,022 feet long and 301 feet high, said to have been the highest bridge in the United States at the time. Ten- and sometimes twelve-car excursions were run to the bridge during summer months, with low fares in effect. These trips were quite lucrative to train butchers and were generally grabbed, or claimed, by the senior men. I made the excursion run a number of times, once as head butcher, for it took several of us to work the huge crowds.

"In addition to the usual lines supplied by the company, we had, on the excursions, plenty of our own goods, including a barrel of alleged lemonade in the baggage car. This stuff was concocted of one barrel of water, two dozen lemons, and a sizable dose of tartaric acid. We butchers made certain, just before the excursion train pulled out, that all of the water coolers were drained dry. Pretty soon the kids would begin to yell for something to drink, and even the adults got pretty thirsty. Then we'd go through the cars with our lemonade and glasses.

Cab of a diesel switch engine in Rock Island freight yards. Note two-way radio system.

After freight trainmen had been enjoying a superior view from caboose cupolas for eight decades, the Burlington Lines produced the Vista Dome car, in 1945.

"Excursion days were usually hot ones. All the car windows would be wide open. Smoke and cinders poured in in clouds. The pretty starched and frilly maids of the morning would be a sight long before the trip was done. Young married couples, for some reason I could never fathom, never missed an excursion and brought with them their babies of six months or a year.

"Arrived at Kinzua Viaduct, the cars emptied and the crowd stared at the great sight. Seeing the bridge took only a few moments, no matter how much you liked to look at a bridge. And the bridge was all there was to see. The place was wild and forbidding, with nothing but a small dance platform and a tiny eating place, where the prices were downright out-rageous. In such a spot the excursion crowd remained for five or six hours. They milled around, getting restless by the minute, and the men drank heavily and soon started fighting. On the return trip home the drunks would mostly be asleep, and all the others—tired, irritated, and dirty— swore they would never go on another excursion. But, they were human beings, and the next year would find them riding to the viaduct again, and having a high old time. I cleared $79 on one such excursion."

Train Butch Hayes thoroughly enjoyed his career. In 1898 he entered train service on the Reynoldsville & Falls Creek Railroad in Pennsylvania, and in 1906 went west, to work on the Missouri Pacific and to retire for age as conductor on that line, in 1937. He has wondered, as have I, why no news butcher has ever set down his life and times in a book.

Nor is there anything even approaching a satisfactory account of the inception and rise of what is now the American News Company, Inc., which "Covers a Continent." (The Union News Co. is the wholly owned subsidiary of the American News Co. which services transportation sys-tems throughout the country with reading matter, food, tobacco, etc. It is by far the largest company in the business.) In a handsome brochure the company published in 1944 to observe its eightieth anniversary, a mere nineteen lines of text serves to relate the concern's long history. From the brochure I learn that today the company has nearly 400 branches in the United States and Canada and supplies 90,000 retailers with periodicals, newspapers, candies, tobaccos and other wares; but nothing of its history except for those few lines. The booklet does display portraits of The Founders, seven in number, who were George Dexter, Henry Dexter, Soloman W. Johnson, John E. Tousey, John Hamilton, Sinclair Tousey, and Patrick Farrelly. Two of the founders, Henry Dexter and Sinclair Tousey, rate sketches in the authoritative *Dictionary of American Biog-raphy*.

Mr. William A. Eichhorn, secretary of American News, informs me that the company was organized in 1864 by a merger of the three largest news firms then in business, namely, Sinclair Tousey; Dexter & Hamilton; and Johnson & Farrelly. Into one or another of these firms had been previously merged a number of other agencies, including those of the famed Skelly of the Erie and of L. N. Spear, who seems to have had a monopoly of train butchering on the New York Central & Hudson River Railroad.

Henry Dexter must have been something of a remarkable man. Born in Cambridge, Massachusetts, in 1813, he became a printer and served for some time as second printing foreman at Harvard College. He went to New York in 1836, and there got into the business of handling newspapers and books. He seems to have been the moving spirit in consolidating many small firms into American News, of which he was president until his death in 1896.

No matter that many a train butch for American News had a good side line selling *Boccaccio* and *Fanny Hill*, Henry Dexter was at heart a moralist and reformer, as well as a philanthropist. I find him listed as a director of the American Bible Society, the American Tract Society, the New York Society for the Prevention of Cruelty to Children, St. Luke's Hospital Society, the Children's Aid Society, the Home for Incurables, the Charity Organization Society, the New York Association for Improving the Condition of the Poor, and the Home for Aged Married Couples. Not least, he contributed $225,000 toward building the present home of the New York Historical Society, thus proving, incidentally, he was more interested in history than are the present men of American News.

Sinclair Tousey was another Yankee, typical in that he belonged to almost as many reform groups as did Henry Dexter. Tousey was born in New Haven, in 1815, and worked at many things, including selling patent medicines, newspapers and magazines. On the outbreak of the Civil War he enlisted and served three years, then wrote a book of his life in the Union Army. In 1853 he became a partner in a firm that was merged in 1864 to form American News. He was a hot Abolitionist before the war, and afterward was active in prison reform, the prevention of cruelty to animals, and aid to ex-convicts.

Founder Soloman Johnson was a farmboy from the Catskills, an orphan, who went Algerlike to New York to make his fortune, beginning as a carrier with a newspaper route and becoming subsequently a partner of John Hamilton, another American News founder, who was actually born in New York City and started a news and book business on Ann Street. Hamilton was strong and aggressive, qualities of great aid in getting as many papers as he wanted and in holding good corners for himself and his boys.

Another founder, Patrick Farrelly, born in Ireland in 1840, was probably the only one of the seven who had served as a train butcher. This he did on the Philadelphia & Reading and with such success that he quickly saved sufficient cash to set up as a wholesaler. He was a stripling of twenty-three when he sold out to and became an official of American News.

Such was the genesis and such were the founders of the great concern that now operates on trains and in depots all over North America. Incidentally, it appears to have been an Englishman, a Mr. Whitmore, who first had the idea of supplying all newspapers and magazines in one package to retailers. He started such a business in 1842, at Nos. 8–10 Ann Street, New York, and sold out two years later. By that time the idea had spread and quite a number of news-agency men were active.*

Doubtless a lot of stuff supplied to news butchers in days past was shoddy—cheap imitations of standard products. But I recall a kind of wintergreen (checkerberry) wafers sold by agents on the Maine Central and Boston & Maine that were, or so it seemed to me and other boys of the day, the finest wafers ever made. They came in a roll of violently purple paper, and were so strong as to bite the tongue pleasantly, especially when consumed along with the smoke and gas common to the steamcars of those times. I am unable to remember, if ever I knew, who made them, but there were no others just as good.

Glass revolvers, mentioned by old-time newsboy Hayes, were apparently a standard item of the Union News Company, for I don't seem to recall having seen them elsewhere than on trains or in railroad stations. A glass switchman's lantern filled with candy was another popular number never seen elsewhere than in Union News territory.

My memory of the extracurricular items handled by butchers—that is, unsponsored and unknown to the company—was of a plain, sealed package, which the butch said was "The Paris Package" and contained matter of a nature described as snappy. This package cost one dollar. It was not to be opened until the customer got off the train, for, the butch said, if he were caught selling such lascivious material he would be sent to state's prison for life. On opening the package, the gull found six postcards whose scenes followed the *partial* disrobing of a woman who was obviously going to bed, alone.

Yet, some of the butchers must have handled real dirty stuff, on the side, of course, for I knew a hired man on a farm who returned to northern Vermont from a trip to Boston and had in his possession a copy of *Only a Boy*, which he had purchased on the train and was something lewd beyond compare.

There neither was nor is anything lewd in the paperbacks of Thomas W. Jackson, the man who "libeled the great states of Arkansas and Missouri," to quote one of the charges made against him. Since around 1903 Jackson's books have probably been consistently the best sellers in the literature

---

* The information about Mr. Whitmore who, when he had sold his news business, went "into the milk business" and apparently disappeared forever, comes from an article in the *Brooklyn Union* of February 2, 1867, which lists a score of news-agency concerns that went into the American News consolidation. My favorite agency would have been the one named Noisy Carrier, of San Francisco.

peddled by train butchers. How many copies of his *On a Slow Train Through Arkansas* and *Through Missouri on a Mule* have been sold in the steamcars is beyond knowing. Jackson collected all the gags about slow trains he could find and hung them one and all on lines in Arkansas. To term his humor broad is an understatement; it is about as subtle as the jokes exchanged of yore by Mr. Bones and Mr. Interlocutor, or today by radio's comics. For more than forty years the Jackson books have been peddled by news agents and sold in railroad depots. Arkansas, at least, finally felt the need to combat their influence. In August, 1946, Mr. Glenn A. Green, publicity director of the Resources and Development Commission, Little Rock, sent a letter to newspaper editors throughout the United States, calling attention to an article about his state in the current *National Geographic Magazine,* a "fair exposition of Arkansas." Mr. Green added that "For more than a century Arkansas has been the victim of adverse publicity surrounding its legendary Arkansas Traveler, its backwoods people and the cheap publications of such writers as Opie Read and Thomas W. Jackson. Even today, laughing at Arkansas is a popular, national pastime."

Of late years the news agents on trains still sell Jackson's books, and also handle much the same standard fare that has proved solid merchandise for the past century almost—newspapers, periodicals, cigars, candy, and, of course, cigarettes. They also carry a few numbers not seen in the old days, among them a truly ghastly line of pillow tops, the gaudiest things ever beheld, bright in color and depicting vivid mountains, eye-rocking rivers, flags, entwined hearts, and Mother, good old white-haired mother; and legends and poems of incomparable sentimentality. I trust that these atrocities will sell well and long. I trust the butchers themselves will continue to flourish, both on the branch runs and the main lines. A passenger train without a butch lacks something of the fine flavor of trains in the great days. May the boys ride the steamcars until the last engine has gone to the boneyard and the last rail has been pulled up!

CHAPTER XXXVI

The Biography of a Flagstop

† *Stops on signal to discharge or receive revenue passengers*
—From any railroad timetable

T HE particular flagstop I remember with deep affection was named Columbia Bridge. The depot reared its story-and-a-half up from a meadow along the remote upper reaches of the Maine Central Railroad in northern New Hampshire, and got its name rightly enough from the wooden covered bridge that crossed the Connecticut River to Lemington, Vermont. Under the bridge, every spring for longer than any living man could remember, had passed untold millions of feet of logs, mostly spruce, while on their rolling decks ran and leaped generations of lumberjacks, driving the sticks like wild horses down to the droning mills at Mount Tom in Massachusetts.

Both the bridge and the depot were built before I was born, and in my time they showed their age by the crop of moss on the one and the weathered paint on the other. They were perhaps a hundred yards apart, and both were marked so that the passing traveler, whether by horse or train, might know something of his progress and also something of the customs of the neighborhood. On the little depot, rather faint when I first knew it, was painted COLUMBIA BRIDGE in those fancy letters whose font is called "Barnum," being wonderfully shaded and fairly crawling with curlicues. On both ends of the bridge itself was the typically brief Yankee legend: "Walk or Pay Two Dollars." It might be well, for the sake of a new generation that never knew the horse, to explain that the sign meant you must not trot or run your team across the structure.

For many years the bridge was a toll affair. Most of the old settled families had a yearly pass, costing I believe five dollars, but all other persons had to pay a few pennies each time they crossed it. The tollhouse was kept first by Jed Butler, and when the railroad arrived in 1888, he also kept the post office and, in addition, rented mileage books for passenger travel on the Upper Coös Railroad, for such was the name of the line in its primitive days. Mileage books were used throughout New England for many years, on all lines, and every town had a man like Jed who acted as broker or renter and charged, I believe, at the rate of $\frac{1}{4}$ cent a mile, for his capital and services. I am certain that even a rented mileage book was cheaper than buying tickets, for otherwise Yankees would have had no truck with them.

In Jed Butler's time there was no depot. The tollhouse was invaded by persons waiting for the cars, when Jed would let them, and near the house was a small raised platform for mounting to the train. Trains never stopped, of course, unless someone aboard wanted to get off or unless Jed flew a flag from the tollhouse door; but they carried the mails, and the sacks had to be put off and taken on while the train was in movement. Tossing off a bag was simple. Putting one aboard was another matter, for the Upper Coös Railroad either had never heard of a mailbag standard or, more likely, was not going to waste its dividends on such trumpery. So, for many years Mary, Mrs. Butler, a stout and rugged woman, listened well for the whistle of the oncoming train, then took her bag of letters and stood up firm and solid on the little platform. The railway mail clerk leaned well out of his side door, clung to the rocking car with one hand, and scooped the bag out of Mary's uplifted arms, meanwhile kicking off the Columbia Bridge sack of mail. It was an acrobatic act fit for Sig Sawtelle's Great United Shows and Moral Exhibition.

I regret I never saw that scene, but people who did have told me it was something to remember—Mary, out there in storm or sun, and often in fearfully cold weather, standing staunch against the worst the elements could do, leaning slightly if the wind were hard, watching the train that was bearing down upon her, timing the moment exactly when she must lift up her arms to hold, as if in supplication, the august sack to be caught and whisked away, in order that young men and women in Boston and New York and Beloit and Seattle might know life went on at home—might know, for instance, that George Ramsay had got married, that Bill Simms had bought a new Buckeye mowing machine, that Harry Blodgett was taking orders for enlarged crayon portraits.

Once the sack was safely aboard the train, Mary dusted off her hands, picked up the incoming sack, and returned to the tollhouse, there to sort the United States Mail for Columbia Bridge, New Hampshire—letters, catalogues from the Larkin Company of Buffalo, New York, copies of the *New England Homestead, Hoard's Dairyman,* and *Comfort,* and perhaps announcements of a bargain sale of Estey Organs at Bailey's Music Rooms, Lancaster, New Hampshire.

For seven years Mary the Mail Maid continued to meet all the trains, faithfully and promptly, while Jed made certain that no down-river slicker from Littleton or Concord crossed Columbia Bridge without payment of two pennies. Then, in 1894, the tollhouse, post office, and mileage-book business was taken over by Jim and Dora Russ, who carried on until 1896. In that year Progress arrived. It arrived in the shape and form of Henry Ballantyne, who built a depot and installed in it not only the post office but a store; and the railroad, which had become the Maine Central, stirred no doubt by the great changes at Columbia Bridge, at last built a frame on which to hang the mailbag, an efficient thing of two arms which was coordinated with the iron arm put out by the railway mail clerk. Henceforth Columbia Bridge depot was on a par with any other flagstop in all New England. It sported sockets in which to display the flag, and a platform some sixty feet long, to say nothing of a privy. In the Maine Central timetables the importance of Columbia Bridge was attested by a printers' mark called a dagger, thus †, and the legend: "Flagstop."

There were two trains a day each way, bound north or south, for ten months of the year. But in July and August a third train each way was added. This summer extra was to carry city folks who had discovered the wild beauty and low prices in extreme northern New Hampshire and Vermont, well beyond the farthest fringe of the vulgar White Mountains region where natives had been gouging visitors since long before the Civil War. The only Pullman cars ever seen on this branch of the Maine Central were those on the summer extra in July and August.

The heyday of Columbia Bridge as a depot and store and place of philosophy and entertainment began in 1900 when Will Bailey, a cripple, took over store, post office, and depot. The place got a bright new sign, the structure was painted, and, due to considerable logging in the neighborhood, quite a number of passengers and a vast amount of freight were unloaded regularly from the passenger trains and the daily mixed. Moreover, Will Bailey stocked his store to perfection. I've been in my share of little crossroads stores but never did I see so much and so varied a merchandise in so small a place as Will carried in his emporium. He had everything from overalls and Johnson Pants and Bass' Calked Boots to Clark's Mile-End Thread, everything from Cliquot Club soda pop to Dr. Perry Davis' Painkiller Good for Man or Beast.

To entertain the loafers and waiting passengers, there was also the first slot-machine I ever saw, and a huge Swiss music box. The slot-machine was a five-cent play, and was said to pay off about five or six times a year. I recall that Heman Nason, a talented habitué of The Bridge, as the depot-store was known, once popped his eyes when the little cup rattled furiously and filled to overflowing with nickels; but it was the only time I ever saw it do that.

The monstrous music box played prettily for one cent. The records were at least eighteen inches across, and gave out with "Over the Waves" and "Sweet Rosie O'Grady." Maine Central trains were not noted for promptness, and Will Bailey probably did pretty well with the music and gambling entertainment features of his place. What he made on them, however, he lost by charging too many goods to too many worthless risks. I know of half a dozen families that virtually lived off Will's great goodheartedness, and never, I am certain, paid him more than a dollar or so on account.

When he died, his books showed more than $10,000 in outstanding bills owed him.

Will lost no little money, too, simply because of the fact that he sold candy—or, rather practically gave it away. At Columbia Bridge we could buy a really gigantic bag of mixed chocolates and gumdrops for one cent, a penny; and a dime's worth of stuff at Will's candy counter was about all one boy or one girl could lug off to get a bellyache on. We youngsters walked as much as three miles to and three miles from in order to spend one cent at Bailey's store. Kids always recognize bargains.

If practicable, and sometimes if not, we timed our visits to coincide with the arrival, or more often the passage, of a train. The favorite in summer was the seven-fifteen in the evening, northbound. It might stop, to let somebody off; or, if it was to be flagged, then Will would permit a good boy to stick the flag in its socket. The seven-fifteen ordinarily had three cars—a combination baggage-mail-express car, a smoker, and one day coach. Once in a long time a train might come along with a special car, toting some brass hats from the Maine Central headquarters.

The up, or northbound, trains could be heard when they whistled for Cone's Siding, some four miles off, and could be seen a bit later crossing the handsome broad meadows of Miss Jeanette Holbrook, where they made fast time on the level straightaway. But the southbound trains came around a sharp curve to the depot, and were passing on the fly almost before a boy could dash outside to see if the one-cent piece or two crossed pins he had laid on the rails had remained in place or were thrown off by the vibration.

One of the Maine Central's glories was Conductor Frank Clark, a perfectionist, who tried always to stop his train just right so that his passengers to and from Columbia Bridge, and especially the ladies, could step down direct to the rather short platform and not in the mud. Conductor Clark rated his engineers high or low according to how near they came to stopping at what Clark held to be the right spot. On one occasion when passenger Rufus Jodrie, no lady, wished to be set off at Columbia Bridge, the engineer overshot the mark and the train did not come to a full stop until even the last car had passed the depot and platform. Conductor Clark announced the station sonorously and then, seeing Jodrie make no sign of getting off, urged him to do so. "Hurry up," he said, "I am late already." Mr. Jodrie was in no hurry. "I will be goddammed," he said in a loud tone, "I will be double goddammed if I will get off out here in the suburbs. I bought a ticket to Columbia Bridge and that's where I want to get off—not out here in the back forty." So, Conductor Clark, the perfectionist, backed up the Maine Central's *Coös County Flyer* fifty yards, and Mr. Jodrie stepped down in style to the platform.*

---

* I am indebted for this and certain other incidents to a kinsman, H. A. Holbrook, unofficial but highly competent historian of Columbia Bridge, both the structure across the river and the depot.

The depot was a natural loafing place, and Agent Will Bailey liked loafers. To see the evening train pass, or stop, whichever the case might be, there was pretty sure to be a gathering of the regulars, come from nearby farms and logging camps. Long John Bell, six feet nine inches tall, was likely to be present, and was the reason why passing strangers came to believe that Columbia Bridge harbored a race of giants. Old Charles Morrison was another regular. He was a marked man, a man to be reckoned with, for it was Charles, by his own report, who when captured during the Civil War and taken to General Jubal Early's tent, lectured that tough old Confederate soldier on the arts of war and warned him that a certain piece of woods Early planned to assault was "fairly alive with more goddam Yankees than you ever see." As if this were not enough, Charles Morrison had looked upon Jesse James in the flesh.

Most of the depot gang were native-born and storytellers to a man. To them was added a scattering of Irish from the Old Country, even bigger and better storytellers, men like Barney Rooney and Jim Flynn, wonderful liars, and they all loved, though none would have admitted it, to hear the steamcars whistle and see and smell the smoke, and perhaps catch a glimpse of some pretty face at a window, and to witness the wonder of picking up the mail on the fly.

Like the Grand Central Terminal in New York, like all other railroad stations everywhere, the Columbia Bridge depot was now and then the scene of tragedy. One such event occurred early one morning around 1901, when a number of local sports were leaving to attend the Coös County Fair at Lancaster. Among them was the aforementioned Rufus Jodrie, who apparently liked to ride the cars, and Gene Jordan and Jim McLaughlin. The down-train, the train they must catch or miss half the fair's wonders, was due at six-fifteen A.M. Almost at that hour, on this particular morning, Jim McLaughlin felt the urge to visit the little house just back of the depot, erected there for the comfort and convenience of passengers of the Maine Central Railroad. Knowing full well that the six-fifteen seldom arrived at the flag until six-twenty-five, and reckoning he had plenty of time, Jim was about his business when the sharp blast of the down train sounded from around the curve. A moment later it stopped.

One can appreciate the predicament of Jim McLaughlin, victim of an unprecedented occurrence such as the on-time arrival of the six-fifteen. If the car windows were open that morning, which being early September was not at all unlikely, then the passengers heard shouts coming from somewhere behind the depot: "Hold the train! Hold the train!" But Conductor Clark, if that perfectionist was on the run, and if he was not, it was some other believer in promptitude, shouted his "all-aboard," and away went the train on its way to Lancaster and the marvels of the Coös County Agricultural Association's great annual event, while out back of the Columbia Bridge depot Jim McLaughlin gave voice to his disapproval and chagrin. "You're one hell of a railroad," he told the Maine Central, "you're a jeasley blackhearted railroad that won't wait—you're not accommodating at all."

Jim had to wait for the eleven-fifteen, meanwhile telling Depot Agent Bailey again and again of the shortcomings of the Maine Central, a railroad, he vowed, not to be spoken of in the same breath as the Montpelier & Wells River; a line mean and contemptible compared to the Grand Trunk; a streak of rust and corruption beside which even the Quebec Central, haywire though it was—beside which, in fact, the Quebec Central was a perfect railroad. Will Bailey was glad when the eleven-fifteen arrived on time for once.

Columbia Bridge, both bridge and depot, aged gracefully. The patina of years and weather turned the bridge into a fit subject for picture postcards, much admired by the summer people who see quaintness in everything outside their ken. The structure burned in 1911, quite properly from a shower of Maine Central cinders, hot as all hell; but the new bridge, built in 1913, looked antique almost immediately, and it, too, went onto the postcards.

No matter Mr. Ford, the signs on the bridge ends still said "Walk or Pay Two Dollars." No matter the new popularity of cigarettes, a sign inside the bridge still urged the male men of Vermont and New Hampshire to use the old reliable chewing tobacco, Battle-Axe, A Great Big Piece for Ten Cents—a splendid sign of tin in the form of the classic battleaxe, bright red. In spite of new ideas of therapy for man and beast, Mr. Kendall still had a bold card for his Spavin Cure, and Dr. Arntall told all that his Mandrake Bitters were the same today as they had been in your grandfather's day, as no doubt they were. Dr. Knight still advertised his Opodildoc, an almost miraculous and protean remedy; and those two Old Testament prophets, the Smith Brothers, still eyed all traffic across the bridge and warned travelers that coughs are hard on the system but can be prevented easily. In addition to these and other apparently immutable worthies, Mr. Walter L. Main, for more years than I can remember, advertised that his Mighty Shows would be at North Stratford on July 8th, or some other summer date, to amaze all who beheld them. How sad Mr. Main's faded pictorial one-sheets looked when the bridge cracked with frost in December. . . .

Yet, the horseless carriage was sneaking up on the Maine Central, just as it was on all other railroads, especially those operating in sparsely populated regions. The three trains a day, fixtures for half a century, gave way to two, then to one and that one a mixed train, which never sees the same man twice as passenger, if he can help it. But it makes no difference now to the Columbia Bridge depot. The little structure still stands but it is empty and decaying, its windows staring, sightless. Not for an age has a flag hung there, or a train stopped, other than to set off an empty boxcar on a pulpwood siding.

I regret its passing. Probably we all regret the passing of anything that gave us pleasure in our youth, even though its survival would be an anachronism, as Columbia Bridge depot certainly would be. I don't think I ever knew a railroad station that could change so quickly and so manifestly from deep calm, almost somnolence, to a state of excitement bordering frenzy. The magic of the steamcars was never more apparent than here.

I remember it best of a winter evening, waiting to see the seven-fifteen come in or by. The big stove in the center of the room gave off welcome heat, and the warmth aroused and fused the assorted smells of Will Bailey's store—that mixture of coffee, spices, tea, candy, liniment, kerosene, and wool clothing which tell or told of a country general store, to my mind one of the most powerful nostalgic aromas there is. In winter we had to scrape the windows with a knife to see much of what was going on outside. While we waited frost snapped the nails in the depot, and the single telegraph line hummed desolate in the bitter cold.

If the loafers were many and the talk consequently loud, one of us youngsters kept going outside to listen for the whistle that would well up out of the dark four miles south to tell us that she was passing Cone's Siding and would be along in about twelve minutes. Will Bailey might let one of us hang out the lantern and put the mailbag in its frame, for no matter if the train did stop, the mail was picked up by the mailcar's steel arm.

Then she'd whistle a mile down the track for Columbia Bridge. The rails started to hum, and presently we could see her headlight far across the meadows, gleaming like a bright evening star in a darkling sky. As she came on, the light stabbed the night as clean as though it were a slice made by a gigantic butcher knife. When she came nearer we could see the headlight trembling, rocking with the locomotive, and the engineer whistled for the stop. She'd come up to Columbia Bridge depot pretty fast, then the brakes would go on and half the time the train would skid to a stop, a process said to be terribly hard on wheels and brake shoes.

Once stopped, excitement mounted, for you know how it is when the fireman keeps ringing the bell, with its urgency to passengers to be spry and to get off and get on with speed and order. At Columbia Bridge as many as five persons might get off, but seldom more than two. Now and again a trunk came out of the mysterious recesses of the baggage car. Meanwhile, we boys gaped up at the lighted windows, seemingly a full mile of lighted windows, strange heads and faces at each window—men, women, girls, babies, all strangers, all going somewhere, all impatient to get going again, some looking doubtless with amusement or condescension at the bucolics beside the track, quaint natives who still thought a train of steamcars a sight worth walking three miles to behold, even on a night dark and biting with cold.

They were right, those amused or condescending passengers, those travelers who never knew Columbia Bridge except as a hick depot in the wilderness, a picture suddenly framed by a car window, and just as suddenly dissipated by night as the train resumed its way. They were right, at least so far as I am concerned. Seeing a train of cars pass Columbia Bridge at night remains one of the greatest sights I ever saw. To watch a Constellation take off or land is as nothing in comparison.

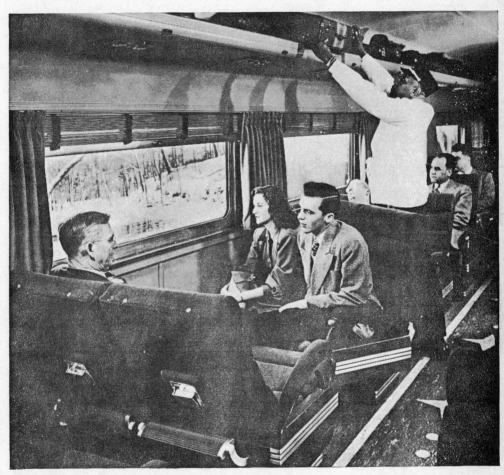

The Great Northern's Empire Builder day coach, air-conditioned, with wide windows, Venetian blinds, indirect lighting, and sponge-cushioned seats that can be swung around at any desired angle.

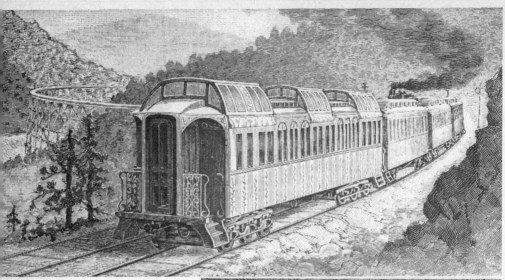

The Vista Dome, publicized as ultra-modern, was conceived and patented by T. J. McBride of Winnipeg, Canada, but never built. McBride's ideas are embodied in these two views from Scientific American of May 2, 1891. Compare with the GM "Train of Tomorrow," below.

(General Motors photo)

CHAPTER XXXVII

The Railroad in the Drama

Villain (looks at watch)—"It is five minutes to midnight. The Lake Shore Express is due on the hour."
—Act 3, *Under the Gaslight*, 1867.

THE drama inherent in railroading must have appealed to American playwrights at an early period, although no play of the rails seems to have made much of an impression until there opened in New York in October of 1867 a show called *Under the Gaslight*, complete with tracks, a steam locomotive, switch, and signal shanty. This play ran for more than one hundred performances in Manhattan, and was a popular number for revival in subsequent years.

The dearth of earlier successful plays dealing with railroads, it seems likely to me, must have been in great part due to the expense and ingenuity involved in making and presenting something that would faithfully represent the railroad's most dramatic object, which is of course the steam locomotive. In those days before the movies, the stage carpenter was a tremendously important person, for it was a time when many playwrights sought to introduce in the theater some of the drama they saw about them on every hand—such as the weird and scary effects of the blast furnaces, the still romantic and appealing steamboats that forever were blowing up, thus making for a nice third act; and naturally, too, the Iron Horse who snorted with fine melodrama across bridges and plains and mountains, breathing fire and smoke, lighting hills and valleys with its great headlamp, and announcing its coming and passing by an exciting cacophony of pounding wheels, and whistles, and bells.

The United States of the nineteenth century was in itself a gigantic theater, putting on a show such as the world had never seen and isn't likely to see again. It was a drama of action, not of talk. Men and women were still engaged in taming a vast expanse of geography, fencing it with territorial, then with state lines, meanwhile killing Indians and bison, cutting the forest, digging ore, blasting the ore into iron to make iron rails and iron horses.

At first no American dramatist could see this great show that was going on right under his nose. He continued to write plays set in England, in

Africa, in Turkey, in France and Russia; but by the time the Civil War was done, and the country leaped again with new life to conquer and to exploit, a number of authors roused to view the stupendous drama that Americans were living.

Writing a good play is an art form to be achieved by comparatively few writing men in any one generation. Writing, or rather putting together, a show that will stun the public and make a lot of money is not a work of genius at all, but a job for shrewd men who understand perfectly the present moment, who comprehend the temper of the public at any given time, and who then fashion a show that is calculated to appeal to the public *now*, and not a hundred years hence, or even ten years hence.

So, the era of melodrama began. It was predicated on the sound supposition that a large number of people will pay cash to be frightened half out of their wits by stage representations of tragedies that few of them have witnessed in real life but of which all of them have read or heard. A bang-up melodrama of the day depended, if not on murder or mystery or both, then on some mechanical device that would raise the hair on the heads of the primates in the galleries and cause cold sweat to break out in the orchestra and the box seats. To contrive these mechanical devices the school of the ingenious stage carpenter came into being and started its long heyday. On the carpenters, more than on the playwrights, depended the success or failure of the show.

That first successful drama of an American railroad, *Under the Gaslight*, had one of the great professors of stage carpentry behind the scenes. The third act revealed a railroad track across the stage, while center stage was one of those clumsy but impressive old-fashioned switches, and back of it a small shanty to protect the switchtender from the inclemencies of the weather. The course of the drama called for the hero to defend the heroine's honor from the villain. This being accomplished in previous acts, it was now time for the silk-hatted one to get the hero into his clutches. This was arranged by the playwright, with little or no trouble, and the hero was bound firmly to the main-line track—just a little to the left of the switch, as viewed from the audience.

Now the villain looks at his watch. "It is five minutes to midnight," he remarks in language no railroad man would think of using. "The *Lake Shore Express* is due on the hour." Then he sneers and laughs simultaneously at the prone and helpless hero. "Heh, heh, heh!" he says, as he sneaks away into the trackside brush, there to await the awful destruction of the curly-haired lad on the track.

A full moon floods the stage. The woods roundabout are dark and forbidding. A cloud starts crossing the moon, dimming the scene. Just then, and not a moment sooner, there comes from some mysterious place in the wings the far-off yet positive whistle of a locomotive. Blood pressures rise in the audience, for this they know from the posters that brought them here is to be the big scene—the scene depicted by the billboards as a truly gigantic engine, begauded with paint and brass but trembling with speed and casting out smoke and sparks, bearing down on the inert figure on the track ahead.

Again the whistle sounds, this time fearfully near. Then a shaft of dazzling light stabs the melancholy scene, lighting the woods, the switch, the shanty, and the hero. With the stab of light comes the unmistakable thunder of the iron horse, pounding louder than the hearts of the boys in the gallery. Just when it seems that the poor hero is a goner, onto the stage dashes the heroine whose virginity, or at least honor, is still intact. In one bound like that of a scared gazelle she reaches the switch, gives it the old heave ho, and just then the forepart of the locomotive emerges into view from the wings. The iron monster is side-tracked, and all is well, as the villain slinks away even farther in the brush.

The iron horse of *Under the Gaslight* must have been a triumph of the stage carpenter's art. It would probably seem crude today, especially to an audience brought up on the movies where the shadows of real locomotives course along the shadows of real rails; but in 1867 it must have been good, for the entire play depended upon the engine's factual appearance, and the play was a thumping success.

Since that day the iron horse, either in full-sized representation or in miniature in the background, has appeared in many an American play, a few of them quite successful. What *Theatre Magazine* said was "One of the most realistic effects of machinery ever seen on any stage" was the locomotive and forest-fire scene from *The Ninety and Nine,* by Ramsay Morris, which appeared in 1902 and was founded on an incident of the Hinckley (Minnesota) fire of 1894, when James Root ran his St. Paul & Duluth engine and train from burning Hinckley through the forest fire to Skunk Lake, where all aboard were saved by the shallow water and muck of the pond.

A photograph of the big scene in *The Ninety and Nine* looks pretty effective. The prop locomotive is full size, and probably exact in copy. The wheels turned. In the picture is the actor, Dore Davidson, at the throttle, peering ahead into the hell along the tracks, while on the platform between tender and cab is his fireman, heaving buckets of water over the brave engineer. Real smoke pours out the stack. Real smoke partially envelops the engine. Speed was simulated by a moving background of flaming trees, the flames being tissue-paper streamers, and lights. It was all quite thrilling and the play enjoyed an excellent run.

There had been at least one earlier stage train in a forest fire, this time in something called *Marked for Life,* produced in New York in 1876. A year later the great Ada Rehan and her leading man, Oliver Doud Byron, appeared in a railroad drama entitled *Across the Continent.* But no rash of railroad shows broke out until the 1890's. In that decade, according to a survey by Harry W. Cole for *Railroad Magazine,* there came *A Mile a Minute, The Limited Mail,* and *The Midnight Special,* all in 1892. Presently people were going to see *Railroad Jack* and two more, *A Railroad Ticket* and *The Pay Train.* Florence Bindley starred in the latter, a real thriller in which robbers attempt to stick up the pay car, only to be foiled at the last moment. Then, in 1899, came that sterling opus *The Fast Mail,* by the master of melodrama Lincoln J. Carter, who capitalized the dramatic possibilities of the new fast mail trains between New York and Chicago.

The Fast Mail had not one but two trains, hence was twice as good as a show with only one. In this play the audience saw a freight pass along back of the footlights and onto an off-stage siding. On top of a boxcar stood a brakeman, lantern and all. The scene was in semi-darkness and the lanterns and headlight were most effective. So were the noises that preceded and accompanied the Fast Mail itself, which tore onto the stage as soon as the freight was out of the way. A mail pouch had been hung on the crane as a build-up, and now the speeding train swept past and the arm put out from the mail car caught the bag neatly and swept it away into the wings, along with the train, which then ran out through the big stage doors and into the street.

Mr. Carter's *Fast Mail* packed them in in New York, then two road companies took it all over the nation, to grand business. Playwright Carter tried to follow up his success with another railroad drama. This was *Bedford's Hope,* in which a tin locomotive was involved. It flopped. Some other author essayed an attempt with *The Denver Express,* and still others sought to ride the bandwagon with patent plagiarisms entitled *The Midnight Mail, The United States Mail,* and *The Orient Express.* But the appeal seemed to have passed for the mails and expresses.

Wondering what plays involving railroads would be remembered by George Jean Nathan, whose alert eyes and retentive mind have been exposed to the drama for half a century, I asked the eminent critic and writer of the theater which ones he could recall offhand. "*Clarice,* by William Gillette," he said promptly, "had remarkably realistic off-stage train sound effects, perhaps the best I ever heard. In *The Fortune Hunter* there was a striking scene of a train by night, crawling across the backdrop. George Cohan's *Forty-Five Minutes from Broadway* had a good depot scene. *Excuse Me,* by Rupert Hughes, took place almost wholly on a transcontinental train, the first two acts in a Pullman sleeper, the third in a combination buffet and observation car. The bell, whistle, smoke, and dust effects all were artfully managed. Rachel Crothers' *The Little Journey* had scenes laid in railroad cars. So did *Twentieth Century,* by Hecht and Mac-

Arthur. *The Whip* and *Life* were two melodramas that had boxcars for the heroic race horses.

"I saw one play about Casey Jones that was all railroad background. Another, *Outside Looking In,* had a crowd of freight-riding hoboes. Unless my memory lapses, George Moore's play *The Strike at Arlington* concerned a railroad. Both *Heavenly Express* and *The Ghost Train* involved railroads in one way or another."

A scene that took the public fancy was that of a railroad-station waiting room, alive with employees, travelers and typical depot-loiterers, which was largely responsible for the success of James Forbes' play *The Traveling Salesman,* in which Frank McIntyre starred for several seasons. In *A Stubborn Cinderella,* featuring John Barrymore and Sallie Fisher, a Pullman car is stranded on a high mountain in Colorado, sidetracked for some reason, and the audience gets a view of a deep canyon running down thousands of feet. The original play, founded on Jules Verne's novel, *Around the World in Eighty Days,* had what theatergoers of the period said was a most impressive railroad scene. One of the favorite revival pieces of the American stage, *Mrs. Wiggs of the Cabbage Patch,* contains an empty freight car in which a drunken and otherwise obnoxious character is put, then the door closed and sealed, and next morning is shunted off to the main line, thus taking the drunk away from the Cabbage Patch for good.

I saw *Mrs. Wiggs,* but did not see another play, *Home, Sweet Home,* which Russell E. Smith, sophisticated in the business of railroads, considered the best rail show he ever saw. "The climax of this play," wrote Mr. Smith for a railroad audience, "was reached in the third act in a small-town railway station, of which the leading juvenile was the station agent and telegraph operator. His sweetheart's father, an ex-convict, appears at the station and meets his daughter, who aids him to escape from town, and shows him a handcar on which he starts away. The fast express is due in a few moments, and the girl suddenly realizes that her father is likely to be killed by the train. Just outside the window of the office is to be seen the semaphore with its arm set to give the express the right of way. The girl, frantic, sets the signal against the train.

"Just then the train is heard whistling for a clear board, but the red ball is set! The engine whistles for brakes, and comes coughing and puffing into the siding, while the crew rush into the waiting room of the little station to find the heroine in a faint upon the floor. The effect of this scene was tremendous, what with the big engine in full sight of the audience, giving out with all of an engine's sounds."

Al Jolson played a Pullman porter in a rather successful comedy, *The Honeymoon Express.* It had one act showing a race between a train and an automobile. The train lights crawling along on a winding mountain road in the background made a pretty scene. The climax came when the stage lights suddenly came on full power, and out of the wings, in full life-size, came the locomotive, to stop to the sound of hissing air. Next to bell and whistle there is probably no sound more typical of the railroad than that of air brakes in operation, and railroaders who saw *The Honeymoon Express* might forget the name of the play and never know who the leading actor was, but they did not forget the sound of that hissing.

In 1937 appeared a show bearing the name of but not about the best-known character connected with American railroading, the late John Luther (Casey) Jones. It failed quickly, although the railroad men who saw it thought it set a new high in authentic railroad realism on the stage. Writing of it in *Railroad Magazine*, in whose pages railroads are to be treated with all technical respect, Harry Cole remarked on the fine cab scenes on a St. Louis-Chicago express, which had Charles Bickford at the throttle and Van Heflin stoking coal. There was also a telegraph operator who pleased the customers immensely by holding up a train order on a loop for the engine crew to snatch at full speed.

The play *Casey Jones* had a number of other scenes so good as to make railroad fans cheer for the play and to mourn its quick demise. One memorable scene was laid in a railroaders' boarding house, where hoggers and shacks and snakes, all recognizable types, sat around and discussed matters of state and of railroading, in the best hot-stove style. There was a fine scene in a railroad yard just outside a roundhouse. There was a nostalgic country depot, by day and by night—faithful to railroad signals, accurate as to the conduct of all railroaders in the play.

"Those of us who saw *Casey Jones*," wrote Mr. Cole, "enjoyed the exciting realism of the engine's noises and motion in her illusory flight past the audience. We liked the yard at night, with familiar lights twinkling far and near; and we think that the station, with the operator's bay and the op at work and the tracks outside and the large water tank, was pretty darned close to the real thing." That is high praise from a railroad man. And Mr. Cole goes on: "The play deals with an engineer who is very loyal to his road. After thirty years of service his eyesight fails and he has to quit the cab. Since he happens to know something about telegraphy, he is given an operator's job. The climax comes when Casey fails to make a go of his job at a quiet country station—he whose very life was the speed of the roaring road."

Well, Casey does something about it. He throws up his job of pounding the key, then flags the limited in defiance of all rules, and climbs into her cab the moment she stops. He is away on a new trail of adventure. "It is a magnificent gesture," Mr. Cole remarks, "if you don't stop to analyze it too closely. Certainly it is dramatic."

But playwrights, no matter how clever, cannot fool customers who are genuine railroad men, and no matter how much Mr. Cole enjoyed the play *Casey Jones,* he finds certain failures in its technical aspects. "There are flaws," he remarks, with obvious reluctance. "For one thing, the whistle signals are carelessly done. Then, one of the trains is Number 8, when any railroader knows it should have carried an odd number. The matter of seniority was handled in a slightly confused manner; and Casey, with his red lantern within reach, should not have used a red flag to stop a train at night. But in spite of these few defects, Robert Ardrey's show set a new record for railroad realism behind the footlights, and we are sorry it folded up."

Another railroad play, which appears to have had some merit, also folded quickly. This was *Heavenly Express,* which opened and closed almost simultaneously at the National Theater in New York in 1940. Its subject is the legendary ghost train that hoboes are said to talk about around their jungle fires, the train that runs to the Big Rock Candy Mountains where the rocks give out with booze and the trees are festooned with cigarettes.* Freeman Hubbard, then editor of *Railroad Magazine,* saw the show and from a railroader's point of view found it very good indeed.

"It is as realistic as stage technique can make it," he wrote. "It is night in the desert at Ash Fork, Arizona. A small group of bindle stiffs is sitting around a fire under a trestle. Snow is falling, and from far in the distance comes the wail of a coyote. The bums have been ditched on a hos-tile pike, the Santa Fe, and they are talking it over.

"We confess we felt like cheering at the grand climax, as the *Super Chief* is shunted onto a siding—even if that was a rather unusual thing to happen to that particular train. Then the mysterious hot shot roars through, 'outward bound,' a load of boes riding her tops into Eternity. Her great yellow headlight floods old Mrs. Graham's boarding house at night with the glare of noontide, while the Overland Kid gives a highball, and the curtain rings down on an evening of choice entertainment."

Heavenly Express was written by Albert Bein, then thirty-three, who acquired his knowledge of railroads in a tragic way. During his youth he lost a leg under a Santa Fe freight while he was hoboing near Ash Fork, scene of the play. Incidentally, Mr. Hubbard remarks that all railroad men who saw *Heavenly Express* much regretted its early closing.

Probably the most famous and durable of shows dealing with a railroad was an A. H. Woods' melodrama that originally appeared as *The Great Express Robbery.* This was a stage show. It had a brief run on the stage, and would never have been heard of again if Thomas Alva Edison, who began life as a train butcher on the Grand Trunk, had not seen it when it

---

* What forgotten hobo invented the Big Rock Candy Mountains is not be known; but the song that made them famous was written by Harry K. McClintock, "Haywire Mac," in 1895, long a wanderer but now more or less permanently a fixture of San Pedro, California.

first appeared in 1897. Edison was crazy about it. A few years later, in connection with his efforts to develop the motion picture, Edison was trying to get away from the prize fights and horse races that up to then had constituted movie fare. He recalled Woods' melodrama and suggested to his camera man, Edwin Porter, that *The Great Express Robbery* might do for a motion picture play.

Up to that time, which was 1903, no attempt to film a play had been made in the United States. Porter got the script of the stage play, read it, and agreed with Edison that it could be made into a moving-picture story. Porter worked it over a bit, then hired a company and went out along some railroad tracks to film it. It was soon ready and late in 1903 appeared as *The Great Train Robbery*.

The Great Train Robbery created a sensation when it flickered across the white sheets of the nickleodeons of the time. It left the audiences with the feeling that they had participated in person in a genuine stickup of a railroad train. They had seen a real express and passenger train—no dummies but the real thing—pounding along a real track, outdoors, the scenery flitting past. They had watched while masked and armed men held up the cars. They could see the smoke from revolvers, even if they could not hear the reports. In spite of the flicker-strain on the eyes, they were greatly moved by this first motion-picture show.

CHAPTER XXXVIII

Ballads of the Rails

He was ditched by a shack and a cruel fate,
The con highballed, and the manifest freight
Pulled out on the stem behind the mail,
And she hit the ball on a sanded rail.
                    —The Gila Monster Route

THE ballad about John Luther Jones, commonly called Casey, is without doubt the most popular railroad song ever written. Just what renders a song popular and keeps it popular is something on which not even experts are in agreement. Part of the appeal of the Casey Jones song may be due to the lyrics, which relate a tragedy in concise, colloquial language, yet it is the lilting and unforgettable melody that is largely responsible for the song's seemingly perennial popularity.

Both the melody and the original lyrics appear to have been the work of one Wallace Saunders, an unlettered (and simple) Negro who worked in the roundhouse of the Illinois Central railroad at Canton, Mississippi, and was much given to the composing of songs about subjects that interested him. Saunders knew Engineer Jones and often cared for his engine. Tragedies, of course, were Saunders' meat, and the collision that removed Jones from the IC payroll fascinated him. Jones was little more than in his grave when Saunders was singing a new number while he wiped the locomotives in their stalls at Canton. This was to become the immortal song of the rails.

Being illiterate, Saunders kept all of his ballads in his head. He'd sing them for his friends among the railroaders. They took a liking to the one on Jones; and John R. Gaffney, an IC locomotive engineer and a friend of the dead Casey, offered Saunders a bottle of gin if he would permit Gaffney to take down the words and melody. Saunders agreed and sang the song over and over until both words and music had been transcribed.

Casey Jones died April 30, 1900. Shortly thereafter Wallace Saunders was singing his song. The mutations of the ballad during the next two years or so must have been many, for when it appeared as a piece of sheet music in 1902 there was hardly a line that had not undergone modification. The first adaptations seem to have been by Bert and Frank Leighton, vaudeville performers, who used a Casey Jones song in their act. No doubt they got it from their brother, Bill Leighton, an Illinois Central engineer. Then, in 1903, appeared a published song *Casey Jones, the Brave Engineer,*" the words credited to T. Lawrence Siebert, the music to Eddie Newton. The Siebert-Newton version departs from the original lyrics almost from the first line. Although its meter is a great improvement over the Wallace Saunders words, it leaves out a great deal of Saunders' authentic railroad language. There just isn't any such thing, as Fred J. Lee points out in his biography of Jones,* as a "six-eight wheeler," which occurs in some versions. The "high right-wheeler" in the Wallace version is good railroad usage. It means unqualified approval.

But the Siebert-Newton song was professionally done, the lines more or less held to the meter, and rhymed after a fashion. But Siebert added not only a chorus, but also a new verse, a verse that understandably shocked and angered the widow, Jane Brady Jones, because it indicated the widow was ready to get a new husband "on the Salt Lake Line."

Mrs. Jones, still hale, still a widow, never had another romance in her life than John Luther Jones. She attends many railroad celebrations where the number is quite likely to be played and sung. She doesn't care much for the Siebert version but will stand for it, all but that last verse which she thinks is a reflection on her. Neither she nor Wallace Saunders ever received a penny from the song which has been published and republished and made into more phonograph records than you could count. Yet, it was Siebert and Newton who, all unwittingly and most efficiently, did for John Luther Jones what Henry W. Longfellow had earlier done for the horseman Paul Revere. Without them and their song, Jones might be only a fading memory along the southern reaches of the Illinois Central. As it is, his is by far the best-known name in American railroad circles, better known even than that of Commodore Vanderbilt. Nor should it be overlooked that Siebert-Newton conjured up one line that will last as long as any steel rail. I mean the immortal: "Number Four stared him right in the face. . ." Only Gussie Davis wrote a line to equal that one, and I shall come to it presently. The truth is, however, that Casey was killed by running into the caboose of a freight train inadequately sidetracked.

A convention of railroad men would probably rate "The Wreck of the Old 97" second only to *Casey Jones* as a classic. This ballad has had a curious history. I don't believe anybody knows just when it was written, although it was inspired by a wreck that occurred on September 27, 1903, to the *Fast Mail* of the Southern Railway on its run between Monroe and Spencer, Virginia. Ninety-seven was an hour late when Engineer Joseph A. Broady and a fresh crew climbed aboard at Monroe. Broady was instructed, so the song has it, to "put her into Spencer on time." Spencer is

---

* *Casey Jones,* Kingsport, Tenn., 1939.

166 miles from Monroe and the *Fast Mail*'s normal running time between those points was about 4 hours 15 minutes.

Broady was given two firemen in order that the steam pressure should hold high, and the challenge of the timecard was all else he needed. He opened her up "rugged like," nor did he cut off power as he approached Stillhouse Trestle, a high structure over Cherrystone Creek, just out of Danville. The combination of a curve and descending grade made Stillhouse Trestle a danger spot, and on both sides of the track at this point were signs: "Slow Up, Trestle!" Joe Broady had an hour to make up, and perhaps he didn't believe in signs, anyway. He paid no heed to the signs or to Stillhouse Trestle and just as Old 97 hit the curve, everything sort of let go at once and an instant later the locomotive had leaped the rails and plowed a hundred feet to bury her nose in the muddy bank of a stream. All five cars followed her. Both firemen were mangled beyond recognition. Conductor Blair died, so did Flagman Moody, and eight others, mostly postal clerks. As for Engineer Broady, much of the United States must know by now that he was "found in the wreck with his hand on the throttle, a-scalded to death with steam."

Such was the wreck that was to put all other wrecks but Casey's into the shadows of memory. The immortalizing agent in this instance was David Graves George, a hillbilly of the region who had worked at braking on the railroad, at farming, and even as a boxer and a revenue agent. He was present at the scene of the wreck while it was still smoking, and went away impressed with the tragedy. When a real hillbilly is impressed with a tragedy, a ballad is likely to be the result. Sure enough, David G. George sat down and composed "The Wreck of the Old 97," then and there. A good melody was handy. This was "The Ship That Never Returned," already an old favorite in the mountain country. George fitted his words to the tune and first sang the number in, appropriately enough, a barber shop at Franklin Junction, Virginia.

Well, *Old Ninety-seven* rolled away from Dave George. It wafted out of the Virginia hills and into the cities. It went across the plains, over the mountains, it permeated all of the United States, in sheet music, phonograph records, finally on the radio. Dave George did not know how far his song had gone until one day in 1927, when he had driven a mule team into some crossroads village in Virginia and heard a phonograph bleating out a familiar song. Yes, it was his song. He was amazed to hear it coming forth from a talking machine, and he went in to ask the man who was playing it how come they had his, Dave George's piece, on a record. Not long afterward he read in a Richmond newspaper that the Victor Talking Machine Company was trying to find the composer of the song. Dave filed a claim, and so did a score, perhaps a thousand others, both hillbillies and lowlanders.

The case meandered through the courts and at last reached the United

States Supreme Court, which upheld George's authorship but subsequently refused to rule on the matter of compensation. The Victor people said they had already paid for rights to Old Ninety-seven to three different claimants. In any case, Dave George never got any of the gravy. The song goes on, year after year, with no sign of abating popularity.

I'm willing to admit that *Casey Jones* and *Old Ninety-seven* are respectively the Number 1 and Number 2 songs of the rails. I'm not sure what a convention of railroad men would vote for as Number 3, but I have my candidate for that spot and I say it is one of the great railroad songs of all time. I refer to the sad and melodious *In the Baggage Coach Ahead*, perhaps the best of the ballads written by Gussie L. Davis, the first Negro to become prominent as a song writer in the United States.

Davis made Cincinnati his headquarters. After several years as a Pullman porter on Midwest and Eastern roads, he returned to his base and got a job sweeping out halls at the Cincinnati Conservatory of Music. Here, by keeping his ears open, he picked up a considerable knowledge of composition, and presently he was writing songs. None appear to have been hits, however, until he rewrote and set to a plaintive melody a poem that had been written by a railroad conductor with whom he had made many runs. The conductor was Frank Archer of Hector, New York. The poem was entitled *Mother* and concerned an incident of a coffin in the baggage car of a train on which both Archer and Porter Davis were working. Here are the lines of the last verse:

> But the father's heart was broken,
> And this was all he said—
> "Their mother is in a casket
> In the baggage coach ahead."

Gussie Davis took Archer's poem and remade it, leaving intact only one of the original lines. Howley & Haviland published it in 1896 on a royalty basis and Davis is said to have been well paid for the song. He should have been, too, for it became a sudden hit and was popular for eight or more years after its appearance. It is also one of the Gay Nineties numbers that survives today as a sort of folksong and is, of course, particularly a favorite with old-time railroaders.

Gussie Davis' masterpiece was the first illustrated song I ever heard, or saw. The event was in Lane's Opera House, Newport, Vermont, the time around 1904. Price Webber's Dramatic Stock Company had a curley-headed tenor, whose name I regret I cannot recall, but whose voice is yet a living memory forty-three years after. It was his duty, between the acts, to sing some ballad and thus soothe in some small part, the customers who had been stirred or frightened by the uncommon amount of shooting that was a portion of all of Mr. Webber's melodramas. On this particular evening his number was *In the Baggage Coach Ahead,* and while he sang from the darkened stage, the great light in the gallery was used to throw on a screen the beautiful image of the *Empire State Express* of the New York Central Railroad, fairly eating up the rails. This was followed by other pictures in sequence, showing the interior of a Pullman, while at the end of each chorus—there were two verses—the screen revealed a tragic-shaped box on the floor of the baggage car. When the song was done, you may be sure—for those were simple times—there was not a dry eye in the house.

Gussie Davis' great song has also been, and still is, one of the really grand numbers for a male quartette. I doubt that any member of such a quartette, who ever used the song, will forget the vast possibilities in the climactic line:

But baby's cries can't waken her

The "her" is held for a moment, or longer, in order to permit the first and second tenors, the baritone and the bass, all to get in a few licks that rise to crescendo, then diminish with sliding minors before going into the final line. It is gorgeous. I trust that railroaders, and others, too, will never let the song die.

Many a wreck has been recorded, and usually with spectacular inaccuracy, in one or more ballads that appear to have been written shortly after the event. Most of these ballads were probably the work of some home-grown bard or other. Many of them are forgotten and are to be found only in the yellowing files of old newspapers and periodicals. There is one, however, that is still verdant, *The Chatsworth Wreck,* known to all railroaders who have any interest in the balladry of the rails. The disaster it celebrated occurred in 1887 to an excursion train of the Toledo, Peoria & Western, near the town of Chatsworth in eastern Illinois. Eighty-two persons died in the wreck, and presently some hillbilly minstrel had his epic ready, grim, dreadful, hopeless except for a line or two devoted to heroism displayed:

THE CHATSWORTH WRECK

From Peoria, town and hamlet,
    There came a joyous throng
To view the great Niagara;
    In joy they sped along,
The maiden and her lover,
    The husband and the wife,
The merry, prattling children,
    So full of joyous life.

Chorus
But oh! how much of sorrow,
 And oh! how much of pain
Awaited those who journeyed
 On that fated railroad train.

With hand upon the lever
 And eye upon the track,
The engineer was standing,
 While the shades of night grew black.
They passed the town of Chatsworth
 And rushing into gloom;
Oh, could some power have saved them
 Ere they had reached their doom!

For see those smoldering embers
 That lie along the ridge;
Oh, God, in pity save them;
 It is the railroad bridge!
Too late to turn the lever,
 Too late to stop the train,
Too late to soothe their sorrow,
 Too late to soothe their pain!

A mighty crash of timber,
 The sound of hissing steam,
The groans and cries of anguish,
 A woman's stifled scream.
The dead and dying mingled
 With broken beams and bars,
An awful human carnage—
 A dreadful wreck of cars.

All honor to the hero
 Who the flame and fury fought
All through that night of horror,
 An honor deadly fraught,
As over land and water
 The thrilling message crossed:
The bridge was burned at Chatsworth
 And a hundred lives were lost!

Here again we have an example of the great strength of folklore as opposed to the fact of history. The record shows that eighty-two people died in this disaster. The ballad has it one hundred. Any old-timer of eastern Illinois will tell you, or anybody else, that "a hundred lives were lost at Chatsworth." Trying to change *that* opinion would be futile.

Southern Pacific's Daylight skirts the Pacific for 113 miles of the 470-mile run between San Francisco and Los Angeles.

The "armstrong" turntable, worked by muscular effort, such as this oldtimer on the Illinois Central at Woodville, Miss., in the 19th century, preceded the electrically-operated type of today. A good example of the latter is shown below at the Turcon, Montreal, engine house of the Canadian National Railways.

Ever since the time, probably in the late 1830's, when railroads first began running trains after sundown, lights have played a big part in the lives of all railroaders. Lights on switches, lights on semaphores, the bobbing, rocking taillights on the last coach or the caboose, and of course the great headlight of the locomotive, one and all have meant a good deal to the men who *read* them and to whom they are something more than merely red and green and amber spots in the dark.

This being so, it is natural that balladists should choose to celebrate the drama of railroad lights, and the number of poems and such in which lanterns and other lights figure must be enormous. Outstanding among them, so I am informed by competent persons, is an anonymous song or poem that has been printed and reprinted in Brotherhood journals and other magazines dealing with the rails and railroadmen. This is "The Red and the Green," and its unknown author was without question a railroad man, for none other would have been likely to think up so pat a situation for two lanterns of different colors:

THE RED AND THE GREEN

A little child on a sick bed lay
    And to death seemed very near;
Her parents' pride, and the only child
    Of a railroad engineer.
His duty called him from those he loved,
    From his home where lights were dimmed.
While tears he shed, to his wife he said,
    "I'll leave two lanterns trimmed."

Refrain
"Just set a light when I pass tonight,
    Set it where it can be seen.
If our darling's dead, then show the red;
    If she's better, show the green."

In that small house by the railroad side,
    'Twas the mother's watchful eye
Saw a gleam of hope in the feeble smile
    As the train went rushing by.
Just one short look, 'twas his only chance,
    But the signal light was seen.
On the midnight air there rose a prayer,
    "Thank God, the light is green!"

There are probably hundreds of songs about the caboose, for that car has played a large part in the lives of railroad men. What no less an expert than Freeman Hubbard considers the most celebrated of all caboose songs, one to which, with a few beers, most any old-timer can give voice, is another anonymous ballad entitled:

THE LITTLE RED CABOOSE BEHIND THE TRAIN *

O, I'm a jolly railroad boy and braking is my trade,
As I run upon the road each day and night,
Throwing switches, making fly-stops, as 'long the road I go,
Taking care to see the train is made up right.
Oh, yes, we're always ready, whene'er we're called to go,
Either in sunshine or the rain,
And you'll always find a jolly crew, if you'll only come and see,
In the little red caboose behind the train.

Refrain
O, the brake-wheel's old and rusty, the shoes are thin and worn,
And she's loaded down with link and pin and chain,
And there's danger all around us as we try to pound our ear
In the little red caboose behind the train.

One red light we hang upon each side, another on behind,
As day goes by and night comes stealing on;
And you bet the boy that rides ahead, he keeps it in his mind,
For to see that all the train is coming on.
And when we're near the station we're startled from our thoughts,
By the sound of the whistle's thrilling scream,
Then we skip out on the hurricane deck and leave our car behind,
That little red caboose behind the train.

There seem to be as many, and probably more, songs about freights than about passenger trains; and one idly wonders if this is so because the caboose supplies a sort of studio-writing room, a place, indeed a flying strip, from which Pegasus can make the needed run to lift his wings. It may well have been a caboose wherein J. N. Stewart raised his voice to tell of the

DRAG FREIGHT

Over the hill at Libertyville, with a jangle of gearing loose,
Comes Forty-eight, the long way freight, with the little red caboose.
'Way up in front, where he bears the brunt of the sleet and swirling snow,
Old Mogul horse plods his weary course, steady and strong, though slow.
With a rattle of slack bumping down the track, Forty-eight takes the siding, clear,
While Number Four, with a deafening roar, whistles by in her mad career.
With a heave and a strain, back on the main, Forty-eight goes gogging along;
While from the frosty rail, in the teeth of the gale, the wheels fling a strident song.

* Copyright 1933 by Bob Miller, Inc. Used by permission.

With a clickety clack, a long mile back, the crummy tails the drag,
And now that night obscures the sight, the lamps replace the flag.
With jolts and jars, on the swaying cars, they're bucking the ceaseless grind,
While a twinkling light laughs at the night, from the little caboose behind.

God grant that they have right of way, with a meet or a pass for all,
Till the home yard light, with a welcome bright, flashes the last highball.

For more years than most men can remember an authentic railroad poem entitled O'Shaughnessy has been going the rounds of the switch-houses, yard shacks, and cabooses. In 1943 the *Railroad Magazine* reprinted it and asked if anyone could name the author. A number of replies were received, among them one from Lee Howard of Portland, Oregon, last surviving grandson of General O. O. Howard of Civil War and Indian campaigns fame. Lee Howard is today(1947) one of the grand old-timers of all the West, four score and more years of age, and among many other things he has served at times as a railroad man. Mr. Howard says that the poem in question was written, about 1880, by one Tommy Miller, with whom Howard worked on the St Paul, Minneapolis & Manitoba Railroad out of Grand Forks, Dakota Territory. Miller had tried braking under a rawhiding conductor named Burbank. He didn't like it. Here is Mr. Howard's version of Mr. Miller's complaint:

O'SHAUGHNESSY

O'Shaughnessy it is me name,
The truth I will relate to ye:
I worked upon the section line,
I am a decent Irishman.
A conductor came to me one day
And to me these words did say:
"Ye must drop your shovel right away
And go braking on me train."

He took me up to the railroad yard,
He put in my hand a big time-card;
He said that braking wasn't hard
If I was only game.
He put on me head a railroad cap,
And said it was wore by all our crap,
And this by a decent Irish chap,
While braking on a train.

They sent me out on the Number Tin,
And then, my boys, me trouble begin;
One would send after a pin,
The other would fire me back agin,

> They kept me running from ind to ind,
> While braking on a train.
>
> I swung the lantern over me head,
> It was a signal, so they said,
> For the ingineer to go ahead,
> And then I were to blame.
> Then I forgot to t'row the switch,
> The cars uncoupled and went into the ditch,
> The conductor called me a son of a bitch,
> While braking on a train.
>
> The cars uncoupled, came down the hill,
> The conductor said that I was a gill
> For smashing the property of Jimmy Hill,
> While braking on a train.

Mr. Howard says that the original of the last verse was entirely too realistic to go through the mails, and that the last four lines as given here were substituted in polite company.

Many songs about hoboes naturally deal in one way or another with trains or railroad yards or railroad police (bulls). There are likely a thousand hobo songs, and most of them have appeared in one or another of the cheaply printed collections. A few have made their way into the sociological documents that are preliminary to the bestowing of the degree of Doctor of Philosophy, and here they are subjected to analysis to "prove" this or that theory regarding the hobo's outlook on life. A vast amount of preciosity has gone into these erudite studies, but I am not at all certain that the total result has added much to knowledge about the footloose men who make a career of riding around in the United States on freight trains. How many actual hoboes, tramps, and bums have written songs is another of my doubts; yet, there are some pretty good numbers in the hobo hymnal, no matter who wrote them. One that has stood the test of years, and is only too likely to be declaimed at musical gatherings of railroad men—and perhaps of hoboes as well—is *The Gila Monster Route*, a ballad whose title relates to a portion of the Southern Pacific railroad. I have seen authorship credited to "Post and Norton," to "T-Bone Slim," of whom there have been many, and also and more often to Anonymous. The versions vary but on the whole they are more nearly alike than is the case with many other such poems.

THE GILA MONSTER ROUTE *

> The lingering sunset across the plain
> Kissed the end of an eastbound train;

* By L. F. Post and Glenn Norton. Used by permission of *Railroad Magazine*.

And shone on a passing track close by,
Where a dingbat sat on a rotten tie.
He was ditched by a shack and a cruel fate,
The con highballed, and the manifest freight
Pulled out on the stem behind the mail,
And she hit the ball on a sanded rail.

As she pulled away in the falling night,
He could see the gleam of her red taillight,
Then the moon arose and the stars came out—
He was ditched on the Gila Monster Route.
Nothing in sight but sand and space;
No chance for a gink to feed his face,
Not even a shack to beg for a lump,
Or a henhouse to frisk for a single gump.

As he gazed far out on the solitude,
He dropped his head and began to brood,
He thought of the time he lost his mate,
In a hostile burg on the Nickel Plate.
They had mooched the stem and threw their feet,
And speared four bits on which to eat,
But deprived themselves of their daily bread
And sluffed their coin for Dago Red.

Down by the track in the jungle's glade,
On the green grass, in the tules shade,
They shed their coats and ditched their shoes,
And tanked up full of that colored booze.
Then they took a flop with their skins plumb full,
And they did not hear the harness bull,
Till he shook them out of their boozy nap,
With a husky voice and loaded sap.

They were charged with "vag" for they had no kale,
And the judge said "Sixty days in Jail."
But the John had a bindle—a worker's plea—
So they gave him a floater and set him free.
They had turned him up, but ditched his mate,
So he grabbed the guts of a west-bound freight,
He slung his form on a rusty rod,
Till he heard the shack say, "Hit the sod!"

The John piled off, he was in the ditch,
With two switch lamps and a rusty switch,
A poor old seedy, half-starved bo,
On a hostile pike, without a show.
From away off somewhere in the dark,
Came the sharp, short note of a coyote's bark,

The bo looked around and quickly arose,
And shook the dust from his threadbare clothes.

Off in the west through the moonlit night,
He saw the gleam of a big headlight—
An eastbound stock track hummed the rail;
She was due at the switch to clear the mail.
As she drew up close, the head end shack,
Threw the switch to the passing track,
The stock rolled in and off the main,
And the line was clear for the westbound train.

When she hove in sight far up the track,
She was working steam, with her brake shoes slack.
She hollered once at the whistle post,
Then she flitted by like a frightened ghost.
He could hear the roar of the big six-wheel,
And her drivers pound on the polished steel,
And the screech of her flanges on the rail,
As she beat it west o'er the desert trail.

Then John got busy and took a risk,
He climbed aboard and began to frisk,
He reached up high and began to feel
For the end-door pin—then he cracked the seal.
'Twas a double-decked stock car filled with sheep—
Old John crawled in and went to sleep,
She whistled twice and highballed out,
They were off—down the Gila Monster Route.

Then, there's *The Phantom Drag* which concerns one of the most cherished of all railroad fantasies—the idea of a ghost train running on through space and time without end. It has been the subject of poems, songs, stories, and even a play or two. It is often the immortal Casey Jones who is at the throttle of this string of cars, as in the following version, which has been credited to Charles Blue:

THE PHANTOM DRAG

It was cold and damp in the hobo camp
  When a tired and hungry bo,
Fretfully slept as the shadows crept
  On his bed in the sleet and snow.
As the cold wind whined, the hobo's mind
  Fled back through the bygone years
When the rumbling strain of a fast train
  Fell on his dreamy ears.

The semaphore dropped, and the rattler stopped,
    Midst the air brakes' shrieks and groans.
In the high cab chair, sitting there
    Was the long dead Casey Jones.
She was a manifest and headed west,
    And a hobo's dream of heaven.
On the engine's side the hobo spied,
    The number Ninety-seven.

With the whistle's scream and the hissing steam,
    The drag got underway.
The bo made a hide for a western ride
    With some pals of another day.
There was Ike the Pike, and Mopey Mike,
    And Little Joe from Nome.
There was the Texas Kid, the Katy-Did,
    All headed westward home.

The drivers chimed, the car wheels whined,
    The smoke rolled from the stack;
The boxcars pitched, and rocked and rolled,
    'Till they nearly left the track.
Through the wintry night she held her flight
    Toward the distant westward shore,
While the frost-bit boes lay nearly froze
    On the cold, hard boxcar floor.

They had staked their souls to reach their goal
    Out in the far off west,
But the bitter night had guided their flight
    Into eternal rest.
At the break of dawn, the train rolled on
    Through the bitter cold and snow;
But no one knew, not even the crew,
    They were hauling a frozen bo.

All in a heap his body lay, on the
    Frost-covered boxcar floor;
That's the first thing the car-toad saw
    When he opened up the door.
The coroner was called and his body hauled
    To a nearby county morgue.
When the inquest was through, all
    The jurymen knew,
That he was only a frozen vag.
    No one will ever know the name of the bo
Who was riding the Phantom Drag.

In nearly all of the twenty-eight editions of the *Little Red Song Book* of the wobblies (IWW) that have appeared in the past thirty years, are two or more ballads dealing with hobo life or railroading. The great bard of the wobblies was Joe Hill (born Hillstrom), whose picture adorns every copy of the *Song Book* and used to be hung on the wall of every IWW hall. Hill was "officially murdered" by the State of Utah on November 19, 1915, for what looked to the State like murder committed by Joe Hill.

Hill became the wobblies' great martyr as well as balladist. Most of his poems were sung to popular tunes. His song *Casey Jones, the Union Scab* is included in all of the nine different editions of the *Song Book* in my possession. It concerns a mythical Casey, who ran his locomotive during a strike and wound up deep in hell.

Although the song as published appears to have a connection with a strike on the Southern Pacific, it was also used in other railroad strikes, and I have one version that refers to Casey "acting like a scab on the DM Line." This was the Duluth, Mesabi & Northern, the famous ore carrier, which continued to operate throughout the great IWW strike on the Mesabi range in 1916. The wobs were great singers, anyway, and though they appear to have turned out no composers of original tunes, they were quick to parody popular songs. They sang these parodies from thousands of moving boxcars, beside uncounted jungle fires, in jails from Lawrence, Massachusetts, to Portland, Oregon, and on the picket lines of strikes across the country. The Red Dawn seemed imminent, and most of the songs of the wobs were to welcome the sun as it came up from back of the crumbling mountain called Capitalism.

The railroad songs I have mentioned are truly folk songs. But in Tin Pan Alley, the realm of the "popular" song, song writers and song pluggers are well aware of the popular appeal of the railroads. "The Chattanooga Choo-Choo" and "The Atchison, Topeka and the Santa Fe" are two fairly recent gems, but any reader who is a radio fan can probably name a dozen others.

Steam-powered railiner, the Baltimore & Ohio's new all-coach Cincinnatian, has been operating since early in 1947 by daylight on the fastest schedule ever established between Baltimore and Cincinnati.

A gleaming, 4000-horsepower, Diesel-electric locomotive wheels the Golden State Limited of the Rock Island Lines between Chicago and the Pacific Coast.

CHAPTER XXXIX

The Second Century

Every little while someone comes along to bury the poor railroads all over again.
—JOHN W. BARRIGER, *President,* Monon Route, 1946

EVERY little while, for at least two decades, some wide-eyed writer has appeared in magazine and Sunday supplement to remark that the railroad was done, obsolete, finished, archaic. More often than not these prophets, at two-cents-a-word and up, belong to the oh-the-wonder-of-it-all school, who point to the sky as the new and sole artery of travel and transportation and marvel, in complete awe—which they indicate by running over with astonishers!—at the thought of monstrous planes hauling the freight and passengers of the nation, even of the world.

No few of these writers, I have noticed, are the same who one month will herald the Air Epoch, a month later inform the housewife of new gadgets that will leave her nothing to do but to play bridge, and in another thirty days tell the world—with the most cruel kind of fatuous optimism—that a quick, certain, and permanent cure for cancer has been discovered.

This sort of quackery, disseminated by periodicals of circulation running into the millions of copies, serves to keep its public competently misinformed, and gullible for more of the same pap. You may be sure they will get more of it, too—sugary, thin, brief from "digesting," and as subtle as a movie script. Meanwhile, most housewives will find enough work to occupy their time, cancers will run their predestined course, and the railroad will carry on a while longer.

The steam railroad in America is a little more than one hundred years old. It overtook and passed the stagecoach and canal in merely the time required to lay the rails, and for the next seventy-five years it dominated inland travel and transportation. It dominates inland travel and transportation in 1947, twenty years or more after the wonder-of-it boys began holding funeral exercises. What its position will be twenty years hence is in the realm of prophecy, and the present writer does not belong to the prophets' union. Yet the present writer believes that 1967 will find trains still rolling in great numbers across and up and down the continent. Whether they will be operated by steam or by Diesel, or by energy released by nuclear fission doesn't matter. If bus, truck and plane can be operated by the new energy, then so can trains on tracks.

In any case, I am happy to leave the future to the professional prophets. What seems to me important in the interim is what the railroads are doing at present to meet the competition that began with the invention of the internal-combustion engine.

For what seemed an age, American railroads apparently paid little heed to the gasoline threat. They remained somnolent when Ford put out the first cheap car. They did not rouse, much, when the Federal and state governments started subsidizing the motorcar industry by building highways. They did grumble a little about it, but at the same time a majority of railroad officials fought introduction of such innovations as light high-speed trains, all-bedroom cars, and air-conditioning, just as their predecessors had fought the introduction of air brakes and automatic couplers.

Perhaps this was unfortunate for the railroads, but it was in perfect accord with human nature. Most of us automatically resist change, and railroads are operated by human beings. Many a cocked-hat man, a relic of an age that was swiftly made an ancient age by the speedy coming of the steam railroad, fought the new carriers savagely, resisting them by every means at their command, on the grounds of economics, safety, and Holy Writ. They abused the railroads as monsters that would one day lay the Republic in ruins. Millions of cocked-hat men, cheered and abetted by canal companies, plank-road companies, stage lines, livery stables, and growers of horse feed, sought the courts and the legislatures, sought Congress itself, to halt the damnable Iron Horse.

Individual man can speed the coming of an innovation; he can do little or nothing to slow its arrival—that is, if the innovation has great merit, such as that of the railroad.

So, the steamcars rolled through, or around, or across all opposition in the space of two decades. More than any other one agency they built the United States into a great and powerful country in a period so brief that anyone who reflects on it cannot help but be astonished, even now, long after the accomplishment.

Successful and unquestioned dominance probably has a tendency, either in human beings or in abstract industry, toward hardening of the arteries and ossification of the mind. A majority of railroad officials, I believe, will admit in private that such has been the case with their industry. But they will tell you, too, that the steam carriers have hardly begun to fight to retain their place.

One of the first indications that the railroads were not giving in to the motor age without a struggle rode across the flatlands of the Midwest in 1934, with the Burlington's streamlined Diesel *Zephyr*. Instigated by

Ralph Budd, head of the CB&Q, an unusual and capable railroad man, the *Zephyr* seemed to mark the railroads' first determined effort to retrieve some of the passenger business they had been losing steadily. It wasn't merely that the new streamliner was fast. Americans had long become accustomed to speed. Speed was good, too, but in addition the *Zephyr* was a piece of superb showmanship—shining, handsome, sleek, gliding almost noiselessly and without smoke or cinders, with great wide windows and an interior *décor* that was luxuriously "modern" compared to the red and green plush of the regulation coaches and Pullmans.

From that point on streamlining advanced rapidly, sometimes in conjunction with Diesel engines, as in the complete streamlined train unit; again simply by streamlined cars operating with steam locomotives sheathed to look like torpedoes. The whole affair caught the public fancy, and a dozen years later the public is still captivated by *Zephyrs*, *Comets*, *Meadowlarks* and *Meteors*, *Super Chiefs* and *Flying Yankees*. More are coming. Early in 1947 both the Northern Pacific and the Great Northern announced they were about ready to inaugurate Diesel streamliners between Chicago and the Pacific Northwest coast.

As for the Diesel itself, it seems certain of a steady advance. Like the steam and the gasoline engines, it is a machine for turning heat into power. The first burns fuel to heat water into steam, then works the steam in a cylinder. The second mixes gasoline and air in a carburetor, compresses the mixture in a cylinder, and explodes it with an electric spark. The Diesel compresses air in a cylinder into which it sprays oil, to be ignited by the heat of compression. The Diesel gets four times as much work out of a pound of fuel as does the steam engine; and perhaps twice as much as does the gasoline engine. Of some 120 streamlined trains now in service, approximately three-fourths are drawn by Diesel locomotives.

The first Diesel built specifically for freight work was put into service in 1941 by the Santa Fe, and before the end of that year other freight Diesels had been ordered by the Great Northern, the Southern, and the Milwaukee. Many railroaders profess to see Diesel as the dominant motive power of the near future of the railroads. The trend to Diesel is accompanied by a trend toward much faster freight trains. The day seems not far when there will be little difference between the speeds of main-line passenger and freight trains.

Five years before the Diesel engine was invented, railroads had begun using electricity as motive power. The first electrified train service opened, on June 28, 1895, on the short Nantasket Branch of the New York, New Haven & Hartford. Two months later the Baltimore & Ohio electrified the 3½ miles of its track that runs through the Baltimore tunnel. Fifty years later, twenty Class 1 line-haul railroads were operating electrically 6,495 miles of track. Today, the two outstanding systems using electrification are the Pennsylvania, with 2,245 miles of track so operated; and the Milwaukee Road, which has 922 miles. The New Haven ranks third with 628 miles.

It is the business of handling *things,* whether freight, mail, or express, from which the carriers receive their chief income. Freight service revenues comprise 85 per cent of all railroad operating revenue. Only about 10 per cent comes from carrying passengers—the Long Island Rail Road excepted. This fact about freight is one the public has never understood. On the contrary, the public judges railroads almost wholly on their performance with passenger trains; and that is unquestionably why so many people came to believe the railroads were dying; they were not paying attention to the passenger public.

So the public was highly critical, and not without a sound base for criticism. The carriers have been prone to devote their interest to getting and holding freight business. Freight service has improved more and much faster than passenger service. During the decade after 1920, when the public was beginning to travel in its own cars, or in buses, and the railroads made no perceptible attempt to prevent it, people said the steam carriers were obsolescent and were determined to stay that way. In this same period the railroad freight business was undergoing a huge program of modernization, both as to equipment and methods, and was more than holding its own in competition with the motor freight-trucking lines. But passenger business did slip away.

In the depression years following 1930, the lines started making gestures of good will to the passenger public. The introduction of fast, light, handsome, stainless-steel or aluminum trains has been mentioned. Accompanying the new trains was a deal of new advertising, all aimed at the potential passenger, telling him how cheap, pleasant, and reliable was the railroad train. Both individual lines and the Association of American Railroads carried on advertising campaigns. After no little arguing among themselves, the roads started to air-condition their cars. In the decade after air-conditioning was introduced in 1931, some 12,500 coaches and Pullman cars were made proof against smoke and cinders, and were equable in any weather.

Passenger train speeds were increased. In 1930 the number of miles operated each day at speeds of 60 miles an hour or better was 1,100. Ten years later daily runs at such speeds averaged 75,000 miles, and 10 per cent of the runs were made at more than 70 miles an hour. In the same period a notable change occurred in the attitude of railroads toward the public. Indifference disappeared. In its place appeared a spirit of warm, even eager, welcome, that made all of us old and true railroad riders very happy. Our favorite carriers were beginning to show good manners along with better service.

Since that period, the steam railroads have never ceased their efforts to get and retain passenger business. World War II years, being what they were to railroads, laid on them a woefully heavy load, yet they acquitted themselves well.

With the end of the war, the railroads could no longer use "emergency" to excuse shortcomings, many of which became apparent during the war years. The carriers were on the spot again, a spot hotter than ever, for now both airlines and truck and bus lines were after the customers in a big way, and were being as aggressive as they were alert. The airlines perhaps got a little cocky about it all. Mindful always of public relations, the airlines erected beautiful buildings, established sleek modernistic offices, and insisted on both courtesy and efficiency in their employees.

For a long time the airlines stressed chiefly, and rightly, the speed of their planes. Then they began to tell the public how cheap flying was also. The railroad worm did not turn until late in 1946, and even then it was only the Southern Pacific worm that turned with a goodly heave. In a milestone advertisement in newspapers and magazines all over the country, the SP came out with a succinct little piece entitled "A short course in Railroading for Airline executives." After stating that the airlines have been progressive and have taken their rightful place in the transportation scheme of things—just as the railroads have theirs—the SP remarked "but we wish they wouldn't spend so much time talking about the railroads in their advertising. They seem to know so many things about railroad service that aren't so!"

Picking up a full head of steam, the SP's man went ahead on a clear track. "We don't like," said he, "to mention a competing service in our advertising but now we're rather forced to talk about the airlines in order to inform the airlines (and the public, too) about some of the facts of the *railroad business.*

"The airlines compare their fares with railroad fares and come to the conclusion that air travel is cheaper. But they always compare *one way* fares. Since airlines make no reductions on round trips for travel in this country, the airline people apparently think the railroads don't either. As a matter of fact, railroads make substantial reductions for round trip tickets. We figure most people have to get home sometimes."

Warming to his subject, the SP teller of truth went on: "The airlines, in comparing fares, always add the cost of a Pullman *lower* berth. A comparison of a seat in a plane and a berth in a train is the same as comparing a chair with a bed. The airlines aren't operating sleeper planes so the services aren't comparable on that point at all. . . .

"In comparing their service with the railroads', the airlines forget to add in the bus fares to and from the airports (and bus travel time as well). Also they overlook their limited baggage allowances, which increase air-travel cost with a normal amount of luggage. These added costs, we think, overbalance the pleasant free meal furnished air-travelers when aloft.

"We accept the fact that airplanes have one primary advantage—*speed*. But we think trains have a lot of advantages, too, including economy and plenty of room to move around." *

Perhaps the SP's simple and good-natured, if edged, statement marks a new era in the railroads' public attitude toward competing services. In any case, it is a corrective needed by both the airlines and the traveling public. Nor is it difficult to think of other advertisements the railroads might be inspired to publish, the most obvious being to remind the public that in railroad wrecks there are commonly many more survivors than victims, whereas. . . .

But the railroads have been doing far more than talking about their services. Inventors, gadget-makers, designers, idea-men, they all have been enjoying a field day in the renaissance of the steam carriers. In the passengers' realm, the Burlington, as usual, has been in the van, this time with its panoramic coach which, in spite of the rather awful name of "Vista-Dome Car," is something to see and to ride in. Basically it is of caboose architecture, with a dome of double-laminated safety glass. A short stairway leads up to the dome compartment in which some twenty passengers have a 180-degree view of the countryside. Below are reclining chair seats in conventional arrangement, and 16 more seats in a cardplaying section. A women's lounge and a men's room are at opposite ends of the car. The whole affair is done up in turquoise green, beige, and lots of plate glass and nickel. Passengers in the dome have as fine a view of the scenery as any bo sitting on a gondola end, or brakeman in the dome of a caboose. The panoramic coach did not appear until 1945, but then it seemed to catch the public fancy much as the first *Zephyr* had many years ago.

High speeds, such as the streamliners are making, have a tendency to increase the number of hotboxes, which are overheated journals or bearings. Roller bearings, which are not likely to turn into hotboxes, were in use in a limited way on the carriers for many years; but recently they have been installed even on freight cars, and delays and accidents due to this cause are disappearing.

Rear-end collisions still trouble the railroads and more often than not are due to emergency stops. To protect the rear end of a stalled train it is the brakeman's duty to hurry back on the track from his last car and to flag down whatever may be approaching. Only too often he has not been quick enough, in these days of many trains. A new development, engineered for the Chicago & North Western by the Mars Signal Light Com-

---

* Apparently many Americans think so too, and were tickled with the SP ad. J. A. Ormandy, general passenger agent of the Southern Pacific at Portland, informed me that the SP had never received so many favorable comments on one of its advertisements as followed this one.

pany, is a powerful electric lamp attached to the rear car. In case of an emergency stop, the brakeman switches on the Mars, and flashing beams of light are set going, visible for many miles either by day or night.

Along with this oscillating taillight is the Mars headlight, set on the front of the locomotive. It remains inoperative until the airhose of the train is broken, or until the pressure of the airhose falls below thirty pounds. In either case the headlight goes into action, flashing word ahead that a train has stopped. Both head and rear lights have already proved their effectiveness and the C&NW is fast equipping all of its trains with them.

Train communication, mentioned in a previous chapter, is being improved steadily. Talking from cab to caboose, and from the moving train to dispatcher, is an accomplished fact. The Santa Fe has pioneered in all kinds of railroad communication, and today requires a staff of 2,700 men and women simply to handle its telephone, radio, and telegraph facilities which, says Kip Farrington in his *Railroading from the Rear End,* cited elsewhere, comprise 139,700 miles of communication lines and is the largest and most modern privately owned system on earth.

The New York Central isn't what one would call a mountain railroad, yet it operates in a region given to sudden and deep snows. To combat these the Central has developed a snow-removal machine that scoops up the snow from the tracks and melts it in a huge steam-charged tank. In operation this machine is pushed by a locomotive at speeds up to six miles an hour. Two endless belt conveyors carry the snow and dump it into a hopper on top of the melter. This machine probably will not revolutionize snow removal work, but it is one of the many innovations of recent years that indicate the steam railroads of the country are not, as so often has been charged, asleep.

Hardly new, yet not ancient and still unknown to the general public, is the dynamometer car, a cabooselike affair that is attached just behind the locomotive and which, with more gadgets than one could well imagine, keeps a record of the locomotive's operating performance. Test engineers ride inside the dynamometer car, watching instruments that chart the pulse of the cylinders, sample smokebox gases, weigh every pound of coal used, and record the continuous yet ever-changing pull on the drawbar. This is the way modern locomotives are tested, and changes in engine construction are made on the strength of the dynamometer's records.

There are more Americans today than ever before who have a direct financial interest in the railroads. At the end of 1944 stockholders, who were mostly individuals, numbered 864,970 in the Class 1 roads, which are lines having operating expenses of more than one million dollars annually. On the same date the holders of Class 1 railroad bonds numbered approximately one million. Both classes of owners have been increasing steadily since 1904, according to the Association of American Railroads.

Indirectly, every American has an important financial stake in the railroads. The major investors in railroad securities are the savings banks and insurance companies of the nation. Their investment portfolios and the portfolios of many trust funds contain a large proportion of railroad mortgage bonds and other rail securities and therefore every savings bank depositor, every policyholder has an indirect stake in the financial welfare of the railroads.

Incidentally, for every dollar that the Class 1 railroads paid to their stockholders in dividends in 1944, they paid $7.61 in taxes to federal, state, and local governments.

A complete realist in the matter of rail transportation is John W. Barriger, head of the Monon Route who, in 1946, was the youngest railroad president in the United States. Mr. Barriger admits that for many years the steam carriers certainly gave the public indifferent passenger service, and he is out to remedy that condition so far as the Monon is concerned. He has started a construction program that will result in grades of 0.5 per cent or less, and in 1 per cent curves. With new locomotives and rolling stock now on order, he plans 100-mile-an-hour passenger trains between Chicago and Louisville. He had purchased 2,000 new freight cars, and a fleet of streamlined passenger coaches.

That is the attitude and the strategy of one of the smaller Class 1 railroads, which probably has been through as much hell and grief as any other carrier and is now on the way to meeting the new conditions facing all steam roads.

The improvements mentioned in this and other chapters will, I think serve to indicate that the roads are seeking to keep abreast of the times, in regard to both passenger and freight services. I think that for the most part they are alert to the threat of motor and air competition. They have now passed through their first century of operation. What the next hundred years will do to or for them lies, as I've said, in the realm of prophecy.

Any informed person, I believe, recognizes that it has been the steam railroads, more than any other one thing, that has made the United States as it is today both possible and almost inevitable. The railroads have been grossly indifferent and abusive in their time, displaying arrogance and defiance that even yet, many years after, is still held against them. The steam railroads have also been grossly abused by legislation that was as vindictive as it was unfair. The roads were often overbuilt, and terribly overcapitalized. These matters have a way of remedying themselves, commonly by receivership, and as everybody ought to know, railroads have not been strangers to the bankruptcy courts.

Now, in postwar years, they seem to have plenty of courage and determination for the hot competition that is theirs. What they will do about it, only time will tell. I imagine they will so change themselves—their engines, their cars, their tracks, almost everything else—that they will hardly be recognizable. Already they have gone through a few stages of metamorphosis. The red and green plush of the old coaches has gone. So have cinders and smoke from the cars. The branch lines, having long since passed into the doldrums of operating Mondays-Wednesdays-Saturdays-Only, bid fair to disappear entirely.

It appears now, and how I do hate even to mention it—it appears now that the steam locomotive itself is on the way out, and so into limbo with the Concord coach and the Erie canal. There is no use protesting against its going, and I shall not protest the inevitable. But I *shall* mutter and complain against the obscene noises and the sheikish appearance of the Diesel locomotive. The Diesel is nothing to offer a man in place of the classic Iron Horse that spanned the continent in less than a man's lifetime, bound it with arteries that carried the blood of life into its most remote and inaccessible parts—that tamed its wildness, softened its savagery, and civilized its places and peoples as nothing else could have done. All of this, I repeat, was done so quickly that the world of reflective men has not yet ceased to marvel.

That is what the Iron Horse did for America. If the steam locomotive must now go to the boneyard, to be supplanted by Diesel, or atomic power, or whatever may be in store, it is quite in keeping with evolutionary process. I doubt that it will disappear in my lifetime. If, however, the present trend should be so speeded that there be danger the last steam locomotive should be making its final run, I shall plan to be on hand to hear and see it. If I should be able to arrange matters at all, I'd like to watch a Last Passenger Train, hauled by a big, snorting Prairie-type engine, head lamp and all car lights on, flitting across the great level open spaces of Nebraska, in the magic twilight of the plains, to pass over the horizon and mark the spot by a white plume from its stack. . . .

And, for *sound,* I'd want to take my stand deep in the northern spruce forest, along the Montreal-Portland Division of the old Grand Trunk, to hear the hoarse cry of a freight climbing through a mountain valley.

No sight, no sound in my native land so stirs my imagination as those do. As symbols of the United States they are better, and more accurate, than the covered wagon and the report of the homesteader's rifle. I think of them as unmistakenly American as the Stars and Stripes and the Constitution.

A Railroad Almanac

1804—Oliver Evans, Philadelphia, builds first American steam locomotive.
1826—Granite Railway Company, Boston, first concern to build and operate a railroad in United States.
1830—First steam locomotive put in regular service, *The Best Friend of Charleston*, South Carolina Railroad.
1830—First common-carrier railroad, Baltimore & Ohio.
1831—First mail carried on railroad, South Carolina.
1837—First locomotive whistle.
1851—First train reaches Lake Erie.
1852—First train reaches Chicago from the East.
1857—First shipment of meat under refrigeration, Chicago.
1858—First Pullman sleeper goes into operation.
1863—First successful rail labor union, The Brotherhood of the Footboard.
1869—First transcontinental completed.
1869—Westinghouse patents air brake.
1870—First through train, coast-to-coast, Boston-San Francisco.
1875—First parlor car by Pullman.
1880—First humane stock car devised, by Alonzo C. Mather.
1883—Standard time belts adopted.
1885—Janney automatic coupler approved by Master Car-Builders.
1893—Federal law provides for air brakes and automatic couplers.
1900—Casey Jones goes to Promised Land.
1905—Fastest run by passenger train, *Broadway Limited* of the Pennsylvania, 127.06 miles per hour.
1931—First air-conditioned train, Baltimore & Ohio.
1934—First streamlined Diesel train.

Bibliography

Books, Pamphlets, Documents, Articles.

Adams, Charles Francis, *Chapters in Erie and Other Essays*, Boston, 1871.
Alexander, E. P., *Iron Horses, American Locomotives 1829–1900*, New York, 1941.
American Railway Association, *The American Railroad in Laboratory*, Washington, 1933.
American Railway Association, *Proceedings of the Protective Division*, New York, 1921.
Anderson, Nels, *The Hobo*, Chicago, 1923.
Andrews, Wayne, *The Vanderbilt Legend*, New York, 1941.
A-No. 1, *Here and There With A-No. 1, The Famous Tramp*, Erie, Pa., n. d.
Association of American Railroads, various pamphlets and bulletins, Washington.
Baker, George Peirce, *The Formation of the New England Railroad Systems*, Cambridge, 1937.
Bangor & Aroostook Railroad Company, *Northern Maine*, Bangor, 1930.
Bangor & Aroostook Railroad Company, *Forty-fifth Annual Report*, 1938.
Bangor & Aroostook Railroad Company, *In the Maine Woods*, 1938.
Baxter, James P., "Reminiscences of a Great Enterprise," in *Collections and Proceedings of the Maine Historical Society*, Second Series, Vol. III, Portland, 1892.
Beebe, Lucius, *Highball, A Pageant of Trains*, New York, 1945.
Berger, Max, *The British Traveller in America 1836–1860*, New York, 1943.
Bishop, Mrs. I. L., *An Englishwoman in America*, London, 1856.
Bowles, Samuel, *The Pacific Railroad—Open. How to Go: What to See*, Boston, 1869.
Bradlee, Francis B. C., *The Boston & Maine Railroad*, Salem, Mass., 1921.
Brady, William A., *Showman*, New York, 1937.
Bridgman, Howard Allen, *New England in the Life of the World*, Boston, 1920.
Buck, Solon J., *The Granger Movement*, Cambridge, 1913.
Buck, Solon J., *The Agrarian Crusade*, New Haven, 1921.
Buckingham, S. G., *The Sabbath and the Rail Roads, A Sermon Preached in the South Congregational Church, Springfield, Mass., June 30, 1872.*
Bureau of Railway Economics, *Arguments For and Against Limitation of the Length of Freight Trains*, Washington, 1916.
Busbey, T. Addison, compiler, *Biographical Directory of The Railway Officials of America*, Chicago, 1896.
Carter, Charles Frederick, *When Railroads Were New*, New York, 1909.

Corliss, Carlton J., *The Day of Two Noons*, Chicago, 1941.

Corliss, Carlton J., *Trails to Rails*, Chicago, 1937.

Covington, Stuart, "The Rebel Route," in *Railroad Magazine*, Jan. 1945.

Crittenden, H. T., *The Two-Footers*, Bulletin No. 57, The Railway & Locomotive Historical Society, Baker Library, Cambridge, 1942.

Cushing, George H., "Hill Against Harriman," in *American Magazine*, Sept. 1909.

Daggett, Stuart, *Chapters in the History of the Southern Pacific*, New York, 1922.

Davies, William Henry, *The Autobiography of a Super-Tramp*, London, 1908.

Dodge, Grenville M., *How We Built the Union Pacific Railway*, Government Printing Office, Washington, 1910.

Engerud, Hal, "Morgan's L&N Raid, Christmas 1862," in *The L. & N. Employes Magazine*, Louisville, Dec. 1932.

Evans, Oliver, *Patent Right Oppression Exposed: or, Knavery Detected*, Philadelphia, 1813.

Everest, Kate A., "How Wisconsin Came by its Large German Element," in *Wisconsin Historical Collections*, Vol. XII, Madison, 1892.

Evidence Showing the Manner Locomotive Engines are Used on Rail-Roads, Boston, 1838.

Farnam, S. E., *Without Due Process, A Typical Tale of Life on the Rail in the Latter Part of the 19th Century*, Columbus, Ohio, 1894.

Federal Trade Commission, *Report on Private Car Lines*, Washington, 1920.

Flynt, Josiah, "The Tramp and the Railroads," in *The Century Magazine*, Vol. LVIII, May–October 1899.

Fischer, Charles E., *Locomotive Building at Taunton, Massachusetts*, Bulletin No. 15, The Railway & Locomotive Historical Society, Boston, 1927.

French, Chauncey Del, *Railroadman*, New York, 1938.

Gates, Paul Wallace, *The Illinois Central Railroad and Its Colonization Work*, Cambridge, 1934.

George, David Robinson, *Growth of the Long Island Rail Road* (mimeographed) New York, 1943(?).

Gilbert, Douglas, *Lost Chords*, New York, 1942.

Gillette, Edward, *Locating the Iron Trail*, Boston, 1925.

Glasscock, C. B., *Bandits and the Southern Pacific*, New York, 1929.

Grattan, T. C., *Civilised America*, London, 1859.

Guide to an Unsurpassed Region in Southern Minnesota and Eastern Dakota Along the Line of the Winona & St. Peter Railroad, Marshall, Minn., 1878.

Hadley, Arthur T., *Railroad Transportation*, New York, 1897.

Haney, Lewis Henry, *A Congressional History of Railways in the United States to 1850*, Madison, 1908.

Hargrave, Frank F., *A Pioneer Indiana Railroad*, Indianapolis, 1932.

Harlow, Alvin F., *Old Waybills*, New York, 1934.

Harlow, Alvin F., *Steelways of New England*, New York, 1946.

Heath, Erle, *Seventy-Five Years of Progress, Historical Sketch of the Southern Pacific*, San Francisco, 1945.

Henry, Robert S., "The Railroad Land Grant Legend in American History Texts," in *Mississippi Valley Historical Review*, Sept. 1945.

Henry, Robert S., *This Fascinating Railroad Business*, Indianapolis, 1943.

Herr, Kincaid A., *The Louisville & Nashville Railroad 1850–1942*, Louisville, 1943.

Hill, Hamilton Andrews, *Seventeenth Annual Report of the Boston Board of Trade*, Boston, 1871.

Hill, James J., *Highways of Progress*, New York, 1910.

Hobart, Charles W., "Nelson Bennett," in *Magazine of Western History*, New York, March, 1891.

Holbrook, Stewart H., *Burning An Empire*, New York, 1943.

Holbrook, Stewart H., *Let Them Live*, New York, 1938.

Horn, Stanley F., *This Fascinating Lumber Business*, Indianapolis, 1943.

House of Representatives, Doc. 203, 26th Congress, 1st Session, *The Hon. Amos Kendall, Postmaster General, reporting on delays in the mails between New York and Boston, July 1839, March 1840.*

Howard, Joseph Kinsey, *Montana, High, Wide and Handsome*, New Haven, 1943.

Howland, S. A., *Steamboat and Railroad Accidents in the United States*, Worcester, 1840.

Hubbard, Freeman H., *Railroad Avenue*, New York, 1945.

Hudson, James F., *The Railways and the Republic*, New York, 1886.

Hungerford, Edward, *Men and Iron, The History of the New York Central*, New York, 1938.

Hunt, Herbert, *Tacoma, Its History and Its Builders*, Chicago, 1916.

Husband, Joseph, *The Story of the Pullman Car*, Chicago, 1917.

James, Thomas L., "The Railway Mail Service," in *The American Railway*, New York, 1897.

Johnson, F. H., *The Milwaukee Road*, Chicago, 1944.

Industrial Workers of the World, *Songs of the Workers*, Chicago, 1945.

Joy, J. F., "A Letter to the Governor of Michigan," in *Michigan History Magazine*, Vol. VIII, p. 395, Lansing.

Kalmbach, A. C., *Railroad Panorama*, Milwaukee, 1944.

Lee, Fred J., *Casey Jones, Epic of the American Railroad*, Kingsport, Tenn., 1939.

Lewis, Lloyd, *Myths After Lincoln*, New York, 1929.

Lewis, Oscar, *The Big Four*, New York, 1938.

Liebling, Abbott J., and Marks, Edward B., *They All Sang*, New York, 1934.

The Long Island Railroad, New York, 1934.

Louisville & Nashville Railroad, *Annual Report*, June 30, 1863.

Love, Robertus, *The Rise and Fall of Jesse James*, New York, 1926.

Markham, C. H., "The Development, Strategy, and Traffic of the Illinois Central System," in *Economic Geography*, Jan. 1926.

Marks, Edward B., and Liebling, Abbott J., *They All Sang*, New York, 1934.

Marshall, James, *Santa Fe, The Railroad that Built An Empire*, New York, 1945.

Martin, Edward Winslow, *History of the Grange Movement; or, the Farmers' War Against Monopolies*, Chicago, 1874.

Mattson, Hans, *Reminiscences, The Story of An Emigrant*, St. Paul, 1891.

Maxwell, A. M., *A Run Through the United States*, London, 1841.

Miller, Francis Trevelyan, *Thomas A. Edison*, Philadelphia, 1931.

Missouri, Kansas & Texas Railway, *The Opening of the Great Southwest*, St. Louis, 1945.

Moody, John, *The Railroad Builders*, New Haven, 1920.

Moody, Linwood W., "Sunset on the Narrow-Gage," in *Railroad Magazine*, Aug. 1941.

Mordecai, John B., *A Brief History of the Richmond, Fredericksburg & Potomac Railroad*, Richmond, 1941.

Mott, Edward Harold, *The Story of Erie*, New York, 1899.

Myers, Gustavus, *History of the Great American Fortunes*, New York, 1936.

Nevins, F. J., *Seventy Years of Service, From Grant to Gorman*, Chicago, 1922.

New York Sabbath Committee, *Railroads and the Sabbath*, Second Document, New York, 1858.

Official Pocket Railway & Navigation Guide to Washington and the Puget Sound Country, Tacoma, 1891.

Overton, R. C., *The First Ninety Years, An Historical Sketch of the Burlington Railroad*, Chicago, 1940.

Pacific Coast Railway & Steamship Guide, San Francisco, 1893.

Pearson, Henry Greenleaf, *An American Railroad Builder, John Murray Forbes*, New York, 1911.

Peck, J. M., *A New Guide for Emigrants to the West*, Boston, 1837.

Pelley, J. J., *Railroads and the Future*, a pamphlet of the Association of American Railroads, Washington, 1946.

Perkins, J. R., *Rails and War, the Life of General G. M. Dodge*, Indianapolis, 1929.

Peterson, Harold F., "Some Colonization Aspects of the Northern Pacific Railroad," in *Minnesota History*, Vol. 10, No. 2, St. Paul, 1929.

Pittsburgh, Ft. Wayne & Chicago Rail Road, *Rules and Regulations for Operating*, Pittsburgh, 1858.

Poor, Laura Elizabeth, *Life and Writings of John Alfred Poor*, New York, 1892.

Prescott, DeWitt Clinton, *Early-Day Railroading from Chicago*, Chicago, 1910.

Pyle, J. G., *The Life of James J. Hill*, New York, 1936.

Quiett, G. C., *They Built the West*, New York, 1934.

The Railway Mail Association and the Railway Postal Clerk, Washington, 1946.

Ray, Clarence Everly, *The Railroad Spotter, An Exposé of the Methods Employed by Detective Agencies and Bonding Companies*, St. Paul, 1916.

Reitman, Ben L., *Sister of the Road*, New York, 1937.

Riegel, R. E., "Standard Time in the United States," in *American Historical Review*, October 1937.

Riegel, Robert Edgar, *The Story of the Western Railroads*, New York, 1926.

Road of Progress, The Story of the New York Central System, New York, 1945.

Roanoke Times, Centennial Edition dedicated to the Norfolk & Western Railway, Sept. 7, 1938.

Robertson, Archie, *Slow Train to Yesterday*, Boston, 1945.

Sabin, Edwin L., *Building the Pacific Railway*, Philadelphia, 1919.

Salmons, C. H., *The Burlington Strike*, Aurora, Ill., 1889.

Smith, J. Calvin, *The Western Tourist and Emigrant's Guide*, New York, 1839.

Smith, Russell E., "Railroads Behind the Footlights," in *Railroadman's Magazine*, 1913.

Spearman, Frank H., *The Strategy of Great Railroads*, New York, 1904.

Starr, John W., Jr., *One Hundred Years of American Railroading*, New York, 1928.

Starr, John W., Jr., *Lincoln and The Railroads*, New York, 1927.

Stevenson, Robert Louis, "Across the Plains" chapter in *Travels and Essays*, New York, 1907.

Stevers, Martin D., *Steel Rails*, New York, 1933.

Tanner, H. S., *A Description of the Canals and Rail Roads of the United States*, New York, 1840.

Thomas, Richard Thomson, *Check List of Publications on Railroads before 1841*, New York, 1942.

Thompson, Jeanette R., *History of the Town of Stratford, New Hampshire, 1773–1925*, Published by Vote of the Town, 1925.

Trottman, Nelson, *History of the Union Pacific, A Financial and Economic Survey, New York, 1923*.

Tuttle, Charles W., "Memoir of John Alfred Poor of Portland, Maine," in *New England Historical and Genealogical Register and Antiquarian Journal*, Vol. 26, No. 4, Oct. 1872.

Villard, Henry, *The Early History of Transportation in Oregon*, Eugene, Ore., 1944.

White, James E., *A Life Span and Reminiscences of Railway Mail Service*, Philadelphia, 1910.

Wilkes, J. G., "Albert Fink, Pioneer Railroader," in *The L. & N., Employes Magazine*, Louisville, Aug. 1927.

Wilkinson, William, *Memorials of the Minnesota Forest Fires in the Year 1894*, Minneapolis, 1895.

Wilson, Neill C., *Treasure Express*, New York, 1936.

Winston, Edmund, "Life of Colonel Falkner," in *Gulf, Mobile & Northern News*, Mobile, Ala., Nov. 27, 1925.

Yellen, Samuel, *American Labor Struggles*, New York, 1936.

Yesterday and Today, a History of the Chicago and North Western System, Chicago, 1910.

Youngmeyer, D. W., "An Excursion into the Early History of the Chicago & Alton Railroad," in *Journal of the Illinois Historical Society*, Springfield, Vol. XXXVIII, March 1945.

Periodicals

The Pathfinder Railway Guide, Boston, various editions.

Railroad Gazette, New York, 1870–1908.

The Railway Monitor, Vol. 1, New York, 1873.

Trans-Continental, Published by Boston Board of Trade, Trans-Continental Excursion, Boston to San Francisco, May 2, July 1, 1870.

INDEX

Clarke, Lewis Gaylord, 163
Clay, Bertha M., 406
Cleveland, Grover, 254
Cleveland, Mt. Vernon & Delaware railroad, 358
Cleveland & Pittsburgh railroad, 83
Cobden, Richard, 100
Coffin, Lorenzo, 11, 140, 289-300
Cohan, George M., 332
Cole, Henry W., 426
Colebrook, N. H., 73
Colfax, Schuyler, 171
Colonization, 98-110
Colorado Midland railroad, 257
Colson, F. W., 327, 328
Columbia Bridge, N. H., 413-420
Columbia, Neb., 350
Combe, George, traveler, 27
Cominsky, John, 375
Compromise cars, 278
Conductors, 340 ff.
Connecticut Western railroad, 282 ff.
Coolidge, Calvin, 332
Cooper, Peter, 6
Corkonians, the, 57 ff.
Corliss, Carlton J., 355
Cornell, Ezra, 14, 64
Corning, Erastus, 8
Corning, John, 106
Coulter, Frank, 384
Coyle, Joe, clown, 284, 286
Cram, Franklin W., 223
Cram, Wingate, 222, 227 ff.
Crawfordsville, Ind., 114, 120
Credit Mobilier, 167 ff.
Crittenden, H. T., 362
Crittenden, John J., 63
Crocker, Charles, 165 ff.
Crook, Gen. George, 169
Crush, William George, 219, 220
Crystal River & San Juan railroad, 365
Culvertown, Ind., 118
Cumberland Valley, railroad, 317

"Daddy Joe", legend, 337, 338
Dalton, Bill, 219, 379, 380
Dalton, Gratton, 219, 379, 380
Daniels, George H., 95
Daniels, Oscar J., porter hero, 333
Darrow. Clarence, 255
Darrow, F. T., 194
Davies, William, tramp, 391, 392
Davis, Gussie, composer, 432, 433, 439 ff.
Davis, Jeff, "King of Hoboes," 393, 396
Davis, Phineas, 22
Davis, W. A., innovator, 311
D'Autremont Brothers, robbers, 387, 388
Dean, Richmond, 338

Dearborn Street station, Chicago, 131
Debs, Eugene Victor, 251 ff.
Dempsey, Jack, 332
Denison, George, 216 ff
Denton, Samuel, 54
Denver & Rio Grande railroad, 191 ff., 207 ff.
Denver & Rio Grande Western railroad, 365
Deposit, N. Y., 51
Detroit, Mich., 401
Detroit & St. Joseph railroad, 47
Dexter, George, 409, 410
Dexter, Henry, 409, 410
Dexter, Mich., 264
Dey, Peter A., 167, 168
Diesel locomotives, 97, 444 ff.
Dining cars, 324 ff.
Dix, Gen. John A., 167
Dixville Notch, N. H., 73, 75-76
Dodge City, Kan., 208
Dodge, Grenville, 8, 167, 168
Dollmer, Charles, 284 ff.
Donnelly, Ignatius, 237 ff.
Douglas, Stephen A., 46, 99, 101
Dowd, Prof. C. F., 355, 356
Doyle, John J., 377
Drag Freight, ballad, 436
Drew, Daniel, 9, 67-68, 302
Dripps, Isaac, 34
Dudley, Plimmon H., 96
Dulany, George M., 333
Duluth, Mesabi & Northern railroad, 442
Duluth, Minn., 150 ff.
Dunkirk, N. Y., 52, 63
Dunlap, George L., 349
Dunlap, James, 136
Dunn, Washington, 201
DuPuy, Charles, 105 ff.
DuQuoin, Ill., 105
Durant, Thomas C., 168
Durham, N. H., 136
Dutch Clock, the, 268, 269
Dynamometer car, 449

Earle Brothers, the, 301
Eastern railroad, of Massachusetts, 278 ff.
Eastern Railway & Lumber company, 274
East Tenn. & Western N. C. railroad, 364, 365
Eccles, David, 365, 366
Edison, Thomas A., 399 ff., 427, 428
Eichhorn, William A., 399, 409
Electrified locomotives, 445
Elgin, Joliet & Eastern railroad, 284
Elizabethtown, Ky., 123, 127
Ellis, J. K., 219
Elmira, N. Y., 63
Elmore, Tom, 282
El Moro, Colo., 212

Vermont & Massachusetts railroad, 234
Vibbard, Chauncy, 85
Villard, Henry, 178, 406
Visalia, Cálif., 378 ff.

Wabash railroad, 95, 137
Wagner Sleeping Car company, 318 ff., 338
Wagner, Webster, 11, 318 ff.
Wallace, Gen. Lew, 120, 189, 190
Ward, Montgomery, 137
Watlington, Charles, 213
Watt, James, 19
Wayzata, Minn., 180
Webster-Ashburton treaty, 223
Webster, Daniel, 46, 62 ff.
Weehawken, N. J., 93
Weitbrec, R. F., 212
Wellington, Arthur Mellen, 191, 192
Wells, Daniel H., 350
Wells, Fargo & Company, 307 ff., 380
Wells, Henry, 302 ff.
Wells, Sam, robber, 374
West Canaan, N. H., 287
Western Union telegraph, 119
Westinghouse, George, 289 ff.
Weyerhaeuser, Frederick, 182
Wheeler, Henry, 373, 374
Wheeling, W. Va., 114, 246
Whisnant, Archibald, 89
White, James E., 312
White Pass & Yukon railroad, 368

White, R. C., 383
Whitney, Alexander F., 403
Whitney, Asa, prophet, 163, 164
Whyte classification, 30
Wilson, John, 106
Winans, Ross, innovator, 47
Winona & St. Peter railroad, 154, 155
Winslow, E. L., 93
Winston, Mo., 374
Wisconsin Central railroad, 156
Wisconsin Union railroad, 137
Woodruff, Sen. Wilfred, 350
Woodruff, T. T., 319
Woods, A. H., 427, 428
Woodward, Sam, 303
Wreck of the Old 97, The, ballad, 430 ff.
Wrecks, accidents, etc., 102

Yakima, Wash., 200 ff.
Yazoo & Mississippi Valley railroad, 337
Yeovil Colony, 155, 156
Yesler, Henry, 397
York & Cumberland railroad, 80
Young, Brigham, 350, 351
Young, Robert R., 141-142
Younger, Bob, 372 ff.
Younger, Cole, 372 ff.
Younger, Jim, 372 ff.
Younger, John, 372 ff.

Zepp, Dick, 246

907002